THE DRUID SOURCE BOOK

FROM EARLIEST TIMES TO THE PRESENT DAY

Edited and Compiled

by

JOHN MATTHEWS

Foreword by Philip Carr-Gomm
Chief of the Order of Bards, Ovates and Druids

BLANDFORD

Dedication

To the memory of Colin Murray (1942-86), founder of the Golden Section Order, who first introduced me to the ideas of Druidism.

A Blandford Book

First published in the
United Kingdom in 1996 by
Blandford
A Cassell Imprint

Wellington House
125 Strand
London WC2R 0BB

Copyright © 1996 Blandford Press

Compilation & original texts copyright © 1996 John Matthews

Foreword copyright © 1996 Philip Carr-Gomm

Distributed in the United States by Sterling Publishing Co., Inc.
387 Park Avenue South, New York, NY 10016-8810

Distributed in Australia by Capricorn Link (Australia) Pty Ltd
2/13 Carrington Road, Castle Hill, NSW 2154

A Cataloguing-in-Publication Data entry for this title is available from the British Library

ISBN 0-7137-2572-9

Typeset by Litho Link Ltd, Welshpool, Powys, Wales
Printed and bound in Great Britain by Hartnolls Limited, Bodmin, Cornwall

CONTENTS

A view of Avebury as it looked in the 1800s.
From The Celtic Druids *by Godfrey Higgins*

FOREWORD

RETURNING TO THE
SOURCE

*The songs of our ancestors are also the songs of our
children*

STUDYING and practising Druidry can be a puzzling affair. Look at it one
day and it seems as if there's nothing there: a few second or third-hand
accounts from biased Greek or Roman observers, a few inferences to be
drawn from linguistic or archaeological research, and a mass of later
material, mainly from the seventeenth century onwards, that is replete with
speculation, fantasy, or downright trickery. Look at it another day and a treasure
chest is opened: the sacred geometry of the megalithic sites built by the proto-
Druids reveals an awesome cosmological understanding, early Irish and Welsh
literature inspires us with tales filled with references to Druidry and paganism,
the classical references reveal tantalizing glimpses of a highly developed
spiritual tradition, and folklore studies show how even today many of our
customs and traditions derive from our Druidic and Celtic heritage. Even the
writings of more recent commentators, however confused with their own
desires to justify their pet theories, and however (as in the case particularly of
Iolo Morganwg) fraudulent their claims to authenticity might be, reveal insights
into Druid philosophy and practice, culled perhaps from historical sources and
elaborated through the workings of their unconscious minds, connected to the
collective and archetypal levels where Druidry exists as an every-present reality.

How are we to approach this wealth of intriguing, yet often confusing,
information, much of which John Matthews has skilfully gathered together in
this volume? Our approach to a subject conditions the way in which we
understand it, and the way in which we are then able to use that understanding
in our research or spiritual practice. The biggest mistake that we can make
when we approach literary source material about Druidry is to believe that this
material is the *primary* source of the Druid tradition, when in fact it is
secondary. The primary source can never be presented in literature, because it
can only be found in places where we must set books aside – in places where
both this world and the Otherworld are strongly present – by sacred springs
and holy wells, by the seashore or in stone circles, beside great trees or strong

mountains. When we open ourselves to these places, to the beauty and the splendour of the natural world, we discover the true source of inspiration for Druidry. It has always been said that the Druid tradition was an oral one, but a more accurate term would be aural, since we learn the most by listening: to our hearts, to others and to the natural world – to the sound of the rivers and the trees, the stars and the night sky. A Druid maxim, therefore, might be: Listen first, read second!

Treating literary sources as secondary rather than primary frees us from the need to treat anything written as sacred, as dogma. The fact that writers have expressed themselves poorly, have confused or misinterpreted facts, have slipped their hidden agendas consciously or unconsciously into their writings, have been overly influenced by contemporary thinking, or have invented material and claimed it to be authentic, rather than disturbing our connection to the primary source, instead becomes a matter for intellectual challenge and discernment.

Most people think that Druidry is something that existed in the distant past, and that some people have tried to re-create it in more recent times from the scattered remnants that we have inherited. But this way of thinking is only meaningful to those who choose to deny the reality of the Spirit. If we believe that the spiritual world exists, then we will also believe that the source of any spiritual tradition lies in that world, rather than in the physical world of effects.

If Druidry exists in the spiritual, archetypal world, and if it exists as potential and ideal in this realm, then each generation must attempt to connect with and express this ideal, potential or archetype as best it can. This is a tremendously exciting idea, because it means that rather than the sources of Druidry moving ever further from us as we move forward in time, the reverse is actually the case – as we move forward in time our increased knowledge of the world and the psyche can enable us to more adequately reflect and express the ideals and images of Druidry that exist so potently in the spiritual realm.

This understanding can help us to make sense of much of the source material presented here. We can see how each generation has been intrigued by the ideas associated with Druidry, and how it has attempted to research and articulate its findings. And as we read, we can sense the outlines forming of a landscape, a Being, a tapestry, that is our heritage, a heritage of spiritual tradition that has existed for millenia and which is now being reclaimed so that the gift of its past can meet the potential of its future in the magic of this present time.

Philip Carr-Gomm
Lughnasadh 1995

INTRODUCTION

THE STORY OF DRUIDRY

HE first thing anyone wishing to know about Druids and Druidry today should recognize is that the only surviving records from the time they originally flourished were written by classical authors, who had no love for them. Thus, the most famous early account – by Julius Caesar – is that of a soldier, who was not only being vigorously opposed by the Druids and who therefore wished to destroy them but who was also writing at the end of their apparently long history. There are, in fact, no records of their origins, nor is it known with any certainty when they were first active. The Druids themselves possessed no writings, preferring to depend on memory and on the oral transmission of their teachings; hence little or nothing can be counted upon – despite claims to the contrary – as having been actually written by them.

The second fact that must be borne in mind is that a great deal of absolute nonsense has been written about the Druids, their origins and beliefs, particularly during and after the eighteenth century, when fashion favoured the pursuit of things ancient and British, resulting in such curious statements as that by Godfrey Higgins in his book *The Celtic Druids* (which was published in 1827) to the effect that the ancient name for the Law in Ireland was 'Tara' and that this was itself a corruption of the Jewish 'Torah'!

Writings of this kind have given rise to a good deal of ridicule, especially among contemporary scholars, of any connection between modern Druid orders and the original Druids. There is, it has to be admitted, some justification for this, but this is not the whole story.

Much of what we can infer about the Druids comes from what is *not* said of them. For instance, they are not vilified by the early Christian writers of the lives of the saints, who record seemingly cordial relations between Druid and Christian (with a few exceptions to be sure). In the end, a good deal of Druidical philosophy seems to have been absorbed by the Christians along with their practices, as has been shown recently in John Minahane's book *The Christian Druids*.

The origin of the name Druid may come from the Celtic word-roots *dru-wid* – oak knowledge – from *dru* meaning 'oak' and *wid* meaning 'to know' or 'to see'. Another possible meaning for this may be simply 'great-knowledge' or 'knowledge as great (old) as the oaks'. However, it has been pointed out that in Irish tradition at least, the rowan and the hazel are more often mentioned in connection with the Druids than is the oak.

One should also note that the Irish word *druidecht* is translated as 'magic' and *druth* as 'fool' or 'madman' (in the sense of inspired madness or inspiration). In addition, in Sanskrit the word *drus* means 'tree' and *duru* means 'wood', and the root *dur* appears in the Celtic *derw* and *darach*, while in Lithuanian *derva* and *doire* mean 'oak'. In Welsh the word *drws* means a door, and we have Gaelic *dorus*, Cornish *daras* and Lithuanian *durys*. There is also Gaelic *druidim*, 'I shut'. From which we may infer if nothing else that the root from which Druid comes is both widespread throughout the Indo-European world and that it had a powerful connection with oak trees and the opening and closing of ways.

An important question arises when one asks: is Druidry a religion or were the Druids rather a priestly caste of the Celtic peoples? In other words, were the original Druids the founders of a religion *per se* or was the term 'Druid' merely a title, used in much the same way that we might use 'priest'? On the whole, I would favour the second option, although the question must be considered in two ways – as a matter concerned, first, with the origins of the Druids and, second, with those who have come to be part of the neo-Druidic revival that began in the sixteenth century.

It should be noted that none of the classical sources refer to the Druids as priests or to Druidry as a religion, and from this one may suppose that neither they nor it were regarded in that light when the original Druids functioned. Today, among those who are part of the Druid revival, Druidry may be clearly perceived as the practice of a form of religion based on the Celtic traditions and, as such, may be seen as the focus of a religious impulse. At the very least it was – and is – a coherent philosophy, offering an approach to life that is distinct from, say, Hinduism, Christianity or Islam.

It can also be said, with a fair degree of confidence, that the Druids were not only priests – perhaps one should, rather, say, that they were only incidentally priests – but were also doctors, lawyers, teachers, psychologists, historians, prophets, astronomers and political advisers. In short, they were the intellectual class of the time.

It has been argued, based on the evidence of Caesar, that Druidism originated in Britain, and this has been, rather oddly, taken to mean that the Druids were here *before* the arrival of the Celts in these lands. It seems an obvious contention that what is really meant is either that the Druids came to the fore in Britain after the coming of the Celts to these islands or that they came with the Celts. A further suggestion has been put forward by Peter Berresford Ellis: that the Druids were present throughout the Celtic world from an early time and that they continued to be active for far longer than is generally accepted but were not always called by the name 'Druid'. This certainly seems to be a reasonable theory and accounts for the apparent disappearance of the Druids after the onset of Christianity. However, it perhaps means no more than the already well-established notion that the Druids, along with other 'pagan' factions, simply went 'underground' as Christianity became the official religion in Britain and remained hidden but still active for a long time after that.

Several often-repeated misconceptions have arisen because of this uncertainty about the time during which the Druids were active. It is, for example, astonishing that many people still believe that the Druids were responsible for the construction of Stonehenge and of most of the other standing stones and circles that pepper the landscape of Britain. The fact that these structures pre-date the arrival of the Celts by several thousand years is often overlooked. Solving this problem depends, of course, on the answer to the question: did the Druids come to Britain with the Celts or were they already present? If the latter view is held then it is perfectly possible to believe that the Druids *were* responsible for Stonehenge and its like. The term 'proto-Druid' has been coined recently by those seeking to prove that the precursors of the classical Druids may have been responsible for the creation of the stone circles, and the term is also used to suggest that a pre-Celtic priesthood existed. The question is, however, by no means resolved.

An accusation frequently levelled against the ancient Druids is that they practised human sacrifice. There is, however, little evidence to support this view. That the Celts, as a race, believed in the willing sacrifice of a life for the good of the people is incontrovertible, but it is often forgotten that such sacrifices were made willingly and were not coerced.

It is also said that the Romans were shocked by the brutality of the Druid religion. This is, of course, an absurd criticism from a race that was famed the length and breadth of the world for its savagery. It is, in fact, true that the Celts were horrified by the barbarity of their Roman 'conquerers'. This is well illustrated in the story of the Celtic hero Caractacus, who, after leading an initially successful uprising against the Romans, found himself trapped and voluntarily gave himself up in order to save his people from slaughter. He was taken in chains to Rome, dragged through the streets and then confined in a cage for two years before being publicly strangled.

I have tried in this book to present a cross-section that goes right through the many layers of the history of Druidism, showing where and when certain ideas originated and how they have contributed to the view of Druidry that is current today. I hold no particular brief for or against much of the material presented here. As a Druid myself, I acknowledge the contribution of writers such as Godfrey Higgins, John Toland and Edward Davies to contemporary practice, while as a writer and researcher into the ancient mysteries of this land, I may have reservations about both their scholarship and the conclusions they draw. Modern-day Druids are not gullible, uncritical beings who will accept any written wisdom as fact. The quality of questioning, combined with an eagerness to learn, are two of the most noticeable characteristics of those with whom I have come in contact.

The element of wish-fulfilment and the desire to live in the past that coloured much early work on the subject are largely absent from the more recent writings on the subject by those who see Druidry as a viable path in today's world, although one has only to turn to the *Druid Journal* for 1930, where the following verse appears, to see that it has not been wholly banished:

Back to the past we all must go! There is
One way for all within the great abyss
In which to-morrow, like to-day, must fall:
Thus Druids turn in faith to Cathoir Ghall.

Except for certain instances of profound inaccuracy, I have forborne to comment on the theories advanced in any of these works. On such questions as the origin and belief of the Druids, much remains to be said, and there are several modern reference books that set out the essentials and exercise their authors' own personal form of deconstructive criticism. Here I have preferred to leave the reader to make up his or her own mind, merely stating the case as clearly as possible in the editorial commentaries that precede each section as well as in this Introduction.

It is my hope that the collection as a whole will not only dispel some of the wilder theories still circulating but also prove a fertile soil upon which the continuing fascination with Druidry will continue to grow and flourish.

John Matthews
Oxford, 1995

Acknowledgements

I owe a debt of gratitude to several people who willingly gave up their time to search for out-of-the-way materials on Druidry. In particular to Philip and Stephanie Carr-Gomm for delving deep into the OBOD archives, and for their hospitality and for allowing me to reprint the essay by Ross Nichols; to my friend Clair North for spending several days at the New York Public Library looking up obscure articles; to Liz Murray for hunting up papers by the late Colin Murray; and to Adam McLean for giving me permission to reprint the essay by Colin, which first appeared in *The Alchemical Journal* for 1988. To all the others who made helpful suggestions – you know who you are – a big thanks. And as ever to my wife, Caitlín Matthews, for support and bibliographic information, and my son Emrys for continuing to be patient when I wasn't around to play.

J. M.

PART ONE

THE DAWN: THE BEGINNINGS OF DRUIDRY IN BRITAIN AND IRELAND

HE mystery of the Druids remains as unsolved today as it was in the seventeenth century, when learned antiquarians first began to study them, or even earlier, when the Romans first encountered them. Were they indigenous to these islands or did they arrive with the Celtic peoples around 600 BC? Were they solely a priesthood or were they also recognized as physicians, lawyers, soothsayers and philosophers? Were there indeed a number of Druid 'colleges' in Britain to which pupils came from the continent of Europe to learn the wisdom of these wise masters? These and other questions will arise throughout this collection. Some answers will be found within these pages; but other extracts will throw up as many questions as they answer.

As already noted in the Introduction, almost everything we know about the early history of the Druids comes from classical sources. These are, for the most part, incidental, little more than casual asides in the works of such writers as Suetonius, Strabo and Pliny. Yet each one helps to build up an overall picture of Druidism that, although by no means complete, has the ring of authenticity about it. The Druids emerge as learned, literate and skilled in many areas.

Almost everything else that has been written since builds on these fragmentary sources, and they will be encountered time and again throughout this volume in one form or another. They will be quoted, misquoted, paraphrased and bent every way possible to prove the pet theory of the particular author in whose works they appear. Thus they are given here first, not only as the earliest written records of the Druids, but in order that the reader can get some idea of the foundation upon which so much other material has been based.

They are given here in more or less chronological order and without commentary, standing witness to the Druids who, since they had no writing, left no account of themselves beyond the memory of the race they served. That memory, which has been kept alive into the present time by a legion of believers and non-believers, is still very much with us in the form of a recent upsurge of interest in Druidry. This has resulted either in the revival or forming of a number of contemporary orders. Some seventeen or eighteen of these currently exist, and there may be others that, because of secrecy or small numbers, exist unacknowledged alongside their larger siblings. (A list of those orders that are known to be active will be found at the back of this volume, while a more serious attempt at a chronological listing appears in the Introduction to Part Three.)

Following the classical accounts will be found a further set of soundings, taken from early Celtic literature, primarily from early medieval Ireland, which preserves among its literary remains a considerable amount of information not found in the accounts of Caesar and his near-contemporaries.

Even to begin to capture the essence of the rich Druidic lore to be found within Celtic literature is beyond the scope of this book (in fact, many of the best quotations will be found within the essays that follow). Instead, I have tried to assemble the widest range of quotations. Here you will find references to several famous Druids, who are often described as – and act like – magicians. They are wondrous beings, filled with wisdom and power, ranging from the art of shape-shifting to that of prophecy. You will find reference to, among others, a female Druid, Gaine, daughter of Gumor (see page 31) and to Cathbad, surely one of the wiliest and most powerful Druids in the tradition. And you will learn something of the skills they possessed and the training they underwent. In short, although this selection represents only the tiniest morsel of the wealth of Celtic literature, it is hoped that it will give both a balance to the more austere classical writings and an idea of the way in which Druids were perceived among their own people.

These writings did not, of course, achieve written form until long after the Druids were suppressed or had perished in the aftermath of Roman rule, but Ireland was never conquered and its traditions were preserved more or less intact. It was another invasion, that of Christianity, that destroyed much that might have remained about the lives of the Druids, although, in fact, there is evidence to suggest that there was a good deal of goodwill between Christian and Druid. An early text describing the life of Saint Bridget includes a Druid prophesy that her birth sees the coming of a remarkable soul into the world. It tells how she became a pupil of the Druids, who quickly discerned that she was meant for other things and that her way lay with Christ. There is no suggestion of enmity, and Druid and Christian exchange views and beliefs as equals.

Despite the ravages of time and custom, there is still a great deal within early and late Celtic literature that offers a fascinating glimpse into a strange and wonderful time, when Druids consulted the spirits and tossed spells at each other before opposing sides joined forces in more physical warfare. They represent another layer in the rich cake that has been systematically nibbled at by generations of those in search of the 'real' Druids.

It must, however, also be said that it is as easy to be misled by the Celtic material as by the classical. We still do not understand much of that marvellous race, and, despite the exhaustive efforts of modern scholarship, they remain as mysterious as they ever were. The word 'Celt' itself comes from a Greek transcription of *keltoi*, an original Celtic word meaning the 'hidden' or 'secret' people, and the Druids themselves are as elusive and hidden in their own right.

Both sets of references include only those that refer directly to the Druids; those of a briefer nature are omitted.

Finally in this opening section, there are a number of commentaries that develop some of the above material in various ways – for the most part serious in intent and bestrewn with fewer of the wilder flights that colour the seventeenth- to early nineteenth-century accounts of Druidry. To begin with there is the chapter on the function and beliefs of the Druids from P.W. Joyce's 1903 book *A Social History of Ancient Ireland*, which assembles most of the important themes and evidence for the tradition of Druidry in the Celtic world. This is followed by Canon MacCulloch's learned account of some of the theories current in 1908 at the time when he was writing, thus setting the scene for much of what was to follow.

Next comes an important article, also published in 1908, by the Celtic scholar Julius Pokorny, which shows the reality behind much of the speculation that arose during the seventeenth, eighteenth and nineteenth centuries. Indeed, Pokorny's article is still one of the least cranky of those reproduced here, although he makes the curious suggestion that the Druids must have originated elsewhere because they are never mentioned in connection with the oak in Celtic literature – a manifestly untrue statement.

Pokorny belongs to the school of 'pre-Aryanists', who believed that the Druids originated earlier than the Celtic peoples and were already here when the latter invaded these islands in the seventh century BC. There is some justification for this idea – such as the fact that there are no classical references to the Druids before the time of the Celtic settlement of Britain and Ireland – but this may mean no more than that the Druids developed as a priestly caste at this time.

T. Rice Holmes, arguably one of the finest scholars of Caesar's writings, discusses the Roman usage of the information currently available on the Druids. Holmes's work has yet to be bettered by more recent scholars, and he offers some remarkable insights into the relationship between the Celts and the Romans.

This section is rounded off by a chapter by the modern antiquarian, Lewis Spence, whose admirable discussion considers some of the many theories that have been developed throughout the ages since the Druids were suppressed by Rome's legions.

With this information taken on board, we will be ready to embark on our voyage through the wilder reaches of romance that characterize so much of what Algernon Herbert, writing in 1891, called 'the neo-Druidic heresy'.

THE CLASSICAL
ACCOUNTS

From Caesar to Clement of Alexandria

Julius Caesar (100–44 bc)

They [the Druids] preside over sacred things, have the charge of public and private sacrifices, and explain their religion. To them a great number of youths have recourse for the sake of acquiring instruction, and they are in great honour among them. For they generally settle all their disputes, both public and private; and if there is any transgression perpetrated, any murder committed, or any dispute about inheritance or boundaries, they decide in respect of them; they appoint rewards and penalties; and if any private or public person abides not by their decree, they restrain him from the sacrifices. This with them is the most severe punishment. Whoever are so interdicted, are ranked in the number of the impious and wicked; all forsake them, and shun their company and conversation, lest they should suffer disadvantage from contagion with them: nor is legal right rendered to them when they sue it, nor any honour conferred upon them. But one presides over all these Druids, who possesses the supreme authority among them. At his death, if any one of the other excels in dignity, the same succeeds him: but if several have equal pretensions, the president is elected by the votes of the Druids, sometimes even they contend about the supreme dignity by force of arms. At a certain time of the year, they assemble in session on a consecrated spot in the confines of the Carnutes, which is considered the central region of the whole of Gaul. Thither all, who have any disputes, come together from every side, and acquiesce in their judgments and decisions. The institution of Druids is thought to have originated in Britain, and to have been thence introduced into Gaul, and even now, those who wish to become more accurately acquainted with it, generally repair thither for the sake of learning it . . .

The Druids usually abstain from war, nor do they pay taxes together with the others; they have exemption from warfare, and the free use of all things. Instigated by such advantages, many resort to their school even of their own accord, whilst others are sent by their parents and relations. There they are said to learn thoroughly a great number of verses. On that account, some continue at their education for twenty years. Nor do they deem it lawful to commit those things to writing; though, generally, in other cases and in their public and private accounts, they use Greek letters. They appear to me to have established this custom for two reasons; because they would not have their tenets published, and because they would not have those, who learn them, by trusting to letters, neglect the exercise of memory; since it generally happens, that, owing to the safeguard of letters, they relax their diligence in learning, as well as their memory. In particular they wish to inculcate this idea, that souls do not die, but pass after death from one body to another; and they think that by this means men are very much instigated to the exercise of bravery, the fear of death being despised. They also dispute largely concerning the stars and their motion, the magnitude of the world and the earth, the nature of things, the force and power of the immortal gods, and instruct the youth in their principles . . .

The whole nation of the Gauls is very much given to religious observances, and on that account, those who are afflicted with grievous diseases, and those who are engaged in battles and perils, either immolate men as sacrifices, or vow that they will immolate themselves, and they employ the Druids as ministers of those sacrifices; because they think that, if the life of man is not given for the life of man, the immortal gods cannot be appeased; they have also instituted public sacrifices of the same kind. Some have images of immense size, the limbs of which, interwoven with twigs, they fill with living men, and the same being set on fire, the men, surrounded by the flames, are put to death. They think that the punishment of those who are caught in theft or pillage, or in any other wicked act, is more acceptable to the immortal gods; but when there is a deficiency of such evil doers, they have recourse even to the punishment of the innocent. . . .

They chiefly worship the god Mercury; of him they have many images, him they consider as the inventor of all arts, as the guide of ways and journeys, and as possessing the greatest power for obtaining money and merchandise. After him, they worship Apollo, Mars, Jupiter, and Minerva. Concerning them they have almost the same opinion as other nations, namely: that Apollo wards off diseases; that Minerva instructs them in the principles of works and arts; that Jupiter holds the empire of heaven; and that Mars rules wars. To him, when they have determined to engage in battle, they generally vow those things which they shall have captured in war. When they are victorious, they sacrifice the captured animals; and pile up the other things in one place.

The Gauls declare that they have all sprung from their father Pluto, and this they say was delivered to them by the Druids.

De Bello Gallico, VI, 13–18
(translated by J. Williams ab Ithel)

Cicero (106–43 BC)

Nor is the practice of divination disregarded even among uncivilised tribes, if indeed there are Druids in Gaul – and there are, for I knew one of them myself, Divitiacus, the Aeduan, your guest and eulogist. He claimed to have that knowledge of nature which the Greeks call 'physiologia,' and he used to make predictions, sometimes by means of augury and sometimes by means of conjecture.

De Divinatione, I, 41
(translated by T.D. Kendrick)

Fourth face (lower section) of stone altar, Mavilly.

Diodorus Siculus (21 BC)

The Pythagorean doctrine prevails among them (the Gauls), teaching that the souls of men are immortal and live again for a fixed number of years inhabited in another body. . . .

And there are among them (the Gauls) composers of verses whom they call Bards; these singing to instruments similar to a lyre, applaud some, while they vituperate others.

They have philosophers and theologians who are held in much honour and are called Druids; they have sooth-sayers too of great renown who tell the future by watching the flights of birds and by observation of the entrails of victims; and every one waits upon their word. When they attempt divination upon important matters they practice a strange and incredible custom, for they kill a man by a knife-stab in the region above the midriff, and after his fall they foretell the future by the convulsions of his limbs and the pouring of his blood, a form of divination in which they have full confidence, as it is of old tradition. It is a custom of the Gauls that no one performs a sacrifice without the assistance of a philosopher, for they say that offerings to the gods ought only to be made through the mediation of these men, who are learned in the divine nature and, so to speak, familiar with it, and it is through their agency that the blessings of the gods should properly be sought. It is not only in times of peace, but in war also, that these seers have authority, and the incantations of the bards have effect on friends and foes alike. Often when the combatants are ranged face to face, and swords are drawn and spears bristling, these men come between the armies and stay the battle, just as wild beasts are sometimes held spellbound. Thus even among the most savage barbarians anger yields to wisdom, and Mars is shamed before the Muses.

Histories, V, 28 and 31
(translated by T.D. Kendrick)

Strabo (64/3 BC–21 AD)

Among [the Gauls] there are generally three classes to whom special honour is paid, viz. the Bards, the Uatis[1] and the Druids. The Bards composed and sung odes; the Uatis attended to the sacrifices and studied nature; while the Druids studied nature and moral philosophy. So confident are the people in the justice of the Druids that they refer all private and public disputes to them; and these men on many occasions have made peace between armies actually drawn up for battle. All murder cases in particular are referred to them. When there are a large number of these cases they imagine that the harvest will be plentiful. Both these and the others (i.e. the Bards and Uatis) assert that the soul is immortal, and that the world is indestructible, although sometimes great changes are brought about by fire and water.

To their simplicity and vehemence they add much folly, arrogance and love of ornament. Around their necks they wear gold collars, on their arms and wrists they have bracelets, and those of good position among them clothe themselves in dyed garments, worked with gold. Their fickle, impressionable nature makes them intolerable in victory and faint-hearted in defeat. Besides their arrogance they have a brutal and senseless custom – common among many northern nations – of hanging the heads of their enemies from the neck of their horses when returning from battle, and of nailing them as an exhibition before their doors when they arrive home.

Poseidonius says that he witnessed this in many different places, and was shocked at first, but in time its frequency made him familiar with it. The heads of illustrious men are embalmed with cedar [oil], and exhibited to strangers; but they would not sell them for their weight in gold. The Romans however put a stop to these customs, as well as to their manner of offering sacrifices and practising divination, which were quite contrary to our established ritual. They would strike the victim in the back with a sword, and divine from his convulsive throes. They never sacrifice without the Druids. They are said to have other manners of sacrificing their human victims; that they pierce some with arrows, crucify others in their temples, and that they prepare a stack of hay and wood which they set on fire after having placed cattle, all kinds of animals, and men in it.

Geographica, IV, 4, 197–8
(translated by W. Dinan)

Ammianus Marcellinus (AD *c*.330–395)

According to the Druids, a part of the population (of Gaul) was indigenous, but some of the people came from outlying islands and lands beyond the Rhine, driven from their homes by repeated wars and by the inroads of the sea . . .

In these regions, as the people gradually became civilised, attention to the gentler arts became commoner, a study introduced by the Bards, and the Euhages [Orates], and the Druids. It was the custom of the Bards to celebrate the brave deeds of their famous men in epic verse accompanied by the sweet strains of the lyre, while the Euhages strove to explain the high mysteries of nature. Between them came the Druids, men of greater talent, members of the intimate fellowship of the Pythagorean faith; they were up-lifted by searchings into secret and sublime things, and with grand contempt for mortal lot they professed the immortality of the soul.

Works, XV, 9, 4–8
(translated by T.D. Kendrick)

Diogenes Laertius (third century AD)

Some say that the study of philosophy was of barbarian origin. For the Persians had their *Magi*, the Babylonians or the Assyrians the *Chaldeans*, the Indians their *Gymnosophists*, while the Kelts and the Galatae had seers called *Druids* and *Semnotheoi*, or so Aristotle says in the 'Magic', and Sotion in the twenty-third book of his 'Succession of Philosophers.' . . .

Those who think that philosophy is an invention of the barbarians explain the systems prevailing among each people. They say that the Gymnosophists and Druids make their pronouncements by means of riddles and dark sayings, teaching that the gods must be worshipped, and no evil done, and manly behaviour maintained.

Vitae, Introduction, I, 5
(translated by T.D. Kendrick)

Suetonius (AD *c.*70–*c.*140)

He (the Emperor Claudius) very thoroughly suppressed the barbarous and inhuman religion of the Druids in Gaul, which in the time of Augustus had merely been forbidden to Roman citizens.

Claudius, 25
(translated by T.D. Kendrick)

Pomponius Mela (AD 18–*c.*75)

There still remain traces of atrocious customs no longer practised, and although they now refrain from outright slaughter, yet they still draw blood from the victims led to the altar. They have, however, their own kind of eloquence, and teachers of wisdom called Druids. These profess to know the size and shape of the world, the movements of the heavens and of the stars, and the will of the gods. They teach many things to the nobles of Gaul in a course of instruction lasting as long as twenty years, meeting in secret either in a cave or in secluded dales. One of their dogmas has come to common knowledge, namely, that souls are eternal and that there is another life in the infernal regions, and this has been permitted manifestly because it makes the multitude readier for war. And it is for this reason too that they burn or bury with their dead, things appropriate to them in life, and that in times past they even used to defer the completion of business and the payment of debts until their arrival in another world. Indeed, there were some of them who flung themselves willingly on the funeral piles of their relatives in order to share the new life with them.

De Situ Orbis, III, 2, 18 and 19
(translated by T.D. Kendrick)

Lucan (AD 39–65)

And you, O Druids, now that the clash of battle is stilled, once more have you returned to your barbarous ceremonies and to the savage usage of your holy rites. To you alone it is given to know the truth about the gods and deities of the sky, or else you alone are ignorant of this truth. The innermost groves of far-off forests are your abodes. And it is you who say that the shades of the dead seek not the silent land of Erebus and the pale halls of Pluto; rather, you tell us that the same spirit has a body again elsewhere, and that death, if what you sing is true, is but the mid-point of long life.

Pharsalia, I, 450–8
(translated by T.D. Kendrick)

Pliny (AD 23–79)

Here we must mention the awe felt for this plant by the Gauls. The Druids – for so their magicians are called – held nothing more sacred than the mistletoe and the tree that bears it, always supposing that tree to be the oak. But they choose groves formed of oaks for the sake of the tree alone, and they never perform any of their rites except in the presence of a branch of it; so that it seems probable that the priests themselves may derive their name from the Greek word for that tree. In fact, they think that everything that grows on it has been sent from heaven and is a proof that the tree was chosen by the god himself. The mistletoe, however, is found but rarely upon the oak; and when found, is gathered with due religious ceremony, if possible on the sixth day of the moon (for it is by the moon that they measure their months and years, and also their *ages* of thirty years). They choose this day because the moon, though not yet in the middle of her course, has already considerable influence. They call the mistletoe by a name meaning, in their language, the all-healing. Having made preparation for sacrifice and a banquet beneath the trees, they bring thither two white bulls, whose horns are bound then for the first time. Clad in a white robe, the priest ascends the tree and cuts the mistletoe with a golden sickle, and it is received by others in a white cloak. Then they kill the victims, praying that God will render this gift of his propitous to those to whom he has granted it. They believe that the mistletoe, taken in drink, imparts fecundity to barren animals, and that it is an antidote for all poisons. Such are the religious feelings that are entertained towards trifling things by many peoples.

Historia Naturalis, XVI, 249

Similar to savin is the plant called *selago*. It is gathered without using iron and by passing the right hand through the left sleeve of the tunic, as though in the act of committing a theft. The clothing must be white, the feet washed and bare, and an offering of wine and bread made before the gathering. The Druids of Gaul say that the plant should be carried as a charm against every kind of evil, and that the smoke of it is good for diseases of the eyes.

Historia Naturalis, XXIV, 103

The Druids, also, use a certain marsh-plant that they call *samolus*, this must be gathered with the left hand, when fasting, and is a charm against the diseases of cattle. But the gatherer must not look behind him, nor lay the plant anywhere except in the drinking-troughs.

Historia Naturalis, XXIV, 104

There is also another kind of egg, of much renown in the Gallic provinces, but ignored by the Greeks. In the summer, numberless snakes entwine themselves into a ball, held together by a secretion from their bodies and by their spittle. This is called *anguinum*. The Druids say that hissing serpents throw this up into the air, and that it must be caught in a cloak, and not allowed to touch the ground; and that one must instantly take to flight on horseback, as the serpents will pursue until some stream cuts them off. It may be tested, they say, by seeing if it floats against the current of a river, even though it be set in gold. But as it is the way of magicians to cast a cunning veil about their frauds, they pretend that these eggs can only be taken on a certain day of the moon, as though it rested with mankind to make the moon and the serpents accord as to the moment of the operation. I myself, however, have seen one of these eggs; it was round, and about as large as a smallish apple; the shell was cartalaginous, and pocked like the arms of a polypus. The Druids esteem it highly. It is said to ensure success in law-suits and a favourable reception with princes; but this is false, because a man of the Vocontii, who was also a Roman knight, kept one of these eggs in his bosom during a trial, and was put to death by the Emperor Claudius, as far as I can see, for that reason alone.

Historia Naturalis, XXIX, 52

It (magic) flourished in the Gallic provinces, too, even down to a period within our memory; for it was in the time of the Emperor Tiberius that a decree was issued against their Druids and the whole tribe of diviners and physicians. But why mention all this about a practice that has even crossed the ocean and penetrated to the utmost parts of the earth? At the present day, Britannia is still fascinated by magic, and performs its rites with so much ceremony that it almost seems as though it was she who had imparted the cult to the Persians To such a degree do peoples throughout the whole world, although unlike and quite unknown to one another, agree upon this one point. Therefore we cannot too highly appreciate our debt to the Romans for having put an end to this monstrous cult, whereby to murder a man was an act of the greatest devoutness, and to eat his flesh most beneficial.

Historia Naturalis, XXX, 13
(translated by T.D. Kendrick)

Tacitus (AD *c.*55–*c.*115)

On the shore stood the opposing army with its dense array of armed warriors, while between the ranks dashed women in black attire like the Furies, with hair dishevelled, waing brands. All around, the Druids, lifting up their hands to heaven and pouring forth dreadful imprecations, scared our soldiers by the unfamiliar sight, so that, as if their limbs were paralysed, they stood motionless and exposed to wounds. Then urged by their general's appeal and mutual encouragements not to quail before a troup of frenzied women, they bore the standards onwards, smote down all resistance, and wrapped the foe in the flames of his own brands. A force was next set over the conquered, and their groves, devoted to inhuman superstitions, were destroyed. They deemed it, indeed, a duty to cover their altars with the blood of captives and to consult their deities through human entrails.

Annals, XIV, 30

The Gauls, they remembered, had captured the city in former days, but, as the abode of Jupiter was uninjured, the Empire had survived; whereas now the Druids declared, with the prophetic utterances of an idle superstition, that this fatal conflagration (of the Capitol) was a sign of the anger of heaven, and portended universal empire for the Transalpine nations.

Histories, IV, 54
(translated by A.J. Church and T.D. Broadribb)

Dion Chrysostom (AD 354–407)

The Persians, I think, have men called Magi . . . the Egyptians, their priests . . . and the Indians, their Brahmins. On the other hand, the Kelts have men called Druids, who concern themselves with divination and all branches of wisdom. And without their advice even kings dared not resolve upon nor execute any plan, so that in truth it was they who ruled, while the kings, who sat on golden thrones and fared sumptuously in their palaces, became mere ministers of the Druids' will.

Orations, XLIX
(translated by T.D. Kendrick)

Lampridius (third century AD)

While he (Alexander Severus) was on his way, a Druidess cried out to him in the Gallic tongue, 'Go forward, but hope not for victory, nor put trust in thy soldiers.'

Alexander Severus, LIX, 5
(translated by T.D. Kendrick)

Vopiscus (third century AD)

When Diocletian, so my grandfather told me, was sojourning in a tavern in the land of the Tongri in Gaul, at the time when he was still of humble rank in the army, and had occasion to settle the daily account for his keep with a certain druidess, this woman said to him, 'You are far too greedy and far too economical, O Diocletian.' Whereto he replied, jestingly, 'I will be more liberal when I am emperor,' to which the druidess answered, 'Laugh not, Diocletian, for when you have killed The Boar, you will indeed be emperor.'

Numerianus, XIV
(translated by T.D. Kenrick)

He [Asclepiodotus] used to say that on a certain occasion Aurelian consulted the Gaulish druidesses to find out whether his descendants would remain in possession of the imperial crown. These women told him that no name would become more illustrious in the state annals than that of the line of Claudius. It is true, of course, that the present Emperor Constantius is of the same stock, and I think that his descendants will assuredly attain to the glory foretold by the druidesses.

Aurelianus, XLIII, 4 and 5
(translated by T.D. Kendrick)

Decimus Magnus Ausonius (AD *c.*310–*c.*395)

Attius Patera, the Elder, the Rhetorician Patera, renowned speaker, although in years you outpassed the men named earlier, yet, seeing that your prime was in the age next before my own, and that in my youth I saw you in your old age, you shall not lack the tribute of my sad dirge, teacher of mighty rhetoricians. If report does not lie, you were sprung from the stock of the Druids of Bayeux, and traced your hallowed line from the temple of Belenus; and hence the names borne by your family: you are called Patera; so the mystic votaries call the servants of Apollo. Your father and your brother were named after Phoebus, and your own son after Delphi. In that age there was none who had such knowledge as you, such swift and rolling eloquence. Sound in memory as in learning, you had the gift of clear expression cast in sonorous and well-chosen phrase; your wit was chastened and without a spice of bitterness: sparing of food and wine, cheerful, modest, comely in person, even in age you were as an eagle or a steed grown old.

Poems Commemorating the Professors of Bordeaux
(translated by H.G.E. White)

Let Macrinus be named amongst these: to him I was entrusted first when a boy; and Sucuro, the freedman's son, temperate and well-suited to form youthful minds. You too, Concordius, were another such, you who, fleeing your country, took in exchange a chair of little profit in a foreign town. Nor must I leave unmentioned the old man Phoebicius, who, though the keeper of Belenus' temple, got no profit thereby. Yet he, sprung, as rumour goes, from the stock of the Druids of Armorica (Brittany), obtained a chair at Bordeaux by his son's help: long may his line endure!

Poems Commemorating the Professors of Bordeaux
(translated by H.G.E. White)

Hippolytus (AD *c.*170–*c.*236)

The Keltic Druids applied themselves thoroughly to the Pythagorean philosophy, being urged to this pursuit by Zamolxis, the slave of Pythagoras, a Thracian by birth, who came to those parts after the death of Pythagoras, and gave them opportunity of studying the system. And the Kelts believe in their Druids as seers and prophets because they can foretell certain events by the Pythagorean reckoning and calculations. We will not pass over the origins of their learning in silence, since some have presumed to make distinct schools of the philosophies of these peoples. Indeed, the Druids also practice the magic arts.

Philosophumena, I, xxv
(translated by T.D. Kendrick)

Clement of Alexandria (AD *c.*150–*c.*216)

Alexander, in his book 'On the Pythagorean Symbols,' relates that Pythagoras was a pupil of Nazaratus the Assyrian . . . and will have it that, in addition to these, Pythagoras was a hearer of the Galatae and the Brahmins . . .

Thus philosophy, a science of the highest utility, flourished in antiquity among the barbarians, shedding its light over the nations. And afterwards it came to Greece. First in its ranks were the prophets of the Egyptians; and the Chaldeans among the Assyrians; and the Druids among the Gauls; and the Samanaeans among the Bactrians; and the philosophers of the Kelts; and the Magi of the Persians.

Stromata, I, xv, 70, 1–71, 3
(translated by T.D. Kendrick)

THE DRUIDS IN
EARLY IRELAND

Extracts from the Earliest Manuscripts

Trostan

The leaders of [the Pictish] fleet were Gud and his son Cathluan; and the reason why Criomhthann entered into friendship with them was because some British nobles, who were called Tuatha Fiodhgha, were making conquests in the Fotharta on either side of the mouth of the Slaney. Such were these people that the weapons of every one of them were poisoned, so that, be the wound inflicted by them small or great, no remedy whatever availed the wounded man, but he must die. Criomhthann heard that there was a skilful druid called Trostan amongst the Cruithnigh who could furnish himself and his people with an antidote against the poison with which the weapons of the Tuatha Fiodhgha were wont to be charged; and he asked Triostan what remedy he should use against the poison of the weapons of those people we have mentioned. 'Get thrice fifty white hornless cows milked,' said Trostan, 'and let the milk got from them be placed in a hollow in the middle of the plain in which you are wont to meet them in battle, and offer them battle on that same plain; and let each one of your followers who shall have been wounded by them go to the hollow and bathe, and he will be healed from the venom of the poison.' Criomhthann did as the druid had advised, and fought the Battle of Ard Leamhnachta against the Tuatha Fiodhgha. He defeated and executed great slaughter on them in that place. From this event, and from the battle which took place, the battle has been called the Battle of Ard Leamhnachta ever since. And in proof of this account the poet has composed the following historic poem:

> Ard Leamhnachta in the southern country
> Each noble and bard may inquire
> Whence is derived the name of the land
> Which it has borne from the time of Criomhthann;

Criomhthann Sciaithbheal it was who fought,
To prevent the slaughter of his warriors,
Protecting them from the sharp poison of the weapons
Of the hateful, horrid giants.

Six of the Cruithnigh, God so ordained,
Came from the land of Thrace,
Soilen, Ulpia, Neachtain the noble,
Aonghus, Leathan, and Trostan.

God granted them, through might
To heal them from the sharp poison of the wounds,
And to protect them from the bitter venom of the weapons
Of the powerful, very fierce giants.

The true knowledge obtained for them
By the druid of the Cruithnigh, at once, was
That thrice fifty hornless cows of the plain
Be milked in one deep hollow.

The battle was pressingly fought
Around the hollow where the new milk was,
And the battle went strongly against

The giants of high Banbha.

from *The History of Ireland* by Geoffrey Keating

Cormac's Druids

It was ordained in Cormac's time that every high king of Ireland should keep ten officers in constant attendance on him, who did not separate from him as a rule, namely, a prince, a brehon, a druid, a physician, a bard, a seancha, a musician, and three stewards: the prince to be a body-attendant on the king; the brehon to explain the customs and laws of the country in the king's presence; a druid to offer sacrifices, and to forebode good or evil to the country by means of his skill and magic; a physician to heal the king and his queen and the rest of the household; a filé to compose satire or panegyric for each one according to his good or evil deeds; a seancha to preserve the genealogies, the history, and transactions of the nobles from age to age; a musician to play music, and to chant poems and songs in the presence of the king; and three stewards with their company of attendants and cupbearers to wait on the king, and attend to his wants. This custom was kept from the time of Cormac to the death of Brian son of Cinneide without change, except that, since the kings of Ireland received the Faith of Christ, an ecclesiastical chaplain took the place of the druid, to declare and explain the precepts and the laws of God to the king, and to his household. Thus does the seancha set forth the matter just stated:

There are ten round the king,
Without rivalry, without anxiety –
I can name them all,
Both prince and official.

There are appointed to attend on gracious kings,
A brehon, a filé, and a prince;
The king who has not the three named,
His honour-price is not sanctioned by Fenian law.

A chaplain to expound the gospels,
A seancha who sets right every mishap,
A musician skilled in harp-strings also:
For these fine and honour-price are appointed.

The fourth person is a physician,
To look to each one's disease;
Three stewards to serve famous companies,
I shall record for the hosts of Erin.

The king who shall not have all these
Has no right to be in the Reim Rioghruidhe;
In the house of Tara shall not pass his time
A king not having the ten.

On account of the excellence of Cormac's deeds, and judgments, and laws, God gave him the light of the Faith seven years before his death. And, accordingly, he refused to adore gods made with hands; and he set himself to reverence and honour the true God; so that he was the third man in Ireland who believed before the coming of Patrick. Conchubhar son of Neasa was the first to receive the faith when he heard from Bacrach the druid that the Jewish people would put Christ to death by torment; Morann son of Maon was the second person; and Cormac son of Art was the third. It was at Tara that Cormac usually resided, according to the practice of his predecessors, until his eye was destroyed by Aonghus Gaoibuaibhtheach, as we have said above; and thenceforward he abode in Achaill, in the house of Cleiteach, and in Ceanannus. For the men of Ireland considered it neither becoming nor auspicious that a king with a blemish should abide in Tara; and for this reason Cormac gave over the sovereignty to his son Cairbre Lithfeachair; and he gave up Tara to him, retiring himself to the house of Cleiteach and to Achaill, not far from Tara. And it was there he composed the Teagaisc Riogh, setting forth what a king should be, as we have said above, and how he should rule the people through their laws. And from the time that Cormac gave over the sovereignty, he believed only in the one God of heaven.

On a certain day, when Cormac was in the house of Cleiteach, the druids were worshipping the golden calf in his presence; and the general body of the people were worshipping it after the manner of the druids. Maoilgheann the druid asked Cormac why he was adoring the golden calf and the gods like the rest. 'I will not,' said Cormac, 'worship a stock made by my own artificer; and it were better to worship the person who made it; for he is nobler than the stock.' Maoilgheann the druid excited the golden calf so that he made a bound before them all. 'Dost thou see that, O Cormac?' said Maoilgheann. 'Although I see,' said Cormac, 'I will worship only the God of heaven, of earth, and of hell.'

After this his food was cooked for the king; and he began to eat a portion of a salmon from the Boinn. Thereupon the demon sprites came, at the instigation of Maoilgheann the druid, and they killed the king. Others say that it was a salmon-bone that stuck in his throat and choked him. For it was eating fish he was when the sprites, or demons of the air, choked him.

When the king was in the throes of death, he directed his officers not to bury his body at the Brugh, where the kings of Tara had been buried up to then. But when the people were conveying his body to the Brugh to be buried, the sprites put it into the greatly swollen river thrice before them; for they did not wish to let his body into the burial-place of the idolaters, since he believed in the true God. And the fourth time its bearers carried the body into the river; and it was snatched away from them by the current of the Boinn, and it reached Ros na Riogh; and it became separated from the *fuad*, or bier, whence the ford Ath Fuaid on the Boinn is named. They mourned for him there; and his grave was made; and he was buried at Ros na Riogh. A long time after this, Columcille came to that place, and found the head of king Cormac there, and buried it. Columcille remained in the place till he had said thirty Masses above his grave, and there is now a church in the place.

As we have spoken of the druids here, I think it will be meet to give some account of them, and especially of their sacrifices, and of their geasa, as will appear below. There are, indeed, to be seen in Ireland to-day in many places, as relics of the Pagan times, many very wide flag-stones, and pillar-stones supporting them; and these are called idol-altars in the old books, while the general populace call them beds of the Fian, as they are ignorant of the reason of their construction. On these altars the druids were wont to make their sacrifices in the olden time, and slay their he-goats, their bulls, and their rams; and the druids themselves went on their knees under the blood as it dropped from their victims, to cleanse themselves from the uncleanness of their sins, as the high priest did among the Jewish people when he went under the sacrificial bridge to let the blood of the victims flow over him, and hence he was called Pontifex, that is, bridgewright.

As to the druids, the use they made of the hides of the bulls offered in sacrifice was to keep them for the purpose of making conjuration, or laying geasa on the demons; and many are the ways in which they laid geasa on them, such as to keep looking at their own images in water, or gaze on the clouds of heaven, or keep listening to the noise of the wind or the chattering of birds. But when all these expedients failed them, and they were obliged to do their utmost, what they did was, to make round wattles of the quicken tree, and to spread thereon the hides of the bulls offered in sacrifice, putting the side which had been next the flesh uppermost, and thus relying on their geasa to summon the demons to get information from them, as the conjurer does nowadays in the circus; whence the old saw has since been current which says that one has gone on his wattles of knowledge when he has done his utmost to obtain information.

from *The History of Ireland* by Geoffrey Keating

The Druids of Erin and Gaine, Daughter of Gumor

Mide, place of the eager steeds,
the road whereon Art the Solitary used to be
the lowland full of the splendour of Lugaid . . .
the level ground of the clan of Conn and Cobthach.

Whence is the name of Meath given to the plain?
to the heritage of the seed of Conn the Hundred Fighter?
what pure bold scion (bright the hero),
what warrior was it when it got its naming?

Mide it was, the ardent son of Brath
the host-leading son of Deaith;
for he kindled a mystic fire
above the race of Nemed, seizer of hostages.

Seven years good ablaze
was the fire, it was a sure truce:
so that he shed the fierceness of the fire for a time
over the four quarters of Erin.

So that it is from this fire in truth
(it is not a rash saying, it is not a falsehood)
that their head-man has a right for ever
over every chief hearth of Erin.

So the right belongs to the gentle heir
of the plain of Mide mirthful and bright;
even a measure of fine meal with a white pig
for every rooftreee in Erin.

And they said (no small grief it was),
the druids of Erin all together,
'It is an ill smoke was brought to us eastward:
it has brought an ill mood to our mind.'

Then Mide the untiring assembled
the druids of Erin into one house,
and cut their tongues (a harsh presage)
out of the heads of the strong and noble druids.

And he buried them under the earth
of Uisnech in mighty Mide,
and sat him down over their tongues,
he, the chief seer and chief poet.

Gaine daughter of pure Gumor,
nurse of mead-loving Mide,
surpassed all women though she was silent;
she was learned and a seer and a chief druid.

And Gaine said with lamentation,
before Mide of the great victory,
'It is *over somewhat* our house was built,
and hence shall Uisnech be named.'

Uisnech and mighty Mide
from which Erin of the red weapons is held,
according as the learned relate the cutting,
hence is derived its story.

Guard, O God, Aed ua Carthaig
from hell with its storms,
God enjoining his clear protection
on the mead-loving king of Meath.

from *The Metrical Dindsenchas*
(edited and translated by E. Gwynn 1903)

Mogh Ruith

The Encampment of Drom Damhghairé took place under the following circumstances. The celebrated Cormac Mac Airt commenced his reign as monarch of Erinn at Tara, AD 213. It would appear that his hospitality and munificence soon exhausted the royal revenues, so that in a short time he found it necessary not only to curtail his expenditure, but to seek immediate means of replenishing his coffers. In this difficulty he was advised to make a claim on the province of Munster for a double tribute, on the plea that although there were properly two provinces of Munster, yet they had never paid more than the tribute of one Cormac therefore, on these very questionable grounds, sent his messengers into Munster to demand a second tribute for the same year. Fiacha

Muilleathan (the son of Eoghan Mór, son of Oilioll Olium) was king of Munster at the time, and he received the messengers of the monarch (at Cnoc Raffann, in Tipperary) with all the usual honours and attention. He denied the justness of Cormac's demands, but offered to send a sufficient supply of provisions to him as a present, for that occasion. The messengers returned to Tara with this answer, but Cormac would not listen to it, and he consulted his Druids on the probable success of an expedition into Munster. They, however, after having recourse (as we are told) to their divinations, gave him an unfavourable answer. Still, he would not be persuaded by them, but insisted on undertaking the expedition. He therefore mustered a large force, and marched directly to the hill of Damhghairé (now Cnoc Luingé, or Knocklong, in the south-east part of the county of Limerick, bordering on Tipperary). Here Cormac fixed his camp; and from this, with the aid of his Druids, by drying up the springs and streams of the province, he is said to have brought that great distress on the people of Munster which was described in a former lecture. Ultimately, the monarch and his Druids were overmastered by the superior power of the great Munster Druid, Mogh Ruith. This celebrated sage, one of the most renowned of those ages, is recorded to have completed his Druidical studies in the East, in the school of no less a master than Simon Magus; and it is even stated in this tract that Simon Magus himself was of the race of the Gaedhils of Erinn.

After Mogh Ruith had relieved the men of Munster from the drought and famine which Cormac's Druids had brought upon them, Cormac again took into council his chief and oldest Druid, Ciothruadh, and inquired of him what was best to be done. Ciothruadh answered that their last and only resource was to make a Druidic fire against the enemy. 'How is that to be made?' said Cormac. 'In this way,' said Ciothruadh.' Let our men go into the forest, and let them cut down and carry out loads of the quickbeam (i.e. the Mountain-ash, or roan-tree), of which large fires must be made; and when the fires are lighted, if the smoke goes southwards, then it will be well for you to press after it on the men of Munster; and if it is hither or northward the smoke comes, then, indeed, it will be full time for us to retreat with all our speed.' So, Cormac's men forthwith entered the forest, cut down the wood indicated, brought it out, and set it on fire.

Whilst this was going on, Mogh Ruith, perceiving what the northern Druids were preparing for, immediately ordered the men of Munster to go into the wood of Lethard, and each man to bring out a faggot of the roan-tree in his hand; and that the king only should bring out a shoulder-bundle from the side of the mountain, where it had grown under three shelters, namely, shelter from the (north-east) March wind, shelter from the sea wind, and shelter from the conflagration winds. The men soon returned with the wood to their camp; and the Druid Ceannmhair, Mogh Ruith's favourite pupil, built the wood up in the shape of a small triangular kitchen, with seven doors; whereas the northern fire (that prepared by Ciothruadh), on the other side, was but rudely heaped up, and had but three doors. 'The fire is ready now,' said Ceannmhair, 'all but to light it.' Mogh Ruith then ordered each man of the host to give him a shaving from the haft of his spear, which, when he had got, he mixed with butter and rolled up into a large ball, at the same time pronouncing those words in rhythmical lines:

I mix a roaring powerful fire;
It will clear the woods; it will blight the grass;
An angry flame of powerful speed;
It will rush up to the skies above.
It will subdue the wrath of all burning wood,
It will break a battle on the clans of *Conn* –

and with that he threw the ball into the fire, where it exploded with a tremendous noise.

'I shall bring the rout on them now,' said Mogh Ruith. 'Let my chariot be ready, and let each man of you have his horse by the bridle; for, if our fires incline but ever so little northwards, follow and charge the enemy.' He then blew his Druidical breath (says this strange tale) up into the sky, and it immediately became a threatening black cloud, which came down in a shower of blood upon the plain of Clāiré before him, and moved onwards from that to Tara, the Druid all the time pronouncing his rhythmical incantations. When the rushing of the bloody shower was heard in the northern camp, Cormac asked his Druid, Ciothruadh, what noise it was. 'A shower of blood,' said the Druid, 'which has been produced by a violent effort of Druidism. It is upon us its entire evil will fall.'

After this (the tale proceeds), Mogh Ruith said to his people: 'What is the condition of the flames from the two fires now?' [for Mogh Ruith was blind]. 'They are,' said they, 'chasing each other over the brow of the mountain, west and north, down to Druim Asail [now Tory Hill, near Croom, in the county of Limerick] and to the Shannon, and back again to the same place.' He asked again the state of the flames. 'They are in the same condition,' said they, 'but they have not left a tree in the plain of middle Munster that they have not burned.' Mogh asked again how the flames were. His people answered that 'they had risen up to the clouds of Heaven, and were like two fierce angry warriors chasing each other'. Then Mogh Ruith called for his 'dark-grey hornless bull-hide', and 'his white-speckled bird-headpiece, with its fluttering wings', and also 'his Druidic instruments', and he flew up into the air to the verge of the fires, and commenced to beat and turn them northwards. When Cormac's Druid, Ciothruadh, saw this, he also ascended to oppose Mogh Ruith; but the power of the latter prevailed, and he turned the fires northwards, and into Cormac's camp, where they fell, as well as [i.e. where also fell] the Druid Ciothruadh. Cormac, on this, ordered a quick retreat out of the province.

They were hotly pursued (we are then told), by the Munster men, led by Mogh Ruith in his chariot drawn by wild oxen, and with his Druidic bull-hide beside him. The pursuit continued beyond the border of the province, and into

Magh Raighné, in Ossory. And here Mogh Ruith asked, though he well knew, who were the nearest parties to them of the retreating foe. 'They are three tall grey headed men,' said they. 'They are Cormac's three Druids, Cicht, Ciotha, and Ciothruadh,' said he, 'and my gods have promised me to transform them into stones, when I should overtake them, if I could but blow my breath upon them.' And then he 'blew a Druidic breath' upon them, so that they were turned into stones; and these are the stones that are called the Flags of Raigné at this day.

The Siege of Drom Damhghairé
(summarized by Eugene O'Curry)

Cathbhadh

One day Conchubhar, king of Ulster, went to partake of a feast to the house of Feidhlimidh son of Dall, storyteller to Conchubhar. In the course of that feast the wife of Feidhlimidh gave birth to a beautiful daughter; and Cathbhadh the druid, who was present at the assembly on that occasion, foreboded and foretold of this daughter that great misfortune and mischief would befall the province on her account. When the warriors heard this, they sought to put her to death on the spot. 'By no means,' said Conchubhar; 'but I will take her and put her to nurse so that she may become my wife.' Deirdre was the name that Cathbhadh the druid gave her. Conchubhar placed her in a dwelling apart, with a tutor and a nurse to bring her up; and no one in the province was permitted to go into her presence but her tutor, her nurse, and Conchubhar's censorious woman, who was called Leabharcham. She continued under these regulations until she was marriageable, and until she excelled the women of her time in beauty. One snowy day it chanced that her tutor killed a calf to prepare food for her; and when the calf's blood was shed on the snow, a raven began to drink it. And when Deirdre observed this, she said to Leabharcham that she would like to have a husband having the three colours she beheld, namely, his hair of the colour of the raven, his cheek of the colour of the calf's blood, and his skin of the colour of the snow. 'Such a man is in the household with Conchubhar; he is called Naoise, son of Uisneach.' 'Then,' said she, 'I beseech thee, O Leabharcham, send him to speak to me in secret'; and Leabharcham informed Naoise of this. Thereupon Naoise came secretly to visit Deirdre, who revealed to him how greatly she loved him, and besought him to elope with her from Conchubhar. Naoise consented to this with reluctance, as he feared Conchubhar. Himself and his two brothers Ainle and Ardan, having Deirdre and thrice fifty warriors with them, proceeded to Alba, where they were maintained in service by the king of Alba till he was informed of Deirdre's beauty, and asked her for his wife. Naoise and his brothers became enraged at this, and fled with Deirdre from Alba to an island in the sea, having previously had many conflicts with the king's party. Now when the story ran in Ulster that the sons of Uisneach were in this sad plight, many of the nobles of the province said to Conchubhar that it was a pity that the sons of Uisneach should be in exile on account of a wicked woman, and that they should be sent for and brought back to the country. Conchubhar consented to this at the request of the nobles; and he gave Fearghus son of Rogh, Dubhthach Daol Uladh, and Cormac Conluingeas as sureties that he would act towards them in good faith. Upon these conditions, Fearghus son of Rogh sent his own son Fiachaidh to the children of Uisneach; and he brought them and their followers to Ireland, and Deirdre with them; and no tidings whatever of them are related till they reached the green of Eamhain.

On the green they were met by Eoghan son of Durrthacht, prince of Fearnmhagh, accompanied by a large host with intent to deal treacherously with the children of Uisneach at the direction of Conchubhar; and when the children of Uisneach arrived, Eoghan went to bid Naoise welcome, and in welcoming him thrust a spear through him. When Fiachaidh son of Fearghus saw this, he sprang between Eioghan and Naoise; and Eoghan dealt his second thrust at Fiachaidh, and slew him, together with Naoise; and forthwith Eioghan and his host fell upon the children of Uisneach, and slew them, and made dreadful slaughter upon their followers.

Now when Fearghus and Dubhthach heard that the children of Uisneach had been slain in violation of their guarantee, they proceeed to Eamhain, and came into conflict with the party of Conchubhar, and they slew Maine son of Conchubhar, together with three hundred warriors of his followers. They burned and plundered Eamhain, and put Conchubhar's women to death; and they and Cormac Conluingeas assembled their supporters from all sides; and their host at that time numbered three thousand warriors; and they thence marched into Connaught to Meadhbh and to Oilill, where they found welcome and were taken into service. When they had arrived there, there was no night that they did not send parties of plunderers to ravage and burn Ulster. They continued to act thus till they ravaged the district of Cuailgne – a deed from which sprang much mischief and contention between the two provinces; and in this manner they passed seven years without an hour's truce between them. Within that time Fearghus knew Meadhbh, and she conceived of him, and bore him three sons at one birth, namely, Ciar, and Corc, and Conmhac, as the poet says:

Meadhbhn conceived in fair Cruachain
Of Fearghus, who deserved not reproach,
And brought forth triplets faultless, strong,
Ciar and Corc and Conmhac.

From this Ciar is named Ciarraidhe in Munster, and O Conchubhair Ciarraidhe is of his progeny. From Corc is named Corca Moraudh; and from Conmhac is named every Conmhaicne in Connaught; and whoever reads the poem composed by Lughair, Oilill's poet, beginning, 'The children of Fearghus, children beyond all,' he will plainly find that these three sons of Meadhbh wielded great power and authority in Connaught and in Munster. This is proved by the territories that are named from them in these two provinces.

Now as to Deirdre, who gave rise to the events we have narrated, she remained with Conchubhar a year after the slaying of the children of Uisneach; and little though it be to raise her head or let a smile cross her lips, she did not do it during that time. When Conchubhar saw that neither sport nor kindness had any effect on her, and neither merriment nor pleasure raised her spirits, he sent for Eoghan son of Durrthacht, prince of Fearnmhagh; and when Eoghan had come into his presence, he said to Deirdre that, since he himself was unable to turn away her mind from her sorrow, she must pass another space of time with Eoghan; and she was thereupon placed behind Eoghan in his chariot. Conchubhar went to accompany them; and as they went along, she cast glances of rage at Eoghan in front of her and at Conchubhar behind her; for there were no two on earth she hated more than these. And when Conchubhar perceived her glancing by turns at himself and Eoghan, he said to her in jest, 'Deirdre,' said he, 'thy glancing at me and at Eoghan is the glancing of a sheep between two rams.' When Deirdre heard this, she started at the words, and sprang lightly from the chariot; and her head struck against a ledge of rock that stood before her on the ground. Her head was broken into fragments, and her brain straightaway issued forth. Thus was brought about the banishment of Fearghus son of Rogh, and of Cormac Conluingeas son of Conchubhar, of Dubhthach Daol Uladh, and the death of Deirdre.

from *The History of Ireland* by Geoffrey Keating

Sencha the Great

'I see another band there. A sedate, gray-haired man in front thereof. A fair bright garment about him, with borders of all-white silver. A beautiful white shirt next to the surface of his skin; a white-silver belt around his waist; a bronze branch at the summit of his shoulder; the sweetness of melody in his voice; his utterance loud but slow.'

'Judicial and sage, by our conscience, is the description,' said Medb.

'Sage and judicial the person whose description it is,' said Cu Roi.

'Who, then, is he?' asked Ailill.

'Not hard to tell. Sencha the Great, son of Ailill son of Maelchloid, from Carn Mag of Ulster; the most eloquent man of the men of earth, and the peace-maker of the hosts of the Ulstermen. The men of the world, from the rising to the setting, he would pacify with his three fair words.'

from *The Intoxication of the Ulstermen*
(translated by T.P. Cross and C.H. Slover)

The Tuatha dé Danann

As for Iobath son of Beothach son of Iarbanel son of Nemed, after his leaving Ireland with his people after the conquest before described, they settled in the northern islands of Greece. They were there till numerous were their children and their kindred. They learned druidry and many various arts in the islands where they were, what with *fithnaisecht*, *amaitecht*, *conbliocht*, and every sort of gentilism in general, until they were knowing, learned, and very accomplished in the branches thereof. They were called Tuatha De; that is, they considered their men of learning to be gods, and their husbandmen non-gods, so much was their power in every art and every druidic occultism besides. Thence came the name, which is Tuatha De, to them.

These were the cities where they were being instructed; Falias, Gorias, Findias, and Murias. They had an instructor of learning in each one of these cities. These are their names; Morfesa in Falias, Esras in Gorias, Uscias in Findias, and Semias who was in Murias. From Falias was brought the Stone of Fal (Lia Fail) which Lug had in Tara; that is what used to scream under every king who took the sovereignty of Ireland from the time of Lug Lamfada to the time of the birth of Christ, and it has never screamed thereafter under any king from that out; for it was a demon that had entrance into it, and the powers of every idol ceased in the time of the birth of the Lord, who was born of the Virgin Mary. From that Lia Fail is called Inis Fail (Ireland), as Cinaeth O'Hartagain proves, having said:

> The stone on which my heels stand,
> From it is named Inis Fail;
> Between two strands of a mighty flood,
> Ireland altogether is called Mag Fail.

From Gorias was brought the spear that Lug had; no battle was maintained against him who had it in his hand. From Findias was brought the sword of Nuada; none used to escape who was wounded by it. From Murias was brought the cauldron of the Dagda; no one came from it unsatisfied.

After they completed their learning, they went between the Athenians and the Philistines, so that they dwelt between them. Now there arose battles and conflicts between those races, and they were evil and maliciously disposed one to the other. Many battles were fought between them, and it was against the Athenians the battles used to be won, until all save a litle remnant were exhausted. Then the Tuatha De joined in friendship with the Athenians, and they formed through druidry demon-spirits in the bodies of the soldiers of the Athenians who were slain, so that they were fit for battle; thus they used to encounter the Philistines again. The Philistines thought it immensely astonishing to see the men they had slain fighting with them the day after. They told that to their druid. Their elder gave them advice, saying, 'Take', said he, 'pegs of hazel and of quicken-tree to the battle on the morrow; and if yours be the victory, thrust the pins in the backs of the necks of the men who shall be slain; and if they be demons, heaps of worms will be made of them.'

from *The Book of Invasions*
(translated by T.P. Cross and C.H. Slover)

Doghra and the Druids of Niall

Niall of the Nine Hostages was succeeded in the monarchy (A.D. 405) by Dathi, the son of his brother Fiachra, king of Connacht; and was, like his uncle, a valiant and ambitious man. It happened that, in the seventeenth year of his reign, king Dathi was induced to go from Tara to Eas Ruaidh, the great cataract of the River Erne (at the present Ballyshannon), to adjust some territorial dispute which had sprung up among his relatives. The time at which this journey was undertaken was the close of the summer, so that the king arrived at his destination close upon November Eve, a season of great solemnity of old among the pagan Gaedhils.

Dathi, having concluded an amicable adjustment among his friends, and finding himself on the eve of the great festival of Samhain, was desirous that his Druids should ascertain for him, by their art, the incidents that were to happen him from that time till the festival of Samhain of the next year. With this view he commanded the presence of his Druids; and Doghra, the chief of them, immediately stood before him. 'I wish', said the king, 'to know my destiny, and that of my country, from this night till this night twelvemonths'. 'Then', said Doghra, 'if you will send nine of your noblest chiefs with me from this to Rath Archaill, on the bank of the river Muaidh [the Moy], I will reveal something to them'. 'It shall be so', said the king, 'and I shall be one of the number myself'.

They departed secretly from the camp, and arrived in due time at the plain of Rath Archaill, where the Druid's altars and idols were. Dathi's queen, Ruadh, had a palace at Mullach Ruaidhé, in this neighbourhood, [a place still known under that name, in the parish of Screene, in the barony of Tireragh, and county of Sligo]. Here the king took up his quarters for the night, whilst the Druid repaired to Dumha na n-Druadh (or the Druid's Mound), near Rath Archaill, on the south, to consult his art according to the request of the king.

At the rising of the sun in the morning, the Druid repaired to the king's bed-room, and said: 'Art thou asleep, O king of Erinn and of Albain?' 'I am not asleep', answered the monarch, 'but why have you made an addition to my titles? for, although I have taken the sovereignty of Erinn, I have not yet obtained that of Albain [Scotland]'. 'Thou shalt not be long so', said the Druid, 'for I have consulted the clouds of the men of Erinn, and found that thou wilt soon return to Tara, where thou wilt invite all the provincial kings, and the chiefs of Erinn, to the great feast of Tara, and there thou shalt decide with them upon making an expedition into Albain, Britain, and France, following the conquering footsteps of thy great uncle, Niall, and thy granduncle, Crimhthann Môr'. The king, delighted with this favourable prediction, returned to his camp, where he related what had happened, and disclosed his desire for foreign conquests to such of the great men of the nation as happened to be of his train at the time. His designs were approved of, and the nobles were dismissed to their respective homes, after having cordially promised to attend on the king at Tara, with all their forces, whenever he should summon them, to discuss farther the great project which now wholly seized on his attention.

Dathi returned home, stopping for a short period at the ancient palace of Cruachain, in Roscommon. From this place he proceeded across the Shannon, and then delayed for some time at the ancient palace of Freamhainn, [a name still preserved in that of the hill of Frewin, in the present parish of Port-Loman, in the county of Westmeath].

The tale goes on to tell, at this place, an anecdote, having reference to the raith or building where the party then were, which is so interesting in itself, and as an example of the kind of informatiom with which these tracts abound, that I may so far digress as to state it to you.

In the course of the. evening, when the fatigues of the journey were forgotten in the enjoyment of the cup and the cheerfulness of conversation, the king asked his Druid, Finnchaemh, who it was that built the noble and royal court in which they were then enjoying themselves. The Druid answered, that it had been built by Eochaidh Aireamh [Monarch of Erinn, about a century before the Christian era]. He then narrated to Dathi how that monarch called on the men of Erinn to build him a suitable residence, which should descend to his own family independently of the palace of Tara, which always Erinn cheerfully consented, and, dividing themselves into seven divisions, they soon built the great rath and the palace within it. The ground upon which the palace was built was the property of the Feara Cul of Teabhtha (or Teffia); and although they formed one of the seven parties who contributed to its erection, the monarch had not asked their consent for the site. This intrusion was so keenly felt by the Feara Cul, and their king, Mormael, that, at the following feast of Samhain, or November Eve, when invited by the monarch to the solemnity of the great festival, Maelmor attended with forty men in chariots, who, in the confusion of the night, murdered king Eochaidh, unperceived by his people, and escaped themselves. The king's death was not discovered till the following morning, and the Feara Cul were the first to charge the murder on the secret agency of the Tuatha Dé Danann, by the hand of Siogmall, of Sidh Neannta (in the present county of Roscommon).

So far the Druid's history of the building of Freamhainn, and the death of the Monarch Eochaidh Airimh. The Feara Cul, however, did not escape detection; their crime was quickly discovered, and, in fact, in order to escape the punishment which awaited them, they fled over the Shannon into Connacht, and settled on the borders of Galway and Roscommon. Here the tribe remained for nearly three hundred years, until the return of Cormac Mac Art from his exile in Connacht, in the year of our Lord 225, to assume the monarchy, when he invited the Feara Cul to accompany him as his body-guard. This service they accordingly performed, and on Cormac's ascending his father's throne he gave them a territory north of Tara, nearly coextensive with the present barony of Kells. And I may observe that since this settlement of the clann by Cormac, they have been always known in Irish history as the Feara Cul Breagh, or the Feara Cul of 'Bregia', a territory comprised in the modern county of East Meath. (This designation seems to have been intended to distinguish their territory from the original one, called that of the Feara Cul of Teabhtha or Teffia, which is in West Meath – a distinction not hitherto accounted for by modern writers.

Let us, however, return to the story of king Dathi himself. On leaving Freamhainn, Dathi came to Ros-na-Righ, the residence of his mother, which was situated north-east of Tara, on the bank of the Boyne. Here he remained for some time, and at last returned to Tara, at which place he had, meanwhile, invited the states of the nation to meet him at the approaching feast of Belltainé (one of the great pagan festivals of ancient Erinn) on May Day.

The feast of Tara this year was solemnized on a scare of splendour never before equalled. The fires of Taillten [now called Telltown, to the north of Tara] were lighted, and the sports, games, and ceremonies, for which that ancient place is celebrated, were conducted with unusual magnificence and solemnity.

These games and ceremonies are said to have been instituted more than a thousand years previously, by Lug, the king of the Tuatha Dé Danann, in honour of Taillté, the daughter of the king of Spain, and wife of Eochaidh Mac Eire, the last king of the Firbolg colony, who was slain in the first great battle of Magh Tuireadh. It was at her court that Lug had been fostered, and on her death he had her buried at this place, where he raised an immense mound over her grave, and instituted those annual games in her honour. These games were solemnized about the first day in August, and they continued to be observed so long as down to the ninth century.

After the religious solemnities were concluded, Dathi, having now discharged his duties to his gods and to his subjects, turned his thoughts to his contemplated expedition; and at a conference with all the great chiefs and leaders of the nation, found them all ready to support him. Accordingly, without further delay, he concluded his preparations, and leaving Tara in the charge of one of his cousins, he marched to Dundealgan (the present Dundalk), where his fleet was ready for sea, at the head of the most powerful army that had ever, up to that time, been known to leave Erinn. He did not, however, embark at Dundalk, but ordering his fleet to meet him at Cuan Snamha Aighnech (now Carlingford), he marched to Iubhar Chinntrachta (now Newry), and from that to Oirear Caoin. On his way to the latter place it appears he passed by Magh Bilé (now Moville), and only at a short distance, (so that Oirear-Caoin may probably have been the ancient name of the place now called Donaghadee.) Here his fleet awaited him, and having embarked all his troops, he set sail for Scotland, which he reached safely at Port Patrick.

Immediately upon his landing, Dathi sent his Druid to Feredach Finn, king of Scotland, who was then at his palace of Tuirrin brighé na Righ, calling on him for submission and tribute, or an immediate reason to the contrary on the field of battle. The Scottish king refused either submission or tribute, and accepted the challenge of battle, but required a few days to propare for so unexpected an event.

The time for battle at last arrived; both armies marched to Magh an Chiarthi (the plain of the Pillar Stone), in Glenn Feadha (the woody glen); Dathi at the head of his Gaedhils, and Feredach leading a large force composed of native Scots, Picts, Britons, French, Scandinavians, and Hebridean Islanders.

A fierce and destructive fight ensued between the two parties, in which the Scottish forces were at length overthrown and routed with great slaughter. When the Scottish king saw the death of his son and the discomfiture of his army, he threw himself headlong on the ranks of his enemies, dealing death and destruction all round him: but in the height of his fury he was laid hold of by Conall Gulban [the great ancestor of Saint Column Cille and of the O'Donnells of Donnegall], who, taking him up in his arms, hurled him against the pillar stone and dashed out his brains. The scene of this battle has continued ever since to be called Gort an Chairthé, the Pillarstone Field; and the glenn, Glenn an Chatha, or Battle Glen.

Dathi having now realized the object of his ambition, set up a surviving son of the late king on the throne of Scotland, and receiving hostages and formal public submission from him, he passed onwards into Britain and France, in both of which countries he still received hostages and submission, wherever he proceeded on his march. He continued his progress, but with what object does not appear, even to the foot of the Alps, where he was at last killed, in the midst of his glory, by a flash of lightning.

The body of this great king was afterwards carried home by his people, and he was buried with his fathers in the ancient pagan cemetery at Raith Cruachain, in Connacht, as related in a very old poem by Torna Eigeas. At this place his grave was still distinguished by the Coirthe Dearg, the Red Pillar Stone, down to the year 1650, when Dubhaltach Mac Firbisigh wrote his first great Book of Genealogies.

from 'The Expedition of Dathi to the Alpine Mountains', *The Book of Leinster*
(translated by E. O'Curry)

3

THE DRUIDS: THEIR FUNCTIONS AND POWERS

P. W. Joyce

From *A Social History of Ancient Ireland*

Druidism No trustworthy information regarding the religion of the pagan Irish comes to us from outside: whatever knowledge of it we possess is derived exclusively from the native literature. Moreover, all of this literature that has come down to us was written – mostly copied from older documents – in Christian times by Christians, chiefly monks: no books penned in pre-Christian ages have been preserved. The Christian copyists, too, modified their originals in many ways, especially by introducing Christian allusions, and, no doubt, by softening down many pagan features that were particularly repellent to them. Yet many passages, and some complete tales, remain thoroughly pagan in character.[2]

So far as we can judge from the materials at our command, which are sufficiently abundant, though scattered and somewhat vague, the pagan Irish appear to have had no well-defined connected system of religion. There were many gods, but no supreme god, like Zeus or Jupiter among the Greeks and Romans. There was little or no prayer, and no settled general form of worship. There were no temples: but it appears from a passage in Cormac's Glossary (as quoted below) that there were altars of some kind erected to idols or to elemental gods, which must have been in the open air. We find mention of things offered to gods or idols. Thus, for instance, in the oldest version of 'The Wooing of Emir,' we are informed that, at Bron-Trogin (the beginning of autumn), the young of every kind of animal used to be 'assigned to the possession of the idol, Bel';[3] and other such examples might be cited. But in all these cases it appears to have been a mere nominal offer or dedication – a matter of words only – and it is doubtful if there was any sacrifice properly so called. We have a few examples where breaches of what were laid down as moral rules were punished. When King Laegaire broke his solemn oath sworn by the sun and wind, which were regarded as gods, he was, as we are told, killed by these two elements . . . from which we can see that there were some rules of conduct which it was dangerous to violate. But, on the whole, the pagan Irish religion seems to have had very little influence in regulating moral conduct. At the same time, it must be borne in mind, that all our very early books have been lost, so that, in great probability, the whole of the evidence is not before us: had we complete information, it might modify our judgment on Irish paganism.

The religion of the pagan Irish is commonly designated as Druidism: and as the druids were a numerous and important class, and as they were mixed up with most of the religious or superstitious rights and observances, it will be best to begin by giving a sketch of their position and functions, which will bring under review a large part of the religious beliefs of the pagan Irish. In the oldest Irish traditions the druids figure conspicuously. All the early colonists had their druids, who are mentioned as holding high rank among kings and chiefs.

Gaulish and Irish Druids   Of the Gaulish druids, their doctrines and worship, detailed accounts have been given by Caesar[4] and other classical writers: and these descriptions are generally supposed to apply to the druids of Britain – a supposition, however, open to doubt. But these writers knew nothing of the druids of Ireland, and of course give no information regarding them. It is pretty certain, indeed, that the druidic systems of Gaul, Britain, and Ireland were originally one and the same. But the Gaels of Ireland and Scotland were separated and isolated for many centuries from the Celtic races of Gaul; and thus, their religious system, like their language, naturally diverged, so that the druidism of Ireland, as pictured forth in the native records, differed in many respects from that of Gaul. Yet, with one exception, all those writers who have hitherto treated of Irish druids have unhesitatingly applied to them Caesar's and other classical writers' descriptions of those of Gaul.[5] O'Curry was the first, so far as I know, to describe in detail (in Lectures ix. and x. of his Manners and Customs of the Ancient Irish) the Irish druids from the native authorities. Certain speculative writers of the last two or three generations, backing up Caesar's description with baseless speculations of their own, have built up a great pagan religious system for Ireland, with druidic temples, druid's altars, the worship of Baal, human sacrifices, divination from the manner in which the blood of victims flowed down the sloping altars, and such like: all quite visionary as being based on insufficient evidence, or rather on no evidence at all. The following account of the Irish druids is derived from the native literature, the only authentic source of information. It will be shown in the next section that, while there are many differences between the Irish and the Gaulish druids, there are also many resemblances and correspondences, and these in some of their most important functions.

Name   The old form of the Irish name for a druid is *drui*, modern *drai* or *draoi* [all pron. dree]; but in the oblique cases it takes a *d*: gen. *druad*, dative *druid*, corresponding with the modern word *druid*. *Drui* is uniformly translated 'wizard' by some of the best modern authorites: and wizards the druids unquestionably were, and are so presented by our earliest traditions, though always called *drui*. The druids of Gaul and Ireland were undoubtedly identical as a class, though differing in many particulars, and they were all wizards; but those of Gaul are always called 'druids': and to apply the term 'druid' to the one class and 'wizard' to the other, might lead to a misconception, as if they were essentially different. That the ancient Irish considered their own druids in a general way identical with those of the Continent appears from this – that they apply the word *drui* to both: and while Latin writers commonly translate *druid* by 'magus', this same word 'magus' is retranslated *drui* by Irish writers. Thus, Simon Magus is called in Irish writings 'Simon Drui.' For these reasons it will be more convenient to retain here the familiar word 'druid.'

Druids, the Sole Men of Learning   In pagan times the druids were the exclusive possessors of whatever learning was then known. They combined in themselves all the learned professions: they were not only druids, but judges, prophets, historians, poets, and even physicians.[6] But as time went on there was a gradual tendency towards specialisation, as we see in some of the learned professions of our own day. 'Until Patrick came,' – says the Brehon Law (1. 19) – 'only three classes of persons were permitted to speak in public in Erin [i.e. their pronouncements received some sort of official recognition], viz. a

Avebury in the 1800s.
From The Celtic Druids *by Godfrey Higgins*

chronicler to relate events and tell stories; a poet to eulogise and satirise; a brehon or judge to pass sentence from the precedents and commentaries.' Here there is a clear intimation that there were three separate persons concerned. Nevertheless, down to the latest period of the prevalence of the Irish customs, two or more professions were often centred in one man, especially those of Poetry, History, and Literature in general.

There were druids in every part of Ireland, but, as we might expect, Tara, the residence of the over-kings of Ireland, was – as the Tripartite Life (p. 41) expresses it – 'the chief [seat] of the idolatry and druidism of Erin.' The druids had the reputation of being great magicians: and in this character they figure more frequently and conspicuously than in any other, both in ecclesiastical and lay literature. So true is this, that the most general Irish word for sorcery, magic, or necromancy, is *druidecht*, which simply means 'druidism' – a word still in use. In some of the old historical romances we find the issues of battles sometimes determined, not so much by the valour of the combatants, as by the magical powers of the druids attached to the armies. They could – as the legends tell – raise druidical clouds and mists, and bring down showers of fire and blood; they could drive a man insane or into idiocy by flinging a magic wisp of straw in his face. In the hymn that St. Patrick chanted on his way to Tara on Easter Sunday morning, he asks God to protect him against the spells of women, of smiths, and of druids. Broichan the druid threatens St. Columba: 'Thou wilt not be able [to voyage on Loch Ness], for I will make the wind contrary to thee, and I will bring a great darkness over thee.' And he did so, as Adamnan's narrative (150) tells us: but Columba removed the storm and darkness by prayer, and made his voyage.

Insanity Perhaps the most dreaded of all the necromantic powers attributed to the druids was that of producing madness. In the pagan ages, and down far into Christian times, madness – Irish *dásacht* – was believed to be often brought on by malignant magical agency, usually the work of some druid. For this purpose the druid prepared a 'madman's wisp' or 'fluttering wisp' (*dlui fulla: dlui* or *dluigh*, 'a wisp'), that is, a little wisp of straw or grass, into which he pronounced some horrible incantations, and, watching his opportunity, flung it into the face of his victim, who at once became insane or idiotic. So generally was insanity attributed to this, that in the Glosses to the Senchos Mór, a madman (Irish *dásachtach* or *fulla*) is repeatedly described as one 'upon whom the *dlui fulla* or magic wisp has been thrown.'[7]

The legend of Comgan illustrates this fell necromantic power. Maelochtair, king of the Decies in Munster, early in the seventh century, had a son named Comgan, remarkable for his manly beauty and accomplishments, who was half-brother by the same mother to St. Cummain Fota. One day, at a great fair held in Tipperary, Comgan carried off all the prizes in the athletic sports: and the spectators were delighted with him, especially the king's druid. But a certain woman, who had before that vainly sought Comgan's love, now revenged herself on him by whispering a false accusation into the druid's ear: whereupon his admiration for the youth was instantly changed to furious jealousy; and when Comgan and his friends retired to a neighbouring river to wash themselves and their horses after the sports, he followed them, and watching his opportunity, flung a magic wisp over him, at the same time pronouncing some fiendish words. When the young man came forth from the water, his whole body burst out into boils and ulcers, so that his attendants had to bring him to his father's house, all diseased and helpless as he was. There he wasted away in body, his mind decayed, his hair fell off: and ever afterwards he wandered about the palace, a bald drivelling idiot. But he had lucid intervals, and then he became an inspired poet, and uttered prophecies; so that he is known in the legendary literature as *Mac-da-cerda*, the 'youth of the two arts,' that is to say, poetry and foolishness.[8]

The invention of the madman's wisp is assigned, by a legend in the Cóir Anmann . . . to a celebrated Leinster druid named Fullon, who lived centuries before the Christian era: – 'Fullon was the first druid who cast a spell (*bricht*) on a wisp, so as to send [by means of it] a human being a-flying (*for foluamhain*). Hence, *dlui fulla*, or "madman's wisp," is a saying among the Scots from that day to this.'

As I am on the subject of madness, it will be better to finish here what is to be said about it. A fit of insanity was often called *baile* or *buile* [ballĕ, bullĕ]: and there was a most curious belief that during the paroxysm a madman's body became as light as air, so that, as he ran distractedly, he scarcely touched the ground, or he rose into the air, still speeding on with a sort of fluttering motion. This was especially the case when madness was produced by the rage of battle. For, during a bloody battle, it sometimes happened that an excitable combatant ran mad with fury and horror: and occurrences of this kind are recorded in the romantic accounts of nearly all the great battles fought in Ireland. We are told, in the historic story of the Battle of Moyrath (175, note v; and 235), fought A.D. 637, that towards the close of the day, a brave young warrior, *Suibne* or Sweeney, became distracted with the horrors he witnessed; and imagining he saw battle-demons hovering and shrieking overhead, he suddenly bounded off the earth, and alighted on the boss of another warrior's shield, from which, after a moment, he laped up again; and so he continued flitting and bounding on the shields and helmet-crests of the combatants and on the tops of the neighbouring trees, till he finally fled from the field; after which he wandered round Ireland, a *gelt* [g hard] or madman. His adventures from the day of battle till his death are told in a romantic tale, still extant in MS., called *Buile Shuibne*, 'Sweeny's frenzy or madness.'

The belief that men were driven mad in battle, and ran and fluttered away in this manner, found its way into the sober records of the Annalists, who relate that at the Battle of Allen in Kildare, fought A.D. 722, nine persons went crazy with terror, or, as Tigernach expresses it, 'Et ix volatiles, i.e. *geltai*': 'and nine persons [went] flying, i.e. madmen.'[9]

Even the Norse visitors to this country took up the legend: and we find it recorded as one of the 'Wonders of Ireland,' in an old Norse Book called

'Kongs Skuggsjo' or 'Speculum Regale,' written about A.D. 1250: – 'There is also one thing which will seem very wonderful, about men who are called *gelt*'; and the writer goes on to tell about men running mad out of battle, and living in woods for twenty years, so that feathers grew on their bodies: and that though they were not quite able to fly, they were incredibly swift, and 'run along the [tops of the] trees almost as swiftly as monkeys or squirrels.'[10] Of this superstition – that frenzied madmen were as light as air, and could climb up precipices – there are many other examples in the ancient tales: we see by the above quotation that it retained its hold till the thirteenth century; and it still lingers among the peasantry in some remote districts.[11]

There is a valley in Kerry called Glannagalt, 'the glen of the lunatics' (Irish, *gleann-na-ngealt*): and it is believed that all lunatics, if left to themselves, would find their way to it, no matter from what part of Ireland. When they have lived in its solitude for a time, drinking of the water of Tobernagalt ('the lunatics' well'), and eating of the cresses that grow along the little stream, the poor wanderers get restored to sanity. It appears by the story of the Battle of Ventry that this glen was first discovered by a youth named Goll, who fled frenzied from that battle, as Sweeny from Moyrath, and plunged into the seclusion of Glannagalt.[12] There is a well in Donegal which was believed to possess the same virtue as Tobernagalt, and to which all the deranged people in the surrounding district were wont to resort. It is situated on the strand, near high-water mark, a third of a mile south of Inishowen Head, near the entrance to Lough Foyle. It still retains its old name *Srubh Brain*, 'Bran's *sruv* or stream,' which is represented in the name of the adjacent hamlet of Stroove.[13]

Various Powers In the Lives of the Saints, the druids and their magical arts figure conspicuously; as, for instance, in the Tripartite Life of St Patrick, and in the earlier memoir of the saint, by Muirchu, as well as in Adamnan's Life of Saint Columba: and not less so in the historical tales. Before the Battle of Cul-Dremne, fought in 561 between the Northern and the Southern Hy Neill, Dermot, king of Ireland, who headed the southern Hy Neill – a Christian king – called in the aid of the druid Fraechan [Freehan], who, just as the armies were about to engage, made an *airbe druad* [arvă drooa] round the southern army to protect it.[14] It is not easy to say what this *airbe druad* was. Stokes translates it 'druid's fence'; and, no doubt, it was a magic fence of some kind: for this is the usual sense of *airbe* in old Irish writings. One man of the northern army, named Mag Laim, sprang across the *airbe*, by which he broke the charm, but sacrificed his own life, for he was at once slain: after which the battle was fought, and Dermot was defeated with a loss of 3000, while Mag Laim alone fell on the other side. All this is related by Tigernach and the other Annalists. In the Agallamh na Senórach, a chief's dun is mentioned as sometimes surrounded by a *snaidm druad* [snime drooa], a 'druid's knot': is this the same as the *airbe druad*, or have the two any connexion?

The druid could pronounce a malign incantation – no doubt, a sort of *glám dichenn* . . . not only on an individual, but on a whole army, so as to produce a withering or enervating effect on the men. Before the Battle of *Mucrimè* (A.D. 250), Ailill Olum's son Eoghan, one of the contending princes, came to Dil, the blind old druid of Ossory, to ask him to maledict the hostile army, as Balak employed Balaam; but on their way towards the place, Dil came somehow to know by Eoghan's voice that he was doomed to defeat and death, and refused to proceed farther (Silva Gad., 354).

The druids could give a drink of forgetfulness (*deog dermaid*), so as to efface the memory of any particular transaction. Cuculainn had fallen in love with the fairy lady Fand, so that his wife Emer was jealous: but Concobar's druids gave each of them – Cuculainn and Emer – a drink of forgetfulness, so that he quite forgot Fand and she her jealousy; and they were reconciled (Sick Bed: Atl., 11, 124). The druids were the intermediaries with the fairies, and with the invisible world in general, which they could influence for good or evil; and they could protect people from the malice of evil-disposed spirits of every kind; which explains much of their influence with the people.

Divination An important function of a druid was divination – forecasting future events – which was practised by the pagan Irish in connexion with almost all important affairs, such as military expeditions. Laegaire's druids foretold the coming of St Patrick (Trip. Life, 33); and the druid Dubdiad foretells the defeat and death of Congal in the Battle of Moyrath. . . . Queen Maive, before setting out on the Táin expedition, confers with her druid to get from him knowledge and prophecy: so he prophesies: – 'Whosoever they be that will not return, thou thyself shalt certainly return.' The druids forecasted, partly by observation of natural objects or occurrences, and partly by cerain artificial rites: and in the exercise of this function the druid was a *fáith* [faw] or prophet.

They drew auguries from observation of the clouds. On the eve of a certain Samain [first of November], Dathi, king of Ireland (A.D. 405 to 428), who happened at the time to be at *Cnoc-nan-druad* ('the druids' hill': now Mullaroe, and often incorrectly called Red Hill), in the parish of Skreen, Sligo, west of Ballysadare Bay, where there was then a royal residence, ordered his druid to forecast for him the events of his reign from that till next *Samain*. The druid went to the summit of the hill, where he remained all night, and, returning at sunrise, addressed the king somewhat as the witches addressed Macbeth: – 'Art thou asleep, O King of Erin and Alban (Scotland)?' 'Why the addition to my title?' asked the king: 'I am not king of Alban.' And the druid answered that he had consulted 'the clouds of the men of Erin,' by which he found out that the king would make a conquering expedition to Alban, Britain, and Gaul: which accordingly he did soon afterwards.[15]

This account of cloud divination is corroborated by the existence in Irish of the word *néladóir* [nailadore] for an astrologer or diviner: and *neladóracht* glosses 'pyromantia' ('divination by fire'), in an old Irish treatise on Latin declension.[16] But the primary meaning of *néladóir* is 'cloud-diviner'; and of *néladóracht*, 'divination by clouds'; for *nél, néul, néll*, means 'a cloud,' even to this day, and not star of fire.

48

Astrology, in the proper sense of the word – divination from the stars – appears, nevertheless, to have been practised by the Irish. Forecasting the proper time for beginning to build a house is alluded to in a short Irish poem contained in an eighth-century manuscript, now in a monastery in Carinthia, having been brought thither by some early Irish missionary: 'There is no house more auspicious, with its stars last night, with its sun, with its moon.'[17] This reference to astrology is in a purely Christian connexion, as it appears from the poem that the house in question was built by the great Christian architect the Gobban Saer. In the legends of the saints we find divination by the heavenly bodies. When St Columkille was a child, his foster-father went to a certain prophet (*fáith*) to ask him when the child was to begin to learn his letters; and the prophet, having first scanned the heavens, decided that the lessons were to begin at once.[18]

For purposes of divination they often used a rod of yew with Ogham words cut on it. When Etain, King Ochy Airem's queen, was carried off by the fairy King Midir, the druid Dallan was commissioned by King Ochy to find out where she was. After much searching he at last 'made four rods of yew, and writes an Ogham on them; and by his keys of knowledge and by his Ogham, it [the fairy palace where the queen was] is revealed to him.'[19] Dr Stokes points out that similarly at Praeneste the oracles were derived from lots consisting of oak with ancient characters engraved on them.

In several of the tales we find mention of a druidic 'wheel divination,' i.e. made by means of a wheel. The celebrated druid Mogh Ruith [Mow-rih] of Dairbre, now Valentia Island, in Kerry, was so called on account of his skill in this sort of divination; for, in the Cóir Anmann (409), we read of him: 'Mogh Ruith signifies *Magus rotarum*, the wizard [or rather the devotee] of the wheels, for it is by wheels he used to make his *taiscéladh druidh-echta* or "magical observation".' In another place[20] we read that his daughter, who went with him to the East to learn magic, made a *roth ramhach* or 'rowing wheel,' probably for the purpose of divination. But the *roth ramhach* figured in other functions, as may be seen in O'Curry's MS. Materials (Index). I have not the least notion of how the druidical divination-wheel was made or how it was used: but it may be of interest to observe here that – as Rhys remarks – the old Gaulish sun-god is represented with a wheel in his hand.[21]

Finn Mac Cumail, besides his other accomplishments, had the gift of divination, for which he used a rite peculiar to himself. A basin of clear water was brought to him, in which, having washed his hands, and having complied with some other formalities, he put his thumb in his mouth under his 'tooth of knowledge', on which the future event he looked for was revealed to him. This is repeatedly mentioned in the Tales of the Fena; and the legend is prevalent everywhere in Ireland at the present day. In the story of 'The Praise of Cormac and the Death of Finn' (Silva Gad., 98), this rite is said to be a sort of *Teinm Laegda* or part of it.

In the Irish Nennius . . . we are told that certain druids taught druidism, idolatry, sorcery, [the composition of] bright poems, divination from sneezing, from the voices of birds, and from other omens; and how to find out by these means suitable weather and lucky days for any enterprise. Before the Battle of Moyrath . . . the druid interprets King Domnall's dream, and advises precautionary measures. Divination by the voices of birds was very generally practised, especially from the croaking of the raven and the chirping of the wren: and the very syllables they utter and their interpretation are given in the old books.[22] The wren in particular was considered so great a prophet, that in an old Life of St Moling one of its Irish names, *drean*, is fancifully derived from *drui-én*, meaning the 'druids of birds.' When St. Kellach, Bishop of Killala, was about to be murdered, the raven croaked, and the grey-coated scallcrow called, the wise little wren twittered ominously, and the kite of Cloon-O sat on his yew-tree waiting patiently to carry off his talons-full of the victim's flesh. But when, after the deed had been perpetrated, the birds of prey came scrambling for their shares, every one that ate the least morsel of the saint's flesh dropped down dead.[23] The Welsh birds of prey knew better when they saw the bodies of the slaughtered druids:-

> Far, far aloof the affrighted ravens sail,
> The famished eagle screams and passes by.
>
> *The Bard* by Gray

Just before the attack by Ingcel and his band of pirates on Da Derga's Hostel, the howl of Ossar, King Conari's *messan* or lapdog, portended the coming of battle and slaughter (Da Derga, 208). The clapping of hands was used in some way as an omen; and also an examination of the shape of a crooked knotted tree-root.[24]

Sometimes animals were sacrificed as part of the ceremony of divination. When King Conari and his retinue were in Da Derga's Hostel, seveal unusual and ominous circumstances occurred which foreboded disaster to the hostel: whereupon the king's chief juggler (who had just failed, for the first time in his life, to perform his juggling feat – one of the omens) said to the druid Fer-Caillĕ, 'Sacrifice thy pig now, and find out who is about to attack the hostel.' Fer-Caillĕ did so, and foretold the impending destruction of the hostel by pirates (Da Derga, 287).

Lucky and Unlucky Days   There were certain *cross* days in every month of the year which were unlucky for undertaking any enterprise, of which a list is given by O'Curry (Moylena, 73, t) from an Irish medical MS. But on individual occasions the druids determined the days to be avoided, often by calculations of the moon's age. A druid predicted that his daughter's baby, if born on a certain day, would turn out just an ordinary person: but if born on the next day, he was to be a king and the ancestor of kings. Accordingly, the poor mother so managed that the birth was delayed till next day, but sacrificed her own life by doing so: and her baby was subsequently Fiacha Muillethan, an illustrious king of Munster.[25] Many examples might be cited where disaster attended an undertaking on account of beginning it on an unlucky day. It is hardly necessary to remark that the superstition of lucky and unlucky days was common amongst most ancient nations, and that it still lives vigorously among ourselves in all grades of society.

Tonsure The druids had a tonsure. The two druids Mael and Calpait, brothers, the tutors of King Laegaire's daughters Ethnea and Fedelma, had their hair cut in a magical figure – 'Norma Magica' – called in Irish *Airbacc Giunnae*; about the meaning of which there has been some doubt. Dr Todd[26] asserts that it means 'as the bond of Gehenna or hell'; but the Rev Dr Hogan[27] questions this, and thinks it may mean simply 'cut of the hair', making airbacc equal caesura, from bacc, 'tonsio' or 'ligo,' with the prep. air. That he is right in making *giunnae*, 'of the hair,' is plain from a passage in the Cóir Anmann (395) which explains *giunnach* as meaning *folt*, i.e. 'hair.' But it seems to me that *airbacc* is merely *airbe* (as in Airbe-druad . . .) with the common termination *-ach*; as we write *smólach* (thrush) for *smól*, and as *giunnach* from *giunnae*, above. For *airbacc* is the way of writing *airbeach* or *airbach* used by Latin writers, as they wrote Fiacc for Fiach. If this is so, *airbacc giunnae* means merely the 'fence-cut of the hair,' implying that in this tonsure the hair was cut in such a way as to leave a sort of eave or fence along some part of the head. St Patrick considered the *Norma Magica* a diabolical mark: for when these two druids were converted, he had their hair cut so as to obliterate it. The very name of one of these brothers, *Mael*, signifying bald, conveys the sense of tonsured: for we see from the narrative that he was not naturally bald. Moreover one of Laegaire's druids at Tara was called Lucet Mael, which name is made by the old Latin writers *Lucet calvus*, i.e. the bald or tonsured.

In connexion with this it will be interesting to mention that in Muirchu's Memoir of St Patrick we read of a certain Ulster chief named Maccuill . . . very tyrannical and wicked, a notorious robber and murderer. This man openly proclaimed his own character by adopting, as an indication of his villanous career, certain marks, usually exhibited by persons of his sort, which are elsewhere explained as *signa diabolica super capita*, 'diabolical marks on the head': no doubt, some special cut of the hair.[28] The adoption of this mark was an indication that the persons devoted themselves to the service of the devil, and became *dibergia*, i.e. people who practised violence, robbery, and murder, as a sort of profession.

Heathen Baptism The druids had a 'heathen baptism' (*baisteadh geinntlídhe*). The three sons of Conall Derg O'Corra were baptised according to this rite, with the direct intention of devoting them to the service of the devil, though they afterwards became three very holy men.[29] So also the celebrated Red Branch hero Conall Kernach. When he was born, 'druids came to baptise the child into heathenism: and they sang the heathen baptism (*baithis geintlídhe*) over the little child; and they said: – "never will be born a boy who will be more impious than this boy towards the Connacians."'[30] When Ailill Olum, king of

Munster in the beginning of the third century, was a child, 'he was baptised [pagan fashion] in druidic streams' (Moylena, 165). In the Gaelic version of the Travels of Sir John Mandeville, where the Scripture account of Isaac and Ishmael is given, the term 'heathen baptism' (*baistedh Genntlidhi*) is applied to circumcision;[31] but this is an exceptional application: and the Irish ceremony was altogether different. The ancient Welsh people had also a heathen baptism: the Welsh hero Gwri of the Golden Hair, when an infant, was 'baptised with the baptism that was usual at that time.'[32] Possibly the heathen baptism of the Irish and Welsh was adopted by the druids of both nations in imitation of the Christian rite, by way of opposition to the new doctrines, devoting the child to the service of their own gods, which in the eyes of the Christian redactors of the tales, was equivalent to devoting him to the devil.

Druids' Robes The druids wore a white robe. We read in Tirechan's Notes that Amalgaid's druid, Rechrad, and his eight companions, on the occasion when they attempted to kill St Patrick, were clad in white tunics:[33] like the Gaulish druid, who, as Pliny states, wore a white robe when cutting the mistletoe from the oak with a knife of gold.[34]

Tees Reverenced We know that the Gaulish druids regarded the oak, especially when mistletoe grew on it, with much religious veneration; but I cannot find that the Irish druids had any special veneration for the oak: although, like other trees, it occasionally figures in curious pagan rites. The mistletoe is not a native Irish plant: it was introduced some time in the last century. The statement we so often see put forward that the Irish druids held their religious meetings, and performed their solemn rites, under the sacred shade of the oak, is pure invention. But they attributed certain druidical or fairy virtues to the yew, the hazel, and the quicken or rowan-tree – especially the last and employed them in many of their superstitious ceremonials. We have already seen ... that yew-rods were used in divination.

In the historic Tale of the Forbais Droma Damhghaire, or Siege of Knocklong, in the County Limerick, we read that when the northern and southern armies confronted each other, the druids on both sides made immense fires of quicken boughs. These were all cut by the soldiers with mysterious formalities, and the fires were lighted with great incantations. Each fire was intended to exercise a sinister influence on the opposing army; and from the movements of the smoke and flames the druids drew forecasts of the issue of the war.[35] On some occasions, as we read, witches or druids, or malignant phantoms, cooked flesh – sometimes the flesh of dogs or horses – on quicken-tree spits, as part of a diabolical rite for the destruction of some person obnoxious to them.[36] Many of thse superstitions have survived to our own day. The quicken is a terror to fairies, and counteracts their evil devices. Bring a quicken-tree walking-stick out at night, and the fairies will take care to give you a wide berth.[37] When a housewife is churning, if she puts a ring made of a twig from this tree on the handle of the churn-dash, no evil-minded neighbour can rob her of her butter through any *pishoges* or other malign fairy influence.

Druids as Teachers and Counsellors   A most important function of the druids was that of teaching: they were employed to educate the children of kings and chiefs – they were indeed the only educators; which greatly added to their influence. King Laegaire's two daughters were sent to live at Cruachan in Connaught in the house of the two druids who had charge of their education: and even St Columba, when a child, began his education under a druid.

The chief druid of a king held a very influential position: he was the king's confidential adviser on important affairs. When King Concobar Mac Nessa contemplated avenging the foray of Queen Maive, he sought and followed the advice of his 'right illustrious' druid Cathbad as to the time and manner of the projected expedition (Ross-naree, p. 9). And on St Patrick's visit to Tara, King Laegaire's proceedings were entirely regulated by the advice of his two chief druids Lucetmail and Lochru.[38] The great respect in which druids were held is illustrated by a passage in the *Mesca Ulad* in the Book of the Dun Cow, which tells us that at an assembly it was *geis* (i.e. it was forbidden) to the Ultonians to speak till their King Concobar had spoken first, and it was in like manner one of Concobar's geasa to speak before his druids. Accordingly, on a certain occasion at a feast, Concobar stood up from where he sat on his 'hero-seat' or throne, and there was instant silence, so that a needle falling from roof to floor would be heard: yet he too remained silent till his druid Cathbad asked: – 'What is this, O illustrious king?' – after which the king, taking this question as an invitation to speak, said what he had to say to the assembly (Mesca, 13).

Druidesses   The ancient Irish had druidesses also, like their relatives the Gauls. In the Rennes Dinnsenchus[39] a druidess is called a *ban-drui*, i.e. a 'woman-druid': and many individual druidesses figure in the ancient writings. According to the same Dinnsenchus,[40] Brigit was a ban-fili (poetess) and ban-drui. These druidesses are also noticed in the ecclesiastical writings: as, for instance, in one of St Patrick's canons, where kings are warned to give no countenance to magi (i.e. 'druids'), or pythonesses, or augurers, in which it is obvious from the connexion that the pythonesses were druidesses.[41] Amongst the dangers that St Patrick (in his Hymn) asks God to protect him from are 'the spells of women,' evidently druidesses. Many potent witches, called ban-tuatha and also ban-sithe, 'fairy-women,' figure in the tales, who were probably regarded as druidesses. Before the second Battle of Moytura the two Ban-tuathaig of the Dedannans promise to enchant (Dolbfamid, 'we will enchant') 'the trees and stones and sods of the earth, so that they shall become a host [of men] against them [the Fomorian enemies], and rout them.'[42]

Chief Points of Agreement   1. They had the same Celtic name in both countries: 'Druid.' 2. They were all wizards – magicians and diviners. 3. They were the only learned men of the time: they were judges, poets, professors of

53

learning in general. 4. They were teachers, especially of the children of kings and chiefs. 5. Their disciples underwent a long course of training, during which they got by heart great numbers of verses. 6. They were the king's chief advisers: they were very influential, and held in great respect, often taking precedence even of the kings. 7. Among both the Irish and Gauls there were druidesses. 8. They had a number of gods. Caesar gives the Gaulish gods the Roman names, Mercury, Jupiter, etc.: but these Roman names do not fit; for the Gaulish gods were quite different from those of Rome and Greece, and had different names, and different functions. Many of the Irish gods, as will be shown farther on, were identical with those of Gaul.

Chief Points of Difference 1. The Gaulish druids were under one head druid, with supreme authority: and they held periodical councils or synods. There was no such institution in Ireland: though there were eminent druids in various districts, with the influence usually accorded to eminence. 2. The Gaulish druids held the doctrine of the immortality of the soul, as applying to all mankind: the soul of every human being passing, after death, into other bodies, i.e. of men, not of the lower animals. There is no evidence . . . that the Irish druids held the souls of all men to be immortal. But in case of a few individuals – palpably exceptional – it is related that they lived on after death, some reappearing as other men, some as animals of various kinds, and a few lived on in Fairyland, without the intervention of death. 3. Human sacrifice was part of the rite of the Gaulish druids, sometimes an individual being sacrificed and slain: sometimes great numbers together. There is no record of any human sacrifice in connexion with the Irish druids: and there are good grounds for believing that direct human sacrifice was not practised at all in Ireland . . . 4. The Gaulish druids prohibited their disciples from committing to writing any part of their lore, regarding this as an unhallowed practice. There is no mention of any such prohibition among Irish druids. 5. The Gaulish druids revered the oak, and the mistletoe when growing on it: the Irish druids revered the yew, the hazel, and the quicken-tree or rowan-tree: but not the oak. 6. The Gaulish druids, as we are informed, were priests: the Irish druids were not: they were merely wizards and learned men. 7. A point of difference regarding druidic literature that ought to be noticed is this: – That while all our knowledge regarding the Gaulish and British druids is derived from Latin and Greek writers, there being no native accounts – or next to none – our information about Irish druids comes from native Irish sources, and none from foreign writers.

4

THE DRUIDS IN
THE LIGHT OF
RECENT THEORIES

J.A. MacCulloch

From *Transactions of the Third International
Congress for the History of Religion*

It is first necessary to discuss recent theories of the origin of the Druids. Of
these M. d'Arbois de Jubainville's theory, based on Caesar's words that 'the
system is thought to have been devised in Britain and brought thence into
Gaul', and alleging that Druidism was the religion of the Goidels of Britain, and
became that of their Gaulish conquerors, passing ultimately to Gaul, is scarcely
likely. Gauls in Britain might have accepted Druidism, but it could hardly have
spread into Gaul and obtained such great influence there. Goidels and Gauls
were akin, and probably possessed the same religion from the first. Caesar's
words suggest that the British origin of Druidism was only an opinion, not a
fact; and in all probability Britain, being less open to foreign influences than
Gaul, had preserved its Druidic cults, etc., intact. Hence Gauls went to Britain
to perfect themselves in Druidism. On the other hand we have Pliny's opinion
(*H.N.* xxx. 1), that it passed from Gaul to Britain.

Another theory, supported on different grounds by Sir John Rhys, Mr
Gomme, and M. Salomon Reinach, is that the Druids were a pre-Celtic
priesthood, who imposed themselves upon their Celtic conquerors. Sir John
Rhys maintains that Celtic polytheism differed from Druidism, which was of a
lower order. But there exists no evidence to show that the Druids ever were
priests of a non-Celtic people, nor is it easy to see how the priests of a
conquered race could ever have obtained such influence over their conquerors
as the Druids certainly possessed. The case of conquering peoples who resort
occasionally to priests or magicians of a subject race because the latter possess

55

more powerful magic, is not really analogous. The Druids were not resorted to occasionally, but dominated the Celts always, in all departments of life. Mr Gomme contends that many Druidic beliefs (e.g. in shape-shifting), practices (e.g. human sacrifices of atonement), nd functions (e.g. judging, arranging boundaries, etc.) were opposed to Aryan sentiment, and seeks an analogous case in the occasional services of a similar kind rendered by un-Aryan tribes to Hindu village communities. But existing evidence shows that the Druids rendered more than occasional services to the Celts, nor was it only among the ruder Celtic tribes that their influence predominated, as Mr Gomme contends. Moreover, the hostility of Rome to the Druids as true Celtic priests is inexplicable if their position only corresponds to that of pariah priests in India. Further, if their beliefs and practices were opposed to 'Aryan sentiment,' why should Aryan Celts so readily have accepted them? The Aryans must have had a savage past, and such practices were still in vogue among them, while recent theories about the Aryans show that they were probably on a lower level than the peoples they conquered. The basis of all Celtic cults was doubtless composed of beliefs and ceremonies akin to those of the aborigines, instead of being of a loftier and purer kind.

M. Reinach argues that the probable lack of images among the Celts before the Roman conquest suggests a religious prohibition and a priesthood powerful enough to enforce it. The existence of such a priesthood he finds implied among certain pre-Celtic peoples by their megalithic structures and lack of images; and therefore reasons that these priests were the Druids, who became the priests of the Celts. But this conclusion is based on negative evidence; there exist no relics of purely Celtic images in Gaul, therefore there never can have been such images. But in other regions, where image-worship was common, images are not now found. If the Celtic images were of wood, their disappearance would be accounted for. Moreover, the Celts in Ireland were certainly image-worshippers, although the Druids were strong among them, and certain of the Gaulo-Roman images show no trace of classical influence, but in their form suggest existing native types. Further, if the Celts were opposed to image-worship as a result of Druidic influence, why should such an outbreak of it have occurred after the Roman conquest? M. Reinach's contention that the Celts adopted Druidism *en bloc* is shown to be incredible, while his supposition that the Celtic military caste had begun to rebel against this *ex hypothesi* foreign priesthood, and that their power was consequently declining, is not supported by evidence. Priest and soldier have always opposed each other wherever such bodies exist as separate castes.

Taking, therefore, these various theories together, there is no historic or epigraphic evidence for them, while the classical evidence contradicts them. Although Druids are not formally connected with certain Celtic regions, it must be remembered that no classical writer has written fully about them. Hence the probability is that the Druids existed wherever the Celts were found, though perhaps not always called Druids. Against the theory that they were pre-Celtic stands the fact that they are not said to have existed in such a non-

Celtic region as Aquitania. The theory demands the supposition that the Celts had no native priesthood or that it was overcome by the Druidic priesthood. Certain Celtic priests were called *gutuatri*, attached to certain temples and to a definite cult. M. d'Arbois de Jubainville considers that these were the only priests known to the Celts before the coming of the Druids. But the probability is that they were a Druidic class, since the Druids were a composite priesthood with a variety of functions. If the priests or servants of Belenus, described by Ausonius and called by him *aedituus Beleni*, were *gutuatri*, then the latter must have been connected with the Druids, since the poet says they were of Druidic stock. Similarly the *sacerdotes* and *antistites* of the Boii, mentioned by Livy, may have been Druids proper and *gutuatri*. Classical evidence suggests that the Druids were a great inclusive priesthood, with a variety of functions – priestly, prophetical, magical, medical, judicial, and poetical. Caesar attributes many of these to the Druids; in other writers they are each in part in the hands of different classes. Diodorus refers to the Celtic philosophers and theologians (Druids), diviners, and bards, as do also Strabo and Timagenes, while Strabo gives in Greek form the native name of the diviners, οὐάτεις, a word akin to the Celtic *vâtis* (Irish *fáith*). These diviners may also have had bardic functions, since *vâtis* means both singer and prophet. Again, Druid and diviner were closely connected, since both studied nature and offered, or assisted in, sacrifice and auguries according to Strabo, Timagenes, and Cicero. Hence, perhaps, Lucan does not mention diviners, but only Druids and bards. Diviners were probably a Druidic sub-class, standing midway between the Druids proper and the bards. Pliny speaks of 'Druids and this race of prophets and medicine-men', and this suggests that some were priests, some diviners, while some practised an empiric medical science. On the whole this agrees with what is met with in Ireland, where the Druids, though appearing in the texts as magicians, were certainly priests and teachers. Side by side with them were the *Filid*, 'learned poets,' occupying a higher place than the third class, the bards. The *Filid*, who may have been known as *Fáithi*, prophets, were also diviners and in certain methods of augury used sacrifice, while the Druids proper also used divination. Thus Druids or Priests, Vates, and Bards in Gaul correspond to Druids or Priests, *Fáithi*, or *Filid*, and Bards in Ireland, their functions in both cases overlapping.

This inclusive Druidic priesthood was a native Celtic priesthood, not an aboriginal priesthood adopted by the Celts. Some have seen in the Druids an esoteric and occult priesthood; but the probability is that they had grown up *pari passu* with the native religion and magic. In certain parts of Gaul, they may have been more civilized as a result of the influence of Greek civilization filtering in through the Massilian colonies, but as a whole they were addicted to magic, and took part in all local, as well as the greater, cults. They had been evolved from primitive medicine-men, later perhaps a series of priest-kings, practising magic and officiating at religious ceremonies. The folk themselves may have practised minor cults, but they doubtless felt that true success depended on the presence of a Druid.

The Druids cannot be regarded as a philosophic priesthood, advocating a pure religion to a polytheistic people; nor was Druidism a formal system outside Celtic religion. It covered the whole ground of Celtic religion: in other words, it was that religion itself. The idea that the Druids possessed esoteric knowledge is due to the idea entertained by a chain of classical writers that they were philosophers. What might be called a 'Druidic legend' was formed, but the basis of it was probably to be found in the fact that the Druids taught immortality, which no classical priest had done. They knew also that the Druids had a certain organization and considered themselves divinely inspired. The eyes of classical observers were dazzled and read much into this priesthood which it did not possess. But side by side with this 'legend' was the fact that the Druidic religion was considered cruel, grossly superstitious, and savage, while on these and other grounds it was attacked by the Roman power. Modern writers in turn have probably exaggerated the force of what classical writers stated. The Druidic associations were probably not much higher than the organized priesthoods of barbarians. Their doctrine of metempsychosis, if it really was taught, involved no ethical content as in Pythagoreanism. Their astronomy was probably astrological: their knowledge of nature a series of cosmogonic myths and speculations. The evidence points in this direction, while, if a true Druidic philosophy and science had existed, it is strange that it exerted no influence on the thought of the time. As to the supposed connexion with Pythagoreanism, while Pythagorean teachings may have reached Gaul, it is certain that the Druidic teaching of immortality in no way resembled the Pythagorean metempsychosis doctrine. There are Celtic myths regarding the re-birth of gods and heroes, but the doctrine taught was apparently this, that the soul was clothed with a body, its own or a new one, in the future state. The Druidic teaching of bodily immortality was mistakenly assumed to be the same as the Pythagorean doctrine. Other points of resemblance were then discovered. The organization of the Druids was assumed by Ammianus to be a kind of corporate life; but those who wrote most fully of the Druids knew nothing of this. The position and power of the Druids demanded some kind of organization, and in Gaul there was a chief Druid wielding authority over the others. Evidence tends to show that the insular Druids were similarly organized and had a chief, as was certainly the case with the *Filid*. M. Bertrand's development of the words of Ammianus, and his theory that the Druids were a kind of monk living a corporate life, while Irish monasticism was a transformation of the system, is opposed to the evidence. Irish Druids had wives and children. Christianity opposed Druidism too much to adopt any part of its system, and there is no doubt that Irish monasticism was modelled on that of the continent. The Druidic organization probably denoted no more than that the Druids were bound by certain ties, and were also more or less graded, with different classes practising different functions, though these were perhaps never very exclusively defined. The religious, magical, and other functions of the Druids are well known; their position as teachers, both in Gaul and Ireland, deserves examination. Their teaching of immortality had the practical end of making men fearless of death. Their scientific teaching was connected with magic and included cosmogonic myths. Their theology was largely mythological; their moral teaching resembled that found in all barbaric societies. Ritual formulae, runes, incantations would also be taught: these were probably the subject of the verses which were never committed to writing and which were kept secret from the people. This secrecy did not involve an esoteric, philosophic, or monotheistic teaching. These secret formulae were magical, and were kept secret lest they should lose their power by becoming too common.

The last point to be discussed is the question raised by some recent writers as to the differences between the continental and insular Druids, viz. that the latter had no organization, no judicial functions, and were magicians, not priests. The Irish Druids have already been shown to have possessed some organization. Judicial functions are ascribed in the Irish texts not to the Druids proper, but to the *Filid*, who have been shown to be a Druidical class. M. d'Arbois de Jubainville suggests that the exercise of such functions by the Christian clergy in Ireland might be due to the fact that the Druids had a judicial position. As to their religious functions, while they appear in the texts rather as magicians, magic and religion were always closely connected, while we know from Tacitus that the British Druids were priests. The absence of reference to their priestly functions in the texts is doubtless due to a deliberate suppression of all that related to religion or the pagan priesthood. Certain rites in which the Druids took part involved the slaughter of animals, and that slaughter must have been sacrificial. In other notices of ritual which have escaped being tampered with, the Druids appear as taking part in sacrifice. The opposition of Christian missionaries to the Druids shows that the latter were priests; if they were not, it remains yet to be discovered what body of men did exercise priestly functions in pagan Ireland. Thus a close examination of the position, powers, and functions of the Druids in Celtic life inevitably leads to the conclusion that no non-Celtic priesthood could ever have attained to these among the conquering Celts. They were from the beginning as Celtic as the Celts who submitted to them and whom 'they tamed as wild beasts are tamed'.

5

THE ORIGIN OF DRUIDISM

Julius Pokorny

From *The Celtic Review*

Schrader says in his *Reallexikon der idg. Altertumskunde*: 'The Celtic Druids are quite different from the other priesthoods of ancien Europe. Where the first beginnings of their origin started from will never be known.' I hope, however, to succeed in throwing some light into that obscurity.

In seeking to determine the origin of Druidism people came to very strange ideas. Some thought the Druids pupils of Pythagoras, others even took them for Buddhists; one thought the origin of Druidism was in Phoenicia, others thought it was in Chaldea or India. The ancients already showed great interest in that priesthood, and in the last two centuries there arose a great literature dealing with them, but it was of no importance as it lost itself in symbolic and occult trifles. Notwithstanding, there was no success in throwing light on the accounts of the Druids nor in explaining the so-called contradictions.

But when in 1906 there appeared a book by the well-known French scholar D'Arbois de Jubainville, *Les Druides et les Dieux Celtiques aux Formes des Animaux*, the scientific world hoped to receive at last some enlightenment regarding that mysterious institution. De Jubainville's book, however, is not much more than a compilation of the most important things we know about the Druids, and he only tells us what we already know from other sources.

In the first chapter of his book De Jubainville speaks of the Gaulish priests: –

They have two kinds of priests, the Druids and the 'Gutuatri.' When Caesar subdued independent Gaul in the first century before our era, the Druids had already gained an important position, but he was told that Druidism originated in Britain and had been transferred from thence to Gaul.

Before the establishment of the Druids on the Continent the Gauls had no other priests than the 'Gutuatri.' He derives their name from the Celtic 'gutu,' Ir. guth (voice), and compares it with our German word 'Gott,' from the Indo-Eur. 'ghutom' (what is invoked), from the root 'ghu'. 'Gutuatri' would then mean, 'the invoking ones,' from the same root as the Goth. 'gudja' (priest). They were all priests of temples or of holy groves. The 'Gutuatri' were still extant during the Roman occupation. We have their name preserved on four inscriptions.

De Jubainville compares the 'Gutuatri' with the Homeric 'ἱερευς,' with Chryses who bears the surname 'ἀρητήρ,' which signifies the same thing as 'Gutuatros' and with the 'Flamines' of the Romans who, like them, formed no corporation.

The Druids, however, formed a corporation and had an Arch-Druid over them, not only in Gaul, but in Ireland, and probably also in England.

In this passage I cannot agree with De Jubainville. In the Irish literature a chief of the Druids is never mentioned, and from the sentence in the *Life of St Patrick*: 'Congregata est multitudo nimis magorum ad primum magum Recradum, nomine,' we are not justified in concluding that the Irish Druids had a head. The passage can also signify, that Recradus was at that time the most famous Druid. It is even very possible that we owe here to the Christian writer, who wished to enhance the glory of the holy man, a little exaggeration, for somewhat later we read how St Patrick killed this Druid by means of a miracle. We have therefore in the Arch-Druid a special Gaulish institution.

In the art of prophecy the Druids had rivals in the 'Vatis,' who by Strabo are called 'οὐάτεις,' by Diodorus 'μάντεις.' St Patrick did not vanquish the Druids till he had associated himself with the 'Vatis,' Ir. fāthi, filid.

De Jubainville, agreeing with Thurneysen, derives the name of the Druids from the root 'dru,' and translates the name 'druis' by 'the most wise one,' the Galatic 'dru-nemeton' by 'arch-sanctuary,' and quotes as the Gaulish synonym 'ver-nemeton.' (Other derivations of the word 'druis' are possible. Cf. Cymr. derwydd; Gaul. dervum.)

The second chapter seems to me to be the most important of the whole book, and therefore I propose to give it word for word in translation:--

It seems that the Druids were known to the Greeks since about 200 B.C. when Sotion mentions them. They existed therefore already at that time in Gaul, on the left side of the Rhine, a country which was very much visited by merchants of Massilia. This happened not long after the Gauls had conquered Britain, which had been occupied first by the Gaels. And it seems, in fact, that the conquest had probably taken place between 300 and 200 B.C. The Gauls had found the Druids in Britain and transferred the institution to the Continent. Caesar says so explicitly. ('Disciplina in Britannia reperta atque inde in Galliam translata esse existimatur, et nunc qui diligentius eam rem cognoscere volunt plerumque illo discendi causa proficiscuntur.') We conclude, therefore, that the Druids were originally a Gaelic institution peculiar to the Gaels. The Gaels are a Celtic tribe, whose language still exists in Ireland and in the Highlands of Scotland. From this tribe, which had during a long time occupied all the British Island, Druidism had been transferred into the large countries which lay spread out to the south of the

Channel between the Atlantic Ocean and the Rhine; but it was unknown in Gallia Cisalpina and in the lands formerly Celtic, to the east of the Rhine, also in the basin of the Danube, and in Asia Minor, where the dru-nemeton (arch-sanctuary) is in no way connected with the Druids.

So far D'Arbois de Jubainville. Before I proceed further I shall shortly summarise what the writers of the ancients tell us about the Druids.

According to Caesar there were two governing classes in Gaul: the warlike aristocracy and the Druids. The latter were free from military service and from all exactions, and through these privileges many of them were drawn to their profession, the more readily as Druidism was apparently not founded upon birth, but merely upon the engagement and training of novices.[43]

The Druids were philosophers and teachers of youth. They gave not only lessons in theology and mythology but also spoke much about the course of the stars, about the nature of all things, and the magnitude of the universe.

From all the ethical doctrines of the Druids nothing but a single sentence is preserved (Diogen, Laert., proem 5): 'To be pious against the gods, not to do injury to any one, and to practise bravery.' But their first doctrine was, that after death they passed into another body. So strong was this belief among the people, that bargains were even made with the promise to pay them in the future life. The novices had to learn by heart a large number of verses, and some spent twenty years in learning them. Almost nothing is preserved to us from the tradition of the Gaulish Druids, for they were not allowed to put down their teaching in writing. It was otherwise in Ireland. The author of the Yellow Book of Lecan tells us that St Patrick burnt a hundred and eighty books of the Druids, and that after his example all Christians did the same, till all Druidical books were destroyed.

The Druids were also soothsayers and assisted at sacrifices.

Every year they met in the territory of the Carnutes, and many cases were brought to them for decision. The most severe punishment they could inflict was exclusion from the sacrifices. Those so punished were cut off from all human society and treated as outlaws. At the head of the Gaulish Druids stood an Arch-Druid, who was elected by the vote of his fellow-Druids on the death of his predecessor.

Caesar seems to include under the name 'Druides' the bards and seers (vā-tis), who were treated by later writers as separate.

The similarity of the Druidical doctrine to that of Pythagoras led to many fables. That the Druids did not live like monks (a theory set forth by Alexander Bertrand) is already clear, as we are told that the Druid Divitiacus, Caesar's friend, had a wife and children, and that the Irish Druids were mostly married.

Criminals were sacrificed to the gods, but also innocent persons. Large figures made of wickerwork were filled with living men and then burned.

The Romans soon prohibited Druidism; but it continued secretly, and Mela tells us (45 A.D.) that the noblest youths of Gaul followed their teachers into secret forests.

Thirty-five years later Pliny the Elder gives us quite another picture of the Druids. He shows them as priests of the oak, as physicians and magicians, as nothing better than common charlatans. They compose the mystic serpent's egg out of snake venom, which assures the success of every action.

How shall we account for this seeming change? Did suppression cause them to set aside their noble teaching in order to earn their livelihood in a less worthy manner? I shall soon have to show that the Druids were already magicians in the earlier times. But how does it happen that they are occupied with mean sorcery as well as with an earnest science? In the meantime we may notice that the most prudent men are often the greatest charlatans, because they know that the great crowd is more easily led by cunning, juggling tricks than by high wisdom.

As to the Druidical belief in the immortality, and their doctrine of the transmigration of souls, D'Arbois de Jubainville quotes many examples of the belief of the Celts in a life in the other world, but he thinks the report of their doctrine of rebirth an error, which had risen owing to the Greeks having heard from the Druids tales of transformations which they misunderstood, and so thought that the Druids taught the transmigration of souls after the doctrine of Pythagoras.

Here I venture to make a conjecture. Have we not in this doctrine a survival of the belief of the pre-Celtic aborigines? It is possible that already the men of the Stone Age believed in metempsychosis, as they often buried their dead in a cowering position. We can detect the belief in metempsychosis chiefly among peoples of a low culture. The next step is the belief in rebirth, of which we have also some examples in Irish mythology.

De Jubainville has shown that the Druids originally had been the priests of only one Celtic tribe – that which conquered Britain first. It is very strange that between brother-nations, whose customs and language differed not very widely, such a fundamental distinction should have existed. For nothing is so characteristic of a people as its religious beliefs. But, as we shall see, Druidism has many features quite alien to the character of an Indo-European religion. There is but one way to account for such a strange and almost fundamental difference as is said to have existed between Gaels and Gauls before the occupation of Gaul by Caesar.

The Gauls certainly took Druidism from their brethren in Britain, but the latter were not yet acquainted with that institution when they crossed the Channel.

For the Druids were the priests of the pre-Celtic aborigines of the British Islands, and it is from them only that the Celts received them.

As the Gaels, the one great nation of the Celts, conquered the British Isles about 1000 B.C., they had already attained a high degree of culture. They brought with them the knowledge of bronze and burnt their dead.[44]

I suppose that they were ruled by priestly kings, whom we find about the same time among the Greeks, Latins, and Germans, who have, in common with the Celts, other characteristics of Indo-European origin. We have no cause whatever to assume that the Celts had differed widely in customs and religion in that early time from the neighbouring Indo-European brother-nations, which we would have to assume if the institution of Druidism had existed among them from the earliest times. Yet in historical times we find among the Irish *kings* traces of the former priestship which had originated in the furthest past ages from the divine adoration of mighty magicians.

For the Indo-European peoples once believed what savages of the present time believe that their divine[45] ruler was the centre of the universe, that he could disturb the course of nature by merely moving his hand; and therefore saved their king from the perils which surrounded him, even after every common mortal had been rendered harmless through numberless taboos (prohibitions). The Indo-European races had given up these beliefs, however, before they had left the common native home.

We detect such traces of the former divinity of the kings, not only in Homer, when he speaks (*Od.* xix. 109) of a ruler who honours the gods and reigns powerfully, so that the earth is fertile and the wealth of the people grows – because of the virtues of the king – but also in Ireland and Wales.

The Celts believed that there would be bad crops as a punishment for bad rulers. In the Book of Leinster we read that under Cairbre Cinnchait, who won the kingdom of Ireland by violence and killed mercilessly the children of the nobles, every ear of corn bore only one grain, and every oak only one acorn. But when the old dynasty came again to the throne, Ireland recovered its fertility. To every new king the Ollamh, the head-bard, sang some verses, wherein he admonished him to reign well, or else famine and diseae would spoil the land; and in a Welsh poem of the twelfth century it is said: 'We shall have bad years and [long] days with false kings and failed crops' (The Black Book of Carmarthen).

We hear besides of many taboos which the Irish kings were obliged to observe even in historical times in order not to ruin their land.[46]

Thus, for example, the sun might not rise on the King of Ireland in his bed at Tara, the old capital of Erin; he was forbidden to alight on Wednesday at Magh Breagh, to traverse Magh Cuillinn after sunset, to incite his horse at Fan Chomair, to go in a ship upon the water the Monday after Bealltaine, and to leave the track of his army upon Ath Maighne the Tuesday after All-Hallows.

The King of Leinster might not go round Tuath Laighean left-hand-wise on Wednesday, nor sleep between the Dothair and the Duibhlinn on Monday, nor ride a dirty, black-heeled horse across Magh Maistean.

The King of Munster was prohibited from enjoying the feast of Loch Lein from one Monday to another; from banqueting by night in the beginning of harvest before Geim at Leitracha; from encamping for nine days upon the Siuir; and from holding a border meeting at Gabhran.

The King of Connacht might not conclude a treaty respecting his ancient palace of Cruachan after making peace on All-Hallows Day, nor go in a speckled garment on a grey-speckled steed to the heath of Dal Chais, nor repair to an assembly of women at Seaghais, nor sit in autumn on the sepulchral mounds of the wife of Maine, nor contend in running with the rider of a grey, one-eyed horse at Ath Gallta between two posts.

The King of Ulster was forbidden to attend the horse fair at Rath Line among the youths of Dal Araidhe; to listen to the fluttering of the flock of birds of Linn Saileach after sunset; to celebrate the feast of the bull of Daire-mic-Daire; to go into Magh Cobha in the month of March, and to drink of the water of Bo-Neimhidh between two darknesses.

Hence it follows, that the kings of the Gaels, like those of other Indo-European peoples, originated in priests and we may conclude, especially as we find the survivals so fresh and vivid in Ireland, that the kings of the Gaels when they conquered the British Islands were at the same time their priests.

In the British Islands the Gaels had found an aboriginal race which had come over from the Continent in early neolithic times when Ireland and England were still connected with the Continent (?). These immigrants were of a small stature, muscular, with dark hair and dark eyes. They were religious, for they buried their dead; and for the nobler ones they erected great stone monuments. Their culture was that of the Stone Age. Tacitus thinks them from their appearance Iberians, and it is at least noteworthy that the skulls which have been discovered resemble strongly those of the Basques, though it is impossible to prove anything from that fact.[47]

Their race is still preserved in the dark-eyed, brown-and-black-haired population in the west of Ireland, in South Wales, in Scotland, in the Isles of Mull and Arran, in Argyll and Inverness, and also in Cornwall.

But if we asume that this race was not wholly crushed out by the invading Celts and that they transmitted their magicians too, then their nationality must have been very strong, as indeed it was, for it has left its traces till to-day on the British Isles. I shall not speak here of the linguistic remains preserved in the topography and in the Celtic languages, nor of the numberless Fetish-stones that are to be met with in the British Isles, where they are worshipped even in our times. I shall only take a few interesting points out of the rich material.

The testimonies of Diodorus and Strabo concerning cannibalism among the Irish is strengthened by St Hieronymus, who says in his writing, 'Adversus Iovinianum': 'Quid loquar de ceteris nationibus, *cum ipse* adolescentulus in Gallia *viderim* Scotos, gentem Britannicam, humanis vesci carnibus? Et cum per silvas porcorum greges et armentorum pecudumque reperirent, pastorum nates et feminarum et papillas solere abscindere et eas solas ciborum delicias arbitrari?' Nobody will contend that we can ascribe such customs to Indo-Europeans. An obscure memory of these times survives still among the Celtic people, and we find in Wales and Scotland tales of giants and ghosts who ate their captives and drank their blood. Also the custom quoted by Strabo, that the old Irish devoured the corpses of their fathers we can hardly ascribe to the Celts. Even to-day we can trace the remains of this custom.

Wood-Martin tells us that the custom, existing still in Ireland, of taking some food in presence of the dead body is but a form of the old custom of consuming food which had been laid on the corpse with the intention of

Reconstruction of the temple of Avebury. From The Celtic Druids *by Godfrey Higgins.*

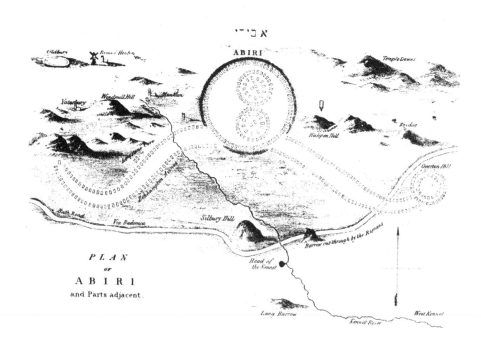

Reconstructed plan of Avebury by Stukeley.

transmitting to those doing so certain faculties of the departed one. I think it to be a survival of the old, barbaric custom of consuming the corpse itself.

Schrader has proved that the idea of family must have been throughout an agnatic one in the primitive ages of the Indo-European people – the principle of relationship in the male line prevailed already in the common past of the Indo-European people the principle of relationship in the male line prevailed already in the common past of the Indo-Europeans. Therefore, if we can detect traces of matriarchy in the British Isles we must ascribe them to a pre-Celtic population.

It has been fully proved by Zimmer that even in historic times matriarchy prevailed among the Picts of Scotland. At any rate the Picts possessed a large substratum of pre-Celtic blood. I think them to have been a non-Aryan race, soon however Celticised, first by the Gaels and then – but in a lesser degree – by the Britons.

In Wales we can detect in the families of the Mabinogion traces of matriarchy, and many may also be found in Ireland. While among the Indo-European peoples it was the father who gave the first food to his child (what for India, the Grihya-Sutras of Apastamba and Hiranyakesin prove[48] and Speijer has proved in Yatakarma . . . for the other Indo-European peoples), Solinus tells us that in Ireland it was the mother who gave to the new-born the first food, on the point of her husband's sword, with the wish that he might die only in battle.

A. Potter ('Description of West-Meath,' 1819) tells us that all married women are called by their maiden names, a custom still extant in Ulster. According to Wood-Martin, women in many English-speaking districts retain their maiden names and follow rather their mother's relations.

The couvade, too, surely a non-Indo-European custom, is to be found all over the British Isles. In Ulster it was known in very olden times, for we read in the Book of Leinster that all men, with the exception of Cuchulainn, lay in their beds unable to fight when Queen Meave of Connacht made a progress to Ulster with her army. A pregnant wife had cursed them, to suffer once a year the throes of women.

In England also the couvade once existed, for in Yorkshire the mother of a girl who has borne an illegitimate child goes out to seek the seducer, and the first man she finds in his bed is held to be the child's father.[49]

Already for the Iberians matriarchy is not only proved, but also the couvade, which we find also among their descendants (?), the Baques. That would make it possible that there was some connections between the aborigines of the British Isles and the Iberians. Moreover we find this custom in Southern India, China, Borneo, Kamtchatka, Greenland, and among many tribes of North and South America.

We have seen now, that the race of the aborigines of the British Islands had not been exterminated by the conquering Celts. It is also certain that it was not wholly suppressed, but that the conquerors intermarried very closely with their subjects. For even in the oldest times we find in Ireland no miserable plebs as in other countries conquered by Indo-Europeans. There were no castes, only different stages of society, and a family could easily, by acquiring fortune, rise from the lowest to the highest rank.

There was perhaps rather an infiltration of the Celts than a real conquest, but perhaps we shall not be astray in seeking the reason of that fact in the great beauty and uncommon loveliness of the women of the aborigines. The beauty of Celtic women is well known, as also the fact that they mostly have dark hair, which indicates apparently a non-Aryan origin.

Among no other people is the 'feminine' of such importance as among the Celts. Their literature is given to the service of women. No literature has so many sweet love-stories as the Irish.

> The absence of feminine interest in the earlier chansons de geste has often been noted. The case is different with Teutonic heroic literature, in which woman's rôle is always great, sometimes preeminently so. The love of man, and immortal, or, if mortal, semi-divine maid is a 'constant' of heroic tradition. Teuton and Celt have handled this theme, however, in a very different spirit. In the legends of the former the man plays the chief part; he woos, sometimes he forces the fairy maiden to become the mistress of his hearth. As a rule, overmastered by the prowess and beauty of the hero, she is nothing loth.
>
> It is otherwise with the fairy mistress of the Celtic hero; they abide in their own place, and they allure or compel the mortal lover to resort to them. Connla and Bran and Oisin must all leave this earth and sail across ocean or lake before they can rejoin their lady-love; even Cuchulainn, mightiest of all heroes, is constrained, struggle as he may, to go and dwell with the fairy queen Faud, who has wooed him. Throughout, the immortal mistress retains her superiority; when the mortal tires and returns to earth she remains, ever wise and fair, ready to welcome and enchant a hero of a new generation. She chooses whom she will and is no man's slave; herself she offers freely, but she abandons neither her liberty nor her divine nature. Even where the love-story passes wholly among mortals, the woman's rôle is more accentuated than in the Teutonic sagas. She is no mere lay figure upon a fire-bound rock, like Brunhild or Merglad, ready, when the destined hero appears, to fall straightaway into his arms. The Celtic woman takes her fate in her own hand, and chooses herself the husband or makes him accept her conditions.[50]

In one of the most ancient Gaelic chronicles we read:–

> But the fairest of the women who came into Erin with the sons of Milidh was Feale, the wife of Luaidh, who have lived alone in the western regions of Spain, in an inland valley, until she was wooed by Luaidh . . . and men said concerning Feale, that she was too beautiful to live.

But the Irish historians called by the name 'Milesians,' or 'Sons of Milidh,' the non-Aryan, dark-haired and dark-eyed Irish race, which on account of their complexion they thought to be immigrants from Spain.

All this makes it possible that the aborigines had influenced the Gaels very strongly, but before we can assume with probability such a great religious influence we must try to find out some analogy for such a fact.

The aborigines of the British Isles stood, as we have seen, on a very low level of culture – they were savages. We shall first investigate what ideas one savage people receives from another.

> Everything new is apt to excite the awe and dread of the savage. So the unusually heavy rains, which happened to follow the English survey of the Nicobar Islands in the winter of 1886–1887 were imputed by the alarmed natives to the wrath of the spirits at the theodolites, dumpy-levellers, and other strange instruments which had been set up in so many of their favourite haunts.[51]

Naturally the savage thinks foreign land to be enchanted too.

> Among the Ovambo of South-Western Africa in time of war the chief names a general who leads the army to battle. Next to the general the highest place in the army is occupied by the 'omunene u oshikuni,' that is, the owner of the firewood, who carries a burning brand before the army on the march. If the brand goes out, it is an evil omen, and the army returns. In that case the fire borne at the head of the army may have been intended to dissipate the evil influences, whether magical or spiritual, with which the air of the enemy's country might be conceived to teem.[52]

All the more the savage believes the inhabitants of another country to be sorcerers, especially if these are of an alien and less civilised race. We not only detect the same fear among savages but also among peoples of a higher culture. In the Ongtong Java Islands strangers, when they land on the islands, are first of all received by the sorcerers, sprinkled with water, anointed with oil, etc. Only after they have been 'disenchanted' can they be introduced to the chief.[53]

It is also known that the Hindu despise the non-Aryan aborigines as unclean, but that they fear them on the other hand, as they consider the Parias to be in possession of secret magic arts and to be associated with the old gods in the country.

It is then very probable that the conquering Gaels thought the aborigines were beings endowed with supernatural powers, who possessed great knowledge of the secrets of nature.

How many superstitions are connected with the so-called fairy-arrows (the arrow-heads of flint which the pre-Celtic aborigines used during the Stone Age) among the Celtic population of Great Britain and Ireland. Perhaps these superstitions go back to the time when the Celts were fighting with a people who used flint-weapons and were then already feared as endowed with supernatural powers. Another belief connected with iron may also be quoted.

Iron is said to possess the power of keeping off bad spirits. In the north-east of Scotland after the death of an inmate of the house a bit of iron is put into all victuals, in order that the 'death may not enter them.'[54] In many Welsh fairy-tales a fairy abandons her lover in the moment when he touches her with iron.[55] On the Western Isles of Scotland it is said that every one who enters a knoll where the faries are dancing must leave a bit of iron on the threshold, for only in this way is he able to prevent the fairies from closing the door and keeping him as a prisoner for ever.

This fear of ghosts seems to be a heritage of the aborigines, who did not know metals, and may often have yielded to the better weapons of the Celts. The savage aborigines of a country appear very often in the later popular superstitions as ghosts, giants, or dwarfs.

Of course the Celts felt especial reverence for the medicine-men of the aborigines, the Druids, for they observed how these were dreaded by their countrymen. Among savage tribes the king develops mostly out of the sorcerer, who can, as they believe, inflict misfortune and death. The Gaels, full of admiration, called these magicians 'Druides,' the very wise ones.

The true character of the Druids was that of mighty sorcerers, and entirely contradicts that of an Indo-European priest. In Ireland, which was least exposed to foreign influence, we can most probably hope to find Druidism in its original form. They appear to us there chiefly as magicians and sorcerers. They change the day into night, wind and wave obey their orders, they pour down fire and blood. Such ideas, that man has power over the elements, we only find among savage peoples who do not possess the idea of the 'supernatural.' That the Druids were physicians is closely connected with their profession as sorcerers, as is also their prophetic faculty. So strong is their power that even St Patrick prays to God that He may protect him against the incantations of the Druids. In the old Irish literature the word 'drui' is always used synonymously with 'magus,' and in the neo-Celtic languages the word for Druid signifies 'sorcerer'.

> The Druids are sorcerers and rain-doctors, who pretend to call down the storm and the snow, and frighten the people with the fluttering wisp and other childish charms. They divined by the observation of sneezing and omens, by their dreams after holding a bull-feast or chewing raw horseflesh in front of their idols, by the croaking of their ravens and chirping of tame wrens, or by the ceremony of licking the hot edge of bronze taken out of the rowan-tree faggot. They are like the Red Indian medicine men, or the Angekoks of the Eskimo, dressed up in bull's-hide coats and bird caps with waving wings."[56]

It was probably in the Highlands of Scotland north of the Grampians that the aborigines maintained their independence the longest time, and therefore preserved best the institution of the Druids as sorcerers, for we read that all who wish to learn very exactly the wicked art of sorcery set out for Scotland. Also Pliny the Elder tells us that Britain was ill-famed on account of its magic, and from the report of Tacitus of the destruction of the isle of Mona we perceive clearly that the Druids were sorcerers.

But how does it happen that they are painted by the writers of the antiquity as also philosophers, as teachers of pure ethics?

In Gaul Druidism was not founded upon birth, but upon the engagement and training of novices. Also in Ireland we find the Druids as teachers of the youth, and of the Druid Cathbad it is expressly stated that he taught his pupils the Druidic science (druidecht). From that we assume as certain that among the aborigines a transference of the magic art also took place by initiation and instruction.

Where the Gaels came into friendly terms with them they certainly were anxious to partake of that instruction, and we find in Ireland no distinct Druidic caste; but we know of poets who were Druids, also of some kings – e.g. the grandfather of the famous Irish national hero Finn and the father of King Connor were members of that priesthood. So the Druids grew by time to be a Gaelic institution, and the priestly power of the king was transferred to them, so that they had finally the highest rank after him; there was even a rule that the king should not speak in the presence of his Druid before the latter had spoken.

An obscure memory of the time when the Druids were the magicians of a hostile race can be detected in the Celtic myths which tell us that the magic power of the Druids had been so great that they won even the victory over the gods – a notion that on the one side reminds us of the 'Shaman,' on the other side can be easily understood if we take into consideration that the Druids originally, as sorcerers of the aborigines, were hostile not only to the Celts but also to their gods. We have also often a curious antagonism to note between the Druids and the Celtic gods which is easily explained in such a way (cf. 'Echtra Condla').

No wonder that the Gaelic poet-prophets (for the Celts had also their own prophets) looked at the new rivals with jealous eyes – a jealousy ending finally with the abolition of the Druids in Ireland, for when St Patrick introduced Christianity into Ireland he found in the Druids his greatest enemies whom he could only vanquish by uniting himself with the 'filid' (637, Battle of Moyrath).

It is not strange that the more highly civilised Celts deemed the priests of the aborigines great sorcerers; we find among the Germans something analogous.

> The Finns, who occupied in the past ages a great part of the Scandinavian peninsula, were deemed by the conquering Germans as endowed with magical powers, so that the old Norse finngerd (literally, a Finn's work) is used for 'sorcery', and also in their own religion the priest-sorcerer, the 'Shaman,' who is the mediator between men and gods, and even by his arts compels the latter to serve him, occupies the foremost place.[57]

Is it too rash to assume that the aborigines of the British Isles had a culture similar to that of the Finnic-Lappic tribes? Similar primitive conditions produce similar cultures, and J.F. Campbell, a prominent connoisseur of Finnic antiquity, was so struck by the surprising similarity of many ancient Scottish dwellings with those of the Finns that he did not hesitate to declare that the aborigines of the British Isles were a people related to the Finns; and, though a primitive Iberian population seems very possible, I have come to the opinion that there may have been also a Finnish race on British soil.

When the Gaels sent their sons to be initiated into the teaching of the Druids, they did not forget their own Indo-European religion, and the same thing took place among the Gauls, who conquered Britain several hundred years later, and adopted Druidism from the inhabitants of the country as the Gaels had taken it from the aborigines. In such a way we can easily explain the strange contrast of noble and mean doctrines which we detect among the Druids. If Pliny the Elder painted the Druids only as magician and priests of the oak, he therewith told to his contemporaries something new: their noble doctrines had been well known long before.

We have also elsewhere sufficient examples of a noble religion tolerating the old, crude faith. We can observe till to-day, in Catholic countries, the feast of Adonis; and the Church tolerates the old, pagan midsummer and harvest customs, and we may safely assume that in the British Isles the pre-Celtic faith existed under the dominion of the Celts.

Andrew Lang quotes, in his *Custom and Myth*, an example of a similar toleration which is related to us by Gercilasso de Vega, the son of a Spanish conqueror and an Inca princess:–

> In the pre-Inca period an Indian was not accounted honourable unless he was descended from a fountain river, or lake, or from a wild animal; but there was not an animal, how vile and filthy soever, that they did not worship as a god. But when the Inca appeared and sun-worship became the established religion, worship of the animal was still tolerated, and the sun-temples also contained images of the beasts which the Indians had venerated.

But I think I have found a sure argument that Druidism took its origin in the British Islands, and was not brought thither by the Celts.

Pliny the Elder describes the Gaulish Druids as priests of the oak-worship, wherein also the mistletoe plays a prominent part. The worship of the oak can be certainly proved to be of Indo-European origin. This is so well known that it is unnecessary to prove it specially. Max. Tyrius says, moreover, that the Celts worshipped Zeus under the image of an oak. In a word, we find the Druids as priests of an Indo-European religion.

But if the Celts had had Druids who were already priests of the oak before the occupation of the British Islands, they certainly would have brought that worship with them to Ireland. For in ancient times Ireland was very rich in oak woods, and we can trace yet over thirteen hundred place-names which begin with 'doire, daire' (oakwood), Anglicised 'derry,' not to speak of the other compositions. The name of the oak occurs in many more names of places than that of any other tree.[58]

How strange must it seem to us, then, that we so seldom hear of the oak in the rich, traditional literature of the Irish. I know no Irish superstition connected with the oak, and *the Irish Druids are never mentioned in connection with the oak*. Their holy tree is the yew, and they bear in their hands wands made of that wood. Also the Druidic fire is kindled with the wood of the yew.

That strange fact, that the oak plays no part in the life of the Irish Druid and a very small one in the popular superstition can be explained only if we assume that the Druids were originally the priests of a people who did not know the oak worship.

The Gauls who had remained in their own country were much less influenced by the pre-Celtic population of Britain than the Gaels, and retained, therefore, besides the new Druidical faith, the old customs of their Indo-European ancestors.

We perceive, then, that the Druids must have been once the priests of a people who did not know the worship of the oak. But the oak-worship of the Celts is vouched for several times, therefore the Druids cannot have been originally a Celtic priesthood. We know also that Druidism took its origin in the British Islands, and it can only have originated among the people who occupied those countries before the Celts. We have seen that such a people existed on the British Islands and that they were a people powerful enough to influence strongly the conquering Celts; we know also that it is possible, and it has often happened, that a people of a lower stage of culture has influenced the religious beliefs of a more highly civilised one.

Besides, Druidism shows so many non-Indo-European features that we must for that reason alone seek the origin of its priesthood among a non-Indo-European people.

We can, therefore, assert with somewhat of certainty that Druidism originated in a people who inhabited the British Islands before the Celts, and who were probably related to those great races who occupied Western and Southern (or Northern?) Europe long before the first Indo-European set his foot there.

6

THE DRUIDS

T. Rice Holmes

From *Caesar's Conquest of Gaul*

The Druids

1   Where and when did Druidism[59] originate? Caesar in a well-known passage remarks that it was believed to have been discovered in Britain and to have been imported thence into Gaul;[60] and some scholars accept this tradition as literally true. The earliest extant mention of Druids, the substance of which was reproduced in Diogenes Laertius's *Lives of the Philosophers*,[61] was made by Sotion of Alexandria[62] about the commencement of the second century before Christ, – not long after the Belgic conquest of Britain began; and it has been supposed that the conquerors found Druidism flourishing there, and made it known in the land from which they had set out. But the Belgae were not the first Celtic conquerors of Britain; and it is reasonable to suppose that if Druidism was of British origin, it had been imported into Gaul before. Maximin Deloche argued that it could not have originated in Gaul, since the Gallic invaders of Italy knew nothing of it:[63] but A. Réville replied, first, that Caesar did not affirm its British origin, but only recorded the belief which he found prevalent among the Gauls; and, secondly, that if the Gauls who invaded Italy had no Druids, Druids may nevertheless have existed in Gaul before the invasion 'à l'état d'humble compagnie de sorciers-médecins'.[64] This of course is a mere conjecture; but the assumption that Brennus and his followers were not accompanied by Druids is only an inference from the silence of the historians and from the statement of Pausanias[65] that the Gallic chief who attacked Delphi did not employ any Greek priests or 'diviners';[66] and in the third cnetury B.C. at all events the Cisalpine Boi had priests.[67] Indeed the prevalent theory is that Druidism was pre-Celtic and developed in the Neolithic Age in Gaul or in Britain, possibly in both; and if this belief were well founded, it would follow that, unless Druidism was a late importation from Britain, the Gallic invaders of Italy must have known it before they left their own country. M. Salomon Reinach[68] attributes the megalithic monuments of Gaul to Druidical influence, arguing that their construction is inexplicable except on the hypothesis of 'a

religious aristocracy exercising an almost absolute dominion over a numerous population'. But is it necessary to suppose that this aristocracy was a hierarchy? And if it is a fair conclusion that the supposed hierarchy was composed of Druids, might it not be argued that Druidism was a world-wide institution, or at least co-extensive with rude stone monuments?[69] M. Jullian,[70] remarking that the Germans, who were congeners of the Celts and had always been more or less closely connected with them, had no priests in Caesar's time,[71] but had a century later,[72] argues that among the Celts also the priestly office had once been exercised by the tribal kings, but had naturally become specialized: in other words, he holds that Druidism was a Celtic institution, which made its appearance comparatively late, – probably in the third century B.C. But Druidism, as we may infer from Caesar's words, had flourished in Britain long before his time, and, as we may infer from the *Annals*[73] of Tacitus, especially in the western and less civilized districts; and it may be doubted whether at the time of its birth remote British tribes were politically or socially more advanced than the German contemporaries of Caesar. M. Jullian indeed urges that if the Druidical doctrine originated in Britain, Druids may nevertheless have first appeared in Gaul; for, he says, 'la doctrine et le clergé d'une religion peuvent avoir des berceaux fort différents: voyez le Christianisme.'[74] But, replies M. d'Arbois de Jubainville, Christianity was introduced into the Roman Empire by Jews, – the disciples of Jesus: besides, how could an unwritten doctrine like Druidism have been imported into Gaul from Britain unless Druids had brought it?[75] M. Jullian's theory implies that in Britain Druidism was a religion without a clergy; that after it was imported into Gaul, a clergy was formed, who were called Druids; and that subsequently Britain, which had given Druidism to Gaul, borrowed from Gaul the idea of appointing Druids. Is not this very improbable?

My own belief is that there will always be room for hypotheses; but that we can never get behind Caesar's report of the Gallic tradition that the *disciplina* – the Druidical doctrine – originated in Britain, and, in the absence of other positive testimony, had better cling to it. Caesar's statement is sometimes explained in the sense that in his time Druidism was more vigorous in Britain than in Gaul, and that Gallic Druids therefore travelled to Britain in order to be initiated into its mysteries;[76] but why should we not accept it in its natural sense?

2 Desjardins[77] points out that there is no evidence that Druidism existed in Caesar's time in Aquitania or in the Roman Province; and, he says, it seems clear from Caesar's narrative that the Romans came in contact with Druids for the first time when they had passed beyond the northern boundary of Roman territory. But neither is there any evidence that Druidism did not exist in the Province; and it seems clear that it must have existed there before the inhabitants became Romanized. Sir John Rhys[75] maintains further, that there is no evidence that Druidism was ever the religion of any Brythonic people; and since he assigns almost the whole of Britain south of the firths of Forth and

Clyde to the Brythons, he appears to restrict the British area of Druidism to a narrow western fringe. This hardly accords with Caesar's statement that Britain was the stronghold of Druidism. Moreover, when Caesar tells us that the Druids were the religious aristocracy of the Gauls, he plainly gives us to understand that Druidism was common to all the peoples who lived between the Seine and the Garonne; and it is certain that among these peoples the Gallo-Brythonic element was predominant. Indeed, although it is commonly assumed that the Belgae had no Druids, there is absolutely no ground for the assumption. Caesar often used the word *Galli* in a comprehensive sense, including the Belgae; and it is not improbable that when he was describing the manners and customs of the Gauls, and Druidism, which was their most remarkable institution, he intended his description to apply to the Belgae.[79]

3   It has often been alleged that Caesar overestimated the power of the Druids.[80] Réville, observing that there is no evidence that Vercingetorix received any support from them, holds that Caesar was misled by Diviciacus, who hoped by exaggerating the importance of his own order[81] to secure for himself 'l'hégémonie spirituelle de la Gaule'.[82] Desjardins,[83] however, points out that by such misrepresentatin Diviciacus would have defeated his own object; and he believes that Vercingetorix regarded the Druids as antagonistic to his own power and therefore would have nothing to do with them. Desjardins's view is that Caesar's account is correct as far as it goes, but that it refers to a state of things anterior to the Roman conquest, especially as regards the custom of human sacrifice. This is a pure guess, based, I suppose, upon the notion that the Gauls, in Caesar's time, were too civilized to sacrifice human victims. But Caesar tells us that it was their custom to torture to death the warrior who was the last to present himself at the general muster which preceded a military expedition;[84] and if the Romans, in the second Punic war, offered human victims to the gods,[85] if suttee prevailed two generations ago in India, why should it be incredible that human sacrifice was practised in Gaul? Moreover, Tertullian[86] affirms that the Druids offered human sacrifices to Mercury, and Suetonius[87] speaks of 'the superstition of the Druids with its terrible cruelty'. Sir John Rhys[88] says that 'in Ireland . . . druidism and the kingship went hand in hand; nor is it improbable that it was the same in Gaul, so that when the one fell, the other suffered to some extent likewise'; while Duruy[89] affirms that the nobles had dealt a fatal blow at the power of the Druids. I cannot find a scrap of evidence in support of this assertion; on the contrary, Caesar expressly says that in 52 B.C. the Aeduan Vergobret, or chief magistrate, was elected by the priests.[90] Mommsen[91] takes a different view from Duruy's. 'It may readily be conceived,' he says, 'that such a priesthood attempted to usurp, as it partially did usurp, the secular government. . . . The Gauls were not much removed from an ecclesiastical state with its pope and councils, its immunities, interdicts, and spiritual courts.' If we are entitled to infer from Caesar's silence that the Druids did not play the part of a national priesthood in the Gallic war, does the truth of the inference prove that their power had been broken by the nobles?[92]

But the silence of Caesar regarding the part which the Druids played in the great rebellion has exercised the ingenuity of many commentators. 'A singularly powerful priesthood,' says Professor Haverfield,[93] 'numbering political leaders, like Divitiacus, among its ranks, might be expected in a national crisis to take some definite line, requiring notice in the *Commentaries*. Yet omit two chapters, and so far as the *Commentaries* go, the Druids might never have existed.' M. Jullian[94] argues that they did take an active part in the rebellion, but that Caesar chose to ignore the fact: Caesar '*a laïcisé à outrance l'ésprit et l'histoire de la Gaule . . . Nul ne croira que la Gaule n'ait pas appelé prêtres et dieux à son secours*'. Professor Haverfield, who naturally asks 'What motive had Caesar for this?' suggests that an analogy 'to these powerful non-political priests . . . is provided by various priestly *collegia* at Rome, which include political teachers, but which in their augural or other capacity take no political action', and maintains that the Druids, 'as Druids, uttered no word against Caesar or for him.' But if so, why, at a time when their power had certainly diminished, did they aid and abet the insurrection of Civilis?[95] To my mind Caesar's attitude hardly needs explanation. Unless he had a motive for concealment, he omitted nothing which had an important bearing upon his operations, but he omitted everything else. I agree with M. Jullian that Druids, as Druids or as individuals, sided with or against the rebels in the movement of 52 B.C.: it is inconceivable that they held aloof.[96] That they interfered as a corporation is, however, most improbable. It is incredible that in the inter-tribal

View of the kistvaen at Rowldrich.
From The Celtic Druids *by Godfrey Higgins*

politics of Gaul they should have habitually acted with unanimity; otherwise, in the event, for instance, of a war between the Aedui and the Sequani, the Druids in one state or the other would have been ranged against their fellow-countrymen. Froude's assertion[97] that, 'So far as can be seen, the Druids were on the Roman side,' is, I suppose, based upon the facts that Caesar's friend and ally, Diviciacus, was a Druid, and that Convictolitavis, whose candidature for the office of Vergobret Caesar supported, was the nominee of the Druids.[98] But one swallow does not make a summer; and even if the Aeduan Druids had been opposed to Caesar, I am not sure that he would have thought it worth while to accentuate their hostility and outrage public opinion by deliberately setting at naught the constitution of his principal allies.[99] I conclude that in the rebellion, save in the case of Convictolitavis,[100] neither the Druids nor any individual Druid exercised an influence which, at all events so far as Caesar knew, sensibly affected the result.[101]

4   Fustel[102] remarks that Caesar does not say that the Druids acted as judges in all suits, but only in almost all (*de omnibus fere controversiis*);[103] and also that he does not say that their jurisdiction, as far as it extended, was obligatory, but rather leaves on our minds the impression that litigants sought it voluntarily. M.G. Bloch[104] argues that the suitors who appealed to Druids probably all belonged to the upper class, who, having unlimited rights over their dependants,[105] doubtless decided their disputes. Moreover, the Aeduan Vergobret had 'the power of life and death over his countrymen,'[106] just as fathers had over their wives and children;[107] and the chief magistrate adjudicated on offences against the state,[108] though the punishment which he inflicted may have been sanctioned and superintended by Druids. Fustel infers, moreover, from Caesar's statement that every one submitted to the verdicts of the Druids,[109] that they had no power of enforcing them. No power, though they could and did excommunicate those who were refractory! Besides, Caesar distinctly says that those who were excommunicated were outside the pale of the law (*neque his petentibus ius redditur*).[110] Whether the law here spoken of was that administered by the Druids themselves or by the secular authorities, matters nothing. Practically, if Caesar was not misinformed, the Druids had the most irresistible power of enforcing their judgements.

5   Desjardins[111] and others hold that the Druids and the oligarchical nobles were leagued together to repress the democratic aspirations of the populace; but, as Fustel points out,[112] there is no evidence whatever in support of his view. Nor, I may add, is there any evidence that such aspirations existed,[113] at all events that any leader had arisen to formulate and sustain them. As the knights, or many of them, sent their sons to be educated by Druids, and as many Druids must have belonged to noble families, it may be reasonably inferred that the two orders had common interests; and when an ambitious noble endeavoured to raise the populace for his own purposes, the Druids may have used their spiritual powers against him: but all this is mere conjecture.

7

THEORIES CONCERNING THE ORIGINS OF DRUIDISM

Lewis Spence

From *The History and Origins of Druidism*

Having reviewed the whole 'document' of Druidism, and epitomized the entire range of information respecting it, we may now summarize the several theories which profess to explain its origin before drawing our final conclusions as to their value.

Mr T.D. Kendrick is of opinion that the main facts associated with Druidism are to be found only in such records as have survived concerning its position in the Gaul of the first century B.C. The Druidism of Ireland, he thinks, is only to be explained incidentally by this governing factor. Celtic doctrine in the Marne area, he believes, must have been 'built up on native faith,' that is the religion of the tribes upon whom the Gauls imposed their rule, after the Gauls had occupied that area for some generations.

This mingled faith was then carried to Britain by those Gauls who had mixed with the native population of the Marne area, and in Britain it blended with the religion of the non-Celtic folk who then peopled our islands. But in the peaceful and appropriate conditions which marked the La Tène period in Gaul, the Celtic settlers there may have developed a priestly caste (the Druidic) at some time in the fourth or third century B.C. Druidism in Gaul, for Mr Kendrick, is therefore Celtic religion after its fusion with 'native' beliefs in the Marne area, while Druidism in Britain was a mélange of this Gaulish system with an aboriginal British cultus which itself had affinities with the native Marne faith with which Celtic belief had blended. The Druids as a hierarchy 'were only subsequent Keltic servants of the Kelticised native faith in Gaul, a separate and accidental phenomenon of Gallic (not British) Druidism.'

79

Sir John Rhys saw fit to alter his views on the origins of Druidism more than once. In an early work he asserted that Druidism had been planted in Gaul by those Belgae who had settled in Britain. Later, he give it as his opinion, that no Belgic or Brythonic people ever practised Druidism. Still later, he concluded that the Goidelic invaders of Britain borrowed their magic and Druidism from the folk of the *sidh* who afterwards became in the popular mind the fairies of folk-lore. Again, he argued that Druidism had been developed by the Goidels of the Continent, or accepted by them from the aborigines. In the last edition of his *Celtic Britain* he affirmed that Druidism had originated among the aborigines both of Gaul and Britain, who inherited it from common ancestors. It was, therefore, so far as he was concerned, not a Celtic cultus at all, but would seem to have been most powerful 'in those districts where a pre-Celtic population may naturally be conjectured to have survived in the greatest numbers, namely in the west of Gaul, in the west of Britain and in Ireland.'

Rice Holmes thought it 'not unreasonable to believe' that the Celts had borrowed Druidism from some non-Aryan people. There was, he thought, 'nothing to show that the Gauls whom the Romans first encountered had ever heard of it.' He denied Rhys's statement that people of Brythonic race did not practise Druidism. Caesar's account, he thought, made it clear that it was common to all the peoples who lived between the Seine and the Garonne, among many of whom 'the Gallo-Brythonic element was predominant.' Holmes quoted as against his own view that Desjardins had pointed out that there was no evidence that Druidism existed in Caesar's time in Aquitania or in the Roman Province and that it seemed clear from Caesar's account that the Romans came in contact with the Druids for the first time when they had passed beyond the northern boundary of Roman territory. But Holmes rightly retorted that there was no evidence that Druidism did not exist in the Province, and that it probably flourished there before the inhabitants became Romanized.

Frazer indicated resemblances between the Druidic religion and that of ancient Latium. The white steers sacrificed on the Alban Mount and in the Capitol at Rome, he says, 'remind us of the white bulls which the Druids of Gaul sacrificed under the holy oak when they cut the mistletoe. . . . When we remember that the ancient Italian and Celtic peoples spoke languages which are nearly related to each other, we shall not be surprised at discovering traces of community in their religion, especially in what concerns the worship of the god of the oak and the thunder.'

M. Camille Jullian holds that Druidism was a Celtic institution of comparatively late appearance, which perhapd had its rise at some time in the third century B.C. He believes that Britain preserved more faithfully than the other Celtic lands the religious habits of the common motherland, retaining their most primitive forms and that this was the reason why the Gaulish Druids sent their novices to Britain for instruction. It may have been that an ancient native community existed in the island with foreign rites and teaching which supplied inspiration to the Druids.

Mr A.H. Allcroft, as we have seen, argues that Druidism was not a religion but 'an organization (*disciplina*) which made of religion a means to political power.' There is, he says, no trace of Druidism among the Celts of Spain, of Italy or of Galatia and it would seem to have been of late introduction in Gaul. In Caesar's time it had small influence in Aquitania and the Narbonnaise. He is of opinion that it originated among the Belgae, as Chartres, its centre, was under 'Belgic hegemony.' The Belgae once conquered, Druidism disappeared as an influence. It probably flourished among the Belgae of Britain, where it was extirpated when Claudius effected the conquest of the island. The Goidelic and Iberian peoples did not readily submit to it. In my view practically none of these assertions can be seriously entertained.

M. Salomon Reinach was of opinion that the Gaulish Celts accepted Druidism from some pre-Celtic people *en bloc*, as the later Romans adopted certain Oriental cults. He further asserted that when the Celts appeared in history Druidism was in its decline.

D'Arbois de Jubainville maintained that the Druids were priests of the Goidels in Briain who imposed their faith upon their Gaulish conquerors, who then introduced Druidism to Gaul at some time about 200 B.C. Sir G.L. Gomme was of the belief that the Druids were a pre-Celtic priesthood, as the faith they practised held much that was 'non-Aryan,' and was indeed the parent of witchcraft.

Another supporter of the theory that Druidism was a 'non-Aryan' faith was Julius Pokorny of Vienna, whose arguments are so interesting as to merit more than passing consideration. 'Druidism,' he thought, 'has many features quite alien to the character of an Indo-European religion,' and this is to be accounted for by the circumstance that the Druids were the priests of the pre-Celtic aborigines of the British Isles. 'In historical times we find among the Irish kings traces of the former priestship which had originated in the furthest past ages from the divine adoration of mighty magicians' – otherwise the doctrine of the Divine King – 'a belief which the Indo-European races had given up before they had left their common native home.' But it is contrary to the evidence to assert either that the doctrine of the Divine King was solely an 'Aryan' one, or that the Indo-European races had relinquished it at a period so early as Pokorny believes they did. So far from being 'Aryan,' it was entertained by the people of ancient Egypt, if indeed it did not originate in that country, as all the evidence goes to show. Pokorny, indeed, destroys his own argument when he states that 'the Celts believed that there would be bad crops as a punishment for bad rulers,' as this alone reveals that Indo-European folk had not deserted the doctrine.

In the British Isles, he continued, the Gauls had found an aboriginal race who had come over from the Continent in early times, and it was among them that Druidism had its rise. The Druids were magicians rather than priests of a well-defined religion, a notion which I have already shown to be ill-founded, if not insupportable. The worship of the oak, he argues, was certainly Indo-European. 'If the Celts had had Druids who were already priests of the oak before the occupation of the British Islands, they certainly would have brought that worship with them to Ireland,' yet we seldom hear of the oak in Irish literature, and 'the Irish Druids are never mentioned in connection with the oak ... The Druids must have been once the priests of a people who did not know the worship of the oak. But the oak-worship of the Celts is vouched for several times, therefore the Druids cannot have been originally a Celtic priesthood.'

... I think Pokorny greatly exaggerated when he asserts that the worship of the oak was unknown in Ireland and that its place there was taken by the yew tree. There are frequent references to sacred oaks in Irish literature. The circumstance that in the *Book of Leinster* we read that during a popular revolt every oak in Ireland bore only one acorn as a punishment for the manner in which the people had treated the King and the nobles, alone makes it plain that the oak was regarded as a sacred food-yielding tree, the central object of a cultus associated with that of the Divine King, as in Gaul. At the same time it must be admitted that the yew appears to have been more prominent in Irish Druidism and that it may have superseded the oak as a symbol. This, however, it seems to me, has no bearing on the question whether the Druids were originally a Celtic or a non-Celtic priesthood. That they were a Celtic priesthood in Gaul, where and when we first encounter them, we know. That they were also servants of the Celtic seasonal festivals in Ireland we are also aware. But the whole argument as to whether they were of 'Aryan' or 'non-Aryan', Celtic or Iberian origin is scarcely relative to the larger view of Druidic beginnings which I hope to be able to maintain in a later chapter.

Having summarized the outstanding theories relating to the origin of Druidism, let us now examine more particularly some of the arguments set forth in them. And first, as to the racial associations of Druidism. We find that Rhys, Kendrick, Reinach, Gomme and Pokorny, with varying degrees of insistence, adhere to the theory that Druidism originated among the 'aboriginal' tribes of the Continent and Britain, that Frazer lays some stress upon its origin among the Latin-Celtic peoples, that Jullian finds that it was wholly a Celtic faith and that Allcroft considers it to have been exclusively a Belgic institution. Rice Holmes goes so far as to assert that there is 'nothing to show that the Gauls when the Romans first encountered them, had ever heard of it.' On the other hand, it may be said, with equal justice, that there is something to show that they had.

If the reference be to the period of the Gaulish invasion of Rome in 390 B.C., it should be remembered that the Romans observed the Gauls on that occasion only as an army and thus not in such circumstances as would be favourable to observing their religious characteristics. If it be to subsequent early contact, the Romans could scarcely have been unaware of the great Druidic settlement at Marseilles. Indeed *a Roman army went to the assistance of the Greek settlers in Marseilles against the Gauls as early as 155 B.C.*, and by 120 B.C. the Romans had acquired the valley of the Lower Rhone by conquest. Druidism in Gaul had been in existence at least a generation or so before this, as Diogenes Laertius's reference to it makes clear, quoting the writings of Sotion of Alexandria, who wrote about 200 B.C. It seems, therefore, idle and even absurd to suggest that Druidism was unknown to the Gauls when the Romans first encountered them in their own land.

More substantial is Holmes's belief, based on the account of Caesar, that Druidism was common to all the peoples who lived between the Seine and the Garonne, and as we know that it was also established on the southern coast of Gaul, there is little question that it was the prevailing religion of the greater part of that country. But, as Desjardins remarks, the evidence for Druidism in Aquitania is lacking. The absence of all proof that it existed in the province is, as Holmes indicates, cancelled by the circumstance that that area had been thoroughly Romanized at an early date.

But there is good reason to believe that Druidism did not function throughout the Belgic portion of Gaul, despite the statements of Allcroft and others that it actually had its rise among the Belgae. Had this people practised it, there can be little question that they would have continued to do so in Britain, where they made extensive settlements in the Southern areas in times immediately preceding the Christian era. But in a prolonged study of the history and general conditions of this Celto-Teutonic folk in Britain I have failed to discover even the slightest evidence that they ever embraced the Druidic cultus, or that they had even the least association with it whatsoever. The one reference which might seem to prove exceptional in this connection is that of Tacitus to the sacrifice or slaughter of the women of Londinium by the host of Boadicea in the grove of Andate or Andraste in the year 61. But as I have already said, the circumstances of dubiety which surround the cult of this goddess make it impossible to judge whether or not she had any associations with Druidism and this seems to me to remove the reference to her and her temple in Romano-Belgic London from the sphere of practical consideration so far as it relates to Druidic origins.

Canon MacCulloch, criticizing the theory of Rhys that the Druids were originally a non-Celtic priesthood, remarks that it fails for lack of historical evidence. 'Everywhere they appear as the supreme and dominant priesthood of the Celts, and the priests of a conquered people could hardly have obtained such power over the conquerors.' He regards such a situation as 'incredible.' He denies that Druidic practice was opposed to 'Aryan' sentiment in its legal and priestly functions. Macbain also maintained the 'Aryan' character of Druidism. He compares it with the Brahman caste of India in its rigidly monopolizing and exclusive spirit.

Such religious ideas as appear to have been known to the Druids were equally familiar to the peoples of other 'Aryan' communities – Germans, Slavs, Greeks, Romans and Hindus. The writers of the Classical period indeed appear to have realized the underlying identity of the more outstanding figures of the several 'Aryan' pantheons in a manner never approached by modern authorities on comparative religion. I certainly do not mean to imply that no leaven of 'non-Aryan' faith or magic found its way into Druidic dogma and ritual. Such a negation would be absurd. Indeed so many religious and magical forms are common to both 'Aryan' and 'non-Aryan' peoples as to make it virtually impossible to distinguish between them at times. Actually the tests by which some traditionalists seek to do so are, in certain circumstances, glaringly incompetent for all practical purposes, and in face of this, I feel it is frequently impossible to draw any hard-and-fast boundaries.

Writing on the subject of the term 'Aryan' in a recent work, Mr Patrick Carleton has sharply criticized the laxity of its employment. 'Probably,' he says, 'no scientific term has been so constantly misused by ignorant persons as has this one. Strictly speaking, the name Âryan ought only to be applied to those ancient European invaders of India and Persia and to their language. But that language is one of the great and important group called (from the fact that its branches extend from England and Germany to India) *Indo-European* or *Indo-Germanic*; and consequently "Âryan" is sometimes stretched to cover the whole of the language-group and all the races who speak any branches of it. . . . The fact of the matter is that we are no more able to speak of an "Indogermanic Race" than of a "Semitic Race".' Nor is it possible, he avers, to identify and separately distinguish any Indo-Germanic race. With his attitude I find myself in perfect agreement.

Whether Druidism were [*sic*] 'Aryan' or otherwise, it is evident that it must have absorbed much of the so called 'Aryan' spirit. But that it also retained much of the character of a more primitive fetishism is clear from the traditions respecting it which we find in Ireland and Scotland. Indeed, we may safely accept it as authoritative that Druidism was, in its beginnings, like the religions of Greece and Rome, a primitive faith of the lower cultus which gradually assumed a more exalted status as it advanced in time, either because of its adoption by a Celtic people, or because of those evolutionary causes which quicken the growth of religious cults.

PART TWO

THE REVIVAL: DRUIDRY IN THE EIGHTEENTH AND NINETEENTH CENTURIES

HE period covered in this section marks the most productive era of Druidic study and speculation until the present. At this time dozens of books and treatises appeared, all claiming to have penetrated the 'secrets' of the Druids and setting forth often nonsensical and far-fetched theories. I have tried to give a representative selection here, while avoiding the more preposterous ideas, although not all of them have been omitted for the simple reason that even the most ludicrous-seeming writings have influenced what Druidry is today and often, indeed, contain material of value.

With the gradual rise of Christianity throughout the Middle Ages, Druidry was almost forgotten, relegated to a distant corner of memory and perceived as a last relic of pre-Christian order. But the memory did not quite die, and during the latter part of the sixteenth century a number of highly speculative works emerged on the Continent. These not only examined the history of Druidism but also claimed the philosophy and wisdom of the Druids for either France or Germany. England followed suit, although it was not until the seventeenth century that the romantic figure of the Druid began to emerge. Poets such as Michael Drayton in his monumental poem on the spirit of Britain entitled *Poly-Olbion* (1596-1622; see pages 92-97) spoke of the Druids in tones of almost breathless respect, while at the same time casting some doubt on their history. Even John Milton mentioned them in his early writings.

Then, in 1689, the antiquary John Aubrey wrote in his preliminary study of Stonehenge that the Druids were most probably its architects and that they must have been mighty in wisdom and skill to achieve such a great feat of spiritual architecture. Aubrey was backed up in his controversial thesis by the eminent Celtic scholar Edward Lhuyd (1660-1709), whose own massive book, *Archaeologica Britannica* (1707), marked one of the first serious attempts to chart the history of Celtic language and belief. Meanwhile the classical sources, such as Caesar, Strabo and Pliny, were becoming more readily available, and these works began to influence the way in which Druids were perceived.

The first serious work on Druidry was a projected history by John Toland (1670-1722). However, the work remained fragmentary and unfinished, appearing finally as a series of letters to Toland's patron Viscount Molesworth in 1726. The work, of which a generous portion is reprinted here (see pages 102-122), is, despite some confusion and an insufficent knowledge of Irish, still an important one and well worth re-reading today. Toland, who is credited with the establishment of the modern order of Bards, Ovates and Druids, had a keen mind and was sceptical of some of the wilder theories put forward by his contemporaries. The notes he wrote in his own copy of Martin Martin's *A Description of the Western Highlands of Scotland* (1716) show that he was scornful of the mystical claims of the religion and culture of the Celts.

Shortly after, in 1740, William Stukeley published a book entitled *Stonehenge, a Temple Restored to the British Druids*. Stukeley was active in the establishment of the Society of Antiquaries, whose member were dedicated to the investigation of just such subjects, and he not only embraced Aubrey's

Title-page of De Dis Germanis, *by Schedius.*

theory, but also considerably elaborated it, describing white-robed Druids worshipping a great serpent named 'Dracontia' at Stonehenge, a temple built by their own hands. His book described a system of Druidry that had never existed, but it was influential at the time and continues, at a popular level and despite the clear refutation of modern scholarship, to influence both the way that Druidry is perceived and the belief that they were in some way responsible for the building of Stonehenge. Stukeley followed up his first book with another, *Abury, a Temple of the British Druids*, which was published in 1743. In this he turned his attention to the great megalithic centre of Avebury in Wiltshire, declaring this to be another of the wonders created by the Druids.

No less a person than the poet and prophet William Blake (1757–1827) was influenced by this book, and his engraving for the poem *Jerusalem* (1804–20) depicts robed Druids worshipping a serpent. In the same poem he wrote, in darker mood, of the bloodier side of Druid history:

O ye sons of the mighty Albion
Planting these Oaken Groves, Erecting these Dragon Temples . . .
Where Albion slept beneath the Fatal Tree
And the Druid's golden knife
Rioted in human gore
In offerings of human life.

Blake has also been claimed as one of the Chosen Chiefs of the Order of Bards, Ovates, and Druids between 1799 and 1827, as was William Stukeley between 1722 and 1765.

The romantic imagery of Druidism was taken up by other eighteenth century poets such as Thomas Gray, whose popular work *The Bard* (1757) drew a picture of a wild and romantic figure who bears all the hallmarks of the revival Druid:

On a rock, whose haughty brow
Frowns o'er Conway's foaming flood.
Robed in the sable garb of woe,
With hagged eyes the poet stood
(Loose his beard and hoary hair
Streamed, like a meteor, to the troubled air);
And, with a master's hand and prophet's fire,
Struck the deep sorrows of his lyre.

The learned Dr John Ogilvie of Aberdeen, in his anonymously published *Fane of the Druids* (1787), described the arch-druid in terms that are familiar to us today from many a romantic painting or photograph of modern neo-Druidic events at Stonehenge:

Though time with silver locks adorn'd his head
Erect his gesture yet, and firm his tread . . .
His seemly beard, to grace his form bestow'd
Descending decent, on his bosom flow'd;
His robe of purest white, though rudly join'd
Yet showed an emblem of the purest mind . . .

However, it was in Wales during the eighteenth century that the revival of Druidry gathered fresh momentum. In 1764 the antiquarian and scholar Evan Evans published a collection entitled *Specimens of the Poetry of the Ancient Welsh Bards*, which generated a good deal of interest among his fellow Cambrians about their own literary history. His work was followed in 1784 and 1802 respectively by Edward Jones's *Mythological and Poetical Relics of the Welsh Bards and Druids* and *The Bardic Museum*.

These works, especially those of Evans, were a major influence on a young man named Edward Williams, who soon began to make a name for himself under the pseudonym of Iolo Morgannwg. Iolo's works, which are voluminous and difficult to read today, nevertheless show a keen mind at work, passionately determined to prove that the literature and philosophy of the Celts were the equal of any others in the world. Unfortunately, what Iolo failed to find among the remains of Welsh bardic literature, he freely invented, thus making much harder the task of succeeding generations of scholars because it is virtually impossible to tell the invented from the real traditions, since many of the manuscripts to which Iolo did have access have vanished.

In 1792 Iolo created a Druidic ritual that was performed on Primrose Hill in London, traditionally, though without any real foundation, said to be a meeting-place for the ancient Druids. On the same occasion Iolo convened the first 'gorsedd' or assembly of the bards of Britain to be held since the Middle Ages, thereby beginning a tradition that continues to this day. Following from this successful venture, Iolo helped to establish the idea of regular Eisteddfods, which would be held in Wales. From 1819 these bardic meetings became regular events, and still take place. Although they are not Druidic in the purest sense of the word, they contain a strong element of Druidic practice, and they represent the most visible aspect of the tradition in the eyes of the world.

I have included here two brief selections from Iolo's work, collected by his son J. Williams ab Ithel, under the title *Barddas*. The first of these, a dialogue between Druid and Teacher, expresses ideas that are still current within revival Druidism. The second, three versions of 'The Gorsedd Prayer', is still in current usage.

Iolo, along with those who came after him, spearheaded what became known as the 'Celtic Revival'. Poets and dramatists such as W.B. Yeats, AE, (G.W. Russell), 'Fiona Macleod' (William Sharp) and others produced a series of brilliant works that captured the romance and mystery of the Celtic traditions and helped to enshrine them in the consciousness of the nineteenty and early twentieth centuries.

Among other pseudo-historians and antiquarians was Edward Davies, whose *Mythology and Rites of the British Druids* (1809) and *Celtic Researches* (1804; see pages 123–153) had a profound and long-lasting effect on the way in which Druidry was perceived, and, indeed, he is still read to this day. Davies, whose work is represented here by an extract from *Celtic Researches*, was a brilliant if erratic scholar, whose misreading of the documents set forth by Iolo Morganwg, led him to some curious conclusions. However, his works still bear re-reading for their insights and (occasionally) inspired guesses, which influenced such modern writers as Robert Graves (see, for example, *The White Goddess*, London, 1957).

Such was the popularity of Davies and of lesser known writers such as Samuel Rush Meyrick and Charles Hamilton Smith, whose *Costumes of the Original Inhabitants of Britain* (1815) described a now familiar image of a bearded, white-robed arch-Druid with a golden breastplate and a sickle with which to cut mistletoe in an ancient and largely spurious ceremony, that Algernon Herbert, the Dean of Merton College Oxford, responded with *An Essay on the Neo-Druidic Heresy in Britannia* (see pages 172–182). Herbert attacked the wilder assertions of antiquarian speculation and went back to the classical sources, although not without adding some of his own curious notions, such as that Druidism bore a strong resemblance to the rites and ritual of the Cherokee tribe of North America!

Other, less well-known writers, such as Godfrey Higgins whose book *The Celtic Druids* (1829; see pages 154-171) traced the Celtic peoples and the Druidic teachings to biblical times, and R.W. Morgan, who sought an equally eastern point of origin for the 'Cimmeranian' race, pushed the boundaries of speculation to the limits. An entire sub-stratum of lore and literature emerged at this time in the shape of the British Israelite movement, which taught that the Celts were one of the twelve Lost Tribes of Israel, who had settled in these islands in the remote past. This led to further speculation and comparison between so-called Druidic rites and those of the Judaic people, a theory that has refused to die, even in our own time, although it is little regarded by modern scholars of Druidry.

Grandiose titles such as the following qualify many of the books on Druidry from the eighteenth and nineteenth centuries: *A Complete History of the Druids: Their Origin, Manner, Customs, Power, Temples, Rites and Superstitions, with an Enquiry into Their Religion and its Coincidence with the Patriarchal*. And all of this in 160 pages! In fact, the volume in question is not a bad summary of what was known, or believed, at the time.

The American Charles de Kay (see pages 230-241) suggested that there were powerful parallels between the Celtic traditions and those of Finland, and he makes some fascinating points in the process. In the meantime the Welsh author writing under the pseudonym Aneurin Vardd (Aneurin the Bard) gave fresh emphasis to the importance of the bardic system within Druidry.

Before we look at the work of some nineteenth-century authors, Part Two opens with a selection from some of the multitude of writers, ranging from 1577 to 1854, who contributed to the vision of the Druid revival. In addition to the authors already mentioned, Part Two also includes an extract from W.A. Winwood Read's 1861 book *The Veil of Isis*, which turns our attention to a less frequented byway, that of folklore, where traces of Druidic tradition still lurk. Charles Mackay adds to this in his somewhat eccentric consideration of the survival of druidic chants in folk-song.

All these and more – many more than I have had space for here – contributed to the recovery of Druid traditions and practices in the twentieth-century. It is their legacy that we have inherited, and their thumbprints are still to be seen in the writings and speculations of contemporary writers such as those we shall be looking at in the third part of this book.

8

EARLY ANTIQUARIAN ACCOUNTS BY VARIOUS HANDS

1577–1854

Raphael Holinshed (d. *c*.1580)

It is not to be doubted, but at the first and so long as the posteritie of Japhet onlye, reigned in this Islande, that the true knowledge and forme of religion brought in by Samothes, was exercised among the Britains. . . . What other learning Magus the sonne of Samothes taught after his fathers death when he also came to the kingdome, beside thys which concerned the true honoring of God, I can not easily saye, but that it shoulde bee naturall Philosophie, and Astrology (whereby his disciples, gathered a kinde of foreknowledge of things to come) the verye use of the worde Magus, among the Persians doth yeeld no incertaine testimony.

In lyke maner, it shoulde seeme that Sarron some unto the sayde Magus, diligentlye followed the steppes of hys fatherm & thereto opened Schooles of learning in sundrie places, both among the Celtes and Britaines, whereby such as were his Auditors, grewe to be called Sarronides, notwithstanding, that as well the Sarronides as the Magi (otherwise called Magusei) & Druiydes, were generally called Samothei, or Semnothei, of Samothies stil among the Graecians, as Aristotle in his *de magia*, doth confesse, and calling them Galles, hee addeth thereunto that they first brought the knowledge of Letters, and good learning unto the Greekes.

Druiyus the sonne of Sarron (as a scholler of his fathers owne teaching) seemed to be exquisite in all things, that pertayned unto the deuine or humaine knowledge: and therfore I may safely pronounce, that he excelled not onely in the skill of Philosophie: and the Quadriualles, but also in the true Theologie, wherby the right seruice of God was kept & preserved in puritie. He wrote moreover sundry precepts, and rules of religious doctrine, which among the Celtes were reserved very religiously, and had in great estimation among such as sought unto them . . .

After the death of Driuyus, Bardus his sonne, and king of the Celtes succeeded not onely over the sayde kingdome, but also in his fathers vertues, whereby it is very likely, that the winding and wrapping up of the sayde Religion, after the afore remembered sorte into Verse, for he was an excellent Poet. . . . But as to procede, as the chiefe estimation of the Druiydes remained in the ende among the Britons only, for their knowledge in religion, so dyd the same of the Bardes for their excellent skill in musicke, and Heroicall kind of song, which at the first contayned only the high misteries of their religion. There was little difference betweene them and the Druiydes, till they so far degenerated from their first institution, that they became to be minstrels at feastes, droncken meetings, and abhominable sacrifices of Idols.

The Chronicles of England (volume 1), 1577

Michael Drayton (1563–1631)

Sometimes within my shades, in many an ancient wood,
Whose often-twined tops, great Phoebus fires withstood,
*The fearelesse British Priests, under an aged Oake,
Taking a milk-white Bull, unstrained with the yoke,
And with an Axe of gold, from that Jove-sacred tree
The Missleto cut downe; then with a bended knee
On th'unhew'd Altar layd, put to the hallowed fires:
And whilst in the sharpe flame the trembling flesh expires,
As their strong furie mov'd (when all the rest adore)
Pronouncing their desires the sacrifice before,
Up to th'eternall heaven their bloodied hands did reare:
And, whilst the murmuring woods even shuddred as with feare,
Preacht to the beardlesse youth, the souls immortall state;
To other bodies still how it should transmigrate,
That to contempt of death them strongly might excite.

from Song IX, *Poly-Olbion*, 1598–1622

Commentary on the above by John Selden (1584–1654)
The fearles British Priests under an aged Oake.

He means the Druids; because they are indeed, as he cals them, British Priests, and that this Island was of old their Mother: whence, as from a Seminary, Gaule was furnisht with their learning. Permit me some space more largely to satisfie you in their name, profession, sacrifice, places of Assembling, and lastly, subversion. The name of Druids hath beene drawne from Δρῦς, .i. an Oake, because of their continuall using that Tree as superstitiously hallowed: according as they are call'd also Σαρονίδαι or Σαρωνίδες, which likewise, in Greeke, is Old Oakes. To this compare the British word **Derw** of the same signification, and, the Originall here sought for, will seeme surely found. But one, that derives all from Dutch, and prodigiously supposes that the first tongue spoken, makes them so stiled from **Trow wis** .i. truely wise, so expressing their nature in their name. Nor is this without good reason of conjecture (if the ground were true) seeing that their like in proportion among the Jewes and Gentiles were call'd (until Pythagoras his time) Wise-men, and afterward by him turn'd into the name of Philosophers. .i. Lovers of wisedome; and perhaps the old Dutch was, as some learned thinke, communicated to Gaule, and from thence hither; the conjecture being somewhat aided in that attribute which they have in Pomponius, calling them Masters of wisedome. A late great Scholler drawes it from **Trutin**, in an old Dutch copy of the Gospel, signifying, as he saies, God; which might be given them by Hyperboly of superstitious reverence: nay, we see that it is justifiable by holy Writ, so to call great Magistrates and Judges; as they were among the people. But that word Trutin or Truchtin in the old Angelicall salutation, Zacharies Song, and Simeons, published by Vulcan, is alwayes Lord; as this **Giwihit si truchtin got Israelo**.i. Blessed be the Lord God of Israel, and so in the Saxon ten Commandements, Ic eom Dpihcen δin Goδ .i. I am the Lord thy God. These are the etymologies which savor of any judgement. To speake of King Druis or Sarron, which that Dominican Frier hath cozened vulgar credulity withall, and thence fetch their name, according to Doctor White of Basingstoke, were with him to suffer, and, at once, offer imposture. Of them all, I incline to the first, seeing it meets in both tongues Greeke and British; and somewhat the rather too, because Antiquity did crowne their infernall Deities, (and from Dis, if you trust Caesar, the Gaules, and by consequence our Britons, upon tradition of these Priests, drew their descent) with Oake; as Sophocles hath it of Hecate, and Catullus of the three Destinies. Neyther will I desire you to spend conceit upon examination of that supposition which makes the name corrupted from **Durcergliis**, which in Scottish were such as had a holy charge committed to them; whereupon, perhaps, Bale sayes S. Columban was the chiefe of the Druids: I reckon that among the infinit Fables and grosse absurdities, which its Author hath, without judgement, stuft himselfe withall. For their profession, it was both of learning Profane and Holy (I speake in all, applying my words to their times:) They sate as Judges, and determined all causes emergent, civill and criminall, subjecting to the disobedient, and such as made default to interdicts, and censures, prohibiting them from sacred assemblies, taking away their capacities in honorable offices, and so disabling them, that (as our now Outlawes, excommunicats, and attainted persons) they might not commence suit against any man. In a multitude of verses they delivered what they taught, not suffering it to be committed to writing, so imitating both Cabalists, Pythagoreans and ancient Christians; but used in other privat and publique busines Greeke letters, as Caesars copies have: but hereof see more to the X.

Song. Their more privat and sacred learning consisted in Divinity, and Philosophy (see somewhat of that to the I. Song,) which was such, that although I thinke you may truely say with Origen, that, before our Saviours time, Britain acknowledged not one true God, yet it came as neere to what they should have done, or rather neerer, then most of other, eyther Greeke or Roman, as by their positions in Caesar, Strabo, Lucan, and the like discoursing of them, you may be satisfied. For although Apollo, Mars, and Mercury were worshipt among the vulgar Gaules, yet it appeares that the Druids invocation was to one All-healing or All-saving power. In Morality, their instructions, were so perswasive, and themselves of such reverence, that the most fiery rage of Mars kindled among the people, was by their grave counsels often quenched. Out of Pliny receive their forme of rituall sacrifice (here described by the Author) thus: In such gloomy shadows, as they most usually for contemplation retired their ascending thoughts into, after exact search, finding an Oake, whereon a Mistletoe grew, on the VI. day of the Moone (above all other times) in which, was beginning of their yeare, they religiously and with invocation brought with them to it a ceremoniall banquet, materials for sacrifice, with two white Bulles, filleted on the hornes, all which they plac'd under the Oake. One of them, honoured with that function, clothed all in white, climbs the tree, and with a golden Knife or Sith cuts the Mistletoe, which they solemnly wrapt in one of their white garments. Then did they sacrifice the Buls, earnestly calling on the All-healing Deity, to make it prosperous and happy on whom soever they shal bestow it, and accounted it both preservative against all Poisons, and a remedy against Barrennes. If I should imagine by this All-healing Deity, to be meant Apollo, whom they worshipt under name of Belin (as I tel you to the VIII. Song) my conjecture were every way receivable; seeing that Apollo had both among Greeks and Latins the Divine titles of Ἀλεξίκακος, Λοίμος, Medicus, and to him the invocation was Ἰὴ Παιάν, all concurring in the same proofe; but also if they had (as probability is enough to conjecture it) an Altar inscrib'd for this devotion, and used Greek letters (which to the next Song shall be somwhat examined) I could well think the dedication thus conceiv'd.

BEΛINΩι.
TΩι.
ΠANAKEI.
OR,
BEΛINΩι. ΘEΩι.[1]

Which, very probably, was meant by some, making in Latin termination, and neerer Apollo's name

DEO
ABELLIONI.[2]

As, an Inscription, in Gaule, to abiding memory committed by that most noble Joseph Scaliger is red; and perhaps some reliques or allusion to this name is in that

DEO
SANCTO BELA-
TUCADRO . . .

Yet remayning in Cumberland. Nor is it strange that Apollo's name should be thus farre of ancient time, before communication of Religion twixt these Northerne parts and the learned Gentiles, seeing that Caesar affirmes him for one of their Deities; and, long before that, Abaris (about the beginning of the Olympiads) an Hyperborean is recorded for Apollo's Priest among the utmost Scythians, being further from Hellenisme then our British. But I returne to the Mistle: Hereto hath some referred that which the Sibyll counsell'd Aeneas to carrie with him to Prosperpine;

> latet arbore opacâ
> Aureas & folis & lento vimine ramus
> Junoni infernae dictus sacer: hunc tegit omnis
> Lucas, & obscuris claudunt convallibus umbrae.[3]

Which may as well be so applied, as to Chymistry; seeing it agrees also with what I spake before of Dis, and that, Virgil expresly compares it to the Mistle,

> quod non sua seminat arbos.[4]

for it springs out of some particular Nature of the Oaken stemme, wherupon it is called by an old Poet Δρυὸς ἱδρως: and although it be not ordinarily found upon Oakes, yet, that oftimes it is, any Apothecary can tell, which preserveth it for medicine, as the Ancients used to make Lime of it to catch birds: of which Argentarius hath an admonitory Epigram to a Blacke-bird, that she should not sing upon the Oake, because that

> ἐπ' Ὀρνίθεσσι φέρει τὸν ἀναρσιον Ἰξόν,[5]

but on the Vine, dedicated to Bacchus, a great favorit of Singers. Upon this Druidian custome, some have grounded that unto this day used in France, where the yonger county fellowes, about New-yeares tide in every Village give the wish of good fortune at the Inhabitants dores, with this acclamation, *Au guy l'an neuf*; which, as I remember, in Rablais is read all one word, for the same purpose. Whether this had any community with the institution of that Temple Ἰξευτηρίας τύχης in Antium, or that Ovid alluded to it in that verse, commonly cited out of him.

At (some read ad) *Viscum Driidae, Viscum clamare solebant*; I cannot assure you, yet it is enough likely. But I see a custome in some parts among us, in our language (nor is the digression too faulty) the same in effect; I meane the yearely **was-haile** in the country on the vigil of the New yeare, which had its beginning, as some say, from that of Ronix (Daughter to Hengist) her drinking

95

to Vortigern, by these wordes **Louerd king was-heil**, he answering her by direction of an Interpreter, **Drink-heile**, and then,

> Kuse hire and sitte hire adoune and glad dronke hire heil
> And that was tho in this land the berst was-hail
> As in language of Saxoyne that me might euere iwite
> And so wel he paith the folc about, that he is not put borpute.

Afterward uit appeares that **was-haile** and **Drinc-heil** were the usuall phrases of quaffing among the English, as we see in Thomas de la Moore, and before him that old Havillan, thus:

> Ecce vagante cifo distento gutture **wass-heil**
> Ingeminant **wass-heil**

But I rather conjecture it a usuall ceremony among the Saxons before Hengist, as a note of health-wishing (and so perhaps you might make it **wish-heil**) which was exprest among other nations in that form of drinking to the Health of their Mistresses and friends,

> Benè vos, benè nos, benè te, benè me, benè nostram etiam Stephanium.

in Plautus, and infinit other testimonies of that nature (in him Martiall, Ovid, Horace, and such more) agreeing neerely with the fashion now used; we calling it a Health, as they did also in direct termes; which, with an Idoll call'd Heil, anciently worshipt, at Cerne in Dorsetshire, by the English-Saxons, in name expresses both the ceremony of Drinking, and the New-years acclamation (whereto in some parts of this Kingdome is joyn'd also solemnity of drinking out of a cup, ritually compos'd, deckt, and fill'd with countrey liquor) just as much and as the same which that All-healing Deity, or All-helping medicine did among the Druids. You may to all this adde, that, as an Earnest of good luck to follow the New-yeare beginning, it was usuall among the Romans, as with us, and I thinke, in all Europe, at this day is, to greet each other with auspicious gifts. But hereof you say I unfitly expatiat: I omit, therefore their sacrificing of humane bodies, and such like, and come to the places of their assembly. This was about Chartres in Gaule, as Caesar tels us; Paul Merula (for affinity of name) imagines it to be Dreux, some eight miles on this side Chartres. And peradventure the Galatians publique Councell called Drymenetum had hence Originall. The British Druids tooke this Isle of Anglesey (then well stored with thicke Woods, and religious Groves, in so much that it was called **Inis-Dowil**) for their chiefe residence; as, in the Roman storie of Paulinus and Agricola's adventuring on it, is delivered. For their sub-version; under Augustus and Tiberius they were prohibited Rome; and Claudius, endevoured it in Gaule; yet in the succeeding Emperors times there were of them left, as appears in Lampridius and Vopiscus, mentioning them in their lives; and, long since that,

Procopius writing under Justinian above D. yeares after Christ, affirmes that then the Gaules used sacrifices of human flesh, which was a part of Druidian doctrin. If I should upon testimony of, I know not what, Veremund, Campbell, and the Irish Cornill, tell you that some C.LX. yeares before Christ, Finnan K. of Scotland first gave them the Isle, or that K. Crathlint in Diocletians persecution, turned their Religion into Christianisme, and made Amphibalus first Bishop of Sodor, I should fabulously abuse time, as they have ignorantly mistooke that Isle of Man, for this. Or to speake of the supposed their **Druttenfuss**.i. a Pentagonall figure, ingravne with 'ΥΓΙΕΙΑ or Ὑγεία. (it is the same, in fashion, with the victorious seale of Antiochus Soter, being admonished by Alexander in adreame, to take it) which in Germany they reckon for a preservative against Hobgoblins, were but to be indulgent to olde wives traditions. Onely thus much for a corollary, I will noteto you; Conrad Celtes observes, to be in an Abbey at the foot of Vichtelberg hil, neer Voitland, six Statues, of stone, set in the Church-wall, some VII. foote every one tall, barehead and foote, cloakt and hooded, with a bagge, a booke, a staffe, a beard hanging to his middle, and spreading a Mustachio, an austere looke and eyes fixt on the earth; which he conjecturse to be Images of them. Upon mistaking of Strabo, and applying what he saith in generall, and bracelets and gold chaines of the Gaules, to the Druids, I once thought that Conrad had beene deceived. But I can now upon better advice incline to his judgement.

Theophilus Gale

Farther, thou mayest demand whence this Oke Religion (of the Druides) sprang? namely from the Okes of Mamre: under which, in times past, those holy men (in whose hands the administration of Divine Service and Worship was) lived most devoutly: the shadow of which Okes afforded an house to Abraham, and a Temple to God. This I sucked from the Dugs of Truth, namely from the sacred Scriptures. Abraham dwelt . . . in, or (as the Arabick has it) among the Okes of Mamre. . . . Under which Oke he fixed his Tabernacle, erected an Altar, and offered to the Lord Calves, Goats, Rams, and other Sacrifices of like kind; and performed all Sacerdotal Offices. Yea under this tree he entertained God himself, together with Angels. He here had conference with God, and entred into covenant with him, and was blessed of him. These are indeed admirable praeconia of Okes. Lo the Oke priests! Lo the Patriarchs of the Druides! For from these sprang the Sect of the Druides, which reached up at least, as high as Abraham's time (for they report that the Druides Colleges flourished in the time of Hermio, who was King of the Germans, immediately after the death of Abraham). For because this holy man and Priest, Abraham lived under Okes, and enjoyed God for his companion, performing worship to him, our Divines (the Druides) from this so famous example, chose Goves of Okes for their Religious Services, etc.

The Court of the Gentiles, Part II, Oxford, 1671

Martin Martin

Before they engag'd the Enemy in Battle, the Chief Druid harangu'd the Army to excite their Courage. He was plac'd on an Eminence, from whence he address'd himself to all of them standing about him, putting them in mind of what great things were perform'd by the Valour of their Ancestors, rais'd their Hopes with the noble Rewards of Honour and Victory, and dispell'd their Fears by all the Topicks that natural Courage could suggest. After this Harangue, the Army gave a general Shout, and then charg'd the Enemy stoutly. This in the antient Language was call'd Brosnichiy Kab, i.e. an Incentive to War. This Custom of shouting aloud is believ'd to have taken its Rise from an Instinct of Nature, it being attributed to most Nations that have been of a martial Genius: As by Homer to the Trojans, by Tacitus to the Germans, by Livy to the Gauls. Every great Family in the Isles had a Chief Druid, who foretold future Events, and decided all Causes Civil and Ecclesiastical. It is reported of them that they wrought in the Night-time, and rested all Day. Caesar says they worshipp'd a Deity under the name of Taramis, or Taran, which in Welsh signifies Thunder; and in the ancient Language of the Highlanders, Torin signifies Thunder also.

Another God of the Britons was Belus, or Belinus, which seems to have been the Assyrian God Bel, or Belus; and probably from this Pagan Deity comes the Scots Term of Beltin, the first Day of May, having its first Rise from the Custom practis'd by the Druids in the Isles, of extinguishing all the Fires in the Parish until the Tythes were paid; and upon payment of them, the Fires were kindled in each Family, and never till then. In those days Malefactors were burnt between two Fires; hence when they would express a Man to be in a great strait, they say, he is between two Fires of Bel, which in their Language they express thus, Edir; da hin Veaul or Bel. Some object that the Druids could not be in the Isles, because no Oaks grow there. To which I answer, That in those days Oaks did grow there, and to this day there be Oaks growing in some of them, particularly in Sleat, the most Southern part of the Isle of Skie. The Houses named after those Druids shall be describ'd elsewhere.

from *A Description of the Western Islands of Scotland*, 1716

John Wood

When I had thus far satisfied myself, I began to take the rise of the British Druids into Consideration; and after collating all the Circumstances touching King Bladud, the reputed founder of the Hot Waters, and the City of Bath, as well as of the ancient University of Stanford, with what is recorded of Abaris, the Hyperborean Priest of the Sun, I could not avoid concluding that they were one and the same Man: Neither could I avoid concluding, that the Britons and the Hyperboreans were one and the same people. . . .

By the circumstances that led me to these Conclusions it appeared, even beyond probability, that Bladud assumed the gift of Prophecy, and became a great Philosopher while he was a Youth. . . . And that he became the favourite Disciple, the Colleague, and in many things, the Master of the Samian Philosopher; since the antient Writers that speak of these celebrated Men, unanimously agree that they reciprocally communicated their Knowledge to each other.

It also appeared that after Bladud had made himself famous all over Greece for his Oracles, he was there dignified with the Title of Abaris; and then built temples in that Country. . . . And it likewise appeared that our British Philosopher, after having been Initiated into the Samothratian Mysteries, and continuing abroad for eleven Years, returned to his native Land about the Year Pythagoras died at Crotona; succeeded his Father soon after in the British Throne; and founded that order of priesthood, which, in the antient times of Paganism, was of such high Renown as to make Cicero himself, on one hand, declare the Druids, or Priests admitted into it, to have been the very Inventors of Mythology; and Pliny, on the other, to suppose them to have been the masters of the Persian magi.

And when the priesthood was founded, Bladud, as arch-Druid, appeared to have seated himself near the Hot Springs of Bath; and to have placed his Grecian Refugees at Stantondrew, as the Heads of so many Orders of Priests to act under him, and instruct the Britons in the Liberal Sciences; making them a stupendous Model of the Planetary World for that purpose, with Blocks of Marble dugg out of Okeyhole to enlarge that dreadful den, and make the Initiating cave really great and tremendous to all that should enter it.

From this Institution the British Fable of Samothes, and the four next Kings in a continued Succession from Father to Son seems to have it's Rise: for Samothes was a Title given to Bladud from his Initiation into Samothration Mysteries; and the Names of Magus, Sarron, Druis, and Bardus, by which the four other Kings were distinguished, express the very functions assigned to each Order of Priests among the Druids; who were so denominated from their esteeming Trees, and particularly Oaks, as Symbols of the Deity. From the same Institution the Fable of Apollo's arrow, concealed by him in the Hyperborean Island, seems likewise to have it's Rise; and Abaris's carrying, or being carried by it through all parts of the World, without eating, seems to imply that Druidism immediately spread itself from Britain Eastward to the utmost Corners of the Earth, instead of coming from the Extremity of the Eastern World to us. The Indian Hylobii seem therefore to have had their Rise from the British Druids; and the Learning of the latter seems to have soon reached China itself, Confucius rising up in that Country, and appearing as a great Philosopher at the Head of four Orders of Priests in about thirty Years after the death of Pythagoras.

Choir Gaure, Oxford, 1747

James Foot

Although some useful truths charm'd in the song
Of Druid wisdom, and with awe their groves
Beheld the natural light through thickest shades
Oft' shew her radiant presence, yet the pomp
Of bloody Altars, knives and death prepar'd
For human victims, where by force compell'd
They shed their blood bewailing, made their groves
The bloody shambles of misguided zeal,
And the vile Priests the butch'ring tools of Heav'n.

Penseroso, 1771

John Smith

Among the *arcana* of nature which our Druids were acquainted with, there are many presumptive, if not positive, proofs for placing the art of gunpowder, or artificial thunder and lightning; though like all other mysteries, they kept the invention of it a secret. Some learned men allow, that the priests of Delphos were in possession of this art. . . . Why may we not suppose, that those great searchers into nature, the Druids, might also light upon the secret? The impressions of which thunder and lightning are so apt to make upon the mind, would certainly induce the Druids to try, if possible, to counterfeit the awful phenomena; as the invention of anything like them would be a most useful engine to keep the wondring world in awe of them. And if we consider the deep and long researches of those colleges of philosophers, their being possessed of the experiments of a series of ages before, and an extensive communication with other countries, we can hardly suppose the mystery of the nitreous grain could escape them.

Galic Antiquities, Edinburgh, 1780

Edward Davies

Many particulars of this allegory may be interpreted from what has gone on before in this essay; and it may be admitted as additional evidence, of two curious facts: namely, that the superstitious rites of Druidism were avowedly practiced, in certain corners of Britain, as late as the close of the sixth century; and that the Bards of that age, used all the means in their power, to conceal their secrets from the knowledge of the populace, to prevent them from the persecution of Christian princes and ministers, and at the same time, to transmit them safe and unblemished, to future ages.

In support of this assertion, I shall produce abstracts from the several stanzas of the *Avallenau*, translated as literally as the darkness of the subject, and the faults of the copies, will permit: and to these, I shall add a few occasional remarks:

'To no one has been exhibited, at one hour of dawn, what was shewn to Merddin, before he became aged; namely, seven score and seven delicious apple trees, of equal age, height, length, and size, which sprang from the bosom of Mercy. One bending veil covers them over. They are guarded by one maid, with crisped locks: her name is Olwedd, of the luminous teeth.'

The Mythology and Rites of the British Druids, 1809

S.R. Meyrick and C.H. Smith

The figures in this plate are an Awenydd or Bardic disciple, and a candidate for that initiatory order. The former having been admitted wears a variegated dress of the Bardic colours, blue, green, and white; while the candidate retains his original habit. . . . In the right hand of the disciple is a cup, which it is conjectured contained some of the sacred juice, the *Gwîn a bragawd* 'wine and bragget', or perhaps only the mead drunk at great festivals; and in his left hand a bird, the symbol of an aspirant, for such Taliesin mystically says he was, when speaking of his initiation. Mr Davies, however, conceives that the bird was the Dryw, a name implying both a wren and a Druid; and if such be correct the bird here represented cannot be this symbol for it is a nearer resemblance to a dove. The dove was the bird of good omen, as the raven was that of bad, among the nations of antiquity, the former having returned to Noah with the olive sprig of peace, when the latter wholly deserted him. The other youth has under his arm a pig, and in the hands of the other a box, perhaps to contain its food. The pig was also a symbol of Druidism. The Druids are frequently termed Swine, the Lunar-arkite goddess is as often alluded to under the character of a mystical sow; and the bard Myrddin commences his address to a disciple with the words Oian porchellan, 'listen, little pig'.

The Costume of the Original Inhabitants of the British Isles, 1821

W. Williams

We have ample proof that during the Arthurian period (that is the fifth and sixth centuries) and probably long after it, there flourished two schools of literature: the one essentially heathenish in creed, although often nominally Christian, and the other blending with Druidic doctrines, the worship of many of the pagan idols of Greece and Rome, and of their own peculiar mythology.

from *Gomer*, London, 1854

9

A CRITICAL HISTORY OF THE DRUIDS

John Toland

The First Letter, to the Right Honourable the Lord Viscount Molesworth

Some men, my Lord, from a natural greatness of soul, and others from a sense of the want of learning in themselves, or the advantages of it in others, have many times liberally contributed towards the advancement of letters. But when they, whose excellent natural parts are richly cultivated by sound literature, undertake the protection of the Muses, writers feel a double encouragement; both as they are happily enabled to perfect their studies, and as their Patrons are true judges of their performances. 'Tis from this consideration alone (abstracted, My Lord, from all that you have already done, or may hereafter deserve from your country, by an unshaken love of liberty) that I presume to acquaint your Lordship with a design, which I form'd several years ago at Oxford, and which I have ever since kept in view; collecting, as occasion presented, whatever might any way tend to the advantage or perfection of it. 'Tis to write the *History of the Druids*, containing an account of the ancient Celtic Religion and Literature; and concerning which I beg your patience for a little while. Tho' this be a subject, that will be naturally entertaining to the curious in every place; yet it does more particularly concern the inhabitants of antient Gaule, (now France, Flanders, the Alpine regions, and Lombardy) and of all the British Islands, whose antiquities are here partly explain'd and illustrated, partly vindicated and restor'd. It will sound somewhat oddly, at first hearing, that a man born in the most northern Peninsula[6] of Ireland, shou'd undertake to set the antiquities of Gaule in a clearer light than any one has hitherto done. But when 'tis consider'd, that, over and above what he knows in common, relating to the Druids, with the learned of the French nation, (whose works he constantly reads with uncommon esteem) he has also certain other advantages, which none of those writers have ever had: when this, I say, is consider'd, then all the wonder about this affair will instantly cease. Yet let it be still remember'd, that whatever accomplishment may consist in the knowledge of languages, no language is really valuable, but as far as it serves to converse with the living, or to learn from the dead; and therefore were that knowledge of times and things contain'd in Lapponian, which we draw from the Greec, and that this last were as barren as the first: I shou'd then study Lapponian, and neglect Greec; for all its superiority over most tongues, in respect of sonorous pronunciation, copiousness of words, and variety of expression. But as the profound ignorance and slavery of the present Greecs does not hinder, but that their ancestors were the most learned, polite, and free of all European nations; so no revolution that has befallen any or all of the Celtic colonies, can be a just prejudice against the truly antient and undoubted monuments they may be able to furnish, towards improving or restoring any point of Learning. Whether there be any such monuments or not, and how far useful or agreeable, will in the following sheets appear.

Among those institutions which are thought to be irrecoverably lost, one is that of the Druids; of which the learned have hitherto known nothing, but by some fragments concerning them out of the Greec and Roman authors. Nor are such fragments always intelligible, because never explain'd by any of those, who were skill'd in the Celtic dialects, which are now principally six; namely Welsh or the insular British, Cornish almost extinct, Armorican or French British, Irish, the least corrupted, Manks or the language of the Isle of Man; and Earse or Highland Irish, spoke also in all the western Ilands of Scotland. These, having severally their own dialects are, with respect to each other and the old Celtic of Gaule, as the several dialects of the German language and Low Dutch, the Swedish, Danish, Norwegian and Islandic; which are all descendants of their common mother, the Gothic. Not that ever such a thing as a pure Gothic or Celtic language either did, or cou'd exist in any considerable region without dialects, no more than pure elements: but by such an original language is meant the common root and trunk, the primitive words, and especially the peculiar contstruction that runs thro' all the branches; whereby they are intelligible to each other, or may easily become so, but different from all kinds of speech besides. Thus the Celtic and the Gothic, which have been often taken for each other, are as different as Latin and Arabic. In like manner we conceive of the several idioms of the Greec language formerly, in Greece itself properly so call'd, in Macedonia, in Crete and the Ilands of the Archipelago, in Asia, Rhodes, part of Italy, in Sicily, and Marseilles; and at this time of the Sclavonian-language, whose dialects not only prevail in Russia, Poland, Bohemia, Carinthia, and Servia, but in a great many other places, too tedious to recite. But of this subject we shall treat professedly in a Dissertation,[7] to be annex'd to the work, whereof I am giving your lordship an account. Neither shall I in this Specimen dwell on some things, whereof I shall principally and largely treat in the designed History; I mean the Philosophy of the Druids concerning the Gods, human Souls, Nature in general, and in particular the heavenly Bodies, their magnitudes, motions, distances, and duration; where of Caesar, Diodorus, Siculus, Strabo, Pomponius Mela, and Ammianus Marcellinus write more specially than others. These subjects, I say, will be copiously handled and commented in my History. In the mean time I do assure you, My Lord, from all authors, that no Heathen Priesthood ever came up to the perfection of the Druidical, which was far more exquisite than any other such system; as having been much better calculated to beget ignorance, and an implicit disposition in the people, no less than to procure power and profit to the priests, which is one grand difference between the true worship and the false. This Western Priesthood did infinitely exceed that of Zoroaster, and all the Eastern sacred policy: so that, the History of the Druids, in short, is, the complete History of Priestcraft, with all its reasons and ressorts; which to distinguish accurately from right religion, is not only the interest of all wise princes and states, but likewise does especially concern the tranquillity and happiness of every private person. I have used the word Priestcraft here on purpose, not merely as being the best expression for the designed abuse, and reverse of religion, (for superstition is only religion misunderstood) but also because the coining of the very word was occasioned by the Druids: since the Anglo-Saxons having learnt the word Dry[8] from the Irish and Britons for a Magician, did very appositely call Magic or Inchantment Drycraft[9]; as being nothing else but trick and illusion, the fourbery of Priests and their confederates.

Now, this Institution of the Druids I think myself, without any consciousness of vanity, much abler to retrieve (as having infinitely better helps in many respects, of which, before I have done) than Dr Hyde was to restore the knowledge of the ancient Persian Literature and Religion; which yet he left imperfect for want of due encouragement, as I have shown in the first chapter of Nazarenus. From undoubted Celtic monuments, join'd to the Greec and Roman remains, I can display the order of their Hierarchy, from the arch-Druid down to the meanest of their four orders of Priests. Of these degrees, the arch-Druid excepted, there's little to be found in the Classic authors, that treat of the Druids: but very much and very particularly, in the Celtic writings and monuments. For many reasons their History is most interesting and entertaining: I mean, as on the one hand we consider them seducing their followers, and as on the other hand we learn not to be so deceiv'd. They dextrously led the people blindfold, by commiting no part of their Theology or Philosophy to writing, tho' great writers in other respects: but their dictates were only hereditarily convey'd from masters to disciples by traditionary Poems, interpretable (consequently;) and alterable as they shou'd see convenient: which is a much more effectual way, than locking up a book from the Laity, that, one way or other, is sure to come first or last to their knowledge, and easy perhaps to be turn'd against the Priests. The Druids, as may be seen in the 6th book of Caesar's Commentaries, drew the decision of all controversies of Law and Equity to themselves, the distribution of all punishmens and rewards; from the power that was first given, or afterwards assumed by them, of determining matters of Ceremony and Religion. Most terrible were the effects of the Druidical Excommunication[10] of any man, that did not implicitly follow their directions, and submit to their decrees: not only to the excluding of private persons from all benefits of society, and even from society itself; but also to the deposing of the princes who did not please them, and often devoting them to destruction. Nor less intolerable was their power of engaging the nation in war, or making a disadvantageous and dishonourable peace while they had the address to get themselves exempted from bearing arms, paying taxes, or contributing any thing to the public but charms: and yet to have their persons reputed sacred and inviolable, by those even of the contrary side, which veneration however was not always strictly paid. These privileges allur'd great numbers to enter into their communities for such Sodalities or Fraternities they had; and to take on them the Druidical profession, to be perfect in which, did sometimes cost them twenty years study. Nor ought this to seem a wonder, since to arrive at perfection in Sophistry requires a long habit, as well as in juggling, in which last, they were very expert: but to be masters of both, and withal to learn the art of managing the mob, which is vulgarly called leading the people by the nose, demands abundant study and exercise.

The children of the several kings, with those of all the nobility, were committed to the tuition of the Druids, whereby they had an opportunity (contrary to all good politics) of moulding and framing them to their own private interests and purposes; considering which direction of Education, Patric, had they been a landed clergy, wou'd not have found the conversion of Ireland so easy a task. So easy indeed it was, that the Heathen monarch Laogirius (who, as some assert, was never himself converted) and all the provincial kings, granted to every man free liberty of preaching and professing Christianity. So that, as Giraldus Cambrensis remarks, this is the only country of Christians, where nobody was obliged to suffer Martyrdom[11] for the gospel. This justice therefore I wou'd do to Ireland, even if it had not been my country, viz. to maintain that this tolerating principle, this impartial liberty (ever since unexampled there as well as elsewhere, China excepted) is a far greater honour to it, than whatever thing most glorious or magnificent can be said of any other country in the world. Girald on the contrary (as in his days they were wont to over-rate Martyrdom, Celibacy, and the like, much above the positive duties of religion) thinks it a reproach to the Irish, That none of their Saints cemented the foundations of the growing Church with their blood, all of them being Confessors, (sayshe,) and not one able to boast of the crown of Martyrdom. But who sees not the vanity and absurdity of this charge? It is blaming the prince and people for their reasonableness, moderation and humanity; as it is taxing the new Converts for not seditiously provoking them to persecute, and for not madly running themselves to a voluntary death, which was the unjustifiable conduct of many elsewhere in the primitive times of Christianity. 'Tis on much better grounds, tho' with a childish and nauseous jingle that he accuses the Irish Clergy of his own time: and so far am I from being an enemy to the clergy, that I heartily wish the like could not be said of any clergy whether there, or here, or elsewhere from that time to this. Well then: what is it? They are Pastors, (says he), who seek not to feed, but to be fed: Prelates who desire not to profit, but to preside: Bishops, who embrace not the nature, but the name; not the burdens but the bravery of their profession.[12] This, My Lord, reckon to be no digression from my subject, since what little opposition there happen'd to be in Ireland to Christianity, was, wholly made, by the Druids, or at their instigation: and that when they perceiv'd this new religion like to prevail, none came into it speedier, or made a more advantageous figure in it, than they. The Irish however have their Martyrologies (lest this shou'd be objected by some trifler) but they are of such of their nation as suffered in other countries, or under the Heathen Danes in their own country, some hundreds of years after the total conversion of it to Christianity.

Those advantages we have nam'd in the two last Sections, and many the like articles, with the Druids pretences to work miracles, to foretel events by augury and otherwise, to have familiar intercourse with the gods (highly confirm'd by calculating Eclipses) and a thousand impostures of the same nature,[13] I can by irrefragable authorities set in such a light, that all of the like kind may to every one appear in as evident a view; which, as I hinted before, cannot but be very serviceable both to religion and morality. For true religion does not consist on cunningly devis'd fables, in authority, dominion, or pomp; but in spirit and in truth, in simplicity and social virtue, in a filial love and reverence not in a servile dread and terror of the Divinity. As the fundamental Law of a Historian is, daring to say whatever is true, and not daring to write any 'falsehood; neither being swayed by love or hatred, nor gain'd by favour or interest; so he ought of course to be as a man of no time or country, of no sect or party; which I hope the several nations concern'd in this enquiry, will find to be particularly true of me. But if in clearing up antient rites and customs, with the origin and institution of certain religious or civil societies (long since extinct,) any communities or orders of men, now in being, should think themselves touched; they ought not to impute it to design in the author, but to the conformity of things, if indeed there be any real resemblance: and, in case there be none at all, they should not make people apt to suspect there is, by crying out tho' they are not hurt. I remember, when complaint was made against an honourable person[14], that, in treating of the Heathen Priests, he had whipt some Christian Priests on their backs; all the answer he made, was only asking, What made them get up there? The benefit of which answer I claim before-hand to myself, without making or needing any other apology. Yet if the correspondence of any Priests with heaven be as slenderly grounded as that of the Druids, if their miracles be as fictitious and fraudulent, if their love of riches be as immoderate, if their thirst after people be as insatiable, and their exercise of it be as partial and tyrannical over the Laity: then, I am not only content they should be touched, whether I thought of them or not; but, that they should be blasted too, without the possibility of ever sprouting up again. For truth will but shine the brighter, the better its counterfeits are shewn: and all that I can do to shew my candour, is to leave the reader to make such applications himself, seldom making any for him; since he that is neither clear-sighted, nor quick enough of conception to do so, may to as good purpose read the Fairy-tales as this history.

Besides this impartial disposition, the competent knowledge I have of the Northern languages, dead and living (though I shall prove, that no Druids, except such as towards their latter end fled thither for refuge, or that went before with Celtic invaders or colonies were ever among the Gothic nations) I say these languages will not a little contribute to the perfection of my work, for a reason that may with more advantage appear in the book itself. But the knowledge of the ancient Irish, which I learnt from my childhood, and of the other Celtic dialects, in all which I have printed books or manuscripts (not to speak of their vulgar Traditions) is absolutely necessary; these having preserved numberless monuments concerning the Druids, that never hitherto have come to the hands of the learned. For as the Institutions of the Druids were formerly better learnt in Britain, by Caesar said to be the native seat of this superstitious race, than in Gaule where yet it exceedingly flourished: so their memory is still best preserved in Ireland and the Highlands of Scotland, comprehending the Hebridae, Hebrides, or Western Isles, among which is the Isle of Man; where they continued long after their extermination in Gaule and South-Britain, mostly by the Romans, but finally by the introduction of Christianity. Besides, that much of the Irish Heathen Mythology is still extant in verse, which gives such a lustre to this matter; and of course to the Greek and Roman Fragments concerning the Druids, as could not possibly be had any other way.

Thus (to give an example in the Philological part) the controversy among the Grammarians, whether they should write Druis or Druida[15] in the nominative case singular, can only be decided by the Irish writings, as you may see demonstrated in the margin; where all Grammatical remarks shall be inserted among the other Notes of the History, if they do not properly belong to the annexed Dissertation concerning the Celtic Language and Colonies. This conduct I observe, to avoid any disagreeable stop or perplexity in the work itself, by uncouth words or of difficult pronunciation. For as everything in the Universe is the Subject of writing, so an author ought to treat of every subject smoothly and correctly, as well as pertinently and perspicuously: nor ought he to be void of ornament and Elegance, where his matter peculiarly requires it. Some things want a copious stile, some a concise; others to be more floridly, others to be more plainly handl'd: but all to be properly, methodically, and handsomely exprest. Neglecting these particulars, is neglecting, and consequently affronting, the reader. Let a Lady be as well-shap'd as you can fancy, let all her features be faultless, and her complexion be ever so delicate: yet if she be careless of her person, tawdry in her dress, or aukward in her gate and behavior, a man of true taste is so far from being touched with the charms of her body, that he is immediately prepossest against the beauties of her mind; and apt to believe there can be no order within, where there is so much disorder without. In my opinion therefore, the Muses themselves are never agreeable company without the Graces. Or if, as your Lordship's stile is remarkably strong, you wou'd, with Cicero[16], take this simile from a man; you'll own 'tis not enough to make him be lik'd, that he has well-knit bones, nerves and sinews: there must be likewise proportion, muscling, and coloring, much blood, and some softness. To relate, facts without their circumstances, whereon depends all instruction; is to exhibit a skeleton without the flesh, wherein consists all comeliness. This I say to your Lordship, not pretending to teach the art of writing to one, who's so fit to be my master; but to obviate the censures of those, and to censure 'em in their turns, who not only do not treat of such subjects as I have now undertaken in a flowing and continu'd stile, but peremtorily deny the fields of Antiquity and Criticism to be capable of this culture: and indeed as suffering under the drudgery of their hands, they generally become barren heaths or unpassable thickets where you are blinded with sand, or turn with bryars and brambles. There's no choice of words or expressions. All is low and vulgar, or obsolete and musty as the whole discourse is crabbed, hobbling, and jejune. Not that I wou'd have too much license taken in this respect; for though none ought to be slaves, to any set of words, yet great judgement is to be employ'd in creating a new, or reviving an old word: nor must there be less discretion in the use of figures and sentences; which, like embroidery and salt, are to set out and season, but not to render the cloth invisible, or the meat uneatable. To conclude this point, we are told by the most eloquent of men, that a profuse volubility,[17] and a sordid exility of words, are to be equally avoided. And now after this digression, if anything that essentially relates to my task can be properly call'd one, I return to the Druids, who were so prevalent in Ireland, that to this hour their ordinary word for Magician is Druid,[18] the art Magic, is call'd Druidity,[19] and the wand, which was one of the badges of their profession, the rod of Druidism.[20] Among antient Classic authors Pliny is the most express concerning the Magic of the Druids, whereof the old Irish and British books are full: which Legerdemain, or secrets of natural Philosophy, as all magic is either the one or the other or both, we shall endeavour to lay open in our history of the Druids; not forgetting any old author that mentions them, for there's something particular to be learnt in every one of them, as they touch different circumstances. Having occasionally spoken of the Wand or Staff which every Druid carry'd in his hand, as one of the badges of his profession, and which in a chpater on this subject will be shewn to have been a usual thing with all pretenders to magic, I must here acquaint you further, that each of 'em had what was commonly call'd the Druid's Egg, which shall be explain'd in the history, hung about his neck, inchas'd in gold. They all wore short hair, while the rest of the natives had theirs very long; and, on the contrary, they wore long beards, while other people shav'd all theirs, but the upper lip. They likewise all wore long habits; as did the Bards and the Vaids: but the Druids had on a white surplice, whenever they religiously officiated. In Ireland they, with the graduate Bards and Vaids, had the privilege of wearing six colours in their Breacans or robes, which were the striped Braccae of the Gauls, still worn by the Highlanders, whereas the king and queen might have in theirs but seven, lords and ladies five, governors of fortresses four, officers and young gentlemen of quality three, common soldiers two, and common people one. This sumtuary law most of the Irish historians say, was enackted under King[21] Achaius the 1st.; tho' others, who will have this to be but the reviving of an old law, maintain it was first established by king Tigernmhas.

As the Druids were commonly wont to retire into grots, dark woods, mountains, and[22] groves in which last they had their numerous schools, not without houses as some have foolishly dreamt, so many such places in France, Britain, and Ireland, do still bear their names as Dreux, the place of their annual general assembly in France; Kerig-y-Drudion, or Druid-stones, a parish so call'd in Denbighshire, from a couple of their altars there still remainining. In Anglesey there is the village of Tre'r Driu, the town of the Druid, next to which is Tre'r Beirdh or Bards-town: as also in another place of the same island Maen-y-Druu, that is, the Druid's stone; and Caer-Drewin, or the city of the Druids, in Merioneth-shire. The places in Ireland and the Hebrides are infinite. The present ignorant vulgar, in the first of the last-mention'd places, do believe, that those inchanters were at last themselves inchanted by their Apostle Patric and his disciples, miraculously confining them to the places that so bear their names; where they are thought to retain much power, and sometimes to appear, which are fancies[23] like the English notion of Fairies. Thus the Druid O Murnin inhabits the hill of Creag-a-Vanny, in Inisoen; Aunius[24] in Benavny from him so call'd in the county of Londonderry, and Gealcossa,[25] in Gealcossa's mount in Inisoen aforesaid in the county of Dunegall. This last was a Druidess, and her name is of the Homerical strain, signifying White-legg'd[26]. On this hill is her grave, the true inchantmant which, confines her, and hard by is her temple; being a sort of diminutive Stone-henge, which many of the old Irish dare not even at this day any way prophane. I shall discover such things about these temples, where of multitudes are still existing, many of them entire, in the Hebrides, in Orkney, and on the opposie Continent, as also many in Wales, in Jersey and Guernsey, and some in England and Ireland, the most remarkable to be accurately describ'd and delineated in our history, I shall discover such things, I say, about the famous Egg of the Druids to the learned hitherto a riddle not to speak of their magical gems and herbs: as also about their favouite All-heal or Misselto,[27] gather'd with so much ceremony by a Priest in his white Surplice, as Pliny[28] tells us, and with a gold pruning-knife; as well as about the abstrusest parts of their Philosophy and Religion, that the like has not yet appear'd in any author, who has treated of them. The books of such are either bare collections of fragments, or a heap of precarious fables; I mean especially some French writers on this subject, as Picard, Forcatulus, Guenebaut, with others of no better allay in Britain and Germany; for as I admit nothing without good authority, so I justly expect, that, without as good, nothing will be admitted from me.

But, My Lord, besides these Druids, the antient Gauls, Britons, and Irish, had another order of learned men, call'd Bards, whereof we shall sufficiently discourse in our propos'd work. Bard is still the Irish and Scottish word, as Bardh; the Armoric and British. There's no difference in the pronunciation, tho', according to their different manner of writing in expressing the power of the letters, they vary a little in the orthography.[29] The Bards were divided into three orders or degrees; namely, to give an example now in the British dialect, as I shall give their turns to all the Celtic colonies, Privardh, Posvardh, and Aruyvardh: but, with regard to the subjects whereof they treated, they were call'd Prududh, or Tevluur, or Clerur; which words, with the equivalent Irish names, shall be explain'd in our history, where you'll find this division of the Bards well warranted. The first were Chronologers, the second Heralds, and the third Comic or Satyrical Poets among the vulgar: for the second sort did sing the praises of great men in the heroic strain, very often at the head of armies, like him in Virgil.

And the first, who likewise accompany'd them in peace, did historically register their genealogies and atchievments. We have some proofs that the panegyrics of the Gallic Bards did not always want wit no more than flattery; and particularly an instance out of Atheneus, who had it from Posidonius, the Stoic, concerning Luernius,[30] a Gallic Prince, extraordinary rich, liberal, and magnificent. He was the father of that same Bittus, who was beaten by the Romans. Now this Luernius, says my author,[31] 'Having appointed a certain day for a feast, and one of the Barbarous Poets coming too late, met him as he was departing; whereupon he began to sing his praises and to extol his grandeur, but to lament his own unhappy delay. Luernius being delighted, call'd for a purse of Gold, which he threw to him, as he ran by the side of his chariot: and he taking it up, began to sing again to this purpose: 'That out of the tracks his chariot had plow'd on the ground, sprung up gold and blessings to mankind.' As some of the Gallic Bards were truly ingenious, so were many of them mere quiblers: and among the bombast of the British and Irish Bards, there want not infinite instances of the true sublime. Their Epigraphs were admirable, nor do the modern Italians equal them in conceits. But in stirring the passions, their Elegies and Lamentations far excede those of the Greecs, because they express nature much more naturally. These bards are not yet quite extinct, there being of them in Wales, in the Highlands of Scotland, and in Ireland: nor did any country in the world abound like the last with this sort of men, whose licentious panegyrics or satyrs have not a little contributed to breed confusion in the Irish history. There were often at a time, a thousand Ollaws[32] or graduate Poets, besides a proportionable number of inferior Rhymers, who all of 'em liv'd most of the year on free cost: and, what out of fear of their railing, or love of their flattery, no body durst deny them any thing, be it armour, fewel, horse, mantel, or the like: which grew into a general custom, whereof the Poets did not fail to take the advantage. The great men, out of self-love and interest, encourag'd no other kind of learning, especially after they professed Christianity: the good regulation, under which they were in the time of Druidism, as then, in some manner belonging to the temples, having been destroyed with that religion. In a small time, they became such a grievance, that several attempts were made to rid the nation of them, and, which is something comical, what at least our present Poets would not extraordinarily like, the orders for banishing them were always to the Highlands of Scotland; while they were as often harbour'd in Ulster, till upon promise of amendment of their manners I mean and not of their poetry, they were permitted to return to the other provinces. At last, in a general national assembly, or parliament, at Drumcat,[33] in the country we now call the county of Londonderry, under Aidus

Anmireus,[34] Xith. Christian king, in the year 597, where was also present Adius[35] king of Scotland and the great Columba,[36] it was decreed: that for the better preservation of their history, genealogies, and the purity of their language, the supreme monarch and the subordinate kings, with every lord of a cantred, should entertain a Poet of his own, no more being allowed by the antient law in the iland; and that upon each of these and their posterity a portion of land free from all duties, shou'd be settl'd for ever that, for encouraging the learning these Poets and Antiquaries profest, public Schools shou'd be appointed and endow'd, under the national inspection; and that the Monarch's own Bard should be Arch-poet[37] and have super-intendency over the rest. 'Tis a common mistake, into which father Pezron has fallen among others, that the Bards belonged to the body of the Druids: but this is not the place to rectify it. They made hymns for the use of the temples, 'tis true and manag'd the music there; but they were the Druids that officiated as Priests, and no sacrifices were offer'd but by their ministry.

In the History likewise shall be fully explain'd the third order of the Celtic Lilerati, by the Greecs called Ouateis, and by the Romans Vates; which yet is neither Greec nor Roman, but a mere Celtic word, *viz* Faidh, which signifies to this day a prophet in all Irish books, and in the common language, particularly in the Irish translation of the Bible; where Druids[38] are also commonly put for Inchanters, as those of Egypt, and especially for the Mages, or as we translate, the wisemen[39] that came from the East, to visit Jesus in his cradle. So easily dolmen convey their own ideas into other men's books, or find 'em there; which has been the source of infinite mistakes, not onely in Divinity, but also in Philosophy and Philology. The Celtic Vaids[40] were Physicians and Diviners, great proficients in natural Philosophy, as were likewise the Druids, who had the particular inspection of Morals, but Cicero, who was well acquainted with one of the prime Druids, remarks, that their predictions were as much grounded on conjecture,[41] as on the rules of Augury: both equally fortuitous and fallacious. For the saying of Euripides will ever hold true, that[42] the best guesser is the best Prophet. He that is nearly acquainted with the state of affairs, that understands the springs of human actions, and, that, judiciously allowing for circumstances, compares the present time with the past: he, I say, will make a shrewd guess at the future. By this time, My Lord, you begin to perceive what is to be the subject of the History I intend to write, which, tho' a piece of general learning and great curiosity, yet I shall make it my business so to digest: as to render it no less intertaining than instructive to all sorts of readers, without excepting the ladies, who are pretty much concern'd in this matter throwing, as I told you before, all my Critical observations, and Disquisitions about words, into the margin, or the Dissertation annext to the History. As to what I say of the ladies being concern'd in this History, there were not only Druidesses; but some even of the highest rank, and Princesses themselves were educated by the Druids: for in our own Annals we read that the two daughters of king Laogirius,[43] in whose reign Patric preach'd Christianity, were educated by them; and we have the particulars of a long dispute those young ladies

111

maintained against this new Religion, very natural but very subtil. Several other ladies bred under the Druids become famous for the writings and proficiency in learning, of some of whom we shall occasionally give an account: but lest I should be thought in every thing to flatter the Sex, how muchsoever I respect them, I refer the reader to a story in my third Letter. But, in order to complete my design so as to leave no room for any to write on this subject after me; and also to procure several valuable Manuscripts, or authentic copies of them; well knowing where they ly, I purpose towards the Spring to take a journey for at least six months: which, at our next meeting, I shall do myself the honour to impact to your Lordship very particularly.

The Irish, a few Scandinavian and Danish words excepted, being not only a Dialect of the antient Celtic or Gallic, but being also liker the mother than her other daugher the British; and the Irish Manuscripts being more numerous and much antienter than the Welsh, shows beyond all contradiction the necessity of this language for retrieving the knowledge of the Celtic Religion and Learning. Camden and others have long since taken notice of the agreement between the present British and those old Gallic words collected by learned men out of Greec and Roman authors: and the industrious Mr Edward Lhuyd, late keeper of the Museum at Oxford, perceiv'd this affinity between the same words and the Irish, even before he study'd that language, by the demonstration I gave him of the same in all the said instances. Nor does he deny this agreement in the comparative Etymologicon he afterwards made of those languages, where he quotes Camden and Boxhornius affirming it about the Gallic and British; but there being, says he[44] no Vocabulary extant, meaning no doubt in print, of the Irish, or antient Scottish, they cou'd not collate that language therewith, which the curious in these studies will now find to agree rather more than ours, with the Gaulish. That it does so, is absolute fact, as will be seen by hundreds of instances in this present work. I am aware that what I am going to say will sound very oddly, and see, more than a paradox; but I deserve, My Lord, and shall be content with your severest censure, if, before you have finish'd reading these sheets, you be not firmly of the same mind yourself: namely, that, without the knowledge of the Irish language and books, the Gallic Antiquities, not meaning the Francic, can never be set in any tolerable light, with regard either to words or to things; and numerous occasions there will occur in this History of illustrating both words and things even in the Greec and Roman authors. I shall here give one example of this, since I just come from treating of the several professors of learning common to the antient Gauls, Britons, and Scots, viz. the Druids, Bards, and Vaids. Lucian[45] relates that in Gaule he saw Hercules represented as a little old man, whom in the language of the country they call'd Ogmius; drawing after him an infinite multitude of persons, who seem'd most willing to follow, tho' drag'd by extreme fine and almost imperceptible chains: which were fasten'd at the one end to their ears, and held at the other, not in either of Hercules's hands, which were both otherwise imploy'd; but ty'd to the tip of his tongue, in which there was a hole on purpose, where all those chains center'd. Lucian wondering at this manner of portraying Hercules, was inform'd by a learned Druid who stood by, that Hercules did not in Gaule, as in Greece, betoken Strength of Body, but the Force of Eloquence; which is there very beautifully dusplay'd by the Druid, in his explication of the picture that hung in the temple. Now, the Critics of all nations have made a heavy pother about this same word Ogmius, and laboriously sought for the meaning of it every where, but just where it was to be found. The most celebrated Bochart, who, against the grain of nature, if I may so speak, wou'd needs reduce all things to Phenician; says it is an oriental word, since the Arabians[46] call strangers and barbarigans Agemion; as if, because the Phenicians traded antiently to Gaule and the British Ilands, for Colonies in them they planted none, they must have also imported their language; and, with their other commodities, barter'd it for something to the natives, naming their places, their men, and their Gods for them. Our present Britons, who are at least as great traders, do not find they can do so in Phenicia, nor nearer home in Greece and Italy, nor yet at their own doors in this very Gaule: besides that Lucian does positively affirm Ogmius was a Gallic word, a word of the country.[47] This has not hinder'd a learned English Physician, Dr. Edmund Dickenson, from hunting still in the East for a derivation of it; conjecturing Hercules to be Joshua,[48] who was surnamed Ognius, for having conquer'd Og King of Bashan:

O! sanctas gentes! quibus haec nascuntur in hortis Numina.

Juvenal. Sat. 15 ver. 10

I could make your Lordship yet merryer, or rather angrier, at these forc'd and far-fetch'd Etymologies, together with others hammer'd as wretchedly out of Greec, nay even out of Suedish and German. But the word Ognius, as Lucian was truely inform'd, is pure Celtic; and signifies, to use Tacitus's phrase[49] about the Germans, the Secret of Letters, particularly the Letters themselves, and consequently the learning that depends on them, from whence the Force of Eloquence procedes: so that Hercules Ogmius is the learned Hercules, or Herculus the protector of learning, having by many been reputed himself a Philosopher.[50] To prove this account of the word, so natural and so apt, be pleas'd to understand, that, from the very beginning of the Colony, Ogum, sometimes written Ogam, and also Ogma,[51] has signify'd in Ireland the Secret of Letters, or the Irish Alphabet; for the truth of which I appeal to all the antient Irish books, without a single exception. 'Tis one of the most authentic words of the language, and originally stands for this notion alone. Indeed after Patric had converted the nation, and, for the better propagating of Christian books, introduc'd the use of the Roman letters, instead of the antient manner of writing their primitive letters, very different from those they now use, began by degrees to grow obsolete; and at last legible only by Antiquaries and other curious men, to whom they stood in as good stead as any kind of occult characters: whence it happen'd that Ogum, from signifying the secret of writing, came to signify secret writing, but still principally meaning the original Irish Characters. There are several Manuscript Treatises extant, describing and teaching the various methods

113

of this Secret Writing; as one in the College-Library of Dublin,[52] and another in that of his Grace the Duke of Chandois.[53] Sir James Ware, in his Antiquities of Ireland, relating how the antient Irish did, besides the vulgar characters, practise also divers ways and arts of occult writing, call'd Ogum, in which they wrote their secrets; I have, continues he,[54] an antient parchment book full of these, which is the same just now said to belong to the Duke of Chandois; and Dudley Forbes,[55] a hereditary Antiquary, wrote to the rather laborious than judicious Chronologist O Flaherty,[56] in the Year 1683, that he had some of the primitive Birch-tables,[57] for those they had before the use of parchment or paper, and many sorts of the old occult writing by him. These are principally the Ogham-beith, the Ogham-coll, and the Ogham-craoth[58] which last is the old one and the true. But that the primary Irish letters, the letters first in common use, which in the manner we have shown, became accidentally occult, were originally meant by the word Ogum; besides the appeal made above to all, antient authors, is plain in particular from Forchern, a noted Bard and Philosopher, who liv'd a little before Christ. This learned man ascribing with others the invention of letters to the Phenicians, or rather more strictly and properly to Phenix, whom the Irish call Fenius farsaidh, or Phenix the antient, says, that, among other Alphabets, as the Hebrew, Greec, and Latin, he also compos'd that of Bethluisnion an Oghum,[59] the Alphabet of Ogum, or the Irish Alphabet, meaning that he invented the first letters, in imitation of which the Alphabets of those Nations were made. Ogum is also taken in this sense by the best modern writers: as William O Donnell,[60] afterwards Archbishop of Tuam, in his preface to the Irish New Testament, dedicated to King James the First, and printed at Dublin in the Year 1602, speaking of one of his assistants says, that he enjoin'd him to write the other part according to the Ogum and propriety of the Irish tongue; where Ogum must necessarily signify the Alphabet, Orthography, and true manner of writing Irish. From all this it is clear, why among the Gauls, of whom the Irish had their Language and Religion, Hercules, as the protector of Learning, shou'd be call'd Ogmius, the termination alone being Greec. Nor is this all. Ogma was not only a known proper name in Ireland, but also one of the most antient; since Ogma Grianann, the father of King Dalboetius,[61] was one of the first of the Danannan race, many ages before Luican's time. He was a very learned man marry'd to Eathna, a famous Poetess, who was besides the fore-mention'd Monarch, Cairbre likewise a Poet: insomuch that Ogma was deservedly surnamed Griannan,[62] which is to say Phebean, where you may observe Learning still attending this name. The Celtic Language being now almost extinct in Gaule, except onely in lower Britanny, and such Galic words as remain scatter'd among the French; subsists however intire in the several dialects of the Celtic Colonies,[63] as do the words Ogum and Ogma particularly in Irish. Nor is there any thing better known to the learned, or will appear more undeniable in the sequel of this work, than that words lost in one dialect of the same common language, are often found in another: as a Saxon word, for example, grown obsolete in Germany, but remaining yet in England, may be also us'd in Switzerland; or another word grown out of date in England, and flourishing still in Denmark, continues likewise in Iceland. So most of the antiquated English words are more or less corruptly extant in Friezland, Jutland, and the other Northern countries; with not a few in the Lowlands of Scotland, and in the old English Pale in Ireland.

Now, from the name of Hercules let's come to his person, or at least to the person acknowledg'd to have been one of the Heros worship'd by the Gauls, and suppos'd by the Greecs and Romans to be Hercules. On this occasion I cannot but reflect on the opposite conduct, which the learned and the unlearned formerly observ'd, with respect to the Gods and divine matters. If, thro' the ignorance or superstition of the people, any fable, tho' ever so gross, was generally receiv'd in a Religion; the learned being asham'd of such an absurdity, yet not daring openly to explode anything wherein the Priests found their account, explained it away by emblems and allegories importing a reasonable 'meaning,' of which the first authors never thought: and if the learned on the other hand, either to procure the greater veneration for their dictates, or the better to conceal their sentiments from the profane vulgar, did poetically discourse of the elements and qualities of matter, of the constellations or the planets, and the like effects of nature, veiling them as persons; the common sort immediately took them for so many persons in good earnest, and render'd 'em divine worship under such forms, as the Priests judg'd fittest to represent them. Objects of divine worship have been coin'd out of the rhetorical flights of Orators, or the flattering addresses of Panegyrists: even metaphors and epithets have been transform'd into Gods, which procur'd mony for the Priests as well as the best; and this by so much the more, as such objects were multiply'd. This is the unavoidable consequence of deviating ever so little from plain Truth, which is never so heartily and highly reverenc'd, as when appearing in her native simplicity; for as soon as her genuine beauties are indeavour'd to be heightn'd by borrow'd ornaments, and that she's put under a disguise in gorgeous apparel: she quickly becomes, like others affecting such a dress, a mercenary prostitute, wholly acting by vanity, artifice, or interest, and never speaking but in ambiguous or unintelligible terms; while the admiration of her lovers is first turn'd into amazement, as it commonly ends in contemt and hatred. But over and above the difficulty, which these proceedings have occasioned in the history of antient time, there arises a greater from time itself destroying infinite circumstances, the want whereof causes that to seem afterwards obscure, which at the beginning was very clear and easy. To this we may join the preposterous emulation of nations, in ascribing to their own Gods or Heros, whatever qualities were pre-eminent in those of others. That most judicious writer[64] about the nature of the Gods, commonly call'd Phurnutus, tho' his true name was Cornutus, a Stoic Philosopher, whom I shall have frequent occasion to quote hereafter, 'Owns the great[65] variety, and consequently the perplexedness and obscurity, that occurs in the history of Hercules; whereby it is difficult to know certainly what were his real atchievements, or what were fabulously fathered upon him: but having been an excellent General, who had in diverse countries signaliz'd his valor, he thinks it not probable, that he went onely arm'd with a Lion's skin and a Club; but that he was represented after his death with these, as symbols of generosity and fortitude, for which reason he was pictur'd with a bow and arrows.' To this let me add, that several valiant men in several nations having, in imitation of some one man any where, been called or rather surnam'd Hercules; not only the works of many, as subduing of Tyrants, exterminating of wild beasts, promoting or exercising of commerce, and protecting or improving of learning have been ascrib'd to one: but that also wherever any robust person was found represented with a skin and a club, a bow and arrows, he was straight deem'd to be Hercules; whence the Egyptian, the Indian, the Tyrian, the Cretan, the Grecian or Theban, and the Gallic Hercules. This was a cosntant way with the Greecs and Romans, who, for example, from certain resemblances perfectly accidental, conjectur'd that Isis was honour'd by the Germans,[66] and Bacchus worship'd by the Jews,[67] which last notion is refuted even by their enemy Tacitus.[68] Such superficial discoveries about the Celtic Divinities I shall abundantly expose. Yet that Ogmius might be really the Grecian Hercules, well known in Gaule, it will be no valid exception that he was by the Druids Theologically made the symboll of the Force of Eloquence, for which that country has been ever distinguish'd and esteem'd: since even in Greece he was, as Phurnutus assures us mystically accounted that Reason which is diffus'd thro' all things, according to which nature is vigorous and strong, invincible and ever generating; being the power that communicates virtue and firmness to every part of things.[69] The Scholiast of Apollonius affirms, that the natural Philosophers understood by Hercules, the intelligence and permanence of beings:[70] as the Egyptians held him to be that Reason, which is in the whole of things, and in every part.[71] Thus the learned allegoriz'd away among others, as I said before, the fabulous atchievments and miraculous birth of this Hero, on which we shall however touch again, when we come to explain the Heathen humor of making all extraordinary persons the Sons of Gods, and commonly begoton Virgins; tho' this last is not the case of Hercules, who was feign'd to be the Son of Jupiter by Alcmena, another man's wife. This wou'd be reckon d immoral among men, but Jupiter, said the Priests, can do with his own what he pleases: which reason, if it contented the husbands, could not displease the batchelors, who might chance to be sometimes Jupiter's substitutes. The Druidical allegory of Ogmius, or the Gallic Hercules, which in its proper place I shall give you at large, is extremely beautiful: and as it concerns that Eloquence whereof you are so consummate a master, cannot but powerfully charm you.

In the mean time 'tis probable your Lordship will be desireous to know, whether, besides the language and traditions of the Irish, or the monuments of stone and other materials which the country affords, there yet remain any Literary records truly antient and unadulterated, whereby the History of the Druids, with such other points of antiquity, may be retriev'd, or at least illustrated? This is a material question, to which I return a clear and direct answer; that not only there remain very many antient Manuscripts undoubtedly genuine, besides such as are forg'd, and greater numbers interpolated,[72] several whereof are in Ireland itself, some here in England, and others in the Irish Monasteries abroad: but that, notwithstanding the long state of barbarity in which that nation hath lain, and after all the rebellions and wars with which the kingdom has been harass'd; they have incomparably more antient materials of that kind for their history, to which even their Mythology is not unserviceable, than either the English, or the French, or any other European nation, with whose Manuscripts I have any acquaintance. Of these, I shall one day give a catalogue, marking the places where they now ly, as many as I know of them; but not meaning every Transcript of the same Manuscript, which wou'd be endless, if not impossible. In all conditions the Irish have been strangely sollicitous, if not in some degree superstitious, about preserving their books and parchments; even those of them which are so old, as to be now partly or wholly unintelligible. Abundance thro over care have perished under ground, the concealer not having skill, or wanting searcloth and other proper materials for preserving them. The most valuable pieces, both in verse and prose, were written by their Heathen ancestors; whereof some indeed have been interpolated after the prevailing of Christianity, which additions or alterations are nevertheless easily distinguish'd: and in these books the rites and formularies of the Druids, together with their Divinity and Philosophy; especially their two grand doctrines of the eternity and incorruptibility of the universe, and the incessant Revolution of all beings and forms, are very specially, tho' sometimes very figuratively express'd. Hence their Allanimation and Transmigration. Why none of the natives have hitherto made any better use of these treasures; or why both they, and such others as have written concerning the History of Ireland, have onely entertain'd the world with the fables of it, as no country wants a fabulous account of its original, or the succession of its Princes, why the modern Irish Historians, I say, give us such a medley of relations, unpick'd and unchosen, I had rather any man else shou'd tell. The matter is certainly ready, there wants but will or skill for working of it; separating the Dross from the pure Ore, and distinguishing counterfeit from sterling coin. This in the meantime is undeniable, that learned men in other places, perceiving the same dishes to be eternally serv'd up at every meal, are of opinion that there is no better fare in the country; while those things have been conceal'd from them by the ignorant or the lazy, that would have added no small ornament even to their classical studies. Of this I hope to convince the world by the lustre, which, in this work, I shall impart to the Antiquities not only of Gaule and Britain, but likewise to numerous passages of the Greec and Latin authors. How many noble discoveries of the like kind might be made in all countries, where the use of Letters has long subsisted! Such things in the mean time are as if they were not: for

Paulum sepultae distat-inertiae
Celata virtus.

Horat. *lib*. 4. *Od*. 9

117

The use of letters has been very antient in Ireland, which at first were cut on the bark of trees,[73] prepar'd for that purpose; or on smooth tables of birchwood, which were call'd Poets tables;[74] as their characters were in general nam'd twigs and branch-letters,[75] from their shape. Their Alphabet was call'd Beth-luis-nion, from the three first letters of the same, B, L, N, Beth, Luis, Nion;[76] for the particular name of every letter was, for memory-sake, from some tree or other vegetable; which, in the infancy of writing on barks and boards, was very natural. They had also many characters signifying whole words, like the Egyptians and the Chinese. When Patric introduc'd the Roman letters, as I said above, then, from a corruption of Abcedarium, they call'd their new Alphabet Aibghittir;[77] which, by the Monkish writers, has been Latiniz'd Abgetorium.[78] But there florished a great number of Druids, Bards, Vaids, and other authors in Ireland long before Patric's arrival; whose learning was not only more extensive, but also much more useful than that of their Christian posterity this last sort being almost wholly imploy'd in scholastic Divinity, Metaphysical or Chronological Disputes, Legends, Miracles, and Martyrologies, especially after the eighth century. Of all the things committed to writing by the Heathen Irish, none were more celebrated, or indeed in themselves more valuable, than their laws; which were deliver'd, as antiently among some other nations, in short sentences, commonly in verse, no less reputed infallible. Oracles than the Lacedemonian Rethrae[79]: and, what's remarkable, they are expresly term'd Celestial Judgements;[80] for the pronouncing of which, the most famous were Forchern, Neid, Conla, Eogan, Modan, Moran, King Cormac, his Chief Justice Fithil, Fachma, Maine, Ethnea the daughter of Amalgad, and many more. The Celestial Judgements were only preserv'd in traditionary poems, according to the institution of the Druids, till committed to writing at the command of Concovar[81] king of Ulster; who dy'd in the year of Christ 48, whereas Patric began his Apostleship but in the year 432. The Poets that wrote were numberless, of whose works several pieces remain still intire, with diverse fragments of others. The three greatest incouragers of learning among the Heathen Irish monarchs were, first, King Achaius,[82] surnamed the Doctor of Ireland, who is said to have built at Tarah an Academy, call'd The Court of the Learned.[83] 'Twas he that ordain'd, for every principal family, hereditary Antiquaries; or, in case of incapacity, the most able of the same historical house, with rank and privileges immediately after the Druids. The next promoter of Letters was King Tuathalius,[84] whose surname is render'd Bonaventura, tho' not so properly, and who appointed a triennial revision of all the Antiquaries Books, by a committee of three Kings or great Lords, three Druids, and three Antiquaries. These were to cause whatever was approv'd and found valuable in those books, to be transcribed into the royal *Book of Tarah*;[85] which was to be the perpetual standard of their history, and by which the contents of all other such books shou'd be receiv'd or rejected. Such good regulations I say there were made, but now how long or how well observ'd: or, if truth is to be preferr'd to all other respects, we must own they were but very slightly regarded: and that the Bards, besides their poetical license, were both mercenary and partial to a scandalous degree. The ordinance however is admirable, and deserves more to be imitated, than we can ever expect it to be so any where. The third most munificent patron of Literature was King Cormac, surnamed Long-beard,[86] who renew'd the laws about the Antiquaries, re-built and inlarg'd the Academy at Tarah for history, law, and military prowess: besides that he was an indefatigable distributer of justice, having written himself abundance of laws still extant. So in his Institution of a Prince[87] or his Precepts[88] to his son and successor Carbre Liffecair,[89] who in like manner was not superficially addicted to the Muses. Cormac was a great proficient in Philosophy, made light of the superstitions of the Druids in his youth; and, in his old age having quitted the scepter, he led a contemplative life: rejecting all the Druidical fables and idolatry, and acknowledging only one Supreme Being, of first Cause. This short account of the primevous Irish Learning, whereof you'll see mant proofs and particulars in the more than once mention'd Dissertation concerning the Celtic Language and Colonies, to be annext to our Critical History, will I am confident, excite your curiosity.

The custom therefore, or rather cunning of the Druids, in not committing their rites or doctrines to writing, has not deprived us as some may be apt to imagine, of sufficient materials to compile their History. For, in the first place, when the Romans became masters of Gaule, and every where mixt with the natives; they cou'd not avoid, in that time of light and learning, but arrive at the certain knowledge of whatever facts they have been pleas'd to hand down to us, tho' not alway rightly taking the usages of other nations: as it must needs be from a full conviction of the Druidical fraudulent superstitions, and barbarous tyranny exercis'd over the credulous people, that these same Romans, who tolerated all religions, yet suppress this instituion in Gaule and Britain, with the utmost severity. The Druids however were not immediately extinguish'd, but only their barbarous, tyrannical, or illusory usages. And indeed their human sacrifices, with their pretended Magic, and an authority incompatible with the power of the magistrate, were things not to be indured by so wise a state as that of the Romans. In the second place, the Greec colony of Marseilles, a principal mart of Learning, could not want persons curious enough, to acquaint themselves with the Religion, Philosophy, and Customs of the country, wherein they liv'd. Strabo and others give us an account of such. From these the elder Greecs had their information, not to speak now of the Gauls seated in Greece in self and in Lesser Asia, as the later Greecs had theirs from the Romans; and, by good fortune, we have a vast number of passages from both. But, in the third place, among the Gauls themselves and the Britons, among the Irish and Albanian Scots, their Historians and Bards, did always register abundance of particulars about the Druids, whose affairs were in most things inseparable from those of the rest of the inhabitants: as they were not only the judges in all matters civil or religious, but in a manner the executioners too in criminal causes; and that their sacrifices, were very public, which consequently made their rites no less observable. One thing which much contributed to make them known, is, that the King was ever to have a Druid about his person; to pray and sacrifice, as well as to be judge for determing emergent controversies, tho' he had a civil judge besides. So he had one of the chief Lords to advise him, a Bard, to sing the praises of his ancestors, a Chronicler to register his own actions, a Physician to take care of his health, a Musician to intertain him. Whoever was absent, these by law must be ever present, and no fewer than three Controllers of his family: which Decemvirate was the institution of King Cormac. The same custom was taken up by all the Nobles, whereof each had about him his Druid, Chief Vassal, Bard, Judge, Physician, and Harper; the four last having lands assign'd them, which descended to their families, wherein these professions were hereditary, as were their Marshal, and the rest of their officers. After the introducing Christianity, the Druid was succeeded by a Bishop or Priest, but the rest continued on the antient foot: insomuch, that for a long time after the English Conquest, the Judges, the Bards, Physicians, and Harpers, held such tenures in Ireland. The O Duvegans were the hereditary Bards of the O Kellies, the O Clerys and the O Brodins were also hereditary Antiquaries: the O Sheils and the O Canvans were such hereditary Doctors, the Maglanchys such hereditary Judges, and so of the rest; for more examples, especially in this place, are needless: it wou'd be but multiplying of names, without ever making the subject clearer. Only I must remark here, from the very nature of things, no less than from facts, that, tho' Caesar be silent about it, there were civil Judges in Gaule just as in Ireland, yet under the direction and controll of the Druids. This has led many to imagine, that, because the Druids influenc'd all, there were therefore no other judges, which is doubtless an egregious mistake.

Further, tho' the Druids were exemted from bearing arms, yet they finally determined concerning Peace and War: and those of that order, who attended the King and the Nobles, were observed to be the greatest make-bates and incendiaries; the most averse to Peace in Council, and the most cruel of all others in Action. Some of them were ally'd to Kings, and many of them were King's sons, and great numbers of them cull'd out of the best families: which you see is an old trick, but has not been always effectual enough to perpetuate an order of men. This however made Historians not to forget them, and indeed several of them render'd themselves very remarkable; as the Druid Trosdan, who found an antidote against the poyson'd arrows of certain Brittish invaders: Cabadius,[90] grandfather to the most celebrated champion Cuculand;[91] Tages[92] the father of Morna, mother to the no less famous Fin mac Cuil:[93] Dader, who was kill'd by Eogan, son to Olill Olom King of Munster; which Eogan was marry'd to Moinic, the daughter of the Druid Dill. The Druid Mogruth, the son of Sinduinn, was the stoutest man in the wars of King Cormac: nor less valiant was Dubcomar,[94] the chief Druid of King Fiacha; and Lugadius Mac-Con the abdicated King of Ireland, was treacherously run thro' the body with a lance by the Druid Firchisus.[95] Ida and Ono, Lords of Corcachlann near Roscommon, were Druids; whereof Ono presented his fortress of Imleach-Ono to Patric, who converted it into the religious house of Elphin, since an Episcopal See.[96] From the very name of Lamderg,[97] or Bloody-hand, we learn what sort of man the Druid was, who by the vulgar is thought to live inchanted in the mountain between Bunncranach and Fathen in the county of Dunegall.[98] Nor must we forget, tho' out of order of time, King Niall[99] of the nine hostage's Arch-Druid, by name Lagicinus Barchedius;[100] who procured a most cruel war against Eocha King of Munster, for committing manslaughter on his son; and which the Druids making a common cause, there was no honor, law, or humanity observ'd towards this King; whose story, at length in our book, will stand as a lasting monument of Druidical bloodiness, and a Priest-ridden State. I conclude with Bachrach, chief Druid to Conchobhar Nessan King of Ulster, who is fabl'd by the Monks long after the extinction of the Druids, to have before it happen'd, others say at the very time, describ'd the Passion of Jesus Christ, in so lively and moveing a manner; that the King transported with rage drew his sword, and with inexpressible fury fell a hacking and hewing the trees of the wood where he then was, which he mistook for the Jews: nay, that he put himself into such a heat as to dy of this frenzy. But even O Flaherty fully confutes this silly fiction,[101] not thinking it possible that such circumstances cou'd be any way inferr'd from an Eclipse, which is the foundation of the story, nor that a clearer revelation shou'd be made of those things to the Irish Druids, than to the Jewish Prophets; and, finally, by shewing, that Conchobhar dy'd quietly in his bed fifteen years after the crucifixion of Christ. Bachrach however was a great man, and the King himself had a Druid for his step-father and instructor.

It can be no wonder therefore, that men thus sacred in their function, illustrious in their alliances, eminent for their learning, and honour'd for their valor, as well as dreaded for their power and influence, should also be memorable both in the poetry and prose of their country. And so in fact they are, notwithstanding what Dudley-Forbes, before mention'd, did, in a letter to an Irish writer,[102] in the year 1683, affirm: namely, that, in Patric's time no fewer than 180 Volumes, relating to the affairs of the Druids, were burnt in Ireland. Dr Kennedy says,[103] that Patric burnt 300 volumes, stuft with the fables and superstitions of Heathen Idolatry: unfit, adds he, to be transmitted to posterity. But, pray, how so? why are Gallic or Irish superstitions more unfit to be transmitted to posterity, than those of the Greecs and Romans? Why shou'd Patric be more squeamish in this respect than Moses or the succeding Jewish Prophets, who have transmitted to all ages the Idolatries of the Egyptians, Phenicians, Caldeans, and other Eastern nations? What an irreparable destruction of history, what a deplorable extinction of arts and inventions, what an unspeakable detriment to Learning, what a dishonor upon human understanding, has the cowardly proceeding of the ignorant, or rather of the interested, against unarm'd monuments at all times occasion'd! And yet this book-burning and letter-murdring humor, tho' far from being commanded by Christ, has prevail'd in Christianity from the beginning: as in the Acts of the Apostles[104] we read, that many of them which believ'd – and us'd curious arts, brought their books together, and burnt them before all men; and they counted the price of them, and found it fifty thousand pieces of silver, or about three hundred pounds sterling. This was the first instance of burning books among

Christians; and ever since that time the example has been better follow'd, then any percept of the Gospel.

From what we have hitherto observ'd, you see that our Historians, My Lord, do, in spite of all chances, abound with matter enough to revive and illustrate the memory of the Druids. Besides that the rites and opinions of other nations serve not only to give light to theirs, but were many of them of Druidical or Celtic extraction. This no body will deny of the Aboriginal Italians, who having been often overrun by the Gauls, and having several Gallic Colonies planted among them, they partook both of their Language and Religion; as will be very easily evinc'd in our Dissertation, and has been already tolerably done by father Pezron in his Celtic Originals. Diogenes Laertius, in the Proem of his Philosophical History, reckons the Druids among the chief Authors of the Barbarous Theology and Philosophy, long anterior to the Greecs, their disciples: and Phurnutus, in his treatise *of the nature of the Gods*, says most expresly, that among the many and various fables which the antient Greece had about the Gods, some were derived from the Mages, some from the Egyptians and Gauls, others from the Africans and Phyrgians, and others from other nations:[105] for which he cites Homer as a witness, nor is there any thing that bears a greater witness to it self. This however is not all: for, over and above the several helps I have mention'd, there are likewise numerous monuments of the worship of the Druids, their valor, policy, and manner of habitation, still remaining in France, in Britain, in Ireland, and in the adjacent Islands; many of 'em intire, and the rest by the help of these easily conceiv'd. Most are of stone, as the lesser ones are of glass, and others of earth bak'd extremely hard. The two last kinds were ornaments or magical gems, as were also those of Chrystal and Agat, either perfectly spherical, or in the figure of a lentill; or shap'd after any of the other ways, which shall be describ'd and portray'd in our book. The Glass Amulets or Ornaments are in the Lowlands of Scotland, call'd Adderstanes, and by the Welsh Gleini na Droedh, or Druid-Glass, which is in Irish Glaine nan Druidhe, Glaine in this language signifying Glass, tho' obsolete now in the Welsh dialect, and preserv'd only in this Gleini na Droedh. But the more massy Monuments shall, in a day or two, be the subject of another Letter from, My Lord,

Your Lordship's most oblig'd and very
Humble Servant
June 25, 1718

10

CELTIC RESEARCHES

Edward Davies

*On the Antiquity of the Druidical order, amongst the Celtae – Specimens of
Druidical traditions preserved by the Welsh – Remarks upon them – The
professors of Druidism anciently known by the name of Hyperboreans.*

The order of Druids, under the name, do not appear to have been traced, or
known, out of Gaul and the Islands of Britain. The name seems to have
belonged exclusively to the British order, and to have extended only where that
order was acknowledged. The original and primitive inhabitants of this Island,
at some remote period of antiquity, revised and reformed their national
institutes. Their priest or instructor had hitherto been simply named Cwyz or
Gwydd, as the term is retained by Taliesin – 'A Bûm Gwydd yngwarthan.' But
it was deemed adviseable, to divide the sacred office between the national or
superior priest, and a subordinate character, whose influence was more limited.
From henceforth, the former became Der-wydd or Druid, which, in the
language of the people to whom we owe the term, is a compound of Dar,
Superior, and Gwydd, a Priest or Inspector: The latter was Go-wydd or Ovydd,
a Subordinate Instructor; and was sometimes called Syw or Sy-wydd, names
familiar to the Bards, Taliesin and Aneurin.

These very terms, as well as Greeks and Romans could spell them, have
been recognized by the oldest people and religion of Europe, and in that very
country from whence the Celtae came.

The name then of Druid was local, but the Religion had a very deep root.
Indeed under this name, the influence and authority of the order once extended
over the whole of Gaul. It covered this extent of territory, as one nation. The
seat of general concourse and Great Session, was fixed in what the Druids
deemed a central spot[106] – a choice that would have been absurd, as well as
inconvenient, if the institution had been confined to any particular district.

These Druids themselves were Celtae, of the Patriarchal or Equestrian
order. Their disciples were nobilissimi Gentis,[107] Sons of the noblest families in
the Nation. These alone could, in their turn, become teachers. The order did not
then consist of Strangers, but of the most illustrious descent which the Celtae
could boast. They were studious to confine their mysteries in the Celtic pale,
where their opinions were respected, and exclude from them all but those who
had been duly initiated.

123

In Caesar's time, the inhabitants of Gaul had been disturbed, in some degree, by the intercourse of strangers. Their sacred groves had been traversed and violated by feet, which they considered as profane. Druidism, therefore, was not so pure in that country as in Britain, the source of the reformed institution, and many sons of the nobles in Gaul were sent hither to finish their Education. De. Bell. Gall. L. VI.

When the Romans acquired a footing in Britain, they found the country possessed by two nations; the Belgae, originally Celtae, but somewhat intermixt with strangers, and an indigenous race, who declared they were born in the Island. The title of Native is a distinction claimed by the first race of a country, and justly – a family had originally settled; but the nation was born in the land. Among these pure descendants of the Celtae, the Druidism of Britain was in the highest repute. The principal seat of the order was found in Mona, an interior recess of that ancient race, wich was born in the Island.

Into that sequestered scene, the Druids, who detested warfare, had gradually retired, after the irruption of the Belgae, and the further incroachment of the Romans. They had retired from their ancient, magnificent seat at Abury, and from their Circular, Uncovered Temple on Salisbury Plain, in which the Hyperborean sages had once chaunted their hymns to Apollo, or Plenyz.

An order thus cautiously withdrawing itself, into the bosom of its primitive nation, of whom it consisted, and for whom it was calculated, could not have owed its fundamental principles to any foreigners, or have been willing to adopt their tenets. The Celtae must have received this institution from their very earliest parents.

A mysticism similar to that of the Druids, appears to have prevailed, amongst the Western Cimmerii or Celtae, from the remotest antiquity.

Some of their most prominent features were – the intercourse they held with souls, after death – the judgment which they passed on the actions of men, and the inference they drew, from their lives, respecting the changes they would undergo, and the mode of their ultimate renovation.

In the court of Pluto, which always held its justicial seat, in the land of the Celtae or Cimmerii, causes of this kind were determined by incorruptible Judges, and there could be no higher compliment paid to the most sacred characters, than to enrol them into this high trust of Judicature. We read of three personages thus promoted, each of whom appears, from his birth, from his place of nativity, and from the history of his life, to have been eminent as a Κοης.

When Homer sends Ulysses to consult the dead, he does not make him touch upon the celebrated shores of Egypt or Phoenica, though he had sailed by them. He directs him to the coast of the Western Ocean – to Portugal or Spain – to the land of the Cimmerii or Celtae, and the Dominions of Pluto or Dis, whom the Celtae acknowledged as their father. In this devious course, the poet must have been guided by ancient and prevailing opinion.

The descent of Aeneas into the Regions below, in which he learns the mysteries of the Metempsychosis, the fortunes – the changes – the renovations of his descendants – Doctrines of pure Druidism – is from a part of Italy, in which, not only the researches of Strabo, but, perhaps, Virgil himself placed one branch of the Cimmerii.

This great Bard was born in Cis-Alpine Gaul, and seems, in his youth, to have courted the Gaulish Muse, till he found that she would not advance his fortune – a very unpoetical ground of desertion –

> Galatea reliquit:
> Namque – fatebor enim – dum me Galatea tenebat,
> Nec spes libertatis erat, nec cura peculî.

'Galatea was the mother of the Celtae.'

Appian. Bell. Illyr.

The same poet mentions the Gallicum Tau, in a passage of his Catalecia, which Ausonius, the Gaulish Bard, proposes as an aenigma to his learned friends. This Tua was the symbol of the Druidical Jupiter. It consisted of a huge, giant oak, deprived of all its branches, except only two large ones, which though cut off and separated, were suspended from the top of its trunk, like extended arms.[108]

Whether, from these passages, we do, or do not infer that Virgil had studies in the mysticism of Druid lore, he, at least, intimates clearly, in the Sixth Aeneid, that he was touching upon Druidical mysteries.

It was necessary the hero should obtain a branch of misseltoe, as the means of his introduction to the court of Pluto. The poet minutely describes this plant, but instead of risking a full explanation, by fixing its name, he says it resembled the misseltoe.

> Discolor unde auri per ramos aura refulsit,
> Quale solet sylvis, brumali frigore, viscum
> Fronde virere nova, quod non sua seminat arbor,
> Et croceo foetu teretes circumdare truncos;
> Talis erat species auri frondentis, opaca
> Ilice.

Aen. VI. 204

This was not only misseltoe, but the misseltoe of the oak, which few, besides Aeneas and the Druids, have had the good fortune to find. The Prince was directed in his search for it, by those sacred birds which fed upon its fruit, and in whom the seed was again prepared, for future vegetation.

All the accounts of Orpheus agree with Druidism: and we could expect no less; for the Celtae or Cimmerii were the first inhabitants of the country in which Orpheus flourished, and some of them continued their abode, in the same region, till this renowned character was no more.

Eusebius mentions an irruption of the Cimmerii into Asia, about 100 years after the war of Troy, and Eustathius, alluding to this irruption, in his comment upon Dionysius, quotes the authority of Arrian for proof, 'That not only the

Mysi and Phryges, but also the Thracians went out of Europe into Asia, with Patarus their leader, when the Cimmerii over-ran Asia.' Under this Generic name, then, the tribes of Thrace had hitherto been included.

Herodotus, L. IV. 13. cites the testimony of Aristeas the Proconucsian, that the Commerii had once dwelt επι τη γοτιη Ιαλαςςη, 'On the South sea,' or 'On the South side of the sea' till they left that country, when disturbed by the Scythians, who were pushed forwards by other Northern invaders. – This Aristeas lived before Homer.

Under the name of Orpheus, who flourished in so many ages, and taught so many things, may be understood, a sacred order of men, similar to the Magi, the Druids, and others. – This celebrated character is represented as having lost his wife. The wife of an order of Sages would, in the language of mythology, imply their Science, their doctrine or their discipline. The very name Eurydice, which appears to be a compound of Ευζυς Latus, and δικη mos jure receptus, will perhaps justify a conjecture, that in the image of Orpheus' wife, is typified his comprehensive discipline.

The bereft husband goes not in search of his wife, into Phoenicia, Egypt, Chaldea or India. He descends into the Dominions of Pluto, into the Country of the Cimmerii or Celtae; though Virgil, to diversify his picture, sends him to the Cimmerii who dwelt upon the North of the Euxine. – Amongst them, Orpheus discovered his Eurydice, and might have restored her to Thrace, if he had not failed in a material part of his probation.

It is acknowledged that such tales are not History; but they are founded upon traditions of the mythological and heroic ages – traditions which existed long before Greece could boast of a single historian, and which uniformly intimate, that a mystical doctrine, similar to that which Druids of the historical ages are known to have taught, had prevailed amongst the Celtae, or Cimmerii of Europe, from the remotest periods.

These are some of the reasons which induce me to be of opinion, that our Druids, either under that name, or the more ancient and general appellations of Bards and Gwyddion, had been the wise men of the West, ever since that continent was first peopled; and that our Celtic parents brought the fundamentals of their religion, when they imported their own persons and families, into Gaul: though, at later periods, they modified some particulars, and adopted some innovations.

The monuments, now remaining, of the Celtae, are such as can be ascribed only to an original and primitive race. Their Cromlechs, their Logans, the rough pillars, that are still found, as well in Britain, as upon those parts of the Continent which the Celtae once occupied, are the erections of an early age, or at least, of a people who had retained the simplicity of patriarchal times.

The inhabitants of Syria, taken in its most ample extent, erected unhewn pillars in their sacred groves: – they had, therefore, once, a custom that was common to them, with many other primitive nations.

But had the works at Abury or Stonehenge displayed their rude magnificence, in Syria, in Egypt, Chaldea or India – not in Britain; critical discernment would have pronounced them, of antiquity superior to that of sculptured and lettered columns, the pyramids and their highly polished marbles, or any other surviving miracles of those renowned and opulent countries.

To those antiquaries, who ascribe our British monuments to any Eastern race whatsoever, I would therefore take the liberty of recommending a more accurate regard for historical truth.

Works like these must have been formed, in the taste of the age, and the country, of their constructors. None would have taken such incredible pains to exhibit, in a land of strangers, a mode and style of architecture which had become obsolete in their own; and which their ancestors had abandoned for a course of ages.

These monuments, thus rude in their workmanship, display that species of Great and Simple united, which is the character of such designs, at an early age. They must therefore have been the work of the natives, not of others. For, however the arts may have sunk in the later Celtae, their patriarch, as well as the father of the Egyptian, Chaldean or Indian, was the son of a civilized family: and in the line of his descendants, the science of the Noachidae was, unquestionably, in great measure, preserved.

If the Celtae then wanted artificers to execute with elegance, they could not want masters of design, or of power to devise plans of edifices like these, with judgment and skill.

The nature of Druidical traditions demonstrate, that the Druids were Celtae, and that their progenitors had been present with this nation from its very source. Thus, for instance, we are told by Caesar – 'Galli se omnes ab Dite patre prognatos praedicant, idque à Druidibus proditum dicunt.' The Gauls affirm that Pluto or Dis was their common progenitor, and refer this account of themselves to the tradition of the Druids.

Had the original Druids been any other than Celtae or Gauls, they would rather have preserved the history or tradition of their own origin. They could have given no account of the father of a nation whom they found, already formed. But this was a Celtic and national tradition, and such as could not have been preserved by strangers.

Yet so much were the Druids interested in this account, that we find them providing for its perpetuity by incorporating it with a national custom, and thus impressing upon the mass of the people, the memory of their descent – 'Ob eam causam, spatia omnis temporis, non numero dierum sed noctium, finiunt: dies natales, et mensium et annorum initia, sic observant, ut noctem dies subsequatur.'

The custom of measuring periods, by the number of nights, in preference to that of days, may not have been peculiar to the Celtae: but the inference they drew from it is clear – That in the West their common ancestor found his portion assigned.

In order to show the nature and the authenticity of this account, respecting the origin of the Gauls, it will not be improper to observe, that, under the character of Saturn, the heathens preserved the history of Noah. Saturn divided the world amongst his three sons. The eldest of these was Dis or Pluto, and for his share he had Europe – the Western or lower region. Thus he became the parent of the first Europeans, and consequently of the Gauls.

This exactly falls into the Mosaic history.

The whole Earth was divided between three sons of Noah. Japheth, who was the eldest of them, inherited Europe; or the Isles of the Gentiles. He was therefore progenitor of the Gauls.

Here we have a real history which the Druids, as Celtae, preserved, ever since the period of the primary allotment: and the device by which it was imprest, prevails amongst the Welsh to this day. They call a week, wyth-nos, Eight nights: a fortnight, pythewnos, Fifteen nights – that is, they circumscribe their periods by the night on which they commence and expire, according to the usage of the ancient Gauls.

'But what – it may be asked – is the peculiar connection between the night and the portion of Dis?'

I answer, that, as the whole of Europe lay directly west of Asia, it was overshadowed by the darkness of the night, when the morning arose upon the Eastern habitations of the Noachidae: and the evening sun would appear to descend, in its progress towards the western continent, as to a lower sphere. Hence the portion of Japheth, or of Dis, obtained the description of a lower Region – the land of Shades and of Night.

Such was the land of the Cimerii, the children of Dis.

It has frequently been remarked, that in the general mysticism of the Druids, and in many of their customs, there is close analogy to those of the Magi, the Brachmans, the Egyptian Priests, etc. I do not deny the fact, but I conceive that these traits of analogy were impressed upon mankind, before the families of the Earth were divided. And I cannot but regret, that when pains have been taken, and Fancy called in, to shew what the Aborigines of Europe may have borrowed from the East, it has hardly been the object of a moment's attention, amongst the learned, in this peculiar class, to ascertain what those Europeans had of their own. – Many of the fundamental customs, and inveterate opinions of the Celtae, appear to have been once universal. I would not therefore, unless compelled by the unequivocal decree of historical proof, refer them to any particular source. And, as to their general mysticism, I have quoted already a well accredited fragment of Sanchoniathon, which contains the elements of all the mystical theology in the ancient world. – It is there told us, that the History, Theology and Philosophy of the first ages had been converted into mystic allegories, and this, at so early a period, that Isiris, or Mizraim, the Brother of Canaan, was amongst those who received them in that form. The Patriarchs of the other Nations, whether in the East or in the West, had an equal opportunity of doing the same.

But, if it must be insisted upon, that a chain of communication united the Magi, Brachmans and our Druids, it must, I think, be a chain drawn through Asia Minor, and Thrace or Macedon, the countries through which the

Celtae came, and in which tradition acknowledges the remains of their family and religion.

* * *

The Druids are not represented as Inventors. They were the jealous preservers of early and primitive discipline, traditions, doctrines, customs and opinions. Their method of instruction was by symbols and by enigmas, or dark allegories,[109] by ancient songs, and maxims orally delivered, and in private; but which they deemed it unlawful to reduce into writing, or communicate out of their own pale.[110]

Of the lessons thus habitually, and by system, concealed, few specimens are to be found in ancient authors. Mela, L. iii. c. 2. has preserved one of them . . .

'to act bravely in war;
that souls are immortal,
and there is another life after death.'

Diog. Laertius presents us with another.

To worship the Gods,
to do no evil,
and to exercise fortitude,

Both of these precepts are Triads; and we may hence conjecture, that such was the general form of their moral and historical instructions. Ausonius, who respected, and seems occasionally to imitate the Bards of his country, has a whole poem of Triads.

The philosophy, the comprehension and good sense of the sentences before us, are such as to inspire a wish, that we could obtain something more, from the hand of those masters.

Amongst the descendants of those who were Professors of Druidism, it would not be unreasonable to expect this gratification. A national institute, which had been so deeply rooted, was not likely to be obliterated from the memory and regard of the people.

The interdict of Gallic Councils would, of itself, prove the lingering obstinacy of Druidism, amongst the people of Gaul, to the end of the sixth century – 'Veneratores lapidum, accensores facularum, et excolentes sacra fontium et arborum, admonemus'[111] – Concil. Turon. A.D. 567.

In Britain, it continued longer still, as appears from the Law of Canute – Prohibemus etiam scriò – quod quis adoret Ignem vel Fluvium, Torrens vel Saxa vel alicujus generis arborum Ligna. – Wilkins, Leg. Aug. Sax. p. 134.

These were not Roman or Gothic, but Celtic superstitions, of Druidism.

He who is at all conversant with the remains of ancient Welsh literature, cannot be at a loss for the reason of these prohibitory Laws. Our oldest authors avow the most pious veneration for the Druids – give themselves credit, as initiated into their mysteries, and profess to deliver their genuine maxims and traditions.

As Druidism had so many real, though concealed partizans, long after its public authority was abolished, may we not suppose, that some attempts would be made, when the use of the pen was no longer interdicted, to cherish and preserve its most valuable relics?

This order, for instance, taught the people something of their own history. The conversion of the native to the Religion of Christ, could not have rendered that history uninteresting. The people would naturally wish to perpetuate some account of their ancient independence. Accordingly we find, amongst the oldest Welsh manuscripts, many historical notices upon the model of the Druidical Triads, and purporting to be the remains of Druidical ages.

Their contents furnish, in my opinion, strong evidence in support of their authenticity. I cannot account for them at all upon other grounds. Many collections of these Triads are preserved, at this day, in old copies upon vellum.

Four of these copies, beside transcripts upon paper, were collated for the Welsh Archaeology. London. 1801.

The old copies, now preserved, are not immediately taken from one original collection. They vary in the selection, the number and the order of their Triads. But when the same Triad occurs, in different copies, it is given to the same effect and, generally, in the same words. We must not then look to known authors, for the origin of these records. Like the old histories of Greece, collected by Apollodorus, they must be carried further back, to remote periods and primitive traditions.

I shall now lay before my Reader, a short selection, translated from a series, in the second volume of the Welsh Archaeology. p. 57.

That series bears the following title.

> These are Triads of the Island of Britain – that is to say, Triads of memorial and record, and the information of remarkable men or things, which have been in the Island of Britain; and of the events which befel the Race of the Cymry, from the age of ages.

To the copy, from which a transcript was made for the London edition, the following note is annext.

> (Translation.) These Triads were taken from the book of Caradoc of Nantgarvan, and from the book of Jevan Brechva, by me, Thomas Jones of Tregaron – and these are all I could get of the three hindred – 1601.[112]

I   The three pillars of the Race of the Island of Britain.

The first, Hu Gadarn, who first brought the Race of the Cymry into the Island of Britain; and they came from the land of Hâv called Defrobani [where Constantinople stands][113] and they passed over Môr Tawch[114] (the German ocean) to the Island of Britain, and to Llydaw,[115] where they remained.

The second, Prydain, the son of Aedd-Mawr, who first established regal government in the Island of Britain [Before this, there was no Equity but what was done by gentleness, nor any Law but that of force.]

The third, Dyvnwal-Moelmud, who first discriminated the laws and ordinances, customs and privileges of the land and of the nation. [And for these reasons they were called the three pillars of the nation of the Cymry.][116]

II   The three benevolent tribes of the Island of Britain.

The first were the stock of the Cymry, who came, with Ilu Gadarn, into the Island of Britain: for He would not have lands by fighting and contention, but of Equity, and in peace.

The second were the race of the Lolegrwys,[117] who came from the land of Gwas-gwyn, and were sprung from the primitive stock of the Cymry.

The third were the Britons. They came from the land of Llydaw, and were also sprung from the primordial line of the Cymry.

[And they are called the three peaceful tribes, because they came by mutual consent and permission, in peace and tranquillity. – The three tribes descended from the primitive race of the Cymry, and the three were of one language and one speech.] (5)

III   Three tribes came, under protection, into the Island of Britain, and by the consent and permission of the nation of the Cymry, without weapon, without assault.

The first was the tribe of the Caledonians, in the North.

The second was the Gwyddelian Race, which are now in Alban (Scotland.)

The third were the men of Galedin, who came in the naked ships (Canoes?) into the Isle of Wight, when their country was drowned,[118] and had lands assigned them by the Race of the Cymry.

[And they had neither privilege nor claim in the Island of Britain, but the land and protection that were granted, under specified limits. And it was decreed, That they should not enjoy the immunities of the native Cymry, before the ninth generation.] (6)

IV   Three usurping tribes came into the Island of Britain, and never departed out of it.

The first were the Coranied, who came from the land of Pwyl.[119]

The second were the Gwyddelian Fichti, who came into Alban, over the sea of Llychlyn (Denmark).

The third were the Saxons.

[The Coranied are about the river Humber, and on the shore of Môr Tawch, and the Gwyddelian Fichti are in Alban, on the shore of the sea of Llychlyn. – The Coranied united with the Saxons; and being partly incorporated with them, deprived the Lloegrwys of their government, by wrong and oppression: and afterwards, they deprived the Race of the Cymry of their crown and sovereignty. All the Lloegrwys became Saxons,[120] except those who are found in Cornwall, and in the Commot of Carnoban, in Deira and Bernicia.

The primitive Race of the Cymry have kept their land and their language; but they have lost their sovereignty of the Island of Britain, through the treachery of the protected tribes, and the violence of the three usurping tribes.] (7)

V   The three awful events of the Island of Britain.

First, the bursting of the lake of waters, and the overwhelming of the face of all lands; so that all mankind were drowned, excepting Dwyvan and Dwyvach, who escaped in a naked vessel (without sails) and of them the Island of Britain was re-peopled.

The second was the consternation of the tempestuous fire, when the Earth split asunder, to Annwn (the lower region) and the greatest part of all living was consumed.[121]

The third was the scorching summer, when the woods and plants were set on fire, by the intense heat of the Sun, and multitudes of men, and beasts and kinds of birds, and reptiles, and trees, and plants were irrecoverably lost. (13)

VI   The three chief master works of the Island of Britain.

The ship of Nevydd Nav Neivion, which carried in it a male and a female of all living, when the lake of waters burst forth;

The drawing of the avanc to land out of the lake, by the branching oxen of Hu Gadarn, so that the lake burst no more;

And the stones of Gwyddon Ganhebon, on which were read the arts and sciences of the world. (97)

VII   The three great Regulators of the Island of Britain.

Hu Gadarn, bringing the Race of the Cymry out of the land of Hâv, which is called Defrobani, into the Island of Britain;

Prydain, the son of Aedd-Mawr, establishing government and law over the Island of Britain;

And Rhitta Gawr, who made himself a robe, of the beards of kings, whom he caused to be shaved (reduced to vassalage) for their oppressions, and contempt of justice. (54)

VIII   The three happy controulers of the Island of Britain.

Prydain, the son of Aedd-Mawr, suppressing the Dragon tyranny [This was a tyranny of pillage and contempt of Equity, that sprung up in the Island]

Carador, the son of Brân, the son of Llyr, checking the oppression of the Caesars;

And Rhitta Gawr, controuling the tyranny and pillage of the tumultuary kings. (55)

IX   The three benefactors of the Race of the Cymry,

The first, Hu Gadarn, who first shewed the Race of the Cymry the method of cultivating the ground, when they were in the land of Hâv [namely, where Constantinople now stands] before they came into the Island of Britain;

Coll, the son of Coll-Frewi, who first brought wheat and barley into the Island of Britain, where, before, there had only been Oats and Rye;

And Elldud the Knight [a holy man of Côr Dewdws] who improved the manner of cultivating the ground, taught the Cymry a better method than what had been known before, and shewed them the art of plowing which now prevails. [For before the time of Elldud, land was cultivated only with a mattock and a spade, after the manner of the Gwyddelians.] (56)

X   The three primary Sages of the Race of the Cymry.

Hu Gadarn, who first collected the race of the Cymry and disposed them into tribes;

Dyvnwal-Moelmud, who first regulated the Laws, privileges and institutions of the country and nation;

And Tydain tâd Awen, who first introduced order and method into the memorials and preservation of the Oral art (poetry) and its properties.

And from that order, the privileges and methodical usages of the Bards and Bardism (Druidism) of the Island of Britain, were first devised. (57)

XI   The three primary Bards of the Island of Britain.

Plennydd, Alawn and Gwron.

These were they who devised the privileges and usages, which belong to Bards and Bardism.

[Yet there had been Bards and Bardism before: but they were not completely methodized, and they enjoyed neither privileges nor established customs, but what they obtained through gentleness and civility, and the protection of the country and the nation, before the time of these three.

Some say they were in the time of Prydain, the son of Aedd Mawr, others, that they were in the time of his son, Dyvnwal-Moelmud, whom some of the old books call Dyvnvarth, the son of Prydain.] (58)

XII   The three Elementery masters of Poetry and Memorial, of the Race of the Cymry.

Gwyddon Ganhebon, the first man in the world who composed poetry;

Hu Gadarn, who first adapted poetry to the preservation of record and memorials;

And Tydain Tâd Awen, who first developed the art and structure of poetry, and the due disposition of thought.

And, from the labours of these three personages, sprung Bards and Bardism, and the regulation of their privileges, and established discipline, by the three primary Bards, Plennydd, Alawn and Gwron.

XIII   The three primary Baptized (or Christian) Bards.
Merddin Emrys,
Taliesin, the chief of the Bards,
And Merddin, the son of Madawe Morvryn.

XIV   The three mighty Labours of the Island of Britain.
Erecting the stone of Ketti,
Constructing the work of Emrys,
And heaping the pile of Cyvrangon.

XV   The three happy astronomers (Seronyddion, Saronides) of the Island of Britain.
Idris Gawr,
Gwyddion, the son of Don,
And Gwyn, the son of Nudd.
[So great was their knowledge of the stars, and of their nature and situation, that they could foretel whatever might be desired to be known, to the day of doom.] (89)

XVI   The three masters of mysterious and secret science, of the Island of Britain.
Mâth, the son of Mathonwy, and he disclosed his secret to Gwyddion, the son of Don.
Mengw, the son of Teirgwaedd, who taught his secret to Uthyr Bendragon.
And Rhuddlwm Gawr, and he learned his mystery of Eiddic, Gôr and Coll, the son of Coll Frewi. (90)

XVII   The three great modellers of the Island of Britain.
Corvinwr, the bard of Ceri Hîr, of Llyngwyn, who first made a ship, with a sail and a helm, for the race of the Cymry.
Mordial Gwr Gweilgi, the architect of Ceraint, the son of Greidial, who first taught the race of the Cymry, the work of stone and lime, [at the time when Alexander the Great was subduing the world.]
And Coll, the son of Cyllin, [the son of Caradawc, the son of Brân,] who first made a mill with a wheel, for the race of the Cymry. And these three were bards. (91)

* * *

In these documents, as they now stand, some degree of confusion may be detected. It is the inevitable effect of transcript and comment, in ages, from which the key of the knowledge contained in them was, by the mysteries of time, withheld; but, upon the whole, they appear to be genuine memorials of remote antiquity.

From the personifications, which occur in several of them, it may be inferred, that something more is implied, than a series of historical events, and that frequently they consist of such allegories, or oenigmata, as Druids are known to have employed, in teaching their disciples.

Thus the three primary bards, or Druids, Plennydd, Alawn and Gwron, No. XI. are, in their literal import, light, harmony, and energy.

In their national prepossession, they resemble the genuine traditions of many other primitive people. The patriarchs are made, almost exclusively, the fathers of the Cymry, and the general events of early ages, are consigned particularly, to the Island of Britan. This may be exemplified in the account of the deluge, No. V.

'The waters burst forth – all lands were covered – all mankind were drowned, except only two persons, who escaped in a boat. Of them was repeopled the Island of Britain.' Even the vessel, which carried a male and a female of all that lived, was, it seems, one of the masterworks of the Island of Britain.

This, which is contradictory to the more temperate accounts of the real progress made by the Cymry, illustrates the nostra-tism of all national traditions.

The personage who survived the deluge, is called Dwyvan, or Dwyvawn, and his wife Dwyvach – the godlike man and woman. His name, (No. VI.) is Nevydd Nâv Neivion – the celestial one, the Lord of the waters. Our old bards call him, Dylan ail Mor; Dylan, or Dyglan, – son of the sea, from Dy-glaniaw, to land, or come to shore – whence perhaps, Deu-calion. – Hu Gadarn, the mighty inspector, is a very high personage, and supreme agent in these Triads. He was the God of the Druids. As such, he has always been acknowledged by the Welsh. A Christian bard thus marks the religion of his votaries, put in opposition to that of Christ. –

> Two active impulses truly there are
> In the world, and their course is manifest:
> An impulse from Christ; joyful is the theme –
> Of a right tendency, an energetic principle.
> Another impulse there is (indiscreetly sung)
> Of falsehood, and base omens:
> Thus, has been obtained by the men of Hu,
> The usurping bards of Wales.

He was not, however, without his partizans long after the introduction of Christianity. He is thus elevated, in the Orphic style, by Jolo Goch, the bard of Owen Glandwr.

> Hu Gadarn, the sovereign, the ready protector,
> A king, distributing the wine, and the renown,
> The emperor of the land and the seas,
> And the life of all in the world, was he.

After the deluge, he held
The strong beam'd plough, active and excellent:
This did our Lord of stimulating genius,
That he might shew to the proud man, and to the humbly wise,
The most approv'd art, with the faithful father.

See O. Dict. V. Hu.

He is thus described by Rhys Brydydd, in the fifteenth century.

The smallest, if compared with small,
Is the Mighty Hu, in the world's judgment
And he is the greatest, and Lord over us,
And our God of mystery:

Light is his course, and swift:
A particle of lucid sunshine in his car;
He is great on land and seas,
The greatest whom I shall behold –
Greater than the worlds – Let us beware
Of mean indignity, to him who deals in bounty.

See O. Dict. V. Mymryn.

Though Hu Gadarn primarily denoted the Supreme Being. I think his actions have a secondary reference to the history of Noah. The following particulars are told of him in the above cited selection.

1   His branching, or elevated oxen, (perhaps his offering) at the deluge, drew the destroyer out of the water, so that the lake burst forth no more. (No. VI.)

2   He instructed the primitive race in the cultivation of the earth. (No. IX.)

3   He first collected and disposed them into various tribes. (No. X.)

4   He first gave laws, traditions, etc. or adapted verse to memorials. (No. XII.)

5   He first brought the Cymry into Britain and Gaul, because he would not have them possess lands, by war and contention; but of right, and in peace. (No. II.)

* * *

The account before us, of the settlements in Britain, gives precedency to the Cymry, who came from Gwlad yr Hâv, called Defrobani. These, at present, are very obscure names; but some commentator, at least, as old as the middle of the twelfth century, explains them, and repeatedly, as meaning 'Where Constantinople now stands.' This comment would not have been made, without some authority, and it belongs to an age which possessed many documents, relating to the history of the Britons, which are no longer extant.

Hâv, in our old orthography, (as in Lib. Land.) would be Hâm; it may import Haemus, or Haemonia. Defrobani may either be Dy-vro-banau, the land of eminences, or high points, Thrace in general; or else Dyvro-Banwy, the land or vale of the Peneus, Thessaly, Haemonia. I have shewn elsewhere, that our ancestors, the Celtae, in their line of march, traversed those regions.

But though the Cymry remained some time in that country, where they began the tillage of the earth, (No. IX.) it was not their ultimate, their destined, and proper home. It was not a land they could possess, 'of right, and in peace.'

That part of the family which first came to Gaul and Britain, in search of lasting possessions, probably withdrew towards the Danube, – ascended even to the souce of that river, – and stretched over to the Rhine; which river some of them perhaps may have crossed, whilst others followed the main stream, to its mouth, upon the German Ocean, or Môr Tawch. We are told (No. I.), that they came over that sea, to the Island of Britain, and Llydaw, or the coast of Gaul, where they remained.

It appears then, by these documents, that Gaul and Britain were peopled, originally, by the same race, and about the same time.

The extent of Britain being imperfectly known, when its coast was discovered, perhaps only a few of the Cymry volunteered themselves to settle there, and these appear to have entered the country in detached, as well as little families not under any one patriarch, of acknowledged authority; for Hu Gadarn was only their figurative conductor, to their western settlement, and the Draig Ormes, or tumult of their leaders, threw them into confusion, till the arrival of another colony. These were the Lloegrwys, or those who dwelt upon the Loire. They came under the conduct of Prydain, the son of Aedd the Great, a prince of the chief branch of the Celtae in the West.

I am very much deceived, if this Aedd was not the Αιδης of Greek mythology, the acknowledged patriarch of the Gauls, and he from whom the ΑΙΔΟΥΟΙ, Aedui, the first and principal race in Gaul, took their name.[122]

Prydain, or Pryd, who came into this island, could not have been his immediate son, but a lineal representative, or descendant of Aides, Dis, or Japheth.

The institution of British Druidism, having been completely established, in the time of a sovereign, who was of the governing family in Gaul, (No. XI.) that circumstance may account for its favourable reception there.

The Brython, who gave its (existing) name to this island, and to its inhabitants, according to some of these Triads, and the venerable Bede, – came from Llydaw; or, in other words, from Armorica. They were probably of Pryd's retinue; for he brought his fleet, and his Llogerwys, 'O Dir Gwas Gwynt,' from the land of the Veneti, or the mouth of the Loire, adjoining to Armorica – Gwas Gwynt was the country to which Britain sent its fleet, for the assistance of the Gauls, against the Romans. Compare Triad XIV. of the orginal series, with Caesar, B.G. III. 8, 9.

The Aedui and Veneti, or Aeddwys and Gwynet, were of the same stock; for Gwyn, the son of Nudd, or Nevydd, king of the lower regions, was the same personage with Aedd Mawr.

These three colonies of the Cymry, arrived in Britain, before their divided families had forgotten their primitive tongue, or had lost the original and sound principle of just and peaceable possession. (No. II.)

* * *

The account of Druidism, which these triads present, has evidently, a mixture of allegory, and it involves ideal, or mythological characters. The following particulars, however, may be remarked, as worthy of notice.

The Celtae regarded the materials of this legendary system, as the relics of the first ages of mankind.

Gwyddon Ganhebon, was the first of the human race who composed poetry, (No. XII.) and he described, by engraving upon stones, the arts and sciences of the world. (No. VI.) This character, who forcibly reminds us of the inscribed pillars of Seth, Thoth, or Hermes, preceded Hu Gadarn, who was present at the deluge – He took the Cymry under his protection – He taught the arts of peace, and principles of justice; – He adapted poetry to memorials and records.

Tydain, or in more ancient orthography, Titain Tâd Awen, Titan, the father of inspiration or genius, introduced order and method, into the poetry and memorials of the Cymry.

This personage, who is identified, by name, and character, with Titan, or Apollo, of the Orphic hymns, and of Greece, forms a connecting link, between the mythologies of eastern and western Europe.

From the labours of those three mastes, sprung British Druidism, with all its privileges, usages, and rules of discipline. (No. X. XII.)

In this island, was Druidism first regularly established, and in the time of princes, who are acknowledged as great legislators, and benefactors of their country. (No. 1.).

The names which honour them, are connected with mythology.

Prydain, from Pryd, which is Time, Season, Due time – Beauty, Comeliness, and from Ain, a source or principle – seems to have been primarily designed as an epithet of the sun – Father of beauty, – and principle of the seasons.

Prydain is the son of Aedd Mawr, the great Αιδης, father of the Aedui, and of the Gauls.

The name of the other prince, Dyvnwal Moelmud, seems to be obliterated in the Celtic – דר חד צל מלמד may signify, the judge, presiding over instruction. His other name, Dyvn Varth ab. Prydain, is, the profound bard or priests, the son of Prydain.

The occasion of the institution, may be collected from the great act of Prydrain, in suppressing the dragon tyranny, or the turbulence and confusion which had risen amongst the heads of families, (No. VIII.) and this he effected, by investing a sacred order of men, from whose definitive sentence there was no appeal, with an authority and jurisdiction to determine all disputes; or, in other words, by committing to the office of priesthood, the administration of civil power.

The leading principles, upon which these patriarchal sages began their functions, are highly laudable, if judgment is to be formed of them by the characters first put into the judicial chair. – 'Plennydd,' – 'Alawn,' – a 'Gwron,' – light, – harmony, – and energy, or virtue. – (It has the same relation to gwr, a man, as virtue has to vir.)

'Plennydd,' is, I think, a name of the 'Sun,' or 'Apollo.' The sunbeams which appear to vibrate in a hot day, are called, 'Tês ys Plennydd,' – the beams of the radiant one. 'Eithinen neud gudd Blennydd.' Tal. 'A furzebush would truly hide the sun.' And again, – 'Blin blaen blen Blennydd.' 'Irksome in front is the radiance of the sun.'

But, though Prydain, or Dyvnwal, invested his Druids with all that civil authority which they exercised, under these Presidents, yet their principles of religion did not originate here. – There had been Bards, or Druids, before, though not completely incorporated, or vested with judicial authority, and with exclusive privileges. (No. II.)

The names of primary bards intimate, that an ostensible design of Druidism was, to enlighten the understanding, promote harmony in society, and encourage virtue.

In the institutional triads, published by Mr E. Williams, the design is thus declared. Tri diben Barddoniaeth: Gwellhau moes a devod; cynnal heddwch, a moli pob daionus a rhagor.

'The three ultimate intentions of bardism: To reform the morals and customs; to secure peace; to celebrate (or encourage) all that is good and excellent.'

Druidism, then, in its primitive and pure state, may be regarded as an edifice, raised upon the basis of the patriarchal religion, for the purpose of superseding the necessity of recourse to arms, in the contentions of independent states; and of restraining the excesses of individuals – without the aid of penal statutes.

It governed men, by taking hold of their minds, and of their imaginations; – by suggesting laws which had their sanction in general opinion – and by teaching its votaries to expect, in a future state, a just recompence of their actions; – an apprehension, which, might serve to regulate their conduct in their present life.

A system thus constructed, probably attained its meridian prevalence at an early age, and amongst the first unmixed colonies of the Cymry. It could operate with effect only amongst the people for whose opinions it was calculated, and who held the sanctions of it in the most profound veneration. When strangers, who paid little deference to the sacred code of these Druids, began to intrude, necessity would gradually put arms into the hands of the Cymry, for self-defence. From that moment, of course, pure Druidism began to decline. The inherent principle of securing peace, must have been occasionally abandoned, and many emendations proposed, for the purpose of declaring, in what cases it would be lawful to unsheath the sword, which the institutional triads describe as a necessary but reluctant exercise of duty, against the lawless and depredatory.

Amongst their disciples, these Druids could, at all times, ensure peace, by holding up the rod of excommunication, their most rigorous instrument of doom; the wretch on whom it fell, was not only menaced with severe punishment hereafter, but was deprived, in the mean time, of all social comfort and benefit.

But, in the eyes of strangers, who confided in their own strength, this weapon was disarmed of all its terrors, and their presence must have opened a secure asylum to the turbulent amongst the Celtae. In the hour of invasion, Druids could only withdraw from the field, and permit the military chiefs, and the people, to defend the region. Their power, as Druids, and the purity of their discipline, must, therefore, have been on the decline, long before the time of Caesar.

In favour of this institution, considered in a political view, little can be said. As our nature is constituted, it seems neither to have been calculated for the liberty of the individual, or the independence of the nation: and I regard its prevalence, as one main cause of the general subjugation of the Celtae. Their country was large and populous. The inhabitants, trained up to the exercise of that principle which they called fortitude, could not be deficient in courage. And we read of several amongst their families, who emigrating with a view of conquest, made good their establishment, in the midst of contending, fierce, and warlike nations. But these, were not attended by their Druids, who deemed conquest unlawful. Within their jurisdiction, arms and warfare in general were in disgrace. As a consequence of this principle, the sword was not ready, nor the soldier expert, in the day of necessity. Much of their best possessions was generally lost, before they looked up to the painful duty, or qualified themselves to discharge it with due effect.

Just so, we may suppose it would happen, to a nation, composed of a religious tribe, well known, and much respected in England. Though friends of peace, they would probably evince, on trying occasions, that the sentiment did not arise from a defect of courage. Yet, they would not overcome their scruples, and begin to exert that courage, till an enemy should have gained such advantage, as would frustate and baffle their utmost efforts.

No. XV. mentions the astronomers, or Seronyddion (the Saronides of the ancients.) The name is British, being a compound of sêr, stars, and Honydd, (Pl. Honyddion,) one who discriminates and points out.

Of those great astronomers, the first named is Idris the giant, whose memory is perpetuated by one of the highest and most pointed mountains in North Wales, called Cader Idris, the chair, or keep, of Idris. It may, perhaps, have been an observatory, in ancient periods. On the very summit, we are told there is an excavation in the solid rock, resembling a couch, and it is pretended that, whoever should rest a night in that seat, will be found in the morning, either dead, raving-mad, or endued with supernatural genius.

By the side of a lake, near the foot of the mountain, are three gigantic stones, called Tri greienyn, which the fable of the populace describes, as three grains of sand which the giant shook out of his shoe, before he ascended the chair. (See Wyndham's Tour, 4to.) I rather think they obtained their name from Greian, the sun. Ιδρις, in Greek, implies, an expert, or skilful person, and דרשׁ', Idresh, in Hebrew, from דרשׁ, Dresh, to seek, search, inquire diligently. Hydres has a similar meaning in Welsh.

Idris, or Edris, is well known to the Arabians. They regard him as the prophet Enoch, and say, that he was a Sabean, the first that wrote with a pen after Enos, the son of Seth.

The Eastern Christians tell us, that Idris was the same with Hermes, or Mercury, the famous Trismegistus of the Egyptians. See Vallencey's Prospect. V. Dres.

Grecian mythology gives a similar name to Atlas, the inventor of the sphere, and this personage is the character with whom I think our British Seronydd, Idris the giant, has much connection.

The second astronomer is Gwyddion, the son of Don. – The Sage, the son of Genius. Without inquiring after the person dignified by this title, I shall just remark, that our old bards distinguished the Galaxy by his name, calling it, Caer Gwyddion.

The last of these luminaries was a person of no small importance; Gwyn, the son of Nudd, the same as Aedd, or Αιδης, father of the Celtae, and king of the lower regions. His dignity is thus acknowledged in a very old mythological tale, called, Buchedd Collen.

A govyn a oedd gwr o vown, yna i dywawd Collon, 'Ydwyv; pwy ai govyn?' – 'Myvi, cenad i Wyn ab Nudd, Brenin Annwn.'

And he asking if there was a man within, Collen replied, 'I am; who asks it?' – 'It is I, the messenger of Gwyn, the son of Nudd, king of the lower regions, or of Annwn.'

By this term, which denotes the deep, the low part, I think the Celtae, primarily understood a western situation; towards which there was an apparent fall, in the course of nature, and in this primary sense, the term, I think, may be understood in that remarkable triad, (No. V.)

When the opinion first prevailed, that souls of men descended for a time, to a lower state of existence, the west, or low region was consecrated peculiarly to them, – Annwn was applied figuratively to the condition of the dead, or the infernal regions, which comprehended the Elysium, and the Tartarus of antiquity. Thus we say, 'Nid eir i Annwn ond unwaith.' There will be but one journey to Hell. Cwn Annwn, are Hell-hounds. Plant Annwn, the children of the deep, certain wandering spirits.

As Annwn, or the west, was the peculiar land of the dead, we find sepulchral monuments most frequent in the western extremities of those countries, where Druidism was professed, as in Britany, Cornwall, and Mona.

There was perhaps a time, when these Druids regarded Ireland as the land of spirits. The Mabinogion, or institutional tales, represent Annwn as lying somewhere off Dyved, or Pembrokeshire; and the Irish acknowledge Annan; or Annun, as an old name of their country. See Shaw, Llwyd, etc.

According to our Bardic documents, the Cymry have preferred their claim to an ancient connection with not only the territories, but the mythology of Greece. It will add much to the influence and credit of British histories, if it shall appear, that ancient Greece acknowledged the same acquaintance with our Cymry, and their institutes of religion.

This acknowledgment is clearly intimated in the persons and characters of the Hyperboreans, a people who revered the sacred places, the Gods, and the religious rites of ancient Greece. To them, in return, Greece confessed her obligation for some objects of her own worship. Her ancestors had, therefore, been connected intimately with such a distant country, and with its inhabitants.

Though once acknowledged, as forming prominent features in Europe, it must be confessed, the latter Greeks were but imperfectly informed of local facts respecting them. However, some of their best authors, do furnish us with particulars, which may assist us in our search for their abode.

Dr Percy,[123] in his inimitable preface to the *Northern Antiquities*, p. 7, points out a remarkable passage of this kind, in Strabo, who there informs us, 'That, although the old Greek authors, gave to all the northern nations, the common name of Scythians, or Celto-Scythians; yet, that writers still more ancient, divided all the nations who lived beyond the Euxine, the Danube, and the Adriatic sea, into the Hyperboreans, the Sauromatae and Arimaspians; as they did those beyond the Caspian sea, into Sacae and Massagetae. These last, the Sacae and Massagetae, might possibly be the ancestors of the Saxons and Goths, (as these last are proved by indisputable evidence, to have been the Getae of the ancients) who, in the time of those remote Greek writers, possibly had not penetrated so far westward, as they did afterwards: for as it is well known the Germanii are considered by Herodotus as a Persian people. Now the most authentic historians, and poets, of the Gothic, or Teutonic nations, agree, in representing their ancestors to have come as emigrants from the more eastern countries. But as to those three other nations, the Hyperboreans, the Sauromatae, and the Arimaspians; if credit be due to Pelloutier, when he asserts, that, under the two former, the Celts and Sarmatians are plainly designed; yet, when he contends that Arimaspians are a fabulous race, which never existed, who does not see that he is blinded with hypothesis? Why may not the ancient Finns and Laplanders have been intended by this term, which he himself interprets, from Herodotus, one-eyed, and supposes it was descriptive of some nation that excelled in archery, as closing one eye, for better aim? Tacitus expressly assures us, that the Finni were great archers; and as it is observed in the following book, it is highly probable, that at some early period of time, both Finns and Laplanders possessed much larger and better tracts of country, than the northern desarts to which they are now confined.

The Sauromatae, and Arimaspians, were clearly inhabitants of eastern

Europe, as they are described by Strabo; and the west has been assigned, by the oldest Greek writers, to the Hyperboreans. Before the Goths penetrated into the west, this was the land of the Celtae, whom we must endeavour to identify in those ancient inhabitants of that region.

The name Hyperborei, has the import of Trans-Boreani, or men who lived beyond the north, who resided therefore, beyond certain districts, or nations to the north, well known to the ancient Greeks. Yet were they not within the arctic circle, or in the extremities of the north, as comparatively recent authors have supposed. For the wheaten straw was indispensible in their sacred mysteries; and this was no produce of high latitudes. According to Herodotus, the women of Thrace, and Paeonia, never made oblations to Diana, a divinity of the Hyperboreans, without recourse to this emblem. From thence it may be inferred, that Hyperboreans, and the inhabitants of these countries, were originally the same.

The father of history describes the sacred gifts of the Hyperboreans, as having been sent from one people to another, in their way to Greece, εγδεδυμενα, or εγδεδεμενα εν καλαμη πυρι, covered or bound by a wheat straw. L. IV. 33.

Perhaps ratified or confirmed by a wheat straw, in conformity with an ancient custom, to which an old bard alludes. –

Oni 'myddyddan ychwaneg,
Tor y gwelltyn ain dyn tèg.

'If she converses no more, break the straw with my fair one.' That is – break off all connection with her.

If he that broke that straw dissolved a compact, he that gave, joined, or exchanged it, made or confirmed a covenant, which the Hyperboreans may have done, when they entrusted their sacred gifts into the hand of strangers. It is in allusion to some habit of this kind, that we have stipulor from stipula; and, perhaps, Foedus, foederis, from the Irish, Fodar, straw.

The ancient Britons, called Helmstraw, Cloig, from Clo, a lock, a conclusion, a confirmation. They had also Belys, from Beli, their Apollo. Beli seems to be derived from Balu, to shoot, spring or issue forth. – Εχαεζγος.

Herodotus having understood that it was the custom of the Hyperboreans, to deliver their sacred gifts into Scythian hands, for the purpose of better forwarding them into Greece, enquired from the Scoloti of Little Tartary, whom the Greeks of his age eminently termed Scythians, respecting the Hyperboreans. But neither could this branch of the Scythians, nor any of their neighbours, the Essedones execepted, give the least account of them, and their trace of them, in his opinion, amounts to nothing. It therefore is clear, that no such people resided in the North East of Europe.

The Essedones, who had this imperfect knowledge of the Hyperboreans, were, probably, an eastern branch of the people who used the war chariot, called Essedum, or Essedon; and this was the national distinction of the Sigynae,[124] or the Celto Scythians, who occupied the South West of Germany, as it was also of their unquestioned Relations, the British Belgae: which carries us to the North West from Greece, and at once into contact with Celts, who were professors of Druidism.

And it was to the North West, from Greece, that we find the region of the Hyperboreans lay.

In the time of Aristeas, (who wrote before Homer) the Hyperboreans dwelt upon the sea, beyond the Arimaspi, and their neighbours, the Essedones. Herod, iv. 13. Hercules went from Greece, to the Hyperboreans, through Illyrium, and by the river Eridanus, or Po. Apollod, L. ii. C 4.

Posidonius and Protarchus, placed them near the Alps. (Gale in *Ant. Liberal*, p. 144), but they were not generally recognised on the south of these mountains, or very near them.

After passing from one people to another, their gifts arrived far in the West, upon the Adriatic, from whence they were carried in the first period, or stage, of their progress, to Dodona, but ultimately to Delos. Herod. iv. 33.

They came, then, from the land of the Celtae, whom Heraclides of Pontus calls Hyperboreans. Plutarch, in Camillo.

It may be asked, how happens it, if the Hyperboreans were Celtae, that the Greeks did not generally recognise them all over Celtica?

It may be answered, that it seems they had conceived a peculiar character of this people, and which appears to have been correct, as bearing upon their primary families, or tribes; but these, were followed by others, of a different character, and which materially changed the manners, previously impressed. The original idea which had been formed of the nation, was not realized by the Greeks, till they reached the interior districts, in which the former inhabitants remained unmixed.

The most considerable of these has been described by Hecateus, and by other celebrated authors upon ancient tradition, cited by Diodorus Siculus.

According to this ancient writer, the country of the Hyperboreans, in his day, was a large and fruitful island, in the ocean, lying to the North, off the coast of Gallia Celtica. This description, which I shall presently adduce at large, can agree with no other spot but Britain. Hecateus places the Island αντιωςζαν, opposite to, the coast of Celtica, without one intervening region: and should we seek it further North, a competent fertility of the land, and the essential wheat straw, will not be found.

Neither in this Island, itself, nor in contiguous parts of Europe, can we find a religious order of ancient celebrity, except our Druids, whose Theology conformed, in general, to that of Greeks and Romans, (Caes. B. G. vi. 17.)

The religion of the Germans was perfectly dissimilar, (Ibid 21.) besides, that, in that part of Europe, their establishments, were comparatively recent, and posterior to the age of Hecateus.

Hence it should seem, the Hyperboreans, who brought their gifts to Apollo, in the Vale of Tempe, down to the last ages of Paganism, (Ael. Var. Hist. L. iii. C. 1.) were our Druids of Britain.

But let us examine if their characters are incorporated. The chief outline of the Hyperborean ethics, was piety, inoffensive as well as peaceable conduct, and fortitude. The favorite maxim of Druids, who abstained from contest, and allayed every popular ferment, was, according to Diog. Laert (already cited for another purpose,) To worship the Gods – to do no evil – and to exercise fortitude; or, as the original British runs – 'Tri chynnorion doethineb: ufuddhâd i ddeddfau Duw; ymgais a llês dyn; a dioddef yn lew pob digwydd bywyd.'

'Three first principles of wisdom: Obedience to the laws of God; concern for the good of mankind; and bravely sustaining all the accidents of life.'

The sacred rites of the Delians, originated in the Hyperboreans: Their virgins came to Delos, accompanied by their Gods. Herod. iv. 35.

Tertius (Apollo) Jove et Latonâ natus, quem ex Hyperboreis Delphos ferunt advenisse – Reliqui (Apollines) omnes silentur, omnesque res aliorum gestae ad unum Jovis et Latonae filium referuntur. Cic. de. Nat. Deor. L. iii.

The legitimate Apollo of Grecian worship is, therefore, an accredited Hyperborean.

According to Gaulish tradition, in the time of Caesar, Druidical discipline originated in Britain. The same account is confirmed by the institutional Triads of that British order.

'Yn ynys Prydain, y cafwyd Barddoniaeth gyntaf – am na chafwys un gwlad arall erioed ddeall cyfiawn ar farddoniaeth – o ba wlâd bynnag y bônt, Beirdd wrth fraint a defod Beirdd ynys Prydain au gelwir.'

'Bardism, or Druidism, originated in Britain – pure Bardism was never well understood in other countries – of whatever country they may be, they are entitled Bards, according to the rights and the institutes of the Bards of the Island of Britain.'

Tydain, or Titain Tâd Awen, Titan the Father of Genius, the same as Apollo, is claimed as one of the Cymry, and as British. See above, (No. X. XII.)

The Hyperboreans used the wheat straw in the rites of Apollo and of Diana.

The old Britons ascribed peculiar virtues and powers to this very symbol. 'Gwrnerth Ergydlym a laddes yr arth mwyaf ac a welwyd erioed, a saeth wellten.' 'The keen-darting Gwrnerth, (perhaps another title of Apollo) slew the largest bear that was ever seen, with an arrow of straw.' W. Arch. V. 2. p. 68.

The arrow which Abaris, the Hyperborean priest of Apollo, carried round the earth, fasting (Herod, L. iv. 36.) was probably of this kind.

As the ancients often played upon words, particularly in their mystical accounts of things, ὄιστος, derived from ὄιω to think or opine, may have conveyed the opinions, as well as the arrow of Abaris; and by what Herodotus expresses, in the terms, ουδευ σιτεομενος, it may not have been originally meant, that he eat nothing. but that he made no provision for his journey, as Druids never did, regarding it as one of their sacred privileges, to find –

'Trwyddedogaeth ble'r elont.'

145

'maintenance wherever they went.' [Institutional Triads.]

It appears, from several passages in Taliesin, that our Druids made use of straw-reeds, and the points, or spicula of certain trees, in all their sacred rites. Perhaps he alludes to the Delian gifts, in telling us –

Bûm ynghaer Fefenydd. (*L.* Felenydd.)
Yt gryssynt wellt a gwydd.

W. Arch. V. I. p. 29.

'I have been in the city of Belenydd, whither the straws and sprigs were hastening.'

Pythagoras, whose philosophy bore a wonderful resemblance to that of Druids, is represented expressly to have heard the Gauls and Brachmans:[125] the former, as it should seem, in the person of Abaris, who delivered his arrow to him, in other words, made a covenant with him, and at the same time, instructed him in his doctrine. The philosophy of Greece, originated in the Celtae.[126]

The name of Abaris belongs to the Cymry. Αβζοικιμbζοι, ως τινες φαςι, κεμμε, ειε.

Steph. Byzant. De Urb.

Abaris may have been one of the Abroi; but the term does not so properly appertain to the Nation, as to the religion of the Cymry. Abarui, or Avarwy, the Contemplative, is a familiar name in the old Welsh. Abaris, considered as the character, I regard not as a personal name, but as a description of the order. In short, as I would understand Magus, or Druida, I think a short summary of Druidism, extracted from the institutional triads, of the order in Britain, will justify this acceptation.

Druids divided the whole of existence into three circles, or spheres. 1. Cylch y Ceugant, The circle of space, which none but God alone can pervade. 2. Cylch yr Abred, or, as the continental Cymry would say, – Aberes, 'The circle of courses,' which comprehended the material creation, and the condition or state of humanity. 3. Cylch y Gwynfyd, the circle of happiness, which man would ultimately attain.

But most of their philosophy respected the Abred, or the changes and revolutions to which nature and man were exposed. That circle of existence embraced their famous doctrine of the Metempsychosis, which they reconciled with apparently ingenuous efforts, to the immortality, and the ultimate felicity of the soul. The circle of Abred was that, in which men, with all the works of nature, began in the Great Deep, or in the lower state of existence. – It contained a mixture of good and evil.

But man, endued with a power of choice, between the evil and the good, by the exercise of his religion – of the relative duties – of pure virtue and fortitude, could bring all the passions or propensities of his nature, to a just balance. This condition of man was termed, the point of liberty, – he passed from thence, through the gate of mortality, into the circle of happiness: no more the victim of adversity, want, or death.

But if he permitted evil affections to govern and predominate, such as pride, falsehood, or cruelty; that bias would sink him down from the circle of happiness. Death would return him to the circle of courses, allotting him a punishment, in due proportion to his moral turpitude. Here the soul was to do penance in a beast, or in a reptile, or in several of them successively. From this degradation it rose, at length, and reassumed the human form. Repeated probations and corrections would, ultimately, subdue all evil propensities. The point of liberty would be attained and the divine particle would be introduced, by death, to infinite happiness.[127]

It has been a litigated question amongst the learned, whether Pythagoras received the doctrine of the Metempsychosis from Druids, or communicated this doctrine to them. But as Greeks acknowledge that he was a disciple of the Celtic Sages – as it is avowed, that he received the arrow of Abaris, which has been carried round the world – evident allusions to the mystery of the Abred, which is the corner stone of Druidism, – and as Aristotle has owned, that philosophy did not emigrate from Greece to Gaul, but vice versa, I think it safer to conclude, that one individual foreigner borrowed from this national institute, than to conceive, that he should have communicated his own speculations, upon this very mystical topic of religion, to an order of men, who were always jealous of novelties.

It may be added, that some of the very oldest Greek writers refer to similar opinions, as already established, and prevalent in the north west of Europe.

Atlas, the son of Japetus, was an Hyperborean, – he was also, a neighbour of the Hesperides. It was, consequently, in the north west corner of the world, that he supported the heavens. It was in the same tract, that fountains, and the origin of the earth, of hell, of the sea, of the sidereal heaven, and of all things, were placed in the great deep. Hesiod. Theog. 736.

It was here that Styx resided, in a magnificent house, composed of huge stones, connected, or covered at the top, (just in the style of our British monuments) and punished, even the Gods, by degrading them, for a time, to a lower state of existence, from whence they were to pass, through a variety of arduous probations, before they could recover their primitive divinity.

It was here also, at the ends of the earth, in the islands of the blessed, and by the deep ocean, that Jupiter assigned, as the reward of the just and the good, – as a recompence and crown to the heroes who had fallen before Thebes, and before Troy, – a residence of tranquillity, after death, in which the fertile soil produced its fruits, thrice every year. Hesiod. Egy a. 155, to 171.

These, must not only have been prevalent opinions, in the age of Hesiod, but must have been considered, by him, as maxims, rooted in the periods he describes. The road of the ancient Greeks, to the court of Pluto, to the land of just retribution, and therefore, the paradise and the hell of their mythology, pointed at the Islands of Britain.

The country, it is true, as we find it, will not answer the description, either of wretchedness or felicity; but those pictures referred, in their colouring, to religious faith, and they are verified in the different states of retribution, which Druidism conferred upon the virtues and vices of men. All that fair criticism demands, may be attested, and confirmed in the unequivocal remains of such monuments, and of such opinions, as the ancients ascribe to our distant progenitors.

Upon the whole, then, I cannot but apply to our Druids of Britain, the description preserved by Diodorus Siculus, L. ii. C. 47, which I here insert, with a few remarks.

Hecateus, and some others, who treat of ancient histories or traditions, give the following account.

'Opposite to the coast of Gallia Celtica, there is an island in the ocean, – not smaller than Sicily, – lying to the north, – which is inhabited by the Hyperboreans, who are so named, because they dwell beyond the north wind. This island is of a happy temperature, rich in soil, and fruitful in every thing, yielding its produce twice in the year.

'Tradition says, that Latona was born there, and for that reason, the inhabitants venerate Apollo, more than any other God. They are, in a manner, his priests, for they daily celebrate him with continual songs of praise, and pay him abundant honours.

'In this island, there is a magnificent grove τεμενος, (or precinct) of Apollo, and a remarkable temple, of a round form, adorned with many consecrated gifts. There is also a city sacred to the same God, most of the inhabitants of which are harpers, who continually play upon their harps in the temple, and sing hymns to the God, extolling his actions.

'The Hyperboreans use a peculiar dialect, and have a remarkable οικειοτατα, attachment, to the Greeks, especially to the Athenians, and the Delians, deducing their friendship from remote periods. It is related, that some Greeks formerly visited the Hyperboreans, with whom they left consecrated gifts, of great value, and also that in ancient times, Abaris, coming from the Hyperboreans, into Greece, renewed their friendship, (γυγγυεαι) family intercourse, with the Delians.

'It is also said, that, in this island, the moon appears very near to the earth, that certain eminences, of a terrestrial form, are plainly seen in it, that the God (Apollo) visits the island, once in a course of nineteen years, in which period, the stars complete their revolutions, and that for this reason, the Greeks distinguish the cycle of nineteen years, by the name of the great year.

'During the season of his appearance, the God plays upon the harp, and dances every night, from the vernal equinox, till the rising of the pleiades, pleased with his own successes.

'The supreme authority, in that city, and sacred precinct, is vested in those who are called Boreadae, being the descendants of Boreas, and their governments have been uninterruptedly transmitted in this line.'

The topography of this island accords, precisely and exclusively, to the local position of Britain. Some have objected that the words, κατα τας αξυτους, do not simply mean, lying towards the north, but imply a higher latitude, than that of Britain. But this island, viewed from the coast of Gaul, appears to be under the Bear, and the same Diodorus, L. V. 21, when speaking expressly of Britain, describes it as, 'ναι αντηγ την αζχτον χεβμενην. – Ipsi ursae subjectam. In the same chapter, he compares the island's form to that of Sicily; he asserts that, in ancient periods, it had remained unmixed by foreign power, for neither Bacchus, nor Hercules, nor any other hero or potentate of whom we have read, had molested it by war. He remarks the simple manners, and singular integrity of the inhabitants: he adds, that their numerous princes generally cultivated peace amongst themselves. These, are distinguishing features of the Hyperboreans. Hecateus was unacquainted with an accurate and real survey of Britain, but he compares it, naturally and properly, to the largest island that was known to the Greeks.

As the Celtic year began in July,[128] Britain may have been described as producing two harvests, one at the commencement, and the other, at the end of each year; but, in the time of the Britons, its most important produce was pasture, and of this, it continued eminently to afford a second crop.

The honour of Apollo is not forgotten, in the ancient monuments of the Cymry. The first name of Britain, after it was inhabited, was Vel ynys, the island of Bel. W. Arch. V. 2. P. 1. Belennydd or Plennydd, was a founder of Druidism, (No. XI.) It was afterwards called ynys prudain, the island of the regulator of seasons. W. Arch. ubi. sup. See also a fragment of a Druidical prayer. W. Arch. V. 1. P. 73.

Llad yn eurgyrn,
Eurgyrn yn llaw, Llaw yn ysci
Ysci ym modrydav
Fûr iti iolav, Buddyg Veli,
A Manhogan Rhi
Rhygeidwei deithi, Ynys Vel Veli.

'The gift in the golden horn – the golden horn in the hand – the hand on the knife – the knife on the leader of the herd – sincerely I worship thee, Beli, giver of good, and Manhogan, the king, who preserves the honurs of Bel; the Island of Beli.'

The sacred precinct, and the temple, in its ancient form, are to be seen, at this day, upon Salisbury plain. It was called (No. XIV.) Gwaith Emrys, or Emreis, the structure of the revolution, evidently that of the sun, for the name has been so contrived, that the letters which form it, when valued as the Celtic or Greek numerals, mark the day on which that revolution is completed, viz.

ή 8, μ̇ 40, ζ 100, ή 8, ἰ 10, ξ 200 = 366.

The account given of the inhabitants of the city of Apollo, might be deemed sufficient of itself to settle this point. We discover no considerable Druidical monument, where the language of Britain is preserved, without finding also, Tre'r Beirdd, the town of the Bards, or a name of similar import, in its vicinity.

The Bards were Priest and Poet. The Harp was their inseparable attribute, and skill upon this instrument was an indispensible qualification for their office.

The ancient friendship and consanguinity of the Hyperboreans and Greeks, are again, strong circumstances.

The Cymry derive their very origin from the neighbourhood of Greece, and they left, as they tell us, the country in peace. These Islanders, who can, I think, be no longer mistaken, claim Abaris as their countryman. The intercourse and friendship which he came to renew, refer to the first ages of Grecian history – to the days of Argis and Opis, of whom Greece received the Gods, and learnt the rites from the Hyperboreans.

The notice which modern discovery has verified so amply, respecting the appearance of the moon, must be very interesting, in an ancient author, concerning any people whatsoever. It seems to indicate the use of something like telescopes; and whatever may have been intended by it, our triads mention Drych ab Cibddar, or Cilidawr, the speculum of the son of pervading glance, or of the searcher of mystery, as one of the secrets of the Island of Britain. W. Arch. V. 2.

It has been acknowledged, by ancient authors, that our Druids professed astronomy. This elevated science is positively insisted upon, in those triads which I have selected. Learned men are of opinion that even the monuments of Druidism, in Britain, bear indisputable evidence of their proficiency in the science. The Greeks call the Cycle, here mentioned, the metonic, from the name of its publisher, about the eighty-fifth Olympiad; but Hesiod mentions the Annus Magnus, as known, long before his time, in the regions of Pluto. Theog. 799.

The music, and the nightly dance of Apollo, were, perhaps, pageants of Druidical device, to celebrate the completion of this period.

Diodorus, and his authorities, did not regard the power and the institution, of these priests as recent, but as what had continued, without interruption, in the descendants of Boreas. Our British name of Stonehenge, Gwaith Emrys, and the name of the neighburing village, Ambresbury, connect this Boreas, with a character well known in Greek mythology.

* * *

It has become a fashion, amongst the learned of this age, to derive all knowledge and religion, prevalent in the west of Europe, from Hercules.

This opinion, appears to me, no less inconsistent with Grecian Mythology, than with Celtic Tradition.

The errands of Hercules to the west, are not for the purpose of introducing to the natives, but for that of procuring from them, what was deemed valuable.

It was to carry off the herds of Geryon – to rob the orchard of the Hesperides – or steal the guard of Pluto's gate.

These tales, though literally fables, must have meant something: let us try if the two last cannot be explained by the mythologies of Britain.

Hercules had the task of procuring three yellow apples, from the garden of the Hesperides. These apples were metaphorical, and pointed at science, discipline, or mystery.

The hero receives directions from Prometheus, how to obtain the fruit, namely, that he should attend his brother Atlas, the Hyperborean, and get him to fetch it, out of the neighbouring garden of the Hesperides. *Apollodor.* L. ii. C. 4.[129]

It will be recollected, that Prometheus was one of the Iapetidae, and son, or native inhabitant, of Asia Propria who had been expelled from thence to the neighbourhood, of Mount Caucasus, in Asiatic Scythia, as Atlas himself, had been driven from the same native spot, into the west of Europe. It appears from hence, to what family these apples belonged.

We are informed, by our British triads, that the first name given to this island, before it was inhabited, was Clâs Merdin, the garden of Merddin. *W. Arch.* V. 2. P. 1. The name of Merddin has been conferred upon old bards, but is originally, a mythological term. His twin sister is Gwenddydd, or the morning star: He must have been himself some luminary, in a similar character.

Merddin, if Mer-Din, be its root, is dweller of the sea; if Mer-dain gives it birth, it is, the comely one of the sea.

It implies, in either sense, the evening star, or Hesperus, the western luminary.

The apple-trees and yellow apples of Merddin's garden, that were given to him by his Lord, Gwendolleu ab. Ceidio, the master of the fair bow, the son of preservation, are famous in British Mythology. In the *W. Arch.* V. 1. P. 150, there is a mystical poem, given under the character, of Merddin, from which it appears, that, by these trees, and their fruit, the whole system of Druidical divination was implied and covered. The first pennill runs thus.

To no one has been shewn, in one season of twilight
What Merddin received before he became old,
Seven fair apple-trees, and seven score,
Of equal age, equal height, length, and size:
One maid, with crisped locks, guards them –
Olwedd is her name – of the form of light are her teeth.

Ola, Olwen, or Olwedd is Venus. Were not those trees, constellations, and may not the apples have been stars, which after they were committed into the charge of the most pre-eminent in the order, could be discovered by none till Merddin, or Hesperus appeared?

From hence it should seem, as if the golden apples, which Hercules procured from the garden of the Hesperides, pointed at the science of astronomical divination.

The guard of Pluto's-gate, or three headed Cerberus, may signify the mystical doctrines of the Hyperboreans, guarded by their three orders – their Druid, their Bard, and their Ovydd. And what renders this, not a little probable is, that Kelb, or Kelv, in many ancient languages, means a dog, and that, in British, the same word imports a mystery or science.

In the volume above cited, p. 45, an old Bard alludes, perhaps, to this enterprize of Hercules, whom, according to the doctrine of the Metempsyshosis, he supposes to have reappeared, in the person of Alexander.

Rhyveddav na chïawr, etc.

'I wonder it is not perceived, that Heaven had promised the Earth, a mighty chief, Alexander the Great, the Macedonian.

'Hewys, the iron genius, the renowned warrior, descended into the deep. – Into the deep he went, to search for the mystery, (Kelv-yddyd). In quest of science, let his mind be importunate, let him proceed on his way, in the open air, between two griffins, to catch a view. No view he obtained. – To grant such a present would not be meet. He saw the wonders of the superior race, in the fishy seas. – He obtained that portion of the world, which his mind had coveted, and, in the end, mercy from the God.'

If Prometheus, or the Iapetidae of Caucasus, could instruct the Greeks how to obtain the desired fruit from the garden of the Hesperides, it may be suspected, that the mystical doctrines of the western creed were known to Asia. And something of this kind must be intimated by the tale of Abaris, who is allegorically represented, as having carried his arrow round the whole world.

It appears, from *Anton. Liberal.* C. 20. (writing after Bosus, and Simmias Rhodius) that the inhabitants of Babylon, in Mesopotamia, often visited the temple of Apollo, in the land of the Hyperboreans, during mythological ages, and attempted, even to introduce their sacrifices, into their own country.

An ingenious friend of mine suggested, that menw ab Teirgwaedd, or Menw of the three Veds, one of the masters of the mysterious and secret science, amongst the Cymry, (No. XVI.) is the same character and personage with Menu, author of the Vedas, in the mythology of the Hindus.

This conjecture seems to have much verisimilitude, and may be extended, perhaps, to Minos, King of κζητ, (which, in the old Cottian Celtic, is the earth,) who was constituted one of the judges in the court of Pluto.

Menu, and Minos, may be referred, ultimately, to the patriarch Noah, whose decrees formed the basis of jurisprudence in the east and the west.

If so, there was, at least, a connection between Druidism, and the religion of India; and it may not be an improbable conjecture, that it was by those Galatae, or Druids, under whom Pythagoras had studied, that he was recommended to the school of the Brachmans.

This idea of a mutual intercourse, between the Sages of the east and the west, is countenanced by Mr Wilford's incomparable dissertation, upon Egypt and the Nile. Asiat. Rec. V. 3.

That masterly writer informs us, that much intercourse once prevailed, between the territories of India, and certain countries in the west. – That the old Indians were acquainted with our British Islands, which their books describe as the sacred Islands in the west, calling one of them Bretashtan, or the seat and place of religious duty. – That one of these Islands, from the earliest periods, was regarded as the abode of the Pitris, who were fathers of the human race. And that, in these Islands, were two places, in which those Pitris could be seen.

That the old Hindus visited them accordingly, for this purpose, and that even a certain Yogi, who was living when Mr Wilford wrote, A.D. 1791, had set out upon that very design, with his attendant pilgrims, and had proceeded in his journey, as far as to Moscow.

In the same volume, that luminary of science, public spirit and virtue, Sir William Jones, 'on the lunar year of the Hindus,' – tells us, that, 'On the day of the conjunction, obsequies are performed (as offerings) to the manes of the Pitris, or progenitors of the human race, to whom the darker fortnight is peculiarly sacred,' – just as the night, or dark season is consecrated, in Druidical worship.

On these passages I would remark.

That the Pitris of the west, and these honours to them, could not have sprung originally from India.

From the earliest periods, their abode had been in the sacred Islands of the west, in which Islands, we find the Cymry, who emphatically call themselves the first, or the oldest race.

These Islands could not have been consecrated by the Indians. Had the mysteries of the Pitris originated with Hindus, their sacred abode would unquestionably have been fixed in a recess of their own country, to which an habitual access would be competent, and of which their own tribes would be the political masters. Whereas, the Hindus could hold no communication with such oracles in the west, and, in a land of strangers, unless they took upon themselves a toilsome pilgrimage, over half the globe, through many barbarous countries, which intervened, before they could reach the sacred Islands.

This veneration, then, for the Pitris, and the usage of consulting them, were necessarily derived, by the Hindus, from the religion of that race, in whose land those consecrated personages were acknowledged, uniformly, to have resided.

And this, was the country of the same people, to whom the ancient poets of Greece and Rome, conducted their heroes, when they were to consult the manes of the dead.

11

MORAL DOCTRINES
OF THE DRUIDS

Godfrey Higgins

From *The Celtic Druids*

I
The Hierarchy of the Druids

The priesthood of the Celtic nations, called in Gaul and Britain Druids, was divided into three orders of men, Druids, Bards, and Eubages or Vates. The first was the men of highest rank and authority, the Bards the second, and the Eubages, Vates, or Prophets, the third. These bear a strong similitude to the hierarchy of the Jews, but the order of the three ranks does not seem to be the same. The Jews had their Priests, their Levites, and their Prophets. The Levites of the Jews answer to the Bards, but the Prophets do not answer to the Eubages – for they certainly in the Jewish hierarchy took the precedence of the Levites. The Jewish prophets seem to have been a regular order, and to have had colleges or monasteries, or something answering to the modern institutions of that kind. We read of them in considerable numbers at a time, and they were inducted into their office by the ceremony of anointing with oil; from this it is pretty clear that they were a regular order. We read in the sixth chapter of Numbers a variety of laws for the regulation of Nazarites. These men, were, in my opinion the persons afterward called prophets, and they are the persons whom the Roman church considers the originals of their orders of Monks, particularly of the order of the Carmelites. I quite agree with the Roman church at this point; and I think that the prophets of the old Jews are to be found again in the Essenes of Philo and Josephus, who were, in fact, the Carmelites who turned Christians. Having already noticed this subject, I shall say no more respecting them, as I am not treating of the Jews but the Druids; and the field with respect to the former is very wide and extremely curious; but it would require a treatise to itself.

The constitution of the order of Druids was in some respects like that of the monastic orders. One general of the order, as he might be called, in each country, was at the head of them, and with him all authority in the order rested.

Although the Gallic Druids were in the habit of sending their youth to Britain for education, and of requiring from its seminaries information upon difficult points, there is no evidence to justify a belief that the Arch-druid of Britain possessed any authority out of his own country, like that of the Pope, or of the Lama of Tibet. It is said by some authors that the order in Britain was governed by twenty-five flamens, over whom were placed three arch-flamens. This is disputed by Dr Borlase: it does not seem very easy to determine the question, nor is it very important. However, as the Doctor justly observes, there is authority enough to remove all doubt of the existence of an annual assembly for the administration of justice in Gaul; and it is not very probable that Britain, to which, as we have seen the Gauls looked up as a pattern, should have been without a similar institution. Caesar states this assembly to have been held in the middle of Gaul, in the country of the Carnutes, between the rivers Loire and Seine, where they approach nearest to each other. Here there was a place consecrated to that purpose, to which all persons having controversies, which could not be otherwise decided, came to have them determined. When it is considered that these countries were divided into separate, independent principalities, tribes, or clans, this assembly looks very like the assembly of the Amphictyons of Greece: it has very little of the character belonging to a nation of uncivilized barbarians. There are said to be some remains in the country between the Loire and Seine, where it is supposed the meetings of this assembly were held, but they are very trifling, if they be genuine. Dr Borlase infers from this Gallic institution, that there must have been one similar in Britain; but of this, as I have just observed, there is no positive evidence.

Mr Rowland has observed, that the travelling of Samuel every year to Bethel, Gilgal, and Mispeh, to judge Israel, is an exact prototype of the Druids meeting once a year in a central part of Gaul to judge the people, as described by Caesar.

Dr Borlase says, 'When we are therefore inquiring into the antiquity of Druidism, it is into the antiquity of that religious sect, that order of priests and philosophers, and not into the antiquity of their religion, which in the principal parts is certainly as old as the first idolatry.' I cannot think that the priests can be separated from the religion. There is not the least evidence to justify such separation. As is the case with all orders of priesthood, they rose with the religion; with it they flourished, and with it they decayed.

In the works of the Greek historians we constantly read of oracles being settled by Hyperboreans, or of communications of some kind or other from them. Now I apprehend I have proved, that by these Hyperboreans were generally meant the swarms from the Oriental hive residing to the North of Greece, Italy, etc.; or passing along to the West, and finally remaining in Gaul, Britain, or Germany: and amongst these tribes no doubt the worshipers of Iou, and the other gods adopted by the Greeks, had their priests, and these priests were the predecessors or ancestors of the Druids of Caesar's time; so that to pretend, as Dr Borlase does, that because we have no historical record of their having been established any where else, they must have arisen or been

155

established first in Britain, is a theory without any solid foundation, and contrary to all probability. That they became more methodically arranged or organized, is very possible, indeed is very certain; but this is no evidence of the order being first invented or instituted here. All orders and institutions of this kind are the produce of accident and circumstance, of a concatenation of small favourable events, uniting to produce the great effect. Dr Borlase has very truly observed, that the omission of the Greeks, when speaking advantageously of them, to claim them as their imitators, sufficiently proves that they had no pretensions to them. If there had been the semblance of probability for such a claim, Grecian vanity would not have permitted it to escape. Certainly various passages of Caesar, the best witness, prove that the order was here in its highest state of perfection and prosperity. . . . This is no doubt in favour of the argument of Dr Borlase; and if it were originally instituted either in Gaul or Britain, the latter would have the best pretension to it. Caesar also says, that the institution of the Druids were maintained with greater strictness and purity in Britain than in Gaul, and that when the Gauls were at a loss in any point relating to their discipline, their custom was to go over to Britain for information. From all this it is apparent that, in the time of Caesar, the great metropolis of the Druids was Britain. It was probably, in this respect, something like the Rome or Tibet of the West of Europe, and this the remains of its gigantic establishments tend strongly to confirm.

II
The Druids Obtained the Chief Power

From Caesar we learn, that in Britain they had obtained, in a very high degree, what all priests attempt in every state; that is, the controul of the civil power and the possession of all real authority.[130] This is no reflection on individual priests; it is a necessary consequence of a privileged order organized like a priesthood. The same spirit always has accompanied such a state of things, and always will accompany it. Caesar says, 'There were two sorts of nobles in Britain, the one sacred, the other civil, or rather military; for most of their civil disputes were decided by the Druids. The first order of the British nobility was that of the Druids, the second that of the Equites. The presence of the Druids was necessary in all acts of devotion.'

They had not only the regulation of all matters relating to religion, but they engrossed to themselves the adjudication of all disputes and the administration of criminal justice.[131] Farther even than this, they are represented as being the judges of merit and the distributors of rewards. The mode by which they succeeded in obtaining this overgrown power is very evident. Their power of excommunication gave them the whole. If any one fell under their displeasure, he was excommunicated, by which he was excluded from the sacrifices, and being looked on as impious and detestable was shunned by all his countrymen as a man infected by the plague. As divination constituted a great part of the religion of the times, and no observation could be taken but by them, they had, by this means, the complete controul of the government; no important affair could be undertaken except with their consent and approbation. For, of course, when they disapproved a measure, they took care that the auspices should be unfavourable, and then nothing could be done. The result of all this was what might be reasonably expected, they lived in luxury and in as much splendour as the manners of the times admitted.

From Dion Chrysostom we learn, that they were attended in the performance of their judicial functions with great magnificence, sitting on thrones of gold; and that they were accustomed to be most sumptuously entertained in the residences of the sovereigns of the country.

In order to obtain and to retain, for any length of time, this power, their conduct must in general have been good, and there is reason to believe that they were often the pacificators of the civil wars of their countrymen, having been known to step in between the two parties drawn up for battle, and to have effected a reconciliation. It is not improbable, as corrupt as the Roman Papacy became in the dark ages of Christianity, that the popes and bishops, if they often caused dissensions, also often succeeded in allaying them and, like the Druids, probably arrived at the acquisition of their enormous power, in part, by standing in the gap between the tyranny of princes and the sufferings of the people. It is generally by conduct of this kind, that priests have acquired power, which once obtained is usually abused, and thus usually, by its abuse, it is lost. It is a map of human nature; it is nothing new or extraordinary.

I have stated, that the Eubages or prophets were the third order, but this is not universally allowed. Mr Rowland thinks they were the second: if this were the fact, they would then answer to the Jews in a manner which seems to me to be surprisingly near. The Levites were particularly employed as singers. This every one knows was the great occupation of the Bards. The Levites I conceive also exactly answer to the Bards, in being employed to record the transactions of the state.

The prophets of the Druids foretold future events and settled the times of the festivals, which they ascertained from their knowledge of magic and astrology. When the order became extinct, these men dwindled down into mere charlatans, and may be probably found in the present Dervises of the East. The third order was of the first consequence in the state, and sometimes, like the Melchizedek of the Jews, united both priest and king. This was the case with Divitiacus, the Gaulish king of the Aedui, the friend and ally of Caesar. When the two offices of chief Druid and King were not united, they had an Arch-druid like the Archimagus of the Persians and the Jewish Chief-priest. He sometimes succeeded to his situation by the election of his fellows; but in general the order was hereditary, like the priesthood of the Jews. They were exempt from all burthensome civil offices, and from all military duties, except that sometimes, on occasions of great emergency, the Arch-druid commanded the armies of his country. They were looked up to with the most profound veneration, and the persons of the chiefs of the order were held sacred, so that

The Celtic Druids

BY

Godfrey Higgins Esq F.S.A

of Skellow Grange near

Doncaster Yorkshire

LONDON.
R. Hunter 72 S.t Pauls Church Yard 1827

Frontispiece to The Celtic Druids *by Godfrey Higgins*

their power was enormous; and at times when they chose to exercise it, they domineered over both people and kings. The effect of the power of excommunication which they possessed, was attended, as it was observed before, with consequences to the full as extensive as those of the communication of the Roman Church in the utmost plenitude of its power – a power which, in fact, laid all orders of the state prostrate at their feet. The Welsh have subdivided the Druids into several other orders, but I think with Dr Borlase, that this is only what we may call a modern invention.

III
The Druids the Assertors of Their Country's Liberty

The Druids were the most strenuous assertors of their country's liberty (in which their own power was intimately blended and united) against the Romans, constantly exciting their countrymen, after every defeat, to fresh insurrections.

This was the true reason why they were, in a particular manner, sought after by the Romans, and put to the sword wherever they could be taken. So determined were they, that neither by Romans, Saxons, Danes, nor Normans, could they ever be conquered either in Britain or Ireland; but as they could not successfully resist the overwhelming numbers and superior discipline of their enemies in the plain country, they retreated, with the highest spirited and most intractible of their countrymen, into the mountains of Wales, Scotland, and Ireland, where they successfully defied the legions of the Roman and Saxon barbarians. It was not until the insidious arts of the Christian priests had destroyed their influence and unnerved the arms of their gallant followers, that they could be tamed. For more than a thousand years they maintained their country's independence in the mountains of Wales and Scotland, whence they constantly made incursions upon their enemies. Here it was where, with their native, wild, and beautiful music, and in poetry, which would not disgrace a Homer (being the produce of passion, not of art,) their venerable Druids deplored their country's misfortunes, or excited their heroes to the fight. But with respect to Ireland, though the harp of queen Erin be gone, the battle is not yet won. The war can never be said to have ceased there, and time has yet to shew to whom will be the victory.

Whatever might be my feelings, the laws of my country would prevent my expressing a wish for the success of the Irish, in, I fear, the certainly approaching war; but yet, I hope the philosopher in his closet may breathe a sigh for the happiness of the generous, open-hearted, hospitable inhabitants of the Emerald isle, whose miseries it is impossible not to pity, whose amiable qualities it is impossible not to admire.

IV
Celtae and Druids in Germany

Dr Borlase is of opinion, that there were no Druids anywhere but in Gaul and Britain; and he draws this conclusion, because they are nowhere proved to have existed. This is not, in a case like this, a fair conclusion. There were, no doubt, many facts relating to the ancients which have not been handed down to us, which, therefore, may be said not to be proved to exist, and of many of which we should have been ignorant but merely for accidental circumstances. For instance, the Magusan Hercules would never have been known, if a tablet, with an inscription, had not been found in Belgium. The Druids were, in fact, only priests; in general character the same as all other priests throughout the world: Bramins in India, Magi in Persia, Ἱερεες in Greece, Sacerdotes in Italy. Nor, because the letters which constitute the name are different in different languages, will there be any difference in the fact – in the nature of the thing itself. With all, the adoration of the Supreme Being was the primary object, although the circumstances in each were different. This was an effect which must necessarily take place from the vast variety of accidents to which each branch was liable, when it became separated from the parent stock by rivers, mountains, seas, and long periods of time. It has been thought that there were no Druids in Germany. Caesar has clearly said so; and I shall be told that I must not be permitted to take him as an irreproachable witness when it suits me, and cast him off when he does not serve my purpose: and this is quite fair. But let us examine this evidence of Caesar's. I am of opinion that his evidence is as good, in its nature in general, as that of any individual can be; but there never was an individual who was not liable to error and mistake. And it must be recollected, that Caesar was not giving evidence in a court of justice, or in any manner in which great care and precision were necessary. When he tells his countrymen that there were Druids in Britain, and that there were no Druids in Germany, he was evidently relating circumstances the truth or falsity of which at that time could be of very little consequence. No doubt he meant to speak the truth, but he probably would not take much trouble on the subject. If the Druids of Germany retired from the seat of war, or had not their establishments where it happened to take place, he might readily be deceived. Tacitus has been thought to contradict Caesar. The latter says, that the Germans had no Druids; the former, that they had priests: Dr Borlase has taken much unnecessary trouble to reconcile the two by explaining that they had priests, but not Druids. The whole question is of no value; and if it were, it never could be satisfactorily determined. The admission of Dr Borlase is quite sufficient. He says,

'But the truth of it is, although the Germans had no Druids – although that order of priests was not established among them, and consequently their religion wanted many superstitious ceremonies, and much of that erudition in idolatry which the authority, learning, and invention of that priesthood had introduced into Britain and Gaul, yet the religion of the Germans was, in the fundamentals, one and the same with that of the Gauls and Britons. Their principal deity was Mercury; they sacrificed human victims; they had open temples, and no idols of human shape; they consecrated groves worshipped oaks, were fond of the auspicial rites, computed by nights, not by days.'

But although Caesar says they had neither priestsd nor sacrifices, he does not deny them religion; for he expressly says that they worshipped the sun, moon, and fire.

This is quite sufficient; whether the priests and priesthoods were a little better organized in one place than the other will make no difference: they were in fact all the same; and I have no doubt that a very intimate relation, and probably correspondence, existed in those days amongst the priests, of whom the Druids were a part, from India to Thule.

After examining the arguments on both sides, and considering the circumstances of the remains of temples, of language and names of countries, and in short all the evidence as well as I am able, I think the difficulty seems capable of very easy solution. In the greatest part of upper and middle Germany, into which the Celtae had never penetrated, or at least where they had never made settlements, as Caesar says there were no Druids, but in the lower parts, wherever the Celtae had established themselves, the remains of them are to be found – and in these countries in greater or less power, according to circumstances. In some, indeed in most of them, what might be called the Gothic or Teutonic sect of the religion almost entirely superseded them; and as may well be expected, in none would they have the same paramount authority as in Britain, where foreign conquerors and foreign priests had not much interfered with them. It must be recollected that amongst the ancients the religious generally exercised a great degree of toleration of one another; (there was nothing like our sectarian bitterness), an effect arising from their being all at the bottom worshipers of the sun, for the most part as the Shekinah of the Supreme Being. The principal exception is to be found in the Iconoclasts of Persia; but probably at the times of which I am now speaking, these nations had not proceeded beyond the stone pillar and the circle, even if they acquired graven images afterward, as we must suppose some of them did, from the expression of Caesar, 'Deum maxime Mercurium colunt: Hujus sunt plurima simulacra.'

It is not improbable that the Teutonic priests, when conquering a country, might admit the Celtic Druids whom they found, into their system, in an inferior rank to themselves, adopting the use of their ready-built temples. This may account for Druid temples and Druid rites without Druids.

Many persons have maintained that the Germans were Celtae, because they find traces of them in some parts of Germany: but what says Caesar? That, in former times, some of the Celtae overcame the Germans, carried war into their territory, and settled colonies there. In the same way he tells us, 'that formerly a number of the Germans passed the Rhine into Belgium, and, expelling the Gauls on account of the fertility of the country, settled there.' Can any thing be more probable than all this? And this is surely sufficient to account for traces of Celtae in Germany, and Germans in Belgium. Dr Percy has justly observed, 'Caesar, whose judgment and penetration will be disputed by none but a person blinded by hypothesis, and whose long residence in Gaul (upwards of ten years) gave him better means of being informed than almost any of his countrymen, expressly assures us, that the Celtae, or common inhabitants of Gaul, "differed in language, customs, and laws," from the Belgae, on the one hand, who were chiefly a Teutonic people, and from the inhabitants of Aquitain on the other. Caesar also says, that the nations of Gaul differed from those of Germany in their manners, and in many other particulars, which he has enumerated at length.' From the expression respecting the Belgae, it is evident that their country was possessed by the Celtae before they occupied it, or they could not have expelled the Celtae. Now during the time that the Celtae occupied it, they may have readily sent colonies to the British Isles; nay indeed they may have fled from thence to Britain, to avoid these very Germans here spoken of. Strabo says, 'That the people of Aquitain only differed in language a *little* from the other Gauls.' This is what might naturally have been expected if these Aquitanians were of the same race with the Celtae, coming into Gaul after a separation of many centuries through Spain, as it is probable that they were.

V
Same Priests in Persia, Judea, and Britain

Upon this subject I think Dr Borlase has wasted a good deal of labour, in order to make a distinction where there was no substantial difference. It seems to be a mere play upon words. His admissions, before quoted, seem to be quite sufficient: he says, 'But the truth of it is, although the Germans had no Druids – although that order of priests was not established among them, yet the religion of the Germans was, in the fundamentals, one and the same with that of the Gauls and Britons.' Again he says, 'No one that observes this great conformity, in such essential points, can doubt but that the religion of the Germans was at the bottom the same as that of Britain and Gaul, although all the tenets and customs which were introduced by the Druids, and distinguished them from any other priesthood, had not taken footing in ancient Germany. If we find, therefore, the same kind of monuments in Denmark, Sweden, Norway, and in Germany, properly so called, as we find in Britain and Gaul, we may attribute them all to a religion essentially the same, although it cannot be proved that the Druids were established, nor the priesthood equally dignified and learned in all.' In fact it is evident that they were the same patriarchal order of priesthood in Gaul and Germany, with some trifling variations, which had been produced by the change of circumstances in long periods of years, many of which have been pointed out in the course of this work. The Curetes or Hirpins in Italy, shew that this religion was the religion of the Celtae, previous to their arrival in Britain. The difference is merely in the form of a word; in Persia he was Arch-magus; in Judea High-priest; and in Britain Arch-druid. There can be no doubt, I think, that amongst the Greek and Roman writers they were spoken of precisely in the loose way in which our similar order is spoken of, who are called priests, clergy, parsons, etc. Thus we read of Druids, Saronides, Courbs, Corybantes, Curetes, Culdees, Magi – not differing so much probably as our orders of the same genus of men at the present day in Greece, Rome, and England; and in the same manner they would be more enlightened in some countries than in others. I think it is not unlikely that the British and Irish Druids might rank with the first.

Dr Borlase maintains that the religious tenets and ceremonies which we find in Germany were common to all the North of Europe, and consequently to the Druids; but that the converse is not true – the tenets and ceremonies of the Druids were not common to them; that what we find recorded of the Druids can by no means be asserted of the Germans and northern nations: in some trifling particulars perhaps not. He says, 'The Druids built much upon, and improved the Celtic plan, added science and contemplation, separated themselves into a distinct and noble order, held annual councils about sacred things, refined the plain, homely rites of their forefathers, and carried the erudition of their mysteries to a height unknown to nations invariably retentive (as the Germans were) of their first simplicity; content to make war and hunting the principal aim of their lives – affording to religion, arts, and speculation, but a small, if any, portion of their time and thoughts.' All this is mere idle theory, arising from the doctor's wish to make the Druids an order of enlightened saints, and then appropriate them to Cornwall, as the Irish do to Ireland, and the Scotch to their Islands. The simple fact is, the men were warriors and hunters, and the priests men of peace, eating the venison, and generally receiving, when taken, the tithes of the spoils of war – let who would be victor, profiting by the brawl.

Dr Borlase wishes to draw a line of distinction between the Druids and the religion, and thus to pave the way for the opportunity of giving Britain, perhaps Cornwall, the honour of being the first parent of Druidism. The striking marks of similarity so evident in all the rites and ceremonies, the festivals, etc., etc., between the Eastern nations and those of the Druids, sufficiently prove their common and simultaneous origin. How can the Tauric festival of the Naurutz be supposed to have been established, if there had not been from the earliest time an order of priests to preserve it, and bring it and its appurtenances along with the wandering tribes? All that can be said is, that the oldest writers, and perhaps Aristotle is the oldest, speak of them as an order of the most remote antiquity in their time.

Dr Borlase admits that it is a vain attempt to fix the aera of their antiquity; but he says, that 'if they had really been Celtic priests, they would have spread with the several divisions of that mighty nation, and their traces would have been found equally strong and lively in every country where the Celtae settled; but that we have no warrant from history to suppose this priesthood settled any where but in Gaul and Britain.' Because we have no history, it does not therefore follow that they did not exist. But their doctrines and festivals are found in every country. The traces of them are found stronger in the British isles than any where else, because, probably in consequence of the secluded situation, after being once brought there, they were less disturbed by conquests and revolutions of various kinds. Have we not found their festivals in India, their circular temples in Judea, their rites at Delphi and Soracte? In short, have we not found them every where?

VI
Druids Superintend the Education of Youth

In all ages and nations priests have been well aware of the influence of education. We need not, therefore, be surprised to find the Druids seizing possession of this powerful engine. No persons were permitted to have any share in the public employments who had not been educated in their establishments. It is not therefore an extraordinary thing that persons of the higher classes of society should be desirous of sending their children to them to be educated, and of having them admitted into the order. It has been thought that institutions of the nature of monasteries or colleges may be perceived amongst them. 'Academia amplissima existimatur fuisse in sylva Carnotensi, eo loco ubi nunc urbs a Druidibus nuncupata Gallicè Dreux, et in Pagis sylvae vicinis (ut Rovillardus) Druidarum domus dicuntur: et non procul Augustoduno (ubi imagines Druidarum de Montfaucon erutae sunt), altera Academia in Monte Gallicè Montedru.' But Ammianus Marcellinus has a passage much more important on many accounts: 'Druides ingeniis celsiores (ut authoritas Pythagorae decrevit) sodalitiis astricti consortiisque, quaestionibus occultarum rerum altarumque erecti sunt, et, despectantes humana, pronunciarunt Animas immortales.' Dr Borlase truly observes that it is difficult to imagine how they could educate youth on any large scale without some institution of the kind.

The youths whom the Druids educated are said to have been taken to the most secluded situations, to caves, or woods, or rocky carns, and their education not to have been completed in less than twenty years. All this applies evidently to young Druids educated for particular purposes, probably those of the Bardic order, of whom we are told it was required that they should learn to repeat twenty thousand verses before their education was complete. Children of this description were not permitted to have any intercourse with their parents till they were turned fourteen years of age. This was evidently good policy to attach them to the order, and to prevent the influence of natural affection from interfering with its interest. It would not admit a divided empire over the minds of its members. This is the policy of all monastic institutions. A good Monk has but one object in the world – the Order. To this, too often, every principle is sacrificed. The practice of committing their doctrines to memory is very similar to that of the Pythagoreans, and, unfortunately, to that of most of the other ancient philosophers. It is to this pernicious and unprincipled desire of monopolising power, that the loss of their learning is to be attributed. Feeling that knowledge is power, they wished to keep all knowledge to themselves.

Numa is said to have ordered his sacred books and writings to be buried with him. Pythagoras was an Essenian philosopher. It is not surprising that he should have followed the monastic practice. In consequence of this pernicious system, Porphyry tell us that when the disciples of Pythagoras perished, during the Metapontine tumults, the discipline and science of that philosopher expired for the most part with them, for their memories were the only repositories in which they had preserved those treasures of knowledge which their great founder had left them. The same thing happened in Egypt when Cambyses destroyed the temples of the Egyptians.[132] Much of the practical part of the religion of the Druids consisted of songs or hymns, which they sung to their harps. In this again we are reminded of the Israelites. Of these verses some remains are supposed to be yet in existence amongst the bardic songs of the Cornish, the Welsh, and the Scottish harpers. In their discipline they are represented to have been exceedingly strict, and that it was a maxim, that all fathers of families were esteemed as kings in their family, having power of life and death over wives, children, and slaves. This is again very like the patriarchal discipline of the Israelites.

Mr Davies remarks, that 'Amongst other nations, the dispersed and scattered members of the system appear as fragments of high antiquity, in terms, customs, and superstitions; but its fundamental principles of remote antiquity were either forgotten, or locked up amongst the mysteries of the sacred orders. The secrets of the Magi, the Orpheans, the priests of the Cabiri, and of Egypt, perished with each of their institutions. We cannot, therefore, expect from Greece and Rome, and much less from the sacred volume, a complete elucidation of their arcana. But, abating for some instances of local improvements and corruptions, we may at once pronounce the Druids to have been of the same class. The discipline they enforced, the sciences they taught, and the opinions they inculcated, were in general the same. The source from whence they had professed uniformly to have derived them was the same; viz., from the ship of Dylan, the son of the sea, who survived, with his single family, when the world was drowned.' That is to say, if this learned gentleman's whimsical theory about the ship be left out, from the first persons who escaped from the effects of the deluge.

In the doctrines of the Druids a wonderful similarity seems to have existed between them and those of the Magi of Persia, which was so strong in the case of magic, as to induce Pliny to observe, that in his day Britain celebrated the magic rites with so many similar ceremonies, that its natives might be taken for Persians. Their reverence for fire, their hatred for images, and of temples closed at the top, are precisely the same as the doctrines of the Magi, as well as many other of their doctrines.

VII
Immortality of the Soul and Metempsychosis

The Druids were not of the Epicurean school, but were firm believers in a Supreme Being, as I have shewn in a former part of this work, and in general held the doctrines of Pythagoras. They believed in a future state of rewards and punishments – in the immortality of the soul, and in the metempsychosis, or the soul's transmigration after death from one body to another.

Of the vast variety of religious opinions which have prevailed at different times in the world, perhaps there is no one that has been more general than that of the Metempsychosis. There was scarcely a country or a sect, in former times, in which traces of it may not be found. It was received by the Bramins, the Magi of Persia, and by numbers of the Greeks and Latins; by the followers of Pythagoras generally, and by the Pharisees, as is remarkably proved by many of them supposing that Jesus Christ was Elias. After the time of Christ it was believed by some of the early fathers and by several large sects. Persons who have taken a fancy to exalt the Druids to the perfection of human nature have denied that it was held by them; but in doing this, they have shut their eyes to the clearest evidence. Caesar says, 'In primis hoc volunt persuadere non interire animas, sed ab aliis post mortem transire ad alios putant.' – They do not think that after death souls cease to exist, but that they pass into other bodies. Nothing can be clearer than this evidence. It is a fact which must have been well known, and of such a nature, that he could not well be mistaken. There are no grounds whatever for disputing his statement. This doctrine was held by the Chaldeans; and it has been observed by an ingenious writer, that in the colleges of these persons much useful learning must have been taught or Daniel would not have consented to preside over them.

As much as this doctrine is now scouted, it was held not only by almost all the great men of antiquity, but a late very ingenious writer, philosopher, and Christian apologist, avowed his belief in it and published a defence of it, namely, the late Soame Jenyns.

On the subject of the metempsychosis, or transmigration of souls, the Bishop of Dromore very truly observes, that 'the Druids taught and the Celtic nation believed the metempsychosis, or a transmigration of the soul out of one body into another; this is so positively asserted of them by Caesar, who had been long conversant among them and knew them well, that it is not in the power of any of the modern system-makers to argue and explain his words away, as they have attempted to do in every other point relating to the Celtic antiquities;' however, they endeavour to qualify it by asserting, that the Celtic nations believed only that the soul passed out of one human body into another, and never into that of brutes.

VIII
Druids had an Excellent System of Morals

According to Valerius Maximus, it was no unusual thing for the Gauls to lend money to be repaid again in some kind of way in another life. Our priests are firm believers in the doctrine of a future state, but I should be sorry to put their faith to this kind of test; I suspect they would rather have their money in the three-per cent consols. The account given by Ammianus Marcellinus of the Druidical doctrines is extremely flattering to them, and I can see no reason to dispute his authority; he comes strongly in confirmation of what we know from Origen that Celsus had been saying of them. He says, that the Druids were men of exalted genius, ranged in regular societies, who, by the advice of Phythagoras, raised their minds to the most sublime inquiries, and despising human and worldly affairs, strongly pressed upon their disciples the immortality of the soul. Lucan says, that, according to the Druid opinion, the ghosts of the dead descended not to Erebus, or the empire of Pluto, (there to remain in a state of separation from all body, as the Greeks and Romans thought,) but that the same soul actuated another body in another world.[133] Pomponeus Mela declares, that the Druids maintained that the souls were immortal, and that there was another life after this, wherein they existed among other departed ghosts; and that they did, for this reason, burn and inter with the dead what suited their rank and inclinations when they were alive. The authors lately alluded to, who wish to make the Druids all perfection, have endeavoured to overturn the evidence of Caesar; but Dr Borlase has shewn, that the attempt is without any success. For my own part, I am of opinion, that the burying along with the body, trinkets or other property, was done for the same reason that the bodies in Siberia are found covered with plates of gold, and rich persons in England are buried in expensive shrouds, namely, to do them honour – to shew them respect. In general, I think, it may be admitted, that in the time of Caesar they held the doctrines of Pythagoras; but, probably, from the length of time which had passed since that philosopher had lived, some, at least, trifling deviations had taken place; and, perhaps, some difference of opinion might exist amongst them upon speculative and philosophical points. Their moral doctrines seem to have been short and simple – to worship the gods, to do no evil, and to be valiant in battle. This code of moral law is very short, but it is very comprehensive; and it may be a question whether, if every individual in a society acted up to these precepts, the society would not be the happiest of any that ever existed. In these three pithy sentences are included our whole duty to God, our whole duty to man, and our whole duty to our country. Without any very violent extension every thing necessary seems to be included.

The Druids are said to have set aside one day in seven for the purpose of religion: the sunday, or day of the sun, has been supposed to be the day; and Clemens Alexandrinus has been quoted in support of this opinion. I think, from their veneration for the sun, and from their known custom of naming the days of the week after the planets, it is very likely that this might be the case. But the Rev Mr Hughs, in his liberal and gentlemanly reply to my book, entitled, Horae Sabbaticae, has shewn, that all the quotations of Clemens, from Homer and Hesiod, are false – nothing but pious fraud.

IX
Judges and Administrators of the Law

As the Druids were the sole depositaries of the laws of their country, which, being unwritten like our common law, were retained in memory, they were obliged to be very well skilled in every thing relating to them. I have little doubt that an unwritten law has continued in Britain from their day to ours. They had a curious mode of trial by the oaths of a certain number of men, who were brought together to swear that they believed the man charged with an offence to be innocent. But it appears that, before they took their oaths, all the witnesses whom the prisoner could bring were examined by him, and the judge was bound by their decision. I call this trial, not by adjuration, as it has been inadvertently called, but trial by jury; and good trial too. Thus we may trace to them both the practice of trial by jury and an unwritten law.

The law was called Tara in Ireland, and was the Tora of the Hebrews. Dr O'Brien translates the word Coisde, a jury of twelve men to try, according to English law. – It will appear, by the following laws, that in cases of disputed property, the ancient Irish did also try by twelve men, whose sentence must be unanimous. Coisde is an original word implying a trial by law; in many parts of Ireland it is still used in that sense, as *Cuirfidh me thu ar coisde*, I will bring you to trial; Sclavonicè Kuekja, the hall of justice; Persicè Cucheri, a code of laws.'

The Mancksmen ascribe their code of laws, which is allowed to be very good, to the Druids. It was their practice, though not actual combatants, to accompany their countrymen to battle, and to animate and encourage them with the expectation of future happiness, if they fell in the contest. An account is given by Tacitus of the advance of the Romans to storm the last strong hold of the Druids, whom they had proscribed, in the Isle of Anglesey. The Druidesses are represented to have acted like furies, running about amongst the soldiers in black garments with dishevelled hair, and even sword in hand, forcing them, when retreating, back to the fight. They are thus looked upon with detestation by those who, at Eton or Westminster, imbibe the notion, that every thing is good which a Greek or Roman could do, who triumph with Aeneas over the unfortunate Turnus, or glory with the Romans could do, who triumph with Aeneans over the unfortunate Turnus, or glory with the Romans over the fall of Carthage. But if these women had been Roman matrons defending the capitol, we should never have heard the last of their gallantry and patriotism.

X
Misletoe and Other Sacred Plants

The Druids are said to have been much addicted to the study of the qualities of vegetables, plants, and herbs. Vervain was amongst their greatest favourites; they used it in casting lots and foretelling future events; they used it to anoint persons to prevent fevers, etc.; but it was to be gathered with certain ceremonies and at certain seasons of the year. 'They deified the misletoe, and were not to approach either that or the selago, or the samolus, but in the most devout and reverential manner. When the end of the year approached, they marched with great solemnity to gather the misletoe of the oak, in order to present it to Jupiter, inviting all the world to assist at this ceremony, with these words: The new year is at hand, gather the misletoe.'

Pliny says, 'The Druids (as the Gauls call their magicians or wise men) held nothing so sacred as the misletoe, and the tree on which it grows, provided it be an oak. They make choice of oak groves in preference to all others, and perform no rites without oak leaves; so that they seem to have the name of Druids from them, if we derive their name from the Greek. They think whatever grows on these trees is sent from heaven, and is a sign that the Deity has made choice of that tree. But as the misletoe is seldom to be met with, when found, it is fetched with great ceremony, and by all means on the sixth day of the moon, which with them begins the months and years, and the period of thirty years, which they term an age: for at that season the moon has sufficient influence, and is above half full. They call this plant in their own language all heal, and after preparing for the sacrifice and feast under the tree, they bring up two white bulls, whose horns have been then bound for the first time. The priest, habited in white, mounts the tree, and with a golden hook cuts the misletoe, which is received in a white cloth. They then sacrifice the victims, praying the Deity to render this his gift favourable to those to whom they distribute it. They suppose it renders every animal fruitful which drinks a decoction of it, and that it is a remedy against all sorts of poisons. So much does the greatest part of national religion consist of trifles.'

The selago, a kind of hedge hyssop, resembling the savine, and the samolus, or marsh-wort, or the round-leaved water pimpernel, were also supposed to have supernatural powers, to prevent evils and cure diseases, and were gathered at particular times with great ceremonies. They were great anatomists, and are said to have given lectures on the bodies of living men, to an extent that is quite incredible.

We have the authority of very respectable writers of the Romans to the physical knowledge of the Druids; Caesar and Mela say, that they reason much, and instruct their youth in many things relating to the planets and their motions. Caius Sulphicius, tribune of the soldiers in the Macedonian war, a Gaul by nation, foretold an eclipse of the moon to the Roman army, upon which Livy adds, that thenceforth Gallos Romanis militibus sapientia prope divina visos. Astronomy and geography seem to have been the particular department of the Eubages or Vates, that is, they were astrologers and magicians. It was their business, no doubt, to watch the wandering stars, the disposers of the affairs of men. They were the acting, observing, and recording part of the Druids in astrological affairs; they might be prophets, like the companies of them of whom we read in the Old Testament, but the chief Druid, with his rod, was the great prophesier and performer of miracles.

XI
Worship of the Serpent and the Anguinum

An infinity of learning has been displayed by Dr Stukeley, to prove, that the Druids worshiped serpents. And I should suppose, that every thing which any one of the ancients has ever said upon the subject of serpent worship, may be found in his book upon Abury. I think the shape of that temple must satisfy any one, that they did pay it some kind of adoration. The brazen serpent set up by Moses in the wilderness, to which the Jews offered incense all the days of Samuel, David, and Solomon, seems to shew, that the Israelites paid a certain kind of adoration or worship to the serpent, and that without any offence to God. From this serpent it is supposed, that a sect of early Christians called Ophites took their origin. They called themselves Christians, but they must have been of an odd kind. They venerated the serpent of Genesis, by whom they denied that sin was brought into the world; maintaining, that it was a personification of the good principle, who instructed Eve in all the learning of the world which has descended to us. Most of the ancient idolaters had a great veneration for this creature. Dr Borlase allows, that if the Druids had groves consecrated to Mithras, a God whose common symbol was a serpent, and temples in a serpentine form, they must have been worshipers of serpents. Now since Dr Borlase's time, many remains of temples of Mithra have been found in Britain, but whether they were Roman or British it may be difficult to determine so satisfactorily as that there shall not remain some doubt. The serpentine form of the temple at Abury, has been so fully confirmed by the examination and measurement of the celebrated antiquarian, Sir R.C. Hoare, Bart., that I should think there could remain no doubt on the subject. And Dr Borlase considerably strengthens Stukeley's doctrine by the fact which he points out, that a mound on the Karnbré hill is thrown up in a serpentine form. In addition to all which we must not forget the famous Anguinum, of which Dr Borlase has given a particular description in the following words:

'Besides the secret virtues attributed by the Druids to their Misletoe, Selago, and Samolus, which were looked upon, when ritually gathered and preserved, as so many powerful charms to keep off sickness and misfortunes; their opinion concerning the Anguinum was altogether extravagant. The Anguinum or serpent's egg, was a congeries of small snakes rolled together, and incrusted with a shell, formed by the saliva and viscous gum, froth, or sweat, of the mother serpent. The Druids say, that this egg is tossed in the air by the hissings of its dam, and that before its fall again to the earth it should be received in the Sagus, lest it be defiled. "The person who was to carry off the egg must make the best of his way on horseback, for the serpent pursues this ravisher of its young ones, even to the brink of the next river; they also pretend, that this egg is to be taken off from its dam only at one particular time of the moon. The trial whether this egg was good in its kind, and of sufficient efficacy, was made by seeing whether it would swim against the stream, even though it were set in gold." Such absurdities did they propagate, in order to set a price and value upon trifles, and no doubt to make the credulous multitude purchase them from their own order only, as by them only regularly and ritually procured, and of full virtue at no other time, or from the hands of any other person than those of a Druid. "I have seen, says Pliny, that egg; it is about the bigness of a moderate apple, its shell a cartilaginous incrustation, full of little cavities, such as are on the legs of the polypus; it is the Insigne or badge of distinction, which all the Druids wear. For getting the better of their adversaries in any kind of dispute, and introducing them to the friendship of great men, they think nothing equal to the Anguinum; and of my own knowledge, I can say, that Claudius Caesar ordered a Roman knight, of the Vecontian family, to be put to death, for no other reason, but that, when he had a trial at law before a judge, be brought into court, in his bosom, the Anguinum." This Anguinum is, in British, called Glain-neidr, that is, the serpent of glass: and some remains of that superstitious reverence, formerly paid it by the Britons, is still to be discovered in Cornwall. Mr Edward Lhwyd says, that he "had no opportunity of observing any remains of Druidism among the Armorican Britons; but the Cornish retain a variety of charms, and have still towards the Land's End the amulets of maen magal, and glain-neidr, which latter they call a melpreo" (or milpreo, i.e. a thousand worms), "and have a charm for the snake to make it, when they have found one asleep and stuck a hazel wand in the centre of her spira."

'In most parts of Wales, and throughout all Scotland, and in Cornwall, we find it a common opinion of the vulgar, that about Midsummer Eve, (although in the time they do not all agree), it is usual for snakes to meet in companies; and that, by joining heads together, a kind of bubble is formed, which the rest, by continually hissing, blow on till it passes quite through the body, and then it immediately hardens, and resembles a glass ring; which whoever finds (as some old women and children are persuaded) shall prosper in all his undertakings. The rings thus generated, are called Gleineu Nadroeth; English, Snake Stones.[134] They are small glass amulets, commonly about half as wide as our finger rings, but much thicker, of a green colour usually, though sometimes blue, and waved with red and white.'

The opinion of the Cornish is somewhat differently given us by Mr Carew: 'The country people (in Cornwall) have a persuasion, that the snakes here breathing upon a hazel wand, produce a stone ring of blue colour, in which there appears the yellow figure of a snake, and that beasts bit and envenomed, being given some water to drink, wherein this stone has been infused, will perfectly recover of the poison.'

The Druids were also wont to consecrate some particular rocks and stones, and then persuade their devotees, that great virtues were to be attributed to them. Of this kind was the fatal stone, called so as supposed to contain the fate of the Irish royal family. On this the supreme kings of Ireland used to be inaugurated on the hill of Tarah; and the ancient Irish had a persuasion, that in what country soever this stone remained, there one of their blood was to reign.

The rocking-stones, called in Cornwall, logan stones, are also thought by some to be engines of the same fraud, and the Druids might probably have recourse to them and pretend, that nothing but the holy hands of a Druid could move them, when they wanted to confirm their authority and judicial decisions, by any such specious miracle.

From these fooleries of different kinds, practised upon the credulous and ignorant populace, there can be no doubt that the serpent came in for a share of the common adoration, most likely as an emblem of some kind of mysterious doctrine.

It has been said, that they were not idolaters; this certainly cannot be supported. The evidence of Caesar is clear upon that point; but yet I think it may be inferred, that the worship of idols was only beginning to prevail in Gaul, and was not in universal practice. There are no signs of it in England.

12

AN ESSAY ON THE NEO-DRUIDIC HERESY

Algernon Herbert

The barbarous nations (meaning those, who partook not of the arts and policy of Southern Asia, Greece, Italy, and Aegypt) were warlike, pastoral, and venatic; and so irregularly[135] agricultural, as scarcely to give rise to the sanctions of private property. Their polity extended no farther than was indispensable for keeping up the rudest of societies, of which the wealth consisted in not wanting rather than in having, and the security of life in utter contempt of death and almost daily self-defence, the happiness of Diogenes, and the safety of Ishmael. Of all these races, there did not exist one more fierce, capricious, and untameable than the Celtic. Yet we find with much surprise, in two great portions of the ancient Celtica, Gallia or Galatia and Alouion or Alwion, a complicated system of government, exhibiting the morbid ingenuity and corrupt fraud of pagan civilization, and savouring of the stench of Chaldaea, Aegypt, and Etruria, rather than the austere bitterness of the nomadic and purely martial system. Yet the countries in which we find it were not civilized in any considerable degree, and continued to rank with barbarians, some of them tattooing their bodies, and all of them exercising a fierce anarchy, furious in their excitement, supinely indolent in their quiet, boisterous in debauchery, and inflamed by the irrational impulses of music and song. The famous Druidism seems as though it had been organized on a sudden, as a sort of civilization hath among the Cherokees, in Otaheite, and in Sandwich; and by the strange union of knavish urbanity and philosophical trumpery with wild atrociousness, it seems to have made a compound worse than either of the discordant elements by itself, a monster hideous and ridiculous. If the methods, arts, and impostures of paganism of its civil and settled state, not martial or nomadic, had grown up with time and as new wants and propensities were unfolded, either the system would have been less advanced or the people more so. We have observed that the word Gaul (cultivator or settled inhabitant) distinguished the half-reclaimed tribes from those who were still Celts or woodlanders. And we know the change took place at no very remote period; for

172

Pausanias was aware that they had all been Celtic before any of them became Gaulish, and says that the latter term came late into vogue. His important remark was pointed out in *Brit. A. R.* p. lxxix. And, seeing that Druidism was not one element of Celtic civility, but constituted the entirety and sole element thereof, that was in effect saying that the Druidical method came late into vogue.

Society in Gaul and Britain was divided into the nobility, the hierarchy, and a degraded commonalty. The nobles, or equites, had the civil power ostensibly in their hands; and of that order many were called kings in various districts. But monarchy was of a very unsettled kind among them. In Gaul some one nation, either the Bituriges, the Arverni, the Aedui, or the Sequani, as each was for the time preponderant, enjoyed what the Grecians in their imperfect confederacy termed the hegemonia, and their king or ruler[136] was for all common and federal purposes king of all Gaul. In Britain it was the like; there were kings in the various tribes, and one ruler was appointed to conduct the more arduous[137] affairs of the whole nation. Within Caesar's memory, as he[138] says, Divitiacus king of Soissons and Rheims was not only the most powerful of the Gaulish kings, but also enjoyed the monarchy of Britannia. In almost every war[139] between the Romans and the Gauls assistance was sent over to the latter from Britannia. We may hence infer that the Gauls and Britons were not entirely regarded as different nations. In one of the principal tribes of Gaul, the Aedui, it was customary to elect a king for one[140] year only. It is evident, that as the civil power became thus weakened the Druidical must have been more absolute. The latter was so constituted as to realize the tyranny, both mental, and positive, which the Romish church in its ascendant never completely achieved, and which forms the long-cherished dream both of Jesuits and Illuminati.

The Druidical organization and attainments exceeded any thing that the savageness of the Celtae is likely to have struck out by the mere energy of their sylvan meditations, or that Teutonic, Hunnish, or Sarmatic barbarism ever, in fact, did excogitate, from its origin down to its invasion of the falling Western Empire. And as it surpassed them in method and profundity, so it differed from them in the temper of its immorality, by adding more fraud and speciousness to violence.

From these two data; that the system was not one of barbarism, but of a superadded civilization; and that the partial change in question fell within historical memory; we may solve the problem. Celtica was first colonized (so far as we know) by civilized inhabitants, where the Ionian Greeks of Phocaea came from Asia Minor and settled at Marseilles; which took place in the reign of Cyrus the Great. They obtained by their skill in arms and superior knowledge an ascendancy over the Celtiaid or men of the woods. 'A part of the Phocaeans found Massylia,' (saith Ammianus) 'and afterwards, as their numbers increased, divers other towns which I will not enumerate to avoid being tedious. When the people in that neighbourhood had been gradually civilized, the laudable studies of learning flourished, being commenced by the bards, euhages, and druids.' Here is a plain and probable assertion, by an exact and honest writer. 'Sometimes ago (Strabo[141] writes) the city of Marseilles was like a school opened for the education of the barbarians, and by means of it the Gauls became such lovers of every thing Greek, that they even write their accounts and private contracts in Greek.' Justin observes,[142] that 'the Gauls learnt from the Massylian Greeks under Protis the use of more civilized manners, laid aside and mitigated their barbarity, and began to cultivate their lands and wall in their towns. They learnt also to live by law and not by war, to prune the vine, and to plant the olive; and so greatly embellished were the people and their concerns, that Gaul seemed to have travelled into Greece, not Greece into Gaul.' Here the abbreviator of Trogus directly tells us when those manners came into vogue which Pausanias had intimated came late into vogue. The Celts had no letters but Greek ones, and were previously as ignorant of letters themselves as the other clans of barbarians were 800 years later. They acquired the use of the Greek alphabet from the Massylians. Caesar visiting Gaul, in the 6th century after the foundation of Marseilles, found its people lettered; and that, not only upon the neighbouring coast, but among the Helvetian Gauls, whose intercepted documents were written in the Greek alphabet. But the use of the alphabet does not at all imply a knowledge of the language, which latter it positively appears they did not possess. For Caesar, wishing to communicate privately with Quintus Cicero, and knowing that Latin was not wholly unknown among his enemies, wrote his epistles in Greek that no Gaul might be able to[143] understand them; and in Hadrian's time the learned Favorinus boasted of three wonderful peculiarities, that he was a Gaul and yet understood Greek, that he was an enemy to the emperor and yet was alive, and another which need not be mentioned. The druids (Caesar says) forbade their religion and philosophy to be committed to writing, lest their secrets should be disseminated among the vulgar: but in all their ordinary transactions whether private or public they made use of Greek letters. And as he had just before stated that Britannia was the grand seat of the druidical discipline, to which the druids of Gaul resorted for instruction, it must be understood that Greek writing was the only writing known to the learned in either territory.

It is a hard thing for any persons, admitting this truth, that the only letters[144] known to the Gauls and Britons were the Greek, to persist in refusing a Greek origin to their literature and philosophy. And in making that observation we may introduce another. Religion, philosophy, and polity could not be modelled, and an alphabet taught, by persons of that nation, without also adding words to the imperfect vocabulary of barbarism. Therefore, when verbal conformities[145] appear between the Greek and Gallo-British tongues, critics will not be straightaway justified in deducing schemes concerning the primeval Celts or Pelasgi, or, as Vallancey has it, 'their Pelasgian and Magogian ancestors.' For it may chance, that Pelasgus and Magog are no more concerned in it than the kings of Lavinium and Alba Longa are with the Latinity which has overrun our insular Celtic. Ov, raw or crude, exhibits the word ὠμος with the mutation that usually indicates a borrowed word; the Celts received it from the foreign Orpheus who deterred them caedibus et victu foedo; and it does not lie at the mercy of the Pezrons, Gebelins, Vallanceys, or other quodlibetarians.

Some ten or twenty years after the founding of Marseilles, a most extraordinary and ambitious sect of united philosophers appeared in the Greek colonies of Italy, called Pythagoreans, from the name or title of their master, who pretended to be an incarnation of the god Apollo. They not only obtained[146] such power in their own cities as to render it necessary to overturn them by force, but obtained great credit and celebrity among the barbarous nations. Some of those who escaped from the destruction of their college became (say the Philosophumena[147]) the instructors of the Celtic druids. A channel was opened to them through Marseilles for organizing in Gaul and Britain the philosophical tyranny, to which they could not render the Greeks obedient. The testimony of Ammianus is sufficiently express to the point; 'the druids who were of a loftier genius, were bound together in unions of sodality, as the authority of Pythagoras decreed.[148] The Pythagoreans are most likely to have turned their steps towards Marseilles after the violent dissolution of their establishments in Italy, that is to say, after the 3d year of the 67th Olympiad or the 510th before our aera.

The testimony of Ammianus and the Philosophumena is confirmed by the striking similitude of the organic Druidism to Pythagorism; a similitude distinct in its character and degree from that resemblance which all heathen institutes bear to one another, and which enables systematists to derive any one from any other. Its alphabet was Greek and so was the Pythagorean. Its three orders or ranks tally with the three orders of Pythagorics, Pythagoreans, and Pythagorists. The members of the higher order in both systems were united in the strictest free-masonry, and aspired by means of it to engross all power; which attempt, failing among a more enlightened people, as it was successful among uncultivated barbarians, was the ruin of the philosophical confederates in Magna Graecia. The multifarious studies of theosophy, metaphysics, ethics, physics, 'the magnitude and form of the earth and the world, and the motions of heaven and the stars,' medicine, magic, and 'the secret counsels of the Gods,' were pursuits aliene from the occupation and ideas of the barbarian nomades (except some rude endeavours at divination or sortilege) and moreover were most of them uncultivated by the civil and literary commonwealths of Europe, till the Pythagoreans brought them forward, and first introduced the phrase 'the world.' The druidical rule of concealing philosophy, committing it to the custody of the memory, and forbidding[149] it to be written down, was that which Pythagoras enjoined, and which was observed by his disciples until after the destruction of his college. One tenet of the Druids (and only that one, as Mela declares) transpired and was publicly known; and that one was the doctrine of metempsychosis, stolen by Pythagoras from Egypt, and (considered as a European doctrine) exclusively Pythagorean. It not only does belong to Pythagoras, but it did not belong to the bards of the Celtiaid, so far as we can judge. They seem to have had a rude and simple notion, though fashioned so as to give themselves importance and power. By those of Erin or the Gaelic Caledonia we are repeatedly told,[150] that the shadowy and disembodied ghost wandered in the air, either hovering in low mists and vapour, or riding on the winds of heaven. 'Ghosts fly on clouds and ride on winds, said Connall's voice of wisdom.' But without the song of the Bard, the airy ghost remained entangled in fogs. 'He shall hear the song of bards, Cairbar shall rejoice on his winds.' Oak-worship or the belief that those trees were gods or oracles, unknown to all the world beside, was cherished in one famous sanctuary of Greece, and the mystery of the misletoe (the ramus aureus) in Italy. The golden verses of the Pythagoreans were hexameters. That metre was the invention of the god Apollo when he had slain Python, and his own peculiar rhythm when he sung to the Gods or gave oracles to men. It was therefore of necessity the verse of Pythagoras, inasmuch as that aspiring knave passed for Apollo himself. But Ammianus informs us, that 'the bards used to chaunt the brave deeds of illustrious men, composed in heroic verses, and accompanied with the sweet modulations of the lyre.' If it be true that heroicis composita versibus may anywhere signify verses in praise of heroes and not in heroic metre, which I do not believe, still the frame of the above sentence precludes such an interpretation. It assures us, that the Druidical Bardi had acquired the use of the spondaic and dactylic rhythm, which was exclusively named heroic, and was sometimes pentameter or tetrameter, but generally speaking hexameter. When Mr Edw. Williams said, that Taliesin first introduced the hexameter and pentameter verse,[151] unknown to every other modern tongue, he shewed the inadequacy of his researches and, at the same time, the nullity of that uninterrupted Bardic tradition which he imagined that he in conjunction with Mr Evan of Aberdar had received from the ages of antiquity. Owen's dictionary introduces without remark the two following extraordinary glosses; pythagoras, explanation of the universe, cosmogony, and pythagori, to explain the system of the universe. He derives them from pyth, period of time, and agori, to open. No authority, or even apology for one (such as Barddas), is subjoined to these glosses. The instances to prove the existence and meaning of the words are entirely omitted. To satisfy sceptical minds, it would be well if the authorities for these words were produced with accurate references. Dr Owen's literary friends[152] must know whence he had them and will come forward to supply his omission. Meanwhile, I will just observe that Pythagoras of Samos and many other Greeks of the same name bore a purely Greek appellation, signifying Pythius concionator, speaking like Apollo Pythius. It is scarcely doubted among the learned that Zoroaster and Pythagoras borrowed some of their learning from the Jews, which connects itself with the abstinence of the Druids from the hare, the hen, and the goose. That could be no article of discipline among venatic and martial Celtiaid, barbarians of the woods, for such people can not afford to restrain their ill-supplied appetites, by inventing a fanciful class of unclean beasts. That Britannia was for the most part peopled by Gauls who passed over the narrow sea, was the prevalent opinion[153] in the time of Agricola. Yet Caesar[154] says, 'the discipline of the Druids is considered to have been invented in Britannia, and brought over from thence into Gaul, and even now those Gauls who desire to study it with great care go over to Britain for the sake of learning.' But if the course of druidism was generally reputed to have been the exact inverse to the course of population, it seems to follow that it was notoriously an introduced and not an aboriginal system. At first sight, the origin of the system being referred to Britain rather than Gaul may not seem to square with Strabo's and Justin's assurances that all cultivation whatsoever came to the Celts through Marseilles, and those of Ammianus, that the triple organization of druidism did so. But Ammianus says, and reason shews, that it could not be the work of a day. And it probably is true as stated, that in this island the system was first completed and its chief seat established. The security of its insular position would combine with the prevalent superstition of the Hespersia or sacred isle in the west to recommend it for that purpose. This is may have actually been the earliest seat of the Druids as an organized college. But one Celtic word expresses both first in rank and first in time.

Not a single author extols the antiquity of these institutions. But, on the contrary, Strabo says, that Marseilles imparted her learning to the barbarians only 'a little before' the Romans frequented that city: Ammian places 'the gradual culture' of the neighbouring Celts as a process intermediate between the landing of the Phocaeans and the inchoation of the druidical studies. It appears from Caesar's account of what he observed, that the imperfect though complicated social system of the Gauls worked so ill for the people, that the latter were converting themselves into the clans or followings of powerful knights in order to escape the oppression and cruelty of the great, and the change was in actual process when he came and imposed the pacifying yoke of Rome upon them. This argues their system to have been as old, as a vicious system requires, in order first to establish itself, and then to be falling into confusion and decay, and not older. If any one takes upon him to affirm, that either Gaul or Druid had been heard of more than about four centuries B.C., he has no sort of authority, and moreover but little probability, on his side. Ireland has a tradition (how preserved I know not, but modest in itself, and militating against Celtic chimaeras) that the Druids first set foot[155] there 700 years before Patrick or about 270 B.C. It surprises me, that theorists should have assumed and imagined so much concerning the remote and almost Diluvian antiquity of druidism; not only in the face of Strabo, Justin, Pausanias, Pseud-Origenes, Ammianus, and the Irish, some of whom assert, and the others seem to imply, the contrary; but also (as I believe) without so much as the vague epithet ancient being applied to it in prose or verse.

It is further observable that the Celts of Iberia,[156] occuyping Lower Arragon and Old Castile, and having no communication with Gaul or with the sea, were a race of savages without learning or Druids, and of whose religion nothing could be ascertained except that they danced at the full moon. It was scarcely possible for them to possess the learning borrowed from Marseilles; and, on the other hand, their instance proves that the Celts did not inherit the Druidical institutes from a patriarchal antiquity.

The origin, authors, and comparative recency of the system are sufficiently shewn, to make us proof against any vague and fanciful boasting about the patriarchs, the Titans, or the Corybantes. The Grecian philosophers found, however, among the savage Celts one element of intellectual culture, the same which is so simple, natural, and independent of letters, that scarce any tribe possessing the use of language has been found entirely to want it, and by which those nations are most influenced which are least improved. Tacitus[157] says of the Germans, 'they have songs at the rehearsal of which, called barritus,[158] they inflame their courage, and augur the fortune of the approaching fight from the song itself.' The Pythagoreans retained what they found, not only because it was a thing difficult to abolish, but as being one so peculiarly suited to their scheme, that had they not found it they would have formed it. 'They thought that the first appeal was to be made to the senses of men,[159] and therefore they began their teaching with music and the use of song and rhythmus.' In this manner the Bad, part fanatic and priest, part poet, and part buffoon and parasite, became the third degree of dignity and the first of admission in their system. That name and office became of greater importance long afterwards, when the destroyed system made an effort to revive itself, without the formal restoration of the two higher orders.

Silbury Hill, Wiltshire, in the 1880s.
From The Celtic Druids *by Godfrey Higgins*

The principle of toleration among men may be resolved into compatibility, although their passions will sometimes hurry them away from it on lighter grounds. God is intolerant and a jealous God, because all worship but that of him is at variance with his unapproachable supremacy. So men will not tolerate that, which would destroy what they uphold. The necessity or propriety of upholding our system must regulate the justice or injustice of intolerance in each case. But positive compatibility is apt to govern the practice of politicians. Slight variations in the names and idle ceremonies of polytheism did not so much affect the constitutions of the pagan kingdoms and republics, as to make their professors very violent against each other. But Druidism was unlike the religions of the other heathen countries which Rome subjugated. It was not mere paganism. It was not a mere formality which gave subsistence to a certain number of priests, and validity to laws, oaths, marriages, etc. But it was a combination similar enough to Carbonarism, or any other active and ambitious species of free-masonry; and the monopoly of power and entire preponderance in the social system which the members of it enjoyed were such, that they could never be brought sincerely to tolerate any effective civil power, foreign or domestic, and such as an imperious conqueror like the Roman never could permit to exist. Pythagorism was incompatible with the social polity of the Magna-Graecian commonwealths, and consequently its association was violently broken up. It was of equal and stronger necessity, that the Romans should extirpate Druidism, if they would peaceably retain the Gauls and Britain, and convert them into harmonious parts of their general and magnificent system. And the necessity was more urgent, rather than less so, if their acquisition of those countries was tainted with injustice. Augustus Caesar went no farther than to prohibit Roman citizens from obtaining initiation into Druidism. Tiberius made an effort to destroy it. 'The magical art (says Pliny)[160] had possession of the Gauls even to within our memory. For Tiberius Caesar when he was emperor cut off (or took away, sustulit) their Druids, and all that class of prophets and physicians.' Suetonius[161] relates that 'Claudius Caesar entirely abolished the dreadfully atrocious religion of the Druids among the Gauls, which Augustus had merely prohibited to Roman citizens.' However in the rebellion of the Gaulish tribes which occurred during the struggles of Vitellius and Vespasian, when the Capitol was burnt, 'the Druids sang[162] with vain superstition, that the Gauls had anciently taken Rome, but, since the seat of Jove had remained intact, her empire had also remained. Now the Gods had given a sign of their wrath by a fatal conflagration, and portended to the nations north of the Alps the supremacy over human affairs.' This fact shews that Claudius had not succeeded entirely in eradicating the inveterate evil; it demanded, and assuredly produced, a more effectual removal thereof. The same Claudius must have had yet stronger reasons to proscribe and hunt Druidism out of his British conquests, when he visited the island in person and 'crushed[163] the parts of Britannia;' for the island being quite independent,[164] must have furnished an asylum to the fugitive druids, and so have abounded with them more than ever. And he prosecuted Pomponia Graecina, wife of Plautius whom he had employed in the conquest of Britannia, upon her return from that island, as externae superstitionis ream.[165] Paulinus and Agricola by the conquest of Mona, the slaughter of the Druids in that island, and 'cutting down the groves that were sacred to their cruel superstitions,' struck the fatal blow to their craft. The three centuries and upwards that intervened between Vespasian and Honorius consigned to silence the Druidical system in the Roman provinces of Gaul and Britain; the religion of Rome first, and then that of Christ, being established in them, and the Latin language extensively prevalent.

But in the very height of their Roman civilization, when the vicious empire was tottering, a pagan apostasy crept into Gaul and Britain, which ended in establishing in the latter country that Neo-Druidism to which the fables of Ambrosius and Arthur relate. Gaul was exempted from the complete predominancy of that pest, both by the prolongation of the Roman powere therein for about seventy years longer; and also by the permanent Latinization of all its parts, except the continental Britain of Cynan Meriadawg (now called Britanny,) which relapsed into Celticism after the reign of Gratian. Whereas Caledonia, Man, and Ireland were a fomes in which heathenism and barbarism had ever nestled in close contact with the British province. From the Isle of Man, Cynedda Wledig came into Wales in the time of Maximus, and his posterity never quitted Britannia. The success of the Baguadae, had fortune smiled upon their efforts, might have in some measure assimilated the destinies of Gaul and Britain.

A sort of magical association had grown up in the eastern parts of the Roman dominions, founded upon the doctrines and mysteries of the Persian Magi. These wee the Mithriacs, followers of the ineffable orgies of Mithras, concerning which many curious details with illustrative engravings are collected in Montfaucon.[166] The earliest account of these magical initia is the practice of them by the formidable Cilician pirates,[167] who for some years bade defiance to the power of Rome; and the captive pirates brought home by Pompey first tainted the Roman commonwealth with this odious novelty. To what an extent it spread, may be learned from the diligent Benedictine above cited. Very early in the Christian aera this pagan sect began in a measure to play the part of heretics,[168] and under their name of Mithriacs imitated and parodied the rites of Christianity. They worshipped the sun by his Persian title of Mithras, but pretended that it was Christ they worshipped and that Christ was the spirit of the Sun. Thus travestied, the system came to differ in so many of its ceremonies from true Persic magianism, that Julius Firmicus[169] enquired of his countrymen why, since they would serve Mithras, they did not serve him aright; at Persarum legibus sequantur. The Aurelian family, devoted from the earliest ages to the worship of the Sun and named from it, seem to have conjoined their ancient domestic sacra with this influx of Orientalism, in their college of the synodites of Apollo. The δια-παντων of their Apollo would seem to be none other than the trials of torments (80 in number[170]) and transformations practised in the Mithriac initia. Commodus son of M. Aurelius 'polluted the Mithriac rites with homicide.'[171] The obscure fraternity of the Mithriacs grew into more importance when their doctrine (both as opposing, and as affecting to sanction, Christianity) had been seated on the Roman throne by the two Syrian priests of the sun Heliogabalus and his kingsman Alexander. In their days, the Pythagorean system and oriental philosophy were revived, both as a matter of doctrine and as a masonic discipline, by Ammonius Saccas at Alexandria. From him the English free-masons[172] seem disposed immediately to derive their own tenets. Plotinus, one of his successors sworn to secresy, transmitted the system to a long series of pagan adepts; and Origen, another of his disciples,[173] infected many professing Christians with the spirit of it, and made them under a pretence of orthodoxy more than heretics. Ultimately, we shall see some of his followers to all appearance much implicated in the affair of the Neo-Druidic heresy. While Plotinus acknowledges the worship of the Sun, he seems to have avoided publishing (as Plato had) that the sun was the second person in his great triad and his Nous or Demiurgus. Together with the priests of the sun from Emesa reigning in Rome, and Ammonius presiding over the eclectics or syncretists in Egypt, we find, in an important and triple synchromism, a Persian priest erecting the standard of revolt against the Parthians, setting on foot an active scheme of religious impostures and forgeries, and establishing a new sect or modification of the famous Magi. All these movements bear the impress of one motive principle, one mystery of iniquity working far and wide, with perhaps more of personal connection than we can discern; and they all contributed to promote the Mysticism of Solar Worship, with its apparatus of emanative demonolatry and pantheistic atheism, slightly varied, or faintly disguised.

But there was one particular code of magic which affected the name of Mithras and enjoined peculiar usages. The emperor Julian was by far the most memorable of those who were devoted to that scheme of philosophy religion and magic. And that was the apostacy which, I said, crept into Gaul (under no more probable date and circumstances than the government of that country by Julian,) and which established itself openly and ran riot in Britannia. The descendants of the Druids were well adapted to receive it, on two grounds, their Pythagorean tenets, and their masonic organization. Ausonius the preceptor of Gratian and cotemporary of Maximus, himself a faintly professing Christian, was intimate with some of the Mithriacal Druidists in Gaul, and introduces us to them. He says to the rhetorician Attius Pateras,

Thou, born at Bayeux, with Druids for thy ancestors
   If report does not deceive our belief,
Derivest thy sacred race from the temple of Belenus.
   Thence do ye receive your names.
Thou, that of Pateras; for so their ministers are called
   By the Apollinar Mystics.
Your father and brother had their names for Phoebus,
   And your son, from Delphi.

And, in a similar poem,

> Nor will I be silent concerning the old man
> > By name Phoebicius
> Who was a hymner[174] of Belenus,
> > And did not enrich himself thereby.
> But nevertheless, being, as it is agreed,
> > Descended from a family of Druids
> Of the Aremorican nation,
> > Obtained by aid of his son
> A professor's chair at Bordeaux.

The Mithriacs of Rome had no less than eight different titles,[175] under one or other of which they received initiation. One of these (perhaps the highest) was that of Pater, or, as Porphyry, has it, ὁι πατερες. or, as an inscription, Patres Dei Solis Invicti. From them, one course of Mithriac solemnities was called the Patrica. Even at Rome they affectedly retained the use of Greek appellations. The eight titles Corax, Niphus (Montf. Cryphius,) Miles, Leo, Perses, Helios, Bromius, Pater, are all except Miles Greek words. Patēr (not Patĕr) is Πατηρ, and accounts for the prosody of the name Pateras in Ausonius. The use of Greek appellatives such as Phoebicius, Delphidius, etc. points to an eastern not a Gaulish source. And, since the name Pateras was expressive of Attius's rank and office among the Apollinar Mystics, it affords some evidence of their specific (and not merely essential) identity with the Mithriacs. The sect diffused itself over Britannia, and established the worship of the sun under his name of Melen in syntax Velen, i.e. the Yellow, or among the Gaelic tribes, Buidhe, also meaning the Yellow. At Lyons in Gaul the same sect placed an image and inscription Deo Invicto Mithr. Its doctrines, except so far as they may be inferred from similar sects, such as the Orientalizing heretics, the Neo-Platonists of Egypt, and the Neo-Magic Persians, must be collected from the remains, chiefly poetical, of the British islanders who were tainted with that superstition.

13

DRUIDRY IN FOLKLORE

W.A. Winwood Read

From *The Veil of Isis, or the Mysteries of the Druids*

It is strange with what pertinacity the ignorant retain those customs which their fathers observed, and which they hold sacred without understanding either their origin or their purpose.

It is an attribute of human nature to hallow all that belongs to the past. It is impossible to look without admiration upon a venerable building which has lived through centuries, an immortal work of art; it is natural that we should also revere those customs which have descended to us by no written laws, by no kingly proclamations, but simply from lip to ear, from father to son.

Before I enter the homes of our peasants however, come with me to the mountains of Wales where we shall find the true descendants, not only of the ancient Britons but also of the Holy Druids themselves.

I mean the Bards, or harpers, who still continue to strike melodious notes in this land of music and metheglin, and who still convey to their hearers the precepts of their great ancestors.

The Bards were always high in high reverence in Wales, and that is why they have lived so long. When the priests had been swept away by the sword of the new religion, this glorious association of musicians remained, and consented to sing praises to Jesus Christ the Redeemer, instead of to HU the pervading spirit.

Indeed it was said of Barach, who was chief Bard to Conchobhar Nessan, King of Ulster, that he described the passion of Jesus in such moving words that the king, transported with rage, drew his sword and fell to hacking and hewing the trees of the wood in which he was standing, mistaking them for Jews, and even died of the frenzy.

By studying the old Welsh laws of Howel the good king (A.D. 940), one finds some curious matter respecting the position which the Bards held at that time in the Court and country.

Y Bardd Teulu, or Court Bard (an appointment from which that of our poet laureate probably originated) on receiving his commission, was presented by the king with a silver harp, by the queen with a gold ring. He held the eighth place at Court. He possessed his land free. At the three great festivals of the year, Christmas, Easter, and Whitsuntide, he sat at the prince's table. On these occasions, he was entitled to have the disdain's or steward-of-the-household's garment for his fee. In addition to these perquisites, the king found him in woollen robes, and the queen in linen, and he received a present from every maiden when she married, but nothing at the bridal feasts of women who had been married before.

At regal feasts the guests were placed in threes; a tune called Gosteg yr Halen, 'the prelude of the salt,' was sung as the salt-cellar was placed before the king, and as they were served with meats, etc., upon platters of clean grass and rushes, the harp played all the while.

When a song was called for after the feast, the Oadeir-fardd, or the bard who possessed the badge-of-the-chair sang a hymn to the glory of God, and then another in honour of the king. After which, the Teuluwr, or Bard of the Hall sang upon some other subject.

If the queen wished for a song after she had retired to her apartment, the Teuluwr, might sing to her, but in a low voice, lest he disturb the other performers in the hall.

If a Bard desired a favor of the king, he was obliged to play one of his own compositions; if of a nobleman, three; and if of a villain, till he was exhausted.

His person was held so sacred that whoever slightly injured him was fined VI cows and CXX pence, and the murderer of a Bard was find CXXVI cows. The worst murder in those days, like criminal conversations in the present age, only needed pecuniary atonement.

On a plundering expedition, the Bard received a large portion of the spoil. He preceded the warriors to battle, reciting a poem called *Unbenaeth Prydain*, 'the glory of Britain.'

An edict was issued by King Edward I authorizing the massacre of the Bards, one of them having prophesied the liberation of Wales. The murder of the last bard has been beautifully described by Gray in one of his poems.

Queen Elizabeth also issued a proclamation, but of a less sanguinary character against certain wandering minstrels, who appear to have been among the musicians of those days what quacks are among our modern M.D.s. It also commissioned certain gentlemen to inquire into the various capabilities of the Welsh Bards, and to license those who were most fit to represent the musical talent of their country.

This profound question was settled at an Eisteddfod, or a musical meeting of the Bard who contested once a year for a silver harp. This practice which had existed from time immemorial is still continued in Wales, and the transactions of the Aberffraw Royal Eisteddfod were published in the year 1849.

I know little of the peculiar character of Welsh music except that it is executed mostly in B flat. Part-singing may be considered as a peculiarity of the Welsh bards. Extempore performances were common to all the ancient minstrels of the world.

A king of extempore composition is still exercised among the Welsh peasantry, and is called Penillion singing. The harper being seated, plays one of his native airs while the singers stand round him and alternately compose a stanza upon any subject they please.

There are many clerwyr, or wandering minstrels still in Wales. Like their predecessors, they are in the habit of going from house to house, and of officiating, as our gypsy fiddlers do at all rustic festivals and weddings.

They have a curious tradition, that Madoc, a brother of one of the Kings of Wales, sailed from that country in the year 1171 A.D. and was the first European settler in Mexico. Sir Thomas Herbert who wrote a scarce book of travels in 1665, mentions it as a fact, and in Hackett's Collection of Epitaphs (1757) is this one:–

Found at Mexico

Madoc wyf mwydic ei wedd
Iawn genau Owain Gwynedd
Ni fynnwn dir fy awydd oedd
Na da mawr ond y Moroedd.

Madoc I am – mild in countenance
Of the right line of Owen Gwynedd
I wished not for land; my bent was
For no great riches, but for the seas.

We have it on the authority of a Captain Davies, and Lieutenant Roberts of Hawcorden in Flintshire, and from a MS. entry in William Penn's journal, evidence collected by the famous Dr Owen Pughe, that the tribes of the Illinois, Madocautes, the Padoucas and Mud Indians spoke the Welsh language.

Without entering into a useless dissertation upon this subject, I will note a curious custom in which the American Indians resemble the Welsh, viz., in the habit of carrying their canoes upon their backs from rapid to rapid. Giraldus Cambrensis informs us that the Welsh used to carry their triangular boats from river to river, which occasioned a famous dealer, named Bledherc, to say: 'There is amongst us a people who when they go out in search of prey carry their horses on their backs to the place of plunder; in order to catch their prey, they leap upon their horses, and when it is taken, carry their horses home again upon their shoulders.'

They worshipped the same symbols of God as the ancient British – the sun, the moon, fire, water, the serpent, the cross, etc., and in the course of this chapter I shall mention other customs common to both nations.

* * *

Among the peasantry of Great Britain and Ireland, there are observed not only those traditional customs which are meaningless because they are out of date, but actual idolatries.

It may surprise the reader that the worship of fire with which our preachers and tract-writers jeer the inhabitants of Persia, is not yet extinct among us.

Spenser says that the Irish never lighted a fire without uttering a prayer. In some parts of England it is considered unlucky for the fire to go out. They have a peculiar fuel with which they feed it during the night. The Scotch peat-fires are seldom allowed to die out.

There are three days in the year on which the worship of fire is especially observed – May-day, Midsummer Eve and Allhallow E'en.

On the first of May which is called Beltan, or Beltein-Day from the Druidic Beltenus, the Phoenician Baal, the Highland herdsmen assemble on a moor. They cut a table in the sod, of a round figure, by casting a trench in the ground of such circumference as to hold the whole company. They kindle a wood fire and dress a large caudle of eggs, butter, oatmeal and milk, taking care to be supplied with plenty of beer and whiskey as well. The rites begin with spilling some of the caudle on the ground by way of a libation; on that, every one takes a cake of oatmeal, upon which are raised nine square knobs, each dedicated to some particular being, the supposed preserver of their flocks and herbs, or to some particular animal the real destroyer of them. Each person then turns his face to the fire, breaks off a knob and flinging it over his shoulder, says: This I give to thee, preserve thou my horses; this I give to thee, preserve thou my sheep, and so on. After that, they use the same ceremony to the noxious animals. This I give to thee, oh fox! spare thou my lambs! this to thee, oh hooded crow; this to thee, oh eagle!

They then knead another cake of oatmeal which is toasted at the embers against a stone. They divide this cake into so many portions (as similar as possible to each other in size and shape) as there are persons in the company. They daub one of these portions all over with charcoal until it is quite black. They put all the bits into a bonnet and every one, blind-folded, draws. He who holds the bonnet is entitled to the last bit. Whoever draws the black morsel is the devoted person who is to be sacrificed to Baal, and is compelled to leap three times through the fire, after which they dine on the caudle.

When the feast is finished, the remains are concealed by two persons deputed for that purpose, and on the next Sunday they re-assemble and finish it.

This, you see, is a relic of the Druidic human sacrifices as well as of their fire-worship. I will give two more examples of the former.

I have noticed the custom of the Druids in great extremities of constructing a large wicker engine, of filling it with sheep, oxen and sometimes men, and setting light to it, as a mammoth sacrifice. Dr Milner in his History of Winchester, informs us that at Dunkirk and at Douay there has existed an immemorial custom of constructing huge figures of wicker-work and canvas, and moving them about to represent a giant that was killed by their patron saint. And St Foix, in his Essay on Paris, described a custom which is not yet abolished in some of the small towns in France, viz., for the mayors on the Eve of St John to put into a large basket a dozen or two cats, and to throw them into one of the festive bonfires lighted upon that occasion.

To return to May Day. In Munster and Connaught the Irish peasants drive their cattle between two fires, as if for purposes of purification. In some parts of Scotland they light a fire to feast by, and having thrown a portion of their refreshments into the flames as a propitiatory sacrifice, deck branches of mountain-ash with wreaths of flowers and heather, and walk three times round it in a procession.

Precisely the same custom is observed by the natives of America and at the same period, i.e., that of the vernal equinox.

In India there is a festival in honor of Bhavani (a Priapic personification of nature and fecundity), which the Hindoos commemorate by erecting a pole in the fields, and by adorning it with pendants and flowers round which the young people dance precisely the same as in England.

The Jews also keep a solar festival at the vernal equinox, on which occasion the Paschal lamb is sacrificed.

The Floridians and Mexicans erect a tree in the centre of their sacred enclosures around which they dance.

On May Eve the Cornish erect stumps of trees before their doors. On the first of the month the famous May-pole is raised, adorned with flowers and encirlced by the pretty country lasses who little know of what this pole, or φαλλος is an emblem.

On Midsummer Eve an involuntary tribute is paid by the peasants of Great Britain and Ireland to the shades of their ancient priests, and to the Gods whom they worshipped, by lighting bonfires. The word bonfire, I may observe, is by some called bone-fire because they believe (without any particular reason), that their fuel consisted of bones; by others boon-fire, because the wood was obtained by begging. Ultrum horum marvis accipe.

The cooks of Newcastle lighted fires on Midsummer Day in the streets of that town; the custom is general almost all over Ireland, and as late as the year 1786, the custom of lighting fires was continued in the Druidic Temple at Bramham, near Harrowgate in Yorkshire, on the eve of the summer solstice.

The 'Cymric' people arriving in Britain (from The British Cymry *by R.W. Morgan, 1857).*

In the Cornish tongue, Midsummer is called Goluan, which means light and rejoicing. At that season, the natives make a procession through the towns or villages with lighted torches.

The Irish dance round these fires, and sometimes fathers, taking their children in their arms, will run through the flames.

In Hindostan it is the mother who performs this office.

On all sacred days among the Druids, they resorted to their different kinds of divination, and I should tire the reader were I to enumerate half the charms and incantations are made use of in the country on Midsummer Eve.

I have always remarked that those divinations which were probably used by priests to foretell the fate of a kingdom, or to decide upon the life or death of a human being, have now become mere methods of love prophecies with village sweethearts.

One will sow hemp-seed on Midsummer Eve, saying, Hemp-seed I sow, hemp-seed I hoe, and he that is my true love come after me and mow. She will then turn around, and expects to see the young man who will marry her.

Another will pick a kind of root which grows under mug-wort, and which, if pulled exactly at midnight on the Eve of St John the Baptist and placed under her pillow, will give her a dream of her future husband.

Another will place over her head the orphine-plant, commonly called Midsummer-men: the bending of the leaves to the right or to the left will tell her whether her husband was true or false.

Bourne cites from the Trullan Council a species of divination, so singular, that it is impossible to read it without being reminded of the Pythoness on her tripod, or the Druidess on her seat of stone.

'On the 23rd of June, which is the Eve of St John the Baptist, men and women were accustomed to gather together in the evening at the sea-side or in certain houses, and there adorn a girl who was her father's first-begotten child after the manner of a bride. They then feasted and leaped after the manner of Bacchanals, and danced and shouted as they were wont to do on their holy-days; after this, they poured into a narrow-necked vessel some of the sea-water, and also put into it certain things belonging to each of them. Then as if the devil gifted the girl with the faculty of telling future things, they would enquire with a loud voice about the good or evil fortune that should attend them; upon this the girl took out of the vessel the first thing that came to hand and showed it, and gave it to the owner, who, upon receiving it, was so foolish as to imagine himself wiser, as to the good or evil fortune that should attend him.'

The Druidic vervain was held in estimation on this day as we read in Ye Popish Kingdome.

> Then doth ye joyful feast of John ye Baptist take his turne,
> When bonfiers great with lofty flame in every town doe burne,
> And young men round about with maides doe dance in every streete,
> With garlands wrought of mother-wort, or else with verwain sweete.

188

The following extract from the Calendar of the Romish Church, shows us what doings there used to be at Rome on the Eve and Day of St John the Baptist – the Roman Pales – the Druidic Belenus.

June

The Virgil of the Nativity of John the Baptist.
Spices are given at Vespers.
Fires are lighted up.
A girl with a little drum that proclaims the garland.
Boys are dressed in girl's clothes.

Carols to the liberal: imprecations against the avaricious.
Waters are swum in during the night, and are brought in vessels that hang for
    purposes of divination.
Fern in great estimation with the vulgar on account of its seed.
Herbs of different kinds are sought with many ceremonies.
Girl's Thistle is gathered, and a hundred crosses by the same.
The Nativity of John the Baptist.
Dew and new leaves in estimation.
The vulgar solstice.

It was on Hallow-E'en that the Druids used to compel their subjects to extinguish their fires, which, when the annual dues were paid, were relighted from that holy fire which burnt in the clachan of the Druids, and which never died.

Even now all fires are extinguished on Hallow-E'en, and a fire being made by rubbing two sticks together they are relighted from that, and from that alone.

The same custom is observed among the Cherokee Indians.

At the village of Findern in Derbyshire, the boys and girls go every year on the 2nd of November and light a number of small fires among the furze growing there, which they call Tindles. They can give no reason for so doing.

Throughout the United Kingdom there are similar divining customs observed to those which I have just described as exercised on Midsummer Eve.

There are miscellaneous vestiges of fire-worship besides those already noticed.

In Oxfordshire revels, young women will sometimes tuck their skirts (twisting them in an ingenious manner round the ankles, and holding the ends in front of them) into a very good resemblance of men's trousers, and dance round a candle placed upon the floor, concluding by leaping over it three times. The name of this dance, too coarse to be written here, as the dance is to be described, betrays its phallic origin.

Then there is the 'Dance round our coal fire,' an ancient practice of dancing round the fires in the Inns of Court, which was observed in 1733, at an entertainment at the Inner Temple Hall on Lord Chancellor Talbot's taking leave of the house, when 'the Master of the Revels took the Chancellor by the hand, and he Mr Page, who with the Judges, Sergeants and Benchers danced round the Coal Fire, according to the old ceremony three times; and all the time the ancient song with music was sung by a man in a bar gown.'

Last and most singular of all the Tinegin, or need-fire of the Highlanders.

To defeat sorceries, certain persons appointed to do so are sent to raise the need-fire. By any small river or lake, or upon any island a circular booth of turf or stone is erected, on which a rafter of birch-tree is placed and the roof covered over. In the centre is set a perpendicular post, fixed by a wooden pin to the couple, the lower end being placed in an oblong groove on the floor, and another pole placed horizontally between the upright post and the leg of the couple into both of which the ends being tapered are inserted. This horizontal timber is called the auger, being provided with four short spokes by which it can be turned. As many men as can be collected are then set to work. Having divested themselves of all kinds of metals, they turn the pole two at a time by means of the levers, while others keep driving wedges under the upright post so as to press it against the auger, which by friction soon becomes ignited. From this the need-fire is instantly procured, and all other fires being quenched, those that are rekindled both in dwelling houses and offices are accounted sacred, and the diseased and bewitched cattle are successively made to smell them.

This contrivance is elaborate and its description not unnaturally awkward. It is however worthy of remark that in the initiation of Freemasons all metals are taken from them.

* * *

Water was worshipped by the Druids, and was used by them for purification. The Welsh peasantry hold sacred the rain-water which lodges in the crevices of their cromleachs or altars, and the Irish proverb 'To take a dip in the Shannon,' would seem to show that its waters were held in the same superstitious reverence as are those of the Ganges by the natives of Hindostan.

The Druids besprinkled themselves with dew then they went to sacrifice, and it is a belief among the English lasses that those who bathe their faces in the dew on May Day morning will have beautiful complexions.

It is a belief in Oxfordshire that to cure a man bitten by a mad dog, he should be taken to the sea and dipped therein nine times.

The regard still paid, however, to wells and fountains by the peasantry is the most extraordinary feature of water-worship. In the early ages it prevailed with such strength, that the Roman Catholics fearing to combat the custom christianized it by giving the holy wells the names of popular saints, and by enjoining pilgrimages after the Pagan fashion to their shrine.

In some parts of England it is still customary to decorate these wells with boughs of trees, garlands of tulips, and other flowers placed in various fancied devices.

At one time, indeed it was the custom on Holy Thursday, after the service for the day at the church, for the clergyman and singers to pray and sing psalms at these wells.

Pilgrimages are still made by invalids among the poor Irish to wells, whose waters are supposed to possess medicinal properties under the influence of some beneficent saint.

The well of Strathfillan in Scotland is also resorted to at certain periods of the year. The water of the well of Trinity Gask in Perthshire is supposed to cure any one seized with the plague. In many parts of Wales the water used for the baptismal font is fetched from these holy wells.

Not only a reverence, but actual sacrifices are offered to some of these wells and to the saints which preside over them, or to the spirits which are supposed to inhabit them.

In a quillet, called Gwern Degla, near the village of Llandegla in Wales there is a small spring. The water is under the tutelage of St Tecla and is esteemed a sovereign remedy for the falling sickness. The patient washes his limbs in the well, makes an offering into it of fourpence, walks round it three times, and thrice repeats the Lord's prayer. If a man, he sacrifices a cock; if a woman a hen. The fowl is carried in a basket first round the well, after that into the churchyard and round the church. The votary then enters the church, gets under the communion table, lies down with the Bible under his head, is covered with a cloth and rests there till break of day. When he departs, he offers sixpence and leaves the fowl in the church. If the bird dies, the cure is supposed to have been affected and the disease transferred to the devoted victim.

The custom of sticking bits of rag on thorns near these wells is inexplicable, as it is universal. Between the walls of Alten and Newton, near the foot of Rosberrye Toppinge, there is a well dedicated to St Oswald. The neighbors have a belief that a shirt or shift taken off a sick person and thrown into the well will prognosticate his fate. If it floats the person will recover, if it sinks he will die. And to reward the saint for his intelligence, they tear a rag off the shirt and leave it hanging on the briars thereabouts, 'where' says Grose, citing a MS. in the Cotton Library, marked Julius F. VI. 'I have seen such numbers as might have made a fayre rheme in a papermyll.'

That the Highlanders still believe in spirits which inhabit their lakes is easily proved. In Strathspey there is a lake called Loch nan Spiordan, the Lake of Spirits. When its waters are agitated by the wind and its spray mounts whirling in the air, they believe that it is the anger of this spirit whom they name Martach Shine, or the Rider of the Storm.

The Well of St Keyne in the parish of Keyne, in Cornwall, is supposed to possess a curious property which is humourously explained in the following verses:–

The Well of St Keyne

A well there is in the west country,
And a clearer one never was seen –
There is not a wife in the west country
But has heard of the Well of St Keyne.

An oak and an elm tree stand beside,
And behind doth an ash tree grow,
And a willow from the bank above
Droops to the water below.

A traveler came to the Well of St Keyne,
Pleasant it was to his eye;
For from cock-crow he had been traveling,
And there was not a cloud in the sky.

He drank of the water so cool and clear,
For thirsty and hot was he;
And he sat him down upon the bank,
Under the willow tree.

There came a man from a neighboring town,
At the well to fill his pail;
On the well-side he rested it,
And bade the stranger hail.

Now, art thou a bachelor, stranger? quoth he,
For an if thou hast a wife,
The happiest draught thou hast drank this day
That ever thou didst in thy life.

Or has your good woman, if one you have,
In Cornwall ever been?
For an if she have, I'll venture my life,
She has drunk of the Well of St Keyne.

I have left a good woman who never was here,
The stranger he made reply;
But that my draught should be better for that,
I pray thee tell me why.

St Keyne, quoth the countryman, many a time,
Drank of this chrystal well;
And before the angel summoned her,
She laid on the water a spell.

If the husband, (of this gifted well),
Shall drink before his wife,
A happy man thenceforth is he,
For he shall be master for life.

But if the wife should drink of it first,
God help the husband then!
The stranger stooped to the well of St Keyne,
And drank of its waters again.

You drank of the well I warrant betimes?
He to the countryman said,
But the countryman smiled as the stranger spoke,
And sheepishly shook his head.

I hastened as soon as the wedding was done.
And left my wife in the porch,
But i'faith I found her wiser than me,
For she took a bottle to church.

I must not omit to mention a method of divination by water, which is practiced at Madern Well in the parish of Madern, and at the well of St Ennys, in the parish of Sancred, Cornwall. At a certain period of the year, moon or day, come the uneasy, impatient and superstitious, and by dropping pins or pebbles into the water, and by shaking the ground round the spring so as to raise bubbles from the bottom, endeavor to predict the future. This practice is not indigenous to Britain. The Castalian fountain in Greece was supposed to be of a prophetic nature. By dipping a mirror into a well the Patraeans received, as they supposed, omens of ensuing sickness or health from the figures portrayed upon its surface. In Laconia, they cast into a lake, sacred to Juno, three stones, and drew prognostications from the several turns which they made in sinking.

I will translate at length a pretty French story which I have met with, and which will adorn as well as illustrate the present subject.

The Legend of the Pin

In the West of France the pin is endowed with a fabulous power, which is not without a certain interest. One of its supposed attributes is the power of attracting lovers to her who possess it, after it has been used in the toilet of a bride. Consequently it is a curious sight in La Vendée or Les Deux–Sèvres, to see all the peasant girls anxiously placing a pin in the bride's dress: the number being often so considerable that she is forced to have a pin-cushion attached to her waist-band to receive all the prickly charms. At night, on the threshold of the bridal chamber, she is surrounded by her companions, each one easily seizing upon the charmed pin, which is kept as a sacred relic.

In Brittany the pin is regarded as the guardian of chastity, a mute witness which will one day stand forth to applaud or condemn in the following manner:–

Some days before the wedding, the betrothed leads his future bride to the edge of some mysterious current of water, and taking one of her pins drops it into the water. If it swims, the girl's innocence is incontestable – if on the contrary it sinks to the bottom, it is considered the judgment of heaven; it is an accusation which no evidence can overcome. But as the peasant girls in Brittany never use any pins heavier than the long blackthorn, which they find in the hedges, the severity of the tribunal is not very formidable.

On the 7th of December, a young peasant mounted on a strong cob, full of hope and gaiety, was seen urging his way towards Morlaix with a handsome girl of twenty on a pillion behind him, her arm tenderly clasping his waist. It was easy to see in their happy faces that they were two lovers, and from the direction which they took, that they were going on a pilgrimage to try the charm of the pin at the fountain of St Douet. Jean's father was one of the richest land-holders in the neighborhood, but above all the young ladies round him, he had chosen Margaret, whose sole wealth consisted in her beauty and virtue.

Through all the glades of the wood with wild thyme and violets beneath their horses feet, they journeyed on till they came to a wild and deserted plain, whence they plunged once more into the dark forests of Finisterre filled with Druidical memories. It might have been those sombre shades which saddened them for a moment, but it was only for a moment. Jean feared not the trial, for he loved Margaret, and believed her to be an angel. And Margaret feared it not, for she knew that she was innocent.

Now they were close to the sacred fountain, which burst through the crevices of a rock overgrown with moss into a natural bason, and thence like a thread of silver through the forest.

They dismounted, and Margaret, kneeling down, prayed fervently for some moments. Then rising, she gave her left hand to her lover, and full of confidence, advanced towards the well. Alas! she had too much faith in the virtue of the legend. Instead of a thorn pin, she took from a neckerchief one with a silver head which he had given her. He pressed her fingers affectionately as he took it from her hand and dropped it into the well. It disappeared instanteously. Margaret sank to the ground with a heart-broken groan.

He raised her and placed her on his horse, but he did not speak to her, he did not caress her. In mournful silence he walked by her side. Her arm could no longer embrace him. She was not his Margaret now. She was a guilty wretch who had dared to tempt the judgment of God.

He placed her down at her father's door, and stooping he kissed her on the forehead. It was a silent adieu he was bidding her; it was his last kiss – it was the kiss of death.

Next morning her corpse was found underneath his window. There were no marks of violence upon her body; the wound was in her heart; she had died a victim to a destestable superstition.

* * *

To the element of air we do not find our peasants pay any particular homage, unless the well-known practice of sailors of whistling for the wind in a dead calm, and of the Cornish laborers when engaged in winnowing may be regarded as such.

But the worship of the heavenly bodies has not yet died out among us. The astrologers of the middle ages were but copyists of the ancient Chaldeans, and the lower classes to this day draw omens from meteors and falling stars. General Vallancey, by the way, records a curious instance in his *Collectanea de rebus*

Hibernicis, of an Irish peasant who could neither read nor write but who could calculate eclipses.

When we consider how universal and how prominent was the worship of the sun in the world, it is almost surprising that we do not find more vestiges of this idolatry. There are some few however.

It was once a custom of the vulgar to rise early on Easter Day to see the sun dance, for they fancied that the reflection of its beams played or danced upon the waters of any spring or lake they might look into.

In the British Apollo, fol. Lond. 1708, vol. i. No. 40, we read;

Q   Old wives, Phoebus say
    That on Easter day,
    To the music o' the spheres you do caper,
    If the fact, sir, be true,
    Pray let's the cause know,
    When you have any room in your paper.

A.   The old wives get merry,
     With spic'd ale or sherry,
     On Easter, which makes them romance
     And whilst in a rout,
     Their brains whirl about,
     They fancy we caper and dance.

The sun shining on the bride as she goes to church is a good omen. The cloudy rising of the sun is a presage of misfortune. The Highlanders, when they approach a well to drink, walk round it from east to west, sometimes thrice.

The Orkney fishermen, on going to sea, would think themselves in imminent peril, were they by accident to turn their boat in opposition to the sun's course; and I have seen many well-educated people seriously discomfited if the cards from the pack, the balls from the pool-basket, or the decanters at the dining-table had not been sent round as the sun goes.

All the ancient dances were in imitation of the revolutions of the heavenly bodies, and were used in religious worship. Such were the circular dances of the Druids – the slower and statelier movements of the Greek strophe – the dances of the Cabiri or Phoenician priests, the devotional dances of the Turkish dervishes, the Hindoo Raas Jattra or dance-of-the-circle, and the war dances of the American and other savage nations round their camp-fires, lodges, or triumphal poles.

Such also is the Round About, or Cheshire Round, which is referred to by Goldsmith in his Vicar of Wakefield, and which is not yet extinct in England.

But the best instance of sun-worship is found in the fires lighted by the common Irish on Midsummer's Eve, and which they tell you candidly are burnt 'in honor of the sun.'

The fires which the Scotch Highlanders light on May Day are to welcome back the sun after his long pilgrimage in the frosts and darkness of winter.

Crantz in his History of Greenland, informs us that the natives of that country observe a similar festival to testify their joy at the re-appearance of the sun, and the consequent renewal of the hunting season.

In matters of divination, the moon is supposed by the vulgar to possess a peculiar power. She was supposed to exercise an influence not only over the tides of the sea, and over the minds of men, but also over the future, in weather, cookery, and physic.

When the moon is encircled by a halo, or is involved in a mist, when she is called 'greasy,' it portends rain – when she is sharp horned, windy weather. It is also a general belief among all classes that as the weather is at the new moon, so it will continue during the whole month.

In many of the old almanacs and books of husbandry, it is directed to kill hogs when the moon is increasing, and the bacon will prove the better, in boiling; to shear sheep at the moon's increase; to fell hand-timber from the full to the change; to fell frith, coppice, and fuel at the first quarter; to geld cattle when the moon is in Aries, Sagittarius, or Capricorn.

In *The Husbandman's Practice, or Prognostication for ever*, the reader is advised 'To purge with electuaries the moon in Cancer, with pills the moone in Pisces, with potions the moone in Virgo,' and in another place, 'To set, sow seeds, graft, and plant, the moone being in Taurus, Virgo or Capricorn, and all kinds of corne in Cancer, to graft in March, at the moone's increase, she being in Taurus or Capricorn.'

Werenfels in his Dissertation on Superstition, speaking of a superstitious man, writes, 'He will have his hair cut either when the moon is in Leo, that his locks may stare like the lion's shag, or in Aries that they may stare like a ram's horn. Whatever he would have to grow he sets about when she is in the increase; for whatever he would have made less he chooses her wane. When the moon is in Taurus, he can never be persuaded to take physic, lest that animal which chews its cud should make him cast it up again; and if at any time he has a mind to be admitted to the presence of a prince, he will wait till the moon is in conjunction with the sun, for 'tis then the society of an inferior with a superior is salutary and successful.'

The islanders of Skye will not dig peats (which is their only fuel) in the increase of the moon, believing that they are less moist, and will burn more clearly if cut in the wane.

In the parishes of Kirkwall and St Ola, Orkney, none marry or kill cattle in the wane.

In Angus it is believed that if a child be put from the breast during the waning of the moon, it will decay all the time that the moon continues to wane. I will mention two more instances of divination, one from Thomas Hodge's *Incarnate Divells*, viz., 'That when the moone appeareth in the springtime, the one horn spotted and hidden with a blacke and great cloude from the first day of her apparition to the fourth day after, it is some signe of tempests and troubles in the aire the summer after.'

When the new moon appears with the old moon in her arms, or in other words when that part of the moon which is covered by the shadow of the earth is seen through it, it is considered not only an omen of bad weather, but also of misfortune, as we learn from the following stanza in the ballad of *Sir Patrick Spence*:

Late, late yestreen I saw the new moone
Wi' the auld moone in her arme;
And I feir, I feir, my deir master,
That we will come to harm.

One might enumerate examples of this kind to volumes, and I fear I have already passed the limits of human endurance; I must, however, write a few words upon the subject of moon-worship.

The feminine appellation is traditionally derived from the fable of Isis, who was entitled the wife of the sun. The superstition of the man-in-the-moon, is supposed to have originated in the account given in the Book of Numbers, XV. 32 et seq. of a man punished with death for gathering sticks on the Sabbath Day, though why, it is difficult to explain. In Ritson's Ancient Songs we read, 'The man-in-the-moon is represented leaning upon a fork, on which he carries a bush of thorn, because it was for "pycchynde stake" on a Sunday that he is reported to have been thus confined.' And in Midsummer Night's Dream, one of the actors says, 'All I have to say is to tell you that the lantern is the moon, I the man-in-the-moon, this thorn bush my thorn bush, and this dog my dog.' Vide also Tempest, act. ii. sc. 2.

The new moon still continues to be idolatrously worshipped by the vulgar of many countries.

On the night of the new moon, the Jews assemble to pray to God under the names of the Creator of the planets, and the restorer of the moon.

The Madingoe Tribe of African Indians whisper a short prayer with their hands held before their face; they then spit upon their hands and religiously anoint their faces with the same.

At the end of the Mahometan Feast of Rhamadan (which closely resembles the Romish Carnival) the priests await the reappearance of the moon, and salute her with clapping of hands, beating of drums and firing of muskets.

In the 65th Canon of the 6th council of Constantinople, A.D. 680, is the following interdiction: 'Those bone-fires that are kindled by certaine people on new moones before their shops and houses, over which also they are more foolishly and ridiculously to leape by a certaine antient custom, we command them from henceforth to cease. Whoever therefore shall do any such thing, if he be a clergyman let him be deposed – if a layman let him be excommunicated.'

No bonfires are not lit in honour of the new moon, but the common Irish on beholding her for the first time cross themselves, saying:

'May thou leave us as safe as thou hast found us.'

English peasants often salute the new moon, saying: 'There is the new moon, God bless her,' usually seating themselves on a stile as they do so.

They also believe that a new moon seen over the right shoulder is lucky, over the left shoulder unlucky, and straight before good luck to the end of the moon.

That if they look straight at the new moon (or a shooting star) when they first see it, and wish for something, their wish will be fulfilled before the end of the year.

The peasant girls, in some parts of England, when they see the new moon in the new year, take their stocking off from one foot and run to the next stile; when they get there, they look between the great toe and the next, and expect to find a hair which will be the color of their lover's.

In Yorkshire, it is common enough for an inquisitive maid to go out into a field till she finds a stone fast in the earth, to kneel upon this with naked knees and looking up at the new moon to say:

All hail, new moon, all hail to thee,
I prithee, good moon, reveal to me
This night, who shall my true love be,
Who he is, and what he wears,
And what he does all months and years.

She then retires backwards till she comes to a stile, and goes to bed directly without speaking a word.

The Irish believe that eclipses of the moon are effected by witchcraft, and this occasions me to narrate a curious custom of the ancient Peruvians who were the Egyptians of the New World.

When the moon became eclipsed, they imagined that she was ill and would fall down and crush the world. Accordingly as soon as the eclipse commenced, they made a noise with cornets and drums, and tying dogs to trees beat them till they howled in order to awake the fainting moon who is said to love these animals, for Diana and Nehalenna are seldom represented without a dog by their side.

Since we find in a book, called Osborne's Advice to his Son, p. 79, that 'the Irish and Welch during eclipses ran about beating kettles and pans, thinking their clamor and vexations available to the assistance of the higher orbes,' it is probable that they made use of the same canine resources as the natives of Peru, and that such is the origin of the Irish proverb that 'dogs will bark at the moon.'

* * *

Having thus considered the worship of the elements and of the heavenly bodies extant among us, let us pass on to those minor idolatries which are still retained among the lower orders.

There is no religious custom of the Russians so celebrated as that of presenting each other with eggs dyed and stained, saying, 'Christ is risen.' To which the other replies 'He is indeed,' and they exchange kisses.

An egg was the Egyptian emblem of the universe, and it was from the Egyptians that all the Pagan nations, and afterwards the Greek Christians derived this ceremony. They are used also by the Roman Catholics and by the Jews in their Paschal festival.

It is probable that it was also a Druidic ceremony, for it prevails in Cumberland and many other counties of England. On Easter Monday and Tuesday the inhabitants assemble in the meadows, the children provided with hard boiled eggs, colored or ornamented in various ways, some being dyed with logwood or cochineal; others tinged with the juice of herbs and broom-flowers; others stained by being boiled in shreds of parti-colored riband; and others covered with gilding. They roll them along the ground, or toss them in the air till they break when they eat them – a part of the ceremony which they probably understand the best. They are called pace-eggs or paste-eggs, probably corrupted from pasche.

This reminds us of the strange fable of the serpent's eggs. As I mentioned in an earlier chapter many of these eggs or adder-stones are preserved with great reverence in the Highlands. There are also some traditions upon this subject which are worth narrating.

Monsieur Chorier in his *Histoire de Dauphiné* informs us that in the divers parts of that county, especially near the mountain of Rochelle on the borders of Savoy, serpents congregate from the 15th of June to the 15th of August for purposes of generation. The place which they have occupied after they have gone, is covered with a sticky white foam which is indescribably disgusting to behold.

Camden relates that in most parts of Wales and throughout Scotland and Cornwall, it is an opinion of the vulgar that about Midsummer Eve the snakes meet together in companies, and that by joining heads together and hissing, a kind of bubble is formed which the rest by continual hissing blow on till it quite passes through the body, when it immediately hardens and resembles a glass ring which will make its finder prosperous in all his undertakings. The rings thus generated are called *gleinu madroeth*, or snake stones. They are small glass amulets commonly about half as wide as our finger rings, but much thicker, of a green color usually though sometimes blue and waved with red and white.

Careu in his *Survey of Cornwall* says that its inhabitants believe that snakes breathing upon a hazel wand produce a stone ring of a blue color, in which there appears the yellow figure of a snake, and that beasts which have been bit by a mad dog or poisoned, if given some water to drink wherein this stone has been infused, will perfectly recover.

The following custom is evidently a dramatic representation of the rape of the serpent's eggs à la Pliny:

On Easter Monday, in Normandy, the common people congregate *à la motte de Pougard* which they surround. They place at the foot a basket containing a hundred eggs, the number of the stones of the temple of Aubury. A man takes the eggs and places them singly on the top of the tumulus, and then descends in the same manner to return them to the basket. While this is doing, another man runs to a village half a league off, and if he can return before the last egg is restored to the basket, he gains a barrel of cider as a prize, which he empties with the co-operation of his friends, and a Bacchanalian dance round the tumulus ends the proceedings.

Serpent-worship is almost extinct, if not entirely so; and the belief of the lower orders in Ireland that St Patrick expelled all the snakes and other reptiles from the island is perhaps derived from his having extinguished their adorers.

However, it is considered unlucky in England to kill the harmless green snake; and there is a superstition almost universally present, that it will not die till the setting of the sun, of which it was an emblem.

Its tenacity of life is indeed something marvelous. Mr Payne Knight, in his work on Phallic worship, (which I read at the British Museum, but which is somewhat absurdly excluded from the catalogue) states that he has seen the heart of an adder throb for some moments after it had been completely taken from the body, and even renew its beatings ten minutes afterwards when dipped in hot water.

Many of our ladies wear bracelets in the shape of a snake, as did the Egyptian dames of old. The lower orders believe that a serpent's skin will extract thorns, and its fat is sold to London chemists at five shillings a pound for its medicinal properties.

Most curious of all, is the superstition that by eating snakes one may grow young, and of which the three following passages are illustrations.

> A gentlewomen told an ancient bachelor, who looked very young, that she thought he had eaten a snake. No mistress, (he said) it is because I never meddled with any snakes which maketh me look so young.
>
> Holy State, 1642, p. 36

> He hath left off o'late to feed on snakes,
> His beard's turned white again.
>
> Massinger, Old Law. Act V. Sc. 1

> He is your loving brother, sir, and will tell nobody
> But all he meets, that you have eat a snake,
> And are grown young, gamesome, and rampant.
>
> Ibid, Elder Brother, Act IV., Sc. 4

Of stone worship there are still many vestiges. In a little island near Skye is a chapel dedicated to St Columbus; on an altar is a round blue stone which is always moist. Fishermen, detained by contrary winds, bathe this stone in water, expecting thereby to obtain favorable winds; it is likewise applied to the sides of people troubled with stitches, and it is held so holy, that decisive oaths are sworn upon it.

There is a stone in the parish of Madren, Cornwall, through which many persons are wont to creep for pains in the back and limbs, and through which children are drawn for the rickets. In the North, children are drawn through a hole cut in the Groaning Cheese, a huge stone, on the day they are christened.

To go into the cleft of a rock was an ancient method of penitence and purification. It may be remembered that in the tradition of Hiram Abiff, the assassins were found concealed in a hollow rock, in which they were lamenting their crime.

To sleep on stones on particular nights is a cure for lameness with our peasants, though perhaps a hazardous one, especially if the disease originated from rheumatism.

A Druidic monument of great historical interest is to be seen under the coronation chair in Westminster Abbey. Originally called *Liag-fial*, the Fatal Stone, by others *Cloch na cineamhna* or the Stone of Fortune, it was that upon which the Kings of Ireland used to be inaugurated, and which, being enclosed in a wooden chair, was, by the ingenuity of the Druids, made to emit a sound under the rightful candidate, and mute under a man of bad title. It was superstitiously sent to confirm the Irish colony in Scotland, and it continued at Scone as the coronation of the Scotch Kings, from the commencement of the Christian Era till 1300 A.D., when Edward I imported it into England. It is still a superstition in the Highlands that those who lay their hands against the Druids' stones will not prosper.

Many of these monuments are approached with great reverence by the natives of Scotland and the Isles, especially the *Tighte nan Druidhneach* in the Isle of Skye, little arched, round stone buildings capable of holding one, where the contemplative Druid sat when his oak could not shelter him from the weather. The common people never pass these without walking round them three times from east to west.

In Chartres, which teems with Druidic vestiges, a curious specimen of stone worship remains. At the close of service in the cathedral, no one leaves the church without kneeling and saying a short prayer before a small pillar or stone – without polish, base or capital – placed in a niche, and much worn on one side by the kisses of the devout. This stone is rumoured to be of high antiquity, even earlier than the establishment of Christianity – for many centuries to have remained in a crypt of the cathedral where lamps were constantly burning – but the stairs having been much worn on one side by the great resort of pilgrims to the spot, the stone had been removed from its original site, to avoid the expenses of repairs. It was said to be a miraculous stone, and that its miracles were performed at the intercession of the Virgin Mary.

There is a certain reverence paid by the peasantry to those caves in which the Druids held their initiatory rites. Many of them are said to be inhabited by spirits, and there is one in the neighborhood of Dunskey, Scotland, which is held in peculiar veneration. At the change of the moon it is usual to bring even from a great distance infirm persons, and particularly rickety children whom they supposed bewitched, to bathe in a stream which flows from the hill, and then to dry them in the cave.

As among the Druids it is still customary to place a platter of salt and earth upon the breast of the corpse in many parts of Britain. Salt was held in great reverence by the Eastern nations as an emblem of incorruptibility. So among us to spill salt is considered unlucky; it was only the other day that I saw a talented and well educated lady overwhelmed with consternation at this mishap, but with admirable presence of mind she flung a pinch over her left shoulder and so recovered her self-possession.

Hare was forbidden to the ancient Britons by their religion, and to this day the Cornish eat it with reluctance. Boadicea also augured from the running of a hare; and a hare that runs across a path (to any one but a sportsman, or rather a pot-hunter) is an omen of ill-luck.

The onion was an emblem of the deity among the Egyptians, perhaps also among the Druids, for it is a custom in some parts of England for girls to divine by it, as Barnaby Googe in his translation of Naogeorgus' Popish Kingdome informs us.

> In these same days young wanton gyrles that meete for marriage be,
> Doe search to know the names of them that shall their husbands bee;
> Four onyons, five, or eight, they take, and make in every one
> Such names as they do fancie most, and best to think upon,
> Thus nere the chimney them they set, and that same Onyon then
> That firste doth sproute, doth surely bear the name of their good man.

In matters of dress, there are not many traces of the Druids and the ancient Britons to be found.

The caps of rushes, however, which they wore tied at the top and twisted into a band at the bottom, may still be seen upon the heads of children in Wales and some parts of England. In Shetland, the ancient sandals of untanned skins are worn, and also, by fishermen in cold weather, the Druidic wooden shoes. I could not discover their real origin during my visit there: some said they had been imported by the Dutch, others that the Dutch had borrowed the idea from them; but in any case these wooden shoes, the sabots of the lower orders of France, are derived from the Druids.

The best instance of dress however, is the Highland plaid, which was the very garment worn by the Druid Abaris, on his visit to Athens, and which is an extraordinary example of savage conservatism. From the *breachan* of the Gauls and Britons, is derived our word breeches and also that inelegant but necessary article of clothing.

Upon the subject of words I will also remark that our word fortnight or fourteen nights, is derived from the Druidic habit of counting time by nights instead of days; and the word *dizzy* from their *deisul*, or circular dance, (in Hebrew *dizzel*). I could give a multitude more, but *ohe! jam satis est*.

A very curious memorial of Druidism in the very bosom of victorious Christianity was discovered a few years ago by the well-known French Antiquary, M. Hersart de la Villemarqué. It is a fragment of Latin poetry which all the children in the parish of Nizon, Canon de Pont-Aven, are taught to sing at school and in church. The original poetry is almost the same as its Latin adaptation, except that in the latter various biblical allusions have been slipped in.

I will give the first strophe of the original, then its translation in the French of M. Villemarqué[176] which is too good for me to meddle with, and then the Latin hymn as sung by the children:–

Ann Drouiz
Daik mab gwenn Drouiz; ore;
Daik petra fell d'id-dei
Petra ganinn-me d'id-de.

Ar Map
Kan d'in euz a eur raun,
Ken a ouffenn breman.

Le Druide
Tout beau enfant blanc du Druide, tout beau réponds-moi; que veux-tu? te
   chanterai-je?

L'Enfant
Chante-moi la division du nombre un jusqu'à ce que je l'apprenne aujourd'hui.

Le Druide
Pas de division pour le nombre un, la nécessitéuni que; la mort père de la douleur;
   rien avant, rien après. Tout beau, etc.

L'Enfant
Chante-moi la division du nombre deux, etc.

Le Druide
Deux boeufs attelés à une coque; ils tirent, ils vont expirer – Voyez la merveille!
Pas de division, etc.

L'Enfant
Chante-moi la divison du nombre trois, etc.

Le Druide
Il y a trois parties dans le monde; trois commencements et trois fins pour
   l'homme, comme pour le chêne, trois cêlestes royaumes de Merlin; fruits d'or,
   fleurs brillantes, petits enfants qui rient.
Deux boeufs, etc.
Pas de division, etc.

The christianized version in Latin is as follows:

L'Enfant
Dic mihi quid unus,
Dic mihi quid unus.

Le Maitre
Unus est Deus,
Qui regnat in Coelis.

L'Enfant
Dic mihi quid duo.
Dic mihi quid duo.

Le Maitre
Duo testamenta,
Unus est Deus,
Qui regnat in Coelis.

L'Enfant
Dic mihi qui sunt tres
Dic mihi que sunt tres.

Le Maitre
Tres sunt patriarchae,
Duo sunt testamenta;
Unus est deus,
Qui regnat in Coelis.

Both of these dialogues are continued to the number twelve. In the Druidic version containing precepts on theology, cosmogony, chronology, astronomy, geography, magic, medicine and history. The Latin version teaching that there is one God, two testaments, three prophets, four evangelists, five books of Moses, six pitchers at the marriage of Cana, seven sacraments, eight beatitudes, nine choirs of angels, ten commandments, eleven stars which appeared to Joseph, and twelve apostles.

The resemblance of style and precept throughout is very striking, and a discovery which I have made of the same nature renders it still more surprising.

There is a peculiar song of the Oxfordshire peasants, the meaning of which had often perplexed me and which of course those who sung it were the least able to explain.

It is sung in this manner. One of them begins:–

I will sing you my one O!

To which the rest sing in chorus.

What is your name one O!

And he sings.

One is all alone,
And ever doth remain so.

The song continues to the number twelve, each verse repeated after each as in the original versions above. Most of these verses are local corruptions, and it is probable that in some parts of England a purer version is retained. However, since the first refers to the One Deity, the second to 'two white boys clothed in green,' the fourth to 'four gospel preachers,' the seventh to the 'seven stars,' etc., there can be no doubt as to its origin.

There is so superstitious a reverence paid by the lower orders in many parts of Britain to bees, that one is almost inclined to suppose that they also were held sacred by the Druids.

The Cornishmen consider bees too sacred to be bought. In other counties, on the death of their proprietor, a ceremonious announcement of the fact is made to them and a piece of funeral cake presented to them. It is believed that were this omitted they would fly away. In Lithuania a similar practice prevails.

There is no clue to this, except in the circumstance that the bee-hive is one of the emblems of Freemasontry, and like many other Druidic and Masonic symbols, e.g. the seven stars, the cross-keys, etc., a favorite tavern sign. For instance the one at Abingdon, under which is written the following jocose distich:

Within this hive were all alive,
Good liquor makes us funny,
So if your dry, come in and try,
The flavor of our honey.

From the apple-tree the Druids were wont to cut their divining rods. And to this tree at Christmas, in Devon, Cornwall and other counties a curious ceremony is paid. The farmer and his laborers soak cakes in cider, and place them on the trenches of an apple tree, and sprinkling the tree repeat the following incantation:

Here's to thee, old apple tree!
Whence thou mayst bud, and whence thou mayest blow.
Hats full! Caps full?
Bushel, bushel, sacks full!
And my pockets full too! Huzza!

After which they dance round the tree and get drunk on the cider which remains. They believe that if they did not do this the tree would not bear.

I have now to consider the vestiges of mistletoe-worship extant among the descendants of the Druids.

On Christmas Eve it was lately the custom at York to carry misletoe to the high altar of the Cathedral, and to proclaim a public and universal liberty, pardon and freedom to all sorts of inferior and even wicked people at the gates of the city towards the four quarters of heaven.

The misletoe was considered of great medicinal virtue by Sir John Coldbatch for epilepsy and other convulsive disorders. The misletoe of the oak is used by the common people for wind ruptures in children.

Like the *houzza!* of the East, the misletoe would seem to have a religious exclamation, as I judge from finding it so often the refrain to old French songs, especially this one:

O gué la bonne adventure, O gué.

205

And in one celebrated English ballad:

O the misletoe bough! and O the misletoe bough!

It is still a custom in many parts of France for children to run down the street on New Year's Day, and to rap the doors crying '*Auf gui l'an né*, or *Au gui, l'an neuf.*'

In the island of Sein, there is a misletoe feast which it is believed has been perpetuated by the Bas Breton tailors who, strange to say, have been formed from time immemorial into a fine association. They are poets, musicians and wizards who never contract marriages with strangers, and who have a language of their own, called *lueache* which they will not speak in the presence of foreigners.

At this feast there is a procession. An altar covered with green boughs is erected in the centre of a circular space of ground. Thence they start, and thither marching round the island return. Two fiddlers form the vanguard; they are followed by children carrying bill-hooks and oak-branches, and leading an ox and a horse covered with flowers. After them a huge crowd which stops at intervals crying *Gui-na-né voilà le Gui.*

There is one more mistletoe custom which I had almost forgotten. Let us imagine ourselves in the hall of some old-fashioned country mansion. Let it be Christmas-night, and at that hour when merriment and wine has flushed every face, and glowed into every heart.

And now I will paint to you a young maiden who embraced in the arms of her lover is whirled round the hall, her eyes sparkling, her white bosom heaving and her little feet scarce seeming to touch the floor. They pause for a moment. An old lady with an arch twinkle in her eye whispers something to her partner, he nods and smiles; she blushes and turns her eyes, pretending not to hear.

They join the dance again, when suddenly he stays her in the centre of the hall. Above their heads droops down a beautiful plant with pale white berries and leaves of a delicate green. He stoops and gives her the kiss-under-the-mistletoe. All laugh and follow his example till the scene vies the revels of the ancient Bacchanals.

It is this picture which awakes me from a reverie into which I have long been buried. Reader! you have sought with me for the first germs of religion in the chaos of youthful Time; you have dived with me into those mysteries which the Veil of Isis held secret from our sight; you have sojourned with me among the tombs of the past, and trod upon the dust of a fallen World.

Let us now return from these caverns of learning to the glorious day-light of the Present, and to the enjoyments of a real existence.

14

DRUIDISM

Iolo Morgannwg and J. Williams ab Ithel

From *Barddas: The Bardo-Druidic System*

Disciple and Teacher

This is the Druidism of the Bards of the Isle of Britain, with their opinion respecting God and all living beings, of whatsoever grade or kind they may be. It is rudimentally taught as follows:–

1 Question. What is God?
Answer. What cannot be otherwise.
Q. Why cannot it be otherwise?
A. Could it be otherwise, we should have no knowledge of any animation, being, existence, or futurity, in respect of any thing now known to us.
Q. What is God?
A. Complete and perfect life, and the total annihilation of every thing inanimate and death, nor can any species of mortality concur with Him. And God is life, full, entire, imperishable, and without end.

2 God is perfect life, which cannot be limited or confined, and, in virtue of His proper essence, is possessed of perfect knowledge, in respect of sight, sufferance, and intention, having His origin in Himself, without communion with any thing else whatsoever, and wholly free from all participation in evil.

3 God is absolute good, in that He totally annihilates all evil, and there cannot be in Him the least particle of the nature of evil.

4 God is absolute power, in that He totally annihilates inability, nor can power and will in Him be restrained, since He is almighty, and allgood.

5 God is absolute wisdom and knowledge, in that He totally annihilates ignorance, and folly; and therefore no event can by any chance happen, which He knows not of. And in view of these qualities and properties no being or animation can be conceived or contemplated other than coming from God, except natural evil, which annihilates all life and goodness.

6   What would utterly annihilate and reject God and life, and therein all goodness, is absolute and natural evil; which is thus in complete opposition, and of a contrary nature, and essence, to God, life, and goodness.

7   And by means of this direction, may be seen two things existing of necessity, namely: the living and dead; good and evil; God and Cythraul, and darkness in darkness, and powerless inability.

8   Cythraul is destitute of life and intention – a thing of necessity, not of will, without being or life, in respect of existence and personality; but vacant in reference to what is vacant, dead in reference to what is dead, and nothing in reference to what is nothing. Whereas God is good with reference to what is good, is fulness in reference to fulness, life in life, all in all, and light in light.

9   And from what has been said, it may be seen that there can be no existence of original nature but God and Cythraul, the dead and living, nothing and occurrence, issue from what is issueless, and existence from mutual union.

10   God mercifully, out of live and pity, uniting Himself with the lifeless, that is, the evil, with the intention of subduing it unto life, imparted the existence of vitality to animated and living beings, and thus did life lay hold of the dead, whence intellectual animations and vitality first sprang. And intellectual existences and animations began in the depth of Annwn, for there is the lowest and least grade, and it cannot but be that there and in that state intellectual life first began, for it cannot be otherwise than that the least and lowest grade of every thing should be the original and primordial one. The greatest cannot exist in an intellectual existence before the least; there can be no intellectual existence without gradation, and in respect of gradation there cannot but be a beginning, a middle, and an end or extremity, – first, augmentation, and ultimate or conclusion. Thus may be seen that there is to every intellectual existence a necessary gradation, which necessarily begins at the lowest grade, progressing from thence incessantly along every addition, intervention, increase, growth in age, and completion, unto conclusion and extremity, where it rests for ever from pure necessity, for there can not be any thing further or higher or better in respect of gradation and Abred.

11   All intellectual existences partake of good and evil, and that, more or less, according to their degree in Abred, from the dead in the depth of Annwn, to the living in the extremity of goodness and power, even so far as would not be at all possible for God to conduct them further.

12   Animations in Annwn are partakers of life and goodness in the lowest possible degree, and of death and evil in the highest degree that is possibly compatible with life and personal identity. Therefore, they are necessarily evil, because of the preponderance of evil over the good; and scarcely do they live and exist; and their duration and life are necessarily short, whilst by means of dissolution and death they are removed gradually to a higher degree, where they receive an accumulation of life and goodness, and thus they progress from

grade to grade, nearer and nearer to the extremity of life and goodness, God, of His merciful affection for animated beings, preparing the ways along Abred, out of pure love to them, until they arrive at the state and point of human existence, where goodness and evil equiponderate, neither weighing down the other. From this spring liberty and choice and elective power in man, so that he can perform which ever he likes of any two things, as of good and evil; and thus is it seen that the state of humanity is a state of probation and instruction, where the good and evil equiponderate, and animated beings are left to their own will and pleasure.

13   In every state and point of Abred that is below humanity, all living beings are necessarily evil, and necessarily bound to evil, from utter want of will and power, notwithstanding all the exertion and power put forth, which vary according as they are situate in Abred, whether the point be high or low. On this account God does not hate or punish them, but loves and cherishes them, because they cannot be otherwise, and because they are under obligation, and have no will and choice, and whatever the amount of evil may be, they cannot help it, because it is from obligation, and not willingly, that they are in this condition.

14   After having arrived at the point of humanity in Abred, where evil and good equiponderate, man is free from all obligation, because goodness and wickedness do not press one upon the other, nor does either of them preponderate over the other. Therefore, the state of man is a state of will and freedom and ability, where every act is one of project and selection, consent and choice, and not of obligation and dislike, necessity and inability. On this account man is a living being capable of judgment, and judgment will be given upon him and his acts, for he will be good or bad according to his works, since whatever he does he could do differently; therefore it is right that he should receive punishment or reward, as his works require.

The Gorsedd Prayer

The Gorsedd Prayer, called the Prayer of the Gwyddoniaid, from the Great Book of Margam.

> God, impart Thy strength;
> And in strength, power to suffer;
> And to suffer for the truth;
> And in the truth, all light;
> And in light, all gwynvyd;
> And in gwynvyd, love;
> And in love, God;
> And in God, all goodness.
> And thus it ends.

The Gorsedd Prayer, from the Book of Trahaiarn the Great Poet.

> Grant, God, Thy protection;
> And in protection, reason;
> And in reason, light;
> And in light, truth;
> And in truth, justice;
> And in justice, love;
> And in love, the love of God;
> And in the love of God, all gwynvyd.
> God and all goodness.

The Gorsedd Prayer, from another Book.

> Grant, O God, Thy protection;
> And in protection, strength;
> And in strength, understanding;
> And in understanding, knowledge;
> And in knowledge, the knowledge of justice;
> And in the knowledge of justice, the love of it;
> And in that love, the love of all existences;
> And in the love of all existences, the love of God.
> God and all goodness.

Talhaiarn's Prayer, called by some, the Gorsedd Prayer, composed by Talhaiarn, the father of Tanwyn.

> God, impart strrength;
> And in that strength, reason;
> And in reason, knowledge;
> And in knowledge, justice;
> And in justice the love of it;
> And in that love, the love of every thing;
> And in the love of every thing, the love of God.

15

BARDISM

Aneurin Vardd

From *The International Review*

Bardism, and the Druids of Ancient Britain, to whom we trace its origin, are subjects concerning which many erroneous impressions prevail, and of which readers in general have very little knowledge. Few are aware, for example, of the fact that, among the descendants of the ancient Britons, there exists to-day an order whose origin is involved in the mysteries surrounding a race, which was coeval with the Jewish nation, and whose history is lost in remotest antiquity. To dispel the prevailing prejudices concerning the Druids of Britain, and to cast new light upon Bardism, will be the chief province of this review.

Bardism of the Druidic Period

By Bardism is meant the primitive system of instruction, knowledge and morals, among the Britons. The only part of this system which has been continued in public use is its literature, the chief representative of which, at the present time, is the Bard, in the character of poet. It is true that the poet held an important place in the ancient system, and there is no doubt that the greater part of the instruction conveyed from age to age by tradition, was in the metrical form, as the one best calculated to impress it upon the memory. Nevertheless, the office of the poet was but a part of the Bardic system, carrying with it special and peculiar duties in the Circle of Judicature. The officers of the Circle were the Druid, the Bard, and the Ovite. The Druid was the priest and the divine, the superintendent of religion and morals; or, according to ancient authority: 'The Druid is a bard, according to the reason, nature, and necessity of things; and his office is to instruct.' The 'Bard' was the instructor, whose duty it was to administer lessons of wisdom, and his 'Avenite' was the one who received instruction in introductory studies, art and the natural sciences.

We find that among the Britons, not only were instruction and religion under the superintendence of the Druids in conjunction with the Rites of Bardism, but that the political concerns of the nation were also in their hands; for, besides being the ministers of religion, they were juridical magistrates, and the chief advisers of the State. With a sphere of influence so extensive as to include its political and religious government, it is clear that the welfare of the nation was also almost entirely in their hands. If, therefore, we compare the national status of the Britons under the control of the Druids, with the condition of contemporary nations, we shall obtain more intimate knowledge of the influence of their rites in the pre-christian period. The advance made by the Britons in the path of civilization by means of Bardism, together with the position taken by the Britons through its instrumentality in the Christian era, will best indicate the character and extent of its influence.

In following this comparative method, we shall not be drawn aside to consider the creed of the early Britons as on a par with that of the Patriarchs, who were influenced by divine guidance; nor shall we be misled by those who would lower their character, through want of knowledge concerning them, and whose ignorance has produced the well-known prejudice occasioned by the charge that they were low and savage idolaters, without a virtue to qualify their condition.

It is an important fact in British history, that, while the Welsh have been deprived of their independence, they are still a distinct nation, whose history is interwoven with the threads of the world's civilization, from the spot where rested the Ark on Oriental Ararat to the Western parts of the American Continent. They speak the same language on the coast of the Pacific, where the sun daily smiles his parting gleam, before going to his watery bed, – as if in approval of the ancient saying, 'In the face of the sun and the eye of light,' – as that which their forefathers spoke on the shores of the Euxine, where they imparted a meaning to the mountains of the Crimea, which made them eternal pyramids, toward which the nation may again turn to make researches into 'The learning of the good old Kymmry.'

These thoughts lead us back to an early period of the world's history, to the Kymmric primitive estate, in reaching which, we pass by, and leave behind us, the cemeteries of whole nations – born after the Kymmric nation was fully-grown – whose languages, like themselves, are dead, while, behold, the Kymmric race, an eye-witness erst of their pomp and greatness, still lives to tell their story.

We cannot regard this national endurance without perceiving in it the hand of divine Providence; and we know of no reason to which we can better attribute it, than to the fact that the Sustainer of the Universe regarded the customs of our ancestors in pre-christian ages, as calculated to prepare them for the reception of Christianity in the way in which they received it. Their unexampled adherence to the purity of their established principles, and their zeal for them, favors this supposition, as does also the fact that nothing is to be regarded as truly Kymmric which will not bear inspection in the light of Christianity. The consideration of these facts leads us directly to Christianity as the test-tone of Bardism. And we find, upon inquiry, that Bardism has been the chief medium to which the British Kelts owe their privileged position among the nations of the world, and that it was a leader by the light of nature to the brighter and purer splendor of the Sun of Righteousness.

As already mentioned, the only fair method of estimating the worth of the British character under Druidic rule, is by a comparison of the condition of the Britons with that of contemporary races. In making such comparison, we ought not to divest the Britons themselves of the imperfections incident to humanity; nor would it be fair to attribute the corruption of the masses to the Druids, as the result of their principles, any more than it would be fair to charge the immorality and savagery of the lower orders at the present time, to the defects of Christianity. Before the Christian era, every nation, but the Jewish, was considered as pagan. This nation had the true religion, with the ten commandments of the Law, together with all their ceremonies, divinely given, and was attended by God's particular care, support and guidance. Nevertheless we find the Jews deviating from God's commandments, and corrupting themselves, with superstition and idolatry, to such an extent as to bring upon them the divine displeasure in severe judgments. They, had a revealed Law as their instructor. The instructor of the Druids, was Nature; she was their Bible, and its pages were her statutes, read 'In the Face of the Sun and the Eye of Light,' while the seasons were its contents, and the stars its index.

Our task now will be to trace the parallel between the Jewish nation, – God's own people, – and the Druids, in respect to learning, morals, and ceremonies, as contrasted with other pagan nations who had a like origin and possessed the same natural advantages.

Such merits as the Britons possessed under Druidic instruction we must attribute to their means of government – the Bardic Rites. This we demand, for it would be the extreme of inconsistency to glory in a national antiquity, while despising the medium through which its characteristics have been preserved from age to age. This would be like despising the metal ark which has inclosed historical treasures intact from the destructive conflagration; or the ship which has borne national heritages over stormy billows against the rude cross-winds of the ages. For it is evident that these national characteristics have been preserved in the bond of Bardism, as the life-boat which the storms of forty centuries have failed to destroy.

Bardism directs us toward her Neptune, landing on the Armenian Mount after being a year and a day in his ship of gopher wood, greeting him in the words of the Christian Bard, Davydd Jonawr, with a Happy New Year and also a New world. Here we have a special promise of God's enlargement of Japheth, eldest son of Noah, father of the new world; and in connection with the descendants of his sons Gomer and Javan, it is said, 'By these were the Isles of the Gentiles divided in their lands; every one after his tongue, after their families in their nations.'[177]

In order to trace accurately the descent of the Kymmry through the line of Gomer, it would be difficult to find any thing more comprehensive and significant than that which we find in the tenth chapter of Genesis on the generations of Noah. No other tribe has realized this spreading abroad, to such an extent as have the sons of Gomer. The Keltic race had, at the time of authentic history's dawn, so thoroughly spread over and occupied Europe, that the Greek geographers called that quarter of the world 'Keltica.'

Pharaoh was a name or title belonging to all the kings of Egypt, and was derived from 'Phra,' the Sun. After death, the Pharaohs were worshiped, together with the sun, and moon, and wild animals, as is shown by the hieroglyphics. To Moses, a man learned in all the wisdom of the Egyptians, was intrusted the work of leading forth the children of Shem from under the tyranny of their oppressors. In reading the history of this race, we discover a remarkable similarity between their customs and rites and those of the Druids.

The practice of using stones at various ceremonies has continued since the age of the Patriarchs. We find that Jacob arose early, taking the stone which he had placed as a pillow under his head, and placed it for a pillar, pouring oil upon it. It is said of Joshua, when he made a covenant with the people at Sechem: 'And Joshua wrote these words in the Book of the Law of God, and took a great stone, and set it up there under an oak that was by the sanctuary of the Lord. And Joshua said unto all the people, Behold this stone shall be a witness unto us; for it hath heard all the words of the Lord which he spake unto us; it shall be therefore a witness unto you, lest ye deny your God.'[178] On the same stone, on another occasion, Abimelech was made king. Stones were erected to mark places of victory, as at Mizpeh, where the stone was entitled 'the stone Ebenezer.'[179] We read also of a stone that was made famous by the resting of the Ark of the Covenant upon it – a stone that was previously known by the name of the 'Great Stone of Abel.'[180] The most distinguished example of a monumental circle is furnished us by Joshua at Gilgal, and the word Gilgal itself signifies Circle. The stones, twelve in number, were brought from the bed of the river, and within the circle composed of them, Samuel held his yearly court. Here Saul was made king, and here Elijah occasionally tarried.

What wonderful histories tell these stones! and yet the surrounding people were not so conversant with the ceremonies connected with them as were the Druids. That is a remarkable coincidence where the Druidical ceremonies before the Sun are found, copied, in the arrangement of the tribes in their tents at the camp, when Moses and Aaron received commandment to place the ensign-bearers of Judah's camp to the East, the Rising Sun.[181]

The universal inclination of nations to idolatry is worthy of remark. This tendency was so strong in the Jews, that we find even the serpent raised by Moses in the desert, becoming an object of worship, and incense burnt to it by the Israelites.[182] It is a remarkable fact that there is hardly a nation on the face of the earth which has not been given to serpent-worship, and several examples are extant at this day. But there is no proof that the Druids of Britain were serpent-worshipers, though the serpent was employed by them emblematically. Researches into their ceremonies have shown the contrary. Idolatrous corruptions, such as those of Egypt, were corruptions of the pure religion of Noah, and when we compare the nations of the world, we find that besides being free from false gods, the Druidical Kelts were less addicted to these corruptions than any other race. The only evidence of Druidical superstition is found in connection with Gaulish priests bearing the name of Druids; a corruption that had been introduced among them by the Greeks.

The Kelts, in accordance with prophecy, extended their boundaries farther than any other people, and therefore traveled further from their national cradle in their migration from Deffrobani across the continent of Europe, along the line of the Black Sea and the mountains of the Crimea, to their destination of the Isle of Britain. Nevertheless, when Caesar landed on the eastern shore, and planted his silver eagle on the Kentish hill-side; and even when Suetonius Paulinus massacred the Druids of Mona; there, far away from the turmoil and struggle of the outer world, the natives had lived on through ages, from a time far beyond the scope of any chronology, continuing the simple customs and ceremonies of the patriarchs. Although Nineveh carved her winged cherub, and bent the knee to the eagle-headed Nisroch, and Egypt worshiped her Isis and her Apis, there was neither an altar nor idol in any part of the west of Britain, from Anglesea to the end of the Cornish promontory. There were only the green sward, and the logan-stone and cromlech, to bear witness to the same God whom Noah acknowledged when he went forth from the Ark.

Bearing in mind the allusions already made to the Druidical altars of worship, we shall now approach a subject that has caused much anxious inquiry and perplexity in the minds of men, and the misunderstanding of which has created so much prejudice against Druidism and the Bardic Rites. We refer to the 'Runic Nôd.'

This Nôd, or Sign, however, presents itself with a duplicate claim for our consideration; there is a Bardic, and also a Judaic, or a physical and a Biblical, view of it. It should be understood that it is God's own peculiar 'Name' which is a mystery – an unspoken word; that is to say, the burden of the sacred motto, the 'Divine Name,' consists of /I\, or the unutterable name.

When the Israelitish race was in cruel bondage under the iron hand of the Egyptian, and Moses, a refugee of forty years in consequence of the outburst of his patriotic feelings, was tending the flock of Jethro in Midian; this Moses saw a bush in flames, but without being consumed. And when he turned to behold the sight, 'God called unto him out of the midst of the bush, and said, Moses! Moses! And he said, Here (am) I. And he said, Draw not nigh hither; put off thy shoes from off thy feet; for the place whereon thou standest is holy ground.'[183] Subsequently, Moses was commanded by the same authority to go to Pharaoh, and take measures for leading the children of Israel out of Egypt. In that conversation, Moses said unto God, Behold (when) I come unto the children of Israel, and shall say unto them, The God of your fathers hath sent me unto you; and they shall say to me, What is his name? what shall I say unto them? And God said unto Moses, I am that I am; and he said, 'Thus shalt thou say unto the children of Israel, I am hath sent me unto you. And God said moreover unto Moses, Thus shalt thou say unto the children of Israel, The Lod God of your fathers, the God of Abraham, the God of Isaac, and the God of Jacob, hath sent me unto you; this is ny name forever, and this is my memorial unto all generations.'

The people of the present age have a better opportunity to understand the meaning of what is called the 'Unutterable Name,' than that afforded in former times; for now we have authoritative works on Biblical Proper Names, and treatises on various Scripture topics; and to add to this, we have historical information concerning the mode of preserving, as a mystery, the peculiar Name of God among the Jews, according to the provisions of the Kabbala, or Secret Literature, and are acquainted with the fact that pagan nations were in possession of similar mysteries. But it is worthy of remark that these authorities, so far at least as we have observed, make no allusion to the Bardic mysteries, a circumstance that goes to prove how independent of, and separate from other nations, the Kymmry have been in respect to their literature and ceremonies.

Learned men, who have given attention to this subject, are agreed that the word, translated above, 'I am,' is not a verb of the present tense only, in the original language, but that it represents at least two tenses, the present and the future, as, 'I am and I shall be,' and, in the form of a special verb, the word signifies 'I am that which I shall be.' Bengel attributed to the word three tenses, as embracing the words of John the Divine, 'which is, and which was, and which is to come,'[184] but his opinion does not receive the support of the most critical scholars. It is written in the Chaldee, 'I am the one who is, and the one who is to be'; and, with this, the best Hebrew scholars agree, rendering the passage, 'I am he who shall be, hath sent me unto you.'[185]

This is the name 'Jehovah.' It occurs in the Old Testament in two forms, 'Jehovah,' and 'Jah'; and this name is the original of the word 'Lord,' wherever that word is found printed in capital letters in our Bible. This name is exclusively applied to the Supreme Being, as his own peculiar name, having never been conferred on any other being, real or fabulous; while the other names, 'El' and 'Elohim,' synonymous with the word God, as we find in Gen. 1, I., have been used for the names of false gods and inferior beings. There is in this something significant, as if the Infinite guarded, with terrible jealousy, his own name, so that the name 'Jehovah,' divinely protected, should not at any time be otherwise applied.

Although the verb *Byddwyv* (I am), in the Kymmric language, is assigned by grammarians to the present tense; it appears that the composition of the word, as a form belonging to that language when contemporary with the Hebrew, corresponds with the double-tensed verb in question, as, 'Byddwyv (I am who shall be) hath sent me unto you.' This formation pervades the syntax of the Kymmric, as if to contradict the hypercritical minuteness of those grammarians who adopt foreign languages of the modern period as standards by which to form their opinion, rather than the ancient characteristic resources of their own mother tongue.[186]

The Hebrew scholars give the syntactic construction of the verb 'to be,' in that sense. Wilkinson in his work entitled 'Personal names in the Bible,' gives an example of a similar construction in the English language, to illustrate the same subject, as 'Next week I proceed to London,' meaning 'I shall proceed;' or having done this he 'proceeded to London.' Like other languages, the Hebrew passed through many changes from Abraham's time to that of Ezra, and after that, suffered such fortune as to be lost in the Aramean, and to become a dead language. The vowel points were not in use in the Hebrew before the Christian era, so that the writing of it before that time was entirely in consonants; and we learn that the consonants making up the word translated above, 'I am he who shall be,' are the very letters of the name Jehovah, I. V. In addition to the interpretation of this Name, there is in the Iolo Manuscripts, a note referring to the following line in the ode of 'The Secret,'

The best portion of Scripture, the word unknown,

The import of which, – according to this note,[187] is, as generally rendered, in perfect accordance with our authorized translation; 'This is my name for ever, and this is my memorial unto all generations.' Now according to the Rabbins, this is a false translation; for the word עֹלָם which we render 'ever,' signifies also 'hidden' and 'secret'; so that the interpretation of the passage, as they contend, is, 'Let this my name be secret; keep this in remembrance for all generations.'[188]

Gesenius says that the Jews, for centuries before the Christian era, either through misinterpretation of articles of the law, such as 'Thou shalt not take the name of the Lord thy God in vain' (Exod. 20. 7), which is given thus in Levit. (24, 16), 'And he that blasphemeth the name of the Lord, he shall surely be put to death'; or through ancient custom, considered that name too sacred to be pronounced. It is written in the Talmud, a book of Jewish laws and traditions, 'He who utters the name of the Lord (Jehovah), there is no part for him in the world to come.'

Now, besides the philological consideration of this word in its ordinary form among the Jews, the name is worthy of our regard as a theological and religious monument. Bearing in mind the fact that the original form of the commemorative name 'Iahvch,' is derived from an old form of the verb *to be*, which is supposed to have become obsolete before the time of Moses, and is scarcely to be found in the Scriptures, we discover this name in the poetic words of Isaac in his blessing of Jacob, 'That thou mayest be a multitude of people' (Gen. 28, 3), and previously, in the mouth of Eve at the birth of her first-born. In the latter instance, it is acknowledged that the ordinary translation, 'I have gotten a man from the Lord' (Gen. 4, I), is not correct, but that it should be, 'I have gotten the Man, the Jehovah;' and it is the opinion of the ablest commentators, ancient and modern, that Eve believed that the promise of a Saviour, or the seed of the woman who was to bruise the serpent's head, was then being fulfilled in the birth of her first-born. The theology of our first parents concentrated in this promise, and as Fagius adds, If we accept this view, that Eve saw in her seed Him who was to bruise the serpent's head, there is clear and evident premonstration of the Divinity of Christ in the word 'Lord.' Luther translates the passage, 'I have gotten the Man, the Lord,' and notes in the margin that it was he, whom Eve thought to be identical with the seed which the Lord had declared would bruise the serpent's head. That Eve was disappointed in her expectation of the 'Iahveh,' in the person of Cain, is indicated, it is believed, by the fact that she called her second son 'Abel,' meaning vanity. Human hope was now beginning to fade away in the expectation of the fulfillment of the promise by the birth of children, and we find that the human race in the third generation, in the days of Enos, began to call upon the name of the Lord (Iahveh), and to look directly to him for the fulfillment of the promise; and their hope having been transferred from the human medium to the divine. The Deluge washed away from the face of the earth all hope of the restoration of Eden according to the first expectation, but we find Him who revealed Himself by the name 'Iahveh,' renewing His promises to men. He appeared to Abraham under the name of 'El-Shaddai,' God Almighty; which name was acknowledged by the patriarchs Abraham, Isaac, and Jacob; and when He renewed the Covenant to Moses, He did it through his name of 'Jehovah,' the memorial and mystic name. We trace this name through the whole of the Old Testament. It is the 'Lord (Iahveh)' of Eve; the 'Jehovah' of Moses's flaming but unconsumed bush; the 'Iah' of David, the sweet singer-bard of Israel (Psalm lxviii. 4); and Malachi closes the Old Testament with the same subject which the angel of the covenant used in opening it, the announcement of the Divine Son. Thus, the whole Bible, in its historical as well as prophetical parts, has every where, like precious gems on the threads of the written volume, these promises of a Saviour, or, of 'Him who is to be.'

The New Testament opens with a noble realization of the expectations which the Old had created, and that, in connection with the Memorial Name. As the Old Testament begins with the promise of 'Him who is to be,' the New opens with the announcement of the consummation of 'God with us.' John begins his history with the Memorial Name, the Logos, or the Word, the interpretation of which has been the occasion of so much perplexity to scholars, but which has the same meaning as the Bardic 'Llog.' In the mouth of the same Apostle, as he closes the Book of Revelation, we find the ancient word 'Iaveh,' I am He who shall be, christianized into 'Alpha and Omega, the first and the last.' Whether this was the result of his knowledge of the original name, or of the influence of divine inspiration, we can not determine. The concluding lines of John of Kentchurch on the names of God, regarded as in harmony with Kymmric Bardism, bearing the initials 'O.I.W.,' seem to partake of the signification of these words; or of the fashion in which they are sometimes inscribed; save that the Bard's O is angular according to the manner of cutting letters on the bars of the Bardic wooden frame, thus ◇, i.e., I A ◇; and this seems to assert the ancient community of Bardism with the Alpha-Omega – the Jesus – of the Revelation.

Thus throughout the Scriptures, we meet with the Memorial Name, or the Bardic Secret; to Eve it was the 'One who shall be'; to Jacob, the 'Angel of the Lord,' to Moses, 'I am He who shall be,' as a Memorial Name; to Malachi, the

'Lord whom ye shall seek,' and the Angel of the Covenant; to Matthew 'God with us,' to John, 'the Word that was made flesh,' and in his Revelation, 'Alpha and Omega,' or the Iahveh, whom every believer, in faith, is expecting; and there can be no better proof of the Divinity of the Messiah, and of the error of Unitarianism, than is given in connection with the history of the Memorial and Runic Name which, rightly understood, accords to Bardism an exalted character. Many theologians have been accustomed to regard the Divine appearances and communications recorded in the Old Testament, as those of the First Person of the Holy Trinity. It is plain, however, that it was the Second Person who gave the promise concerning himself; who appeared and spake as we have mentioned; and who, in harmony with his own promise, became incarnate in the fullness of time. This is a fact too much overlooked in the treatment of the Old Testament promises. Paul has given Bardic testimony (Rom. 16, 25), to the same effect, when referring to 'the revelation of the mystery which was kept secret since the world began.'

In an old manuscript in the library of Raglan castle, which has been published with the Iolo Manuscripts, (p. 424) under the title of 'The Roll of Tradition and Chronology,' it is said:

> First of all, an account is here presented of the occurrences transmitted by oral tradition, before the commencement of chronological computation. The announcement of the Divine Name is the first event traditionally preserved; and it occurred as follows: God, in vocalizing his Name, said /I\, and with the Word, all worlds and animations sprang co-instantaneously to being and life from their non-existence; shouting, in ecstasy of joy, /I\, and thus repeating the name of the Deity. Still and small was that melodiously sounding voice (i.e., the divine utterance), which will never be equaled again until God shall renovate every pre-existence from the mortality entailed on it by sin, by re-vocalizing that name from the primary utterance of which emanated all lays and melodies, whether of the voice or of stringed instruments; and also all the joys, ecstasies, beings, vitalities, felicities, origins, and descents, appertaining to existence and animation.

In the vocalizing of his Name as above mentioned, we have Creator, Death, and Resurrection. The account of the Creation, coming into existence at the harmonious and sweet repeating of the Name, if not so authentic as the 'Let there be' of Genesis, is fully as imaginative, to say nothing of its poetic beauty; for from the expression 'Let there be,' we have only the idea of will, and power. In the account contained in the above extract we find, also, decline and death through sin, with restoration from the effects of death to original purity, as an echo to the utterance of this name by its Owner and Author.

Like a Bard of the Mystery, Job, in whose book are to be seen several characteristics of Druidical import, wonderfully concurs with the idea that creation echoes the name of God 'in the still and small melodiously sounding voice,' in those words of his, 'When the morning stars sang together, and all the sons of God shouted for joy.'[189] Thus, according to Bardism, no attempt should be made to utter the pure and holy Name by a sinful man, until the time of his restoration 'from the mortality entailed on him by sin' when the /I\ will Himself re-vocalize it for the renovation of every pre-existence.

The /I\ further denotes the three Rays of Light. As the Sun gives life and light to nature, it came to be regarded as a symbol of the Creator, having power to effect the restoration of the physical world to the productiveness of spring, after it had subjected it to the mortality of winter, because of the withholding of its rays. The Druids possessed a considerable knowledge of astronomy, and especially of the course of the sun through the twelve signs of the Zodiac. We perceive from these facts, the appropriateness of the Kymmric word *amser*, signifying time. It is descriptive of the revolution of the year through the signs of the Zodiac, *am* (= around), and *ser* (stars), signifying the circle of the stars. The Bardic Throne, in its formation, corresponds to the passage of the sun through the signs.

The summer solstice furnishes a representation of the Creation; the winter solstice represents Him as withholding His benefits, or in the character of Destroyer; and the middle staff, or ray,[190] is a duplicate sign representing first, the renovation of Spring (Spring Equinox), and secondly, the fruitfulness of Autumn (Autumnal Equinox), which respectively show forth the Creator as Father and Sustainer. We have here a remarkable correspondence between the facts of Nature as presented to us, and the Bible Runic Sign, when the latter is subjected to the light of the /I\ of Bardism, and interpreted as symbolical of 'Him who is and shall be.' The 'Resurrection and Life' Himself makes use of Nature to elucidate this subject: 'Except a corn of wheat fall into the ground and die, it abideth alone but if it die, it bringeth forth much fruit.'[191] And Paul adds, '(Thou) fool, that which thou sowest is not quickened except it die.'[192]

It was the belief of the Bardic Gwyddonites[193] that there is a correspondence between things earthly and things spiritual, and that this world, in its cyclic revolution, is a type of the world to come. The estates of being were divided and differently designated, as various circles revolving one into the other. We have for example the 'Circles of Existence,' containing the 'Circle of Inchoation,' and belonging more particularly to living things here upon the earth. The 'Circle of Felicity' is that wherein the good are for ever happy; and of the 'Circle of Infinitude,' it is said that none but God can pervade it.[194]

The Bard, as he stood facing the East, on the Logan-Stone, where, at the Eye of Light, the three rays converged, was looked upon as the moral sun of the world, and also, according to Christian Bardism, as an emblem of the Trinity.

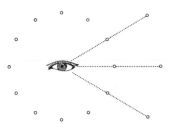

It is worthy of note here, that the Bards had a theory connected with the sun, which, according to their mysteries, makes the age of the world correspond to the Mosaic period. It is well known that the sun does not pass through the same space in the zodiac every year, a fact which involves a change in the reckoning of time. In conformity with this change, according to Bardic chronology, it is said that conventional session was in action when the sun was, in the spring, at the Point of Liberty, or the Line of the Equinox, having returned from winter solstice, or Celestial Hades,[195] to Paradise, immediately over against the Horns of Taurus. This event, according to the calculation of the Albannau, by the 'Precession of the Equinoxes,' could not have occurred less than 5800 years ago – very nearly the period which has elapsed since the time of Adam, according to Biblical chronology.

Another characteristic of the /|\ is that it comprised every form by which the Bardic alphabet can be cut, and therefore contained within itself all the elements of learning; for the letters could only be cut on wood, transversely or obliquely, and never in the direction of the grain. From the same root came the term *egwyddor*, a name applied to the Kymmric alphabet, and which also signifies principle. The element of the character, or the instinct of the mind, was called *egwyddor*, and *kelv a gwyddor* signified 'art and science.' So deep-rooted is the old Gwyddonic custom in the nation of the Kymmry, that the expression among them, at this day, for writing one's name, is to 'cut' one's name. Hence came the expressions synonymous with 'carpentering a song,' or 'hewing poetry,' and the characterization of Llawdden's reformation of the Kymmric poetic metres, as the work of his 'axe.'

What we have already adduced is sufficient to refute the charge of idolatry made against the Druids of Britain. The belief in Creator and Sustainer, a being infinite and invisible; together with the conception of man's degeneracy through sin, which rendered him too foul of lip to utter the name of that Being until the time when He himself would proclaim the /|\, when all things responding to the sound would return to original purity – these facts demonstrate that, whatever their defects, the Druids of Britain were not idolaters. However lightly those who live in the nineteenth century of the Christian era may esteem the cabalistic traditions of the Jews, and the 'heathen rites' of the Druids; whatever may be thought of their custom of keeping the Name of God unuttered; and we may ask if, after all, there is not something like an upbraiding voice arising out of these 'heathen rites,' to rebuke their enlightened Christian despisers who roll in their mouths the name of the Holy Trinity with such nonchalance? The truth from the Logan-Stone might well, indeed, put to the blush many supporters of Christianity, and many promoters of orthodox faith.

According to the testimony of Caesar, the inhabitants of Gaul sent their youth to Britain to perfect their education, a fact which shows that the Druids possessed extensive knowledge, as well as purity of morals.

There is nothing incredible in the supposition that the descendants of Gomer retained the conception of the Being of God, when we remember that, on account of longevity, few generations had passed away from the time of Adam to Noah. The contemporaneous living of the patriarchs with their ancestors and descendants for centuries, afforded excellent facilities for the transmission of histories and traditions from one age to another. According to Dr Adam Clarke's interesting table,

	Years
Noah and Lamech were contemporary	595
Noah and Methuselah were contemporary	600
Noah and Enos, of the third generation	84
Japheth, father of Goner, was contemporary with Lamech	93
Japheth, father of Gomer, was contemporary with Methuselah	98
Japheth, father of Gomer, was contemporary with Noah	448
And after the Deluge Japheth was contemporary with Abraham	150
And after the Deluge Japheth was contemporary with Isaac	50

Japheth lived contemporary with the antediluvian patriarchs, longer than Shem, for he was the eldest son of Noah; though Moses names Shem first, possibly because he was considered the progenitor of the Hebrews. Japheth thus had an opportunity to transmit all the mysteries of the antediluvian world to his children and race, for it is likely that the dispersion was effected but gradually in accordance with the increase of population.

If we examine the philological coincidents in the Kymmric and Hebrew, and other ancient languages, as recorded by scholars, these, with what we have already shown, will prove that there is nothing in Druidism necessarily incompatible with Christianity; but that, on the contrary, there was much in its ceremonies common to Judaism, and which made it typical of the Gospel of Christ; thus preparing the nation, under Bardic instruction, to embrace that Gospel. In agreement with this theory, we find that the Kymmry willingly received the Gospel upon its first presentation to them, adapting their circumstances to the Christian service; and there is credible proof that Christianity met with neither opposition nor persecution in Britain, save from pagan Rome and the infidel Saxons.

The religions of the Hindoos and Brahmins are corruptions of the old patriarchal religion of Noah. When we compare the condition of the ancient idolatrous nations, which had a like ancestry, with that of the Kymmry, and remember the manner in which Christianity, upon its first offer, was received by the latter, while the former are still clinging to their false gods; when we remark the adherence of the Kymmry to Christianity from the time of its dawn among them, and the fact that they are to-day among the most eminent defenders of its principles; what a subject is presented for our meditation! It was to the efforts of Thomas Charles, John Owen, and Thomas Hughes, descendants of the Kymmry, that the British and Foreign Bible Society owed its origin. Thus the children of those who were worshipers in the temple of Nature in the White Isle, in the language of Williams of Pantycelyn, the Kymmric Watts, have united to

'Let the Gospel
Loud resound from pole to pole.'

In the midst of this Kymmric glory, Bardism, as the medium for the transmission of morals and learning among the descendants of Gomer, the son of Japheth, lifts up her voice from the ancient past. She claims, from the descendants of the Kymmry, acknowledgment of her services as their trusty leader through the clouds and darkness of pagan ages, until she brought them, in spite of hostile influences, safely to the noonday of Christian light, where she still would keep their feet steady and firm in the paths of civilization, 'In the Face of the Sun and the Eye of Light.'

Bardism of the Christian Period

It may be possible that those who doubt the national claims of the Kymmry to religious, political, and literary distinctiveness, have considered our Biblical and Judaic investigations as foreign to the question. They may argue that we have no right to link together Bardic characteristics of Druidic origin, and facts in the history of the Jewish nation, the latter being looked upon as a chosen and peculiar people, and instruments in the hands of the Almighty to work out his purposes and promises touching the Saviour. But the Gentiles may claim, as has often been remarked by Christian writers, a certain degree of consanguinity with the Head of the Church, as a Root of the Stock of David through his ancestress, Ruth the Moabitess. The political estate of the Jews was on the eve of decay, and the sceptre was to depart from Judah, upon the advent of Shiloh, in the reign of Herod the Edomite. It is a fact recorded to the praise of the Gentiles, that those who had the privilege of first offering tribute to the Young Babe, were pagans, influenced not by knowledge of promises and prophecies possessed by the Jews, but by their own pagan philosophy and native inclinations, in connection with their astronomical studies. We have in this fact a strong argument pointing to the higher government of Him whose Name is Jah, indicating the manner in which he works to fulfill his purposes, using men and nations as His unconscious instruments. If it was in accordance with divine Providence that the three Magi, Gaspar, Melchior, and Balthasar, as wise men and astronomers, should be conducted to the Babe by means of their own traditions and ceremonies, it was equally in accord with the workings of Providence, that the Britons should be led to believe in the doctrines of the Gospel, having nothing in their own belief and customs to prevent such a result, and much, as we have shown, to fit them for it. Concurrently with this, as early as 175, A.D., the Bardic Rites had been wholly transferred, at least in outward appearance, to the service of Christianity; and through the earlier centuries of the Christian era, we find these Rites employed in connection with the church.

It is not within the province of this paper to inquire when and how Christianity was first introduced into Britain; but the testimony of Tertullian, in the second century, that the Britons who had not been reached by the Romans had submitted to Christ, indicates that the Kymmry never succumbed to physical weapons. Origen, writing about forty years later, referring to the Kymmry of Caledonia, says, that 'The power of the Lord, the Saviour, is among those in Britain, who are separated from our world.' These early testimonies are incontrovertible proofs that some power, independent of external circumstances, had previously prepared the Kymmry for the reception of Christianity; and to what can we attribute this tillage of the Kymmric field for the reception of Christian seed, if not to previous cultivation under Bardic 'Privilege and Custom' and Druidic instruction?

Not only did the Kymmric Christians for four centuries hold their religious services in conjunction with the Bardic Rites; but worthy priests and ministers in every subsequent age, while perhaps dividing the ecclesiastical from the congressional regulations, have been supporters of the Bardic cause in conjunction with literature. We could present a long list of famous poets and *literati* for thirteen centuries, who were zealous supporters of Bardic customs, while chief ornaments of the Church.

Rudston Standing Stone, East Riding, Yorkshire.

In the sixth century, a Chair was instituted called the Baptismal Chair, and a profession of the Christian religion by baptism was made a requisite of membership. As a result of this institution, Christianity and Baptism became synonymous terms in the Kymmric language; and to bring 'Faith and Baptism' to any place, signified the introduction there of the Christian religion, as is made evident by many allusions in the works of the poets, and the old writings on the genealogy of the British Saints.

The motto of this Baptismal Chair was 'Good is the Stone with the Gospel,' which at once unfolds its purpose – of utilizing, for the service of the Gospel, that tribunal Stone which was formerly used in the service of Druidism. The general motto of the Bards of the Isle of Britain was 'The Truth against the World.'

In the eleventh century, the Bard was a necessary element in society, as is easily proved from the Laws of Howel the Good. We refer to this fact to show that Christianity had an influence upon the literature of that period, contrary to the impressions of writers like the Rev. Edward Davies, author of the 'Mythology of the Druids,' who, misunderstanding certain writings, endeavoured to prove from them that in the eleventh century there was an attempt to revive Druidism. A conciliatory address by Cynddelw to Rhys ab Gruffydd, Prince of South Wales, together with some poems of Howel ab Owain, have been used as the basis of such a supposition; but all of the Druidism of that period, is contained in Mr Davies's erroneous rendering of the original. We may take Cynddelw's address as an example:

> O thou consolidator of the comely tribe! since I am returned home in thy
>   dominion,
> To celebrate thee under heaven,
> O thou with the golden protecting spear, hear my Bardic petition.
>   In peace let us taste the cauldron of Prydain's tranquillity,
> Round the sanctuary of the uneven number, thy sovereign power to extend.
>   It (the Bardic sanctuary) loves not vehement loquacity;
> It is no cherisher of useless sloth,
> It opposes no previous concealed mysteries (Christianity).
> Disgrace alone is excluded from the Bardic worship.
> It is the guardian bulwark of the breaker of shields.
> It is wise and zealous for the defense of the country, and for decent manners.
> A foe to the hostile aggression, but the supporter of the faint in battle.[196]

It seems that an attempt had been made to prejudice the Prince against the Christian ritual of the Bards, and the poet implores his protection of the Bardic order, showing the superiority of the worthy poets over the false bards, and defends the order on the ground that it is not at variance with Christianity. This also shows that Christianity had a strong hold upon the Kymmric princes of that time, for it is represented as the chief object of defense. Mr Stephens, author of 'The Literature of the Kymmry,' claims, that besides being more classical, the Bards of those days excelled the Church in learning.

The office of the Bard had a direct tendency to foster heroism, and transmit the history of the magnanimous and brave knights from one age to another, as a national inheritance to the end of time. To be well-versed in the history of the nation was one of the indispensables of the Bardic chair, and to descant upon the brave deeds of ancestors, thus to kindle the patriotic flame in the hearts of Britons, was one of the Bard's duties. But besides inspiring patriotism, we find the ancient Bards themselves in the thick of the fight, as is indicated by their literary remains. Aneurin, in the sixth century, says in his 'Gododin,' that he was at the Battle of Cattraeth, and that only two others escaped beside himself:

> Three hundred and sixty-three chieftains wearing the golden torques,
> Of those who hurried forth after the excess of revelling,
> But three escaped by valor from the funeral fosse.
> The two war-dogs of Aeron and Cynon the dauntless,
> And myself from the spilling of blood, the reward of my candid song.[197]

Gwalchmai, a Bard of the twelfth century, says in 'Gwalchmai's Delights':

> I am of the golden order fearless in battle.
> I am a lion in the front of the army – ardent in my advance,
> Anxiously have I, at night, watched the boundary
> Fords of the murmuring waters of Dygen Vreiddin
> Where the untrodden grass was supremely green, the water limpid
> And excessively talkative the nightingale well-versed in odes.

The principles of their system after the introduction of Christianity taught the Bards to look to the true God for the gifts of the *awen* (genius) and not to pagan gods, as is shown by the following triad: 'The three foundations of genius: the gift of God, the exertion of man, and the events of life.[198]

One of the important results of the Bardic Institute has been indicated by Rev. Thomas Price, who says that

> In addition to their work of exciting and fostering patriotism, we are indebted to the Bards for another valuable service; they have preserved our language in a condition of purity and fullness without parallel in the later ages. Not only is this an honour to our nation, but it has also been an invaluable profit, and that in things which are of the utmost importance; for when the Protestant Reformation shone upon the world, and the Sacred Scriptures were offered to the public in popular translations, the Kymmry were in possession of a language cultivated, rich, and beautiful, as a vehicle wherein the Holy Word might appear in a form as worthy of the original as perhaps can be seen in any other translation whatever. The Bishop Richard Davies was a Bardic disciple of Lewis Dwnn, and the venerable Archdeacon Edmund Prys was himself a Bard, and the other translators were very conservant with the works of the Bards, especially Dr John Davies. When we contemplate this transaction, we can not but wonder at the abundance of words and richness of language and expression at the command of those noble writers, and that in an age when they had neither lexicon nor any thing else of the kind to help them.[199]

In the teachings of the Bards, we are led to the fountain source of that spirit of heroism which characterized Caswallon, and inspired him to his bold stand against the Roman invaders. Indeed we know that though Caesar completely subjugated other nations, he was unable to exact from the Britons more than a promise to pay tribute; and there is no evidence during Caesar's life, nor for nearly a hundred years after his death, of the fulfillment of this promise. It is evident that the Kymmric nation did not improve in knowledge and morals while under the Roman dominion; but they kept their language uncontaminated by the Latin, with the exception of the Latin introduced through the church-ritual, as shown by the works of the Bards.

Were we to compare the Bardic regulations with the 'Parliamentary Rules,' which form the standard for the regulations of the generality of associations to-day, the uninitiated would be surprised by the excellence of those of the Bardic Conventions, in respect to equity, liberality and common sense.

The Kymmric traditions so far influenced the revival of the literature of Europe in the twelfth century, that we find the legends of Arthur and the Knights of the Round Table, constituting the groundwork of the romance, legends, and literature of that Continent.[200]

Among the remains of the Privilege and Institute of the British Bards, there is nothing that exhibits the antiquity of Bardism more clearly than the Chair.[201]

The principal church of a Bishopric, or Diocese, is called the Cathedral church. The English word Cathedral is derived from the Greek $\kappa\alpha\theta\varepsilon\delta\rho\alpha$, compounded from two words, $\kappa\alpha\tau\alpha$, and $\varepsilon\delta\rho\alpha$, a seat, or chair.

The chair, here referred to, chiefly denotes a source of authority, and seat of instruction and guidance, as in Matth. 23, 1–2, where it is recorded that Jesus spake to the multitude and to his disciples, saying, 'The Scribes and the Pharisees sit in Moses' seat.' The word for 'seat' in the Welsh version of the New Testament is cadair – chair. The accepted meaning of the passage is, that the Scribes and Pharisees taught the law of Moses to the multitudes, and took upon themselves the Cathedrate office of teaching.

The first historical account of the origin of the Bardic chair, is in connection with a chair which was restored at Caerlleon-upon-Usk, over which the two Merddins, Taliesin and Mabon, and others, presided. It was here that the system of the Round Table was formed which was 'a system of the arts and sciences, rites and privileges of Bards and Minstrels, and the preservation, where such was deemed necessary, of the worthiest of old traditions, and the discrimination of all innovations that would be considered of a nature calculated to improve and enlarge honorable sciences, with reference to the wisdom and interest of country and nation.'[202]

A prayer, composed by Talhaiarn, has always been used at the Bardic Congress of the chair of Glamorgan. The following is one of its forms:

God! impart they strength;
And in that strength, reason;
And in reason, knowledge;

And in knowledge, justice;
And in justice, the love of it;
And in that love, the love of everything;
And in the love of everything, the love of God.[203]

Each Bardic chair had its distinct territory, to which its privileges were confined. The following are the mottoes of the different chairs of the Island of Britain:

1 The chair of the Bards of the Island of Briain – 'Truth against the World.'
2 Glamorgan or Siluria – 'God and all goodness.'
3 The Round Table of Arthur of Taliesin, and of Tir Iarll, (Earl's Land) – 'Nothing is truly good that may be excelled.'
4 Powis – 'Who slays shall be slain.'
5 South Wales – 'Heart to heart.'
6 North Wales (Venedotia) – 'Jesus,' or, according to an old traditional record – 'O! Jesus, repress injustice.'
7 Bryn Gwyddon (Abury) – 'Hearing is believing, seeing is truth.'
8 Devon (Damnonium) in the chair of Beiscawen (hodiè Boscawen, in Cornwall) – 'Nothing is for ever that is not for ever and ever.'
9 Urien Rheged (at Loughor) under the presidency of Taliesin – 'Truth will have its place.'
10 Raglan Castle, under the patronage of Lord William Herbert 'Awake, it is day!'
11 The Chair of Neath – 'God's peace and his heavenly tranquillity.'

The canons of proficiency in the art of poetry were given in triads, some of which we append:

'The three primary requisites of poetical genius, – an eye that can see nature, a heart that can feel nature, and a resolution that can follow nature.

'The three final intentions of poetry, – increase of goodness, increase of understanding, and increase of delight.

'The three properties of just imagination, – what may be, what ought to be, what is seemly to be.

'The three indispensables of poetical language, – purity, copiousness, and ease.

'Three things that ought to be well understood in poetry, – the great, the little, and their correspondents.

'The three dignities of poetry, – the praise of goodness, the memory of what is remarkable, and the invigoration of the affections.

'The three purities of poetry, – pure truth, pure language, and pure conception.

'Three things that poetry should thoroughly be, – thoroughly learned, thoroughly animated, and thoroughly natural.'

As to the genuineness of the compositions of the ancient British Bards, we presume there are, at present, no disputants; especially since the futile efforts, of

Mr Malcolm Laing and the 'Critical Review' to discredit their authenticity. On the contrary, an appreciation of the poetic remains of the Kymmry has been manifested by some of the most eminent literati in England, and on the Continent of Europe. Passing by Aneurin and the works of the earlier poets, we come to Gwalchmai ab Meilir's Epic to Owain Gwynedd, Prince of North Wales, which was presented to the English public by the Rev. Evan Evans (Prydydd Hir).

The occasion of the composition of this poem was Owain's victory over the armies of Henry the Second on the shore of the Menai. Mr Evans's free translation attracted the attention and won the admiration of several literary men, among others, the poet Gray, who produced it in metre under the title of 'The Triumphs of Owain.' Bishop Percy characterized it as 'Gwalchmai's very sublime and animated ode,' and in a letter to the Rev. Evan Evans with reference to Bards of the same period, he remarked: 'I have lately been collecting specimens of English Poetry, through every age, from the time of the Saxons down to that of Elizabeth, and I am ashamed to show you what wretched stuff our rhythmers produced, at the time that your Bards were celebrating the praise of Llywelyn with a spirit scarce inferior to Pindar.'[204]

Sharon Turner's 'Vindication of the British Bards' is widely known. Robert Southey,[205] the Poet-Laureate of England, was so captivated by these works that he made his arrangements to reside in the country which gave birth to such gifted poets, but his intention was frustrated through the parsimony of one of the lords of Glamorgan, who failed to make the necessary repairs in the kitchen of the Maes Gwyn, in the Vale of Neath. The Laureate was a great admirer of the Bard of Privilege and Usage, 'Old Iolo,' who, before the submarine cable, united Great Britain and America in the spirit of the Bardic motto, 'God's peace and His heavenly tranquillity,' by coupling together in capital letters, in the list of subscribers to his poems, the names of General Washington and Humanity's Wilberforce. The Laureate was far too much of a Liberal to induce the parsimonious Tory of the Vale of Neath to add to his culinary comforts.

To the same bard, Leigh Hunt paid his poetical tribute; nor are we to forget the acknowledgment due to the fair sex, as represented by Felicia Hemans. Sir Walter Scott was on intimate terms with the Cambrian Lexicographer, Dr W.O. Pughe, and he has inserted in his notes to several of his poems, extracts from Kymmric documents furnished him by the inquiring savan.

In connection with these words, it is a fact worthy of remark that the School of the Round Table has been one of the principal topics of Alfred Tennyson's poems, for the past forty years.

In this brief treatise the reader will perceive that we have been able to present only a partial view of an extensive subject, and that there are wide and interesting fields within its compass, worthy of more extended investigation.

16

FAIRIES AND DRUIDS OF IRELAND

Charles de Kay

From *Century Magazine*

The trouble with the old archaeologists was, and it remains the trouble with those Irishmen who refuse to look at their island as a part of Europe subject to the laws governing humanity everywhere, that they treated Erin as if it belonged to some other planet. This comes from the great wealth of legend with which the country teemed after it had almost vanished from the larger part of the rest of Europe – at least from that part which was educated. If in 'Pagan Ireland' I have asserted that we have strong evidences in the island of the primeval warfare between intrusive Kelts and the Turanian or Finno-Ugrian tribes which at one time held all Europe, it is not done to belittle the Irish, as some of that sensitive folk may suppose. The Turanian element is not wanting in Germans, Frenchmen, and Italians; it is present among the English in a very marked degree, and will be acknowledged some day when prejudices based on false teachings, ignorance, or pride shall give way before the arguments of scholars. The selection of Ireland as the place where these arguments are applied brings into relief the now well-known value of her old literature, manners, customs, and myths as documents in reading the past of our common family of nations.

The Fenians have always been a stumbling-block to native and foreign students, owing largely to the oriental allusions in the old literature and the similar sound of Phoenicians, but also to ignorance of the literature itself. So with Druidism. It has been denied to Ireland outright, because in the records that came through Christian hands there were fewer allusions to the order than were to be expected. As definite facts about these bodies of men were wanting, the native archaeologists drew on their imagination, having always behind them, however, the traditions that lurk obscurely in the people. The distinction between historical figures enveloped in an atmosphere of myth, and mythical figures to whom historical events have been fitted, is naturally difficult to draw; it is hard enough with all the facts that are now at our command, and was manifestly impossible in previous periods. The earliest records of Ireland refer to bands of settlers coming from the mainland, to gods and guardian deities so closely connected with places and specific human acts that their divinity is almost gone, and to historical tribes and men to whom semidivine or magical attributes have been given. Where are we to draw the line between man and myth, between fact of history and shadow of some old superstition? It will be something gained if we can assign the chief fairies of Ireland to those invading swarms whose deities they appear once to have been. For be it known to those little read in Irish literature that of old the fairies were not trivial folk at all, but powerful champions and wizards who lived in great state inside the hills with their horses and hounds, banquets and retinues, like the nobles they were. Fairy princesses had too often a leaning for mortal heroes, and lured them into their palaces for a year and a day. It seems at one time to have been the fashion in Ireland to couple the name of a fairy with each hero or great chief, as we find Latin legendary giving Egeria the nymph to the wise Roman king. It will be a gain, too, if we can connect Druidism by the aid of languages with a simple religion that lies at the bottom of all the old pagan faiths, just as the Turanian race seems to enter into the composition of most of the peoples of Europe. I shall continue to draw attention to the analogies between the Finnic past as seen in the Kalewala and the Irish past as shown by her literature, because the Finns have kept themselves least mixed with other stocks and therefore represent best the population of Ireland when the Kelts arrived. But we must not understand this arrival in the sense of sudden conquest by an entirely different race. The Kelts would conquer Turanians in Gaul and Holland, and the first swarm into Ireland would be a mixed swarm. At a later date came the horde of purer Kelts.

In 1857, while living in Brooklyn, L.I. John O'Mahony translated a history of Ireland written in Gaelic by Geoffrey Keating. It is only one of many instances of his wisdom that he should have put his finger on the key to the meaning of many obscure points concerning the earliest inhabitants of Ireland. Speaking of Cichol Gri the footless, a chief of the Fomorians, he says: 'There are traces of such people, living by fishing and fowling, by people of perhaps Lapponian type, and they it was that probably left those stone implements improperly called Celtic.' And again, speaking of those who think the Fomaraigh came from the Baltic, he says: 'They must have been Finns or Laps, who perhaps were the predecessors of both Celts and Teutons in Western Europe, for in those times it is not likely that there were any Gothic or Teutonic nations in North-western Europe. It is remarkable that the Welsh, Gaelic, and Breton resemble the Uralian dialects in one or two important points wherein all three differ from their kindred Indo-European tongues.' Had he lived he would have found so many proofs of this guess by comparing the old literature of Ireland and the manners and customs of its more or less purely Keltic tribes with those of Finland that he would have avoided certain minor errors and spoken with certainty on the subject.

The Finnic harpers and dispensers of magic are Irish Druids of a very primitive type, such as Caesar came too late to find in Gaul. Waïnamoïnen makes a great harp from the head of the monster pike – the Salmon of Knowledge of the Irish tales – and with it either delights the world or renders his foes powerless. Lemminkaïnen is a younger, less wise, Druid, who falls into mishaps, is sliced to pieces by a blind beggar whom he scorns, as Balder is slain by the blind god who was overlooked; he is thrown into the River of Death and fished out piecemeal by his mother. With his harp he puts his enemies to sleep or drives them like cattle into the River of Death. He journeys westward to an island where every good thing exists and all the women fall in love with him. This is the Tir na n'óg or Land of the Young visited by Fion, Cuchulinn, Oisîn, and other heroes. It is a later version of the Isles of the Blessed or Paradise of the Kelts, where pigs trot about roasted and the streams run with beer, of which place modern Germany has a humorous reminiscence in Schlaraffenland. Reports of this cloudland, hidden land, or vanishing achipelago in the Atlantic may really have induced St Brendan of Kerry to cross the ocean during an epoch when holy men sought the most inaccessible places. They were discovered by the Norse even in Iceland. Such firmly seated traditions may well have induced Columbus to try the solution of the enigma of the Atlantic. It is Madoc's land and the fabled Atlantic.

The foes of the Kaleva heroes are like the magicians who interrupt Fion and his comrades in their hunts. The Lapp of Pohjola is even more malignant than the Sidhé or fairy of the Irish, who is generally considered a survival of the Dé Danann people, one of primitive swarms from over-sea. Fion and his comrades lived the life of hunters and their methods of cooking were extremely archaic. A pit was dug and a fire built therein to heat stones. Then the fire was drawn off, flesh wrapped in leaves placed in the pit, hot stones laid on, another layer of meat added, and thus the pit filled. The practice is still found among some savage tribes; it is still with us a favorite process for a clambake. Parallels between the Kalewala and Irish legends are endless. Magic horses that carry men off like the wind, nymphs who become the wives of heroes, archers who knock enchanted pins from the hair and save people from magic, wizards who cast men into a 'Druidic sleep' to force them to reveal the truth, boats of skin or copper that go of themselves, runners who have to bind one leg for ordinary occasions lest they go too fast, enchanted boars or elk that only talking weapons can slay, and swords which have a life and vengeance of their own – these and other singular fancies in Irish literature can be found with little radical difference in the Kalewala. We associate these ideas with pagans or simply enjoy them in the nursery for their wild, preposterous boldness. Oscar pursues a fairy who has bewitched Fion, follows him to a mound, digs after and finally captures him. Shiefner has published a similar story among Siberian tribes. Bearing in mind the eternal quarrel of Iran against Turan in Persia and the battles of Gaels on two Tura-Plains in the west of Ireland, mentioned in 'Pagan Ireland,' and recalling, the hatred shown by the Gaels for the wicked, misshapen, giant-like or pigmy Fomoraigh, we can understand better how gods and heroes of the conquered Finno-Ugrians appear in Gaelic stories with non-Aryan traits.

The Fomorians have been sometimes explained as the Fir-muir, or men of the ocean. We have a ballad in English, found in the Shetlands, which does something to support the view that the Fomorians belonged to the same race as the Finns, though it will also aid Professor John Rhys in his argument that Fomor means under the sea, and refers to an entirely mythical race of submarine fairies. The two ideas are not incompatible; for in popular tales a detested and feared race of sea-robbers holding islands off the coast might readily merge into baleful fairies after they had been destroyed and time had been allowed for myths to grow up round their former sites. But to the Shetland story. According to a ballad in Professor Child's collection there is a human race of seals in Shetland, who come on shore, throw off their skins, and enjoy themselves in the dance. If you can secure the skin, its owner, man or woman, is your booty. This is the familiar idea of swan-maidens and fairies, whose feathery dress, whose green or red cap, you must try to seize. But the singular part of the Shetland story is that they are called Finns.

Another explanation of Fomoraigh is Firmorca, men of horses, and the old histories indeed speak of a King Horsehead among their leaders. Giraldus de Barry reported in the twelfth century a 'New and Monstrous Way of Inaugurating their Kings' practiced by a tribe in Donegal, the very part of Ireland where Christianity least penetrated and the non-Kelts must have survived in largest numbers. A new king had to bathe in broth made from the flesh of a white mare, and feast on the flesh and broth with his people. This story is probably one that was handed down from heathen days and from malice or ignorance told to Giraldus when in Leinster as a practice of his own epoch.

However this may be, these and other primitive inhabitants are strangely like the Finnic heroes. Fintann, the only man who survived the deluge, was such an early Irishman with pronounced Finnic traits. He partakes of some of Waïnamoïnen's characteristics, for he is a Methuselah, lives in the shape of a fish through the flood, passes into other disguises, and is thus able to form the bridge whereby knowledge of the past is handed down to the true Gaels. He recalls Japanese legends of transformations at the other side of Asia. He crops up in St Finnian's day just as Oisîn returns to quarrel with St Patrick and delight him with 'Fenian tales.' He brings us naturally to the Salmon of Knowledge already mentioned, for he and it was probably one and the same.

Fion the hero comes as a lad to the river Boyne in search of a teacher of poetry. His youth has been unfortunate, for his father Cumhal is killed and he is hidden and reared by a Druidess. The poet is fishing the Boyne for a magical creature called the Salmon of Knowledge, which gives prophetic and poetic genius to him who eats it. The Salmon once caught, the pupil is ordered to prepare it for the table; but in cooking it he burns his hands, puts the finger to his mouth, and receives the gift his master intended for himself. At once he knows the past and future and understands the speech of animals. His master sees that Fion is destined to greatness. Taking far distant ideas from Finno-Ugrian sources, Oannes of the Chaldeans, the adventures of Waïnamoïnen the

Finnic god with various magic fish, and still others, we can form at least some idea of the meaning of this, one of the most mysterious passages in Irish legend. The trail goes back to some primeval god of the Turanians who united the attributes of Apollo, science and prophecy, with the habitat of Poseidon.

In this way Fion gained a 'magic thumb'. When the Fianna are disturbed by portents or do not recognize a giant or goblin coming towards them, they ask their leader Fion to put his thumb in his mouth and prophesy. Later bards represent him chewing his thumb to the blood, to the bone, and finally to the marrow in the fury of his prophetic trance. We know the old English phrase used by hectoring fellows, 'Do you bite your thumb at me, sir?' It suggests that biting the thumb at a man was at one time a piece of dumb show, meaning clearer than print that the victim of that gesture was held by the man who made it no better than a foul, sinful Druid. It explains, perhaps –

By the pricking of my thumbs,
Something wicked this way comes –

an idea found in Rune 26 of the Kalevala:

Comes the hour of the departing
Of the hero Lemminkaïnen,
Right hand ready, left unwilling,
All his anxious fingers pain him,
Till at last in full obedience
All his members give permission.

Fion is a race-hero of the subdued but not obliterated Ugrians of Ireland. We may well imagine that the Fianna, of whom he was captain, represent a militia formed by some ancient statesman from this nomadic hunterstock to keep turbulent tribes at peace and the sea-robbers off the shores of Erin. Growing too strong and arrogant to suit a powerful ruler, the Fenians were destroyed like the Mamelukes in Egypt. Fion's harper and jester is a dwarf of the fairy stock. In the Kalevala a curious effect is produced by the sudden appearance of some pigmy to do tremendous labors, or to stop the path of a hero. Or again it is an infant, not a pigmy, who suddenly speaks up and rebukes or rails or scoffs at a powerful wizard. The name of Cumhal, Fion's father, means 'bondage' in Gaelic, and may refer to the enslaved condition of his stock. An uncle has survived the slaughter of that father and of the clan. When Fion discovers him in the extreme west, whither the Firbolgs retired when defeated, he is very old, 'and some of the old Fianna along with him who were wont to chase for him.' This raises Fianna from the name of the militia to the wider meaning of the tribe or nation from which they were recruited.

In many regards the Gaelic stories, treasuring, as they do, ideas of a vanished race which peopled Europe in remote epochs, contain customs far more archaic than anything in the Kalevala. A bath is prepared for Cuchulinn by heating pieces of metal red hot and casting them into water. This has gone out in all but a few parts of the world. He and his men are called 'the distorted ones,' owing to their frantic behavior when filled with battle rage. He becomes deformed as if he were a goblin. This allies him with the Fomorians and other non-Keltic monsters and giants; it also recalled the grimaces, contortions, and accouterments of savages whereby they hope to terrify the foe. As the war-witches of Irish legend are far more primitive than the Valkyrs of the Norse, so the frenzied fighters of Ireland are more archaic than the Berserkers of Norway. As a rule in Irish poems the magic-making and slaughter are divided between Druids and heroes, while in the Kalevala both occur in the same person; yet occasionally Vaïnamoïnen, Lemminkaïnen, and Ilmarinen cease their magic, lay aside their harps, and drawing sword whip off somebody's head. An Irish Druid such as Cathbad, however, is like Vaïnamoïnen in his mastery of swordsmanship as well as witchcraft; he goes on 'Fenian' expeditions about Ulster, and is a very bloody and disagreeable person to meet. The heroes who fight for or against Queen Meave, who has been assigned to the earlier cycle, rely more on magic than do those of the Fion cycle. One of Fion's sisters is Fairy, famous for supernatural speed; another is Goat, married to Hound of the World. His aunt is turned by a wizard into a dog, and his wife is transformed into a doe by a Druid whose love she rejects, whereupon she gives birth to the hero Oisîn, 'little fawn.' In Irish ballads, as in the Kalevala, we have the enchanted house into which the hero penetrates. In Finland he confounds the

Malabar cromlech.
From The Celtic Druids *by Godfrey Higgins*

wizards there assembled; in Ireland he is generally enchanted until released by the sword of a comrade. It must always be remembered that these resemblances do not suggest the influence of Finland on Ireland or the reverse; they are rudimental, as we may expect in long-separated branches of the same race which in one case, certainly, has suffered overwhelming mixture with an Aryan stock. Irish legends are profoundly influenced by the overbearing and bloodthirsty Aryan. These characteristics are as strong in the Kelt as they are weak in the Finn.

Cuchulinn represents a Finno-Ugrian demigod who has been so completely absorbed by the Gael that the name has been altered to a Gaelic meaning, then a story fabricated to account for it. Doubtless we get it nearer the original in Cichol, the Fomorian king, round whose name the Gaels placed attributes of gods mixed with memories of past race conflicts. A diminutive of affection, owing to his great popularity in song, made him Cicholîn. As the Gaels did not know what they meant, they invented the story of the boy Setanta, who destroys the watch-dog (cu) of his host (Culann) and promises thenceforth to be his guardian in the place of the dog. Hence his name arose as Cuchulinn, dog of Culann. The etymology was popular because of the great respect the Gaels had for the dog, the defender of sheep against the wolf – a respect shown in the number of tribes and heroes who have the dog's term, cu, cyn, or con, in their names. A more striking veneration of the dog among Aryans is found in the Avesta of the primitive Parsees, also of Aryan races.

Druidism appears to have made a profound impression on the Irish and Britons. We learn how a poet in the Christian age sought Druidic powers. While performing the rite he recited the incantation, Imbas Forosnai, 'Illumination by the Palms,' or the Teinm Laegha, 'Illumination of Rhymes,' which were forbidden by St Patrick.

> This is the way it is to be done: the poet chews a piece of the flesh of a red pig, or of a dog or cat, and he brings it afterwards on a flag behind the door and chants an incantation upon it and offers it to idol gods; and his idol gods are brought to him, but he finds them not on the morrow. And he pronounces incantations on his two palms; and his idol gods are also brought to him in order that his sleep may not be interrupted; and he lays his two palms on his two cheeks, and thus falls asleep; and he is watched that no one may disturb or interrupt him, until everything about which he is engaged is revealed to him, which may be a minute, or two, or three, or as long as the ceremony requires.

Lessons by Christians and their denunciations will not account for the abhorrence for Druidism which has cut its way into the language of the Gaels, and even into English, if we imagine that the Druids were as Lucan and Caesar described them. Druidism must have been greatly modified for the better in Gaul when Caesar arrived, but at the same epoch it might easily retain its worst features in an island apart. Lucan drew his knowledge of Druids from Spain, and his picture of them is consequently more savage and uncivilized. And it was the Spaniards who in after-centuries burned heretics by the thousand. In moral vileness as well as fiendish cruelty seems the origin of such words. With time all Druids became more philosophers, less necromancers; but the bad odor of their deeds hung round the name. Those of Gaul disappear from history suddenly because they were on the wane. Pliny tells us that the Druids made much of the serpent. He was the lucky one who found a mass of adders bringing forth the Mystic Egg, which must be caught in his cloak as it rose up from their coils. He must then spring on his horse and race for his life to the nearest stream, like Tam o'Shanter to escape the goblin snakes. If overtaken, he was enveloped and bitten to death. Pliny saw such an egg 'about the size of a large round apple; it has a cartilaginous rind studded with cavities like those on the arms of a polypus.' Apparently it was an oak-apple of unusual size. That excrescence was a mysterious one to the ancients, and we know that other things like mistletoe, when found on the oak were sacred. The Druids taught in forests and used the awe of mighty trees to enhance reverence for their lessons and rights. The religion is one that belongs to a hunter race living in woodlands, and has many points foreign to the Keltic character. But Druidism, especially on its necromantic side, fits well to the strange scenes of the Finnic epic and some of the oldest lays of Ireland. The magician who throws a mist round the strong fighter, makes the champions of Ulster as weak as women, brings on a hero the pains of childbirth, or enchants the weapons of his enemy, and the satirist who compels men, in dread of his occult power, to deliver up to him their wives and choicest possessions – these are persons who have little but a name in common with the respectable and comparatively stately Druids of Gaul in Caesar's time.

To bring back to life the pagan past of Ireland, and with it that of Britain, philology is not without its use. The Greek word for the oak, drus, with its captivating derivative, Dryads, the nymphs of the oak tree, is no longer accepted as the origin of Druid. But a satisfactory explanation has not, so far as I know, been offered. Bearing in mind the Finno-Ugrian and Irish tendency to slur out a harsh consonant between vowels, we may readily suspect between the two syllables of Gaelic Dráoi a rough breathing which took the place of an earlier guttural. The plural is Dráoite. Inserting the guttural, Dragoit would give a word whose first syllable, 'drag,' contains the meaning 'fire' and 'anger.' Droch, chariot-wheel, sun-wheel, and troghain, sunrise, are other helps, connecting the word with the celestial bodies worshiped by the Finno-Ugrians and pagan Gaels. Dragart, a flint or firestone, Dragaigean, a fire shovel, are other Gaelic words in point.

The sentiment inspired by the Druids was that of fear, horror, wrath. They were the executioners in pagan Europe and burned in osier frames those who were accused of crimes against the state. Hence 'burning in effigy' remains the popular form of threat against political offenders. They superintended the burning of the firstborn of men and cattle to propitiate the sun, moon, and elemental influences. In modern times the hangman is the only person who enjoys or suffers the same distinction of abhorrence from the people, and it is well known how much magic is attributed by the ignorant to the hangman. Owing to this feeling towards the Druid, languages are full of words referring to him which have been misunderstood because they retain that guttural which dropped out of 'Druid' before the Latins fixed it as we see it now. Whence came into Welsh droog, wickedness; into German Trug, deception; in French dialects truc, fraud; in English trick, truck, truckle. But there are others presenting the fire-meaning only, such as drought, dry, drug (herbs that are dried), dree or dry (wizard), and others. So that we have not far to seek as to the meanings underlying Dráoi. Here is the root of dragon, Greek drakon, the fiery monster with the terrific side of sun-worship uppermost. A root like *drag* will always be found as darg. In Sanskrit *târkshya* is a dragon representing the sun-wheel, and tarka adds another element of Druidism, being a philosophical system. Thus in many directions are words that throw light on the hated priesthood as fire-worshipers, philosophers, and tyrants, justifying the tradition that they were the Magi of the West. Men of the classic epoch and the Middle Ages sought ever a direct transfer from east to west to explain such resemblances, but the analogies sprung from roots far back in the past, namely, the religious ideas of the same widely separated stock.

The pagan past of this singular bit of Europe may be divided tentatively into four epochs:

I   The primeval, represented by an aboriginal race of cave-dwellers completely in the stone age, cannibals, who used paint in place of clothes, and moon-worshipers.

II   The Ugrian, in which an unsubtantial form of architecture existed along with subterranean dwellings, grave mounds, cromlechs, stone circles, crannogs, and lake dwellings, and remains like Stonehenge in Britain, pointing to star and sun worship. Shamanism and a very crude Druidic type of religion obtained among people mainly hunters, fishers, and pirates. Slavery, polygamy, and occasional cannibalism existed along with burning as a punishment for offenses to the tribe.

III   The Firbolg-Danann, in which Ugrians from the mainland, much mixed with Kelts, reached the island by north and south Britain, bringing a higher type of Druidism and belief in the immortality of the soul. A wood and wattle architecture suited to a partly pastoral, partly agricultural, people, and the raths, lioses, duns, and 'Danes' forts' of earth, thickly scattered over Ireland, may be assigned to them.

Architecture for palaces and temples lacks the arch and is similar to remains in Yucatan. Remains in Ireland are the 'bee-hive' huts of the Aran islands, the type surviving under Christianity in the Church of Glendalough, oddly enough in connection with the round tower, which is also a pagan survival among Christian architects.

These art and song loving mixed tribes brought horses and war-chariots, beautiful objects in gold and silver, bronze weapons and tools of exquisite workmanship. The Bolg-men were those who left on the Continent the name of Belgium to their former seats in the rich country to the south of the Rhine. The men of the goddess Danann, pushed out by Keltic swarms of purer stock, or it may be by the Teutonic advance-guard, left the name Denmark to the country near the Baltic over against Britain. They had slavery, polygamy, burning as punishment, and burning as voluntary or forced honors to the gods. IV   Lastly we reach the epoch of Miledh (Latin miles, soldier), when the purest Keltic swarm, pushed without doubt by Roman conquests, crossed from south France and northern Spain into Munster, and with superior brains and weapons succeeeded for a time in subjugating the kindred but mixed tribes already amalgamated into the Irish folk. They formed a governing caste, and were in all probability at once in antagonism with the Druidic profession, whose grossness and tyranny could not please them. Iron as well as bronze was now in use, but bronze is more plentiful in the finds because it rusts less. Laws were made and intrusted to a special class, the newcomers being influenced by the example of the Romans before whom they fled. Probably they used some stone in their forts and houses, but the true arch and stone architecture of an elaborate sort were not general in Ireland till the Normans. The Milesians were more warlike than art-loving; probably the Firbolg-Dananns surpassed them in almost all branches of art. But they brought letters to Ireland, such as they were, though writing did not thrive under the adverse teachings of the Druids, who objected to it as weakening to the memory and allowing laymen to pry into their mysteries and loosen their hold on the ignorant. It was this caste, hating Druids and ready for a better law, that governed Ireland after a fashion when Christianity arrived.

The aristocracy was largely in favor of Christianity, which might curb the Druids and make subjects more content with their lot. Nevertheless people might be baptized in shoals and driven to chapel, but not lose consciousness of paganism. Few peasants like to put a spade into a so-called 'Dane's fort' for fear of the wrath of the 'good people' who dance there of moonlight nights. The fort, like the tradition, existed long before the eighth-century Danes appeared. On the 24th of June thousands of fires blaze from the hills in honor of – St John! They descend from the pagan festival of the summer solstice. Burning brands are seized by the fleetest boys and carried to arable fields; if the embers are alive when the field is reached, a good crop is assured. The Shetland fisherman thinks he will have bad luck if he cannot turn his boat with the sun. To make a vow he marches round a well in the same direction. In the Hebrides fire is carried in the right hand round homesteads and round young mothers to scare the fiends of darkness with the symbol of the sun. In Ireland it is bad luck to meet a hare; it is a demon that loves to sport in moonlight, is able by day to vanish into its form and start up like magic from the plowed field where no one saw it. It is bad luck to meet a red-haired woman. Why? Badb the war-witch used to meet heroes in the guise of a red-haired woman. Red of head was the unscrupulous Queen Macha, who beat in war certain princes, drove them into exile, followed and cajoled them with the charms of her person, and brought them back to toil at her fortress on the hill of Navan near Armagh. Popular prejudice against red hair points to a hated race that showed more than the usual number of red-haired men and women. The fishermen of the Claddagh, a suburb of Galway, led by a priest who has taken the place of a Druid, repeat yearly a ceremony at sea intended to bring success to the fisheries. The mayor of Limerick takes possession of the Shannon's mouth by throwing a spear into the sea. Hundreds of 'holy wells' shows by the rags or round pebbles thrown about or into them that nature worship is not dead; these propitiate nymphs, nixies, and gods of healing. Old querns in which grain was broken by hand, as well as spangles of gold for personal decoration, bear a cross on them. . . .

Claimed as Christian, they are really pagan, and symbolize the fertile sun, like the Sampo or wonder-mill of the Finns. A weird quern is that which the heroes of Kaleva rescued from the cavern where the foul hostess of Pohjola locked it. Its broken fragments were enough to bring back light, fertility, and wealth to Kaleva-land. In Ireland sun-worship lurks traditionally round the 'hag's beds,' Druid altars, or 'beds of Grainné,' was a maiden who had grian, the sun, in her name. During her elopement from Fion, son of Cumhal, she slept at the places marked by cromlechs with her lover Diarmuid, the Irish Adonis, who had a beauty-spot which deprived women of their reason. Mr Wakeman reports that in Fermanagh a peasant who is about to be evicted has been known to meet his persecutor with a fire of stones. He fills his hearth with stones, as if they were peats, and kneeling down prays that evil luck attend his landlord and family forever. Then he scatters the stones far and wide in fields and streams lest they be collected and a counter-curse be uttered over them. In the island Innismurray is an ancient stone fort with three 'beds,' or Cyclopean dwellings. On the largest are certain round stones. The person who wishes to curse an enemy makes the circuit of the bed nine times, reciting the prayers of the Catholic Church used at the 'stations' about a cathedral. He then turns the stones:

> They loosed their curse against the king,
>   They cursed him in his flesh and bones,
> And daily in their mystic ring
>   They turned the maledictive stones.[208]

If guilty, the enemy will die or go mad. Here again Christianity of no uncertain kind has been ineffectual to remove the paganism rooted in the people.

Thus we can learn more of the religion of our pagan ancestors from the Irish records than from any other source; for a conservatism which is a trait of the Irish as a whole – shall we say a trait derived from the Finno-Ugrian substratum? – caused them to treasure the echoes of heathenism in histories, annals, ballads, customs, and traditions handed down from generation to generation among the illiterate. The old gods have been degraded into ghosts or demons, or else humanized and connected with heroes and heroines like Cuchulinn, Queen Mab, Fion mac Cumhal, Grainné the beautiful, and Diarmuid the irresistible; or again baptized into saints and put in the calendar. Some are retired into mounds and Dane's forts; and others have gone to Tir na n'òg, the elysium beyond the setting sun, the Indian's happy hunting-ground.

Putting minor divisions aside, and keeping in mind the two grand divisions among the old Irish, namely, the imaginative, persistent, stolid, revengeful, superstitious Ugrian, and the quick-tempered but kind-hearted, generous, unsteady, quick-tongued, pleasure-loving Kelt, we can understand perhaps better than before the reason for anomalies in the national character. We may perceive in the individual Irishman, it may be, the contest still going on between Aryan and Ugrian, between Iran and Turan. Have we not here a clue to contradictions in Irish natures, their fiery threats and actual peaceableness, their turbulence and relative freedom from crime, their reputation for ferocity among those who do not know them, and the charm they exercise through kindliness and hospitality when treated with regard? It is not fanciful to trace here the singular mixture of sharpness and stupidity in the peasant, nor will it be found on reflection hazardous to assert that the Irish owe to the sturdy, plodding Ugrian element their ability to support suffering and their dogged love for the soil – traits hitherto given to the Kelt, although history is full of examples of the Keltic passion for roving about the world. It is an element that gives the counterpoise to the hot-headedness natural to those in whom Keltic blood is strong; it explains the caution of many Scots and Irishmen, for both are apt to talk with violence but to act with great circumspection. It may also supply the sad poetical side of the Irish. It accounts best of all for their essential law-abiding character when humanely treated, their freedom from crimes other than agrarian, to which the latest trials in London bear testimony. It may offer an explanation for the petty though vindictive nature of misdemeanors like moonlighting, houghing cattle, and destroying crops – traits which seem foreign to the Keltic genius. Moreover it affords a reason for the virulence of class hatred in Ireland and for anomalies like the siding of the Roman Catholic upper classes with the enemies of the nation, though the enemies are all that is most bigoted in contempt of their old faith. But it must also be obvious to those who have followed me through these two papers full of strange-looking names and, it is to be feared, wearisome arguments, that the key to the Irish nation fits more or less well the lock of many other peoples. The ancestors of every one of us have fought, conquered, and suffered in that endless quarrel between Aryan and Turanian which took place all over Europe and a large part of Asia, and which still goes on in the breast of every American who is descended from that primeval mixture of races.

17

DRUIDICAL CHANTS
PRESERVED IN THE
CHORUSES OF POPULAR
SONGS IN ENGLAND,
SCOTLAND, IRELAND
AND FRANCE

Charles Mackay

From *The Celtic Magazine*

The learned Godfrey Higgins informs us in his *Anacalypsis* that 'every word in every language has originally had a meaning, whether a nation has it by inheritance, by importation, or by composition.' He adds that it is evident if we can find out the original meaning of the words which stand for the names of objects, great discoveries may be expected. The Duke of Somerset, in our day, expresses the same truth more tersely when he says that 'every word in every language has its pedigree.'

All who are acquainted with the early lyrical literature of England and Scotland, preserved in the songs and ballads of the days immediately before and after Shakspere, must sometimes have asked themselves the meaning of such old choruses as 'Down, down, derry down,' 'With a fal, lal, la' 'Tooral, looral,' 'Hey, nonnie, nonnie,' and many others. These choruses are by no means obsolete, though not so frequently heard in our day as they used to be a hundred years ago. 'Down, down, derry down,' still flourishes in immortal youth in every village alehouse and beershop where the farm labourers and mechanics are accustomed to assemble. One of the greatest living authorities on the subject of English song and music – Mr William Chappell – the editor of the Popular Music of the Olden Time, is of opinion that these choruses, or burdens, were 'mere nonsense words that went glibly off the tongue.' He adds (vol. i., page 223), 'I am aware that "Hey down, down, derry down," has been said to be a modern version of "Ha, down, ir, deri dunno," the burden of an old song of the Druids, signifying, Come let us haste to the oaken grove (Jones, Welsh Bards, vol. i., page 128), but this I believe to be mere conjecture, and that it would now be impossible to prove that the Druids had such a song.' That Mr Chappell's opinion is not correct, will, I think, appear from the etymological proofs of the antiquity of this and other choruses afforded by the venerable language which was spoken throughout the British Isles by the aboriginal people for centuries before the Roman invasion, and which is not yet extinct in Wales, in Ireland, in the Isle of Man, and in the Highlands and Islands of Scotland.

Julius Caesar, the conqueror of Gaul and Britain, has left a description of the Druids and their religion, which is of the highest historical interest. That system and religion came originally from Assyria, Egypt, and Phoenicia, and spread over all Europe at a period long anterior to the building of Rome, or the existence of the Roman people. The Druids were known by name, but scarcely more than by name, to the Greeks, who deprived the appellation erroneously from *drus*, an oak, under the supposition that the Druids preferred to perform their religious rites under the shadows of oaken groves. The Greeks also called the Druids Saronides, from two Celtic words *sar* and *dhuine*, signifying 'excellent or superior men.' The Celtic meaning of the word 'Druid' is to enclose within a circle, and a Druid meant a prophet, a divine, a bard, a magician; one who was admitted to the mysteries of the inner circle. The Druidic religion was astronomical, and purely deistical, and rendered reverence to the sun, moon, and stars as the visible representatives of the otherwise unseen Divinity who created man and nature. 'The Druids used no images,' says the Reverend Doctor Alexander in his excellent little volume on the Island of Iona, published by the Religious Tract Society, 'to represent the object of their worship, nor did they meet in temples or buildings of any kind for the performance of their sacred rites. A circle of stones, generally of vast size, and surrounding an area of from twenty feet to thirty yards in diameter, constituted their sacred place; and in the centre of this stood the cromlech (crooked stone), or altar, which was an obelisk of immense size, or a large oblong flat stone, supported by pillars. These sacred circles were usually situated beside a river or stream, and under the shadow of a grove, an arrangement which was probably designed to inspire reverence and awe in the minds of the worshippers, or of those who looked from afar on their rites. Like others of the Gentile nations also, they had their 'high places,' which were large stones, or piles of stones, on the summits of hills; these were called carns (cairns), and were used in the worship of the deity under the symbol of the sun. In this repudiation of images and worshipping of God in the open air they resembled their neighbours and Germans, of whom Tacitus says that from the greatness of the heavenly bodies, they inferred that the gods could neither be inclosed within walls, nor assimilated to any human form; and he adds, that "they consecrated groves and forests, and called by the names of the gods that mysterious object which they behold by mental adoration alone."

'In what manner and with what rites the Druids worshipped their deity, there is now no means of ascertaining with minute accuracy. There is reason to believe that they attached importance to the ceremony of going thrice round their sacred circle, from east to west, following the course of the sun, by which it is supposed they intended to express their entire conformity to the will and order of the Supreme Being, and their desire that all might go well with them according to that order. It may be noticed, as an illustration of the tenacity of popular usages and religious rites, how they abide with a people, generation after generation in spite of changes of the most important kind, nay, after the very opinions out of whch they have risen have been repudiated; that even to the present day certain movements are considered of good omen when they follow the course of the sun, and that in some of the remote parts of the country the practice is still retained of seeking good fortune by going thrice round some supposed sacred object from east to west.'

But still more remarkable than the fact which Doctor Alexander has stated, is the vitality of the ancient Druidic chants, which still survive on the popular tongue for nearly two thousand years after their worship has disappeared, and after the meaning of these strange snatches and fragments of song has been all but irretrievably lost, and almost wholly unsuspected. Stonehenge, or the *Coir-mhor*, on Salisbury Plain, is the grandest remaining monument of the Druids in the British Isles. Everybody has heard of this mysterious relic, though few know that many other Druidical circles of minor importance are scattered over various parts of England, Scotland, and Ireland. In Scotland they are especially numerous. One but little known, and not mentioned by the Duke of Argyll in his book on the remarkable island of which he is the proprietor, is situated between the ruins of the cathedral of Iona and the sea shore, and is well worthy of a visit from the thousands of tourists who annually make the voyage round the noble Isle of Mull, on purpose to visit Iona and Staffa. There is another Druidic circle on the mainland of Mull, and a large and more remarkable one at Lochnell, near Oban, in Argyllshire, which promises to become as celebrated as Stonehenge itself, combining as it does not only the mystic circle, but a representation, clearly defined, of the mysterious serpent, the worship of which entered so largely into all the Oriental religions of remote antiquity. There are other circles in Lewis and the various islands of the Hebrides, and as far north as Orkney and Shetland. It was, as we learn from various authorities, the practice of the Druidical priests and bards to march in procession round the inner circle of their rude temples, chanting religious hymns in honour of the sunrise, the noon, or the sunset; hymns which have not been wholly lost to posterity, though posterity has failed to understand them, or imagined that their burdens – their sole relics – are but unmeaning words, invented for musical purposes alone, and divested of all intellectual signification.

The best known of these choruses is 'Down, down, derry down,' which may either be derived from the words *dun*, a hill; and *darag* or *darach*, an oak tree; or from *duine*, a man; and *doire*, a wood; and may either signify an invitation to proceed to the hill of the oak trees for the purposes of worship, or an invocation to the men of the woods to join in the Druidical march and chant, as the priests walked in procession from the interior of the stone circle to some neighbouring grove upon a down or hill. This chorus survives in many hundreds of English popular songs, but notably in the beautiful ballad 'The Three Ravens,' preserved in Melismata (1611):–

There were three ravens sat on a tree,
  Down-a-down! hey down, hey down.
They were as black as black might be,
  With a down!
Then one of them said to his mate,
Where shall we now our breakfast take,
  With a down, down, derry, derry, down!

A second well-known and vulgarised chorus is 'Tooral looral,' of which the most recent appearance is in a song which the world owes to the bad taste of the comic muse – that thinks it cannot be a muse until it blackens its face to look like a negro:–

  Once a maiden fair,
  She had ginger hair,
With her tooral looral lá, di, oh!
  And she fell in love
  Did this turtle dove
And her name was Dooral,
Hoopty Dooral! Tooral looral, oh my!

This vile trash contains two Celtic or Gaelic words, which are susceptible of two separate interpretations. *Tooral* may be derived from the Celtic *turail* – slow, sagacious, wary; and *Looral* from *luathrail* (pronounced *laurail*) quick, signifying a variation in the time of some musical composition to which the Druidical priests accommodated their footsteps in a religious procession, either to the grove of worship, or around the inner stone circle of the temple. It is also possible that the words are derived from *Tuath-reul* and *Luath-reul* (*t* silent in both instances), the first signifying 'North star,' and the second 'Swift star;' appropriate invocations in the mouths of a priesthood that studied all the motions of the heavenly bodies, and were the astrologers as the astronomers of the people.

A third chorus, which, thanks to the Elizabethan writers, has not been vulgarised, is that which occurs in John Chalkhill's 'Praise of a Countryman's Life,' quoted by Izaak Walton:–

Oh the sweet countentment
The countryman doth find.
High trolollie, lollie, lol: High trolollie, lee,

These words are easily resolvable into the Celtic; *Ai!* or *Aibhe!* Hail! or All Hail! *Trath* – pronounced *trah*, early, and *la*, day! or '*ai, trǎ là, là, là*' – 'Hail, early day! day,' a chorus which Moses and Aaron may have heard in the temples of Egypt, as the priests of Baal saluted the rising sun as he beamed upon the grateful world, and which was repeated by the Druids on the remote shores of Western Europe, in now desolate Stonehenge, and a thousand other circles, where the sun was worshipped as the emblem of the Divinity. The second portion of the chorus, 'High trolollie lee,' is in Celtic, *Ai, tra la, la, li*, which signifies, 'Hail early day! Hail bright day!' The repetition of the word *la* as often as it was required for the exigencies of the music, accounts for the chorus, in the form in which it has descended to modern times.

'Fal, lal, là' a chorus even more familiar to the readers of old songs, is from the same source. Lord Bathurst, afterwards Earl of Dorset, wrote, in 1665, the well-known ballad, commencing:–

To all you ladies now on land,
 We men at sea indite,
But first would have you understand
 How hard it is to write.
With a fal, lal, lá, and a fal lal, lá,
 And a fal, lal, lal, lal, là.

Moles saxiae stone circle, prope Helmstadium.
From The Celtic Druids *by Godfrey Higgins*

Fal is an abbreviation of *Failte!* welcome! and *là* as aleady noted signifies a day. The words should be properly written 'Failte! la! la!' The chorus appears in the 'Invitation to May,' by Thomas Morley, 1595:–

> Now is the month of Maying,
> When merry lads are playing,
>   Fal, la, lal!
> Each with his bonnie lass,
> Upon the greeny grass,
>   Fal, la, là!

The Celtic or Druidical interpretation of these syllables is, 'Welcome the day.'
'Fal, lero, loo,' appears as a chorus in a song by George Wither (1588–1667):–

> There was a lass – a fair one
>   As far as e'er was seen,
> She was indeed a rare one,
>   Another Sheba queen.
> But fool, as I then was,
>   I thought she loved me true,
> But now alas! she's left me,
>   Fal, lero, lero, loo.

Here *Failte*, as in the previous instance, means welcome; *lear* (corrupted into *lero*), the sea; and *luaidh* (the d silent), praise; the chorus of a song of praise to the sun when seen rising above the ocean.

The song of Sir Eglamour, in Mr Chappell's collection, has another variety of the Failte or Fal, la, of a much more composite character;–

> Sir Eglamour that valiant knight,
>   Fal, la, lanky down dilly!
> He took his sword and went to fight,
>   Fal, la, lanky down dilly!

In another song, called 'The Friar in the Well,' this chorus appears in a slightly different form:–

> Listen a while and I will tell
> Of a Friar that loved a bonnie lass well,
> Fal la! lál, lal, lal, lá! Fal la, langtre down dilly!

Lan is the Gaelic for full, and *dile* for rain. The one version has *lanky*, the other *langtre*, both of which are corruptions of the Celtic. The true reading is *Failte la, lan, ri, dun, dile*, which signifies 'Welcome to the full or complete day! let us go to the hill of rain.'

Hey, nonnie, nonnie. 'Such unmeaning burdens of songs,' says Nares in his Glossary, 'are common to ballads in most languages.' But this burden is not unmeaning, and signifies 'Hail to the noon.' *Noin* or noon, the ninth hour was so-called in the Celtic, because at midsummer in our northern latitudes it was the ninth hour after sunrise. With the Romans, in a more southern latitude, noon was the ninth hour after sunrise, at six in the morning, answering to our three o'clock of the afternoon. A song with this burden was sung in England in the days of Charles the Second:–

> I am a senseless thing, with a hey!
> Men call me a king, with a ho?
>   For my luxury and ease,
>   They brought me o'er the seas,
> With a heigh, nonnie, nonnie, nonnie, no!

Mr Chappell cites an ancient ballad which was sung to the tune of *Hie dildo, dil.* This also appears to be Druidical, and to be resolvable into *Ai! dile dun dile!* or 'Hail to the rain, to the rain upon the hill,' a thanksgiving for rain after a drought.

Trim go trix is a chorus that continued to be popular until the time of Charles the Second, when Tom D'Urfrey wrote a song entitled 'Under the Greenwood Tree,' of which he made it the burden. Another appears in Allan Ramsay's Tea-table Miscellany:–

> The Pope, that pagan full of pride,
>   He has us blinded long,
> For where the blind the blind does guide,
>   No wonder things go wrong.
> Like prince and king, he led the ring
>   Of all inquitie.
> Hey trix, trim go trix!
>   Under the greenwood tree.

In Gaelic *dream* or *dreim* signifies a family, a tribe, the people, a procession; and *qu tric*, frequently, often, so that these words represent a frequent procession of the people to the hill of worship under the greenwood tree.

In Motherwell's 'Ancient and Modern Minstrelsy,' the ballad of Hynd Horn contains a Celtic chorus repeated in every stanza:–

> Near Edinburgh was a young child born
>   With a Hey lilli lu, and a how lo lan!
> And his name it was called young Hynd Horn,
>   And the birk and the broom bloom bounie.

Here the words are corruptions of *aidhe* (Hail); *li*, light or colour; *lu*, small; *ath*, again; *lo*, day-light; *lan*, full; and may be rendered 'Hail to the faint or small light of the dawn'; and 'again the full light of the day' (after the sun had risen).

In the Nursery Rhymes of England, edited by Mr Halliwell for the Percy Society, 1842, appears the quatrain;–

Hey dorolot, dorolot,
  Hey dorolay, doralay,
Hey my bonnie boat – bonnie boat,
  Hey drag away – drag away.

The two first lines of this jingle appear to be a remnant of a Druidical chant, and to resolve themselves into,

Aidhe, doire luchd – doire luchd,
Aidhe doire leigh, doire leigh.

Aidhe, an interjection, is pronounced Hie; *doire*, is trees or woods; *luchd*, people; and *leigh*, healing; and also a physician, whence the old English word for a doctor, a leech, so that the couplet means

Hey to the wood people! to the woods people!
Hey to the woods for healing, to the woods for healing.

If this translation be correct, the chorus would seem to have been sung when the Druids went in search of the sacred mistletoe, which they called the 'heal all,' or universal remedy.

There is an old Christmas carol which commences –

Nowell! Nowell! Nowell!
This is the salutation of the Angel Gabriel.

Mr Halliwell, in his Archaic Dictionary, says 'Nowell was a cry of joy, properly at Christmas, of joy for the birth of the Saviour.' A political song in a manuscript of the time of King Henry the Sixth, concludes –

Let us all sing nowelle.
Nowelle, nowelle, nowelle, nowelle,
And Christ save merry England and spede it well.

The modern Gaelic and Celtic for Christmas is *Nollaig* – a corruption of the ancient Druidical name for holiday – from *noamh*, holy, and *la*, day, whence 'Naola!' the burden of a Druidical hymn, announcing the fact that a day of religious rejoicing had arrived for the people.

A very remarkable example of the vitality of these Druidic chants is afforded by the well-known political song of 'Lilli Burlero,' of which Lord Macaulay gives the following account of his History of England:–

Thomas Wharton, who, in the last Parliament had represented Buckinghamshire, and who was already conspicuous both as a libertine and as a Whig, had written a satirical ballad on the administration of Tyrconnel. In his little poem an Irishman congratulates a brother Irishman in a barbarous jargon on the approaching triumph of Popery and of the Milesian race. The Protestant heir will be excluded. The Protestant officers will be broken. The great charter and the praters who appeal to it will be hanged in one rope. The good Talbot will shower commissions on his countrymen, and will cut the throats of the English. These verses, which were in no respect above the ordinary standard of street poetry had for burden some gibberish which was said to have been used as a watchword by the insurgents of Ulster in 1641. The verses and the tune caught the fancy of the nation. From one end of England to the other all classes were constantly singing this idle rhyme. It was especially the delight of the English army. More than seventy years after the Revolution a great writer delineated with exquisite skill a veteran who had fought at the Boyne and at Namur. One of the characteristics of the good old soldier is his trick of whistling Lilliburllero. Wharton afterwards boasted that he had sung a king out of three kingdoms. But, in truth, the success of Lilliburllero was the effect and not the cause of that excited state of public feeling which produced the Revolution.

The mysterious syllables which Lord Macaulay asserted to be gibberish, and which in this corrupt form were enough to puzzle a Celtic scholar, and more than enough to puzzle Lord Macaulay, who, like the still more ignorant Doctor Samuel Johnson, knew nothing of the venerable language of the first inhabitants of the British Isles, and of all Western Europe, resolve themselves into *Li! Li Beur! Lear-a! Buille na la*, which signify, 'Light! Light! on the sea, beyond the promontory! 'Tis the stroke (or dawn) of the day!' Like all the choruses previously cited, these words are part of a hymn to the sun, and entirely astronomical and Druidical.

The syllables *Fol de rol* which still occur in many of the vulgarest songs of the English lower classes, and which were formerly much more commonly employed than they are now, are a corruption of *Failte reul!* or welcome to the star! *Fal de ral* is another form of the corruption which the Celtic original has undergone.

The French, a more Celtic people than the English, have preserved many of the Druidical chants. In Beranger's song 'Le Scandale' occurs one of them, which is as remarkable for its Druidic appositeness as any of the English choruses already cited:–

Aux drames du jour,
  Laissons la morale.
Sans vivre à la cour
  J'aime le scandale;
    Bon!
Le farira dondaine
  Gai!
La farira dondé.

These words resolve themselves into the Gaelic *La! fair! aire! dun teine!* 'Day! sunrise! watch it on the hill of fire (the sacred fire)'; and *La! fair! aire! dun De!* 'Day! sunrise! watch it on the hill of God.'

In the Recueil de Chanson's Choisies (La Haye, 1723, vol. i., page 155), there is a song called Danse Ronde, commencing *L'autre jour, pres d'Annette* of which the burden is *Lurelu La rela!* These syllables seem to be resolvable into the Celtic:– *Luadh reul! Luadh!* (Praise to the star! Praise!); or *Luath reul Luath* (the swift star, swift!); and *La! reul! La!* (the day! the star! the day!).

There is a song of Beranger's of which the chorus is *Tra, la trala, tra la la,* already explained, followed by the words – *C'est le diabh er falbala.* Here *falbala* is a corruption of the Celtic *falbh la!* 'Farewell to the day,' a hymn sung at sunset instead of at sunrise.

Beranger has another song entitled 'Le Jour des Morts,' which has a Druidical chorus:–

> Amis, entendez les cloches
> Qui par leurs sons gemissants
> Nous font des bruyans reproches
> Sur nos rires indecents,
> Il est des ames en peine,
> Dit le pretre interessé.
> C'est le jour des morts, mirliton, mirlitaine.
> Requiscant in pace!

Mir in Celtic signifies rage or fuss; *tonn* or *thonn*, a wave; *toinn*, waves; and *tein*, fire; whence those apparently unmeaning syllables may be rendered – 'the fury of the waves, the fury of the fire.'

Tira lira la. This is a frequent chorus in French songs, and is composed of the Gaelic words *tiorail*, genial, mild, warm; *iorrach*, quiet, peaceable; and *là*, day; and was possibly a Druidical chant, after the rising of the sun, resolving itself into *Tiorail-iorra la*, warm peaceful day!

Rumbelow was the chorus or burden of many ancient songs, both English and Scotch. After the Battle of Bannockburn, says Fabyan, a citizen of London, who wrote the 'Chronicles of England,' 'the Scottes inflamed with pride, made this rhyme as followeth in derision of the English':–

> Maydens of Englande, sore may ye mourne
> For your lemans ye've lost at Bannockisburne,
>   With heve a lowe!
> What weeneth the Kyng of Englande,
> So soone to have won Scotlande,
>   With rumbylowe!

In 'Peebles to the Play' the word occurs –

> With heigh and howe, and rumbelowe,
> The young folks were full bauld.

There is an old English sea song of which the burden is 'with a rumbelowe.' In one more modern, in Deuteromelia 1609, the word dance the rumbelow is translated –

> Shall we go dance to round, around,
>> Shall we go dance the round.

Greek – *Rhombos, Rhembo*, to spin or turn round.

The word is apparently another remnant of the old Druidical chants sung by the priests when they walked in procession round their sacred circles of Stonehenge and others, and clearly traceable to the Gaelic – *Riomball*, a circle; *riomballach*, circuitous; *riomballachd*, circularity.

The pervasion of so many of these once sacred chants ot the service of the street ballad, suggests the trite remark of Hamlet to Horatio:-

> To what base uses we may come at last! . . .
> Imperial Caesar, dead and turned to clay,
>> May stop a hole to keep the winds away.

The hymns once sung by thousands of deep-voiced priests marching in solemn procession from their mystic shrines to salute with music and song, and reverential homage, the rising of the glorious orb which cheers and fertilises the world, the gift as well as the emblem of Almighty Power and Almighty Love, have wholly departed from the recollection of man, and their poor and dishonoured relics are spoken of by scholars and philosophers, as trash, gibberish, nonsense, and an idle farrago of sounds, of no more philological value than the lowing of cattle or the bleating of sheep. But I trust that all attentive readers of the foregoing pages will look upon the old choruses – so sadly perverted in the destructive progress of time, that demolishes languages as well as empires and systems of religious belief – with something of the respect due to their immense antiquity, and their once sacred functions in a form of worship, which, whatever were its demerits as compared with the purer religion that has taken its place, had at least the merit of inculcating the most exalted ideas of the Power, the Love, and the Wisdom of the Great Creator.

18

DRUIDICAL MAGIC

James Bonwick

From *Irish Druids and Old Irish Religions*

As to magical arts, exercised by Druids and Druidesses, the ancient Irish MSS. are full of stories about them. Joyce has said, 'The Gaelic word for Druidical is almost always applied where we should use the word magical – to spells, incantations, metamorphoses, etc.' Not even China at the present day is more given to charms and spells than was Ireland of old. Constant application of Druidic arts upon the individual must have given a sadness and terror to life, continuing long after the Druid had been supplanted.

It was a comfort to know that magician could be pitted against magician, and that though one might turn a person into a swan or horse, another could turn him back again.

Yet, the chewing of one's thumb was sometimes as effectual a disenchanter as the elevation or marking of the cross in subsequent centuries. Thus, when Fionn was once invited to take a seat beside a fair lady on her way to a palace, he, having some suspicion, put his thumb between his teeth, and she immediately changed into an ugly old hag with evil in her heart. That was a simple mode of detection, but may have been efficacious only in the case of such a hero as Fionn. Certainly, many a bad spirit would be expelled, in a rising quarrel, if one party were wise enough to put his thumb between his teeth.

Charm-mongers, who could take off a spell, must have been popular characters, and as useful as wart-removers. It is a pity, however, that the sacred salmon which used to frequent the Boyne is missing now, when examinations are so necessary, as he or she who bit a piece forgot nothing ever after. Balar, the Fomorian King, was a good-natured fellow, for, finding that a glance from his right eye caused death to a subject, he kept that eye constantly closed.

One way of calling spirits from the deep, to do one's will, was to go to sleep with the palms of both hands upon the cheek. The magic cauldron was not in such requirement as with the Welsh. But it was a Druidic trick to take an idol to bed, lay the hands to the face, and discover the secret of a riddle in dreams. Another trick reminds one of the skill of modern spiritualistic mediums, who could discover the history of a man by a piece of his coat; for, Cormac read the whole life of a dog from the skull.

Healing powers were magical. Our forefathers fancied that a part of enjoyment in heaven was fighting by day and feasting at night, the head cut off in daylight conflict resuming its position when the evening table was spread. The rival forces of Fomorians and Danaans had Druids, whose special work was to heal the wounded at night, so as to be ready for the next morning's battle.

In the *Story of Deirdri* it is written, 'As Conor saw this, he went to Cathbad the Druid, and said to him, "Go, Cathbad, unto the sons of Usnach, and play Druidism upon them."' This was done. 'He had recourse to his intelligence and art to restrain the children of Usnach, so that he laid them under enchantment, that is, by putting around them a viscid sea of whelming waves.'

Nothing was more common than the rising of Druidic fogs. It would be easier to do that in Ireland or Scotland than in Australia. The *Story of Cu* speaks of a King Briudin who 'made a black fog of Druidism' by his *draoid-deacht*, or magic. Druidic winds were blasting, as they came from the East. The *Children of Lir* were made to wander on the Irish Sea till the land became Christian.

A wonderful story in an old MS. respecting Diarmuid is connected with the threatened divorce of the lovely Mughain, as no prince had appeared to her husband the King. 'On this,' says the chronicler, 'the Queen went to Finnen, a Magus (Druid) of Baal or Belus, and to Easbad, named Aedha, son of Beg, and told them she was barren. The Reataire (chief Druids) then consecrated some water, of which she drank, and conceived; and the produce of her womb was a white lamb. "Woe is me!" said Mugain, "to bring forth a four-footed beast." "Not so," replied Finnen, "for your womb is thereby sanctified, and the lamb must be sacrificed as your first-born." The priests blessed the water for her, she drank, and conceived. Say the priests, "You shall now bring forth a son, and he shall be King over Ireland." Then Finnen and Easbad Aedha blessed the Queen and the seed of her loins, and giving her more consecrated water, she drank of it, and called his name *Aedh Slaines*, because he was saved from the sacrifice.'

Well might Vallencey exclaim, 'The whole of this story is strong of Chaldaean Paganism, and could not have been invented by any Christian monks whatever.'

Cuchulainn of Ulster was much given to magic. He caught birds by it. He left his wife to be with a lady in fairy-land. Caught by spells, he was brought back home. He drank the draught of forgetfulness that he might not remember fairy-land, and she drank to forget her jealousy. All this is in *Leabhar na-h-Uidhré*.

When the Danaans raised a storm to drive off the invading hosts of Milesians, this was the spell used by Milesius, as told in the *Book of Invasions*: – 'I pray that they reach the land of Erinn, these who are riding upon the great, productive, vast sea that there may be a King for us in Tara, – that noble Erinn be a home for the ships and boats of the son of Milesius.'

By the 14th Canon of the Synod of Armagh, as asserted for the year 448, a penance was exacted for any soothsaying, or the foretelling of future events by an inspection of animals' entrails, as was the practice with the Druids. It is curious to see how this magic was, by the early writers, associated with Simon

Magus; so much so, that as Rhys observes, 'The Goidelic Druids appear at times under the name of the School of Simon Druid.'

Fionn was once coursing with his dog Bran, when the hare suddenly turned into a lady weeping for the loss of her ring in the lake. Like a gallant, the hero dived down and got it; but all he had for his trouble was to be turned by her into a white-haired old man. On another occasion he was changed into a grey fawn. But Fionn endured the metamorphoses of twenty years as a hog, one hundred a stag, one hundred an eagle, and thirty a fish, besides living one hundred as a man. The heroine Caer had to be alternate years a swan and a woman.

The *Kilkenny Transactions* refer to one Liban, transformed for three hundred years as a fish, or, rather a mermaid, with her lap-dog in the shape of an otter after her. Bevan, however, caught her in a net, had her baptized, and then she died. In the *Fate of the Children of Lir*, we read of Aoife, second wife of Lir, jealous of her husband's children by his first mate, turning them into four swans till her spell could be broken. This happened under the Tuath rule, and lasted nine hundred years. They are reported to have said, 'Thou shalt fall in revenge for it, for thy power for our destruction is not greater than the Druidic power of our friends to avenge it upon thee.' However, having musical qualities, they enjoyed themselves in chanting every night. At last they heard the bell of St Patrick. This broke the spell. They sang to the High King of heaven, revealed their name, and cried out, 'Come to baptize us, O cleric, for our death is near.'

An odd story of the Druid Mananan is preserved in the *Ossian Transactions*. It concerned a magical branch, bearing nine apples of gold. They who shook the tree were lulled to sleep by music, forgetting want or sorrow.

Through that, Cormac, grandson of Conn of the hundred fights, lost his wife Eithne, son Cairbre, and daughter Ailbhe. At the end of a year's search, and passing through a dark, magical mist, he came to a hut, where a youth gave him a pork supper. The entertainer proved to be Mananan. The story runs, 'After this Mananan came to him in his proper shape, and said thus: "I it was who bore these three away from thee; I it was who gave thee that branch, and it was in order to brign thee to this house. It was I that worked magic upon you, so that you might be with me tonight in friendship."' It may be doubted if this satisfied King Cormac.

A chessboard often served the purpose of divination. The laying on of hands has been from remote antiquity an effectual mode for the transmission of a charm. But a Magic Wand or Rod, in proper hands, has been the approved method of transformation, or any other miraculous interposition. Here is one Wand story relative to the romance of Grainne and Diarmuid:– 'Then came the Reachtaire again, having a Magic Wand of sorcery, and struck his son with that wand, so that he made of him a cropped pig, having neither ear nor tail, and he said, "I conjure thee that thou have the same length of life as Diarmuid O'Duibhne, and that it be by thee that he shall fall at last."'

This was the boar that killed, not the Syrian Adonis, but a similar sun-deity, Diarmuid. When Fionn, the disappointed husband, in pursuit of the runaway, found the abductor dying, he was entreated by the beautiful solar hero to save him. 'How can I do it?' asked the half-repentant Fionn. 'Easily,' said the wounded one; 'for when thou didst get the noble, precious gift of divining at the Boinn, it was given thee that to whomsoever thou shouldst give a drink from the palms of thy hands, he should after that be young and sound from every sickness.' Unhappily, Fionn was so long debating with himself as to this gift to his enemy that, when he walked towards him with the water, life had departed from the boar-stricken Irish Adonis.

Dr W.R. Sullivan has a translation of the *Fair of Carman*, concerning three magicians and their mother from Athens:–

> By charms, and spells, and incantations, the mother blighted every place, and it was through magical devastation and dishonesty that the men dealt out destruction. They came to Erin to bring evil upon the Tuatha de Danann, by blighting the fertility of this isle. The Tuatha were angry at this; and they sent against them Ali, the son of Allamh, on the part of their poets, and Credenbel on the part of their satirists, and Lug Baeban, i.e. the son of Cacher, on the part of their Druids, and Becuille on the part of the witches, to pronounce incantations against them. And these never parted from them until they forced the three men over the sea, and they left a pledge behind them, i.e. Carman, their mother, that they would never return to Erin.

A counter-charm is given in the *Senchus Mor*. When the Druids sought to poison St Patrick, the latter wrote over the liquor:–

> Tubu fis fri ibu, fis ibu anfis,
> Fris bru uatha, ibu lithu, Christi Jesus.

He left it on record that whoever pronounced these words over poison or liquor should receive no injury from it. It might be useful with Irish whisky; only the translator adds that the words of the charm, like most of the charms of the Middle Ages, appear to have had no meaning.

Spiritualism, in all is forms, appears to have been practised by the Irish and Scotch Druids. Dr Armstrong's *Gaelic Dictionary* has an account of the Divination of the Toghairm, once a noted superstition among the Gaels, and evidently derived from Druid-serving ancestors. The so-called prophet 'was wrapped in the warm, smoking robe of a newly slain ox or cow, and laid at full length in the wildest recess of some lonely waterfall. The question was then put to him, and the oracle was left in solitude to consider it.' The steaming body cultivated the frenzy for a reply, although 'it was firmly believed to have been communicated by invisible beings.'

Similar traditions are related by Kennedy, in *Fictions of the Irish Celts*. One of the tales is of Sculloge, who spent his father's gold. While out hunting he saw an old man betting his left hand against his right. At once he played with him for sixpence, but won of the ancient Druid a hundred guineas. The next game won, the old fellow was made to rebuild the Irishman's mill. Another victory

Cheese wring near Liskeard, Cornwall.
From The Celtic Druids *by Godfrey Higgins*

brought him as wife a princess from the far country. But Sabina, when married, besought him to have no more to do with old Lassa Buaicht of the glen.

Things went on well a good while, till the man wanted more gold, and he ventured upon a game. Losing, he was directed to bring the old Druid the Sword of Light. Sabina helped her husband to a Druidic horse, that carried him to her father's castle. There he learned it was held by another brother, also a Druid, in an enchanted place. With a black steed he leaped the wall, but was driven out by the magic sword. At last, through Fiach the Druid, the sword was given to Lassa Buaicht. The cry came, 'Take your Sword of Light, and off with his head.' Then the un-spelled wife reappeared, and the couple were happy ever after.

Conn of the Hundred Battles is often mentioned in connection with Druids. One of the Irish MSS. thus introduces the Magical Stone of Tara: 'One evening Conn repaired at sunrise to the battlements of the Ri Raith or Royal fortress at Tara, accompanied by his three Druids, Mael, Bloc, and Bluicné, and his three poets, Ethain, Corb, and Cesare; for he was accustomed every day to repair to this place with the same company, for the purpose of watching the firmament, that no hostile aerial beings should descend upon Erin unknown to him. While standing in the usual place this morning, Conn happened to tread on a stone, and immediately the stone shrieked under his feet so as to be heard all over Tara, and throughout all Bregia or East Meath. Conn then asked his Druids why the stone had shrieked, what its name was, and what it said. The Druids took fifty-three days to consider, and returned the following answer: – "Fal is the name of the stone; it came from Inis Fal, or the Island of Fal. It has shrieked under your royal feet, and the number of the shrieks, which the stone has given forth, is the number of Kings that will succeed you."'

At the Battle of Magh Tuireadh with the Fomorians, it is said that the chief men of the Tuatha de Danann 'called their smiths, their brass-workers, their sorcerers, their Druids, their poets, etc.' The Druids were engaged putting the wounded in a bath of herbs, and then returning them whole to the battle ranks.

Nash, who showed much scepticism respecting Druids in Britain, wrote:– 'In the Irish tales, on the contrary, the magician under the name of Draoi and Drudh, magician or Druid, *Draioideacht, Druidheat,* magic plays a considerable part.' The Cabiri play a great part according to some authors; one speaks of the 'magic of Samhan, that is to say, Cabur.' A charm against evil spirits, found at Poitiers, is half Gallic, half Latin. Professor Lottner saw that 'the Gallic words were identical with expressions still used in Irish.'

We are told of a rebel chief who was helped by a Druid against the King of Munster, to plague the Irish in the south-west by magically drying up all the water. The King succeeded in finding another Druid who brought forth an abundant supply. He did but cast his javelin, and a powerful spring burst forth at the spot where the weapon fell. Dill, the Druidical grandfather of another King of Munster, had a magical black horse, which won at every race.

Elsewhere is a chapter on the Tuatha de Danaans, concerning whom are so many stories of Druids. Attention is drawn by Rhys to 'the tendency of higher races to ascribe magical powers to lower ones; or, rather, to the conquered.'

A Druid's counsel was sometimes of service. A certain dwarf magician of Erregal, Co. Derry, had done a deal of mischief before he could be caught, killed, and buried. It was not long before he rose from the dead, and resumed his cruelties. Once more slain, he managed to appear again at his work. A Druid advised Finn Mac Cumhail to bury the fellow the next time head downward, which effectually stopped his magic and his resurrection powers.

Fintain was another hero of antiquity. When the Deluge occurred, he managed by Druidic arts to escape. Subsequently, through the ages, he manifested himself in various forms. This was, to O'Flaherty, an evidence that Irish Druids believed in the doctrine of metempsychosis. Fintain's grave is still to be recognized, though he has made no appearance on earth since the days of King Dermot.

It is not safe to run counter to the Druids. When King Cormac turned against the Craft, Maelgenn incited the Siabhradh, an evil spirit, to take revenge. By turning himself into a salmon, he succeeded in choking the sovereign with one of his bones. It was Fraechan, Druid of King Diarmaid, who made the wonderful Airbhi Druadh, or Druidical charm, that caused the death of three thousand warriors.

A King was once plagued by a lot of birds wherever he went. He inquired of his Druid Becnia as to the place they came from. The answer was, 'From the East.' Then came the order – 'Bring me a tree from every wood in Ireland.' This was to get the right material to serve as a charm. Tree after tree failed to be of use. Only that from the wood of Frosmuine produced what was required for a charm. Upon the dichetal, or incantation, being uttered, the birds visited the King no more.

In the *Book of Lecan* is the story of a man who underwent some remarkable transformations. He was for 300 years a deer, for 300 a wild boar, for 300 a bird, and for the like age a salmon. In the latter state he was caught, and partly eaten by the Queen. The effect of this repast was the birth of Tuan Mac Coireall, who told the story of the antediluvian colonization of Ireland. One Druid, Trosdane, had a bath of the milk of thirty white-faced cows, which rendered his body invulnerable to poisoned arrows in battle.

A Druid once said to Dathi, 'I have consulted the clouds of the man of Erin, and found that thou wilt soon return to Tara, and wilt invite all the provincial Kings and chiefs of Erin to the great feast of Tara, and there thou shalt decide with them upon making an expedition into Alba, Britain, and France, following the conquering footsteps of thy great-uncle Niall.' He succeeded in Alba, but died in Gaul. A brother of his became a convert to St Patrick.

Grainne, the heroine of an elopement with the beautiful hero Diarmuid, or Dermot, fell into her trouble through a Druid named Daire Duanach MacMorna. She was the daughter of King Cormac, whose grave is still shown at Tara, but she was betrothed to the aged, gigantic sovereign Fionn the Fenian. At the banquet in honour of the alliance, the Druid told the lady the names and qualities of the chiefs assembled, particularly mentioning the graceful Diarmuid. She was smitten by his charms, particularly a love-mark on his shoulder, and readily agreed to break her promised vows in order to share his company. When she fled with him, Fionn and his son pursued the couple who were aided in their flight by another Druid named Diorraing, styled a skilful man of science.

A fine poem – *The Fate of the Son of Usnach* – relates the trials of Deirdri the Fair. Dr Keating has this version: 'Caffa the Druid foreboded and prophesied for the daughter (Deirdri, just born), that numerous mischiefs and losses would happen the Province (Ulster) on her account. Upon hearing this, the nobles proposed to put her to death forthwith. "Let it not be done so," cried Conor (King), "but I will take her with me, and send her to be reared, that she may become my own wife."' It was in her close retreat that she was seen and loved by Naisi, the son of Usnach, and this brought on a fearful war between Ulster and Alba.

The *Book of Leinster* has the story of one that loved the Queen, who returned the compliment, but was watched too well to meet with him. He, however, and his foster-brother, were turned, by a Druidic spell, into two beautiful birds, and so gained an entrance to the lady's bower, making their escape again by a bird transformation. The King had some suspicion, and asked his Druid to find out the secret. The nextr time the birds flew, the King had his watch; and, as soon as they resumed their human appearance, he set upon them and killed both.

The *Book of Leinster* records several cases of Druids taking opposite sides in battle. It was Greek meeting Greek. The northern Druids plagued the southern men by drying up the wells; but Mog Ruth, of the South, drove a silver tube into the ground, and a spring burst forth. Ciothrue made a fire, and said a charm with his mountain-ash stick, when a black cloud sent down a shower of blood. Nothing daunted, the other Druid, Mog Ruth, transformed three noisy northern Druids into stones.

Spiritualism, as appears by the *Banquet of Dun na n-Gedh*, was used thus:– 'This is the way it is to be done. The poet chews a piece of the flesh of a red pig, or of a dog or cat, and brings it afterwards on a flag behind the door, and chants an incantation upon it, and offers it to idol gods; and his idol gods are brought to him, but he finds them not on the morrow. And he pronounces incantations on his two palms; and his idol gods are also brought to him, in order that his sleep may not be interrupted. And he lays his two palms on his two cheeks, and thus falls asleep. And he is watched in order that no one may disturb or interrupt him, until everything about which he is engaged is revealed to him, which may be a minute, or two, or three, or as long as the ceremony requires – one palm over the other across his cheeks.'

The author of *The Golden Bough*, J.G. Frazer, judiciously reminds us that 'the superstitious beliefs and practices, which have been handed down by word of mouth, are generally of a far more archaic type than the religions depicted in the most ancient literature of the Aryan race.' A careful reading of the chapter on the 'Superstitions of the Irish' would be convincing on that point.

Among ancient superstitions of the Irish there was some relation to the Sacred Cow, reminding one of India, or even of the Egyptian worship of Apis. The *Ossianic Transactions* refer to this peculiarity.

There was the celebrated *Glas Gaibhne*, or Grey Cow of the Smith of the magical Tuaths. This serviceable animal supplied a large family and a host of servants. The Fomorians envied the possessor, and their leader stole her. The captive continued her beneficent gifts for many generations. Her ancient camps are still remembered by the peasantry. Another story is of King Diarmuid Mac Cearbhail, half a Druid and half a Christian, who killed his son for destroying a Sacred Cow. But Owen Connelan has a translation of the *Proceedings of the Great Bardic Institute*, which contains the narrative of a cow, which supplied at Tuaim-Daghualan the daily wants of nine score nuns; these ladies must have been Druidesses, the word *Caillach* meaning equally nuns and Druidesses. As W. Hackett remarks, 'The probability is that they were pagan Druidesses, and that the cows were living idols like Apis, or in some sense considered sacred animals.'

One points out the usefulness of the Irish Druids in a day when enchantments prevailed. Etain, wife of Eochaid, was carried off by Mider through the roof, and two swans were seen in the air above Tara, joined together by a golden yoke. However, the husband managed to recover his stolen property by the aid of the mighty spell of his Druid.

PART THREE

THE RECOVERY: DRUIDRY IN THE TWENTIETH CENTURY

N our own time Druidry has become one of the fastest growing spiritual movements in the world. The reasons for this are not hard to discern. There are many starry-eyed, born-again Celts who are often shocked to learn that the world in which the original Celtic peoples lived was frequently both bloody and barbarous. Not without culture, it is true, nor without love and valour and comradeship and the many other values that have been recorded in the tales and legends left behind by the Celtic story-tellers. But it was also savage, careless of life and property, and possessed of just as many 'bully boys' as there were artists, warriors and noble kings.

In much the same way, those who call themselves by the name 'Druid' today often seem unaware that the heritage into which they have come is largely the invention of antiquarian romantics from the seventeenth to the nineteenth centuries and that what little we do know of the Druids is anything but cosy or comfortable, any more than it is necessarily enlightened, beautiful or inspired. Our heritage is frequently bloody and barbarous, and as downright unpleasant as much of twentieth-century life. In short, it is very human!

The humanity – as opposed to humanism – of the new Druid orders is self-evident. They are concerned with ecology, with establishing a harmonious relationship with the natural world and with honouring the seasons and patterns of life at every level and in whatever form, winged, furred, clawed or scaled. They are also concerned with discovering the truth about their origins, hard though that may often prove, and with establishing a lineage that reflects as faithfully as possible the original practices and beliefs of the Druids. What is more, they are, in general, able to see past the historical framework to the spiritual reality to adapt that reality to fit the century in which we live. Of their history, a less clear picture emerges.

Ross Nichols, Chosen Chief of the Order of Bards, Ovates and Druids, which he established after a split with the Ancient Order in 1964, put the case for revival Druidry and its lineage in a letter to *The Times* in 1965. He was responding to a somewhat peevish attack on the proliferation of various Druid orders by a professor of archaeology at the University of London.

This Order, using some ancient sites, aims to recall to the natural seasonal pieties a generation by whom they are particulaly needed, since mankind has largely lost its way in technological know-how. One of the best ways to stir people into re-thinking their attitudes is by demonstration in ritual. Bardic and Druidic observances, whether more or less open, have been widespread in comparatively recent times. The modern form of Druidry may have been shaped about and since 1717, but delegates in that year came from circles in York, Oxford, Wales, Cornwall, the Isle of Man, Anglesey, Scotland, Ireland and Brittany, as well as London; so that in all those places it had already a certain degree of vigour. Evidently the Universal Bond then declared under the leadership of John Toland sprang from widespread and old roots. Within the Bond, Druids and Bards are of various persuasions, since any group of qualified senior members has always had the recognized right to form a separate working. In 1964 the late Chosen Chief, Robert MacGregor Reid, established a group separate from what appeared to be the correct succession, that of 'Smith of Clapham'; it was MacGregor Reid's Order which was later recognized as being the main body. History repeats itself with the establishment in correct form of the Order of Bards, Ovates and Druids in September 1964.

A brief glance at the genealogy of modern Druidry shows a tangled web of decent and cross-tracking, which is difficult, if not impossible, to entangle. Various recent historians of Druidry, including Ross Nichols and Michel Raoult, have attempted to sort out the origins and connections that exist between the various orders.

What becomes increasingly clear is that there is no single Order that one can name the 'first' of the new Druids. John Toland has precedence in all of the current works dedicated to the origins of the neo-Druidic movement, despite the fact that no simple chronology has as yet been satisfactorily worked out and most dates are hesitant and suspect. What follows is, therefore, offered with extreme caution; it is likely to be inaccurate as accurate, and other scholars would doubtless produce a completely different list. I am grateful to the work of the above-named writers for much of the information included here, which I have only slightly modified from my own researchers (see in particular "The Revival of Druids on the European Continent, in France and in Brittany' by Michel Raoult in the forthcoming collection, *The Druid Renaissance*, edited by Philip Carr-Gomm.

A Partial List of Druid Orders and Affiliates

1717   An Druidh Uileach Braithreachas (The Druid Circle of the Universal Bond) founded by John Toland along with representatives of Druid groves from London, York, Oxford, Wales, Cornwall, Isle of Man, Anglesea, Scotland, Ireland and Brittany.

1781   Ancient Order of Druids founded in London by Henry Hurle.

1792   The first Druidic/Bardic gorsedd established by Iolo Morgannwg (Edward Williams). This leads to the founding of Bardic/Druidic Eistedfoddau in Wales.

1833   The United Ancient Order of Druids founded after a split with the original Ancient Order.

1838   The Breton scholar and antiquarian Hersant de la Villemarque initiated at Anglesa Gorsedd. He establishes a Druidic/Bardic grove in Brittany in 1855, named Breuriez Drarzad Bried (The Fraternity of Bards of Brittany).

1869   Nicholas Drummer, an American member of the United Ancient Order, founds a lodge in Paris. Afterwards, lodges are established in Sweden, Norway, Denmark, Germany, Switzerland, Australia, Tasmania and New Zealand.

1885   The Druidic and National Church founded in Paris by Henry Lizeray.

1908	The international Grand Lodge of Druidism is founded, combining elements of both the Ancient Order and the United Ancient Order.
1908	Winston Churchill is initiated into the Albion Lodge.
1928	Cornish gorsedd founded.
1933	Bardic College founded in Gaul by Phileas Lebesque under the aegis of the Welsh and Breton gorsedds.
1936	The Kredenn Giltiek (Celtic Belief) founded in Brittany.
1942	A second Druidic College of Gaul established by Paul Bouchet (Bod Koad), independent of the earlier groups and not recognized by them.
1950	The Great Oak Forest Celtic College of Broceliande founded by Goff ar Steredennou.
1960	The Great Oak Order re-established in France by Mic Goban, claiming descent from the ancient 'Order of Gawre'.
1963	The Carleton Grove of the Reformed Druids of North America founded.
1964	Order of Bards, Ovates and Druids founded by Ross Nichols (Nuinn) after a schism within the Druid Order.
1975	Golden Section Order active (founded by Colin Murray in 1966).
1975	The Philosophical Brotherhood of Druids founded in Brittany by Coaver Kalondan after a schism with the Breton gorsedd.
1976	A Universal Fraternity of Druids established in France, independently of the earlier groups. They are the first modern group to be lead by a female Druid.
1978	Druid Order of Avernia founded in the Auvergne region of Gaul.
1979	The British Druid Order founded by Philip Shallcrass.
1982	Oaled Drwized Kornog (Hearth of the Western Druids) founded in Brittany by Goff ar Steredennou.
1983	Ar nDraiocht Fein (A Druid Fellowship) founded in the USA.
1988	École Druidique des Gaules founded by the Allobragmatos, Boduogmatos and Catuvolus.
1990	Cornardiia Druvidiacta Aremorica (Druid Brotherhood of Armorica) founded in Brittany after a split with the Kredenn Gieltiek.
1992	The Druid Clan of Dana established in Ireland. It is founded on the work of the Fellowship of Isis, established in 1976 by Rev. Lawrence Durdin-Robertson, Pamela Durdin-Robertson and the Hon. Olivia Robertson.
1993	A further split in the Cornardiia Druvidiacta Aremorica results in the founding of the Armorican Brotherhood of the Sacred Law.
1993	The Druidic Federation of Gaul founded by Pierre de la Crau out of the Druidic Church of Gaul and the Green Druidic Order of Ronan ap Lugh.

1993   The Insular Order of Druids founded at Stonehenge by Dylan ap Thuinn.

1993   Order of Druids of Ireland founded by Michael Mile McGrath.

It will be seen from the above that not only is there a great variety of 'types' of Druidism currently available, but that many are natural outgrowths from one another. The widespread resurgence of interest seems to have begun in the 1960s and to have continued in an ever-widening ripple until the present, when there are more Druid orders flourishing than at any time previously – or at least, since the original Druids were active.

The selection that follows is, therefore, largely idiosyncratic. Another writer would undoubtedly choose a very different set of reference points – and there is certainly no shortage of available material.

The first three chapters that can be seen to develop out of the wilder fantasies of the preceding ages, and to advance gradually towards a more historically informed position. Dudley Wright, in 'Initiatory Ceremonies and Priesthood' of 1924, still looks backwards towards the writings of Bonwick, Higgins and Davies, and is at times just as fantastic as they, while Sir John Daniel and more particularly T.D. Kendrick – both writing in 1927 – move us out of the age of antiquarian fancy into that of modern scholarship. Kendrick, who was the Keeper of Antiquities at the British Museum, was among the first writers in the twentieth century to look back at the original sources and to make new and accurate translations of them for a modern audience.

Lewis Spence, who probably made one of the greatest contributions to the interest and understanding of Druid history, follows, in a second extract from his seminal book, *The History and Origins of Druidism*. The collection is rounded off by short articles from the pens of two respected 'elders' of modern Druidry, Ross Nichols, of the Order of Bards, Ovates and Druids, and Colin Murray, who founded the Golden Section Order in 1966 and who first introduced the editor of this collection to the concepts of Druidry in the 1980s.

The sheer variety of material contained here promises a healthy future for Druidry, both in Europe and the United States, with more members joining the various orders daily. The focus on ecology, spiritual philosophy and the respect for tradition that most of these orders display promises something else – that the Celtic traditions from which they sprang are as relevant today as they ever were; perhaps more so as we move towards the end of the twentieth century and look forward to a more hopeful, integrated and holistic future in which Druidry may once again find its true place.

19

THE INITIATORY CEREMONIES AND PRIESTHOOD

Dudley Wright

From *Druidism: The Ancient Faith of Britain*

The mode of life adopted by the Druidical priests made easy the transition from Pagan to Christian monasticism. To all intents and purposes the Druids formed a Church, and their ecclesiastical system seems to have been as complete as any other system of which records have been preserved, whether Christian or non-Christan. The word 'Church', it is interesting to note, is by many etymologists derived from the Greek word *kirkos*, meaning 'a circle'. It appears in varied, though similar forms in different languages: Welsh, *cyrch*; Scotch, *kirk*; Old English, *chirche*, *cherche*, or *chireche*; Anglo-Saxon, *circe* or *cyrice*; Dutch, *kerk*; Icelandic, *kirkja*; Swedish, *kyrka*; Danish, *kirke*; German, *kirche*; Old High German, *chirihha*.

The rank of the Arch, or Chief, Druid was that of *pontifex maximus*, and, apparently, he held his position until death or resignation, when his successor appears to have been elected in a manner similar to that in which the Pope of the present day is elected, although some writers assert that the Arch Druid was elected annually. Caesar states that 'when the presulary dignity becomes vacant by the head Druid's death, the next in dignity succeeds; but, when there are equals in competition, election carries it.'

Many Druids appear to have retired from the world and lived a hermit existence, in order that they might acquire a reputation for sanctity. Martin, in his *Description of the Western Isles*, has pointed out that, in his time, in the most unfrequented places of the Western Isles of Scotland, there were still remaining the foundations of small circular houses, intended evidently for the abode of one person only, to which were given the name of 'Druids' Houses' by the people of the country. The Druids were great lovers of silence, and if any one was found prattling during their assemblies or sacrifices he was admonished; if, after the third admonition, he did not cease talking, a large piece of his garment was cut off; and if, after that, he again offended, he was punished in a more rigorous manner.

The majority of the Druids, however, appear to have lived a communal life, uniting together in fraternities and dwelling near the temples which they served; each temple requiring the services of several priests, except, perhaps, in isolated districts. In Wales, one Druid resided in every *Cwmwd* to offer sacrifices and to instruct the people. In addition to the portion of land to which every freeborn Cymro was entitled, and the immunities and privileges belonging to his class, this local priest could claim a contribution from every plough used in the hamlets of his Cwmwd. Ammianus of Marseilles describes these early priests of Britain in the following words:

> 'The Druids, men of polished parts, as the authority of Pythagoras has decreed, affecting formed societies and sodalities, gave themselves wholly to the contemplation of divine and hidden things, despising all wordly enjoyments, and confidently affirmed the souls of men to be immortal.'

Not a few, however, lived in a more public and secular manner, attaching themselves to kingly courts and the residences of the noble and wealthy. The Druids have thus a close affinity with both the monastic orders and religious congregations of the Church of Rome, known as the regular clergy; and those living unrestricted by special vows, known as the secular clergy.

The period of novitiate and the character of the training of an aspirant to the Druidical priesthood was as lengthy and as rigorous as that of an aspirant to membership of the Society of Jesus, better known as the Jesuit Society. It lasted for twenty years and, although the candidates were, in general, enlisted from the families of nobles, many youths in other ranks of life also entered voluntarily upon the novitiate, and very frequently boys were dedicated to the priestly life by their parents from an early age. None but freemen were admitted as aspirants, so that a slave seeking admission into the Order had first to obtain his freedom from his master.

The ceremony of initiation, so far as can be gathered from the records, was solemn and arduous. The candidate first took an oath not to reveal the mysteries into which he was about to be initiated. He was then divested of his ordinary clothing, crowned with ivy, and vested with a tri-coloured robe of white, blue, and green – colours emblematical of light, truth and hope. Over this was placed a white tunic. Both were made with full-length openings in front and, before the ceremony of initiation began, the candidate had to throw open both tunic and robe, in order that the officiating priest might be assured that he was a male. This divesture was also to symbolise his extreme poverty, which was supposed to be his characteristic prior to initiation.

The tonsure was one of the ceremonies connected with initiation. As practised in the Roman Church the tonsure, the first of the four minor orders conferred upon aspirants to the priesthood, is undoubtedly a Druidical survival.

There is evidence of its practice in Ireland in A.D. 630, but it does not appear to have become a custom in England until the latter part of the eighth century. The tonsure was referred to by St Patrick as 'the diabolical mark,' although, according to Druidical lore, St Patrick himself was tonsured; and in Ireland it was known as 'the tonsure of Simon the Druid.' The Druidical differed greatly from both the modern monastic and secular form. All the hair in front of a line drawn over the crown from ear to ear was shaved or clipped. All Druids wore short hair, the laymen long; the Druids wore long beards, the laymen shaved the whole of the face, with the exception of the upper lip. The tonsure was known also in Wales as a sign of service in a kingly or noble family. In the Welsh romance known as the *Mabinogion*, we find among the Brythons a youth who wished to become one of Arthur's knights, whose allegiance was signified by the king cutting off the youth's hair with his own hand.

The initiation took place in a cave, because of the legend which existed that Enoch had deposited certain invaluable secrets in a consecrated cavern deep in the bowels of the earth. There is still to be seen in Denbighshire one of the caves in which Druidical initiations are said to have taken place. The caves in which the various ceremonies were performed were, like the over-ground Druidical temples, circular in form. The underground rooms of the Red Indians, where their secret councils were held, were also circular in form, with a divan running around them. After taking the oath the candidate had to pass through the Tolmen, or perforated stone, an act held to be the means of purging from sin and conveying purity. Captain Wilford, in *Asiatic Researches*, says that perforated stones are not uncommon in India, and that devout people pass through them, when the opening will admit it, in order to be regenerated. If the hole be too small to permit of the passage of the entire body, they put either the hand or foot through the hole; and, with a sufficient degree of faith, this answers nearly the same purpose. Among the Namburi of the Travancore State a man is made a Brahman by being passed through the body of a golden cow, or being placed in a colossal golden lotus flower, which article then becomes the property of the priests. The individual is, by this act, said to acquire a new birth of the soul, or have become twice-born. Passing persons through holed stones is also practised in other parts of India, as it is in the East Indies. In some parts of the north of England children are drawn through a hole in the 'Groaning Cheese' on the day on which they are christened. All rocks containing an aperture, whether natural or artificial, were held to possess the means of transmitting purification to the person passing through the hole. At Bayons Manor, near Market Rasen, Lincolnshire, there is a *petra ambrosiae*, consisting of a gigantic upright stone resting upon another stone and hollowed out so as to form an aperture sufficiently large for a man to pass through. This stone is believed to have been used by the Druids in the performance of their sacred rites. The celebrated Purgatory of St Patrick, at Lough Derg, in Ireland, is also thought to have been a place of Druidical initiation, and even in ante-Druidical times no person was permitted to enter the enclosure without first undergoing all the ceremonies of preparation and purification. Some writers have conjectured that the prophet Isaiah was referring to a practice similar to this when he wrote (1, 19): 'And they shall go into the holes of the rocks and into the caves of the earth for fear of the Lord, and for the glory of His majesty, when He ariseth to shake terribly the earth.' All such orifices were consecrated with holy oil and dedicated to religious uses, hence the distinguishing name of *lapis ambrosius* which was given to each.

Forling, in *Rivers of Life*, throws much light upon this custom. In one passage he says:

> The superstition of passing through natural, or even artificial, clefts in trees and rocks, or, failing them, caves and holes, has scarcely yet left the most civilised parts of Europe, and is firmly maintained throughout the rest of the world, and, in India, takes the thoroughly literal aspect of the question, viz., of being really 'born again,' the person to be regenerated being actually passed through the mouth and organ of a properly constructed cow – if the sinner be very rich, of a gold or silver cow, which is then broken up and divided among the purifying priests. A wooden or lithic perforation, that is an *I Oni*, is, for ordinary men, however, a sufficient 'baptism of grace'. and in these islands the holy ash, or Ygdrasil, is the proper tree to regenerate one. Major Moor describes his gardener in Suffolk as splitting a young ash longitudinally (the oak is its equivalent) and passing a naked child through it three times, 'always head foremost for rickets and rupture.' The tree is bound up again, and if it heals, all goes well with the child. The operation is called drawing in Suffolk, and, in 1834, seems to have gone beyond the spiritual and passed into the sphere of a medical luxury. In England the ash is for drawing preferred to the oak; it should be split for about five feet, as closely as possible east and west, and in the Spring, or fertilising season of the year, before vegetation has set in, and just as the sun is rising. The child must then be stripped quite naked, and some say passed feet, and not head, foremost, through the tree three times, and it should then be carefully turned round, or, as the Celts say, deasil-ways, that is with the sun, after which, the cleft of the tree must be bound up carefully. Here we see the tree as a thing of life, and forming the very *IOni-ish*, 'door of life,' and in the presence of Siva, or the Sun, without whom regeneration of old, or the giving of new life is known by all to be impossible.

Bottrell, also, in his *Traditions of West Cornwall*, says that children were at one time brought to Madron Well to be cured of shingles, wild fires, tetters, and various skin diseases, as well as to fortify them against witchcraft and other mysterious ailments. The child was stripped naked, then it was plunged or popped three times through the water against the sun; next it was passed quickly nine times round the spring, going from east to west, or with the sun; then dressed, rolled up in something warm, and made to sleep near the water; if the child slept and plenty of bubbles rose in the water, it was a good sign.

The candidate was next placed in a chest or coffin, in which he remained enclosed – apertures being made for the circulation of air – for three days, to represent death. From this chest he was liberated on the third day to symbolise his restoration to life. The Bard, in describing the initiation of Arthur, says that at his (mystical) death the 'three nights was he placed under the flat stone of Echmeint.' When the aspirant emerged from the tomb in which he had been immured he was pronounced regenerated, or born again. Dr George Oliver, in *Signs and Symbols*, says that in all ancient Mysteries before an aspirant could claim to participate in the higher secrets of the Institution he was placed within the Pastos, or Bed, or Coffin; or, in other words, was subject to a solitary confinement for a prescribed period of time, that he might reflect seriously, in seclusion and darkness, on what he was about to undertake, and be reduced to a proper state of mind for the reception of great and important truths, by a course of fasting and mortification. This was symbolical death and his deliverance from confinement was the act of regeneration, or being born again. The candidate was made to undergo these changes in scenic representation and was placed under the Pastos in perfect darkness.

The sanctuary was then prepared for the further ceremonies in connection with the intiation, and the candidate, blindfolded, was introduced to the assembled company during the chanting of a hymn to the sun and placed in the charge of a professed Druid, another Druid, at the same time, kindling the sacred fire. It is said that we still retain in some old English choruses the odes which those Phallo-Solar worshippers used to chant. Thus: 'Heydown, down derry down,' is held to be *Hai down ir deri danno*, signifying: 'Come, let us haste to the oaken grove'; or, if taken from the Celtic, Dun dun daragan dun, it would mean, 'To the hill, to the hill, to the oaks, to the hill.' Another chant: 'High trolollie, lollie loi, or lee,' is said to come from the Celtic *Ai tra la, la, li*, which would be an address to the rising run as 'Hail! early day.'

Still blindfolded, the candidate was taken on a circumnambulation nine times round the sanctuary in circles from East to West, starting at the South. The procession was made to the accompaniment of a tumultuous clanging of musical instruments and of shouting and screaming, and was followed by the administration of a second oath, the violation of which rendered the individual liable to the penalty of death.

Then followed a number of other ceremonies, which typified the confinement of Noah in the Ark and the death of that patriarch, the candidate passing eventually through a narrow avenue, which was guarded by angry beasts, after which he was seized and borne to the waters, symbolical of the waters on which the Ark of Noah floated. He was completly immersed in this water, and, on emerging from the water on the bank opposite to that from which he had entered, he found himself in a blaze of light. The most dismal howlings, shrieks, and lamentations are said to have been heard during the progress of this ceremony, the barking of dogs, the blowing of horns, and the voices of men uttering discordant cries. These were made partly for the purpose of intimidating the candidate, and partly with the design of inspiring with terror any uninitiated persons who might be within earshot, and so deter them from prying into the secrets. Some writers assert that the sound of thunder was heard, which is not improbable: the art of making artificial thunder was known to the priests of Delphos. The candidate, on arriving at the opposite bank, was presented to the Arch Druid, who, seated on his throne or official chair, explained to the initiate the symbolical meaning of the various ceremonies in which he had just taken an active part.

Taliesin, in his account of his initiation, says:

> I was first modelled into the form of a pure man in the hall of Ceridwen, who subjected me to penance. Though small within my ark and modest in my deportment, I was great. A sanctuary carried me above the surface of the earth. Whilst I was inclosed within its ribs, the sweet Awen rendered me complete; and my law, without audible language, was imparted to me by the old giantess darkly smiling in her wrath; but her claim was not regretted, when she set sail. I fled in the form of a fair grain of pure wheat; upon the edge of a covering cloth she caught me in her fangs. In appearance she was as large as a proud mare, which she also resembled: then was she swelling out, like a ship upon the waters. Into a dark receptacle she cast me. She carried me back into the sea of Dylan. It was an auspicious omen to me, when she happily suffocated me. God, the Lord, freely set me at large.

The ceremony of initiation was similar to that of the Egyptian rites of Osiris, which were regarded as a descent into hell, a passage through the infernal lake, followed by a landing on the Egyptian Isle of the Blessed. By this means men were held to become more holy, just, and pure, and to be delivered from all hazards which would otherwise be impending. The cave in which the aspirant was placed for the purpose of meditation before he was permitted to participate in the sacred Mysteries was guarded by a representation of the terrible divinity Busnawr, who was armed with a naked sword, and whose vindictive wrath, when aroused, was said to be such as to make earth, hell and even heaven itself, tremble.

Dionysius tells us that when the Druidesses celebrated the mysteries of the great god, Hu, the Mighty, they passed over an arm of the sea in the dead of the night to certain smaller contiguous islets. The ship or vessel in which they made the passage represented the Ark of the Deluge; the arm of the sea that of the waters of the Flood; and the fabled Elysian island, where the passage terminated, shadowed out the Lunar White Island of the ocean-girt summit of the Paradisiacal Ararat.

After the initiation was completed the novice retired into the forest, where the period of his novitiate was spent, his time being devoted to study and gymnastic exercises. The Druids encouraged learning, and candidates for the priesthood passed first through the courses assigned to those who were to become Ovates or Bards. Four degrees were conferred during the long novitiate; the first being given after three years' study in the arts of poetry and music, if the candidate, by his capacity and diligence, merited the honour. The second was conferred after six years' further study, if merited; the third after a further nine years' study; and the final degree, equal to a doctorate, was bestowed two years later, on the completion of the twenty years' course.

The *Book of the Ollambs* gives the following as the course of study for the first twelve years. The Druids, it may be remarked, have been claimed as the originators of the collegiate system of education.

First year. – Fifty oghams, the Araicecht, or grammar, twenty tales, and some poems.

Second year. – Fifty more oghams, six minor lessons in philosophy, thirty tales, and some poems.

Third year. – Learning the correct diphthongal combinations, the six major lessons of philosophy, forty tales, and various poems.

Fourth year. – Fifty tales, Brèthà Nemidh, or law of privileges, twenty poems called 'Enan'.

Fifth year. – Sixty tales, critical knowledge of adverbs, articles, and other niceties of grammar.

Sixth year. – Twenty-four great Naths, twenty-four small Naths (this was a name given to a certain kind of poems), the secret language of the poets, and seventy tales.

Seventh year. – The Brosnacha of the Sai (professor) and the Bardesy of the Bards.

Eighth year. – Prosody or Versification of the poets, meaning of obscure words (or glosses), the various kinds of poetry, the Druidical or inchantatory compositions called Teinm Laeghdha, Imbas Forosnai, Dichetal di channaibh, the knowledge of Dinnseanchus or topography, and all the chief historical tales of Ireland, such as were to be recited in the presence of kings, chiefs, and goodmen.

Ninth and tenth years. – Forty Sennats, fifteen Luascas, seven Nenas, an Eochraid of sixty words with their appropriate verses, seven Truths and six Duili Fedha.

Eleventh year. – Fifty great Anamains, fifty minor Anamains. The great Anamain was a species of poem which contained four different measures of composition, viz., the Nath, the Anair, Laidh, and Eman, and was composed by an Ollamg only.

Twelfth year. – Six score great Ceatals (measured addresses or Orations) and the four arts of poetry, viz., Laidcuin Mac Barceda's art; Ua Crotta's art, O'Briene's art, and Beg's art.

J.W. Arch, in *Written Records of the Cwmry*, says that the Druids, unlike the hereditary priest castes of the Eastern world, owed their sacro-sanct character, not to blood and race, but to a long continued course of instruction, from which they were supposed to emerge a wiser, more sober, a better informed, and a more learned class than any other portion of the community.

The presiding officers in all Druidical ceremonies and Mysteries were three in number. They were named Cadeiriaith, the Principal, who was stationed in the East; Goronwy, who represented the moon, and occupied a position in the West; and Fleidwr Flam, the representative of the meridian sun, and was stationed in the South. Other subordinate officers were necessary for the due celebration of the mysteries. The principal of these were Sywedyad, or the mystagogue, who assisted the Arch-Druid in the illustration, and Ys yw wedydd, the revealer of secrets, who communicated to the initiated the mysterious tokens of the Order and their meaning. The two great lights of heaven were of no little importance in these rites and ceremonies. The Sun was a symbol of the superior god Hu, because he is the great source of light and the ruler of the day. The mild sovereign of the night typified the supreme goddess Ceridwen, in whose sacred cauldron were involved all the mysteries of this religion.

The Druids ascribed the origin of all things to three principles, therefore during the initiation ceremony three hymns were chanted to the Deity. These hymns were called by the name of Trigaranos, or 'the triple crane.'

> The Druids [says Hollinshead] applied themselves as earnestly to the study of philosophy, as well natural as moral, that they were held in no small reverence of the people, as they were both accounted and known to be men of the most perfect life and innocence, by means whereof their authority daily so far increased that, finally, judgements in the most doubtful matters were committed unto their determination, offenders by their discretion punished, and such as had well deserved accordingly by their appointments rewarded. Moreover, such as refused to obey their decrees and ordinances were by them excommunicated, so that no creature durst once keep company with such till they were reconciled again and by the same Druids absolved.

Rowlands, in *Mona Antiqua*, bears testimony to the nature of the studies pursued: 'The Druids considered nature in her largest extent; in her systems and in her motions; in her magnitude and powers; in all which they seemed to cabbalize. Their philosophy was so comprehensive as to take in, with the theory of nature, astronomy, geometry, medicine, and natural magic, and all this upon the corpuscularian hypothesis.

They were very studious of the virtues of plants and herbs, and were exceedingly partial to the vervaine, which they used in casting lots and foretelling events. This was gathered at the rise of the Dog-star, and, before digging it up, they described a circle around it. It was gathered with the left hand into a clean, new napkin, the right hand being covered with a sacred vestment kept specially for that purpose. The plant was waved aloft after it was separated from the ground. It was infused in wine and then used as an antidote to the bite of serpents. It was also supposed to possess the virtue of fascination. Medea, in Sophocles, it will be remembered, is described as gathering her magic herbs with a brazen hook. In gathering the selago, a kind of hedge hyssop, the Chief Druid had to be clothed in white, as an emblem of internal purity, after bathing himself in clean water. The herb was gathered in bare feet and the gathering was preceded by participation in a sacrament of bread and wine. The Druids looked upon this herb as a preservative against all misfortune, and the smoke of it was regarded as an excellent cure for, as also a preservative against, sore eyes. The act of going with naked feet was always considered to be a token of humility and reverence, and the priests in the temple worship always officiated with feet uncovered, although frequently it was regarded as inimical to their health. The command thus given to Moses did not represent the civil and legal ceremony of putting off the shoes, as the Israelites were subsequently directed to do, when they renounced any bargain or contract (Deut. 25, 9; Ruth 4, 3); nor yet the sign of grief and sorrow, as when David entered into Jerusalem barefooted (II Samuel 12, 30); but it was enjoined that Moses might approach that sacred place with reverence and godly fear, as if it had been a temple consecrated to divine worship. There was another herb, called by the Gauls 'samolus', which grew in moist places and had to be gathered with the left hand while fasting. He who gathered it must not look upon it before it was plucked, and he was not allowed to place it anywhere save in the canals or places where beasts drank, bruising it before depositing it. It was held to be a prevention of disease among swine and oxen.

The three degrees of Ovate, Bard, and Druid were regarded as equal in importance, though not in privilege, and they were distinct in purpose. There is little doubt that knowledge was confined mainly, if not altogether, to the professed Druids, and it was one of their tenets that the Arcana of the Sciences must not be committed to writing, but to the memory. Caesar says that the Druids disputed largely upon subjects of natural philosophy and instructed the youth of the land in the rudiments of learning. By some writers the Druids are credited with a knowledge of the telescope, though this opinion is based mainly upon the statemnt of Diodorus Siculus, who says that in an island west of Celtae the Druids brought the sun and moon near to them. Hecataeus, however, informs us that they taught the existence of the lunar mountains. The fact that the Milky Way consisted of small stars was known to the ancients is often adduced in support of the claim to the antiquity of the telescope. Idris, the giant, a pre-Christian astronomer, is said to have pursued his study of the science of astronomy from the apex of one of the loftiest mountains in North Wales, which, in consequence, received the name which it now bears – Cader Idris, or the Chair of Idris. The Druids encouraged the study of Anatomy to such an extent that one of their doctors named Herophilus is said to have delivered lectures on the bodies of more than seven hundred men in order to reveal the secrets and wonders of the human frame. Diodorus Siculus is responsible for the statement that the Druids were the Gaulish philosophers and divines, and were held in great veneration, and that it was not lawful to perform any sacrifices except in the presence of at least one of these philosophers.

Sir Norman Lockyer writes:

> The people who honoured us with their presence here in Britain some four
> thousand years ago had evidently, some way or other, had communicated to them
> a very complete Egyptian culture, and they determined their time of night just in
> the same way that the Egyptians did, only of course, there was a great difference
> between the latitude of 25° in Egypt and 50° in Cornwall. They could not
> observe the same stars for the same purpose. They observed the stars which
> served their purpose for one thousand years or so. These stars were Capella and
> Arcturus.

P.W. Joyce, in his *Social History of Ancient Ireland*, says that in pagan times the Druids were the exclusive possessors of whatever learning was then known, and combined in themselves all the learned professions, being 'not only Druids, or priests, but judges, prophets, historians, poets, and even physicians.' He might have added 'and instructors of youth,' since education was entirely in their hands. No one was capable of public employment who had not been educated under a Druid. Children were brought up and educated away from their parents until they reached the age of fourteen. Even St Columba began his education under a Druid, and so great was the veneration paid to the Druids for the knowledge they possessed that it became a kind of adage with respct to anything that was deemed mysterious or beyond ordinary ken: 'No one knows but God and the holy Druids.'

There is a legend concerning St Columba and a Druid which runs: 'Now when the time for reading came to him, the clerk went to a certain prophet (*faidh*, or Druid) who abode in the land to ask him when the boy ought to begin. When the prophet had scanned the sky, he said: "Write an alphabet for him now." The alphabet was written on a cake, and St Columba consumed the cake on this wise, half to the east of a water and half to the west of a water. Said

Festival of the Bards of Kernow in Cornwall.

275

the prophet: "So shall this child's territory be, half to the east of the sea and half to the west of the sea."' This is claimed to have reference to Columba's work in Iona and among the Picts, i.e., one half in Ireland and the other half in Scotland.

The Druids were the intermediaries between the people and the spiritual world, and the people believed that their priests could protect them from the malice of evilly-disposed spirits of every kind. The authority possessed by the Druids is easily understood when it is remembered that they were possessed of more knowledge and learning than any other class of men in the country. 'They were,' says Rowlands, in *Mona Antiqua Restorata*, 'men of thought and speculation, whose chief province was to enlarge the bounds of knowledge, as their fellows were to do those of empire into what country or climate soever they came.'

Kings had each ever about them a Druid for prayer and sacrifice, who was also a judge for determining controversies, although each king had a civil judge besides. At the court of Conchobar, king of Ulster, no one had the right to speak before the Druid had spoken. Cathbu, or Cathbad, a Druid once attached to that court, was accompanied by a hundred youths, students of his art. After the introduction and adoption of Christianity, the Druid was succeeded by a bishop or priest, just as the Druidesses at Kildare were succeeded by the Briggintine Nuns. Martin, who wrote his *Description of the Western Islands of Scotland* in 1703, tells us that:

> Every great family of the Western Isles had a Chief Druid who foretold future events and decided all causes, civil and ecclesiastical. It is reported of them that they wrought in the night time and rested all day. Before the Britons engaged in battle the Chief Druid harangued the army to excite their courage. He was placed on an eminence whence he addressed himself to all standing about him, putting them in mind of all great things that were performed by the valour of their ancestors, raised their hopes with the noble rewards of honour and victory, and dispelled their fears by all the topics that natural courage could suggest. After this harangue the army gave a general shout and then charged the enemy stoutly.

In the time of Tacitus the Gallic Druids prophesied that the burning of the Capitol signified the approaching fall of the Roman Empire.

The position of Arch Druid was, as already stated, at one time held by Divitiacus, the Eduan, the intimate acquaintance and friend of Caesar, who is believed to have inspired the account of Druidism given by Caesar in *De Bello Gallico*. The British Arch Druid is said to have had his residence in the Isle of Anglesey, in or near to Llaniden. There the name of Tre'r Dryw, or Druidstown, is still preserved, and there are also still there some of the massive stone structures which are associated invariably with Druidism. The courts of the Arch Druids were held at Drewson or Druidstown. A short distance from the road leading from Killiney to Bray there stands a chair formed of large blocks of granite, which is called 'The Druid's Judgement Seat.' On occasions of ceremony the Arch Druid's head was surrounded by a oaken garland, surmounted by a tiara composed of adder stones encased in gold. When at the altar he wore a white surplice, fastened on the shoulder by a golden brooch. In Ireland there appears to have been no chief Druid, nor even a Druidical hierarchy or corporation. The Druids acted singly or in twos and threes. They were married and each lived with his family in his own house.

The principal seat of the French Druids was at Chartres, the residence of the Gallic Arch Druid, at which place also the annual convention of Gallic – and some say the British – Druids was held. There was also a large Druidic settlement at Marseilles. It was here that Caesar, in order to put an end to Druidism in Gaul, ordered the trees to be felled.

Dr John Jamieson, in his *Historical Account of the Ancient Culdees of Iona*, published in 1870, says that twenty years previously there was living in the parish of Moulin an old man who, although very regular in his devotions, never addressed the Supreme Being by any other title than that of Arch Druid. He quotes this as an illustration of the firm hold which ancient superstition takes of the mind.

Druids had the privilege of wearing six colours in their robes, and their tunics reached to their heels, while the tunics of others reached only to the knee. Kings and queens reserved to themselves the right of wearing robes of seven colours; lords and ladies five colours; governors of fortresses, four; young gentlemen of quality, three; soldiers, two; and the common people, one colour. When the Druids were officiating in their official capacity they each wore a white robe, emblematic of holiness as well as of the sun. When officiating as a judge the Druid wore two white robes, fastened with a girdle, surmounted by his Druid's egg encased in gold, and wore round his neck the breastplate of judgment, which was supposed to press upon his breast should he give utterance to a false or corrupt judgment. One is reminded by this breastplate of the wonderful collar referred to in Irish lore and legend, known as the Jadh Morain. This collar was attended with a very surprising virtue, for if it was placed on the neck of a judge who intended to pronounce a false judgment it would immediately shrink and almost stop the breath; but if the person that wore it changed his resolution and resolved to be just in his sentence, it would instantly enlarge itself and hang loose about the neck. This miraculous collar was also used to prove the integrity of the witnesses and if it were tied about the neck of a person who designed to give false testimony it would shrink close and extort the truth or continue contracting until it had throttled him. From this practice arose the custom, in the judicature of the kingdom, for the judge, when he suspected the veracity of a witness, to charge him solemnly to speak the truth, for his life was in danger if he did not, because the fatal collar, the Jadh Morain, was about his neck and would inevitably proceed to execution.

Vallancy, in *Collect. de Reb. Hibern*, tells of one of the Druidical breastplates found twelve feet deep in a turf bog in the county of Limerick. It was made of thin plated gold chased in a neat and workmanlike manner: the breast plate was single but the hemispherical ornaments at the top were lined throughout with another thin plate of pure gold; they were less exposed to injury when on the breast than when on the lower part. About the centre of each was a small hole in the lining to receive the ring of a chain that suspended it around the neck, and in the centre in front were two small conical pillars of solid gold, highly polished. The whole weighted twenty-two golden guineas. Another was also found in County Longford and sold for twenty-six guineas.

The Druid sitting as judge also wore a golden tiara upon his head and two official rings on his right hand fingers. On ordinary occasions the cap worn by the Druid had on the front a golden representation of the sun under a half moon of silver, supported by two Druids, one at each cusp, in an inclined position. The Irish Druid wore a long crimson robe over which was a shorter one, and suspnded at his side was his Druid's knife. He wore a white cap, in shape and appearance like a fan: it was ornamented with a gold plate. The British Arch-Druid wore over his ordinary robes a white mantle edged with gold; around his neck was a golden chain from which was suspended a golden plate, inscribed with the words: 'The gods require sacrifice.' J.C. Walker, in his *Historical Essay on the Dress of the Irish*, says that when the Druids were employed in sacrifice and other solemn ceremonies they wore, behind an oak-leaved crown, a golden crescent, with buttons at the extremities, through which a string was drawn that served to fasten it behind. Several of these crescents have been found in Irish bogs. The dress of the Druids was uniformly and universally a white garment, emblematic of the affected purity of their mind. In order to render their appearance more venerable and imposing they encouraged their beards to flow on their breasts.

> His seemly beard, to grace his form bestow'd,
> Descending decent, on his bosom flow'd;
> His robe of purest white, though rudely join'd
> Yet showed an emblem of the purest mind;
> Stern virtue, beaming in his eye, controul'd
> Each wayward purpose, and o'eraw'd the bold.

It is also established that in many instances priesthood was hereditary and that a special name was given to a priestly family. Thus the following was written by Ausonius, in honour of Attius Patera.

> Tu Bajocassis stirpe Druidarum satus
>   (Si fama non fallit fidem)
> BELENI sacratum ducis e Templo genus
>   Et inde vobis nomina;
> Tibi PATERAE (sic Ministros nuncupant
>   Apollinaris Mistyci.)
> Fratri-Patrique nomen à Phoebo datum
>   Natoque de Delphis tuo.

From his verse it is clear that all the family of Attius had a particular name, owing to their deriving their origin from the Druids of Bayeux, and that they were also devoted to the Mysteries of Belenus. The new name of Attius was

Patera: that of his father and brother was derived from Phaebus. The name of the son of Attius was Delphidus, as we read later:

Facunde, docte, lingua et ingenio celer,
Jocis amaene, Delphidi.

Here is another verse from Aysonius in confirmation:

Nec reticedo senem
Nominie Phoebtium,
Qui Beleni aedituus
Nil opis inde tulit:
Sed tamen, ut placitum,
Stirpe satus Druidum,
Gentis Aremoricae,
Burdigalae Cathedram
Nati opera obtinuit.
Et tu Concordi,
Qui profugus patria
Mutasti sterilem
Urbe alia cathedram,
Et libertina, etc.

The following interesting narrative appears in Wilson's *Prehistoric Annals of Scotland*:

In the museum of the Phrenological Society of Edinburgh may be found an interesting group of six skulls brought from the sacred isle of Iona, and each marked as the 'skull of a Druid from the Hebrides.' They were presented to the society by Mr. Donald Gregory, secretary of the Society of Antiquaries of Scotland and of the Iona Club, who procured them under the following circumstances. The institution of a Scottish Club, specially established for the investigation of the history, antiquities, and early literature of the Highlands of Scotland, was celebrated at a meeting held on the island of Iona, upon the 7th September, 1833, when the sepulchres of the Scottish kings were explored. The results were detailed by Mr. Gregory in the following letter addressed to Mr Robert Cox, of the Edinburgh Philological Society.

'Along with this you will receive six ancient skulls procured under the following circumstances. There is a place here called *Cladh na Druineach*, i.e., the burial place of the Druids, in which I have caused some deep cuts to be made. An incredible quantity of human bones has been found: and as it is perfectly certain that this place has never been used as a Christian churchyard, or as a place of interment at all, since the establishment of Christianity here by St Columba, there can be no doubt of the antiquity of the skulls now sent. They are by every one here firmly believed to be the skulls of the Druids, who were probably interred here from distant parts as well as from the neighbourhood, on account of the sanctity of the island, which formerly bore the name of *Innis na Druineach*, or the Druids' Isle. The six skulls herewith sent were selected with care by myself

279

Avebury in the eighteenth century.
From The Celtic Druids *by Godfrey Higgins*

from a much larger number. One you will observe is higher in the forehead than the rest. But this is an exception: for I am satisfied – and others whose attention I directed to the matter agree with me – that the general character of the skulls is a low forehead, and a considerable breadth in the upper and posterior parts of the head, which you will undoubtedly readily perceive. Although, with the exception mentioned, these skulls have the same general character (as far as I can judge), yet there are sufficient differences in the individuals to make them of considerable interest to the phrenologist. I must not omit to mention that the present race in the islands appear to have much better foreheads than the Druids, and independent of intellect and intelligence, are perhaps above the average of the Highlanders and islanders. Some of the skulls did not present such strong individual character as those sent and were more quickly developed. But as I was limited in the number to be taken, I preferred choosing well-marked skulls, particularly as the general character of the whole was so much the same.'

The mode of excommunication from the community was to expose the erring member to a naked weapon. The Bards had a special ceremony for the degradation of their convicted brethren. It took place at a Gorsedd, when the assembled Bards placed their caps on their heads. One deputed for the office unsheathed his sword, uplifted it, and named the delinquent aloud three times, adding on the last occasion the words: 'The sword is naked against him.' After these words were pronounced the offender was expelled, never to be re-admitted, and he became known as 'a man deprived of privilege and exposed to warfare.'

20

THE DRUIDIC CHURCH

Sir John Daniel

From *The Philosophy of Ancient Britain*

Its Origin and Constitution

The term 'Church' may be employed in a number of senses, admittedly, which do not come within the scope of these pages. But if it may be applied to any body of persons professing the same religion, as it certainly is when we speak, for instance, of the Jewish Church, why hesitate to use it of the Ancient Britons? Or if it may be employed to mean the ecclesiastics, priests, clergy, ministers or officers responsible for the government of those professing a common faith, why may it not be applied to the Druids who were both priests and law-givers to those who professed the ancient religion of this country? It would be difficult to find any just reason why the term should be regarded as sacrosanct against any other than its Christian uses. The Druids professed a form of religion which had its distinctive rites and ceremonies, system of doctrine, and organised priesthood. Consequently there is no incongruity in the title of this chapter.

It will now be necessary to turn to what records we have of the origin, establishment and constitution of this ancient system of religion. Before doing so it may not be out of place to observe that, when the reader remembers with what difficulty a foreign language is acquired so as to possess a correct appreciation of its many idiomatic pecularities, he will be prepared to meet with expressions in those records which, in their translated form, may sound strange. To translate one language into another, word for word, may be a simple thing. To transfuse into the new form the exact meaning of the original is quite another and more difficult thing. The labour spent on the translation of the Old and New Testaments, the several versions or renderings through which that translation has passed, and, notwithstanding all this, the numerous commentaries and expositions which have been compiled to elucidate the translated text, are a sufficient demonstration of the difficulty referred to. The older the language, the greater this difficulty becomes. It should not surprise us, therefore, to come across terms in the records under consideration which had for those who first employed them a significance they do not and cannot possess to modern ears.

> Triads of memory, record and knowledge, respecting notable men and things which have been in the Isle of Prydain (Britain), and respecting the circumstances and misfortunes which have happened to the nation of the Cymry from the remotest ages: (literally the age of ages).

Three names given to the Isle of Prydain

Before it was inhabited it was called *Clâs Merddin*; after it was inhabited it was called *Y Fêl Ynys*; and after the regular organisation of Government by Prydain the Son of Aedd the Great, it was denominated the Isle of Prydain. The tribe of Cymry have an inalienable right to it.

(No one has any right to it but the tribe of Cymry, for they first settled in it; no human being previously having lived therein; it being full of bears, wolves, crocodiles, and bisons.)

The three national pillars of the Isle of Prydain

1st. Hu Gadarn who brought the nation of the Cymry to the Isle of Prydain. They came from the land of Summer, which is called Deffrobani (Animative high-places): and they came through the vapoury sea to the Isle of Prydain.

2nd. Prydain the son of Aedd the Great, who first organised a social state and sovereignty in the Isle of Prydain, for before that time there was no justice but what was done from internal probity, nor was there any law but that of superior force.

3rd. Dyfnwal Moelmud, who made the first orderly discrimination of Laws, ordinances, customs and privileges of country and tribe.

The three benevolent tribes of the Isle of Prydain

1st. The tribe of Cymry, that came with Hu Gadarn into the Isle of Prydain, because he would not possss a country and lands by war and contest, but equity and peace.

2nd. The tribe of Sleograins which came from the Land of Gwasgwyn (Gentle ascent), and they were descended from the primitive tribe of Cymry.

3rd. The Brython, that came from the land of Slydau (Flowing Breadth) and who were also ascended from the primitive tribe of the Cymry.

These three were called the peaceful tribes, because they came by mutual consent and permission, in peace and tranquillity; these three tribes had sprung from the primitive race – the Cymry, and the three were of one language and of one speech.

The three awful events of the Isle of Prydain

1st. The bursting forth of Llyn Llion (The lake of the Floods), and the overwhelming of the face of all lands, so that all mankind perished, except Dwyfan (the Divine Principle), and Dwyfach (the offspring of the Divine) who were preserved in a ship without a mast, and of them the Isle of Prydain was repeopled.

2nd. The consternation of the tempestuous fire, when the earth split sunder to Annwn (Hell) and the greatest part of all living was consumed.

3rd. The scorching summer, when the woods and plants were set on fire by the intense heat of the sun, and immense multitudes of men, and beasts, and all kinds of birds, and reptiles and trees, and plants were irretrievably lost.

The three chief work of excellency on the Isle of Prydain

1st. The ship of Nefydd Nâf Neifion (the heavenly Lord of creating power) which carried it in a male and female of every living thing when the lake of the floods burst forth.

2nd. The branching oxen of Hu Gadarn, which drew the afanc (the amphibious) to land out of the waters, so that the lake burst no more.

3rd. The stone of Gwyddon Ganhebon, (knowledge with its utterance) on which are read all the arts and sciences of the world.

Many of the triads given in this and succeeding chapters are taken from 'Celtic Researches' and 'British Druids', two volumes written by the Rev Edward Davies and published respectively in 1804 and 1809, in which are translated a large number from the original Druidic writings. These triads furnish us with the only available information concerning the establishment of the Druidic Church in Britain; and they do so in language which defies ordinary methods of exposition. Taken literally they are meaningless to us. To class them, however, with the histories of the fabulous gods and heroes of antiquity which go under the name of mythology is the refuge of the baffled expositor who has failed to find the key to their solution. Not that mythology is wholly empty, for there is a large amount of hidden instruction in ancient myths; but the ordinary methods of mythological exposition, applied to these triads, give no satisfactory result.

The semblance of history contained in them has given rise to much conjecture and controversy as to the country from which the Druids hailed, some identifying 'Deffrobani' with Gaul, others with Thrace, others with North Africa; and the 'vapoury sea' is supposed by some to refer to the German ocean. It is the writer's opinion that the correctness or otherwise of these geographical surmises is of little concern, and that the account given in these triads of the origin of the Druids has as little historical or geographical significance, in the literal sense, as the story of the Creation given in the first chapter of Genesis. Both are allegories, and, in the primary sense, allegories of spiritual things.

That the spiritual or correspondential import of every term should be now apparent and easy to decipher would be more than one could reasonably expect after such a lapse of time. All that can be attempted is to show, in a general way, that these triads are based on correspondences and can only be understood in that sense.

Let us summarize what they tell us, following the natural sequence of the events depicted.

Hu Gadarn brought the Cymry from the land of Summer called Deffrobani (animative high-places) to the Isle of Prydain, passing in their journey through the vapoury sea. Before being inhabited the isle was called Clâs Merddin; afterwards Y Fêl Ynys; and when Prydain the Son of Aedd the Great organised its government it was named the Isle of Prydain. Dyfnwal Moelmud was its great Lawgiver. Two other tribes which sprung from the primitive Cmyry also came, the Sleogrians from the Land of Gwasgwyn (gentle ascent) and the Brython from the Land of Slydau (flowing breath). These three tribes came by mutual consent in peace and tranquillity. Three great events are given, the Bursting of Llyn Llion, the Tempestuous Fire, and the Scorching Summer; also three great works, that of the Ship of Nefydd Nâf Neifion, that of Hu Gadarn's Branching Oxen, and that of the Stone of Gwyddon Ganhebon.

The personal names given above, Hu Gadarn, Prydain the Son of Aedd the Great, and Dyfnwal Moelmud, will be dealt with in another connection. Deffrobani, Gwasgwyn and Slydau call for attention at this point. It goes without saying that these must have had some reference to place; but it is strange that, in spite of the efforts of capable scholars, their identification with any known part of the world has gone no further than conjecture. The simple reason is that they are not, in the strict sense, geographical terms at all, but terms significant of spiritual experiences and applied to those places which were associated with those experiences. Bible readers will know that this was a common practice among the ancients. Times and seasons as well as material objects were replete with religious symbolism, so that morning, noon, evening, night, spring, summer, autumn and winter had their respective values and uses in the vocabulary of the soul's experienes. Spiritual knowledge, in its early dawn, its ripe fulness, its gradual decline, or its final extinction, had its natural correspondence in one or another of these.

When we are told, therefore, that the Cymry 'came from the land of summer which is called Deffrobani', it must mean a land where the knowledge of God was full and ripe like a fruitful summer. In this connection it is not unworthy of note that the British word Hâf (summer) has the same meaning of fulness. Deffrobani (Deffro – to awake) implies a land whose people were awake to the value of the doctrines entrusted to the Ancient Church. Yet another meaning is given to this word – 'animative high-places'. Scripture says, 'He made him to ride on the high places of the earth, and feedeth him with the produce of the field.' In the language of correspondences making him to 'ride on the high places of the earth' signified spiritual intelligence, to 'ride' signifying to understand, and 'high places' signifying spiritual things. These first comers, then, arrived richly endowed with the treasures of knowledge inherited by the Ancient Church. Those who followed them were not in quite so happy a situation. The Brython came from Slydau, the place of 'flowing breath', where they at least were not hemmed in through total ignorance, but where their minds moved with freedom in the broad fields of truth. They were not 'shut up into the hand of the enemy' but their feet were 'set in a large place'. The truth was theirs although, as yet, they had not begun to climb to the lofty heights attained by their predecessors. The Sleogrians, from the land of Gwasgwyn (gentle ascent) were of another order, for they had taken the first upward steps along the slopes leading from the level of the plain to the 'high-places' above. Here we have presented three grades or degrees of religious knowledge or spiritual intelligence – express it as we like – which the teaching of correspondences tells us these very terms denote; and it might well surprise us to find so clear an illustration of it in the language of the triads, did we not know how near their authors lived to the time when correspondences were the ordinary medium of religious expression.

Interpreted by the same means, the 'vapoury sea' through which they passed is an expression equally significant. The 'sea' signifies the state of those who think of the things of religion naturally, not spiritually, and the 'vapoury' sea that of those who, possessing truth in its lowest or ultimate forms, only apprehend it in its external or literal sense. The British word, 'tawch' (vapour), contains the idea of something offensive to the nostrils, and it may mean that the course taken by these early settlers lay among people where the external things of the Ancient Church had been corrupted into gross superstitions and its truths perverted into false teaching. Such seems to have been the condition of the greater part of Europe, its southern portion in particular, in the early ages when the settlement took place.

The condition of the island when they arrived is described in almost similar language. Before they came to it, it was called 'Clâs Merddin'. 'Clâs' means a region or place; 'Merddin' is a compound of 'Merydd' and 'In'. 'Merydd' (adj.), moist, waterish, slow, sluggish, lazy; it is sometimes used in connection with the noun sin, as Pechod meridd. (T. Richards' Dict.) 'Merydd' (sub.), that which is flaccid or sluggish, a plash, a sluggard. 'In', anything pervading – (Dr W. Richards' Dict.) Hence it is obvious that the compound word Merddin signifies the pervasion of sluggish or stagnant waters. There is nothing, however, in the physical character of the Island to make such a name appropriate, for it is beautifully diversified with hill and dale, watered by silvery streams, perpetually clad in living verdure, and surrounded by a sea sometimes so boisterous around the coast as to make navigation extremely dangerous. But 'Clâs Merddin' is a more intense form of the same idea that is expressed by the words 'vapoury sea'. A place of dead and stagnant waters denotes a region still more remote from the 'animative high places' or spiritual understanding of the church, a region where nothing of the church as yet existed. What a dark and gloomy picture this gives us of the ancient condition of the island we now call our home! And how fit and expressive was its new title! After the Isle was inhabited and the principles of the church implanted, growing and yielding their sweets, it was no more 'Clâs Merddin' but 'Y Fêl Ynys' (The honey Isle). Honey corresponds to what is delightful and pleasant in the spiritual world. The blessings of Jerusalem, by which is understood the spiritual church, are thus decribed by Ezekiel, 'So wast thou adorned with gold and silver; and thy garments were fine linen, and silk, and needlework; fine flour and honey, and oil, didst thou eat, whence thou becomest exceedingly beautiful, and didst prosper even to a kingdom.' – (Ezek. 16.)

The ancient Cymry came under the guidance and protection of Hu Gadarn. 'Hu Gadarn' signifies the Mighty One who pervades, overshadows, inspects. Hu Gadarn, or Huw the Mighty, was one of the many names given the Deity and not a human being to be relegated to any niche in history. 'Hu' differs little from our present name of the Deity, 'Duw.' This name, therefore, denotes the same Divine presence and guidance that were represented by the cloud which went before the Sons of Israel through the wilderness to Canaan. Long before Israel passed through the wilderness, did the Divine Providence lead this ancient people from the regions of the church in Asia to their new possession, where they instituted a church similar to that from which they had come forth, and, according to the instructions received from their forefathers, worshipped the true and living God. Swedenborg informs us that, besides the churches which are mentioned in the Word as having decreased and destroyed themselves, there have existed many others which are not so described. One of these churches, there is strong evidence for believing, existed in Britain.

The Government of this Church was formed by Prydain, the son of Aedd the Great. Prydain the Son of Aedd was not a person, but the personification of a principle. The word is a compound of 'Pryd' (beautiful) and 'ain' (extension), and denotes the order of truth. Aedd (the father of Prydain) denotes din, clamour, confusion: and therefore Prydain the Son of Aedd represents the order produced by truth out of the natural principle which is disorder.

After the organisation of a social state and its sovereignty by Prydain the Son of Aedd the Great, and the Druidicial order of Government was regularly established, the Druids gave the island, the home of their church, and to them the representative of the church as Canaan was of the Hebrew church, a new name. The Isle of Beautiful Extension, beautiful from the order of its government. Here we see a striking instance of the correspondence mentioned in the passage before quoted from Ezekiel: 'Fine flour, and honey, and oil didst thou eat, whence thou becamest beautiful and didst prosper even to a kingdom.'

Another name mentioned is 'Dyfnwal Moelmud' who made the first orderly discrimination of the laws, and ordinances, customs and privileges of country and tribe. This name signifies 'a deep laid rampart' and 'the removal of nakedness', and therefore is representative of truth as a defence. He is said to be the Son of Prydain, signifying that the defence of truth springs or is derived from the order of truth. The correspondence of this name, and of the office attributed to it is given in the following words of Swedenborg, 'By a wall, a rampart, gates, and bars, are meant doctrinals.' By doctrinals we discriminate truths and defend against the false, for without doctrine we have no understanding of truth, and therefore no defence.

Further, what is said by Swedenborg concerning the Doctrines and origin of the Ancient Church, is in agreement with what is said by the Druids in some of their poems. Taliesin, a chief Bard or Druid, in a poem descriptive of Druidism – the system being personified in him as the High Priest, as was the case in the Ancient Church – speaks as follows:

> I was happiness to the man,
> Of wisdom in the primitive world,
> For then I had a being,
> When the world was in dignity, and was beautiful,
> The glory of the Bard was I made,
> I incite the songs of praise,
> Which the tongue utters.
> Truly I was in safety,
> Amid the sea-like deluge
> Encompassed and protected
> Between the royal knees,
> When from Heaven came,
> With a dissolvent throe,
> The Inundation to the great abyss.

In another passage the Bard says that Druidism was

> The greatest of the three mental exertions
> That have disported in the world,
> And the one that was formed
> From the stores of the deluge.

From these verses we learn that the Druids had a knowledge of the Most Ancient Church and knew that the Church was then in a far more elevated state than was the Ancient which succeeded it, for they represent that period as being the time when the world was 'in dignity, and was beautiful.' 'I,' says Taliesin, 'was happiness to the man of wisdom in the primitive world.' These principles which, as we shall show, were love and charity, were preserved amid the deluge which swept the evil to the great abyss.

This poem of Taliesin evidently refers to the preservation of the sacred principles which were to constitute the foundations of the re-formed Church when all falsities and evils had been swept away. It is clear then that the Druids regarded themselves as part of the Church so preserved. What other meaning can with equal justice be attached to their language? The Bards simply clothed in the language of correspondence doctrines and sentiments well known, received in the Church, and professedly derived from heaven in the manner already explained.

Historians have debated and continue to debate as to whether Taliesin lived in the sixth, ninth or some other century of the Christian era. But Druidic doctrine was often rendered in poetic form, the verses ending 'I am Taliesin' in much the same form as the Scripture rendering of 'Thus saith the Lord.' Historian for once may therefore agree, for Taliesin belonged to the sixth, ninth and every other century before or since. Taliesin was evidently a name common to the chief Druid in the British Church, as Melchizedek was a name common to the king and priest of the Ancient Church, each being representative of the Divine Principle which constitues the Church. The word is a compound of *Tal* (front, forehead), and *Iesin*, (radiant, glorious, fair) and therefore literally means, the Radiant or Glorious Front; a name by no means inappropriate to the High Priest who was representative of the Divine, also represented by the sun. Aaron, the high priest of the Jewish Nation, signified 'lofty', 'mountainous', or 'mountain of strength'; for he represented the Lord as to the principle of divine goodness, to which the mountain corresponds; while Taliesin, like the Melchizedek of the ancient church, represented the Lord as to both principles, goodness and truth. The throne of Taliesin, by correspondence, denoted the spiritual church, which also, in the Scriptures, is called the throne of God, the throne being predicated of Divine Truth by which the Lord governs the church. In the language of the Druids, this church is personified and represented as speaking of itself; and may be understood as speaking of itself either in its collective capacity or in the individual man, the Druidicial temple being representative of either, or of both.

As a further illustration we shall now give some extracts written purely in the language of correspondence. In a poem entitled 'The Seat, or Throne of Taliesin', the Bard speaks of the Druidic Church, and gives a description of its internal qualities and principles.

Stonehenge reconstructed.
From The Celtic Druids *by Godfrey Higgins*

The Throne of Taliesin

Surrounded by the sea, I am
To the praise of God the Governor.

Profound is the all-sufficient source
Which fully supplied me, the sacred circle,
In every evening festival,
When the calm dew descends,
With the blessing of wheat and the suavity of bees,
And incense, and myrrh, and aloes, from beyond the sea;
And the gold pipes communicating,
And glad precious silver, and the ruddy gem;
And berries, and the ocean wave;
And cresses, – the virtue watered by the gushing spring,
And a joint multitude of the herbs of the gentle flood,
And, borne by the effusive moon, placid, cheerful vervain,
And stars of intelligence diffused around the moon,
And the wide spread aspect of the pure element;
And below in the moving atmosphere,
The moisture, and the falling drops;
And the increase which succeeds;
And the vessel of glass in the hand of the Pilgrim,
And the strong youth with the rosin of pine,
And the exalted one free from guile,
With the healing herbs where no delusion is,
And Bards with flowers.
Meet for a sovereign is the Druidic lore.

From a purely literary point of view the above poem has little or no merit, its only value being in the correspondence it contains and without which it is meaningless. In tracing these out, we refer the reader to the Dictionary of Correspondences for the correctness of our interpretation.

This is a Hymn of Praise to God the Governor sung by His Church, enumerating the blessings derived from the profound and all-sufficient source, God Himself; for the sacred circle or temple represents the Church and in 'every evening festival' we have the Church engaged in worship.

Glad in the knowledge he possesses of those correspondences by which every natural object spoke to him of the sublime things of His Church, the Bard in his exultation fittingly exclaims 'Meet for a sovereign is the Druidic lore'.

A poem of still more significant language calls for explanation in this connection; one which it is easy to understand would mystify those who knew nothing of the laws of correspondences nor of the relation of the Druidic Church to the Ancient. Before giving the poem, the reader's attention is drawn to the 21st verse of the 10th chapter of Genesis. 'Unto Shem also, the father of all the children of Eber, the brother of Japheth the elder, even to him were children born.' Swedenborg informs us that by Eber is signified a new church, and that by Shem being the father of all the sons of Eber, is signified that this second ancient church and the things appertaining to it had existence from the former ancient church – (A.C. 1217). As will be seen the Druids must have had a knowledge of this church, must have known it to be a reform of the ancient church which had preceded it, for they speak of their own system as being the same as that of the church Eber.

> My afflictions have been related in Ebrew in Eber,
> A second time have I been formed,
> I have been a blue salmon; I have been a dog;
> I have been a stag, and a roe-buck on the mountain;
> I have been the stock of a tree; a spade; and axe in the hand;
> I have been a pin in a forceps for eighteen months;
> I have been a variegated cock –
> I have been a stud
> I have been a bull; I have been a buck
> Of yellow hue, yielding nourishment;
> I have been a grain concealed
> Which vegetated on a hill;
> And the reaper placed me in a smoky recess
> That by means of tribulation my virtue may be brought forth;
> A fowl with a divided crest and ruddy feet received me;
> Nine nights I remained in her womb – a male child;
> When I came forth from my entombment
> I was presented an offering to the Sovereign.
> I was dead, I have been vivified;
> And rich in my possession, I am made a medium of conveyance.
> In my prior state I was poor,
> For the heat-enkindling re-instruction
> Of the ruddy rooted I was received,
> Scarcly can be expressed the great praise which is due;
> I am Taliesin.

Some have found it the simplest thing in the world, on reading the above poem, to conclude that the Druids believed in and taught the transmigration of the soul. The evident stumbling-blocks to that conclusion have been hastily passed over; for it is difficult to conceive the human soul passing into 'the stock of a tree', 'a spade', 'an axe' or 'a pin in a forceps'. The series of metamorphoses these words speak of are of a very different kind. In the correspondences of the above poem, may be traced the process of regeneration in man as an individual of the ancient church; or the development of the church itself, viewed collectively. The Bard, in his description, commences with the scientific principle and passes through phase after phase of experience until he reaches the highest. The first thing mentioned is a species of fish; 'Fishes in the Word, signify scientifics, which have their birth from things sensual; for there are scientifics of three kinds, intellectual, rational, and sensual, all of which are sown in the memory – or rather in the memories, and in the regenerate are thence called forth of the Lord by the internal man' – (A.C. 991). The salmon consequently is a species of these scientifics appertaining to the sensual principle. Dog denotes the lowest things of the church placed, as it were, between the good and the evil, as a guard to prevent the profanation of holy things. This principle, though the lowest, is absolutely necessary for the safety of the church.

The limits of this volume will not admit of our giving the meaning of every word used in the poems quoted. The reader can himself discover such by appeal to the works on Correspondence already alluded to; in which case instead of being the meaningless effusions they on the surface appear to be, they will be found to give forth gems of true wisdom.

It must be admitted the writings of the Druids present us with such a weight of accumulative evidence in favour of their derivation from the Ancient Church of God that it must be only the stubbornness of prejudice that can possibly resist it. The religion which the British Bards inform us was derived from the primitive world, the principles of which were preserved amid the deluge and afterwards formed into a system, was from that time handed down among them from age to age by memorial. Their governing orders, form of worship, temples, theology and general philosophy harmonise with it.

The system of Church Government described in the present chapter furnishes evidence of the lofty regard in which its ministers were held, their training, mode of appointment, functions, obligations and privileges as well as what character of men they must have been.

The three following historical triads will explain the origin and nature of the various offices held.

1   The three primary sages of the race of the Cymry

Hu Gadarn (the mighty one who pervades, covers, inspects), who first collected the race of Cymry, and disposed them into tribes.

Dyfnwal Moelmud (a deep laid rampart or defence) first regulated the laws, privileges and institutions of the country and nation; (this name is significative of the defence of the truth or of the law: Dyfnwal, a deep laid rampart, and Moelmud, the removal of nakedness).

Tydain Tâd Awen (the central fire, father of inspiration), who first introduced order and method into the memorials and preservation of the oral art and its properties; and from that order, the privileges and methodical usages of the Bards and Bardism of the Isle of Britain were first devised.

2   The three primary Bards of the Isle of Britain

Plenydd (Light or Radiance).

Alawn (Harmony).

Gwron (Energy or Virtue).

These were they who devised the privileges and usages which belong to Bards and Bardism.

3   The three elementary masters of poetry and memorial of the race of Cymry

Gwyddon Ganhebon (knowledge or wisdom with its language or utterance), the first in the world who composed poetry.

Hu Gadarn (the mighty one who pervades, covers, inspects) who first adapted poetry to the preservation of record and memorials.

Tydain Tâd Awen (the central fire and father of inspiration), who first developed the art and structure and poetry, and due disposition and thought.

The personification of abstract principles is here again plainly seen. Not only are principles so treated, but the conceptions the Druids had of the various phases of God's dealings with them as a people are also personified. The providence which collected the Cymry, disposed them into tribes, and taught them the use of poetry as a means of preserving their records and memorials is Hu Gadarn (the mighty one who pervades, covers, inspects). The divine love of right and order which laid down laws by which, instead of being naked and exposed to the evils of lawlessness, they were covered as with a defence and sheltered as by a rampart is Dyfnwal Moelmud. The inspiration which taught them how to set in order their memorials, their oral arts, their privileges and usages, as well as to develop the art and structure of poetry is Tydain Tâd Awen, the central fire, the father of inspiration. Who were Hu Gadarn, Dyfnwal Moelmud and Tydain Tâd Awen? Certainly neither legendary gods nor heroes; but they were one and the same Deity under different aspects; the one God to whom this ancient people ascribed all praise for the good they possessed. To themselves they take no praise. Even the first in the world to compose poetry is not one of themselves, but Gwyddon Ganhebon, knowledge with its utterance; and the three primary Bards of the Isle of Britain bear not the proud names of men but those of the three principles which were God's gifts and which in their belief shone like three bright stars in the firmament of British Bardism: – Gwron (energy or virtue), Plenydd (Light), and Alwan (Harmony).

Nothing can be clearer than that the Druidic orders were regarded as a divine institution just as the Christian ministry is regarded to-day. No modern minister believes more firmly in his divine call to the office than did the Druid Bard. It is evident the Druids believed as strongly as did the Ancient Hebrews that God alone was Head of the Church; that in its inception, its establishment in the Isle of Prydain, its constitution and its government all that pertained to the Church was from Him. The Divine Love of which 'the central fire', according to correspondence, was the representative or symbol, was the source of all their inspiration or, as they express it in another place, 'poetic genius from God'. The Divine Might and all pervading Presence were their shelter, their rampart and defence. Instinctively occur to our minds similar terms used by Old Testament writers, which sound like echoes of the thoughts which had stirred the Druids long before either Moses or David had committed them to writing. 'The rock of my strength'; 'a shelter for me and a strong tower from the enemy'; 'a sun and a shield'; these, beautiful as they have become to the ear of the Bible reader, are no more expressive than some found in Druidic writings.

The language of the triads just given point back to a remote period of antiquity when Druidism was first brought forth out of chaos and reduced to a system.

The various offices and their functions are further described in the 'Laws of Dfynwal Moelmud' as follows: – 'There are three orders of the profession of Bardism: first, the Chief Bard, or the Bard of full privileges, who has acquired his degree and privilege through discipline under a master duly authorised, being a Conventional Bard. His office is to preserve the memory of all arcana and knowledge whilst he shall continue in his office of Bard regularly instituted, and also to preserve every record and memorial of the country and tribe respecting marriages, pedigree, arms, inheritance and rights of the Country and Nation of Cymry.

'Second, the Ovate, whose degree is acquired in right of his possessing natural poetic genius, or praise-worthy knowledges, which he shall prove by the correctness of his answers when examined before a customary and honourable congress of Bards; or where there is no such congress, by a lawful session granted by the tribe of the Lord of the District; or by twelve of the judges of his Court; or by the twelve jurors of the Court in the customary manner. The Ovate is not to be interrogated respecting anything else, except his proficiency and accuracy in knowledge. This is so regulated for the maintenance of knowledges, lest there should be a deficiency of regular teachers, and thus knowledges, and the Art of memory, and wisdom, through the deficiency of regular instruction should be lost; and also for the further improvement of the Arts and sciences, by the addition of every new discovery approved by the judgment of the masters and wise men, and confirmed as such by them; and also lest the advantage airising from the powers of natural genius and invention should be repressed.

'Third, the Druid-Bard; who must be a Bard regularly initiated and graduated, of approved wisdom and knowlege, and language to make known judgment and reason founded upon knowledge. He is raised to his office according to the privilege granted by reason and the regular court of the tribe, being elected by ballot and his election being warranted by the vote of the Convention. His duty is to teach and make known the knowledges and wisdom and godliness in the convention of the Bards, in the Palace, in the place of worship, and in every family in which he has full privilege.

'Each of these three has a just and lawful claim to five free acres of land in right of his profession, exclusive of what he is entitled to as a free-born Briton: for the right of profession does not abrogate that by nature, nor the natural right the professional.' – Triads of the Social State.

As seen in the Institutional triads the Chief Bard, besides discharging the duties mentioned above, was also governor of the ruling order, and, by virtue of his office, was called the presiding Bard.

'The three orders of the primitive Bards: –

'The Presiding Bard, or Primitive Bard Positive, according to the rights, voice, and usage of the Bardic convention, whose office is to superintend and regulate.

'The Ovate according to poetical genius, exertion and contingency, whose function is to act from the impulse of poetical inspiration; and

'The Druid according to reason, nature, and necessity of things, whose office is to instruct.' – Institutional Triads.

The Druid Bard, though mentioned last in both these triads, was nevertheless the most honourable of the three, being elected to his office from amongst the Presiding or Chief Bards. From among the Druidicial order was elected the Chief Priest of the Nation, or the Arch Druid, who in his person united the priestly and kingly offices. Originally the Druid-Bard was the Patriarch of the Nation, in whom was vested all power temporal and spiritual. As this term of patriarch was in the Scripture confined to fathers of families and tribes in antediluvian times, and to those progenitors of the Israelites who preceded Moses, such as Abraham, Isaac and Jacob, the fact provides another interesting index to the great antiquity of the Druidic Church. At a later period it became necessary to separate the sacred from the secular duties, and the subordinate or secular office became that of the Ovate. With the exception of those mentioned, we read of no distinctions among the orders of the Druidical Priesthood. They were distinguished according to their respective functions, the most honourable among them being, not the ruling priest, but the teacher in the convention of Bards, in the palace, in the place of worship, and in the private family.

The derivation of the word Derwydd or Druid has been erroneously traced to Derw – oak, and Gwydd – a man of wisdom. The error is partly due to the similarity of the words Derw and Derwydd, and partly to the supposed custom of the Druids of worshipping in oak groves. This, however, can scarcely be sustained, for the Druids did not always worship in Oak groves, but in the open, sometimes on mountain tops and sometimes on the open plains – Salisbury Plain for instance, where there were no oak groves. The correct derivation of the word Derwydd is undoubtedly that given by Davies in his 'Celtic Researches.' He says, 'The order of the Druids, under that name, do not appear to have been traced, or known, out of Gaul and the Islands of Britain. The name seems to have belonged exclusively to the British Order, and to have extended only where that order was acknowledged. The original and primitive inhabitants of the Island, at some remote period of antiquity, revised and reformed their national institutes. Their priest or instructor had hitherto been simply named Gwyz or Gwydd, as the term is retained by Taliesin – "Bum Gwydd Yngwarthan"; but it was deemed advisable to divide the sacred office between the national or superior priest, and a subordinate character whose influence was more limited. From henceforth, the former became Derwydd or Druid, which in the language of the people to whom we owe the term, is a compound of Dâr, Superior and Gwydd, a Priest or instructor: the latter was Go-wydd or Ovydd, a subordinate instructor; and was sometimes called syw or sy-wydd, names familiar to the Bards – Taliesin and Aneurin.'

Sir John Morris-Jones in Y Beirniad 1911 – Pages 66–72, seems to have overlooked this derivation of Ovydd, and seeks to ascribe it to Henry

Rowlands 'Mona Antigua', as a Welsh rendering of Strabo's *ovaties*, which is somewhat far fetched.

Mr Davies is not quite correct in his translation of Gwydd as 'Priest': 'sage' or one possessed of superior wisdom would have been more apt a term.

Myfyr Morgannwg traces the root of the word as follows:

Welsh: – Gwyddon, wisdom: Gwyddoniaith, science.
Erse: – Fodh, knowledge.
Sanskrit: – Budh, sage, from which 'Buddha' is derived.
Persian: – Wudd, to know.
Latin: – Vid-ere, to see.
Danish: – Vidi, to know.

The derivation of the word might also be traced to 'gwydd' – trees or wood. Before paper was invented Druidic characters were carved or cut in wood. Hence a man able to carve or read such wooden characters became one versed in 'wooden knowledge' or 'gwydd-on': a literary man is now known as llenor, *llen* a sheet, llenor, a *littérateur*. Even to-day the idiomatic Welsh form of 'write your name' is *torrwch eich enw*, or cut your name, and without a doubt is derived from this ancient practice.

Hutchinson remarks, 'It is singular that the Magi (or wise men) of Matthew 2.I is rendered by an Irish version, Daraoithe, the Druids, or the true wise men. Magi in the east, Druid in the west.' – History of Cumberland.

Moore, in his 'History of Ireland,' derives the word from Draoid, in Irish signifying a cunning or wise man. The 'Magicians of Egypt', is rendered in the Irish version, 'The Druids of Egypt'.

Borlase, in his 'Antiquities of Cornwall,' writes on the same subject as follows: –

'What the Magi were in Persia, the same were the Druids in Britain. The testimony of Pliny is conclusive on the point: "Why should I commemorate?", says he, "these things with regard to an art which has passed over the seas, and reached the bounds of nature? Britain, even at this time, celebrates Druidism with so many wonderful ceremonies, that she seems to have taught it to the Persians, and not the Persians to the Britons. The Druids were the Magi of the Britons, and had a great number of rites in common with the Persians: the term Magus, among the ancients, did not signify a magician in the modern sense but a superintendent of sacred and natural knowledge."'

The position occupied by the Druids was one of great power and privilege, and the sway they exercised over those whose ministers they were was more marked than has been the case with any hierarchy since. Their office however, carried with it responsibilities and sacrifices commensurate with its lofty dignity. The Druid bearing upon himself the burdens of High Priest, King and Prophet, was of an order similar to if not identical with that of Melchizedek in whom were joined the same three functions. Indeed, Morien in the 'Light of Briozannia' essays to prove that they were one and the same order, and that Melchizedek was a priest of the Druidic Church. The similarity of the two orders is so marked that there seems no reason to doubt the argument. How great, then, must have been the sublime dignity of the office when it is borne in mind that the prophecy of the 110th Psalm, 'Thou art a priest for ever after the order of Melchizedek' is by the writer of the Epistle to the Hebrews applied to Christ Himself! Nothing within the power of human language can more worthily set forth the estimation in which the sacred office of Druid was enshrined.

One of the restrictions of the Druidic office was that he should not bear arms. The injunction was not only rigidly observed, but the mind of the people was so possessed by a sense of its sacred character that none ever dared to unsheathe a sword in the presence of a Druid. Thus we find that at the commencement of every religious service the question was first asked 'A oes heddwch' – 'Is there peace?' – and unless the answer was in the affirmative the service could not proceed. And in cases of tribal differences, should they resort to arms in order to settle them, the appearance on the field of a Druid in his unicoloured robe, even if the battle were at its highest, was an instant sign for both sides to sheathe their swords, and the fighting having ceased their differences were submitted to him for arbitration.

Compare this with the conduct of Christian Nations to-day. Not only do their priests and clergy accompany their armies, but they are enjoined to pray, each for the success of his respective army in its work of blood-shed, death and destruction. We have truly travelled far since the Druidic period, but scarcely in line with the sacred word, 'Thou shalt not kill', in which there is no mention of extenuating circumstances in excuse of war.

The character of these men, as teachers and governors, will appear from the following institutional triads.

'The three ultimate objects of Bardism: to reform morals and customs; to secure peace; and praise all that is good and excellent.

'The three joys of the Bards of the Isle of Britain; the increase of knowledges; the reformation of manners; and the triumph of peace over devastation and pillage.

'The three splendid honours of the Bards of the Isle of Britain: the triumph of learning over ignorance; the triumph of reason over irrationality, and the triumph of peace over depradation and plunder.

'The three attributes (or necessary and congenial duties) of the Bards of the Isle of Britain: to manifest the truth, and diffuse the knowledges of it, to perpetuate the praise of all that is good and excellent; and to make peace prevail over disorder and violence.

'The three necessary, but reluctant duties, of the Bards of the Isle of Britain: secrecy for the sake of peace and public good; invective lamentation required by justice; and the unsheathing of the sword against lawlessness and depradation.

'There are three avoidant injunctions on a Bard: to avoid sloth because he is a man given to investigation; to avoid contention, because he is a man of discretion and reason.' – Institutional Triads.

Another trial which appears in a later chapter requires, as one of three things without which no man can be a Bard, irreproachable manners.

The detractors of the Druids may be justly challenged to a comparison of these objects of the Druidic Bard with those of a Christian legislature and of even a Christian ministry. It is less in the case of Christian Magistrates than Christian Ministers that the comparison shows so much in the favour of Druidism. The calling of the preacher of the Gospel, rightly understood, is undoubtedly the highest to which a human life can be consecrated, but that it is so regarded by the masses of the people of Christian countries is little evident, for side by side with a widespread and, it might be said, inherent reverence for what the calling represents, there is an equally extensive disregard for those who fill it, due perhaps to a variety of causes not the least of which is the narrow interpretation placed upon it by the preacher himself. The importance of human salvation cannot be too strongly insisted upon, but if the need of it is interpreted only in relation to a future life, it falls immeasurably beneath the objects of ancient Druidism, and when unsupported by earnestness and zeal corresponding to the terrors from which man is supposed to be saved, it is not surprising that men regard it with doubt and suspicion. But surely the gospel message of salvation is not merely concerned with Heaven and Hell. The reformation of morals and customs, the security and promotion of peace, the praise of all that is good and excellent, the increase of knowledge, the triumph of learning over ignorance, the manifestation and diffusion of truth, the triumph of reason over irrationality, and courageous invective against injustice and all manner of lawlessness, all of which were among the avowed objects of the Bard are worthy of Christian ministers from the least to the greatest, and should not be delegated to magistrate or politician as outside the sphere of the pulpit. Let the Christian Church continue to divorce these things from the question of human salvation, then not all its evangelical missions or revival campaigns will save it from decline. If too the ancient Bard was enjoined 'to avoid sloth because he is a man given to investigations; to avoid contention, because he is a man given to peace, and to avoid folly, because he is a man of discretion and reason' and if he had to be a man 'of irreproachable manners' are these not also worthy of the emulation of the modern preacher into whose charge has been committed the Christian Gospel?

Druidic Costumes

Any account of the Druidic orders would be incomplete which omitted a description of their costumes. From most ancient times and among almost all races priests have been distinguished by peculiarity of dress. The elaborate instructions given to Moses for the making of the holy garments were a development of a custom which in simple form existed in patriarchal times, and has since descended to the Christian Church in forms varying from the pontifical robes of the Roman Catholic Church to the scarcely less imposing ones of the Protestant Church and, it may be added, still further to the simple garb of a modern clergyman or minister. There can be little doubt of the symbolic character of the ancient priestly dress. That of the Jewish priest was emphatically so, and that of the Druids, although not so imposing, was most strikingly representative. As ministers of religion, governors, and men of science, they wore appropriate robes, each order having its distinctive colour corresponding with and representing its particular function.

These dresses are so well described by Mr James in his treatise, that I cannot do better than transcribe from him.

The Druid Bard

'His dress was pure white. Taliesin calls the dress of this order "the proud white garment which separated the elders from the youth". But several French authors assert that the white garment of the continental Druids had a purple border.'

A Druid in full costume is described thus: – 'On his head, a garland or crown of Oak leaves; in his right hand, the crescent, or the first quarter of the moon, to signify that the time of the festival had arrived; around his neck, a string of white glass beads, called Glain; short hair, long beard, and a linen robe of pure white flowing down from the shoulders to the ankles, differing in shape from the surplices which are now worn by the ministers of religion, in that one side folded over the other in front and was fastened by a loop and button at the shoulder like a cassock; the sleeves were also open on the upper side along the arm as far as the shoulder, disclosing at once, the tunic or white jacket worn underneath, which had tight sleeves with cuffs turned up at the wrists, and cut in points. The crescent was of pure gold.'

The Chief or Privileged Bard

'The distinguishing dress of this order was the unicoloured robe of sky-blue. Thus Cynddelw in his ode on the death of Cadwallon, calls these Bards "wearers of long blue robes". And since the sky without a cloud appears serene, and exhibits to an advantage its vivid blue, this colour was the best that could have been chosen as an emblem of peace, of which the Bards were professedly the advocates and heralds.'

The following is Mr James's account of a Bard in full costume. 'In addition to the robe we have just described, the privileged Bard on all occasions that he officiated wore a cowl or hood of the same colour, as a graduated badge or literarary ornament. This custom was borrowed from the Bards by the Druids of Gaul, and from them by the Romans. Whence this cowl, on its being made use of at Rome obtained the name of "Bardo-cucullus", or the Bard's hood, which was adopted by the monks, and is still worn by the Capuchin friars. But the dress of the Bards differed a little in shape as well as in colour from that of the Druid order. It seems to have been more open in front, and with narrower sleeves, lest they should be in the way when the Bard had occasion to play on the harp. Around his neck was a string of blue glass beads, called, as before, Glain. His hair was short and his beard was long, similar to the Druid or Priest.

'The original British Harp was strung with hair, and consisted probably of the same number of strings as the ribs of the human body, viz. twelve. And such harps were used at first by scholars so late as the tenth century, as appears from the laws of Howel the Good, who directed a fee to be paid to the master of the art when the minstrel left off playing on them.'

The Ovate

'The dress of this order was green, the symbol of nature, the mysteries of which the Ovate was considered more particularly to study, as the physician of the tribe. He studied astronomy, the revolution of the Seasons, and the use of letters, but, above all, the production of nature, with a view to ascertain their medicinal qualities. Taliesin, in one of his poems, makes an Ovate say, "With my robe of light green, possessing a place in the assembly". He also had a cucullus or hood attached to his robe, and a string of green glass beads around his neck, and in his hand a golden topped staff which measured about five feet six inches, a badge of his being an honorary member of the Bardo-Druidic institutions. His beard was also long, and his hair short. With the people it was otherwise. Their hair was allowed to grow like that of Absalom, and their beard was kept close, except on the upper lip.'

The Judicial Costume

'The national Druid in his Judicial Habit was clothed in a stole of virgin white, over a closer robe of the same that was fastened by a girdle on which appeared the crystal stone, which was incased in gold, hence Taliesin says, "O thou with pure gold upon thy clasp." Round his neck was the breastplate of judgment, in the form of a crescent with a full moon or circle fixed to each point, so as to present an even superficies to the spectators. Below the breastplate appeared the string of white glass beads set in gold. Encircling his temples was a wreath of oak leaves, and a tiara of pure gold in the form of a crescent placed behind it, the narrow points of which were concealed behind his ears, whilst the broad or middle part presented a bold front over the crown of the head.

'On the middle finger of the left hand was a ring, and a chain ring on the next to it, while the hand itself rested on the Peithynen or Elucidator, supported by an altar of stone. The Elucidator consisted of several staves called faith-sticks or lots, on which the judicial maxims were cut, and which being put into a frame were turned at pleasure, so that each staff or bar, when formed with three flat sides represented a triplet; when squared or made with four flat sides, a stanza. The frame itself was an oblong with right angles.

'The appearance of the National Priest in his judicial robes was splendid and imposing; inferior certainly to the Jewish High Priest, but not altogether dissimilar in the distant view of him.'

Something more must have been intended by these costumes than the mere distinction of one order from another, an object which could have been gained without the introduction of so many points of difference. Nor can those distinctive features be regarded as simply ornamental. Every detail of the garments of the Israelitish priesthood had a particular signification and was laid down authoritatively as such in the injunction given to Moses. 'And thou shalt make holy garments for Aaron thy brother for glory and for beauty. And thou shalt speak unto all that are wise-hearted, whom I have filled with the spirit of wisdom, that they may make Aaron's garments to consecrate him, that he may minister unto me in the priest's office. And these are the garment which they shall make.' We see no reason for supposing the Druids were left without similar guidance; and when we examine their vestments in the light of Scripture correspondences, sufficient ground is discovered for believing that they were not, and that the same God taught them what they should do as taught Moses.

Very many passages might be cited to prove that, throughout Scripture, such words as clothes, apparel, garments, raiment, indicate truths in the case of the good and falsities in that of the evil, or, in other words the principles of life derived from those truths or falsities. A few examples must suffice. The Jewish Church, in its possession of the truths of the Word and its treatment of them, is referred to in the following or similar language again and again. 'Awake, awake: put on thy strength, O Zion, put on thy beautiful garments, O Jerusalem' (Isaiah 52.I.) 'The king's daughter is all glorious within; her clothing is of wrought gold; she shall be brought unto the king in raiment of needlework' (Ps. 45. 13, 14.) In the New Testament we read of the man without the wedding garment, the false prophets in sheep's clothing, and of putting a piece of new cloth unto an old garment; in the Apocalypse, of the four and twenty elders clothed in white raiment, those who were clothed in white robes, those who washed their robes in the blood of the Lamb, and of the armies in heaven clothed in fine linen, white and clean. The Bible contains repeated references of the kind, and the Book of Revelation is particularly rich in them; but, whether in the Old Testament or the New, they always bear in their inner meaning some relation to truth, it may be the neglect of truth, the corruption of truth, the perversion of truth or, on the other hand, its acceptance, its power to reform, or some other aspect of the benefits which spring from it.

It may be seen that the official robes of the Druids bear a like interpretation. In the first place a point of similarity between them lies in the fact that they were all made of linen. Herodotus, writing of ancient Egypt, says: 'The priests also wear a linen garment and shoes of papyrus, and they are not permitted to put on any other clothing, and no other shoes.' White linen garments were not peculiar to the Egyptians and Israelites but were the common priestly dress throughout the old world. Bahr, in 'Der Symbolik des Mosaischen Cultus', says 'Everywhere from India to Gaul, the priests wear garments of vegetable material, consequently, of linen or cotton, and of white, if possible, of brilliant white colour.' Saubert in his 'De Sacrificiis' shows that everywhere in antiquity the priests were accustomed to clothe themselves with white linen garments. Hengstenberg in his 'Egypt and The Books of Moses', admits the colour taken by itself is not without importance and that white priestly apparel is common among other nations of antiquity. But in its exclusiveness as white linen, he asserts, it is peculiar only to the Egyptians and Israelites. The custom of the Druids contradicts this assertion.

What then was the significance of this general mode of dress? Many think it implied cleanliness. To quote Herodotus more fully: 'The Egyptians are excessively religious above all other people, and consequently practice the following usages: They drink from brazen cups which they wash out thoroughly every day. They wear linen garments always newly washed, with regard to which they take particular care. They also pratice circumcision for the sake of cleanliness, and prefer neatness to decorum. Moreover, the priests shave the whole body each third day, lest either a louse or any other vermin may be found on them while they are engaged in the service of the gods.' Plutarch attributes the custom to the fact that linen is a pure garment which least of all generates vermin. Many writers would have us believe that cleanliness was the object of the Israelitish priesthood in wearing the same material, and others that the wearing of linen by Aaron and his sons indicated and emphasised holiness. Without a doubt both cleanliness and holiness were intended. But they by no means were all that was meant. Cleanliness of body may be served by the wearing of white linen, and cleanliness may be symbolic of holiness, but white linen does not give holiness. Scripture consistently teaches that, apart from the Lord Himself who alone is Holy because He is Divine Truth, everything and everyone sanctified is made holy through relation to Divine Truth. It was not linen that made holy, but that which it represented, namely Truth. The ark in the tabernacle was termed the holy of holies, because it contained the Word of God. Christ said 'Father, sanctify them through the Truth, Thy Word is Truth; for their sakes I sanctify Myself that they also might be sanctified through the Truth.' (Gospel of John 17. 17, 19.)

Not only did the three orders, therefore, symbolise their devotion or consecration to the service of Truth by wearing 'linen', but one order wore 'white', another 'blue' and the other 'green', distinctions again not without their own peculiar significance. Gliddon in his work on Ancient Egypt states: – 'It is proved beyond doubt by Portal that from remotest times, colour had a symbolical meaning; and that remarkable analogies exist in regard to the mystical acceptation of every colour, among the Persians, Indians, Chinese, Hebrews, Egyptians, Greeks and Romans, preserved through the middle ages of Christianity – the last relics of which remain to our day in Heraldry.' The Bible student will admit that Scriptural expressions such as 'walk in white', 'clothed in white' or 'white robes' signify an exalted state of spirituality, or, in other words close relationship with God through His Truth.

'Blue' and 'green' are words which do not so frequently occur. Yet according to Swedenborg each has its peculiar significance in the world of correspondences. I feel it to be somewhat difficult to present in simple language what he says on this subject, and at the same time I appreciate how hard it is likely to be to the uninitiated to follow his own words. Interpreted in ordinary phrase, we are told that the 'ineffable splendour and effulgence' of the Divine Presence appears under three different colours in the three kingdoms, the celestial, the spiritual, and the natural. In the first it appears 'red like a ruby', in the next 'blue like the lazule stone', and in the third 'green like an emerald'. In the spiritual world there are 'two fundamental colours, white and red'. 'White' originates in the light of the Sun in heaven, that is in spiritual light, which is white; and 'red' in the fire of the Sun there, thus in celestial light. The origin of 'blue' is twofold, from whar is red or aflame, or from what is white or lucid. That which is from the red or flaming is the celestial love of truth, and that which is from the white or lucid is the spiritual love of good. 'Green', he tells us, signifies the scientific and 'sensual' principle. The word sensual here means that which is dependent on the senses. We gather then that white is the correspondence of spiritual light, blue the spiritual love of good, and green the scientific principle. The celestial kingdom, obviously, has no relation to the subject before us, and therefore red does not call for our consideration.

There is a remarkable agreement between what Swedenborg says of these three colours, and their selection by the Druids for the distinction of the three orders. There is such special fitness in these colour representations of the functions of the three offices, and such harmony between them and Swedenborg's teaching, that it almost seems as though the Druids were conversant with his writings. It may be asked 'Were they aware of these correspondences?' The founders most certainly were. That they were well known to them naturally follows from what has been said concerning the relationship of Druidism to the Ancient Church.

I have dealt so fully with their robes, their material and colour, that the reader will pardon me if remaining features are given a less lengthy treatment. On the head of the Chief Druid was a garland of Oak leaves and a tiara of pure gold. The head signifies wisdom and intelligence or their opposites, folly and insanity, according to the context in which the word is used. Anything, therefore, of head dress must signify some modification of the representative meaning of head; and as the leaves of the oak, according to correspondences signify 'scientifics' or rational truths, the garland must have been intended to attribute to the wearer wisdom or intelligence of a scientific nature, and as a golden crown signifies wisdom proceeding from love of truth, the tiara of pure gold, like Aaron's mitre with its plate of gold, must have declared the wearer to be wise in the knowledge and exposition of Divine Truth. The breastplate of judgment had not the stones which were in Aaron's and which represented the twelve tribes; but it contained a crystal stone which, encased in pure gold represented transparent truth held in love, the girdle which kept it in place further pointing to the conjunction of truth and goodness. The union of inner and outer principles was also symbolised in the necklace of beads.

The 'crescent shaped tiara' and the 'moon' in the breastplate brings us to one of the 'principle correspondences of Scripture, and I cannot do better than give its elucidation in the language of David Goyder. After describing how the

Sun as the great source of life and centre of the planetary system corresponds to Divine Love, he says: – 'The Moon, as deriving her light from the Sun, corresponds to the Divine Truth. In a primary sense, the moon is the representative of the church, because, as she derived all her light from the sun, on whom she is dependent, so the church derived all her truth and intelligence from the Lord, the Sun of Righteousness, on whom she is dependent. In a seconday sense the moon corresponds to faith; for as faith is the principle which removes darkness from the mind of every recipient of admission into the church, so the moon is the only medium of removing that entire obscurity and darkness of night, which compensates in some small degree for the absence of the more glorious light of the sun.' The correspondence of the moon and faith is more fully illustrated by the same writer. 'The moon depends for her light upon the sun; she is the constant attendant upon the earth, and revolves round it, communicating to it light in darkness, and by her influence moves and purifies the waters of the ocean, rendering it a source of life, instead of a stagnant mass of putridity. And faith or truth performs the same offices, spiritually, to the mind, that the moon does to the earth, deriving all its excellency, in fact its very existence, from Divine Love. It is the constant light of the Christian, cheering him with the "evidence of things not seen" when all else is dark and gloomy around him.' The reader will find it interesting to study scriptural references to the moon in the light of what is here said; and, if satisfied that the correspondence given is correct, he will see a new meaning in the breastplate and tiara of the Druids.

The cucullus or hood must have signified the same as the linen bonnets of the Jewish priests mentioned in Ezekiel 44, 18, and the golden topped staff of the Ovate signified power from the Lord and implied the faculty of knowing and seeing. (Compare Psalm 23, 4; 110, 2; Isaiah 14, 5; Jeremiah 48, 17). Even the harp in the ancient Church had its correspondences which tempt to lengthy treatment, but it must suffice to state them in a few words. Harps signify the religious confessions of those who know God through goodness and truth. Scripture in numerous places bears this out: 'Praise Jehovah with the harp, sing unto Him with the psaltery, and an instrument of ten strings.' 'I will praise Thee on the harp, O God, my God'; 'Sing unto Jehovah with thanksgiving, sing praise upon the harp unto our God'; and in the Apocalypse the word is used with the same meaning.

21

THE DRUIDS IN TRADITION

T.D. Kendrick

From *The Druids: A Study in Keltic Prehistory*

There is little need to remark upon the inextinguishable affection with which the druids are still regarded in the popular imagination. The antiquary in his travels, or for that matter any curious layman, must inevitably be aware of the renown they enjoy; for the signs of it are constantly encountered in the narratives of guides and guide-books, and in the place-names of the country-side: while it is not uncommon to hear that some of the supposed ceremonies of the druids have been reenacted with appropriate pomp by societies professing to continue the ancient functions of the order. A visitor to the Chislehurst Caves in Kent – to take one example out of the many that offer themselves in this connection – will discover that there is attached to these artificial galleries, which are relatively of quite modern date, a complicated system of legend glorifying the druids not only as the singing priests of a subterranean chapel,[1] but also as the makers of the prehistoric flint implements found in the neighbourhood. In fact, it may truly be said that the unlettered public has accepted, as a simple solution of the mysteries of very remote antiquity, a primary division of nearly all our ancient remains earlier than Saxon times into 'Roman' and 'Druidic,' so that the druids are rapidly becoming synonymous with the Ancient Britons, that is to say, the pre-Roman population of this country. As a counter to this, the learned from time to time assert that the current notions concerning the druids are mistaken; but in spite of all their endeavours the priesthood has lost little, if any, prestige, and contines securely enthroned in the fancy of the people.

This general faith in the druids, so widely held throughout the country and so difficult to disturb, invites discussion at the outset of a book dealing with the priesthood as it is known to us in antiquity. For it may reasonably be asked whether the popular beliefs ought not to affect the manner whereby the problem is approached, whether they do not place it in a sense outside the scope of a merely archaeological dissertation. In a word, is it possible that the people possess through the agency of folk-memory a dim and mysterious knowledge of the druids that should over-rule any theoretical conclusions in opposition to the popular notions?

As a matter of fact, it cannot seriously be maintained that such knowledge exists. Folk-memory may, of course, be a significant factor in many of the problems in which the antiquary is interested, but here it would be little short of amazing if it had existed in such a precise and informative manner over a period that is now about 2000 years in length. For it would not be an instance of haphazard memory of forgotten days preserved in names and customs no longer understood, whereby one might conceivably achieve contact with the times of the druids, but an instance of deliberate and uninterrupted knowledge that unfortunately only made itself manifest in quite recent times (as will soon be shown), and that, equally unfortunately, is partly in conflict with the archaeological evidence.

The soundest argument against the possibility that such folk-memory existed is the positive knowledge we possess of the growth of the beliefs in question, and in the first chapter I propose to prove their modernity. This can best be achieved, firstly, by considering one especially deep-rooted notion about the druids, namely, the theory that it was they who built and used prehistoric rough stone monuments; and, secondly, by a general study of their appearances in popular literature.

One reason why archaeologists are not very successful in correcting the general opinion of the druids, or in showing that some of its more extravagant implications are ridiculous, is that it was they themselves, or rather their ancestors in archaeology, who implanted the current notions. Doubtless the culprits did not anticipate the far-reaching results of the magnification of an obscure priesthood, but the fact remains that as the result of an archaeological disclosure the druids at one bound came not only into their own, but into a great deal more than their own; and it looks as though they are likely to hold on to it.

Of course, it is not a very difficult thing to establish eccentric ideas concerning the distant past, but as a rule these find favour only in a strictly limited section of the community: for a time they may be firmly believed, and they may even be persistent, but they are only current among a few dabblers in learning, and seldom attract any wide notice. It is obvious, therefore, that there must be some strong appeal to common sense, or the satisfaction of a solution to a definite puzzle, if an idea is to be popularly comprehended and accepted; and it is because these advantages could be pleaded on behalf of the druids, that they hold their present high place in the general estimate of our ancient history and prehistory.

For there happened to be a focus upon which their claims could be centred, a reason for the revived memory of them, and this was provided by the mysterious but well-known rough stone monuments that are still plentiful throughout the land, chambers built of enormous slabs of stone, and circles and alignments of massive uprights or great recumbent boulders. Nothing was known as to the use of these or their origin, and when the druids were paraded as their probable builders the attraction of priests without temples to temples without priests proved irresistible.[2] And so it came about that all the protests of modern learning are insufficient to re-name the Druids' Altars and Druids' Temples of our country-side; they are the names bestowed by the people at the bidding of earlier archaeologists, and they are at once explanatory and satisfying; wherefore it is evident that dolmen, cromlech, megalithic monument, and the like, have small chance of becoming popular substitues.

This widely held belief that it was the druids who built the stone monuments is the subject that it is convenient to discuss first of all; and to illustrate the genesis of the idea, that is to say, the manner of the druidic revival in its archaeological sense, it is necessary to consider in some detail the historical aspect of a special problem of British archaeology, that of the famous megalithic pile, Stonehenge. Nowadays there is nothing more druidic than Stonehenge; in fact, it is so signally and sacredly druidic that some modern druids think it proper that a portion of the ashes of their deceased brethren should be buried within its precincts. It is all the more interesting, therefore, to find that for a long while its druidic character was absolutely unsuspected, for this must surely rob the modern notion of all traditional value.

The first unmistakable reference to the monument occurs in the 12th century in the writings of Henry of Huntingdon, who was content simply to catalogue it as one of the marvels of this island, though he remarked incidentally that its origin was unknown. But in the same century we come upon the account of the building of Stonehenge related by Geoffrey of Monmouth, an exciting legend about the transport of the stones from Ireland by Merlin to form the memorial erected by Aurelius Ambrosius to the victims of Hengist's treachery in A.D. 470. This story was current for about 500 years, and is repeated in the poetry of Alexander Neckham (1157–1217), in Langtoft's chronicles (c. 1300), and in the works of several much later writers. A slight variation in the legend was made by Polydore Vergil at the beginning of the 16th century, for this writer affirmed that the monument was simply the sepulchre of Ambrosius; but the first published theory running counter to Geoffrey's version is that of Edmund Bolton, who proposed in 1624 that Stonehenge was the tomb of Boadicea.[3] And it is evident that the Merlin story was wellnigh forgotten about this time, because even such an inquisitive and diligent person as the antiquary Camden, who can be trusted to have ferreted out any surviving folklore, was quite at a loss to explain the monument, and had nothing better to repeat than a vague rumour that the stone themselves had been artificially composed of sand and glue.

Therefore, so far as tradition is concerned, all that there is to go upon is this 12th century story recounted by Geoffrey: and, accordingly, it becomes important to enquire whether Merlin was supposed by the medieval historians to have been a druid. I am not disposed to shirk the issue by saying that Merlin was largely a creature of Geoffrey's imagination; but to maintain that this author's account of the origin of Stonehenge is evidence of its traditional association with the druids seems to me, even on the most charitable view of the tale that can be taken, to be absolutely beyond the warrant of the facts.

Actually, the Merlin stories form a group that originally concerned two distinct persons, one a 6th century Welsh prince, Myrddin ab Morfryn, and the other Vortigern's prophet, Ambrosius, who figures in the *Historia Britonum* of 'Nennius.' Geoffrey used the name Merlinus for both these persons, and then proceeded to combine the stories about them as though they referrd to a single individual. The Welsh prince is certainly the hero of his later *Vita Merlini*, but in the earlier *Historia Regum Britanniae* it is Ambrosius who is uppermost in his mind: in fact, in his first work he plainly says that Ambrosius was another name for Merlin.[4]

Now there is not one word about druidical training nor practice either in the *Historia* or in the *Vita*. In the last-named work it is said of Merlin *rex erat et vates*, he was a king and a prophet; while in the *Historia* he is simply a prophet, only distinguished by his strange birth and his superior utterances from the other magicians of Vortigern. And these, it should be noted, share the name magi with other wise men living outside the druidic lands, the soothsayers of the Trojan settlers in Italy, for example.

In order, therefore, to give a druidic flavour to this story about Stonehenge, we must say that the tale relates to the Ambrosius of 'Nennius', and that the dual rôle of sorcerer and adviser played by this person at the court of Vortigern in the 5th century suggests the degraded duties that might have appertained to the surviving druids, if there were any in England, at so late a date. But in 'Nennius', it must be remembered, the word magi is used for such seers, and not druids; so that even if it be granted that this Ambrosius was a druid in its ultimate sense of a simple magiciain, Geoffrey's tale is nevertheless separated by a period of about eight centuries from the last mention of the word druid in Gaul. And we are even further removed from the real and organised druidism that was flourishing in this country before the Roman occupation, of which it is very obvious neither Geoffrey nor 'Nennius' knew anything at all.

But this is not everything. Geoffrey himself describes his Merlin-Ambrosius person as the son of a Christian princess[5] who had been visited by an incubus;[6] and if we go further back for information about his birth, and what manner of man he was, that is to say, if we enquire in the *Historia* of 'Nennius',[7] we get still further away from the druids, for it is therein related that he was sprung from Roman parents of consular rank.

It is almost impossible, therefore, to see any trace in this story of Geoffrey's that can reasonably be held to reflect the tradition of a druidic origin of Stonehenge. Nor, in truth, can it even be said that there is anything in the legend to suggest that the monument was popularly connected with the religious ceremonies of the ancient Britons; for it will have been noticed that in the tale it is explained simply as a memorial to dead heroes.

But whether one attaches any importance to it or not, this story represents the only popular belief ever current, so far as one can tell, about the monument before the beginning of the 17th century. At that time King James I became interested in Stonehenge, and the enquiries that he caused to be made into the origin of this astonishing ruin gave rise to a long series of theoretical disquisitions whose purport has considerable bearing upon our special subject, the growth of the current notion that it was the druids who built it. The first attempt to solve the mystery was made by Inigo Jones, the architect-general, who was ordered to the task by the King himself. Jones prepared a treatise on the subject that was drawn up in 1620 and published some thirty years later. At the outset he discusses the possibility of a druidic origin, but he does not bring this forward as a theory favoured by others or supported by any sort of tradition; he mentions it incidentally as a supposition of his own, and it is dismissed in a page as an exceedingly improbable alternative to his decided opinion that the monument was Roman.

This disquisition was followed in 1663 by the admirable essay of Dr Charleton, a court physician, who, though 'reputed to have over-valued his Parts and Performances', was nevertheless acknowledged to be a person of great learning. He contended that the monument was built by the Danes for the consecration of their kings, a most popular conclusion in the days of a recently revived monarchy:–

> Nor is thy Stone-Heng a less wonder grown,
> Though once a Temple thought, now prov'd a Throne.
> Since we, who are so bless'd with Monarchy,
> Must gladly learn from thy Discovery,
> That great Respects not only have been found
> Where Gods were Worshipp'd, but where Kings were Crown'd.

But Dr Charleton never even bothered his head with a possible druidic origin; he was only at pains to disprove the Roman theory of Inigo Jones, and quite clearly the druids were not reckoned in his day as serious candidates for the honour of having built Stonehenge. Nor are they as much as mentioned in the tremendously vigorous counterblast prepared by John Webb, a relation by marriage and former pupil of Inigo Jones, who undertook to restore Stonehenge to the Romans; this, I think, is really significant, because he goes out of his way to quote Dr Aylett Sammes as supporting the theory of a Phoenician origin. Bishop Nicholson as thinking the monument Saxon, Aubrey as believing it to be British, and Bolton's guess that it was the tomb of Boadicea. Aubrey, as we shall see, did believe that the druids built Stonehenge, but his views and arguments were unpublished, and Webb knew nothing of them; consequently there is not a word for or against the druids in his long and involved work.

The first person, then, to claim Stonehenge for the druids was the excellent and entertaining antiquary, John Aubrey (1626–1697), the portrait of whom is reproduced as the frontispiece. A mere statement of his opinion was published in Gibson's edition of *Camden's Britannia* in 1695, but his celebrated disquisition upon Stonehenge and Avebury was never given to the world, apparently because he was not satisfied with his knowledge of the rough stone monuments in other districts. This is a great pity, since it must have been a refreshing and intelligent document, far pleasanter reading than the angry and laboured arguments of Jones, Charleton and Webb. 'I come in the rear of all,' wrote Aubrey, 'by comparative arguments to give clear evidence that these monuments (Avebury, Stonehenge, and the like) were Pagan temples; which was not made out before; and have also with humble submission to better judgment, offered a probability that they were Temples of the Druids. . . . This enquiry, I must confess, is a groping in the dark; but although I have not brought it into clear light, yet can I affirm that I have brought it from an utter darkness to a thin mist, and have gone further in this essay than anyone before me.'[8] This is an admirable mood, and it is not surprising to find that both in description and conjecture he had written with care and acumen. For he was never obsessed with his druidic theory; indeed, he seems at one time to have decided that the monuments were merely sepulchres, and was propably turned to his final opinion by Camden's remarks on the name Cerrig-y-Drudion. But what we shall notice with interest is that he himself was clearly of the opinion that he was the very first to think that Stonehenge was a druidic temple, for it is unlikely that we should have had such humble talk if there had been a scrap of folklore that could have been used as warrant for his view.

Although it was never completly published and explained, Aubrey's conclusion seems to have had more effect than there is controversy to show. I think there is no doubt that he influenced Dr Plot, the historian of Staffordshire; and Toland (1670–1722), who wrote a curious and rambling history of the druids, pays a pretty tribute to him as the only man he had met in his early days who, beside himself, had a right notion of these matters. And so, when the next and chief protagonist of the druids appears, there was no longer need to prove that Stonehenge was the work of this priesthood; instead, it is tacitly assumed. Part of this assurance may be ascribed to the natural ebullience of the new author; but if views other than his own held the day, he was not the one to pass them by unchallenged, and I am inclined to think that William Stukeley owed something of the startling success of his writings upon the druids to the increasingly favourable reception, just before his own day, of Aubrey's hypothesis. Not that there can have been direct influence, for Stukeley was but ten years old in 1697 when Aubrey died, and when his famous works upon Stonehenge and Avebury appeared in 1740 and 1743, he makes no acknowledgment of indebtedness to his predecessor; indeed, the allusions to Aubrey in Stukeley's abundant writings are few and of the briefest sort.

If Aubrey was a somewhat diffident protagonist, Stukeley, at any rate, was headstrong and whole-hearted. The druids absorbed him. He even erected his own private druidic temple, a sylvan one, in his garden at Grantham; and his friends nicknamed him Chyndonax. With admirable ingenuity he mixed together a splendid hotch-potch of invention and surmise until he had brewed the legend of a community of all-powerful priests of an ultimate Phoenician origin, and professing the patriarchal religion of Abraham, who built stone temples in the form of sacred serpents; *Dracontia*, he said these serpent-fanes were called, though he had no authority at all in antiquity for the word in a temple sense. And not only did he twist words, but he is also said to have twisted the very stones themselves to suit his theory, when he attempted the diagrammatic reconstruction of the remains; even Sir Richard Colt Hoare, who followed Stukeley and accepted most of his conclusions, was sometimes far from satisfied with the doctor's surveys and descriptions. But it is only fair to add that although he has been occasionally convicted of curling a tail out of a straight line of stones, or discovering the head of a snake where others have not been able to find anything at all, he has nevertheless won modern approval as a field-worker, for it is not very long ago that a particular series of measurements made by him had by chance to be repeated, whereupon the surveyors were able to record unequivocal testimony to the accuracy of the 18th century antiquary;[9] and there is certain positive achievement to his credit in this respect, for it was he who first pointed out the existence of the avenue and the curses at Stonehenge, and who first grappled with the problem of the relation between the monument and the adjacent barrows.

But even so, I imagine present-day enthusiasts for the druids are not likely to praise over loudly the man who so nobly furthered the renaissance of their cult, since the imaginative doctor-clergyman is an advocate of dubious repute, and I doubt if any modern druid would be wise to appeal to Stukeley's archaeological authority in the matter of stone monuments; for it would not be difficult to compile an ugly little catalogue of his mistakes, and the outspoken aspersions of his contemporaries[10] and successors upon his over-confident method; and, although he must be freely pardoned for it, it is not easy to forget that it was he who stood sponsor for a document that later proved to be one of the most harmful forgeries that have ever been perpetrated, a none too happy augury for his pet theory.

But whether he was a good or bad antiquary hardly matters; it is enough that he was in earnest and that he was successful in the propagation of his doctrine; more suddenly and completely successful than any other archaeological teacher I can call to mind. No one seems to have disputed his main conclusion, although in the instance of Stonehenge an attempt was made to give it an astronomical flavour in 1771 by the Glasgow vaccinator, John Smith, the first of the exponents of the famous theory that the plan of the monument is in deliberate relation with the movements of heavenly bodies. This author dissented from Stukeley on certain matter points; for instance, he did not believe that the altar stone was used for human sacrifice, his reason being simply that the altar would not bear fire. He tried a fragment of it in a crucible and found that it first of all changed colour and then was reduced to a powder; 'very unfit surely for burnt offerings! 'he says.[11] And there were other variations of Stukeley's thesis, such as that of the Bath architect, John Wood, who hazarded that although Stonehenge was druidical, it was really a lunar temple with Diana as its goddess. In fact, the first directly opposed view was not put forward until almost exactly fifty years after Stukeley had published his book on Stonehenge; this was the theory of John Pinkerton, a Scottish historian, who argued that the monument was Gothic.[12]

It was not only in Great Britain that Stukeley's notion found favour. Toland tells us that in his time none of the French megalithic monuments were attributed to the druids, but in 1805, when Cambry published his famous *Monumens Celtiques*, we find that he advocates the druidic origin of all the continental rough stone monuments. It is true that he does not directly express his indebtedness to Stukeley, but the reverend doctor is mentioned in such a way that there is little doubt that his writings must have provided the mainspring of Cambry's arguments.

If we except Pinkerton's work, we may say that Stukeley's theory held the field without a rival. Certainly no one seriously attempted to challenge the druids as builders of Stonehenge and other monuments, and they continued in splendid possession for wellnigh a hundred years after Stukeley's time. And it was natural enough that during this length of time popular fancy should adopt them as obviously the ideal priests for the tenantless altars and temples; thus, with leisure to work its way unopposed throughout all the land, and with the argument of scholars in its support, the familiar function was formidable indeed; and there is nothing remarkable in its becoming at the beginning of the 19th century an article of general belief.

The moral of this story of the disputed origin of Stonehenge is very obviously that the now famous druidic theory, whether it be right or wrong, is not based on any sort of tradition, but is merely an invention of the late 17th century that was very successfully propagated during the next hundred years. In fact, before this period[13] the only person who seems to have considered it

Stonehenge in the 1800s.
From The Celtic Druids *by Godfrey Higgins*

even as remotely likely was Inigo Jones, and he very summarily rejects it at the outset of his enquiry. It would be possible to cite other instances of what may be termed the pre-druidic notion of our megalithic monuments, such as that of the celebrated Kit's Coty House, near Maidstone in Kent. Quite recently I have seen this once more claimed for the druids, since it has the appearance of being the ruins of a small chamber . . . the kind of thing supposed by the modern friends of the order to have been either a sort of observatory or a cell of initiation. But I would point out that there is at least nothing traditional about this contention, for it differs in toto from the popular belief of other days; this is related to us by Camden and by Stow, and their version is to the effect that the Coty was erected to mark the burial-place of a British prince Catigern, who fell near the site when fighting against the Saxons in the 5th century A.D. The druid theory, therefore, is simply a rival and subsequent guess, and it will later be shown that there are excellent archaeological reasons proving that both guesses are wrong.

It is hardly necessary to add that there is little or no corroborative evidence suggesting that a prolonged folk-memory actually existed.[14] Thus I have not been able to discover any antique place-names embodying the notion of druidic origin attached to sites of megalithic monuments. In this connection the most notorious name is Cerrig-y-Drudion in Denbighshire, for the second word is sometimes mis-spelt Druidion, and an inevitable confusion with the druids, initiated by the celebrated antiquary Camden (1551–1623), has resulted. Actually the name means stones of the heroes, and nothing more; the megalithic monuments to which it refers have now disappeared, but a tradition in respect of one of them has survived, and it has nothing whatever to do with the druids, the legend being that it was used as a prison for the victims of the terrible Cynric Rwth. I have also come across Tre'r Dryw, translated Druidstown, at Llanidan, in Anglesey, recently quoted again as an example, for there were stone monuments near by; but it is hardly possible to admit this instance, because the ancient meaning of Dryw is wren, and not druid, which is a more or less modern connotation.[15] In England we have Stoke Druid in Gloucestershire as a place-name, where megalithic remains are to be found, and if it could be traced back beyond the period of the archaeological advertisement of the druids we might see in it some evidence of folklore. But at the moment I have not succeeded in tracing it back at all, and I am rather impressed by the fact that it seems to have been quite unknown to Seyer, the historian of Bristol, who described this particular ruined structure in considerable detail in the year 1821.

Up to this point I have only attempted to show that in disputing the claim that the druids built the stone monuments one is not adventuring against a formidable display of folk-knowledge. There is, of course, a great deal more to be said on the archaeological aspect of the subject, and it is possible that it may not be necessary to insist upon a complete divorce of the druids from all their 'temples'. But here I am concerned solely with the traditional value of the theory of druidic origin, and it will be convenient to postpone further discussion for a later chapter.

The next point I want to make is that the theories of Aubrey and Stukeley, however well they may explain many modern notions, are not wholly responsible for them. To discover the ultimate cause of the revival of interest in these priests, and the secret of the success of such theories, it is essential to search further than among the pronouncements of individuals and to take stock of the altering outlook of the times in which they were promulgated. This, I think, can best be appreciated after a short survey of the rôle played by the druids in literature.

At the end of the 4th century A.D. the word druid still survived in the general literature of Roman Gaul, for it occurs twice in the poems of Ausonius . . . in an adjectival form that must clearly have been intelligible at any rate to the professors to whom the poem is addressed. But after the decline of the Empire and the passing of Western Europe into the hands of the Teutonic immigrants, the traditional history of Gaul, and the works of the classical historians, were rapidly and completely forgotten; so that as a result the druids do not re-appear again in any literature for a good many hundred years.

The word comes to light once more in 8th century Irish glosses and in the early mediaeval manuscripts of Ireland, where it had never ceased to circulate in the vulgar tongue,[16] while a supposed variant form, *derwydd*, is also found in a few early poems of the Welsh bards. In the 14th century, for example, the Irish scribe who translated the *Historia Britonum* of 'Nennius' uses 'druid' as the equivalent of *magi*, i.e. seers or magicians, in the original; and there is no doubt that at about that time, and before it, the word was well known to the Irish clerks.

But in the original *Historia*, written about A.D. 800, the magicians of the 5th century king Vortigern were not called druids; the Venerable Bede did not write of them in his *Ecclesiastical History*, and there is no mention of them at all in any of the Saxon or early mediaeval chronicles and romances. In England and on the continent, in fact, the Teutonic invasions had effectively obliterated all common knowledge of the ancient priesthood, and it stood little chance of revival as long as the church, the official fount of historical information, ignored the one possible source of enlightenment, the early Roman historians. This state of affairs is plainly revealed in the grossly unhistorical treatment of the subject-matter of the Arthurian cycle, wherein the druids might reasonably have found mention had the mediaeval authors consulted the classical material relating to the periods they were describing.

Thus, except for the occasional use of the name in a debased sense by the Irish schoolmen, and, more doubtfully, by the Welsh bards, it seems safe to say that throughout a long period from the 4th to the 16th century the original druids of antiquity had wellnigh passed from man's memory.

At length, however, the time came that the common classical sources of information were more frequently consulted, and as an inevitable consequence the knowldge that there had once been priests called druids gradually became general among educated folk. And if one watches for the early mentions of the druids in popular work, it can fairly easily be seen that their name creeps in rather as a morsel of this casual erudition than as a concession to vulgar predilection.

In England the period of oblivion from the 4th century onwards is not interrupted, to the best of my knowledge, until the year 1509, when the druids were included in the complement of Barclay's *Ship of Fools*: but thet only get in at second-hand, and four lines is their portion:–

> Or as the Druydans rennyth in vayne about
>> In theyr mad festes upon the hylle of yde
> Makynge theyr sacrafyce with furour noyse and shout
>> Whan theyr madness settyth theyr wyt asyde.

On the continent they were brought once more, after their long oblivion, to the notice of scholars by the *Annales Boiorum* of Aventinus (Johann Turmaier), who completed this celebrated work about the year 1521. The druids are described as Gaulish philosophers driven out of Gaul into Germany by the Emperor Tiberius, and this is really all that Aventinus has to say about them; but the *Annales* are so frequently quoted by later writers,[17] that the book may in justice be signalled as the starting-point[18] of the awakening interest in the druids that resulted from the renaissance of learning.

It would be difficult to imagine Rabelais omitting any discoverable name, so that it is not surprising that he should mention the ancient druids two or three times in *Pantagruel*, that was written about 1532. His source was obviously Caesar, as can be seen from the passage, 'If you fancy Mercury (*sic*) to be the first inventor of arts as our ancient Druids believed of old,'[19] for it is borrowed directly from the Sixth Book of the *Gallic War*.

In the half-century after the appearance of *Pantagruel*, there were published several learned treatises of antiquarian interest in which reference was made to the druids. The first of which I have record was a book in French verse by Jean Le Febure of Dreux, called *Les Fleurs et Antiquités des Gauls*, published in 1532; this must have been a very interesting book, and a very important one in the druidical bibliography, since it is said to have been principally devoted to a description of the druids, or ancient philosophers of Gaul; but, unfortunately, there does not seem to be any copy still existing.[20] The next important book appeared over forty years later;[21] this was the *Historiae Brytannicae Defensio* (1573), by Sir John Price, who suggested that as *pryduides* (*prydydd*, a poet) was an alternative name for the Welsh bards, these must be the same folk as those called druids by the ancients. This volume was accompanied by the *De Mona Druidum Insula* of Humphrey Llwyd, in which one or two of the classical references to druidism were repeated. Four years afterwards, in 1577, Holinshead offered some fanciful remarks about what he termed the *Druyish* religion, but he was evidently aware that ordinary people knew nothing whatever about the priests themselves; and the same may be said of that careful antiquary Camden (1586), who can be trusted to have recorded any folklore that came to his ears.

In the meantime Étienne Forcadel had published his *De Gallorum Imperio* (1579), a book that set forth much of the classical information about the druids; and this was followed in France by the *Histoire de l'Estat et Republique des Druides* (1585) of Noel Taillepied, an amusing book that describes the druids as an aristocracy ruling Gaul from about the year 2800 after the creation of the world (i.e. roughly 1200 B.C.) to the year A.D. 16.

But all these works were heavy antiquarian treatises and the next popular reference to the druids after their mention in the works of Rabelais seems to be that in the *Felicitie of Man* (1598), by Barckley, who speaks of a woman 'that was a Soothsayer of them which were called Druides,' an explanatory remark that illustrates tolerably well my contention that the word druid reappears in literature as the result of the increased attention given by scholars to the classical historians, and not as a contribution from popular traditional knowledge.

As a matter of fact, at this period the only practical interest taken in the druids seems to have been aroused by the French antiquary Guenebauld, who claimed that he had found the tomb of an archdruid called Chyndonax. This discovery was a very exciting affair that attracted considerable attention; it took place in 1598 onh Guenebauld's vineyard near a Roman road in the vicinity of Dijon, and consisted of a cylindrical stone coffer, about a foot in height, that contained a glass cinerary urn. On the base of the coffer was a Greek inscription mentioning Mithras and also a name interpreted by Guenebauld as Chyndonax, who, because he was described as a chief priest, was assumed to have been necessarily an important druid. Guenebauld himself published this find some years later in a delightful little book, complete with illustrations, which seems, since it is of earlier date than Sir Thomas Browne's *Hydrotaphia*, to be one of the first treatises in the history of transalpine archaeology that dealt with the problems of a single excavation. The authenticity of the inscription has been questioned, although it is rather difficult to understand why, and, needless to say, the coffer itself is now lost; but as a Roman cemetery, whose existence was unknown to Guenebauld, was discovered over 200 years later on the site, the funeral apparatus must have been genuine enough. However this may be, Chyndonax the Druid became a real person to a great many people at the end of the 16th century and at the beginning of the 17th; and on more than one occasion he was saluted in verse:–

Felicem Druydam, qui tot post saecula vivit,
Quemque per ora virum fata volare jubent!

But this, as I have said, is the only instance at so early a date where any sort of popular attention seems to have been devoted to the druids; and even after this discovery I daresay that outside Burgundy no one bothered about Chyndonax except a few scholars and theological disputants.

By this time, however, the learned world was beginning to occupy itself seriously in the problems of druidism, and throughout the 17th century, just as in the later half of the 16th, a number of works appeared that dealt with the priesthood. But books of this kind are evidence of nothing more than an academic study of the classical historians; and the manner in which the subject is approached, at any rate in the first half of the century, makes it tolerably clear that it was deemed to be one not as yet generally familiar.

The first work in the new century that treated of the druids was an oration of Francois Meinard, the Frisian, that was printed in 1615,[22] and set forth the claims of the druidic mistletoe to be henceforth regarded as the emblem of jurisprudence. But much more important was the great work *De Dis Germanis*,[23] by the German youth Elias Schedius (1615–1641), in which as many as twenty-six chapters were devoted to a study of druidism; for Schedius believed that the Germans had had their druids just like the Kelts. Two chapters deal with the probable kind of altar used by the druids, and it is important to remark, in view of the modern superstition on this subject, that in the 17th century turf, and not stone, was thought to be the chosen material. This notion of a turf altar in the middle of the grove is re-stated in an engaging pamphlet on the druids by the diplomat Esaias Pufendorf of Chemnitz, a work written as a university thesis, and first printed in 1650.[24] Pufendorf's charming study had the luck to be brilliantly translated in the last century by Edmund Goldschmid,[25] and in its English form his little book deserves to be better known.

The next work of interest here was the *Originum Gallicarum Liber* of the Dutchman Marcus Boxhorn, that was published at Amsterdam in 1654: the greater part of it is philological and not directly connected with the druids, but it contains an appendix in the form of a long Latin poem that purports to set forth a system of druidic philosophy. A continental work of greater significance appeared two years later; this was written by Jean Picard of Tours,[26] who treated the problem of the druids in a severely historical fashion, transcribing in full many of the classical references to them. In the meantime, a short article, *De Origine Druidum*, by Henry Jacob, a Fellow of Merton College, had been published in England in the *Delphi Phoenicizantes* (Oxford, 1655), a work of which Edmund Dickinson claimed to be the author; and a few years later another little book on druidism, also in Latin, came from Oxford; it was written by Thomas Smith of Magdalen,[27] and its principal interest is that it names Camden, the 16th century antiquary, as the pioneer in the revival of the study of the druids. There is yet a third Oxford book to be mentioned, namely, *The Court of the Gentiles*,[28] by Theophilus Gale, for it contained a short section on the druids, and, since it was written in English, may well have given them some publicity.

But at this period the druids were no longer in need of such advertisement – at any rate in this country. For the 17th century had witnessed, as well as the continued interest of scholars, the gradual spreading in England of a vague popular notion of the druids as the ancient poet-priests of Britain. This recognition was not directly due to any one scholar's work, and I am inclind to think it must be almost wholly ascribed to the choice by Beaumont and Fletcher of an Early British theme for a tragedy. The performance in 1618 of *Bonduca* must have presented a picture of the druids in a form that could not fail to win for them a considerable amount of popular attention, and from that date onwards it is idle to pretend that their name could not have been generally familiar. Thus it is possible that when Henry Jacob wrote in the middle of the 17th century that there was no one in whose ears their fame had not resounded,[29] he may well have been referring to something more than their repute in the world of scholars.

Bonduca, then, is certainly a landmark in the story of the revival of popular interest in the druids. Of course, the part played in it by the druids is indirectly a result of the labours of scholars, because these had enabled Fletcher to use the works of the classical writers, especially Tacitus, as sources for his story; whereas Shakespeare, because he had taken the story of his *Cymbeline* largely from mediaeval romances, consequently did not bring the druids at all into his play dealing with the same period.

The first scene of the third act of *Bonduca* is laid in a Temple of the Druids, and begins with a solemn entry of the druids singing; and it will be noticed that song seems to be their principal function. 'Now sing, ye Druides!' commands Caratach; and in another place Bonduca exclaims–

Rise from the dust, ye relics of the dead,
Whose noble deeds our holy druids sing.

And in the first act Caratach refers to

The holy Druides composing songs,
Of everlasting life to victory.

This notion of the druids as being primarily bards gained further currency in Milton's *Lycidas* (1637):–

Where were ye, Nymphs, when the remorseless deep
Clos'd o'er the head of your lov'd Lycidas?
For neither were ye playing on the steep,
Where your old Bards, the famous druids, ly–

and in England it remained firmly established for close upon a hundred years.

In France, on the other hand, it is likely that a popular knowledge of the druids was achieved more slowly, and, when established, it was probably a more precise notion of them than that obtaining in this country. The principal factor must have been the translation of Lucan's *Pharsalia* by de Brebeuf (1656), for this would render the well-known passage describing the druids (p. 88) familiar in substance to a good many Frenchmen. And it is interesting to note, as an appendix to a subject already mentioned, that at this period in the 17th century the current idea in France must still have been that groves, and not stone temples, were the places of worship of these priests.[30]

Au milieu du silence et des bois solitaires
La Nature en secret leur ouvre ses mystères.

As a reinforcement of this view (which was already clearly established in Pufendorf's *Dissertatio*, and in the earlier work of Schedius), the same poem contains the famous and magnificent description of the horrible druidic forest at Marseilles, so fearsome a place that–

Les voisins de ce bois si sauvage et si sombre
Laissent à ses Démons son horreur et son ombre,
Et la Druide craint en abordant ces lieux
D'y voir ce qu'il adore et d'y trouver ses Dieux.

But in England, as I say, the idea of the druids as a kind of prophetic bard prevailed for a hundred years after Milton wrote *Lycidas*. It is true that at the beginning of the 18th century Addison refers once in the *Tatler*[31] to the 'Druid of the family' in a context that shows he was using the word in the sense of a priest; but William Diaper, in 1713, returned to the more popular notion–

With sacred miselto the Druids crown'd
Sung with the Nymphs, and danced the pleasing Round.[32]

And so did Thomas Coke in 1726–

Thrice happy land [Kent], 'tis here the Druids sing,

and–

He walked a God amids't th' admiring Throng,
The darling Subject of the Druids' Song.[33]

In the middle of the 18th century there took place that very remarkable revival of interests in the druids upon which I have already commented in connection with the theories of the origin of Stonehenge. Aubrey, who first suggested the druids as builders of the monument, had died in 1697, and it was not until over forty years later that Stukeley's famous exposition appeared to achieve for this theory almost universal acclamation and acceptance. But in the meantime the ground had been prepared by the publication of several books of antiquarian argument and disquisition that differed from those of the preceding century in that they were intended for a wider public than the few students of the ponderous Latin treatises of earlier days. One of the first was Thomas Brown's dissertation on Mona that was included in Sacheverell's *Account of the Isle of Man* (1702), and another was Henry Rowland's *Mona Antiqua Restaurata* (1723). In 1726 came Toland's *History of the Druids*, and a year afterwards France had *La religion des Gaulois tirée des plus pures sources de l'antiquité*, by Dom Martin (1727). By the turn of the half-century there had also appeared the important work of Frick (1744), that included reprints of several earlier essays on druidism, Sir Thomas Carte's *History of England* (1747), containing a full account of the druidic order as it was known to the ancient writers, and Simon Pelloutier's *Histoire des Celtes*, which, curiously enough, had very little to say about the druids.

A point had clearly been reached, therefore, when a knowledge of the druids was no longer an incidental product of historical research among the classical authors, but was in itself the subject of a fairly general interest, a period, that is to say, wherein most educated folk would have some knowledge of the ancient Keltic inhabitants of the country. Now within twenty years of the publication of Stukeley's book on Avebury in 1743, Gray's famous poem *The Bard*, had appeared, Mason had published his *Caractacus*, and, more important even than *The Bard*, Macpherson's *Ossian* ('Fingal,' 1761) was in circulation, a work there and then destined to compel the chiefs of literary Europe, either in angry defiance or in triumphant delight, to an investigation of the mythology of the ancient Keltic world.

There was nothing about druidism in *Ossian*, there was nothing directly about druidism in *The Bard*, but they advanced the cause of the druids and promoted a popular affection for them more thoroughly than any archaeological treatise could have done. It is, in fact, to this early romantic poetry that we should properly attribute the astonishing success of the laborious theories of Stukeley and other archaeologists. Such poetry was an evidence of the turning of men's minds away from the old familiar classical mythology and the rigours of the classical formulae in letters and art; and the signal for a movement towards the freedom of Keltic wildness, of the chill grand landscapes of the north peopled with hoary bards and with rude chieftains, and the mysterious haunting creatures of Keltic mythology.[34]

The Romantic Movement, then, is the ultimate cause of the revived interest in the druids that we have witnessed in the 18th century, the secret of that strange power they have exercised ever since over popular fancy. The string of books concerning them, and the list of allusions to them in general literature that followed the turning-point in the story of the revival (1750), are much too long to be recited here. But as evidence of their renown soon after this date, it will suffice to mention the production at the Théâtre-Français in 1772 of a tragedy, *Les Druides*, by Le Blanc de Guillet (Antoine Blanc), and of Fisher's *Masque of the Druids*, at Covent Garden (1774 and 1775), and the revival of *Bonduca* in 1778.

Their fame, however, was destined to be even greater than that afforded them by the theatre. For not only was their ancient glory recalled, but their religion also; and it had many votaries. An important factor in the romantic movement had been the renewed study of Welsh bardic poetry,[35] promoted chiefly by Lewis Morris (1700–1765) and Evan Evans (1731–1789), and it was not very long before it was suggested that the mediaeval bards were the repositories and servants of an ancient and mystical religion, of druidism, in fact. The tenets of this Bardism were formulated in 1792 by William Owen

Pugh in *Llyware Hen*, but the chief exponent of the new faith was Iolo Morganwy (1746–1826), who not only accepted the greater part of the bardic traditions as a survival from the days of the druids, but also claimed that he himself was directly descended from them.

The supposed bardic religion was eventually developed into a system in which druidism, so far as it is discoverable in the classical sources, and the patriarchal faith of the Scriptures were ingeniously combined. At the beginning of the 19th century this helio-arkite theology was most successfully championed by the Rev. Edward Davies,[36] and afterwards by Algernon Herbert,[37] who gave it the name by which it is now known, neo-druidism. But there is no need to describe its later progress and complicated ramifications; it will be sufficient to remark that an important general consequence of the movement was the conversion of the ancient bardic gorsedd into a druidic institution, so that the gathering of the poets at the Eisteddfod became a full-dress ceremony of the druids, and was, and still is, particularly effective in keeping their memory fresh in the popular imagination.

It is necessary, however, to say a word about the basic assumption that the mediaeval Welsh bards were a direct continuation of the druidic hierarchy, for this is not by any means an extravagant or ridiculous belief. The druids of old were very closely connected with the bardic profession: much of their lore was doubtless transmitted by means of poetry, they are more than once named together with the bards, and it is even possible that as their sacerdotal powers vanished they may have been to some extent merged in the bardic class. Moreover, as Matthew Arnold pointed out,[38] the very fact of the existence of an elaborate poetical system right at the beginning of the mediaeval literary history of Wales seems to indicate a clear and persistent tradition of an older poetical period, and one is irresistibly led to think of the druidic system described by Caesar. But such considerations cannot be taken to imply that the servile Keltic bard of the kind known to us in the Middle Ages was necessarily descended from bards included in the druidic order. For whatever the druids may have been, or may have become, professional bardism is something recognisable and distinct. Even in their distant past the Kelts seem to have employed poets in a purely secular capacity, and who were in no way concerned with the druidic functions . . . thus it is obvious that the survival of the calling of the professional bard is only a token of ancient Keltic custom, and not a proof of connection with druidism.

The most that can reasonly be claimed is that some bards of special distinction may have been possessed of the remnants of the druidic doctrines. But even on this point the evidence is not convincing, and it would be almost impossible to demonstrate that any of the mediaeval Welsh poets and poetasters were the conscious possessors of a scrap of the ancient druidic lore. The existing manuscripts of their poems do not date back beyond the 12th century, and it may be safely said that there is nothing in the poetry of that period, even in those of the pieces that have a traditional flavour of the earlier centuries, or in those that are ascribed to 6th century bards, to warrant the belief that the poets themselves knew anything at all about ancient druidism as an organised religion. All that can be adduced on this score is that in the 12th century and afterwards the bards sometimes, not very frequently, called themselves *derwyddon*, which may, or may not, be a form of druids; but, to my mind, there is not the slightest suggestion that those to whom the term was applied enjoyed the reputation of being members of, or even connected with, the ancient priesthood.

This question of Bardism and Druidism has already been treated in thorough fashion by writers of much learning,[39] and I do not propose to pursue the enquiry here. But I cannot help remarking with regret that Neo-druidism, with all its extravagances and impostures, has rendered the delightful study of Keltic tradition in Wales a wearisome and ungrateful task for a student in earnest search of druidic survival. I believe myself that bardic tradition and bardic custom is the most important of the several fields in which one might legitimately seek to achieve contact with real druidism. But the blundering enthusiasm that pretends this contact is already proved, and the consequent prejudice of scholars against enquiry in this direction, are indeed formidable obstacles in the way of an ordinary examination of the material.

In this chapter I have tried to test several methods whereby one might forge a link, traditionally, with the druids, and I have not been able to claim any success. It is necessary, therefore, to add that I have no special reason for wanting to prove that such a link cannot exist. But I am impressed by the remarkable stirring of popular opinion engendered by Romanticism, which I believe to be directly responsible for the many druid-cults of to-day; and this must of necessity lead to a profound suspicion of every alleged tradition that has become involved with the movement.

To sum up, I think it may be said that the testimony of the druidicial literature is plain enough. For England it has shown that the Saxon invasion blotted out the memory of the druids, leaving, so far as our records go, no trace of them in popular tradition, either as regards sites of their former worship or vestiges of their lore; and it has shown that a knowledge of the former existence of the priesthood was regained slowly and laboriously in the 16th century as a result of the return to the study of the ancient historians. And it has shown that the theory, now so popular, that the druids built the megalithic monuments, was an invention of the late 17th century, successfully promulgated, in the succeeding century, by Romanticism.

22

DRUIDIC THEOLOGY AND RITUAL

Lewis Spence

From *The History and Origins of Druidism*

Whatever the general theological system of the Druids, it must, if my conclusions are correct, have originated in the worship of the oak tree as a source of provender in early times. In Chapter XVII of his *Commentaries* (Book VI) Caesar wrote that 'they' worshipped gods, including Mercury, Apollo, Mars, Jupiter and Minerva. In the chapter (XVI) which precedes this, he had been dealing with the subject of Gaulish rite and religious belief in connection with which he mentions the Druids as the ministers of Gaulish sacrifices. The personal pronoun 'they' alludes therefore to the Gauls, and, by implication, to the Druids also. The deities in question, although Caesar confers upon them the names of Latin divinities, were certainly the equivalents of gods included in the Celtic pantheon, so that we are left with the inference that the Druids were their priests.

In chapter XVIII of the same book (VI) Caesar tells us that the Gauls assert that they are descended from the god Dis, and says that this tradition has been handed down by the Druids: so that we can only conclude that the Druids were the source of their religious traditions. 'In short,' as Mr. Kendrick observes, 'we must be prepared to believe that druidism professed, or was in sympathy with, all the known tenets of ancient Keltic religion, and the gods of the druids were the familiar and multifarious deities of the Keltic pantheon.' Dis, in Roman myth, is the god of the Underworld and of the dead, the Roman equivalent of the Greek Pluto. For this reason, continues Caesar, the Gauls (in his honour) reckoned time not by days but by nights, so that the night preceded the day. We find much the same conditions in Irish myth, where the gods of the Fomorians, the powers of darkness, are in point of time anterior to the Tuatha Dé Danann, the gods of day and of life. Indeed M. D'Arbois equated the Dis of Caesar with the Irish god Bilé, the root of whose name is associated with the idea of death. The Druids, says Pomponius Mela 'professed to know the will of the gods,' which appears to make it plain that they were expressly the servants of the gods. Here Mela almost certainly refers to their augural capacity and office.

The matter contained in the great number of verses which the Druidic neophytes were compelled to learn by heart was probably, as Professor Macalister observes, contained 'in sacred hymns composed before the introduction of writing, and, like the Vedas in ancient India, preserved by oral tradition, because they would have been profaned were they to be committed to the custody of this novel art.' This body of traditional verse, if it were so great as to engage the study of a man for twenty years, as Caesar tells us it occasionally did, 'must', Macalister thinks, 'have been at least as extensive as the material at our disposal for the study of classical Latin.' We have seen that it probably contained a myth respecting the god 'Dis', but the likelihood is that it embraced an entire mythology, as complicated and as complete in its way as those of Greece and Rome. If Irish myth, as we know it, was the production of Druidism as it survived in the writings of Christian scribes, then its extensive character is apparent and it is not straining the probabilities too far to believe that Gaulish Druidism possessed at least an equally comprehensive mythology.

Strabo tells us the Druids asserted that the souls of men were 'indestructible.' Lucan, in one of his rhapsodies, apostrophizes them as follows: 'It is you who say that the shades of the dead seek not the silent land of Erebus and the pale halls of Pluto; rather, you tell us that the same spirit has a body again elsewhere, and that death, if what you sing is true, is but the mid-point of long life.' 'With grand contempt for the mortal lot,' says Ammianus Marcellinus, 'they professed the immortality of the soul.' This, however, is a subject which will receive the more serious discussion it deserves in a later chapter.

The Gods of Druidism

The question has been posed more than once as to whether the Druidic cultus centred its adoration in any one particular deity. As we shall see, the Druids invoked a god during the mistletoe rite, while Maximus of Tyre speaks of the Celtic image of Zeus as having been symbolized in a lofty oak. The Irish hero Cuchullin is made to say that the Druid Cathbad instructed him concerning the arts of 'the god of druidism' (dé druidechta). This, says Rhys, 'doubtless meant that divinity with whom the druids as magicians had to do and with whose aid they practised their magical arts. We are,' he adds, 'unfortunately not told the name of this god, but it is natural to suppose that it was the chief of the Goidelic pantheon,' whose miracles were mostly of an atmospheric nature associated with the phenomena of the weather. He goes on to say that it is possible to recognize the Welsh counterpart of this Goidelic, or Irish, god of Druidism (who was probably Nuada) in the figure of Math Vab Mathonwy, who appears in a well-known Welsh mabinogi, or tale.

Math was probably superseded as the god of Druidism in Wales by Gwydion, as the former deity is said to have handed on to him the whole apparatus of illusion and fantasy. But it must be admitted that these ascriptions occur in Irish and Welsh accounts which are at least a thousand years in date after Druidism had disappeared as an influence in Gaul, and that therefore it is difficult to believe that they can refer to deities in any way associated with Druidism in that region. The likelihood is that they are racy of a period when Druidism was regarded by Christian scribes as mainly a corpus of magical art and little more, and when a folk-lore interpretation was placed upon its memorabilia. But this is not to say that the details concerning the association of especial gods with Druidism are lacking in a certain degree of authenticity. The great mass of material concerning Druidism which is to be found in Irish Christian writings cannot altogether be regarded as inventive in character, and must in the ultimate have been obtained either from still earlier manuscripts or from tradition, whether official or popular.

It is only proper to state that Professor Macalister is of opinion that Nuada 'is actually the sky-god . . . In fact the equivalence of certain of the legends of Nuada with some of those of Zeus has been pointed out by Rhys, D'Arbois and Cook.' He also indicates that in Irish myth we read of a certain girl called Mess, whose name may be translated as 'Acorns.' 'The king of birds obtains access to her and a son called Conaire is born to her.' We hear of another female personage in Irish mythology known as Odba (i.e., 'Timber-knots') of whom was born three sons, one of them the god Lug, the sun-god. These incidents, thinks Macalister, are fragments of one story. Now 'the oak tree is the tree of the thunder-god, and when a deity is born of wood-knots or acorns as the result of the attention of a bird, we naturally look for the woodpecker. In modern Irish folk-lore, the king of the birds is the wren; he may be a deputy for the woodpecker, which was once a native of Ireland, but is so no longer. . . . This throws some light on the mysterious line in the doggerel rhyme of the wren-boys: "Although he is little his family's great"'. (*Tara*, pp.119–21.)

Professor Macalister's reference is, of course, to the rhyme chanted by boys in Ireland and England at the ceremony known as 'the hunting of the wren,' on December 26th. As we have seen, the name of this bird has been said by some authorities to be associated with the root from which Druidism took its name. It was evidently thought necessary to hunt and kill the wren and to carry it round the district, and then to eat it sacramentally to obtain its divine influence. Macalister suggests that the wren may have been a surrogate of the woodpecker in Ireland. The assumption is that the woodpecker, the bird of the oak, fertilizes that tree, and of this union the sun-spirit is born. The wren was certainly associated with lightning. The Roman god Picus took the shape of a woodpecker, and was also connected with the oak. (Rendel Harris, *The Ascent of Olympus*, pp. 4–5.) So that, were the wren the counterpart of the woodpecker in Ireland, it does not seem to be straining probability too far to see in it the spirit of the oak, and therefore a Druidic deity in bird form. In brief, the Roman myth of the oak and its bird-god appears to have been duplicated in Ireland.

Presently, we may agree that the original god of Druidism was a spiritual conception of the oak tree, like the Greek Zeus and the Roman Jupiter, as

Maximus of Tyre asserts, and that this conception, at a much later date, achieved a more elaborate 'personality'. At the same time, it appears to me as not improbable that the ancient spirit of the oak tree may, at a later stage of Druidic development, have been represented by the Gaulish god known as Cernunnos. A monument at Rheims reveals a sculpture of this deity, horned, and in a squatting posture, holding a bag from which issues a profusion of acorns or beech-mast, the 'fruit' of the oak tree. The acorns drop between a stag and an ox, which was certainly a 'Druidical beast' or symbol. The god, like the animals, he feeds, is horned. Rhys was of opinion that he resembled the god Dis, adored by the Druids, according to Caesar. It has been stated by me elsewhere that the spirit known as 'Herne the Hunter,' who, horned and threatening, haunted an oak in the royal forest of Windsor, is a British form of this deity, and this legend, it seems to me, supports the view that such a god resembling Cernunnos was known also in Britain.

It has been repeatedly asserted that the gods Taranis, Teutates and Belenos were associated with the Druidic cult in Gaul and even in Britain, and a brief examination of the claims of these deities to a Druidic connection seems to be called for. Taranis, who has been identified with Jupiter, was certainly a god of thunder and lightning, so that his status as a Druidic deity seems by no means improbable. To him also is credited the fertility of the soil. Sacrifices were, appropriately enough, made to him by fire. Taranis, I think, may have symbolized the lightning spirit which inhabited the oak in the first and original sense, and in that aspect he may gradually have developed into a god. M. Camille Jullian, a prime authority, definitely identifies all three deities mentioned above as 'The sovereign deities' of the Druids. (J.A. MacCulloch, *Religion of the Ancient Celts*, p.30 f.; Diodorus Siculus, xxxi, 13; C. Jullian, *Cambridge Mediaeval History*, p. 462 ff.)

Teutates, identified by the Romans with Mercury, and sometimes with Mars, was the Gallic war-god. He, too, appears to have been associated with the thunder, and bore the hammer symbolic of the thunderbolt in many mythologies. The name, according to Rhys, has a royal significance. It seems to me that he may also have been connected with the oak cultus. (C. Jullian, *op. cit.*, p. 463; J. Rhys, *Hibbert Lectures*, p. 46.)

Bel, Bilé or Belenos, the last his Gallic appelation, who is associated so frequently with the Druidic faith by writers serious and the reverse, was certainly the god of the *Beallteinn* fire-festival, with which he is definitely connected, as we know, by Cormac's 'Glossary.' It is now merely absurd to attempt to dissociate his Irish and British forms which last are distinctly the same (see W.J. Gruffydd, *Math Vab Mathonwy*, p. 172 ff.) from that by which he was known in Gaul, or to pretend that he had no connection with the *Beallteinn* festival. Beli gave these festivals his name in Britain and in Ireland the Druids are known to have officiated at them, as we have seen. So I cannot see why the Irish form of the god, Bilé, may not be regarded as a Druidic deity. It would seem to follow that in Gaul his worship was also Druidic. (C. Jullian, *op. cit.*, p. 462; Rhys, *op. cit.*, p. 46.)

That the Tuatha Dé Danann of Ireland were gods associated with the Druidic cults may be inferred from the statement in an ancient manuscript that 'all who are adepts in Druidical and magical arts are the descendants of the Tuatha Dé Danann.' The discussion of this part of the subject may perhaps be fittingly concluded by quoting the statement of Diodorus that the Druids alone 'knew the gods and divinities of heaven.'

It appears to have been regarded essential that at least one Druid should be present at every sacrifice. According to Diodorus Siculus, it was 'a custom of the Gauls that no one performs a sacrifice without the assistance of a philosopher, for they say that offerings to the gods ought only to be made through the mediation of these men, who are learned in the divine nature, and so, to speak, familiar with it.' Professor Anwyl constructed this as meaning that the 'philosopher' in question was 'apparently a Druid in addition to the sacrificing seer, the theory being that those who were authorities on the divine nature were to the gods intelligible mediators for the offering of gifts and the presentation of petitions.' But Caesar distinctly avers that the Druids were the performers of such sacrifices. (Book VI, Chap. xvi.)

The Worship of the Oak

It now becomes necessary to examine with close fidelity the whole circumstances of the ancient cultus of the sacred oak in Europe, but before approaching that subject more particularly, it appears essential to say a few preliminary words on the worship of trees in general, so that the reader who has no knowledge of the topic will be enabled to pick up the threads of the general argument. Perhaps no writer has so clearly demonstrated the successive steps in the history of tree-worship as the late Sir James Frazer, and here I propose to summarize his account of it, briefly noting his chief arguments apart from the very numerous examples by which he illustrates his thesis.

The savage, he says, believes the world in general to be animate (that is, with him the law of animism prevails) and trees and plants are no exception to the rule. Trees were regarded by primitive man as ensouled or inhabited by spirits. Sometimes only particular species of trees are so tenanted. In some instances, again, the souls of the dead are thought to animate them. Among some tribes such trees are conceived as the ancestors transformed, and they must not be injured or defaced. In the majority of instances the spirit is viewed as incorporate in the tree. If the tree dies the spirit dies along with it. But according to what seems to be a later form of the belief, the tree is not the body but merely the dwelling of the tree-spirit, which can leave it and return at pleasure. In some cases entire groves are regarded as sacred and inviolable because they are thought to be inhabited or animated by sylvan deities. In this phase, 'an advance has been made in religious thought. Animism is passing into polytheism.' The tree-spirit has become a forest-god. 'He begins to change his shape and assume the body of a man in virtue of a general tendency of early thought to clothe all abstract spiritual beings in concrete human form . . . The powers which he exercised as a tree-soul incorporate in a tree, he still contines to wield as a god of trees.' Trees considered as animate beings are credited with the power of making the rain to fall, the sun to shine, and flocks and herds, and even human beings to increase, and at a later juncture the fully developed tree-god is found to possess the self-same powers. In some parts of the world, too, the belief prevails that tree-spirits have the power to quicken the growth of the crops, thus revealing that they are regarded as gods of growth in general.

There is also good evidence that trees are worshipped not only because they enshrine spirits, but for a more practical reason, one which bears more precisely upon the question at issue – because they are 'food-givers', that is because they or the spirit which animates them furnish primitive man with nuts, or fruit, by way of provender. The idea is entirely similar to that which is associated with the worship of food plants and cereal grain-plants, only it is plain that the adoration of food-bearing trees must have preceded that of grain-bearing plants, a condition which in most instances could scarcely have come into vogue until the period at which agriculture was adopted. Among the people of certain Fijian islands, a man would never eat a coconut without first asking its leave, and addressing it as 'chief', while to cut down a coconut palm among the 'Waniki of East Africa was considered a serious crime.

To acquire palm-wine in Togoland necessitates a felling of the palm-tree, and this is accompanied by an expiatory ceremony. Among the Celts the rowan and hazel were regarded as the bearers of celestial fruits, and their divine exemplars were supposed to be planted in the Celtic paradise. Hazelnuts and rowan-berries were regarded as divine fruit, which yielded, in the first instance, the poetic inspiration, and in the second a wine conducive to longevity, and many legends are told of their virtues. The rowan was, indeed, as Rhys remarks, 'the Celtic counterpart to the soma-plant of Hindu mythology,' with all its associations of mystery and magic. The hazel was indeed a god. It was worshipped as such by one of the eponymous kings of Ireland, MacCuill, 'Son of the hazel.' In the *Rennes Dindsenchas*, an ancient Irish document, we read that a place known as Mag Mugna, 'the greatest of oaks,' bore acorns, apples and nuts, a combination of the three sacred fruits of the Celts. As we shall see, the oak was regarded in the same manner in many parts of Europe, as a sacred food-yielding tree.

Trees, then, are regarded by uncultured peoples as 'the ancestors transformed.' Now we know from the records of tribes in the lower phases of human progress, the Australian aborigines, for example, that trees, rocks and other natural objects are regarded as the dwelling-places of human spirits after death, those spirits indeed which await reincarnation in a new human body and which lie in wait in such receptacles until a possible human mother passes their lair, to enter her body and to be reborn therefrom. (See J.G. Frazer, *The Belief in Immortality*, Vol. I, p. 93 ff.; M.F. Ashley-Montagu, *Coming into Being Among the Australian Aborigines, passim*.) Among some Australian tribes the mistletoe which clings to such trees is believed to contain the souls of spirit children waiting to be reborn. (Ashley-Montagu, *op. cit.*, pp. 78, 79, 91, 94.) This, as Mr Ashley-Montagu indicates, is not necessarily connected with the process of reincarnation, but of ordinary incarnation, and it seems to me not impossible that such an idea may explain the Druidic reverence for the mistletoe.[40]

In this chapter the worship of the oak will be dealt with in a strictly objective manner, in relation to the Druidic and other European cults, all theoretical observations on the subject being omitted until the final and conclusive chapters. In primeval ages the continent of Europe was covered by dense forests, and particularly with those in which the oak tree featured. Indeed, it was not until the late mediaeval period that most of these disappeared, and their presence must have had a profound influence upon the life and habits of European man. Enormous oak-trunks in a petrified state have been excavated from bogs and dried-up lake-dwellings in Europe, and from peat-deposits in Scotland and Ireland, and mosses in Yorkshire. Oak timber was employed in the construction of primitive lake-dwellings and artificial islands, canoes were hollowed from oak-trunks and oak timber was employed for firewood. It is also evident from stores or heaps of acorns which have been discovered in the dwellings in these lake-villages that their inhabitants subsisted upon the acorn as an article of food even at a period when they had adopted the agricultural state of life to some extent and grew wheat, barley and millet. In the valley of the Po great quantities of stored acorns have been found and these were eaten as food by the folk as well as by their swine.

That acorns were an article of diet for human consumption in primitive times can be proved from many a passage in classical literature. Speaking of the manner in which the righteous will be rewarded, Hesiod, in his *Works and Days*, composed in the seventh century B.C., says that for them the earth yields her riches and that the oak in the mountains puts forth acorns. According to Pausanias and Galen, the Arcadians were eaters of acorns. Pliny, in his *Natural History*, says that in his day, in times of death, acorns were still ground and baked into bread. Strabo tells us that the mountain folk of Hispania in his time, the century before Christ, lived upon acorn bread for the greater part of the year. In Greece and Spain the peasantry still eat acorns, and even in England and France they have been regarded as food by the poor in time of famine. Homer, in his 'Hymn to Aphrodite,' alludes to the 'man-feeding' oak. Juvenal, in his first satire, speaks of mankind as born of the opening oak which, mother-like, fed man with her own acorns, while Ovid says that the first human food was supplied by 'acorns dropping from the tree of Jove.' In the Irish *Book of Leinster* we read that during a revolt of the plebs every ear of corn bore but one grain and every oak only one acorn, which seems to reveal that the acorn was regarded as an article of food, classed as it is with grain.

It is scarcely surprising, then, that the oak tree loomed so largely in the religious ideas of early European man. Its mast fed him, its twigs and branches served him for firing, its timber provided him with building material, his swine were fattened upon its acorns. He worshipped the tree itself for its benefactions and doubtless for its favours to come, and, when he came to believe that it was animated by a powerful spirit, he conceived it as the abode of a god.

The worship of the god of the oak was common to most of the peoples of Europe. In ancient Greek the god Zeus was revered in oak-form at the famous shrine at Dodona, in Epirus, which he shared with his spouse Dione, who at this spot was regarded as his wife instead of Hera. The oldest relic in the sanctuary was an oak tree, from the rustling of whose leaves the attendant priests ascertained the will of the gods. Near at hand stood an iron basin or gong, the clanging of which is thought to have mimicked the thunder.

The people of Plataea, in Boeotia, held a movable festival at which they laid before a grove of oaks an offering of meat. Should a raven bear off a portion of this, and settle upon a particular oak, that tree was felled and its wood shaped into an image. This was dressed as a bride, and at the jubilee of the *Great Daedala*, a nature festival, which was celebrated once in every sixty years, all the images collected within that period had animals sacrificed to them by fire, the idols themselves being included in the conflagration. The myth associated with this ceremony recounted that Hera had forsaken Zeus after a quarrel, and that to ensure her return, Zeus circulated the story that he was about to espouse the nymph Plataea, the tutelary genius of the region. He ordered an oak to be cut down and this was dressed as the prospective bride. In jealous wrath Hera tore off the bridal veil which concealed the wooden statue, and thus becoming aware of her husband's stratagem, was reconciled to him. In all likelihood the ceremony represented the marriage of the oak-god with the oak-goddess, while the above story was invented at a later time, to 'save the face' of the goddess Hera. As we shall see, both Greek and Roman kings claimed to be descended from Zeus and Jupiter, and to share their powers of fertility.

Zeus, as the oak-god, wielded the powers of rain, thunder and lightning. Frazer was of opinion that this view of oak-gods generally as rain-bringers and lightning-wielders arose from the notion that as fire on earth was generated by the rubbing together of oaken sticks, so in heaven it was produced in a like manner. Zeus' power as a rain-god was merely consequent upon his aspect as a god of the thunder-and-lightning.

In Italy the oak was sacred to Jupiter and on the Capitolian Hill at Rome he was worshipped as the god of the oak and of the rain and the thunder. The probability is that the sacred tree of Nemi, rendered famous by Frazer in *The Golden Bough*, was an oak, the centre of a similar tree-cult. The Germans certainly worshipped the oak, which was dedicated to the god Donar or Thunar, the Lord of the Thunder, the great fertilizing power. Among the Slavonic peoples the oak was the sacred tree of the thunder-god Perun, whose image at Novgorod represented a man holding a thunder-stone. His priests dare not let the sacred fire of oak wood which burned in the vicinity go out except at the risk of their lives. It is noteworthy that oxen were sacrificed to him.

Among the Lithuanians the god Perkunas, the deity of thunder and lightning, was associated with the oak, and when Christian missionaries cut down his groves, the folk lamented. He also had perpetual fires burned to him.

The Dominican friar Simon Grunau, who for long sojourned in Prussian Poland in the early part of the sixteenth century, mentions these doings as within his knowlege, and although the veracity of his account of them has been questioned, it has been confirmed by Maeletius and Rostowski, and agrees too precisely with what we know of the circumstances of other oak-cults to be in any sense an invention.

Moreover, Peter of Dusburg, whose account dates from 1326, speaks of a High Priest of the Prussians, revered as a Pope, who maintained a perpetual fire at Romow. The Lithuanians sacrificed to oak trees for plentiful crops, says Rostowski. The Esthonians, who are not Slavs, worshipped the oak in the person of the god Taara, and smeared the oaks with the blood of beasts once a year. They also sacrificed oxen to it, praying for rain and good crops. Tylor alludes to a grove in a Siberian forest where gaily decked idols, 'each set up beneath its great tree swathed with cloth or tin-plate, endless reindeer hides and peltry hanging to the trees around, kettles and spoons and snuff-horns and household valuables strewn as offerings before the gods' composed a strange picture of a holy grove at a later stage. (*Primitive Culture*, Vol. II, p. 224.) The close resemblance of all this Slavonic and other evidence to what Pliny has to say concerning the rite of the mistletoe, shortly to be described, led Professor Rhys to remark: 'Seeing, the importance of sacred trees in the ancient cult of the chief god of the Aryans of Europe, and the preference evinced for the oak as the tree fittest to be his emblem, or even the residence of his divinity, I am inclined to regard the old etymology of the word druid as being, roughly speaking, the correct one', that is, 'men of the oaks.' The evidence is, I believe, irrefragable that in ancient times the worship of the oak obtained over a wide area in Europe and that among the Slavonic peoples it survived until the fourteenth century at least.

The oak was by no means the only tree adored by the Celtic peoples, and they appear to have adopted local tree-cults from some of their neighbours, as Canon MacCulloch indicates. He thinks that they accepted the cult of the beech and the god of some coniferous tree from the Ligurians, while 'forests were also personified or ruled by a single goddess, like Dea Arduenna of the Ardennes, and Dea Abnoba of the Black Forest.'

The perpetual fire maintained by the nuns of St Brigit at Kildare, a place whose name means 'church,' or 'shrine of the oak' is reminiscent of those which certain Slavonic peoples burned to the genius of that tree, and the saint's maidens may innocently have preserved, down to the reign of Henry VIII, a fire which glowed to the glory of Brigit, the ancient pagan goddess, the patroness of bards, physicians and smiths. No man might set foot within the fence which surrounded her sanctuary. The oak was certainly a sacred tree in pagan Ireland, but in later times it appears to have been supplanted as a Druidic tree by the yew. Indeed, Dr Pokorny assures us in italics that 'the Irish Druids are never mentioned in connection with the oak.' Their holy tree, he says, was the yew. They bore wands made of its wood and the Druidic fire was kindled by yew faggots. This appears to be the case, indeed it is confirmed by O'Curry, but I think Pokorny exaggerates when he remarks that 'the Druids must have been once the priests of a people who did not know the worship of the oak.' To cut down an oak was an offence in pagan Ireland, and even Colomba deplored the destruction of an oak-grove at Derry and forbade the felling of oaks. So I prefer to believe that the oak was originally the Druidical tree in Ireland and that for some reason unknown the yew superseded it, as the wren superseded the woodpecker as its genius in bird-form.

At least one relic of yew-worship appears to have been known in England. Tupper, in his *Farley Health* (p. 69), mentions that 'on Merroe Downs, in Surrey, are two distinct concentric groves of venerable yews a thousand years old with remnants of little avenues, possibly Druidic.' The age of these may readily be discounted. There are far too many Irish place-names connected with the oak to permit of the belief that it was regarded as a sacred tree in pagan times, and the notion that the Irish Druids had never adored it at any time when all other Druids did so, is one that scarcely commends itself. To fortify such a theory it would also be necessary to explain why so many early Christian churches in Ireland were erected on the site of oak-groves, for it was proverbially customary with the early Christian missionaries to build their churches on the sites of pagan shrines.

Folk-lore of the Oak Cult

In many parts of Europe superstitions concerning the oak strengthen the theory that its worship must formerly have been widespread. As an example of this type of surviving reminiscence, the Copt Oak, of which only the trunk remains, which stands on high ground in Charnwood Forest in Leicestershire, was held by tradition to have been a centre of Druidic worship. In the Middle Ages it appears to have been a place where swainmotes, or lordship courts were held. Near Dolgelly, in Merionethshire, once stood the haunted oak of Nanneu, held to be the abode of spirits and demons. Other examples of this kind will be instanced when we come to consider the subject of sacred groves. What were known as 'Bull oaks' may still be seen in many parts of England. These were very old and hollow trees of which the country folk said that they were so-called because bulls sheltered inside them. That they should have been associated with the bull, the Druidic beast of sacrifice, seems significant. They may have been styled 'bell' oaks, as some trees in Ireland and Scotland were. I have already alluded to Herne the Hunter and the oak which he haunted in Windsor Forest. There was formerly in the park of Sir Robert Vaughan in Wales, a celebrated oak tree named 'The Elf's Hollow Tree.' Oaks such as this were, indeed, regarded as the haunts of spirits, thus revealing that formerly they must have been thought to be ensouled by them and consequently adored or placated. In later times such haunting spirits come to be looked upon as elves, fairies, or demons. An old English folk-rhyme has it:

Turn your clokes,
For fairy folks
Are in old oakes.

That is, one must turn his cloak or coat outside-in to neutralize their harmful magic. Such spirits were capable of entering houses through knot-holes in oak timbers, as did an elfmaid in Smaland, who wed with the son of the house. This belief seems to cast some light upon the significance of the Irish female spirit Mess, whose name, as we have seen, implies 'timber-knots.'

In some districts of Lower Saxony and Westphalia, says Grimm, 'holy oaks' were preserved, to which the folk 'paid a half-heathen half-Christian homage' until 'quite recent times.' In Minden, on Easter Sunday, the young people danced a circular dance round an old oak, and a procession was made to another by the people of Wormeln and Calenberg. A memory of the heathen worship of oaks, thought Grimm, was preserved in the place-name *Dreieich*, that is 'Three Oaks.' In Brittany and France oaks are still associated with saints. One finds such names as 'Our Lady of the Oak' in Anjou and the same at Orthe, in Maine, places famous for pilgrimage. One sees ar various cross-roads in Maine the most beautiful rustic oaks decorated with figures of saints. There are seen there, in five or six villages, chapels of oaks, with whole trunks of that tree enshrined in the wall beside the altar. An oak-coppice or grove near Loch Siant, in the Isle of Skye, was at one time held so sacred that none would venture to cut even the smallest twig from it.

The Mile Oak, near Oswestry, in Shropshire, was deemed sacrosanct, and a local ballad declared of it:

To break a branch was deemed a sin,
A bad-luck job for neighbours,
For fire, sickness and the like
Would mar their honest labours.

To deface the holy oak at Ragnit in East Prussia boded misfortune or bodily ailment for the spoiler. On a rivulet between the governments of Pskov and Livonia, in Russia, stood a stunted and withered holy oak to which homage was paid until at least the year 1874. At a given ceremony there, wax candles were fixed to the trunk and branches, and a priest of the Orthodox Church adjured the tree: 'Holy Oak Hallelujah, pray for us.' The people then worshipped the tree and the proceedings concluded with a drunken orgy.

Old Aubrey tells us that in England 'our late Reformers gave order (which was universally observed accordingly) for the Acorn, the fruit of the oak, to be set upon the top of their maces or crowns, instead of the Cross.' He alludes, of course, to a supposed Puritan decree, but I can find no authority for the statement. In this regard, it is amusing to find so authoritative a student of folk-lore as the late Rev. Sabine Baring-Gould declaring that 'under the name of Methodism we have the old Druidic religion still alive, energetic and possibly more vigorous than it was when it exercised a spiritual supremacy over the whole of Britain.' And who shall dare to say that it does not to a great extent survive in the 'Christianity' of Brittany, or remain as an 'under-current' to that somewhat fuliginous faith?

'When an oake is felling,' says Aubrey, 'before it falls it gives a kind of shriekes or groanes, that may be heard a mile off, as if it were the genius of the oak lamenting. . . . To cut oak-wood is unfortunate.'

In Balkan story we find a holy oak growing out of a slain king's mouth, which seems to reveal an association between the tree and the kingship.

In England the oak was believed to attract lightning.

> Beware of an oak,
> It draws the stroke.

ran an old rhyme. This shows that a belief must once have prevailed that the tree was the abode of the thunder-spirit. The oak tree was thought to exhibit certain omens on occasion. The change of its leaves from their usual colour was more than once regarded as giving a fatal premonition of coming misfortunes during the Great Civil War in England. The Earl of Winchelsea gave orders to fell a curious grove of oaks, whereupon his Countess died and his eldest son was killed in action at sea. I cannot pretend that this category of folk-lore beliefs respecting the oak is either embracive or definitive, but at least it suffices to indicate the survival of religious beliefs concerning the tree.

The Mistletoe as a Druidical Plant

Both tradition and literature have inevitably associated the mistletoe plant with Druidism. This connection, so far as its literary part is concerned, has probably emerged from Pliny's account of the Druidic rite in which the plant figures. 'The Druids,' he tells us, 'held nothing more sacred than the mistletoe and the tree that bears it, always supposing that tree to be the oak. But they choose groves formed of oaks for the sake of the tree alone, and they never perform any of their rites except in the presence of a branch of it.' Everything which grew on the oak, they believed, 'has been sent from heaven.' This last sentence, indeed, appears to me to satisfy all doubts concerning the authenticity of Pliny's account, as it certainly agrees with what we know of most tree-cults. The mistletoe, however, is found but rarely upon the oak, he continues, and when it is, it is gathered with due religious ceremony, if possible on the sixth day of the moon, when her influence is already being felt. They (the Celts) call the mistletoe by a name which in their language means 'all healing.'

After a repast beneath the trees of the sacred grove, they brought forward two white bulls, 'whose horns are bound for the first time.' A white-robed priest then ascended the tree and cut the mistletoe which adhered to it with a golden sickle, so that when it fell it was received by his colleagues in a white cloak. The bulls were then sacrificed and prayers were offered up to the God of the Oak, requesting that he should render the plant propitious 'to those to whom he has granted it.' 'They believe that the mistletoe, taken in drink, imparts fecundity to barren animals and that it is an antidote for all poisons.'

It is not a little extraordinary to discover a similar ritual act in ancient Egypt. At the feast of the first Pachons, associated with the rite of vegetation, the Pharaoh cut with a sickle a sheaf of corn and sacrificed thereafter a white ox consecrated to Min, the god of fecundating energy. The ox was regardesd as one of the forms of Osiris. (J.G. Frazer, *The Golden Bough*, vol. III, pp. 94 ff., and 104 ff.; A. Moret, *Mystères Egyptiens*, pp. 7–8.) The month Pachons fell in summer. The close analogy between this rite and the Druidic one can scarcely be accidental. Probably both cast back to a very ancient ritual associated with the powers of fertility and the rites carried out by a king who represented the earthly form of a god of fertility.

The willow, the poplar and the apple are the trees which chiefly attract the mistletoe as a parasite. Its Druidic name is still preserved in Celtic speech, in words meaning 'all-healer' and 'sap of the oak' and it is also known more familiarly as *Druidh lus*, or 'Druid's weed.'

MacCulloch pregnantly criticizes Pliny's account. He thinks that Pliny was 'relating something of which all the details were not known to him.' The rite 'must have had some other purpose than that of the magico-medical use of the mistletoe, which he describes. 'He is of opinion that the oxen sacrificed may, at a later time, have taken the place of an earlier human victim. Perhaps, according to a more ancient form of the ritual, remarks this authority, a branch of the tree may have had to be captured from its guardian and 'king', that is, the personal representative of the God of the Oak, as was the case in the ritual associated with the Golden Bough at Nemi, in Italy.

But long ago Frazer indicated a Roman equivalent to the Druidic rite. For at the Capitol at Rome and on the Alban Mount white oxen were offered up to the earthenware image of Jupiter (originally a god of the oak) by the Roman consuls, and triumphal processions of victors in war were held there.

I may say, in passing, that the circumstance that the sickle employed by the Druids was actually made of gold has been questioned, and it has been suggested that the Latin word *aurea* has been scribally substituted for *aerea* (brass). It is significant that Vergil expressly remarks that herbs used for magical purposes were cut with sickles of brass. Stukeley, alluding to the rite described by Pliny, says: 'This mistletoe, they (the Druids) cut off the trees with their upright hatches of brass.' In old-time phraseology the term 'brass' usually implies bronze. Towards the end of the eighteenth century a Mr Philip Rashleigh found a brass sickle at the bottom of a mine mear the River Powey.

'The mistletoe or branch,' says MacCulloch, 'was the soul of the tree, and also contained the life of the divine representative. It must be plucked before the tree could be cut down or the victim slain.' This is very well, so far as it goes, but I am of opinion that it is possible to carry the significance of the mistletoe farther. It was, indeed, regarded as the semen or life-essence of the oak, the glutinous matter contained in its berries was thought of as the spermatozoa, or impregnatory fluid of the god, and to such fluid, indeed, it bears a quite remarkable resemblance. This theory is supported by the prevalence of the superstition that the mistletoe was given to barren animals to render them fecund, while the amatory practice of 'kissing under the mistletoe' seems to have some tincture of recollection of a rite which might make a union fertile by 'sympathetic magic.' I think it is further fortified by one of the names conferred upon the mistletoe by the Bretons, *dour-dero*, that is the 'pith', 'vigour', or strength of the mistletoe, but literally 'water of the mistletoe.' (J. Cambry, *Monumens Celtiques*, p. 330.) It seems to me that the slaying of bulls, animals notoriously symbolic of sexual vigour, was regarded as compensation to the God of the Oak for the loss of his vigour, thought to be contained in the berries, or seminal vessels of the plant, and for the removal of his male protoplasm. That the mistletoe was thus not so much the 'soul' of the oak but rather its life-essence, is, I think, demonstrable. But I refer the reader to my remarks concerning Australian beliefs about the connection of the mistletoe with 'spirit children' on a previous page, and I entertain the sentiment that this belief may explain the Druidic reverence for the plant in some degree. The ancient forest folk who adored the oak may well have nourished such an idea concerning the plant which adhered to it, indeed the belief may be so ancient that a universal concept of it may have been entertained in parts of the world very distant one from the other, and it may well have gradually spread from one centre to areas so far apart as Europe and Australia. The Australian belief is that spirit-children are contained in the bunches of mistletoe. There is no evidence that the Druids believed as much; but the two beliefs would appear to have developed from one and the same idea.

That the mistletoe was identical with the silver branch or bough of ancient Celtic tradition, I am also assured. This branch, the especial property of the

Winston Churchill installed in the Albion Lodge of the Ancient Order of Druids on 15 August 1908.

335

Irish god Manannan, a deity intimately associated with Druidic art, was cut from a mystical apple tree. It furnished the bearer with food and drink and emanated enchanting music. It led one to the abode of the god and was the symbol of the divine tree standing in the centre of paradise. It is the equivalent of the Golden Bough mentioned by Vergil as a passport to the Land of the Gods. Indeed, he says that this branch is the mistletoe. A correspondent in *The Gentleman's Magazine* for February, 1791, got very near the truth when he wrote that 'Mistletoe, a magical shrub, appears to be the forbidden tree in the middle of the trees of Eden.' I do not suppose that after what has been said by Rydberg concerning the 'mistletoe' with which the Norse sun-god Balder was slain, anyone will expect a dissertation on that legend. *The Mistleteinn* which took his life was the name of an enchanted sword, *teinn* meaning a 'branch' or 'sword' in the poetic sense, as we speak of a 'brand'.

Folk-lore of the Mistletoe

So far as I am concerned, this concludes the explanatory criticism of Pliny's account. We must now examine what folk-lore has to say upon the question, and whether it supports, or declines to support, my view. Aubrey states that in England a decoction of mistletoe was given to promote the discharge of the placenta in calving cows. In Worcestershire farmers took the Christmas mistletoe bough from the wall and gave it to eat to the first cow that calved after New Year's Day, an act which was supposed to avert ill-luck from the whole dairy, but which must surely have originated in a former notion that it induced fertility in the animal. Elsewhere, in his *History of Surrey*, Aubrey observes that when an oak tree at Norwood was felled about 1657, the mistletoe it bore was sold to some London apothecaries at 'ten shillings each time.' The men who cut it were visited with misfortune. One fell lame, 'soon after, each of the others lost an eye,' while he who felled the tree broke his leg. Sir John Colbatch, in his *Dissertation Concerning Mistletoe*, states that it was used for the cure of animals smitten by various diseases.

In Brittany the mistletoe was believed to give strength and courage to those who engaged in wrestling and athletic sports and this, I think goes far to reveal that it was regarded as a seminal product. In Scotland it was, for this reason, thought of as a cure in case of decline. But it well deserved its name of 'All-heal,' for it was employed as a specific against epilepsy, as a liniment to dispel stiffness, a cure for stitches of the side, a panacea for 'green' wounds, that is gangrene, and a nerve-tonic.

In Sweden the mistletoe is the 'thunder-besom,' or broom, the implement of the thunder-god, which reveals its ancient association with the oak-cultus. Placed on the doors or walls of houses, it protected them from the lightning. A certain oak, entwined with mistletoe, was associated by tradition with the ancient and noble family of the Hays of Errol, in Perthshire. So long as the mistletoe grew on this tree (said a venerable saw, believed to have fallen from the lips of Thomas the Rhymer) the Hays would flourish. But should the oak decay and the mistletoe wither, the grass would grow on the Earl's hearth-stone. It was believed that a sprig of mistletoe cut by a Hay of Allhallowmas eve with a new dirk, and after the gatherer had walked three times round the tree sunwise, was a certain charm against sorcery and fatality in the day of battle.

But we find that quite another vegetable medium had associations with kissing beside the mistletoe. The 'kissing-bush,' hung up in houses in the Cleveland district of Yorkshire (at Christmas, presumably), was an ornamental bush made of holly and evergreens, with 'roses' cut from coloured paper and hung with apples and oranges. When railways made their appearance, the mistletoe was added to the 'bush.' It had evidently been remembered, but had been unobtainable locally before that time. Stukeley says that mistletoe was carried to the high altar of York Cathedral on the eve of Christmas Day, when a 'universal liberty' and pardon was proclaimed to 'all sorts of inferior and even wicked people' (thieves, loose women and so forth) 'at the gates of the city,' and this is corroborated by Leland. Now this was actually the procedure at the Roman 'Saturnalia,' the festival of the Latin agricultural god Saturnus, held on December 17th to 23rd, during which season no criminals were punished. This festival was held on the Capitoline Hill, the home of Jupiter, God of the Oak, and during its incidence the people gambled for nuts.

I think that on the whole a reasonably good case has been made out of the authenticity of Pliny's assertions regarding the Druidic rite of mistletoe, even though it is not referred to elsewhere in classical literature. I am not of opinion that the widely diffused superstitions respecting the mistletoe plant were derived from Pliny's account, more particularly that part of them which deals with the exhibition of mistletoe at Christmastide and its tradition as a lovers' plant. That it was also held as sacred is proved by the superstition which averred that bodily misfortune overtook those who cut it from the tree without sanction. That it was thought of as the life-essence of the oak is revealed by the fact that it was given to athletes and consumptives in Britain. Its all-healing character, as recorded by Pliny, is fully displayed in European folk-medicine. That it is associated with the thunder and lightning is made clear by its being affixed to houses in Sweden as a 'lightning conductor', or protector against the heavenly fire. The associations of its rites as carried out under official religious auspices at York seem to make it evident that the plant must have received ancient reverence in that city and its neighbourhood, though this last may well be a survival of ancient Roman practice in 'Eboracum.'

In a tumulus at Gristhorpe, near Scarborough, only a little more than thirty miles from York there was unearthed in 1834 an oak coffin containing a human skeleton which was covered with oak branches and vegetable matter identified, according to one account, as mistletoe. The burial was of the Bronze Age, and thus of a period greatly anterior to that normally connected with Druidic belief. Yet the discovery seems to show that mistletoe and the oak were known as sacred, protective and allied plants in Britain long before historic times.

Representation of Gods

The question as to whether the Druids did or did not fabricate and worship images or idols of their gods is one which has given rise to some controversy. As we have seen, Maximus of Tyre says that the Celts worshipped Zeus in the form of a great oak. Justin states that a statue of a goddess was to be seen in a shrine at Marseilles (lxiii, 5) and the Galatian Celts had images of their deities (Strabo, XII, 5, 2). Caesar remarked upon the numerous effigies of Mercury in Gaul, and Lucan distinctly states that there were many images in the celebrated Druidic grove at Marseilles. Irish literature almost teems with statements concerning idols. Lucan seems to suggest that the images at Marseilles were tree-trunks roughly carved. Figures of Mercury have been found beneath and upon menhirs or standing stones at Peronne in the Somme country and at Kernuz in Finisterre.

In a well-known essay M.S. Reinach has argued that Druidic sentiment was contrary to the fabrication of idols in human form. On the whole, it would seem that the presentation of the Gaulish deities in human shape was partly an innovation introduced under Roman auspices, as we have already seen in the cases of the god Cernunnos and other deities. Reinach's attitude on the subject is prompted by his theory that the Druids were of pre-Celtic origin and were thus unaware of the use of effigies, and that they favoured Pythagoreanism, which was opposed to the worship of images. But there is no mention of Druidic antipathy to images in classical writings, as surely there would have been had it existed, and animal effigies were certainly adored in Gaul. We read of the image of the goddess Berecynthia in sixth century Gaul, and of the 'Venus of Quinipily' in Brittany, which existed, the one in post-Roman and the other in Roman times (although it may be older, even if it bear part of a Latin inscription). Camille Jullian believed that the majority of such images were 'unformed trunks, rough-hewn pillars, a kind of sheath in wood or stone, analogous to the most ancient *Xoana* of the Greeks, without any of the features of a man, or those fixed attributes which make it possible to distinguish a Zeus from an Apollo.'

O'Curry indicates that in Cormac's *Glossary* there is a passage which mentions that the Druids took idols into their couches at night to influence their visions. There was also an invocation to idols in the rite known as *Teinm Laeghala*. He adds: 'That the people of ancient Erinn were idolators is certain, for they certainly adored the great idol called Crom Cruach.' (A standing-stone.) 'But it is remarkable that we find no mention of any connexion between this idol and the Druids, or any other class of priests, or special idol-servers.' It is worthy of mention that Tara, the capital of ancient Ireland, was known in St Patrick's day as 'the chief seat of the *idolatry* and Druidism of Erin,' although in this instance the term 'idolatry' may here be merely a synonym for 'paganism.' Groups of images existed at Rath-Archaill, 'where the Druids' altar and images are' (Ailred, *Vita St Ninian*, p. 6) The ancient Irish King MacCuil adored for his god a log of wood. (Keating, O'Connor's translation, p. 108.)

Keating recounts a legend which states that in the days of King Cormac one of the idols of the ancient Irish was a golden calf. On one occasion this effigy was brought by the Druids into the presence of Cormac, who had become a convert to Christianity. The Chief Druid, Maoilogeann, inquired of the King why he did not adhere to the religion of his ancestors, whereupon Cormac replied to him in a scornful manner, saying that the idol in question was merely the image of a beast and not the true god. The Druids removed the idol, only to bring it back later bedizened with jewels and covered with ornamental housings, and once more asked the King if it were not worthy of his devotions. But he refused even more strenuously to bow the knee to the image. Resolved on vengeance, the Chief Druid so enchanted a salmon which had been prepared for Cormac's evening repast that one of its bones stuck in his throat and choked him. Miss Eleanor Hull thought that this story was 'a mere adaptation of the Biblical account of the golden calf in the wilderness.' It is true that the main idea of a calf of gold inspires both stories, but otherwise I can trace but little resemblance between them.

A strange case of seeming idolatry in Wales, at a period so late as the reign of Henry VIII, is on record. It occurred in the diocese of St Asaph and is described in a letter from one Ellis Price to Thomas Cromwell, the famous secretary of Henry, dated April 6th, 1538. Price wrote as follows:

'There ys an image of Darvellgadarn within the said diocese, in whome the people have so greate confidence, hope and truste, that they cumme dayly a pillgramage unto hym, somme with kyne, othir with oxen or horsis and the reste with money; in so much that there was fyve or syxe hundrethe pilgrimes to a man's estimacion, that offered to the said image the fifth daie of this present monethe of Aprill. The innocente people hath ben sore aluryd and entised to worship the saide image, in so much that there is a commyn sayinge as yet amongst them that who so ever will offer anie thinge to the said Image of Darvellgadarn, he hathe power to fatche hym or them that so offers oute of Hell when they be dampned.'

This idol was conveyed to Smithfield and incontinently burnt there, along with a 'friar' or priest who bore the same name as itself. The general circumstances surrounding the affair yield the impression that the idol was associated with a surviving cultus of the sacred ox. Oxen were offered up to it, and we shall see that the sacrifice of these animals was fairly common in Wales until a late date. An ancient British deity known as Hu Gadarn was said to have drawn souls out of Annwn, or Hell, and 'Darvellgadarn' had certainly some reputation in Wales as a 'saint.' 'Darvell' may perhaps be a corruption of *tarw*, the Welsh word for a bull. May he not be the same as Gargantua or Cernunnos? It seems to me not altogether improbable that he was.

Numerous objects resembling idols have been recovered in Ireland, chiefly from bogs. Some are garbed in a short petticoat or kilt and wear forked beards. One such, now in the Dublin Museum, was taken from beneath the root of a large tree in Roscommon. It had formerly been gilt and is about five inches in height. A metal idol weighing twenty-four pounds was recovered from the soil at Clonmel. About 1690 a large wooden image was found in the bog of Cullen, in Tipperary. Pins and pegs were stuck in different parts of it, and gold plates found near it seem to have been suspended from these, evidently as offerings. 'The old Tuath, a vaulted stone temple at Knockmay, in Galway, which was afterwards turned into an abbey, had a remarkable figure, like Apollo, bound to a tree, pierced by arrows.' Strabo, as we shall see, mentions that the Druids sacrificed some of their victims by shooting them with arrows, and indeed shooting at tree-trunks is a feature of tree-worship in some countries, as Frazer observes. It may, indeed, have been a part of the ritual of the forest-god or spirit known to later ages as 'Robin Hood' and that of his Swiss 'cousin', William Tell.

At Cashel a stone image was discovered late in the last century. It was about two feet in height, the legs taking the form of serpents crossed.

An image of wood about two feet high, in the likeness of a woman, was piously preserved by one of the family of O'Herleby in Ballyvorney, County Cork, and when anyone was smitten by the small-pox they sent for it, sacrificed a sheep to it and wrapped the skin about the sick person, while the family ate the sheep. Tigernmas, an Irish king, is said to have been slain by lightning for worshipping an idol. Petrie, the great Irish antiquary of the nineteenth century, was of opinion that such effigies had replaced the worship of standing-stones in Erin. He alludes to Kerman Kelstach, the favourite idol of the folk of Ulster, which had for its pedestal the golden stone of Clogher, and which may have resembled in its general shapelessness the Greek *Hermae*. He attributed the introduction of such images to 'the Eastern fire-worshippers.'

It appears to me as not improbable that some of these effigies at least may have been associated with Druidic worship. That such rude images were actually connected with it in Gaul we have seen, and that they were also adored in Ireland it seems scarcely rash to assume, though a number of them may possibly have been worshipped by the adherents of other cults. Yet this seems hardly possible in view of the very exclusive character of the Druidic faith.

The Druidic Idea of Creation

We read that the Druids of Ireland claimed that they were the creators of the world. On one occasion King Connla of Connaught convened a great gathering of the Druids, who in the course of the discussion claimed that they were the creators of the heavens and the earth. But their pretensions were scoffed at by the monarch, who challenged them to alter the courses of the sun and moon so that they should appear in the north, to their complete confusion.

But there seems to be a certain degree of truth in the superstition that the Druids believed themselves to have possessed such creative powers. Professor A.M. Hocart has made it clear that the priesthoods of other races indulged such a notion. The natives of Western Vanua Levu, in the Fiji group, hold installation ceremonies or consecration of the chiefs, at such times as the crops do not flourish. These they call 'creating the earth.' The same ceremony was known in early India, and the book entitled *Satapottia* describes at length the method to be followed in a rite known as 'the creation of the world.' A piece of clay is shaped 'like the world.' By this means, imitating the creative process, the priest or enchanter is thought to gain control over the whole earth, he places plants in the clay model. he mimics the sun by holding fire above it. 'The whole purpose of the king's coronation is to gain control of the world and thus create abundance and creatures.'

The Egyptian Pharaoh did much the same. He 'renewed each day the mystery of the creation.' The same process was carried out in the ritual of the Eleusinian mysteries. Indians and Germans, Scandinavians and Babylonians knew of a myth which told how a god, a monster, or a man had been slain and dismembered and how the universe was subsequently created from his several parts, the soil being composed of his flesh, the rocks from his bones, the sky and clouds from his brains and the sun and moon from his eyes. In some cases a human sacrifice was performed in order to re-enact the process, which was that of renewing the earth's vigour. The king or chieftain then took mystical possession of the essence of the earth for the benefit of the community.

It seems not at all impossible that a Druidic myth and ritual of a similar propensity and significance lay behind this claim of the Irish Druids, who, after all, were, as we shall see, a body of priests chiefly identified with the cultus of the Sacred King. By the time of Connla the belief in this rite may have waned considerably or grown partly discredited, and only the general memory of it may have survived. But that the survival of belief in the creation of the world by the Druidic caste suggests the former existence of such a myth and rite seems clear enough, for the belief could scarcely have existed unless such a ritual practice had once prevailed.

The Druids and Well-worship

We find the Druids mentioned in connection with the worship of wells. In the 'Annotations' of Tirechan on the life of St Patrick, to be found in the *Book of Armagh*, and which contains material at least as old as the latter half of the seventh century, we are told that Patrick came to the fountain of Findmaige, which is called Slan, because it was shown to him that the Magi honoured the fountain and made offerings to it 'as gifts to God,' and that they 'worshipped the fountain as a god.'

As Whitley Stokes points out, this is the only passage which connects the Druids with well-worship. But it is important, as it indicates their association with such spirits or genii as those who presided over wells. The rather elaborate ritual engaged in at some sacred wells is still mimicked in certain children's games surviving in Britain, and these may possibly represent fragments of ancient Druidic ritual. These cannot actually be proved, but the circumstance that such sacred wells are, or were, frequently to be found in the near neighbourhood of venerable oaks, with which they are associated in local legend, seems to support the idea that they were places of Druidic reverence. Moreover, we find distinct traces of official priesthood at such wells. At that of St Aelian, in Denbighshire, a woman resided who officiated as 'priestess'. Evilly-disposed folk, who wished to bring down a curse on an enemy, resorted to her, and for a small sum she registered the name of the blighted one in a book kept for the purpose. A pin was dropped in the well in the name of the victim.

This recalls a Gascon belief that those who wish to revenge themselves upon their enemies may be able to induce a priest to say a mass to their detriment and injury. This rite, known as 'the Mass of St Sécaire,' will, of course, be performed only by a priest of the most abandoned character and such are indeed few. It can be said only in a ruined church at midnight, with an equally depraved woman acting as clerk. A black, three-pointed host is used and water from a well into which the body of an unbaptized infant has been cast. The man against whom the mass is said is supposed to 'dwindle, peek and pine' until he dies. (J.F. Bladé, *Quatorze superstitions populaire de Gascogne*, p. 16 ff.) At St Teilo there is an 'oxen's well,' formerly tended by a family called Melchor, which, says Sir John Rhys in his *Celtic Folklore*, 'may indicate a succession which seems to point unmistakably to an ancient priesthood of a sacred spring.'

It is worthy of notice that the tale known as 'The Lady of the Fountain,' to be found in the Welsh *Mabinogion*, appears to hold a significance connected with the worship of the oak. It recounts how a knight is made aware of an adventure which is to be encountered in the neighbourhood of a tall tree, beneath which stands a fountain bounded by a marble slab. To this is attached a silver bowl. If water be taken from the spring in this bowl and cast upon the slab, a terrific peal of thunder resounds, and a storm of rain follows, so terrible in its fury as scarcely to be endured by flesh and blood. Immediately after the phenomenon a multitude of birds in the tree burst into songs of rhapsody. Then a champion mounted on a black steed appears, with whom the knight must do combat. This defending champion is slain and the knight who slays him marries his wife and rules over his country. But he must defend the fountain, as did his predecessor, or his lady's right to the kingdom will lapse.

The story obviously contains certain elements of Celtic mythology. Within its compass we are confronted with the thunder-oak and the rain-making well. Is the Lady of the country a goddess or 'Sacred Queen'? The combat of the knights under the tree appears as reminiscent of the strife between the priests at Aricia, the shrine of the Golden Bough,' or Nemi, in Italy, and if the interloper conquers the defender, he weds the Queen, or goddess, a proceeding which seems to have been carried out in the ancient ritual connected with the King and Queen of the May, as in that of 'Robin Hood.' The tale appears to contain some of the factors of the Divine King myth as well as those of the sacred oak and fountain. The fountain seems reminiscent of the shrine of Zeus at Dodona, with its oak tree and sacred spring, its oracular birds and iron basin. Indeed, the resemblance seems too close to be a matter of chance.

Druidic Ritual

Apart from the subject of sacrifice, which will be dealt with in the following chapter, objective information concerning Druidic ritual is somewhat hard to come by. We find that, a rite resembling baptism was performed by the Druids in Ireland. Thus it is said of Conall Cernach that when he was born, 'Druids came to baptize the child into heaathenism, and they sang the heathen baptism over him.' When twins were born to two families, a pair of boys and a pair of girls, the boys were baptized first and later the girls, by the Druids, who acted as officiating priests and duly named the children. Ailill, the husband of the famous Medb, was 'baptized in Druidic streams.' Druids also seem to have officiated at burials in Ireland. The Druid Dergdamsa revited a funeral oration over the hero Mog-neid, buried him with his arms and chanted a magical rhyme over him, and it seems probable that the Druid priesthood also carried out sacrifices at the grave on such occasions, as for example, at the burial of Fiachin, when fifty hostages were buried alive and the death-dirge was chanted by a bard. 'The Druidic or other sacred ceremonies' and funeral games, says O'Curry's editor, 'appear to have been included under the collective name of *Nosad*.'

Druidic Philosophy

Doubtless a great deal of extravagance has been indulged in by those writers who made the loftiest claims on behalf of Druidic philosophy. In all likelihood, however, Druidic doctrine of was of not less distinction than the thought of Egypt or of Babylonia in the earlier phases of these civilizations, which is not according it a very high position.

The curiosity of Roman freethinkers was aroused by the discovery that the barbarians of Gaul entertained the doctrine of immortality, and probably the intense earnestness of the Druid caste impressed Caesar, himself a priest, and indeed Pontifex Maximus in the honorary sense. Their somewhat theatrical anathemas also appear to have scared the Roman men-at-arms, when they confronted them in Anglesea. Indeed; the rather blasé Roman of the last century B.C. felt that he was the spectator of a cultus which must have closely resembled that of his own more simple forefathers and the latent sense of virtue, never to be sought for in vain among the best Roman minds, was probably stirred and quickened by the austere habits and bearing of the Druids with whom they came in contact, until at last the seemingly grotesque magical ideas and feitishistic practices which underlay Druidic 'thought' came to be recognized. The ghastly sacrificial system appears to have disgusted Italian sentiment, which properly regarded it as unhealthy and abhorrent. Later, I shall deal more particularly with the theory that certain Druidic ideas had their origin in the Pythagorean philosophy. Here I am concerned merely with the content and nature of Druidic thought, or 'philosophy' or theology in general.

In his homily on Ezekiel, Origen, the Christian apologist, who flourished in the third century, remarked that the people of Britain had 'worshipped the one God' 'previous to the coming of Christ,' and in his Commentary on the same book, he says that the island 'had long been predisposed to Christianity through the doctrines of the Druids and the Buddhists, who had already inculcated the doctrine of the unity of the Godhead.' But although it seems probable that the Druidic system had originally been confined to the worship of one god, that of the sacred oak, we are confronted by a good deal of evidence that other gods, those of the Celtic pantheon, in fact, were also recognized, if not adored by it. The probability seems to be that Druidism, originally the cult of the god of the oak tree, adopted in the course of its existence a great deal of mythical material concerning other deities. Probably those belonged to the general stock of European nature-gods, as their resemblance to Italic, Greek, Teutonic and Slavonic deities appears to bear out, and we seem to be left with the general impression that the original Druidic cult of the oak came to terms with other prevailing cults, as was the case in Greece, Rome and Germany,. but that it still maintained a predominance in the national or tribal worship in certain parts of Gaul, which the oak-worship of Greece and Rome had not succeeded in attaining. The philosophy of Druidism, the spirit which animated it, can, in my opinion, only be surmised from a general review of its history and practice, and this, it seems to me, reveals it as a system in which a mass of myth, magical lore and taboo was slowly being formed into a 'wisdom-religion' somewhat resembling that of the early Semites, or that of the 'Aryans' of India, and which was beginning to entertain views of a moral character derived chiefly from the circumstances of taboo, distinguishing *fas* and *nefas*, dividing right and wrong, into what was 'lawful' and 'not lawful.' 'The *geasa*, or taboos which surrounded the Irish kings seem to reveal such a gradual process.

And as Diogenes Laertius tells us, the Druids inculcated the observation of a rough general maxim: 'to worship the gods, to do no evil, and to exercise courage' – enough, indeed, for a race of men existing in a condition of almost primeval simplicity. It is held in some quarters that the Welsh Triads embrace in their obsure numbers much of the ancient Druidic philosophy and belief. But it is difficult to credit that the remains of a system which had been abolished and evidently extirpated at least seven centuries before the earliest of the Triads was composed could have survived such a passage of time. In any case, the necessity of proof lies with those who infer such survival, and their endeavours to make good their claims impress me as being of about as much value as the reasoning by which their opponents seek to denounce them.

Classical writers speak well of the integrity of the Druidic caste. 'The Druids,' says Strabo, 'are considered the most just of men.' 'They are of much sincerity and integrity,' says Diodorus Siculus, 'far from the craft and knavery of men among us, contented with homely fare, strangers to excess and luxury.' Where such strict discipline was maintained, it could scarcely have been otherwise, and the circumstances that the Druids were not a celibate priesthood must certainly have helped to maintain a high standard of personal morality among them.

23

✲

THE TREE-TRILOTHON OF THE YEAR DUIR - THE MONTH OF THE OAK: 11 JUNE-8 JULY

Ross Nichols

From the *Records of the Order of Bards, Ovates and Druids*, c.1950

> I am a god who sets the head afire with smoke.
>
> *Song of Amergin*

This is pre-eminently the Druidic month of the Druidic tree, standing for eternity and its strengths. The mistleberry upon the oak was the rare finding of the berry of incarnation and instance upon eternity: a kind of centre-point of the dance: 'at the still point, there the dance is' (T. S. Eliot): the point where the upright and the arms of the cross meet. To signify the union of the mother with the father in this, the mistleberry, which to early minds was like the male sperm, was cut by a golden sickle that appears to represent the moon, hence the feminine. So the silver is cut by the gold, the male berry by the female moon. That is the reasonable interpretation of the cutting of the mistletoe on the oak with a golden sickle given by Caesar, for no one would normally cut anything with a sickle of soft gold.

The oak is venerable indeed. It is the tree of Greek Zeus, perhaps of Jewish El or Jehovah, of Roman Jupiter, and of Herakles the hero; in Celtdom, of the Dagda, chief of the older Irish deities, of Scandinavian Thor, and all the thunders. The archaeologists and folklorists agree: and Frazer's great work is based on the sacrifice of the oak-king at Nemi.

Midsummer fires are of oak – so are the need-fires – so was Vesta's fire at Rome, the shrine of the Roman state. So the fires were sacred and their smoke, probably helped by herbs and gums, was inspirational – and the Welsh, saying in its hyperbolical way that Duir 'sets the head afire with smoke', was meaning that sacred oakfires gave poetic inspiration.

In the 'Câd Goddeu' Gwion writes of the oak 'stout guardian of the door, his name is on every tongue.' Duir indeed seems cognate with door in many tongues: Old Goidelic *dorus*, Latin *foris*, Greek *thura*, German *tür*, Sanskrit *Dwr*, Hebrew Daleth (l and r are interchangeable linguistically). Midsummer is the oak's flowering time, hence he is centre of the year.

Duir therefore is a Janus, facing both ways: like Herakles, a door-keeper after death, and there seems to be a link with the goddess of hinges, Cardea, who looked after the unruly winds and further ruled the great hinge, the millstone of the universe. (See Varro, 'De Re Rustica'.) This again links with Scandinavia where we have Fenje and Menje, giantesses who grind round the great earth-millstone Grotte in the circumpolar night: and one remembers that the Pole Star is 'turned' by two astronomical bears.

Like the ash's, the oak's roots go deep into the other world: they go as deep underground as its branches rise in air, so that the god whom it symbolises rules the laws of both heaven and underworld. Possibly the Acheans, who earlier found the beech oracular, transferred its qualities to its nearest likeness when they migrate into Greece: their name for oak, *phegos*, is the same as the Latin for beech *fagus*. Acorns are perhaps not unlike beechnuts in use – both will feed certain animals. Anyway, oaks were linked with lightning and thunder and oracles. The Dodona oracle, which gave answers by the wind in its leaves, was much earlier than Acheabs but continued its reputation. Herodotus linked it with the oak-and-black-dove oracle of Zeus at the shrine of Amûn in the Libyan desert; both, he said, were the same age, and indeed Flinders Petrie thought there was a Libyan-Greek holy league as early as the 3rd millenium. This Amûn-Zeus was a ram-headed Herakles, like Osiris' main form and like Amûn-Rā at Thebes. The stem 'Garama' comes both in Greece and Libya; the Garamantes clan was in charge of the Libyan Amûn, and the Greek ancestor Garamans was 'chief of men'. To this Libyan shrine came Alexander the Great to seek recognition and guidance and found both. He was recognised as son of Amûn and not of Philip of Macedon, and he henceforth wore Amûn's ram-horns, and he was counselled upon his mission, his immediate victories being foretold but his purposes changed – henceforth he is less of a mere conqueror, more the leader of a sacred mission of education.

Returning to Britain, it is thought by Robert Graves that the oak cult came here from the Baltic 1600–1400 B.C. by the amber trading route, with the cult of Arthur, and that this may be about the date of the whole of this Beith-Luis-Nuinn tree alphabet calendar that we may use here. Gwyn, son of Lir, was buried in an oak coffin made boat-shape, and it was an oak-tree hollowed as a coffin that the monks found in 1245 and reckoned as Arthur's. The usual account is that they faked the leaden inscription for the coffin. But, first, we now know that hollowed oak tree coffins are correct for the Arthur period, and that the burial was therefore probably 5th century anyway; second, Mr Raleigh Radford in 1962 showed by excavation that Girald Cambrensis' directions for where Arthur's grave was found were correct; and third, the latest Arthurian period researcher, Count Nikolai Tolstoy, considers that the wording of the inscription as given is quite reasonable for the fifth century.

The archaeologists can now point to a number of hollowed oaktree burials both in Scandinavia and here. The oaktree was a soul-boat; in it the soul voyaged into the next life. At Loose Howe, on the Cleveland Moors, Yorks, are three such boats; at Grisethorpe, Scarborough, was found an oak-boat with a skeleton with oakbranches and mistletoe – surely a Druid? This area is where the amber route from Eire reached the sea from the Pennines: – Irish gold for Baltic amber. The Viking ship-burials are a spectacular later version of this idea. The older folk buried in an oaken ship, like the boat-burials of Ancient Egypt. The less civilised minds of the Viking period would have a body drive out to sea physically on a seaworthy ship. The most substantial treasure reflecting this idea is the rich Sutton Hoo burial of the sixth-century Saxon kings. Last relic is the Up-helly-aa ceremony in the Orkneys. The reference for much of this is Christopher Hawkes' 'Prehistoric Foundations of Europe'.

So this Druid Oak-month has links that are basic to all our western traditional culture. Central to the year, symbol of eternity, sacred to the chief father-god figure, always the door or the hinge, with oracular leaves and inspirational smoke, the oaktree's roots and branches make laws for heaven and earth and its trunk is the burial and rebirth place for death and the new life.

24

❧

THE FOUR CELTIC
FIRE FESTIVALS

Colin Murray[41]

I
Samhuinn: Winter's Dance of Thirteen

According to the best evidence we have of Celtic calendars, the Coligny Tablet, it is established that historical Gaels measured time by the passing of the moon. Consequently, the Old Year was divided into thirteen lunar months. As the solar year only equates with the lunar cycle (the Metonic Cycle) every nineteen years an adjustment was made at the end of each year to bring the two systems into harmony.

It has been shown that the old tree alphabet, the Oghams of the ancient Druids, were a system of passing magical knowledge from one initiate to another. In the slow turning of the year the last of the thirteen lunar months is Ruis and the first Beth, Ruis the elder and Beth the white birch, according to the Welsh calendar poem 'The Song of Amergin' and the tales of Diarmid and Grainne.

At this special junction, with the ending of the old year, the rising of all old thoughts and wishes and the preparation of the rebirth of the new year, great tension arises. This was traditionally released in the form of a festival with fires during the three special days that introduce, balance and close the actual events. In Eire and Alba, you would know the time as Samhuinn; in Mannin as Sauin; in Cymru as Nos Galan Gaeof (the Calends of Winter); and in Breizk (Brittany) as Nos Kentan 'r Bloaz, the first night of the year.

At the time when the sciences, arts and political organizations were under a unified Celtic system of college-trained graduates, the filid or bards, from say 600 B.C. until the descent of the Celtic Culdee Church (composed mainly of old Druids in, say, 1300 A.D.), a systematic harnessing of inner and outer forces would have been commercially ritualized for the whole population. This has now degenerated into folk dances, games and divinatory rites, whose roots lie far back, in a more creative and organised past.

The four Fire Festivals spoken of equate roughly with our modern seasons. Samhuinn starts the new year with a period of throwing out all careworn ideas and influences and, more especially, of direct contact with the spirits of the dead and the 'group mind' of the race, for want of a better word. Let us start, this magical procession with three shouts upon the traditional Cnoc Miodhchaoin, the special hill of Lochlain, reference to which is made in 'The Crane Bag', that special container for the Ogham aphabet that is centered around the Isle of Man. Three is a number that echoes forwards and backwards into our common legacy, you may call it the Trinity in Christian terms or the three aspects of the Goddess in her and many varied forms and many names.

The three worlds of the Celt are Abred, Gwynffrydd and Ceugant, three circles of knowledge that chart the undying soul in its journey through this present world of illusion and the real world of spirit, that lies behind it. Abred is the outer life, the bearing, marrying, dying world that we see all around us; all is change, creation and progression. Gwynffrydd is the second circle, that of illumination, where the 'soul spirit' passes only when it has understood the rite of passage, present behind the everchanging 'real' world. Ceugant is the realm of pure principle. The nearest equivalent to which is the white light of truth in one religious system, or the three rays of light that strike from the risen sun at midsummer, in another older tune. It is Mazda in Persia and Ogmios or Ogma in Eire. The Light is the same, wherever you are.

Now, with this onion skin of reality peeled back for you at Samhuinn time, you may, if you are prepared for it, perceive in a different way. In recent and present folk games these metaphysical ideas have been watered down, but they still show some of the old truths behind the unreality of the present. The Bannoch or bonnach Samhuinn was once a sacramental cake baked at each of the four fire festivals. In St Kilda a large bannoch was made in the form of 'a triangle, furrowed.' In the Lowlands, in the ancient burgh of Rutherglen, 'sour cakes' were ritually made by a group of chosen women, called the queen, the bride and her maidens. The bannoch is rolled by each in turn, Deasul or sunwise, thus giving it the strength of the sun, in its daily course. At a much earlier time, Columba the Celtic saint, learnt his Oghams from a Druid teacher by eating a bannoch a day, with a letter impressed upon it. The cakes might be divided up, one blackened and the group required to make a choice. The person who received the marked cake, would be marked by the darkness of the winter, had to blacken his face and was spoken of as dead, for the three days of the festival.

The other potent symbol at Samhuinn time is the apple. One remembers that Arthur, following his death in this world, went to Avalon, or the apple land. It is no chance that rowan berries are linked as well. You will observe that the inner core of an apple has five pips, forming a pentagram, and that the top of a rowan berry has a similar five-pointed star formation. The structure of the secret Ogham cryptogram language was based on five, as had been the Pythagorean number symbolism, both systems in use at about the same time. The apple represents the five changes of the Holy Grail, in later times, or the five transformations of the Celtic cauldron of rebirth, that predated the Grail.

So naturally, we find many games involving the winning of apples at Samhuinn. For example, in 'The Apple and the Candle', one takes a small rod of wood, suspends it from the ceiling by a cord and, when it is balanced, fixes a lighted candle at one end and an apple at the other. One then sets the rod whirling and requires each of the company to try and bite the apple without getting singed. Another such is known as 'pairing the apple'. This should be performed at the stroke of midnight. Pare an apple carefully so that the skin comes off in one unbroken ribbon and, as the clock strikes, fling it over your left shoulder. In the shape it assumes you will find truth, maybe the name of a bethrothed if you are young, or an answer to a problem, or the key to a personal quest.

The examples are legion, but they all show a heightened awareness of the natural and supernatural worlds that lie closely linked together. The doors to these worlds are always open but never more so than at Samhuinn, the ending of the old king year and the rebirth of the white birch of the new. Drive out your old, bad thoughts with a birch besom, especially if you live in the Isle of Man. The European Court at Strasbourg considers that birching is inhuman. It is no more than the old seasonal dance that links us to the earth and the common sea from which we rise and fall, endlessly.

II
Imbolc – The Festival of Brigantia

Brigantia: Dea Nymphae Brigantiae – The Triple Muse

Your first candle lit, is your sunrise birth; the flame of your house reaching
  Ceugant's bride.
Your second, is the spark of your union with Bress, son of Elathan.
Your third, is the pillar of fire, as you took the veil, rising high and clear.
Your fourth are brothers, with Dagda your father, Broadb the red, Medar Ogma
  and Angus.
Your fifth is eternal life's spring; that sings your name, in crystal gaze.
Your sixth, is the flame of your altar, that never dies.
Your seventh, is the Grove at Llandwynwn, on Mena's shore, where lovers tryst.
Your eighth is the strength of your Oxen of Dil, Fea and Fearna, Red and Black.
Your ninth, is the sigh of your breath, as new life grows from old, your bridge of
  truth.
Your tenth, is a milk white cow, of redden ears, The Earth Mother's Nectar,
  sweet!
Your eleventh, is a girdle, that spans night and day, yet heals and remains.
Your twelfth, is a veil of truth, in a flowering thorn, your wearyall path.
Your thirteenth, is for your son, Ruardan, to be reborn.
Your fourteenth, is the white light of the flowing word, born at sunrise – the
  molten sky.

Your fifteenth, is the Grove at Kildare, with solid Oak and crystal spring.
Your sixteenth, are shrines throughout Albion, in Church, Well and Wall.
Your seventeenth, is your will, of black iron, forged in the determination of a
thousand
Your eighteenth, is a healing, The White Dog at the Portal, the Chalice of your
smile.
Your nineteenth is a Clarsach, which spells and binds, the hours, days and signs,
all in a silver bough.
Your last is your first, the beginning of the turning sea, the ending of the three in
one
The Dancing Sun in the hearts of all! The candle that never dies!

So runs the blue and silver thread of fair Brigid's many guises, in her various
forms, romantic thoughts and fancies and historical truths mixed all together.
There was a factual tribal land of the Brigantes spreading across England, from
the Wirral to the Wash, in pre-Conquest times. Brigit is remembered as a
fertility goddess in every marriage ceremony as 'the Bride'. She appears, like the
solar king and god, Arthur (or perhaps Ar-Tur) at different times and places
both in recorded history and in poetic legend.

Let us take a vision, quoted, according to Moïna MacGregor Mathies, from
a manuscript in the Library of Ireland recording a version of Brigid, the Triple
Goddess of the Gael, as seen by Maud Gonne. This vision occurred at the time
that Yates was experimenting with his 'Castle of Heroes' and other visions,
through the early Celtic influenced Golden Dawn tradition, under MacGregor
Mathers.

The Three Brigids

The Three Brigids guard the entrance to the land of the gods. This entrance
consists of three gateways, formed of heavy beams of wood, inlaid with small
ornaments of silver and brass.

Brigid, the Smith-worker stands strong and alert at the left-hand gate. She
is very dark, with black, wiry hair and restless black eyes. Her tunic is of blue
and purple; her bratta is purple, and a bronze brooch clasps her bratta; and on
her head is a bronze band; beaten bronze-work ornaments her leather belt and
sandles. She governs all handiworks and represents the hard, laborious and
painful side of life.

Brigid of Medicine stands at the right-hand gate. She has a fair and gentle
face; her robes are light blue, embroidered with silver thread, clasped by a silver
winged brooch; another winged ornament rests on her head. She represents the
happy, sympathetic side of life, and so becomes the healer of that which is
bruised and broken by the hammer of the Brigid of Smithwork.

Brigid of Poetry stands over the central gateway. Her robes are more
sombre and cloudy. They are of a dull blue-grey and white; her face is neither
fair or dark, she has soft blue eyes, which sadly look out upon the world, feeling
the joys and sorrows that work therein. She combines the forces of the other

two, being both active and passive, receptive of impressions, and possessing the power of producing form. . . . While she rests, vegetation grows; she blows the blast from her trumpet duing the dead months of winter. The waves of the sea flow towards her when she is at rest, and are driven back when she becomes active. Behind the posts of the gateway lie two hounds, that on the side of Brigid the Smithworker is black, the other is white. They represent life and death, joy and sorrow. Whosoever would enter through this gateway should know the secret of one of these hounds, for a battle takes place between them, and that hound which is known, grows stronger through that knowledge, and when the stronger has devoured the weaker, it becomes the servant of him who knows its nature.

Moïna's vision is a little heavy-handed, but the characteristics are all there. The original mythic Brigid was a solar goddess, wed to a Fomorian, one of the early 'giant' invaders of Eire. Bress, who had married Brigid according to romance, was the son of the Fomorian King Elathan. Their son, Ruardan, becomes trapped in a web of intrigue and is asked to spy on Goibnui and to attempt to kill him. However he fails and is himself mortally wounded. Goibnui is healed at the magical spring of youth, the eternal spring mentioned in the opening poem.

As a fire goddess, Brigid was born at sunrise, in a house which burst into flame, which reaches to heaven. A pillar of fire is said to have risen from her head when she took the veil, and her breath gave new life to the dead. She rules over boiling springs and at her altar an eternal flame is lit, a perpetual fire. The sacred flame at her shrine at Kildare was never allowed to go out. It was extinguished once in the thirteenth century, but after being relit, it burned until the reformation and dissolution of the monasteries under Henry VIII. The same sacred fire might not be breathed on by an impure human breath. For nineteen nights the fire was tended by Brigid's nuns, but on the twentieth night it remained lit in a miraculous manner, though untouched.

The factual Brigid was an abbess, born perhaps at Faughart in about A.D. 450 and dying at Kildare in A.D. 523. The great fact about her life is that she founded a community of women at Kildare. She is properly regarded as the initiator and abbess of the first Christian women's community among the Irish and attained a unique position of authority during her own life time. She died and was buried at Kildare. During the later Danish invasions her remains were removed to Downpatrick to be interned, it is alleged, with St Patrick. The cult of St Brigid spread far and wide and has survived well beyond the emasculation of the primitive orthodox Celtic Culdee church, which was annexed by the Roman Catholic Church in its expansionist phase during the Holy Roman Empire. The fundamental importance and necessity of a woman's spiritual role remains and the dialogue continues fervently among the current patriarchal religions that are prevalent today.

It is interesting that many of the more spiritual of the women's groups that are developing today have, of necessity, to go through a painful rejection of the Christian dogma because of its one-sided nature. What is creative and fecundating among the old religions continues in some fashion as a spearhead of the slowly changing tide that is gradually replacing the aggressive patriarchal, Old Testament vision with the easier earthy and fertile mother image of Brigid, in her several characters.

III
Beltane's Purifying Fires

The Bard addresses his Soul

Soul, since I was made blameless of necessity
True 'tis woe's me that thou didst fashion me;
Neither for my own sake, death's end, nor for beginning
Was I created, seven senses winning,
Seven created things to purify—
In my beginning gleaming fire was I,
I was dust of earth, and then grief could not reach me,
I was high wind, which mostly good did teach me,
I was mountain mist, seeking supplies of deer,
I was blossom of trees which once the earth did wear—
Soul, since it was the Lord himself that blessed me,
It should be well for thee, matter possessed thee.

Black Book of Carmarthen, VI, Sixth Century

'In my beginning gleaming fire was I' . . . from Breton and Gaulish traditions the Celtic year was divided by the four fire festivals into two halves: the dark half from Samhuinn to Beldan or Beltane, 31 October to 1 May in our calendar, and the light half, from 1 May to 31 October again. This yearly pattern closely follows the monthly lunar pattern according to the Coligny Tablet calendar, where the month starts with the last quarter moon, the dark half of the month and culminates with the waxing moon. Thus light flows after a period of darkness. Naturally the pattern of life takes this cue and marriages were not solemnized during the dark half of the year. In the lunar calendar, starting with the 'Old Year' of 31 October, the seventh lunar month straddles May Day. May Day is, therefore, a turning point; its oak name, Duir, reflects the lightning struck oak, the Divine Fire that comes down to burst the oak with superhuman energy.

This quality of illumination, of divine inspiration, takes practical reality in the old custom of fire festivals. Clearly, the fires at Samhuinn are a purgative, the burning sense of removing unwanted dross, the cleaning-up process before the coming rigours of winter. It is quite remarkable how this intention has carried over into the November, the fifth festival, with its ritual effigy burning and spiral catherine wheels of fire. The destroyer of the forces of order is himself burnt in effigy and the onlookers are relieved of their past troubles, in preparation for the coming winter. As is commonly still held in the Celtic homeland, for three days

353

the spirits of the dead world are in direct contact with the living. In Breton traditions, the doors of the Underworld, the sidhe, are ritually opened on the first evening. The next day follows with a vigil, and the last day involves closing the doors of the Underworld. A ritual libation is made to the deceased and the enhanced perception given by this contact between the two halves, the dark and light, that make the world, and produces the inspiration that is reflected in the divine fire. In folklore this has become a series of games played between the questioner and the 'unknown'. Recently these have become less serious, involving questions of future husbands for young girls. At the time when the primitive tribal clans were held together by Druid-trained priests, this perception would have taken on a deeper significance for the whole community. The old groups were held together by participation, in a way that has been totally lost today. The 'magical' perceptions of group release, of inspired guidance, of greatly strengthened powers through coming together are only rarely seen these days, mostly at times of great crisis or rejoicing, such as the winning of wars or the jubilee of the reigning monarch, to quote a recent example.

We do not have so much respect for natural rythms, for seasonal patterns, to relate simply to these underlying patterns any more. Nevertheless, we are biological organisms, closely related to the common whole. Our spiritual eyes open and close like flowers in the rotating pattern of the yearly dance.

The pattern that shows in the old Beltane fires links the individual, the family and the whole community. With fires on the carns or tops of hills throughout the land, all would feel part of the whole. Each family would extinguish its hearth fire before the festival and receive the new fire as a divine gift, as the flower receives the necessary pollen, allowing it to continue until the next seasonal change time.

Each community clearly developed its own special rituals. We hear of fires being built around trees in Eire. Cloghaunnatinny in County Clare takes its name from Clochir-bilé-teine, or 'the stepping stones of the fire tree', from a large tree under which May fires used to be lit. No doubt dances around the fires took place as well as the more common passing through two fires, which purified the person and the cattle against illness. The fire has become a great focus of strength which imparts its knowledge to individuals. The sacred dance might take the form of a Maze dance – as, for example, in Alkborough, Lincolnshire, where villagers, as late as 1866, played May games around the Maze, sometimes called here Gillian's Bore. These May dances on Troy Towns, or Mazes, link back to the close Celtic-Greek links of carn games . . .

To return to our carn fires, it was customary for the Lord of the place, or his son, or some other person of distinction, to take the entrails of the sacrific'd animal in his hands, and walking barefoot over the coals thrice, after the flames had cease'd, to carry them straight to the Druid, who waited in a whole skin at the Altar. If the noble man escaped harmless, it was reckoned a good omen, welcomed with loud acclamations: but if he received any hurt, it was deemed unlucky, both to the community and to himself.

In this example, quoted by John Toland, the community is ritually represented by a lord or noble, who takes on the whole of the burden of the group and whose actions reflect on the future well being of the same group. In order to survive the actual walking on fire, there would have to be complete trust on both sides, of the group in the individual, and of the individual in the group.

The strengthening of the whole is tested in this way with a practical outcome, which uses the special character of the psychic links at the fire festival to demonstrate the balance of forces inherent in the community. This is the link that we have so sadly lost, with our rational scientific community of specialists, who communicate so poorly with each other and with the (supporting) multitude.

At the same time, while the strongest communities could succeed in this show of communal togetherness, it might be more suitable if we concentrated on simpler rituals, which are not so dangerous for the losers! There is a fine tradition of collecting the sacred dew at sunrise, on May morning. The old Druids held that water was especially powerful, and the most powerful was that which appeared so 'magically' on the morning of Beltane. Quite recently on Arthur's Seat in Edinburgh, a traditional Beltane fire hill, young people would come and collect the dew, which traditionally assured health and happiness for the ensuing year.

With this image of clear dew at sunrise on Beltane morning, let the old Druid, William Blake speak:

Youth of delight, come hither
And see the opening morn,
Image of truth new born.
Doubt is fled and clouds of reason,
Dark disputes and artful teazing.
Folly is an endless maze,
Tangled roots perplex her ways,
How many have fallen there!
They stumble all night over bones of the dead,
And feel they know not what but care,
And wish to lead others when they should be led.
'The Voice of The Ancient Bard', *Songs of Experience* William Blake

IV
Lugnassadh Eured Lug
The Marriage of the Sun to the Earth

The eye of the Great God
The eye of the God of Glory
The eye of the King of Hosts
The eye of the King of the living
    Pouring upon us at each time and season
    Pouring upon us gently and generously

Glory to thee, Thou glorious Sun
Glory to thee, thou Sun, Face of The God of Life.

Carmina Gaedelica

The passage of the Sun marks four cycles within the slow turning of the Celtic year. The Old Year started in late October with Samhuinn, passed through Imbolc in February, Beldan or Beltasme in May and produces the ripe fruits on the vision seen at Midsummer, at the harvest festival of Lugnassad. This literally means the wedding of Lugh, the Irish sun god principle, to the Mother earth, personified in Tailltenn: Lugh's foster mother. The power of the male sun gives fertilizing life through a practical chlorophyll cycle and through a symbolic phallus, Lugh's magic spear. This same sun guises under many names in the regions – Lugh, Llyr, Nudd, Noada, Nodens, Llew Llaw Gyffes, Lug Llamfadha (the Long-handed), Ludd, Lot and the triple Cymric transformation of Dylan, Llew and Gwyn.

As the outcome of the union of sun and earth, the future harvest is assured, and Lugnassadh becomes both a celebration of the previous spring's fertility and the future strength of the land, which must survive the coming rigours of the descending year through Samhuinn, to its lowest point at Alban Arthuan – midwinter, when the sun is magically reborn and the day and sun gain in strength again.

The Irish traditions, the festival was first said to be held at Tailltenn, where Lugh's foster mother was buried. Her death is recalled each year with races and circular dances to strengthen the sun by mimicry and to ensure the continuing force of life for another year.

As the sun, through its ritual consumation with the earth produces an actual harvest of produce, so it became natural for handfasting marriages to be celebrated. At Tailltean the young men ranged themselves on one side of the Rath (fortress) and the women on the other. Parents would then arrange brief unions between chosen couples. In order to ensure longevity of marriage, the old Celts had a short form of introductory marriage for a year and a day, during which time the partners could discover if they were compatible or not. If, at the end of the year, the union was decided to be broken, the couple would walk into the Rath Dhu, stand back to back facing north and south, and walk out as free individuals. This same idea was carried on at the church of Stennis, which had a door at each end. The couple wanting to sever their bonds turned back to back in front of the pulpit and walked out through opposite doors. The legend lingers in Kintyre that, once a year, disgruntled husbands and wives met in Kilkevan church, about four miles from Campbelltown, and in the darkness seized hold of a new partner, with whom they lived for another year and a day.

If, during the period of the handfasting marriage, a child was born and the union was not continued, then it would be brought up by the father with equal legal rights as his later legitimate offspring. There was no shame in the handfasting unions, and the arrangement contined well into the sixteenth century, when the reformed church opposed the arrangement and refused to accept the status of the children,

At the same time as this symbolic handfasting, which patterns the union of male sun and female earth, the actual fires become a symbolic manifestation of the hidden god's power. The old Druids certainly practised fire walking. In Eire, a test to establish an accused person's guilt, was by passing three times barefoot through fire – the Gabha-Vheil tradition.

This same power to illuminare life's pattern is manifest in the interlacing of the legends surrounding the magical sun wheel of the Druid Mog Ruith, and the Simon Magus stories. The Roth Fail or Roth Ramach was a sun wheel chariot, an enchanted ship, which in one version contained a thousand beds with a man in every bed. The wheel was said to be wrecked on the pillar stone of Cnomhchoil (near Tipperary), whose chief would slay every warrior it contained. There is an illustration of the symbolic sun wheel under St Columb's church on a pillar stone, underneath the open arch of the tower, in St Columb Major, Kernow.

In Christian legends, Simon Magus, a Samaritan sorcerer, travelled to Rome and demonstrated his power before Nero, including the ability to fly on a magic wheel. His exploits, which match the Daedelus legends, were brought to grief when St Paul prayed for his downfall. Simon is then said to have fallen at Nero's feet and received injuries from which he died. Simon's patronym, Magus, became the Latinized word for Druid, and in Eire Simon became known as Simon the Druid, although this is a simple confusion of names. The construction of a practical sun wheel and the ability to understand the natural solar rythms and seasons may have become intertwined in the confusion of historical legend.

On a more immediate family level, the tradition of Lammas, Scottish Lugnassadh, has links with Bannocks, 'The Lammas Bannock'. This Celtic and Druid tradition consisted of baking cakes which were dedicated during Christian times to Mary and known as 'Moilean Moire', the fatling of Mary. The Bannock is toasted before a fire of rowan sticks. (Rowan gives strong protection against enchantment.) It is then broken in pieces, which are given to the family in descending order of age when all raise the chant 'Iolach Mhoire Mhathar' (The Paean of Mary). All walk sunwise, Deasuil, around the fire, with the father first and then wife and children, following in age order. The embers of the sacred fire are later gathered into a container and carried sunwise around the homestead, fields and flocks of cattle, which are gathered together specially for the purpose.

The Paean of Mary

On the feast day of Mary the fragrant,
Mother of the Shepherd of the flocks,
I cut me a handfull of the new corn,
I dried it gently in the sun,
I rubbed it sharply from the husk,
With mine own palms.

I ground it in a quorn on Friday,
I baked it on a fan of sheep skin,
I toasted it to a fire of Rowan,
And I shared it round my people.

I went sunways round my dwelling,
In the name of the Mary Mother,
Who promised to preserve me,
Who did preserve me,
And who will preserve me.

In peace, in flocks,
In righteousness of heart,
In labour, in love,
In wisdom, in mercy,
For the sake of Thy Passion,
Thou Christ of Grace
Who till the day of my death
Wilt never forsake me!
Oh, till the day of my death
Wilt never forsake me!

Iolach Mhoire Mhather

A feill Moire cubhr,
Mathair Buachaille nan treud,
Bhuain mi beun dhe'n toradh ur,
Chruadhaich mi e caon ri grein,
Shuath mi e gu geur dhe'n ruag,
Le mo bhasa fein.

Mheil mi e'air brath Di-aoine,
Dh'fhuin mi e air cra na craime
Bhruich mi e ri aine caorain,
Sophairtich mi e'n dail mo dhaoine.

Chaidh mi deiseil m' ardrach,
An ainmh Mhoire Mhathar,
A gheall mo ghleidheadh
A rinn mo ghleidheadh
A ni mo ghleidheadh,

Ann an sith, an an ni,
Ann am fireantas eridh
Ann an gniomh, ann an gradh,
Ann am brigh, ann am baigh,
Air agath do Phais,
A Chriosd a ghrais

Gu la mo bhais
Gu brath nach treig mis
O gu la mo bhais
Gu brath nach treig mi.

Carmina Gadelica

The passing around the house and fields in a pattern to match the sun's turning, gives the strength of the solar principle to the land, reinforced by the scattering of ashes from the sacred fire. The rowan tree gave protection against enchantment because its bright scarlet berries match the bright sun in their colour and, more surprisingly, hide a small five-fold pentagram pattern at the top of the berry. The pentagram is well established as the hidden symbol of the old Druids and their fellow Pythagoreans, with which many traditions are held in common. The five-folding of the Grail cup and its earlier counterpart, the Celtic cauldron, is carried forwards into Arthurian tradition with the Holy Grail.

Am I not a candidate for fame
To be heard in the song in Caer Pedryvan
Four times revolving.

The First word from the Cauldron – when was it spoken?
By the breath of nine maidens it was gently warmed.
Is it not the Cauldron of the Chief of Annwyn?

What is its fashion?
A rim of pearls is round its edge
It will not cook the food of a coward or one forswarn
A sword flashing bright will be raised to him,
And left in the hand of Lleuminawg.

Preiddu Annwn, Taliesin

Why pass around three times deasuil? Because three is the number of circles of existence in Celtic Druid cosmogeny: the three worlds of existence: Abred, Gwynffrydd and Ceugant. Before considering these states, consider a Norfolk counting poem from 'Norfolk Life' by Rider Haggard and Henry Williamson, published in 1943, which may be the folk continuation of an old Celtic number pattern;

Three wattles a hound's life	9
Three hounds a steed	27
Three steeds a man	81
Three men an eagle	243
Three eagles a salmon	729
Three salmon a yew tree	2,187
Three yew trees a ridge	6,561
Three ridges from the beginning to the end of the world	19,683

Diagram of the Three Worlds of Existence

The Celtic idea of the conception of the world depended on the creation of two opposites: God and Cythrawl. Cythrawl may be thought of as Chaos, Annwyn in Cymric terms. The World was formed out of this chaos and may be thought of as three concentric circles, Abred, Gwynfydd and Ceugant.

Abred is the present life of evil and suffering, where all is change: birth, becoming, marriage, begetting, dying and rebirth; a continual struggle.

Gwynffrydd is the second circle, where the undying soul passes as a rite of passage after having purified itself by successive passages through the realms of everyday existence in Abred.

Ceugant is the ultimate state of pure rejoicing existence to which life continually aspires.

The following translated extract from the sixteenth-century Cymric collection of Bardic thought, 'Bardas', illustrates the conception:

Question: Whence didst thou proceed?
Answer: I came from the great World, having my beginning in Annwn.
Q: Where art thou now? and how camest thou to what thou art?
A: I am in the little World, whither I came having traversed the circle of Abred and now I am a man, at its termination and extreme limits.
Q: What wert thou before thou didst become a man; in the circle of Abred?
A: I was in Annwn, the least possible that was capable of life and the nearest possible to absolute death; and I came in every form and through every form capable of a body and life to the state of man along the circle of Abred, where my condition was severe and grievous during the age of ages, ever since I was parted in Annwn from the dead, by the gift of God, and His great generosity and His unlimited and endless love.
Q: Through how many different forms didst thou come, and what happened unto thee?
A: Through every form capable of life, in water, in earth, in air. And there happened unto me every severity, every hardship, every evil and every suffering and but little was the goodness of Gwynffrydd before I came a man . . .

Gwynffrydd cannot be obtained without seeing and knowing everything, but it is not possible to see or know everything without suffering everything. . . . And there can be no full and perfect love that does not produce these things which are necessary to lead to the knowledge that causes Gwynffrydd.

Every being we are told, shall attain to the circle of Gwynffrydd at last.

William Blake is one of the few visionary poets of recent times who understood this conception, the world within the Sun that is the Eye of Life, the light that illuminates our continuing struggle for purity.

> Glory to thee, Thou glorious Sun
> Glory to thee, Thou Sun, Face of the God of Life.

The Sun by Colin Murray.

NOTES

Part One

1 The Vates (ed.)
2 *Rev. Celt.*, XI. 443.
3 *Ibid.*
4 Gallic War, VI. xiii–xviii.
5 In Harris's Ware (*Antiqq.*, p. 117) is an excellent essay on Druids, setting forth the testimonies of the principal classical authorities regarding them. It professes to treat of druids in connexion with Ireland: but it is nearly all about Gaulish druids, with merely a few sentences about those of Britain and Ireland.
6 Physicians: see Sick Bed, *Atlantis*, I. 391, verses 3 and 4.
7 *Br. Laws*, I. 84, line 29; 85, 90 (and note); 124 and 126; and Gloss, 143; II. 47: III. 13, 3.
8 Todd, *Book of Hymns*, 90.
9 *Rev. Celt.*, XVII. 229: see also *FM*, vol. I., p. 319, top.
10 *Folklore*, V. 311.
11 Moyrath, 231, 233: see also Sir Samuel Ferguson's *Congal*, 227, 233, 234, 235.
12 Joyce, *Irish Names of Places*, I. 172, 173.
13 MS. Mat., 477: O'Donovan, Suppl. to O'Reilly, '*Sraobh.*'
14 For the *aire druad* ses Stokes, *Lives of SS.*, xxviii.: FM, A.D. 555: Todd, St Patk., 119–122: Silva Gad., 85, and 516, 3.
15 MS. *Mat.*, 285: HyF, 99.
16 Stokes, *Irish Glosses*, in *Treatise on Latin Declension*, 63, 271.
17 O'Curry, *Man. & Cust.*, II. 46, and notet.
18 Stokes, *Three Homilies*, 103.
19 *Rev. Celt.* XXI. 440: O'Curry, *Man. & Cust.*, I. 193.
20 O'Grady, *Silva Gad.*, 511, 38.
21 Rhys, Hibbert Lectures, 55.
22 O'Curry, Man. & Cust., I. 224.
23 *Silva Gad.*, 58, 59, 60.
24 Todd, *St Patk.*, 122.
25 *Rev. Celt.*, XI. 43: *Silva Gad.*, 354.
26 *St Patk.*, 455.
27 *Documenta*, 73, *a.*
28 *Trip. Life*, 286, note 6: Hogan, *Docum.*, 41, 167 ('Diberca').
29 *Rev. Celt.*, XIV. 28, 29: Joyce, *Old Celt. Romances*, 402.
30 Stokes, *Cóir Anmann*, 393: see p. 150, *supra.*
31 *Zeitschr. für Celt. Phil.*, II. 52.
32 Rhys, Hibbert Lect., 499.
33 *Trip. Life*, 325, 326: Hogan, *Docum.*, 83.
34 See de Jubainville, VI. 112.
35 O'Curry, *Man. & Cust.*, I. 213–216.
36 See *Rev. Celt.*, VII. 301: and Miss Hull, *Cuch. Saga*, 254.
37 See *Kilk. Arch. Journ.*, I. (1849–51) 353, 375.
38 Hogan, *Docum.*, 34, 35: *Trip. Life*, 43.
39 *Rev. Celt.*, XVI.34.
40 *Ibid.*, 277.

41 *Trip. Life*, 507.

42 *Rev. Celt.*, XII 93. On druidesses see also O'Curry, *Man. & Cust.*, I. 187: and de Jubainville, VI. 92.

43 Schrader, *Reallexikon der idg. Altertumskunde*, ii. p. 643.

44 Munro, *Prehistoric Scotland*, p. 480, London, 1899.

45 Cf. Frazer, *The Golden Bough*, i. pp. 233, 234, London, 1900

46 *Ibid.*, i. p. 240

47 Cf. Munro, *Prehistoric Scotland*, pp. 460, 480.

48 M. Muller, *Sacred Books of the East*, xix. pp. 213, 281.

49 *The Academy*, xxv. p. 112.

50 A. Nutt, *Studies in the Legend of the Holy Grail*, pp. 231–233: London, 1887.

51 *The Golden Bough*, i. p. 347.

52 *Ibid.*, p. 305.

53 *Ibid.*, p. 303.

54 W. Gregor, *Folklore of the North-East of Scotland*, p. 206.

55 *Transactions of the Hon. Society of Cymmrodar*, vi. p. 2.

56 *Lectures*, O'Curry, who gives also another explanation.

57 R. Much, *Deutsche Stammeskunde*, p. 31.

58 Joyce, *Irish Names of Places*, 3rd ed., p. 487.

59 The etymology of the word 'Druid' is still disputed. M. d'Arbois de Jubainville (*Rev. celt.*, xxix, 1908, p. 83) defends Thurneyson's view – that it was derived from *'dru* (fortement), *uid* (savant)' – against M. Julian (*Hist. de la Gaule*, ii, 85, n. 7).

60 *B.G.*, vi, 13, § 11, – Disciplina in Britannia reperta atque inde in Galliam translata existimatur.

61 Ed. Didot, p. 1, 11. 9–12.

62 Or possibly in the treatise called τὸ Μαγικὺν, once erroneously ascribed to Aristotle. Diogenes cites both.

63 *Rev. des Deuz Mondes*, 3ᵉ pér., xxiv, 1877, p. 466.

64 Ibid., pp. 473–5.

65 *Ibid.*, x, 21, § 1.

66 Cf. C. Jullian, *Hist. de la Gaule*, ii, 80.

67 Livy, xxiii, 24, § 12.

68 *Comptes rendus de l'Acad. des inscr.*, 4ᵉ sér., xx, 1892, pp. 6–7. See also Rice Holmes, *Anc. Britain*, p. 291, n. 2.

69 M. Reinach (*Orpheus*, 1909, p. 177) is now inclined to believe that Druidism originated in the Neolithic Age in the British Isles; that it flourished principally in Ireland; and that it early spread to the Continent. Julius Pokorny (*Celtic Review*, v, 1908–9, p. 19) insists that 'the fact that the oak plays no part in the life of the Irish Druid and a very small one in the popular superstition can be explained only if we assume that the Druids were originally the priests of a people who did not know the oak worship', that is (*ibid.*, p. 6) of 'the pre-Celtic aborigines of the British islands'. I cannot follow this argument. If Pokorny has stated the facts correctly, they only prove that oak-worship was unknown to the Irish aborigines, and that the Celtic invaders of Ireland, who undoubtedly knew it, were unable or unwilling to impose it upon them.

70 *Hist. de la Gaule*, ii, 88–9.

71 *B. G.*, vi, 2, § 1.

72 Tacitus, *Germania*, 10.

73 Ibid., xiv, 30.

74 *Hist. de la Gaule*, ii. 87, n. 3.

75 *Rev. celt.*, xxix, 1908, p. 81.

76 See *Neue Jahrb. f. Philologie*, etc., cxlv, 1892, p. 770.

77 *Géogr. de la Gaule rom.*, ii, 515.

78 *Celtic Britain*, 3rd ed., 1904, p. 69.

79 The political condition of the people of Brythonic Britain,' says Sir John Rhys (*Celtic Britain*, 3rd ed., 1904, pp. 57, 61), 'towards the end of the Early Iron Age and the close of their independence, is best studied in connection with that of Gaul as described by Caesar. . . . The state of things, politically speaking, which existed in Gaul, existed most likely among the Belgic tribes in Britain.' That is to say, Sir John accepts the political part of Caesar's description as applying to the Belgic and the other Brythonic tribes of both Gaul and Britain. Yet he insists that that part of the same description which deals with Druidism, and which is indissolubly connected with the political part, has nothing to do either with the Belgac or the other Brythons.

80   Cf. Roget de Belloguet, *Ethnogénie gauloise*, 1858–68, iii, 310, and *Dict. arch. de la Gaule*, i, 430.

81   Fustel de Coulanges (*Hist. des inst. pol. de l'anc. France,–la Gaule rom.* p. 29, n.2) remarks that Caesar, who knew Diviciacus intimately, does not say that he was a Druid. But Cicero, who conversed with him on matters of religion, says that he was; and Caesar's silence proves nothing. When one reads the passage in Cicero, his testimony appears conclusive: – eaque divinationum ratio ne in barbaris quiden gentibus neglecta est, siquidem et in Gallia Druidae sunt, e quibus ipse Divitiacum Haeduum . . . cognovi, qui et naturae rationem, quam φυσιολογίαν Graeci appellant, notam esse sibi profitebatur et partim auguriis, partim coniectura, quae essent futura dicebat, etc. *De Divin.*, i, 41, § 90. M. Salomon Reinach (*Orpheus*, 1909, p. 179) thinks that we must distinguish between nobles who had been merely educated by Druids, 'comme était sans doute ce Divitiac', and 'the sacredotal body properly so called'; but the fact of Diviciacus's having received a Druidical education does not invalidate Cicero's statement, – that he was himself a Druid.

82   *Rev. des Deux Mondes*, 3ᵉ pér., xxii, 1877, p. 849.

83   *Géogr. de la Gaule rom.*, ii. 532.

84   *B.G.*, v. 56, § 2.

85   Livy, xxii, 57, §§ 1–6.

86   *Apologeticus*, 9, *Adversus Gnosticos*, 7, quoted by M.M.P. Monceaux in *Rev. hist.*, xxxv, 1887, p. 255.

87   *Claudius*, 25, – 'Druidarum religionem dirae immanitatis.' A. Bertrand. remarking (*La religion des Gaulois*, p. 252) that there is no trace of human sacrifice in the history of Ireland – 'le pays druidique par excellence' – argues (pp. 68–73, 386) that the Druids did not originate, but merely tolerated and sanctioned this rite, which he believes to have been a survival of prehistoric times.

88   *Celtic Heathendom*, 1888, p. 231.

89   *Hist. des Romains*, iii, 1889, pp. 119, 131.

90   *B.G.*, vii, 33, § 3.

91   *Hist. of Rome*, v, 1894, p. 20 (*Röm Gesch.*, iii, 1889, p. 237).

92   Michelot (*Hist. de France*, i, 63, ed. 1835) fancies that B.G., vii, 1–2 show that Druids played an important part in initiating the great rebellion; but, as Fustel remarks (*Hist. des inst. pol. de l'anc. France, – la Gaule rom.*, p. 31, n. 2), this whimsical notion is unsupported by any evidence.

93   *Eng. Hist. rev.*, xviii, 1903, p. 336.

94   *Vercingétorix*, pp. 107–11.

95   Tacitus, *Hist.*, iv, 54.

96   Commentators generally forget that Cotuatus, one of the two 'desperadoes' who sacked Cenabum, was a priest (gutuater). See pp. 831–2.

97   *Caesar, a Sketch*, ed. 1886, p. 24.

98   F. de Coulanges, indeed, says (*Hist. des inst. pol. de l'anc. France, – la Gaule rom.*, p. 27, n. 2) that there is no evidence that the priests by whom Convictolitavis was elected were Druids: but I take leave to say that there is, and that of the most convincing kind. Caesar distinctly says (*B.G.*, vi, 13, §§ 1–3) that in the whole of Celtican Gaul there were only two classes of men who were held in any esteem, the 'knights' (*equites*) and the Druids. He mentions no other priests, except the Druids; and he implies (*ib.*, 13, §§ 4–7, 10) that there were no other. The Aedui were in Celtican Gaul. The priests who elected Convictolitavis were certainly important personages. Is it to be supposed that the Druids, to whom Caesar ascribes such importance, would have permitted any other priests, if there were any, to oust them? The only other Gallic word that denoted a priest was *gutuatros*, which occurs (see p. 832, *infra*) in Gallo-Roman inscriptions, and the Latin form of which was *gutuater*. Gutuatri, as M. Salomon Reinach says (*Orpheus*, 1909, p. 179), regulated local cults. I doubt whether it is possible to prove that in pre-Roman times they were not Druids; but if they were a distinct, they were also an inferior order.

99   M. d'Arbois de Jubainville (*Rev. arch.*, nouv. sér., xxxviii, 1879, p. 378) asserts that Caesar 'avait triomphe des chevaliers, grâce à l'appui du sacerdoce qu'il était parvenu à détacher de la cause nationale'. There is simply no evidence for this sweeping assertion except the fact that Diviciacus was on Caesar's side; and if the Druids were so powerful that their alleged support enabled Caesar to triumph over the 'knights', why were they powerless to prevent or even to put the least drag on the insurrection in 52 B.C.?

100   The procedure of the Druids in the election of Convictolitavis is somewhat obscure. Caesar says that he 'authorized Convictolitavis, who had been appointed by the priests, in accordance with tribal custom in a period of inter-regnum (or "when the magistrates failed to attend" [?]), to continue to hold offico' (*Convictolitavem, qui per sacerdotes more civitatis intermissis magistratibus esset creatus, potestatem obtinere iussit* [*B.G.*, vii, 33,§ 4]). Schneider (*Caesar*, ii, 43) interprets *intermissis magistratibus* in the sense that there was regularly a period of interregnum after the expiration of the Vergobret's term of office, in which the priests, acting as *interreges*, appointed his successor; but the words leave on my mind the impression that the right of appointment did not ordinarily belong to the priests, and, moreover, *per sacerdotes* is different from *a sacerdotibus*. M. Jullian (*Hist. de la Gaule*, ii, 48, 103) appears to hold that the right of appointment belonged to the magistrates, or headmen, of the various clans, and that in their default it was exercised by the priests. But why should the magistrates have waived their right? M. Jullian's interpretation of *intermissis* seems to me to conflict with Caesar's use of the word (see Meusel's *Lex. Caes.*, ii, 221–2). *Intermissis magistratibus* must, I think, mean 'when the magistracy was (or remained) vacant'; but who the regular electors were is doubtful.

101   M. Jullian in his *Hist. de la Gaule*, iii, 373–6, suggests that the prominent part which the Carnutes played against Caesar not only in the great rebellion but also in the two years that preceded it may have been due to the instigation of the Druids, whose annual council was held in their territory (*B.G.*, vi, 13, § 10). Perhaps; but how little we know!

102   *Hist. des inst. pol. de l'anc. France – la Gaule rom.*, pp. 19–20.

103   *B.G.*, vi, 13, § 5. Cf. H. d'A. de Jubainville in *Rev. celt.*, viii, 1887, p. 519, and *Les premiers habitants de l'Europe*, ii, 1894, p. 375, and C. Jullian, *Hist de la Gaule*, ii, 100–1. M. Jullian remarks (p. 101, n. 3) that 'la formation des cités [*civitates*] . . . a dû contribuer à affaiblir l'autorité judiciaire du druides'. But were not many of the 'cités' formed by the union, more or less loose, of pagi before the late date to which M. Jullian assigns the rise of Druidism?

104   *Rev. internat. de l'enseignement*, Août 1895, p. 151.

105   *B.G.*, vi, 13, §§ 3, 5.

106   *Ib.*, i, 16, § 5.

107   *Ib.*, vi, 19, § 3.

108   *Ib.*, i, 4: v, 56, § 3; vii, 4, § 1.

109   *Ib.*, vi, 13, § 10.

110   *Ib.*, §§ 6–7.

111   *Géogr. de la Gaule rom.*, ii, 529. Cf. C. Jullian, *Hist. de la Gaule*, ii, 107.

112   *Hist. des inst. pol. de l'anc. France, – la Gaule rom.*, p. 31, n. 1.

113   See pp. 529–41.

Part Two

1   To All-healing Apollo. [To God Belin].

2   To God Abellio.

3   She directs him to seeke a golden branch in the darke woods, consecrate to Proserpine.

4   Sweat of the Oake.

5   Bred Lime to catch her.

6   This peninsula is Inis-Eogain, vulgarly Enis-owen, in whose Isthmus stands the city of Londonderry, itself a peninsula, and, if the tradition be true, originally a famous Grove and School of the Druids. Hence comes the very name Doire, corruptly pronounced Derry, which in Irish signifies a Grove, particularly of Oaks. The great Columba changed it into a College for Monks (who in his time were retir'd Laymen, that lived by the labour of their hands) as most commonly the sacred places of the Heathens, if pleasant or commodious, were converted to the like use by the Christians after their own manner. This Derry is the *Roboretum* or *Campus roborum*, mentioned by Bede in his *Ecclesiastical History*, but not Ardmacha, now Armagh, in the same province of Ulster, as many have erroneously conceived; nor yet Durramh, now Durrough, in that of Leinster, as some have no less groundlessly fancied, among whom Archbishop Usher. Dearmach is compounded of Dair an oak and the ancient word Mach (now Machaire) a field. They who did not know so much, have imagined it from the mere sound to be Armagh, which, far from Campus roborum, signifies the height or mount of Macha (surnamed Mongruadh or redhair'd) a Queen of Ireland, and the only woman that ever sway'd the sovereign sceptre of that kingdom. But Armagh never was a monastery founded by Columba, who in Bede's time was called Coluim-cille, as he's by the Irish to this day: whereas it was from the monasteries of Derry and I-colmkill (which last, though the second erected, became the first in dignity) that all the other monasteries, dedicated to Columba, whether in Scotland or Ireland, were so many colonies. This is attested by the just mentioned Bede, no less than by all the Irish Annalists since their several foundations.

7   *A Dissertation concerning the Celtic Language and Colonies.*

8   Pronounced as Dree in English.

9   Dry magus, Drycraeft incantatio, Aelfric. in Glossar.

10   If the learned reader, who knows any of the passages, or the unlearned reader who wants authorities for proving the following assertions, should wonder I do not always cite them; let it be known to both, that as in this Specimen I commonly touch but the heads of things (and not of all things neither) so I would not crowd the margin with long passages, nor yet curtail what in my History shall be produced at large: and therefore all the following citations (the original manner of writing Celtic words excepted) are either samples of the quotations I shall give, or proofs of what I would not for a moment have suspected to be precariously advanced, or, finally, for the better understanding of certain matters which come in by way of digression or illustration. Otherwise they wou'd not be necessary in a mere Specimen, though in a finished work indispensable.

11   Omnes sancti terrae istius confessores sunt, & nullus martyr quod in alio regno Christiano difficile erit invenire. Mirum itaque quod gens crudelissima & sanguinis sitibunda, fides ab antiquo fundata & semper tepidissima, pro Christi ecclesia corona martyrii nulla. Non igitur inventus est in partibus istis, qui ecclesiae surgentis fundamenta sanguinis fusione cementaret: non fuit, qui faceret hoc bonum: non fuitusque ad unum. Topograph. Hibern. Distinct. 3 cap. 29.

12   Sunt enim pastores, qui non pascere quaerunt, sedpasci: sunt praelati, qui non prodesse cupiunt, sed proesse sunt episcopi, qui non omen, sed nomen: non onus, sed hostis rem amplectuntur. Id. Ibid.

13   The heads of the two last Sections, with these here mentioned (though conceived in few words) will yet each make a separate chapter in the History; this present Specimen being chiefly intended for modern instances, as by the sequel will appear.

14   Sir Robert Howard.

15   The Irish word for Druid is Drui, corruptly Droi, and more corruptly Draoi: yet all of the same sound, which in Etymologies is a great matter: and in the nominative plural it is Druidhe, whence comes no doubt the Greek and Latin Druides; as Druis in the singular was formed by only adding 's' to Drui, according to those nation's way of terminating. But as these words in Irish as well as the British Drudion, are common to both sexes; so the Romans according to their inflection, distinguished Druida for a She-Druid (which sort are mentioned by authors) whereof the nominative plural being Druidae, it ought by us to be used in that sense only: and so I conclude, that in our modern Latin compositions Druides and Druidae should not be confounded; as they have frequently been by the Transcribers of old writings, who mislead others. We are not to be moved therefore by reading Druidae in any Latin author in the masculine gender, or in the Greek writers who certainly used it so. All equivocation at least will be thus taken away.

16   *de Oratore*, lib. 1.

17   *Ibid.*

18   Drui.

19   Druidheacht.

20   Slatnan Druidheacht.

21   Eochaid Eudghathach.

22   These Groves for pleasure and retirement as well as for awe and reverence, were different from the lurking places in forests and caves into which they were forc'd when interdicted in Gaule and Britain.

23 Such fancies came from the hiding of the persecuted Druids, from the reign of Tiberius, who made the first law against them (having been discountenanced by Augustus) but strictly put in execution by Claudius, and the following Emperors, till their utter extirpation by the general conversion of the people to Christianity.

24 Aibhne or Oibhne.

25 Gealchossach.

26 Cnuc na Gealchossaigh.

27 All these heads will be so many intire Chapters.

28 Sacerdos, candida veste cultis, arborem scandit: falce aurea demetit. *Hist. Nat. Lib.* 16, cap. 44.

29 Let it be noted once for all, that as in other tongues, so in Irish and Welsh particularly, t and d are commonly put for each other, by reason of their affinity; and that dh and gh being pronounc'd alike in Irish, and therefore often confounded, yet an exact writer will always have regard to the origin as well as to the analogy of any word: and so he'll write Druidhe (for example) and not Druighe, much less Draoi broadly and aspiratly; nor will he use any other mispellings, tho' ever so common in books. This is well observ'd by an old author, who writing of Conla a heathen freethinking Judge of Connacht, thus characterizes him: Se do rinne an choinbhliocht ris na Druidhibh: 'twas he that disputed against the Druids. These Criticisms, some wou'd say, are trifles; but Hae nugae in seria ducunt.

30 Whether it be Luernius or as Strabo writes it Luerius. the name is frequent either way in the antientest Irish-Writersm, as Loarn, and Luire or Luighaire.

31 Aphorisar tos d'antou prothesmian pote tēs thoinēs, aphysterēsanta tina tōi Barbarōu poiētēn aphikesthai; kai synantēsanta met' ōdes hymncia antou tes hyperochēn, heanton d'hypothrēnrin hoti hysterēke: tonde terphthenta thylakion aitesai chrysion, kai ripsai anto paratreohonti; aneloinenon de ekeion palip hymnein, legonta, dio kaī ta ichnē tēs gēs (eph' hēs harmatēlatei) chrysen-tai energesias anthropois pherei. *Edit. Lugd. Lib.* 4. Pag. 15?.

32 Ollamh' is a Professor or Doctor in any faculty.

33 Druim-ceat alias Druimcheat.

34 Aodhmhac Ainmhire.

35 Aodhanmhac Gaurain.

36 Coluim-cille.

37 Ard-Ollamh.

38 Draoithe. Exod. 7,11. Anois Draoithe na Hegipte dorinnedrusanfosa a modhgceadnal nandroigheachtuibh.

39 Mat. 2,1. Feuch Tangadar Draoithe o naird shoir go Hiarusalem.

40 The word is Faidh (or Vait by the usual conversion of the letters F into V and D into T) whence the Latins made Vates; and their critics acknowledge, that they took many words from the Gauls. The Euchages and Eubages, in some copies of Ammianus Marcellinus, are false readings, as in time will appear. So are Drusi, Drusides and Drusiades for Druides; as likewise Vardi, from the British and Irish oblique cases of Bard.

41 Siquidem & in Gallia Druides sunt, e quibus ipse Divitiacum Aeduum, hospitem tuum laudatoremque, cognovi (inquit Quintus) qui & naturae rationem, quam physiologicam Graeci appellant, notam esse sibi profitebatur; & partim Auguriis, partim conjectura, quae essent futura dicebat. *De Divinat, Lib. 1*, cap. 41.

42 Mantis aristos, hostis eikazei kalos.

43 Laoghaire.

44 In the preface to his *Archaeologia Britannica*, page 1.

45 Ton Heraclea hoi Keltoi Ogmion onomazousi phonē tē ephichōriē, et que sequientur in Hercule Gallico Graece etenim longiora sunt, quam ut hic commode inseri possint.

46 *In Geographia Sacra, sive Canaan*, part 2, cap. 42.

47 Phonē te epichorio. *Ubi supra.*

48 Josuam quoque spectasse videtur illud nomen, quo Galli antiquitus Herculem nuncupabant. Under vero Ogmios? Annon ab Og victu? *Delph. Phoenicizant.* cap. 3.

49 Literarum Secretar viri pariter ac foeminae ingnorant. *De moribus Germanorum*, cap. 19.

50 En de tois chronois tēs Basileias tou Phoinicos eū Heraclēs ho Philosophos Tyrios hostis epheure ten congehylēn, &. Palaephati fragmentum in Cronico Alexandrino. Heraclēs ilkmēnēs hyios, Touton Philosophou hystorousi, &. Suidus in Voce Heraclēs. Et diu ante Suidam audiebat apud Heraclitum, in Allegoriis Homericis, Ahēr emphron, kai sophias ouranious mystēs, hōsperei kata Batheias achlyos epithēdykyian ephotize ten philosopian, Kathaper homologousi kai Stōikōn hoi dokimotatoi.

51 As in the Dublin College Manuscript, to be presently cited.

52 'Tis, among other pieces, in the *Book of Ballimore*; being the 255th volume in the Dublin Catalogue, in parchment, folio, D. 18.

53 Anonymi cujusdam Tractatus de variis apud Hibernos veteres occultis seribendi formulis, Hibernice Ogum dictis.

54 Praeter characteres vulgares utebantur etium veteres Hiberni variis occultis scribendi formulis seu artificiis, Ogum dictis, quiibius secreta sua scribebant: his refertum habeo libellum membranaceum antiquum. Cap. 2.

55 Dualtach mhac Firbis.

56 Rudhruigh O Flaith-bheartuigh.

57 Ogygia, part. 3, cap. 30.

58 Ogum-branches.

59 Fenius Farsaidh Alphabeta prima Hebraeorum Graecorum, Latinorum, et Bethluisnion an Oghuim, composuit. Ex Forcherni libro octingentis retro aunis Latine reddito.

60 William O Domhnuill.

61 Dealbhaaoith.

62 Grian is the Sun, and Grianann Sun like, or belonging to the Sun.

63 These are British, Welsh, Cornish, Irish, Manks, and Earse.

64 Phournoutou theoria peri tēs tōn theōn physeōs, vulgo: sed ut Ravii codex & Vaticanus tegunt (notante doctissima Galev) verus titulus est Kornouteu epidromē tōn kata tēn Hellēnikēu theōrian paradidomenōn.

65 To de dysdiakrita gegoneneai ta tou theou idia, apo tōn peri tou Hērōos historoumenōn. Tacha d'an hē leontē kai to ropalon ek tēs palaias theologias epi touton metenēnegmena eiē: stratēgon gar auton genomenon agathon, kai polla merē tēs gēs meta dynameōs epelthonta ouch' hoion te gemnon edoxan perielēlythenai xylō monō hōplismenon: all tois (Alii pisynois) episēmois tou theou, meta tōn apathanatismon, hypo ton euergetoumenon kekosmēsthai; symbalon gar hegateron eiē rōmēs kai gennaioitētos, &c.

66 Pars Suevorum & Isidi sacrificat. Unde causa et briga peregrino sacro parum comperi; nisi quod signum ipsum, in modium Liburnue figuratum, docet advectam Religionem. *Tacit. de mor. German*, cap. 9.

67 Plutarch. *Symposiac*. lib. 4. quem prolixius disserentum otiosus consulas, lector.

68 Quia sacerdotes eorum tibia tympanisque concinebant, hedera vinciebantur, vitisqus aurea templo reperta, Liberum patrem coli, domitorem Ocientis, quidum arbitrati sunt, nequaquam congruentibus institutis: quippe Liber festos laetosque ritus posuit, Judaeorum mos absurdus sordidusque. *Lib*. 5. cap. 5.

69 Hēraclēs de estin lio en tois, holois logos, kath hon hē physis ischyra, kai kratain estin, anikētos kai aperigennētos onsa: metadotikos ischyos, kai tes para meros alkēs hyparchon.

70 Para tois Physikois ho Heracles synesis kai alkā lambanetui.

71 Ton en pasi, kai dia pantōn, logon; non Hēlion, ut corrupte legi cum Galeo suspicor in Macrobio. Saturnal lib. 1, cap. 20.

72 As the Uraiceacht na neigios, i. e., the Accidence of the Artists, or the Poets, which being the work of Forchern before-nam'd, was interpolated, and fitted to his own time, by Ceann Faoladh the son of Oilioll the Year of Christ 628.

73 Oraium.

74 Taibhle Fileadh.

75 Feadha Craobh Ogham.

76 Birch, Quicken, and Ash.

77 At first it was very analogically pronounc'd Ab-ke-dair, since the letter C then in Latin, as still in Irish and British, had the force of K no less before E and I, than before A, O, U; having never been pronounc'd like S by the antient Romans, who said Kikero, kenseo, koecus, but not Sisero, senseo, soecus, when the words Cicero, censeo, coecus, or such like occurr'd: so that Abkedair did naturally liquidate into Aibghittir, in the manner that all Grammarians know.

78 Scripsit Abgetoria [scilicet Patricius] 355, et eo amplius numero. *Nenn. Hist. Britain*. cap. 59.

79 Rētrai.

80 Breatha nimhe.

81 Conchobhar Nessan, i.e. Mac Neassa.
82 Eochaidh Ollamhfodla.
83 Mur-Ollamhan.
84 Tuathal Teachtmhar.
85 Leabhar Teamhra.
86 Ulfhada.
87 'Tis, among other most valuable pieces, in the Collection call'd O Duvegan's, folio 190. a, now or late in the possession of the right honourable the Earl of Clanrickard. There are copies of it elsewhere, but that's the oldest known.
88 Teagarg Riogh.
89 Cairbre Lifiochair.
90 Cathbaid.
91 Cuchulaind.
92 Tadhg.
93 Finn mhac Cubhaill.
94 Dubhchomar.
95 Fearchios.
96 Ailfinn, from a vast Obelisc that stood by a well in that place; and that fell down in the year 1675. The word signifies the white Stone, and was corrupted into Oilfinn. Some wou'd derive the name from the clearness of the fountain, but 'tis by torture: others from one Oilfinn, a Danish commander.
97 Lambhdearg.
98 Taobhsaoil-treach.
99 Niall Naoighi-allach.
100 Laighichin mhac Barrecheadha.
101 Ogyg.
102 O Flaherty.
103 *Dissertation about the family of the Stuarts*, Pref. page 29.
104 Acts 19, 19.
105 Tou de pollas kai poikilas peri theōn gegonenai para tois palaiois Hellēsi mythopoias, hōs allai men epi Magois gegonasin, allai de par' aigyptiois kai Keltois, kai Libysi, kai Phyxi, kai tois allois ethnesi. *Cap.* 17. Thus the Manuscript very accurately: but the printed copy has tois allois Hellēsi superfluously in the end, and wants Phryx. before, which is very essential.
106 Hi (Druide) certo anni tempore, in Finibus Carnutum, quae regio totius Gallia media habetur, consident, in loco consecrato. Huc omnes undique, qui controversias habent, conveniunt, eorumque decretis judiciisque parent. (*Bell. Gall.* VI. 13)
107 Mela iii, 2.
108 See Borlase p. 108, for the authorities.
109 Diog. Laert. L. C. Seg. 6.
110 Caesar, *De Bel. Gal.* L. VI. Mela L. iii. 2.
111 See Borlase p. 110, 121–2.
112 Caradoc of Nantgarvan, or Llangarvan, above mentioned, as the copyist of one of Jones's originals, lived about the middle of the twelfth century. – Jevan Brechva wrote a Compendium of the Welsh Annals down to 1150.
113 The passages inclosed between books appear to be comments upon the original Triads, added by some ancient copyists.
114 The Coritani lay upon Môr Tawch, it was therefore upon the East of Britain –
115 Letavia or Lexovia, the Water-side. This name is confined, at this day, to the description of Brittany; but it covered, anciently, the entire coast of Gaul.
116 The figures annext, refer to their order in the London edition.
117 The dwellers about the Loire or Liger. – Gwas-Gwyn or Gwas-Gwynt the country of the Veneti, about the mouth of the Loire, and not Vasconia. – It was the country to which the Britons sent their fleet, in order to assist the Celtae of Gaul, their relations, against the arms of Caesar. *Triad* 14.
118 Strabo L. VII speaks of the removal, and of the dispersion of the Cimbri, in consequence of an inundation. This tradition was preserved by the Cimbri of the Cerhsonese; but the event must have happened when their ancestors dwelt in a low country.

119 In p. 78 it is added – Ac or Asza pan hanoeddynt. And they originally come from Asia. Jones declared 200 years ago, that he copied the various readings from which this passage is taken, just as he found them, in a copy that was more than 600 years old in his time. See W. Arch. v. 2. p. 80.

120 i.e. Adopted the Saxon language and manners.

121 This conflict of the Elements probably happened, when the Japetidae occupied the inflammable soul of *Asia Propria*. It is perhaps the event so awfully described by Hesiod, *Theog.* 678, etc. and which contributed not only to the defeat, but the removal of the Titans.

122 Docebat etiam ut omni tempore, totius Galliae principatum Aediu tenuissent, Caesar. *B. G. I*. 43.

Summa auctoritas antiquitus erat in Aencuis. *Ib*. VI. 12.

Eo statu res erat, ut longe principes Aenhui haberentur. *Ib*.

Celtarum clarissimi Hedui. *Mel*. III.2.

Divitiacus, prince of the Aedui, had a sovereign principality in Britain, as well as in Gaul. See Borlase, p. 83, and his authorities.

The British Aedui, or Hedui, were in Somersertshire Ric. Corinav. Stukeley.

The Welsh dominate this district, after the cradle of the Celtic nation, Gwlad yr Hâv.

123 Now Bishop of Dromore. 'His Lordship has drawn the line of distinction, between the Goth and the Celt, with a hand so judicious, and guided by so comprehensive a knowledge of the subject, that he has left no ground for debate; but I cannot help adding, in support of his doctrine, that similar points of demarkation have, in a general manner, been perceived and acknowledged by the Welsh.'

124 Herodot. L. V. 9.

125 Clem. Alexand. Strom. L. i. Ex. Alex. Polyhist.

126 Diog. Laert. Ex. Aristotele. *Borlase*, p. 73.

127 The triads from which this epitome is compiled, may be seen in the original, and in its version. Ed. *William's Poems*, V. ii. P. 227.

Of the copy from which they are taken, that ingenious poet and writer gives the following account.

'The triads that are here selected, are from a manuscript collection, by Llywelyn Sion, a bard, of Glamorgan, about A.D. 1560. Of this manuscript, I have a transcript. The original is in the possession of Mr Richard Bradford, of Bettws, near Bridgend, in Glamorgan. This collection was made from various manuscripts of considerable and some of great antiquity. These, and their authors, are mentioned, and most, or all of them, are still extant.'

128 Pliny. L. XVI C. 44. The Welsh call this month Gorpheahav, the conclusion of the summer, or year.

129 Several of the ancients, who wrote after the Carthagenians had extended their voyages, describe the seat of Atlas and the Hesperides, as attached to Africa. It is very usual to distinguish newly discovered places, by familiar names. Thus we have New England, in America; New Holland, and New South Wales, amongst the Antipodes.

Apollodorus, the accurate recorder of tradition, corrects the error.

Atlas, and the gardens of the Hesperides, were not, as some represeus them to have been, in Lybia; but amongst the Hyperborcans.

130 Strabo, lib. iv. says, that it was a general opinion that the greater number of Druids there were in a country, the greater would be their harvests and abundance of all things.

131 Grotius, *de Jure Belli et Pacis*, II. cap. xxxiii. says, that our Christian bishops derived their authority in their ecclesiastical courts from the imitated power of the Druids.

132 The spirit of Cambyses, by metempsychosis, passed to John Knox: thus we have nothing but the Ruins of Melrose.

133 Mela, the geographer says, the Thracians held one of the doctrines of the Druids as a common, national persuasion, and it is not improbable that they may have learnt it from them; that souls, after being purified by their transmigration, attained a condition of endless felicity.

134 Instead of the natural one (which surely must have been very rare), artificial rings of stone, glass, and sometimes baked clay, were substituted in its room, as of equal validity.

135 'The lands are occupied collectively by each tribe according to the number of its husbandmen, and they divide them again among themselves according to their dignity. The extent of their land renders the partition easy. They change the land every year, and they have more than they can use.' Tacit. *Germ*. c. 26.

136 Celtillus ... Arvernus ... principatum totius Galliae obtinuerat. Caesar. 7.4.

137 Summa imperii permissa Cassivelauno. Caesar. 5.11.

138 Caesar. 2.4.

139 Caesar. 4.20.

140 Caesar. 7.32.

141 Geogr. 4. p. 248.

142 Hist. 43. c. 4.

143 Caesar, 5.48.

144 The authenticity of the coelbren y beirdd is now openly renounced, not a particle of evidence being brought to support it. See Poems of Glyn Cothi, p. 260, note. Were it an authentic document, it would make no difference; it would rank with Druidistic, not with Druidic, remains.

145 Some are pointed out by Lhuyd and others, as morv, μνϱμηξ, golvan, γολμις, heddychu, ησυχεω, haul, ἅλιος, digon, ἱκανος, mer, μεϱος, achlud, ἀχλυς, pwyll, pwyllaw, βουλη, βουλενω, garan, γεϱανος, dagr, dagru, δακϱυ, δακϱυω, cylch, κυκλος, holl, ὅλος, medd, meddw, meddwi, μεθυ, μεθυω, etc. However, a portion of Owen's Greel and Welsh vocabulary is frivolous and fantastic.

146 See Justin. 20. c. 4. *Appian. Mithrid.* c. 28.

147 *Pseud-Origenes Philos.* p. 46.

148 Compare Diodorus *L.* 5. p. 309, line 10. Bipont.

149 This prominent feature of Druidism suffices to overturn the story of the Coelbren, as applied to those times.

150 We must regard those ideas, as being adopted from the ancient popular minstrelsy; whatever person may have vamped up any given Ossianic poem. The subject is full of obscurity. The Gaelic poems would tend to discredit the importation of Druidism into Ireland. But perhaps it would be nearest the truth to say that the Belgians introduced it, but could not bring over the Gael to its views.

151 Poems, etc. vol. 2. I should wish to gratify the reader with a specimen of those verses, but do not understand the British metres enough to distinguish which they are.

152 The death of this author was announced in the public journals, with an encomium on him by a writer using the title of Bardd Alaw, and whose real name is doubtless known in his own country. 'He was (says Alaw) ever ready to impart information from his rich stores of literary lore.' What was in him a merit is to us an advantage, for it entitles us to look for explanations of the various and curious things which the deceased advanced, but omitted to substantiate in his lifetime. The inscription mentioned in the last edition of the *Dict. art. Gwynedd* should certainly be produced, if it has not been so already.

153 Tacit. *Agr.* c. 11. This island was named Alouion or Alwion; and Tzetzes quoting from one Dionysius (not Periegetes) makes Aloubion of it. Chil. 8. 719. Not only was it so named for reasons unconnected with the Latin colour albus of its Kentish cliffs, or with the mountains which formed no conspicuous feature of its surface, 'being for the most part champaign and woody, but with many small hills,' (Strabo. iv. 219); but that appellation was not, I believe, anciently confined to this portion of Celtica. By anciently, I mean before any part of Celtica was Galatized. Celt was a descriptive or epithetic name, and not a mere name nominative. That name (equivalent to Gaidheal, or in contraction Gael) was once used by the Gauls to describe all the midland tribes of Europe, western and eastern, Cis-Rhenane and German, even to the Riphean mountains; (See Dion. Hal. 14. c. 1, 2, 3. ed. Maio) and rightly so used: for then they all were Sylvestres, and far removed from the ways of civil life. And it is not to be taken as though, because they all were such, they all called it by that name, and consequently spoke the language to which that name belongs. In fact, when all were in the Celt condition none would have so styled themselves; unless in the Cisalpine country, where they came close to civilized states. People never will begin to go right on these points, until they make it their care to distinguish names epithetic from names absolute. See the remarks in Br. A.R. p. lii. liv. lv. Galatae or Galli, names of the opposite meaning, are more distinctly recorded to be of modern origin; but their very opposition or correlation renders it probable that neither style was common till the other was. There is reason to believe, that the great country from which this island was chiefly peopled was also, and previously, Alwion; and that that name (national in its purport, and not topographical) was co-extensive with the territories of the now-called Cymmraeg tongue. On the plains between Marseilles and the mouths of the Rhone Hercules gained an important victory over Albion and

Bergios otherwise Dercynus. See Pomp. Mela 2. c. 5. and the author bearing the name of Apollodorus, 2. p. 188. Since nearly all other authors depose that the Ligyes, Ligystini, or (in Latin) Ligures, were opposed to him in that battle; and since only three nations are known to have ever flourished in, or close to, that corner of Europe, viz. the Celto-Galatian natives, their Ligyan neighbours, and the Phocaean Greeks; we are led to conclude that Bergios represents the Ligistic people, whose language is unknown. And so he does, in fact; for the scholiast of Dionysius terms the two champions, Albion (spelt by him Alebion), and Ligys founder of the Ligyan state. In Perieg. v. 76. Tzet. in Lycophr. 1312. In the war waged by Hercules on the fields of Crau against Albion and Bergios Ligys, the Massylian poets seem to have mythologized the early struggles which are known to have occurred, between the intruding Greeks and the united Ligyes and Segobrigian Alwioniaid, in the plains which adjoined the new city; magna cum Liguribus, magna cum Gallis bella.' See Justin. 43. cc. 4, 5. Before Druidism or Galatism, before improved husbandry, and before any literature at all, had entered this country of sought-for name, it was, as well as our country, Alouion; and perhaps the desired name is found. Ingenious must he be, who can bring the white cliffs of Kent to the delta of the Rhone, to fight against the Greeks conjointly with the savages of the Maritime Alps. The western exploits of Hercules in Erythea, Tartessus, Gaul, etc. seem to relate to the voyages of the Phoenicians and Massylians. This story belongs more naturally to the affairs of the latter. But it is immaterial to which.

The field Albiona beyond the Tiber derives its name (says Pompeius Festus) from the grove of the Albionae, where a white ox was sacrificed. Here we have the usual Latin spelling, and the association of albus. But that hurts me less, than this curious passage helps me. The Cisalpines crossed the Alps about B.C. 600, that is, long before they were Druidized, before Marseilles was built, and before the habits of agriculture were advanced among them. How that was, appears not from Justin only but from the name of the chief city they built, Medi-o-lân, 'the harvest of the tilth' or 'cultured land.' Those who practised husbandry were still compelled to hoard its produce in their fortified towns: Medi-o-lân in Merioneth and fortresses of the same name in Transalpine Gaul and in Belgica shew not only similar manners, but exact identity of language from Wales and Ardennes to the Po. The Cisaplines were dangerous neighbours to old Tuscany and young Rome. Not only from vicinity and intercourse, but on the principles of placation, averruncation, or evocation, their sacra are likely to have been cultivated by the Tuscan wizards. The Jupiter Vimineus or wicker-work Jove of Mount Viminal was borrowed from the horrid rites of the Gauls. A Gaul was annually sacrificed as a victim at Rome. And this field was a sacred glebe attached to the grove of the Alvionae, the goddesses of Alwion. The profound silence of all antiquity beside, and the sacrificabatur of Festus, argue the obsoleteness of those rites. The Alwionesau therefore could not be goddesses of that remote island which the Romans knew not personally till Caesar's time, nor even from the study of Greek books till about a century before. They were rather goddesses whose altars were on the Rubicon, and whose sorceresses had howled their war-song at the foot of the besieged Capitolium. When the Phocaeans first issued from their new-built walls they met the warriors of Alwion; and Alwion was the nation whose hostile genii the Etruscan augurs deprecated.

The Gauls and Britons had one language, one system of religion, and were united in one alliance so strict, that they had no separate unbennaeth, and a king of the Rhemi, Suessones, etc. could wear the insular crown as well as a king of the Iccni or Ordovices. They certainly had been one political body, one state and nation. Therefore they ought to have had one name. And the name is before the reader. It may be taken the other way. Since they possessed this ancient name in common, they ought to have been one state or nation, and not two as vulgarly supposed. And we see that they had been so. The whole hangs together.

Conjectures may make what it will, or the best it can, of the old word Alouion. At any rate, it is effectually disconnected from the local peculiarities of Britannia. It is a name once used and revered by the great Celto-Galatian body of mankind, even to their utmost southern habitations. I should cling less to the opinion I propounded, were it not for the entirely lost and obsolete etymology of Gwion. For a name without an imaginable etymon or meaning is rare, and for ought I know quite unique, in the mystical or superstitious nomenclature of that language. See *Br. A.R.* p. lxiv–viii.

154   Caesar. 6. 13.
155   Beauford in *Collect. Hibern.* 2. p. 208.
156   See Strabo, 3. p. 225.

157 *Germ.* c. 3.
158 See Ammian. xvi. 12. 43. xxxi. 7. 11. Vegetius, iii. 18.
159 Jambl. *Pythagorica Vita*, c. 15.
160 *Hist. Nat.* 30. c. 4.
161 *Vit. Claud.* c. 25. *Aur. Vict.* in Claud. p. 114. Delph.
162 Tacit. *Hist.* 4. 54.
163 *Aur. Vict.* p. 115.
164 The non-payment of the tribute imposed by Julius Caesar should not have been presumed in Br. A. R. p. 2, but distinctly averred. For Strabo discusses the matter, and owns that no tribute was paid or could be extorted without more expense than it was worth. And argues, by way of apology, that the export and import duties levied in Gaul upon the transit of bridles, necklace, amber, and import duties levied in Gaul upon the transit of bridles, necklaces, amber, and glass was more profitable. He also speaks of certain dynasts, as sending embassies and presents to Augustus, on the foot of independence. iv. p. 280 *Oxon.*
165 Tacit. *Annal.* 13. 32.
166 Montf. *Ant. Expl.* 1. p. 367–84, 2. p. 16–18.
167 Plutarch. *Vit. Pomp.* p. 631.
168 See Justin Martyr *Apol.* 1. p. 97. et *Dial. cum Tryphone*, p. 289. Thirlby. Tertuallian Praescript, c. 40.
169 *De Erroribus*, p. 21, ed. Munter.
170 See *Eudociae Violarium*, p. 291.
171 Lampridius in *Comm.* p. 278. ed. 1661.
172 See Dr Ashe's *Masonic Manual*, p. 163.
173 For a summary of his doctrine (or so much of it as he suffered to appear) see Brucker *Period.* 2. part 2. lib. 1. cap. 3.
174 Aedituus. See Hor. *Ep.* 2. 1. 230.
175 Hieronym. *ad Laetam de Inst. Filiae.*
176 For a translation of the complete text see *Merlin Through the Ages: A Chronological Anthology and Source Book*, edited by R.J. Stewart and John Matthews (Cassell, 1995).
177 Genesis 10, 5.
178 Joshua 24, 26–27.
179 1 Sam. 7, 12.
180 1 Sam. 6, 15–18.
181 Num. 2, 1–3.
182 2 Kings 18, 4.
183 Exod. 3, 4–5.
184 Rev., 4, 8.
185 Exod. 3, 14.
186 An example of this error will be found by referring to H. Tegai's Grammar, p. 137.
187 Referring to Exodus 3, 15.
188 Iolo MSS. p. 691.
189 Job 38, 7.
190 The three divergent rays in the accompanying cut are here referred.
191 John 12, 24.
192 1 Cor. 15, 36.
193 The Kymmric term 'Gwyddon,' signifies philosopher; a man of science, from the primitive mode of the aboriginal Britons inscribing their knowledge on wood – *gwydd*, or billets. From this the alphabet is called in the Welsh language *egwyddor*. *Gorsedd blyn gwyddon* was one of three primary places of meeting of the Bards of the isle of Britain.
194 The word circle is too limited a term to express the Bardic meaning of the Kymmric word *cylch*, especially as the residence of the Deity. '*Cylch*' is druidically used, in the sense that 'state' is used, in the expressions, state of Felicity, state of Infinitude, and state of Inchoation – except that it is also a symbol of endlessness – Note to Iolo MSS. p. 424.
195 The words coelus and hell were originally one and the same term.
196 'Literature of the Kymmry', p. 118.
197 Ab Ithel's Gododin.
198 Triads of Bardism.

199   Hanes *Cymru*, p. 53.
200   Vide Essays of the Abergavenny Eisteddfod on the 'Influence of Welsh Traditions on the Literature of Europe.'
201   Cadair, (chair). A seat of authority or presidency, but more particularly among the Bards; and figuratively the qualification which entitled a candidate to preside. Hence, Cadeirdraw, cadair-traw. A doctor or professor of science. Also, Cadeirfardd, (chair-bard). A bard that is entitled to preside at a Gorsedd. And, Cadeiriol. Belonging to a chair or seat; cathedral.
202   Edward Williams, Preface to *Cyfrinach y Beirdd*.
203   Iolo Mss. p. 469.
204   Price *Lit. Rem.*, vol. 1, p. 196.
205   Robert Southey, in a letter expressing his gratification at having been elected an honorary member of the Cymrodorion Society in Gwynedd, in the spirit of poetic fellowship, said: 'This honour is peculiarly gratifying to me, because one of the works by which I hope to be remembered hereafter, relates mainly to Welsh tradition and Welsh history.'
206   'Lays of the Western Gael,' by S. Ferguson.

Part Three

1   Cf. the description of the caves in *Journ. Brit. Arch. Assoc.*, IX (1903), 147.
2   Dr Joseph Anderson noted the significance of the entries for stone circles in the early indexes to Archaeologia; in 1809 it was simply Stones, Circles of, but in 1844 this was altered to Stones, Circles of, v. Druids.
3   The name is, I admit, indefensible, except on the grounds of euphony and popularity. But though I am prepared to champion most forlorn causes, I confess it seems hopeless now to substitute the appalling, yet more correct, Boudicca or Buddug.
4   *His. Reg. Brit.*, VI, 19. On this subject see J. J. Parry, *The Vita Merlini*, Illinois, 1925, p. 113; Hans Matter, *Englische Gründungssagen von Geoffrey of Monmouth bis zur Renaissance in Anglistische Forschungen*, Hft. 58, Heidelberg, 1922, pp. 149 ff.; W. W. Newell, *Publications of the Modern Language Assoc. of America*, XX (N.S. XIII), Baltimore, 1905, No. 19 – 'Doubts Concerning the British History attributed to Nennius', pp. 647 ff.
5   *Hist. Reg. Brit.*, VI, 17.
6   Ibid., VI, 18.
7   Nennius, *Hist. Brit.*, 42 (Stevenson, 1838).
8   Aubrey, *Topographical Collections*, ed. J. E. Jackson, Devizes, 1862, p. 317.
9   See Mr O.G.S. Crawford's remarks in *The Observer*, 23 September 1923.
10   The poet Gray, for instance, more than once refers uncompromisingly to Stukeley's 'nonsense.'
11   Poor Stonehenge! John Evelyn found the stone so hard that all his strength with a hammer could not detach a fragment. – *Diary*, July 22, 1654.
12   Pinkerton was not really the first in the field with an alternative opinion, for John Bryant, in his *Analysis of Antient Mythology* (1776), suggests Stonehenge was much older than the druid theory implied; but he only devoted a line or two to the subject, and can hardly be called the champion of a rival theory.
13   Cf. the testimony of Schedius and of Pufendorf (p. 21) and my remark about de Brebeuf (p. 24).
14   This has, of course, been tested several times. In 1692 Professor Garden of Aberdeen, describing the stone circles of his district, treats the question of their origin in scientific fashion. He concludes: 'I have found nothing hitherto, either in the names of these monuments or the tradition that goes about them, which doth particularly relate to the Druids or point them out.' – *Archaeologia*, I, 341.
15   There is, however, a connection between wrens and druids, since the wren was a prophetic bird (see *Cormac's Glossary*, 60; on the word *dryw* see *Rev. Celtique*, XC, 340, and XLIII, 453). Rowland (*Mona Antiqua*, pp. 84, 89) translated the name Druid's Mansion, claiming it was the site of the Archdruid's dwelling. The word Drew does, of course, occur in the names of places

where there are megaliths, as at Stanton Drew, but it should be no longer necessary to point out that it is merely a personal name, and not a variant of druid. There are three examples, and in each instance it can be shówn that the land belonged to a family called Drew (see Rev. J.E. Jackson in *Aubrey's Topographical Coll. for Wilts*, Devizes, 1862, p. 103, for the references to all three sites; also Thurnam, in *Wilts. Arch. Mag.*, III (1856), 168; and Crawford, *Long Barrows of the Cotswolds*, 231). The only place I know where tradition may really keep alive the memory of a druidic place of worship is at Chartres, and there it has nothing to do with megalithic remains. But it is a fact that in the cathedral crypt one may visit a recess in the foundation of the masonry now called the Druids' Grotto, and, more important, a stela probably of Gaulish, i.e. druidic, date. Legend has it that in pagan times the druids worshipped here the Mother of God (*la Vierge devant enfanter* or *Virgo paritura*), and up to the end of the 18th century a wooden image existed that was supposed to be the object of their adoration, though it was really of early mediaeval date. Legend also places the site of this druid worship at Fermincourt, near Dreux (Cochin, *Mem. Acad. Celt.*, IV, 1809), and this must surely add considerable interest to the fact that the first printed book dealing with the druids . . . was written by a priest of Dreux. It must also be remembered that this is the district wherein the ancient druids held their annual assemblies (Caesar, *B.G.*, VI, 13).

16 It is to my mind much less likely that it was merely a borrowing by learned scribes from classical sources, or that the word was in any sense a Gallo-roman importation. I am quite prepared to believe that in one form or another the name druid may have remained current in common Keltic speech; but from the 5th century onwards there is no evidence that it had any significant traditional association with the ancient druids; it merely referred to a person pre-eminent for magic or poetry. The etymology of the word is still uncertain. The old orthodox view (cf. Holder, *Altceltische Sprachschatz, s.v. druida*, D'Arbois de Jubainville, *Cours de la littérature celtique*, VI, 93; n. 2, and *Revue Celtique*, XXXI (1908), p. 83) takes *dru* as a strengthening prefix and *uid* as 'knowing,' but this has lately been abandoned by the propounder (Thurneysen, *Zeit. f. Celtische Philologie*, XVI (1926), p. 276) who now inclines to a derivation from an oak-word. M. Camille Jullian had already remarked (*Hist. de la Gaule*, II, p. 85, n. 7) that one should not exclude the significance of Pliny's fanciful derivation from the Greek δρῦς (see p. 89); for who knows, he asks, that the Gauls did not use a radical sounding like δρῦς as a word for oak. Dr R. Much is of the same opinion, and called attention (*Mitt. Anthr.*, Wien, XXXVIII (1908), p. 46) to the Welsh *derw* (= oaks) (cf. Evans, *Welsh Dict., s.v. Derwydd*). On the other hand, Dr Goldman suggested (*Mitt. Anthr.*, Wien, ib., p. 47) an Etruscan origin for the word.

17 It seems to have been Aventinus who started the curious legend about the druid's shoe. See *Annales*, ed. Cisner, Frankfurt, 1627, p. 68; and, in the same work, *Nomenclatura, s.v. Druides*.

18 There was nothing about the druids in the *Germaniae Exegeseos* (Hagenoae, 1518) of Franciscus Irenicus.

19 Rabelais, *Oeuvres*, ed. Moland, Paris, 1884, p. 454. Cf. *B.G.*, VI, 17, 'Minervam operum atque artificiorum initia tradere.'

20 See *Bibliothèque de la Croix du Maine* (ed. de Juvigny, Paris, 1772, I, 495). Le Febure was a priest and a native of Dreux. The work was apparently unknown to Cochin, who wrote an article on the antiquities of Dreux (*Mem. de l'Acad. celtique*, IV (1809), 453).

21 In the meantime Leland had compiled an excellent summary of the classical references to druids and druidism, but this had remained in MS. until the 18th century (*Commentarii de Scriptoribus Britannicis*, Oxford, 1709, Chs I–III). Leland assumed that druidism flourished in England until the conversion of Lucius Magnus to Christianity (see Geoffrey of Monmouth, *Hist. Reg. Brit.*, IV, 19–VI, 1); Merlin he classed as a bard, or possibly (he suggests) a *vates*. Another work that appeared in this interval was the *De Prisca Celtopaedia* of Picard de Tontry (1556); it is cited by Jullian, *Hist. de la Gaule*, II, p. 86, n. 2 (5th ed.), but I have not seen it myself.

22 *Orationes Legitimae*: I. *Oratio solemnis de visco Druidarum juris prudentiae symbolo*, Poitiers, 1615.

23 Amsterdam, 1648. The earlier and gloriously illustrated book by Cluverius, *Germania Antiqua* (Lugduni Batavorum, 1616), contains only two or three brief references to the druids.

24 It was later included in the *Opuscula a iuvene lucubrata*, Halae Hermundurorum, 1699.

25 Privately printed, Edinburgh, 1886.

26 *De Prisca Celtopaedia*, Paris, 1556.

27 *Syntagma de Druidum moribus ac institutis*, London, 1664.

28 Oxford, 1669 and 1671. See Pt. II, Bk. I, Ch. V, 78–82. There were one or two other works on the druids published in the closing years of the century. Of these the *De Philosophia Celtica* of J.C. Kuhn (1676) is a dull tact of fourteen pages; there was also the *Disputatio de Gallorum veterum Druidibus* (Upsala, 1689), by Peter Lägerlof (a work I have not seen). More interesting than Kuhn's book, though not much longer, was the *Veterum Instituta Druidum*, by Elias Eyring (1697); this includes a reading of the suspected inscription (Orelli, 2200) from the Moselle (p. 100).

29 *Loc. sit.*, p. 33.

30 The grove idea was always more popular in France than in England. Courier, for instance, in one of the *Censeur* letters of 1819, mentions a 'M. Marcellus' who regarded his native forests as a memorial of the druids, and would not allow a single tree to be cut. P.–L. Courier, *Lettres au rédacteur du Censeur*, V, Nov. 1819. For that matter, it is still current in France and in the wooded districts of Northern Spain (especially in Galicia, so my friend Dr Pericot tells me).

31 *Tatler*, No. 255 (1710).

32 *Dryades: or the Nymphs' Prophecy*, London, 1713, p. 15.

33 *The Bath*, Dublin, 1726, p. 3.

34 On this subject see the excellent little book, *The Celtic Revival in English Literature*, by E.D. Snyder (Cambridge, Mass., 1923). I most gratefully acknowledge my indebtedness to this work for many of the references quoted here.

35 The story of this revival is outlined by Sir J. Morris-Jones in *Y Cymmrodor*, 28 (1918), p. 10 ff.

36 *Celtic Researches* (1804); *Mythology of the British Druids* (1809).

37 *The Neo-Druidic Heresy* (1838).

38 *On the Study of Keltic Literature* (Works, ed. 1903, V. p. 45).

39 D.W. Nash, *Taliesin: or the Bards and Druids of Britain*, London, 1858, esp. pp. 330 ff.; Matthew Arnold, *loc. cit.*, pp. 26 ff.; Jules Leflocq, *Etudes de mythologie celtique*, Orleans, 1869, pp. 115 ff.; Thomas Stephens, *Literature of the Kymry*, London, 1876, pp. 84 ff.

40 As will be seen, I have in a later passage explained the Druidic adoration of that plant as arising out of a belief that it symbolized the male essence of the god or spirit of the oak. This notion of mine, however, might appear to be vitiated by the circumstance that some of the Australian aboriginal tribes do not regard paternity as a factor in the birth of children and that among them the belief prevails that the human mother is impregnated solely by the type of ancestral spirit alluded to above. May not the Druidic idea have been a distortion or adaptation of the older notion, as found among the Australian tribes and other primitive folk, adopted at a later period when human paternity came to be recognized as a fact? That European man believed that men were born from trees seems established. The god of the oak was certainly a male spirit. This, I think, fortifies my argument that the fact of paternity was known to the people who worshipped the oak, even in early times. In Greece, Rome and among the Celts the oak-spirit was a male. We seem, indeed, to encounter here a later phase of the idea which inspired Australian notions of birth. Nor, I may add, do all Australian tribes believe that paternity plays no part in the begetting of children.

41 A revised version of this chapter was originally published in the *Hermetic Journal*, 1979.

FURTHER READING

A complete listing of books on Druidry would fill a small volume in itself and is, in any case, beyond the scope of this book. Those readers who are interested in finding out more are recommended to the bibliographies in the works of Berresford Ellis, Nichols and Spence shown below and in the listing, compiled by George F. Black in 1920, of references to books relating to Druidry and Druidism in the New York Public Library. The titles included below are those that I have consulted in the compilation of this collection and those that I have found to be particularly helpful to my own studies in this area.

Aneurin Vardd, 'Bardism', *The International Review*, New York, vol. 3, 1976

Anonymous, *A Complete History of the Druids: Their Origin, Manner, Customs, Power, Temples, Rites and Superstitions, with an Enquiry into Their Religion and its Coincidence with the Patriarchal*, T.G. Lomas, Lichfield, 1810

Anonymous, *A Druid History of Creation*, Richardson, Carlton Vic, 1906

Anwyl, Edward, *Celtic Religion in Pre-Christian Times*, London, 1906

Archbishop of Wales, 'Druidism', *Journal of the Chester and North Wales Architectural, Archaeological and Historical Society*, vol. xxviii, 1928

Berresford Ellis, Peter, *The Druids*, Constable, London, 1994

Bonwick, James, *Irish Druids and Old Irish Religions*, Griffin, Fanwick & Co., 1894; reprinted Dorset Press, 1986

Bowles, William Leslie, *Hermes Brittanicus*, J.B. Nichols, London, 1828

Broome, J.H., *Astronomy and Druidic Worship at Stonehenge*, London, 1870

Butt, Martha, *The Druids of Britain*, London, 1840

Carr-Gomm, Philip, *The Elements of the Druid Tradition*, Element Books, Poole, 1991

Carr-Gomm, Philip, *The Druid Way*, Element Books, Poole, 1993

Carr-Gomm, Philip (ed.), *The Druid Renaissance*, Harper Collins, London, 1996

Chadwick, Nora K., *The Druids*, University of Wales Press, Cardiff, 1966

Cooke, William, *an Enquiry into the Druidical and Patriarchal Religion*, London 1747

Cooper, Captain George H., *The Druid Bible: Universal Key to Prehistoric Symbolic Records*, Victor Hillis & Sons, San Jose, California, 1936

Cromwell, Thomas, *The Druid*, London, 1832

Daniel, Sir John, *The Philosophy of Ancient Britain*, 1927; reprinted Kennikat Press, New York, 1970

Darkstar, Erynn, *Ogam, Tree Lore and the Celtic Oracle*, Inis Glas Productions, Seattle, 1993

Davies, Edward, *Celtic Researches*, J. Booth, London, 1804

Davies, Edward, *The Mythology and Rites of the British Druids*, J. Booth, London, 1809

de Jubainville, Henri d'Arbois, *Les Druides et les Dieux Celtiques aux Formes des Animaux*, Paris, 1906

de Kay, Charles, 'Fairies and Druids of Ireland', *Century Magazine*, New York, vol. 37, 1889

Elynd, *Travels of a British Druid*, J. Hatchard, London, 1811

Evans, D.D., *Dewi Hiraddug: The Ancient Bards of Britain*, Education Publishing Co., Merthyr Tydfil, 1906

Fisher, P., 'Blake and the Druids', *Journal of English and Germanic Philology*, vol. liv, 1959, pages 48–64

Frazer, James George, *The Golden Bough* (12 vols), London, 1890–1915

Frick, J.G., *Commentatio de Druidis*, Ulm, 1744

Herbert, Algernon, *An Essay on the Neo-Druidic Heresy in Britannia*, H.G. Bohn, London, 1838

Higgins, Godfrey, *The Celtic Druids*, London, 1827

Holmes, T. Rice, *Caesar's Conquest of Gaul*, Oxford University Press, Oxford, 1911

Hopman, Ellen Evert, *A Druid's Herbal for the Sacred Earth Year*, Destiny Books, New York, 1995

Hurd, William, *The Religious Rites and Ceremonies of the Druids*, London, 1800

Hutton, Ronald, *The Pagan Religions of the Ancient British Isles*, Oxford University Press, Oxford, 1991

James, David, *The Patriarchal Religion of Britain; or, a Complete Manual of Ancient British Druidism*, J. Brook, London, 1836

Joyce, P.W., *A Social History of Ancient Ireland* (2 volumes), Longman, Green & Co., London and New York, 1903

Kendrick, T.D., *The Druids: A Study in Keltic Prehistory*, Methuen & Co., London, 1927

King, John, *The Celtic Druids' Year*, Cassell, London, 1994

le Roux, Françoise, *Les Druides*, Paris, 1961

Macbain, Alexander, *Celtic Mythology and Religion*, Eneas Mackay, Stirling, 1917

MacCulloch, J.A., 'The Druids in the Light of Recent Theories', *Transactions* of the Third International Congress for the History of Religion (2 volumes), 1908

Mackay, Charles, 'Druidical Chants Preserved in the Choruses of Popular Songs in England, Scotland, Ireland and France', *The Celtic Magazine*, vol. i, Inverness, 1876, pages 57–65

Macclaglan, R.C., *Our Ancestors: Scots, Picts and Cymry*, T.N. Foulis, London and Edinburgh, 1913

Matthews, Caitlín and John, The *Encyclopaedia of Celtic Wisdom*, Element Books, Shaftesbury, 1994

Mercurios, *La Magie des Druides*, Guy Tredanial Editeur, Paris, 1992

Minahane, John, *The Christian Druids*, Sanas Press, Dublin, 1993

Morgan, R.W., *The British Cymry*, H. Humphries, Caernarvon, 1857

Morgannwyg, Iolo, *Barddas: The Bardo-Druidic System* (vol. 1, translated, with notes, by J. Williams ab Ithel), Longman, Green & Co., London, 1822

Murray, Liz and Colin, *The Celtic Tree Oracle*, Rider and Co., London, 1988

Nichols, Ross, *The Book of Druidry*, Aquarian Press, London, 1990

Ogilivie, John, *The Fane of the Druids*, London, 1787

Owen, A.L., *The Famous Druids*, Oxford University Press, Oxford, 1962

Piggott, Stuart, *The Druids*, Thames & Hudson, London, 1968

Piggott, Stuart, *Ancient Britons and the Antiquarian Imagination*, Thames & Hudson, London, 1989

Pim, Herbert M., *A Short History of Celtic Philosophy*, Dundalk, 1920

Pokorny, Julius, 'The Origin of Druidism', *The Celtic Review*, 15 July 1908

Raoult, Michel, *Les Druides*, Editions du Rochers, Monaco, 1988

Reade, W. Winwood, *The Veil of Isis*, or, *the Mysteries of the Druids*, C.J. Skeet, London, 1861

Ross, Ann, and Robins, Don, *The Life and Death of a Druid Prince*, Rider & Co., London, 1989

Rust, J., *Druidism Exhumed*, Edmonston & Douglas, Edinburgh, 1871

Rutherford, Ward, *The Druids and Their Heritage*, Gordon & Cremonesi, London, 1978

Ryan, Marah Ellis, *The Druid Path*, London, 1917

Shallcross, Philip, *A Druid Directory, 1995*, British Druid Order, St Leonards-on-Sea, Sussex, 1995

Smiddy, Richard, *An Essay on the Druids, the Ancient Churches and the Round Towers of Ireland*, Dublin, 1871

Smith, John, *Gallic Antiquities*, T. Cadell, Edinburgh, 1780

Smith, Thomas, *Syntagma de Druidism Moribus*, Oxford, 1664

Spence, Lewis, *The History and Origins of Druidism*, Rider & Co., London, 1949; reprinted Aquarian Press, London, 1971

Stukeley, William, *Stonehenge, a Temple Restored to the British Druids*, London, 1740

Stukeley, William, *Abury, a Temple of the British Druids*, London, 1743

Toland, John, *A Critical History of the Druids*, Lackington, Huges, Harding & Co., 1740

Vallencey, Charles, *Collectanea de Rebus Hibernicis*, Dublin, 1781

Wiese, H., and Frick, H., *Handbuch des Druiden Ordens*, Munich, 1931

Wright, Dudley, *Druidism: The Ancient Faith of Britain*, E.J. Burrow & Co. Ltd, 1924; reprinted E.P. Publishing Ltd., 1976

MAJOR DRUID ORDERS

There are a number of thriving Druid orders in the world today, and the major ones are listed below. (The addresses are in England unless otherwise indicated.) A fuller listing, with additional membership details, will be found in Philip Shalcross's *A Druid Directory, 1995* (see Further Reading). When writing to any of these addresses, please enclose a stamped addressed envelope.

Ancient Order of Druids
174 Tomkinson Road
Nuneaton
Warwickshire CV10 8BW

Aos Dana
Dun Cauld Cottage
Cauldhame
Kippen FK8 3HL
Scotland

Ar nDriaiocht Fein
ADF, PO Box 516
East Syracuse
New York
NY 13057
USA

British Druid Order
Philip Shalcross (BDO)
PO Box 29
St Leonards-on-Sea
East Sussex TN37 7YP

Council of British Druid Orders
125 Magyar Crescent
Nuneaton
Warwickshire CV11 4SJ

Druid Clan of Dana
Clonegal Castle
Enniscorthy
Eire

École Druidique des Gaules
The Secretary
Bernard Jaquelin
Villa Montmorency
75016 Paris
45 27 74 79
France

Glastonbury Order of Druids
Rollo Maughfling
Dove House
Barton St David
Somerset TA11 6DF

Henge of Keltria
PO Box 33284
Minneapolis
MN 55433
USA

Insular Order of Druids
c/o Labyrinth
2 Victoria Road South
Southsea
Hampshire PO5 2DF

London Druid Order
(formerly the Universal Druid Order)
Membership Secretary
Council of British Druid Orders
125 Magyar Crescent
Nuneaton
Warwickshire CV11 4SJ

Order of Bards, Ovates and Druids
PO Box 1333
Lewes
Sussex BN7 37G

Order of Sula
PO Box 658
Mold
Clwyd CH7 1FB
Wales

Reformed Druids of North America
c/o Carleton College Archive
300 North College Street
Northfield
Minnesota 55057
USA

In addition, John and Caitlín Matthews offer courses on various aspects of the Celtic tradition, including Shamanic and Grail work. For further information on these and other activities, publications and so forth, subscribe to the *Hallowquest Newsletter*, BCM Hallowquest, London WC1N 3XX. At time of writing, the subscription is £6.00 in Britain and Europe, $20.00 in the USA and £12.00 elsewhere in the world. This brings you four quarterly issues. For information only send a large, stamped addressed envelope with five first-class stamps or eight International Reply Paid Coupons (available from main post offices).

INDEX